ARCTIC OCEAN
RUSSIA
FIN.
SWED.
E.
L.
L.
POL.
BEL.
UKRAINE
AUS.
H.
ROM.
YUG.
BUL.
ITALY
GREECE
TURKEY
G.
AR.
AZ.
KAZAKSTAN
MONGOLIA
UZ.
TURK.
KYR.
TAD.
CHINA
N. KOREA
S.
JAPAN
CYP.
SY.
LEB.
ISR.
JOR.
IRAQ
IRAN
KUWAIT
AFGHAN.
PAKISTAN
NEP.
BHU.
BANG.
INDIA
TUNISIA
LIBYA
EGYPT
SAUDI ARABIA
U.A.E.
OMAN
YEMEN
ERIT.
DJIB.
GER
CHAD
SUDAN
ETHIOPIA
SOMALI REP.
C.A.R.
U.
KENYA
GAB.
CONGO
CONGO (DEM. REP. OF THE)
R.
B.
TANZANIA
COMOROS
ANGOLA
ZAMBIA
M.
ZIM.
MOZ.
MADAGASCAR
NAMIBIA
BOTS.
SWAZ.
SOUTH AFRICA
LES.
BURMA
L.
THAI-LAND
CAM.
VIETNAM
TAIWAN
PHILIPPINES
SRI LANKA
MALAYSIA
SING.
INDONESIA
PAPUA NEW GUINEA
PACIFIC OCEAN
Tropic of Cancer
MARSHALL IS.
Equator
KIRIBATI
INDIAN OCEAN
VANUATU
FIJI
Tropic of Capricorn
AUSTRALIA
NEW ZEALAND
THERN OCEAN
tica

WHS

COMPACT WORLD ATLAS

NEW EDITION

WHS

COMPACT WORLD ATLAS

NEW EDITION

Contents

World Statistics

vi–ix Countries
x–xi Cities
xii–xv Physical
xvi Climate

The Earth in Focus

2–3 The Universe and Solar System
4–5 The Changing Earth
6–7 Earthquakes and Volcanoes
8–9 Water and Ice
10–11 Weather and Climate
12–13 Landforms and Vegetation
14–15 Population
16–17 Languages and Religions
18–19 Agriculture and Industry
20–21 Trade and Commerce
22–23 Transport and Travel
24–27 International Organizations
28–29 Regions in the News
30–32 World Flags

Cartography by Philip's

Text
Keith Lye

Picture Acknowledgements
Robert Harding Picture Library /Photri 1
Image Bank /Lionel Brown 10
Rex Features /Sipa 6, 24
Still Pictures 26, /Anne Piantanida 8, /Chris Caldicott 16, /Mark Edwards 18, 20, /Hartmut Schwarzbach 14, 22, /Luke White 4
Tony Stone Images /Kevin Kelley 2, /Art Wolfe 12

This edition first published in the UK in 1999 by George Philip Limited for WHSmith, Greenbridge Road, Swindon SN3 3RX

Cartography by Philip's

George Philip Limited, a division of Octopus Publishing Group Limited, 2–4 Heron Quays, London E14 4JP

ISBN 0-540-07822-0

A CIP catalogue record for this book is available from the British Library.

Printed in China

World Maps

1 General Reference
2–3 Northern Hemisphere
4–5 Southern Hemisphere
6–7 Europe
8–9 Scandinavia
10–11 British Isles
12–13 France
14–15 Germany and Benelux
16–17 Central Europe
18–19 Spain and Portugal
20–21 Italy and the Adriatic
22–23 Greece and the Balkans
24–25 Eastern Europe
26–27 Asia
28–29 Western Russia and Central Asia
30–31 Eastern Siberia
32–33 Japan
34–35 China
36–37 South-east Asia
38–39 Philippines and Eastern Indonesia
40–41 Eastern India, Bangladesh and Burma
42–43 Western India and Pakistan
44–45 Iran, the Gulf and Afghanistan
46–47 The Middle East and Turkey
48–49 Arabia and the Horn of Africa
50–51 Africa
52–53 North-east Africa
54–55 North-west Africa
56–57 Central Africa
58–59 Southern Africa
60–61 Australia
62–63 South-east Australia
64–65 New Zealand, Central and South-west Pacific
66–67 North America
68–69 Eastern Canada
70–71 Western Canada
72–73 North-east USA
74–75 South-east USA
76–77 North-central USA
78–79 Southern USA
80–81 North-west USA
82–83 South-west USA
84–85 Mexico
86–87 Caribbean and Central America
88–89 South America
90–91 South America – North-west
92–93 South America – North-east
94–95 South America – South
96 Antarctica

97–160 **Index to World Maps**

World Statistics – Countries

Listed below are all the countries of the world; the more important territories are also included. If a territory is not completely independent, then the country it is associated with is named. The area figures give the total area of land, inland water and ice. Annual income is the GNP per capita. The figures are the latest available: usually 1997.

Country / Territory	*Area (1,000 sq km)*	*Area (1,000 sq mls)*	*Population (1,000s)*	*Capital City*	*Annual Income US$*
Afghanistan	652	252	24,792	Kabul	600
Albania	28.8	11.1	3,331	Tirana	750
Algeria	2,382	920	30,481	Algiers	1,490
Andorra	0.45	0.17	75	Andorra La Vella	16,200
Angola	1,247	481	11,200	Luanda	340
Argentina	2,767	1,068	36,265	Buenos Aires	8,750
Armenia	29.8	11.5	3,422	Yerevan	530
Australia	7,687	2,968	18,613	Canberra	20,540
Austria	83.9	32.4	8,134	Vienna	27,980
Azerbaijan	86.6	33.4	7,856	Baku	510
Azores (Portugal)	2.2	0.87	238	Ponta Delgada	–
Bahamas	13.9	5.4	280	Nassau	11,940
Bahrain	0.68	0.26	616	Manama	7,840
Bangladesh	144	56	125,000	Dhaka	270
Barbados	0.43	0.17	259	Bridgetown	6,560
Belarus	207.6	80.1	10,409	Minsk	2,150
Belgium	30.5	11.8	10,175	Brussels	26,420
Belize	23	8.9	230	Belmopan	2,700
Benin	113	43	6,101	Porto-Novo	380
Bhutan	47	18.1	1,908	Thimphu	390
Bolivia	1,099	424	7,826	La Paz/Sucre	950
Bosnia-Herzegovina	51	20	3,366	Sarajevo	300
Botswana	582	225	1,448	Gaborone	4,381
Brazil	8,512	3,286	170,000	Brasília	4,720
Brunei	5.8	2.2	315	Bandar Seri Begawan	15,800
Bulgaria	111	43	8,240	Sofia	1,140
Burkina Faso	274	106	11,266	Ouagadougou	240
Burma (= Myanmar)	677	261	47,305	Rangoon	1,790
Burundi	27.8	10.7	5,531	Bujumbura	180
Cambodia	181	70	11,340	Phnom Penh	300
Cameroon	475	184	15,029	Yaoundé	650
Canada	9,976	3,852	30,675	Ottawa	19,290
Canary Is. (Spain)	7.3	2.8	1,494	Las Palmas/Santa Cruz	–
Cape Verde Is.	4	1.6	399	Praia	1,010
Central African Republic	623	241	3,376	Bangui	320
Chad	1,284	496	7,360	Ndjaména	240
Chile	757	292	14,788	Santiago	5,020
China	9,597	3,705	1,236,915	Beijing	860
Colombia	1,139	440	38,581	Bogotá	2,280
Comoros	2.2	0.86	545	Moroni	450
Congo	342	132	2,658	Brazzaville	660
Congo (= Zaïre)	2,345	905	49,001	Kinshasa	110
Costa Rica	51.1	19.7	3,605	San José	2,640
Croatia	56.5	21.8	4,672	Zagreb	4,610
Cuba	111	43	11,051	Havana	1,300

Country / Territory	Area (1,000 sq km)	Area (1,000 sq mls)	Population (1,000s)	Capital City	Annual Income US$
Cyprus	9.3	3.6	749	Nicosia	13,420
Czech Republic	78.9	30.4	10,286	Prague	5,200
Denmark	43.1	16.6	5,334	Copenhagen	32,500
Djibouti	23.2	9	650	Djibouti	850
Dominica	0.75	0.29	78	Roseau	3,090
Dominican Republic	48.7	18.8	7,999	Santo Domingo	1,670
Ecuador	284	109	12,337	Quito	1,590
Egypt	1,001	387	66,050	Cairo	1,180
El Salvador	21	8.1	5,752	San Salvador	1,810
Equatorial Guinea	28.1	10.8	454	Malabo	530
Eritrea	94	36	3,842	Asmara	570
Estonia	44.7	17.3	1,421	Tallinn	3,330
Ethiopia	1,128	436	58,390	Addis Ababa	110
Fiji	18.3	7.1	802	Suva	2,470
Finland	338	131	5,149	Helsinki	24,080
France	552	213	58,805	Paris	26,050
French Guiana (France)	90	34.7	162	Cayenne	10,580
French Polynesia (France)	4	1.5	237	Papeete	7,500
Gabon	268	103	1,208	Libreville	4,230
Gambia, The	11.3	4.4	1,292	Banjul	320
Georgia	69.7	26.9	5,109	Tbilisi	840
Germany	357	138	82,079	Berlin/Bonn	28,260
Ghana	239	92	18,497	Accra	370
Greece	132	51	10,662	Athens	12,010
Grenada	0.34	0.13	96	St George's	2,880
Guadeloupe (France)	1.7	0.66	416	Basse-Terre	9,200
Guatemala	109	42	12,008	Guatemala City	1,500
Guinea	246	95	7,477	Conakry	570
Guinea-Bissau	36.1	13.9	1,206	Bissau	240
Guyana	215	83	820	Georgetown	690
Haiti	27.8	10.7	6,781	Port-au-Prince	330
Honduras	112	43	5,862	Tegucigalpa	700
Hong Kong (China)	1.1	0.40	6,707	–	22,990
Hungary	93	35.9	10,208	Budapest	4,430
Iceland	103	40	271	Reykjavik	26,580
India	3,288	1,269	984,000	New Delhi	390
Indonesia	1,905	735	212,942	Jakarta	1,110
Iran	1,648	636	64,411	Tehran	4,700
Iraq	438	169	21,722	Baghdad	2,000
Ireland	70.3	27.1	3,619	Dublin	18,280
Israel	27	10.3	5,644	Jerusalem	15,810
Italy	301	116	56,783	Rome	20,120
Ivory Coast (Côte d'Ivoire)	322	125	15,446	Yamoussoukro	690
Jamaica	11	4.2	2,635	Kingston	1,560
Japan	378	146	125,932	Tokyo	37,850
Jordan	89.2	34.4	4,435	Amman	1,570
Kazakstan	2,717	1,049	16,847	Astana	1,340
Kenya	580	224	28,337	Nairobi	330
Korea, North	121	47	21,234	Pyŏngyang	1,000
Korea, South	99	38.2	46,417	Seoul	10,550

Country / Territory	*Area (1,000 sq km)*	*Area (1,000 sq mls)*	*Population (1,000s)*	*Capital City*	*Annual Income US$*
Kuwait	17.8	6.9	1,913	Kuwait City	17,390
Kyrgyzstan	198.5	76.6	4,522	Bishkek	440
Laos	237	91	5,261	Vientiane	400
Latvia	65	25	2,385	Riga	2,430
Lebanon	10.4	4	3,506	Beirut	3,350
Lesotho	30.4	11.7	2,090	Maseru	670
Liberia	111	43	2,772	Monrovia	770
Libya	1,760	679	4,875	Tripoli	6,510
Lithuania	65.2	25.2	3,600	Vilnius	2,230
Luxembourg	2.6	1	425	Luxembourg	45,360
Macau (China)	0.02	0.006	429	Macau	7,500
Macedonia	25.7	9.9	2,009	Skopje	1,090
Madagascar	587	227	14,463	Antananarivo	250
Madeira (Portugal)	0.81	0.31	253	Funchal	–
Malawi	118	46	9,840	Lilongwe	220
Malaysia	330	127	20,993	Kuala Lumpur	4,680
Maldives	0.30	0.12	290	Malé	1,080
Mali	1,240	479	10,109	Bamako	260
Malta	0.32	0.12	379	Valletta	12,000
Martinique (France)	1.1	0.42	407	Fort-de-France	10,000
Mauritania	1,030	412	2,511	Nouakchott	450
Mauritius	2.0	0.72	1,168	Port Louis	3,800
Mexico	1,958	756	98,553	Mexico City	3,680
Micronesia, Fed. States of	0.70	0.27	127	Palikir	2,070
Moldova	33.7	13	4,458	Chişinău	540
Mongolia	1,567	605	2,579	Ulan Bator	390
Morocco	447	172	29,114	Rabat	1,250
Mozambique	802	309	18,641	Maputo	90
Namibia	825	318	1,622	Windhoek	2,220
Nepal	141	54	23,698	Katmandu	210
Netherlands	41.5	16	15,731	Amsterdam/The Hague	25,820
Netherlands Antilles (Neths)	0.99	0.38	210	Willemstad	10,400
New Caledonia (France)	18.6	7.2	192	Nouméa	8,000
New Zealand	269	104	3,625	Wellington	16,480
Nicaragua	130	50	4,583	Managua	410
Niger	1,267	489	9,672	Niamey	200
Nigeria	924	357	110,532	Abuja	260
Norway	324	125	4,420	Oslo	36,090
Oman	212	82	2,364	Muscat	4,950
Pakistan	796	307	135,135	Islamabad	490
Panama	77.1	29.8	2,736	Panama City	3,080
Papua New Guinea	463	179	4,600	Port Moresby	940
Paraguay	407	157	5,291	Asunción	2,010
Peru	1,285	496	26,111	Lima	2,460
Philippines	300	116	77,736	Manila	1,220
Poland	313	121	38,607	Warsaw	3,590
Portugal	92.4	35.7	9,928	Lisbon	10,450
Puerto Rico (US)	9	3.5	3,860	San Juan	7,800
Qatar	11	4.2	697	Doha	11,600
Réunion (France)	2.5	0.97	705	Saint-Denis	4,500

Country / Territory	*Area (1,000 sq km)*	*Area (1,000 sq mls)*	*Population (1,000s)*	*Capital City*	*Annual Income US$*
Romania	238	92	22,396	Bucharest	1,420
Russia	17,075	6,592	146,861	Moscow	2,740
Rwanda	26.3	10.2	7,956	Kigali	210
St Lucia	0.62	0.24	150	Castries	3,500
St Vincent & Grenadines	0.39	0.15	120	Kingstown	2,370
São Tomé & Príncipe	0.96	0.37	150	São Tomé	330
Saudi Arabia	2,150	830	20,786	Riyadh	6,790
Senegal	197	76	9,723	Dakar	550
Sierra Leone	71.7	27.7	5,080	Freetown	200
Singapore	0.62	0.24	3,490	Singapore	32,940
Slovak Republic	49	18.9	5,393	Bratislava	3,700
Slovenia	20.3	7.8	1,972	Ljubljana	9,680
Solomon Is.	28.9	11.2	441	Honiara	900
Somalia	638	246	6,842	Mogadishu	500
South Africa	1,220	471	42,835	C. Town/Pretoria/ Bloemfontein	3,400
Spain	505	195	39,134	Madrid	14,510
Sri Lanka	65.6	25.3	18,934	Colombo	800
Sudan	2,506	967	33,551	Khartoum	800
Surinam	163	63	427	Paramaribo	1,000
Swaziland	17.4	6.7	966	Mbabane	1,210
Sweden	450	174	8,887	Stockholm	26,220
Switzerland	41.3	15.9	7,260	Bern	44,220
Syria	185	71	16,673	Damascus	1,150
Taiwan	36	13.9	21,908	Taipei	12,400
Tajikistan	143.1	55.2	6,020	Dushanbe	330
Tanzania	945	365	30,609	Dodoma	210
Thailand	513	198	60,037	Bangkok	2,800
Togo	56.8	21.9	4,906	Lomé	330
Trinidad & Tobago	5.1	2	1,117	Port of Spain	4,230
Tunisia	164	63	9,380	Tunis	2,090
Turkey	779	301	64,568	Ankara	3,130
Turkmenistan	488.1	188.5	4,298	Ashkhabad	630
Uganda	236	91	22,167	Kampala	320
Ukraine	603.7	233.1	50,125	Kiev	1,040
United Arab Emirates	83.6	32.3	2,303	Abu Dhabi	17,360
United Kingdom	243.3	94	58,970	London	20,710
United States of America	9,373	3,619	270,290	Washington, DC	28,740
Uruguay	177	68	3,285	Montevideo	6,020
Uzbekistan	447.4	172.7	23,784	Tashkent	1,010
Vanuatu	12.2	4.7	185	Port-Vila	1,290
Venezuela	912	352	22,803	Caracas	3,450
Vietnam	332	127	76,236	Hanoi	320
Virgin Is. (US)	0.34	0.13	118	Charlotte Amalie	12,000
Western Sahara	266	103	280	El Aaiún	300
Western Samoa	2.8	1.1	224	Apia	1,170
Yemen	528	204	16,388	Sana	270
Yugoslavia	102.3	39.5	10,500	Belgrade	2,000
Zambia	753	291	9,461	Lusaka	380
Zimbabwe	391	151	11,044	Harare	750

World Statistics – Cities

Listed below are all the cities with more than 600,000 inhabitants (only cities with more than 1 million inhabitants are included for Brazil, China and India). The figures are taken from the most recent censuses and surveys, and are in thousands. As far as possible the figures are for the metropolitan area, e.g. greater New York or Mexico City.

Country / City	*Population (1,000s)*
Afghanistan	
Kabul	1,565
Algeria	
Algiers	2,168
Oran	916
Angola	
Luanda	2,418
Argentina	
Buenos Aires	11,256
Córdoba	1,208
Rosario	1,118
Mendoza	773
La Plata	642
San Miguel de Tucumán	622
Armenia	
Yerevan	1,248
Australia	
Sydney	3,770
Melbourne	3,217
Brisbane	1,489
Perth	1,262
Adelaide	1,080
Austria	
Vienna	1,595
Azerbaijan	
Baku	1,720
Bangladesh	
Dhaka	6,105
Chittagong	2,041
Khulna	877
Belarus	
Minsk	1,700
Belgium	
Brussels	948
Bolivia	
La Paz	1,126
Santa Cruz	767
Brazil	
São Paulo	16,417
Rio de Janeiro	9,888
Salvador	2,211
Belo Horizonte	2,091
Fortaleza	1,965
Brasília	1,821
Curitiba	1,476
Recife	1,346
Pôrto Alegre	1,288
Manaus	1,157
Belém	1,144
Goiânia	1,004
Bulgaria	
Sofia	1,116
Burkina Faso	
Ouagadougou	690
Burma (Myanmar)	
Rangoon	2,513
Cambodia	
Phnom Penh	920
Cameroon	
Douala	1,200
Yaoundé	800
Canada	
Toronto	4,344
Montréal	3,337
Vancouver	1,831
Ottawa–Hull	1,022
Edmonton	885
Calgary	831
Québec	693
Winnipeg	677
Hamilton	643
Chile	
Santiago	5,067
China	
Shanghai	15,082
Beijing	12,362
Tianjin	10,687
Hong Kong (SAR)*	6,502
Chongqing	3,870
Shenyang	3,860
Wuhan	3,520
Guangzhou	3,114
Harbin	2,505
Nanjing	2,211
Xi'an	2,115
Chengdu	1,933
Dalian	1,855
Changchun	1,810
Jinan	1,660
Taiyuan	1,642
Qingdao	1,584
Fuzhou, Fujian	1,380
Zibo	1,346
Zhengzhou	1,324
Lanzhou	1,296
Anshan	1,252
Fushun	1,246
Kunming	1,242
Changsha	1,198
Hangzhou	1,185
Nanchang	1,169
Shijiazhuang	1,159
Guiyang	1,131
Ürümqi	1,130
Jilin	1,118
Tangshan	1,110
Qiqihar	1,104
Baotou	1,033
Hefei	1,000
Colombia	
Bogotá	6,004
Cali	1,985
Medellín	1,970
Barranquilla	1,157
Cartagena	812
Congo	
Brazzaville	937
Congo (Zaïre)	
Kinshasa	1,655
Lubumbashi	851
Mbuji-Mayi	806
Costa Rica	
San José	1,220
Croatia	
Zagreb	931
Cuba	
Havana	2,241
Czech Republic	
Prague	1,209
Denmark	
Copenhagen	1,362
Dominican Republic	
Santo Domingo	2,135
Santiago	691
Ecuador	
Guayaquil	1,973
Quito	1,487
Egypt	
Cairo	9,900
Alexandria	3,431
El Gîza	2,144
Shubra el Kheima	834
El Salvador	
San Salvador	1,522
Ethiopia	
Addis Ababa	2,112
France	
Paris	9,319
Lyon	1,262
Marseille	1,087
Lille	959
Bordeaux	696
Toulouse	650
Georgia	
Tbilisi	1,300
Germany	
Berlin	3,470
Hamburg	1,706
Munich	1,240
Cologne	964
Frankfurt	651
Essen	616
Dortmund	600
Ghana	
Accra	949
Greece	
Athens	3,097
Guatemala	
Guatemala	1,167
Guinea	
Conakry	1,508
Haiti	
Port-au-Prince	1,255
Honduras	
Tegucigalpa	813
Hungary	
Budapest	1,885
India	
Bombay (Mumbai)	12,572
Calcutta	10,916
Delhi	7,207
Madras (Chennai)	5,361
Hyderabad	4,280
Bangalore	4,087
Ahmadabad	3,298
Pune	2,485
Kanpur	2,111
Nagpur	1,661
Lucknow	1,642
Surat	1,517
Jaipur	1,514
Coimbatore	1,136
Vadodara	1,115
Indore	1,104
Patna	1,099
Madurai	1,094
Bhopal	1,064
Vishakhapatnam	1,052
Varanasi	1,026
Ludhiana	1,012
Indonesia	
Jakarta	11,500
Surabaya	2,701
Bandung	2,368
Medan	1,910
Semarang	1,366
Palembang	1,352
Tangerang	1,198
Ujung Pandang	1,092
Bandar Lampung	832
Malang	763
Padang	721
Iran	
Tehran	6,750
Mashhad	1,964
Esfahan	1,221
Tabriz	1,166
Shiraz	1,043
Ahvaz	828
Qom	780
Bakhtaran	666
Iraq	
Baghdad	3,841
Diyala	961
As Sulaymaniyah	952
Arbil	770
Al Mawsil	664
Ireland	
Dublin	952
Israel	
Tel Aviv-Yafo	1,502
Italy	
Rome	2,775
Milan	1,369
Naples	1,067
Turin	962
Palermo	698
Genoa	678
Ivory Coast (Côte d'Ivoire)	
Abidjan	2,500
Jamaica	
Kingston	644
Japan	
Tokyo–Yokohama	26,836
Osaka	10,601
Nagoya	2,152
Sapporo	1,757
Kyoto	1,464
Kobe	1,424
Fukuoka	1,285
Kawasaki	1,203
Hiroshima	1,109
Kitakyushu	1,020
Sendai	971
Chiba	857
Sakai	803
Kumamoto	650
Okayama	616
Jordan	
Amman	1,300
Az-Zarqā	609

	Population (1,000s)
Kazakstan	
Almaty	1,150
Kenya	
Nairobi	2,000
Mombasa	600
Korea, North	
Pyŏngyang	2,639
Hamhung	775
Chŏngjin	754
Chinnampo	691
Korea, South	
Seoul	11,641
Pusan	3,814
Taegu	2,449
Inchon	2,308
Taejŏn	1,272
Kwangju	1,258
Ulsan	967
Sŏngnam	869
Puch'on	779
Suwŏn	756
Latvia	
Riga	846
Lebanon	
Beirut	1,900
Libya	
Tripoli	1,083
Madagascar	
Antananarivo	1,053
Malaysia	
Kuala Lumpur	1,145
Mali	
Bamako	800
Mauritania	
Nouakchott	735
Mexico	
Mexico City	15,048
Guadalajara	2,847
Monterrey	2,522
Puebla	1,055
León	872
Ciudad Juárez	798
Tijuana	743
Culiacán Rosales	602
Mexicali	602
Moldova	
Chişinău	700
Mongolia	
Ulan Bator	627
Morocco	
Casablanca	3,079
Rabat-Salé	1,344
Fès	735
Marrakesh	621
Mozambique	
Maputo	2,000
Netherlands	
Amsterdam	1,101
Rotterdam	1,076
The Hague	694
New Zealand	
Auckland	997
Nicaragua	
Managua	864
Nigeria	
Lagos	10,287
Ibadan	1,365
Ogbomosho	712
Kano	657
Norway	
Oslo	714
Pakistan	
Karachi	9,863
Lahore	5,085
Faisalabad	1,875
Peshawar	1,676
Gujranwala	1,663
Rawalpindi	1,290
Multan	1,257
Hyderabad	1,107
Paraguay	
Asunción	945
Peru	
Lima–Callao	6,601
Callao	638
Arequipa	620
Philippines	
Manila	9,280
Quezon City	1,989
Davao	1,191
Caloocan	1,023
Cebu	662
Poland	
Warsaw	1,638
Lódz	825
Kraków	745
Wroclaw	642
Portugal	
Lisbon	2,561
Oporto	1,174
Romania	
Bucharest	2,060
Russia	
Moscow	9,233
St Petersburg	4,883
Nizhniy Novgorod	1,425
Novosibirsk	1,400
Yekaterinburg	1,300
Samara	1,200
Omsk	1,200
Chelyabinsk	1,100
Kazan	1,100
Ufa	1,100
Volgograd	1,003
Perm	1,000
Rostov	1,000
Voronezh	908
Saratov	895
Krasnoyarsk	869
Togliatti	689
Simbirsk	678
Izhevsk	654
Krasnodar	645
Vladivostok	632
Yaroslavl	629
Khabarovsk	618
Saudi Arabia	
Riyadh	1,800
Jedda	1,500
Mecca	630
Senegal	
Dakar	1,571
Singapore	
Singapore	3,104
Somalia	
Mogadishu	1,000
South Africa	
Cape Town	2,350
East Rand	1,379
Johannesburg	1,196
Durban	1,137
Pretoria	1,080
West Rand	870
Port Elizabeth	853
Vanderbijlpark–Vereeniging	774
Spain	
Madrid	3,029
Barcelona	1,614
Valencia	763
Sevilla	719
Zaragoza	607
Sri Lanka	
Colombo	1,863
Sudan	
Nyala	1,267
Khartoum	925
Sharg el Nil	879
Sweden	
Stockholm	1,744
Göteburg	775
Switzerland	
Zürich	1,175
Bern	942
Syria	
Aleppo	1,591
Damascus	1,549
Homs	644
Taiwan	
Taipei	2,653
Kaohsiung	1,405
Taichung	817
Tainan	700
Tanzania	
Dar-es-Salaam	1,361
Thailand	
Bangkok	5,572
Togo	
Lomé	590
Tunisia	
Tunis	1,827
Turkey	
Istanbul	7,490
Ankara	3,028
Izmir	2,333
Adana	1,472
Bursa	1,317
Konya	1,040
Gaziantep	930
Icel	908
Antalya	734
Diyarbakir	677
Kocaeli	661
Urfa	649
Kayseri	648
Manisa	641
Uganda	
Kampala	773
Ukraine	
Kiev	2,630
Kharkiv	1,555
Dnipropetrovsk	1,147
Donetsk	1,088
Odesa	1,046
Zaporizhzhya	887
Lviv	802
Kryvyy Rih	720
United Kingdom	
London	8,089
Birmingham	2,373
Manchester	2,353
Liverpool	852
Glasgow	832
Sheffield	661
Nottingham	649
Newcastle	617
United States	
New York	16,329
Los Angeles	12,410
Chicago	7,668
Philadelphia	4,949
Washington, DC	4,466
Detroit	4,307
Houston	3,653
Atlanta	3,331
Boston	3,240
Dallas	2,898
Minneapolis–St Paul	2,688
San Diego	2,632
St Louis	2,536
Phoenix	2,473
Baltimore	2,458
Pittsburgh	2,402
Cleveland	2,222
San Francisco	2,182
Seattle	2,180
Tampa	2,157
Miami	2,025
Newark	1,934
Denver	1,796
Portland (Or.)	1,676
Kansas City (Mo.)	1,647
Cincinnati	1,581
San Jose	1,557
Norfolk	1,529
Indianapolis	1,462
Milwaukee	1,456
Sacramento	1,441
San Antonio	1,437
Columbus (Oh.)	1,423
New Orleans	1,309
Charlotte	1,260
Buffalo	1,189
Salt Lake City	1,178
Hartford	1,151
Oklahoma	1,007
Jacksonville (Fl.)	665
Omaha	663
Memphis	614
Uruguay	
Montevideo	1,378
Uzbekistan	
Tashkent	2,107
Venezuela	
Caracas	2,784
Maracaibo	1,364
Valencia	1,032
Maracay	800
Barquisimeto	745
Vietnam	
Ho Chi Minh City	4,322
Hanoi	3,056
Haiphong	783
Yemen	
Sana	972
Yugoslavia	
Belgrade	1,137
Zambia	
Lusaka	982
Zimbabwe	
Harare	1,189
Bulawayo	622

* SAR = Special Administrative Region of China

World Statistics – Physical

Under each subject heading, the statistics are listed by continent. The figures are in size order beginning with the largest, longest or deepest, and are rounded as appropriate. Both metric and imperial measurements are given. The lists are complete down to the > mark; below this mark they are selective.

Land and Water

	km²	miles²	%
The World	509,450,000	196,672,000	–
Land	149,450,000	57,688,000	29.3
Water	360,000,000	138,984,000	70.7
Asia	44,500,000	17,177,000	29.8
Africa	30,302,000	11,697,000	20.3
North America	24,241,000	9,357,000	16.2
South America	17,793,000	6,868,000	11.9
Antarctica	14,100,000	5,443,000	9.4
Europe	9,957,000	3,843,000	6.7
Australia & Oceania	8,557,000	3,303,000	5.7
Pacific Ocean	179,679,000	69,356,000	49.9
Atlantic Ocean	92,373,000	35,657,000	25.7
Indian Ocean	73,917,000	28,532,000	20.5
Arctic Ocean	14,090,000	5,439,000	3.9

Seas

Pacific Ocean	km²	miles²
South China Sea	2,974,600	1,148,500
Bering Sea	2,268,000	875,000
Sea of Okhotsk	1,528,000	590,000
East China & Yellow	1,249,000	482,000
Sea of Japan	1,008,000	389,000
Gulf of California	162,000	62,500
Bass Strait	75,000	29,000

Atlantic Ocean	km²	miles²
Caribbean Sea	2,766,000	1,068,000
Mediterranean Sea	2,516,000	971,000
Gulf of Mexico	1,543,000	596,000
Hudson Bay	1,232,000	476,000
North Sea	575,000	223,000
Black Sea	462,000	178,000
Baltic Sea	422,170	163,000
Gulf of St Lawrence	238,000	92,000

Indian Ocean	km²	miles²
Red Sea	438,000	169,000
The Gulf	239,000	92,000

Mountains

Europe		m	ft
Elbrus	Russia	5,642	18,510
Mont Blanc	France/Italy	4,807	15,771
Monte Rosa	Italy/Switzerland	4,634	15,203
Dom	Switzerland	4,545	14,911
Liskamm	Switzerland	4,527	14,852
Weisshorn	Switzerland	4,505	14,780
Taschorn	Switzerland	4,490	14,730
Matterhorn/Cervino	Italy/Switzerland	4,478	14,691
Mont Maudit	France/Italy	4,465	14,649
Dent Blanche	Switzerland	4,356	14,291
> Nadelhorn	Switzerland	4,327	14,196
Grandes Jorasses	France/Italy	4,208	13,806
Jungfrau	Switzerland	4,158	13,642
Barre des Ecrins	France	4,103	13,461
Gran Paradiso	Italy	4,061	13,323
Piz Bernina	Italy/Switzerland	4,049	13,284

Europe (cont.)		m	ft
Eiger	Switzerland	3,970	13,025
Monte Viso	Italy	3,841	12,602
Grossglockner	Austria	3,797	12,457
Wildspitze	Austria	3,772	12,382
Monte Disgrazia	Italy	3,678	12,066
Mulhacén	Spain	3,478	11,411
Pico de Aneto	Spain	3,404	11,168
Marmolada	Italy	3,342	10,964
Etna	Italy	3,340	10,958
Zugspitze	Germany	2,962	9,718
Musala	Bulgaria	2,925	9,596
Olympus	Greece	2,917	9,570
Triglav	Slovenia	2,863	9,393
Monte Cinto	France (Corsica)	2,710	8,891
Gerlachovka	Slovak Republic	2,655	8,711
Torre de Cerrado	Spain	2,648	8,688
Galdhöpiggen	Norway	2,468	8,100
Hvannadalshnúkur	Iceland	2,119	6,952
Kebnekaise	Sweden	2,117	6,946
Ben Nevis	UK	1,343	4,406

Asia		m	ft
Everest	China/Nepal	8,848	29,029
K2 (Godwin Austen)	China/Kashmir	8,611	28,251
Kanchenjunga	India/Nepal	8,598	28,208
Lhotse	China/Nepal	8,516	27,939
Makalu	China/Nepal	8,481	27,824
Cho Oyu	China/Nepal	8,201	26,906
Dhaulagiri	Nepal	8,172	26,811
Manaslu	Nepal	8,156	26,758
Nanga Parbat	Kashmir	8,126	26,660
Annapurna	Nepal	8,078	26,502
Gasherbrum	China/Kashmir	8,068	26,469
Broad Peak	China/Kashmir	8,051	26,414
Xixabangma	China	8,012	26,286
Kangbachen	India/Nepal	7,902	25,925
Jannu	India/Nepal	7,902	25,925
Gayachung Kang	Nepal	7,897	25,909
Himalchuli	Nepal	7,893	25,896
Disteghil Sar	Kashmir	7,885	25,869
Nuptse	Nepal	7,879	25,849
Khunyang Chhish	Kashmir	7,852	25,761
Masherbrum	Kashmir	7,821	25,659
Nanda Devi	India	7,817	25,646
Rakaposhi	Kashmir	7,788	25,551
Batura	Kashmir	7,785	25,541
Namche Barwa	China	7,756	25,446
Kamet	India	7,756	25,446
Soltoro Kangri	Kashmir	7,742	25,400
Gurla Mandhata	China	7,728	25,354
Trivor	Pakistan	7,720	25,328
> Kongur Shan	China	7,719	25,324
Tirich Mir	Pakistan	7,690	25,229
K'ula Shan	Bhutan/China	7,543	24,747
Pik Kommunizma	Tajikistan	7,495	24,590
Demavend	Iran	5,604	18,386
Ararat	Turkey	5,165	16,945
Gunong Kinabalu	Malaysia (Borneo)	4,101	13,455
Yu Shan	Taiwan	3,997	13,113
Fuji-San	Japan	3,776	12,388

Africa		m	ft
Kilimanjaro	Tanzania	5,895	19,340
Mt Kenya	Kenya	5,199	17,057
Ruwenzori	Uganda/Congo (Zaïre)	5,109	16,762
Ras Dashan	Ethiopia	4,620	15,157

Africa (cont.)		m	ft
Meru	Tanzania	4,565	14,977
Karisimbi	Rwanda/Congo (Zaïre)	4,507	14,787
Mt Elgon	Kenya/Uganda	4,321	14,176
Batu	Ethiopia	4,307	14,130
Guna	Ethiopia	4,231	13,882
Toubkal	Morocco	4,165	13,665
Irhil Mgoun	Morocco	4,071	13,356
Mt Cameroon	Cameroon	4,070	13,353
Amba Ferit	Ethiopia	3,875	13,042
Pico del Teide	Spain (Tenerife)	3,718	12,198
Thabana Ntlenyana	Lesotho	3,482	11,424
Emi Koussi	Chad	3,415	11,204
Mt aux Sources	Lesotho/South Africa	3,282	10,768
Mt Piton	Réunion	3,069	10,069

Oceania		m	ft
Puncak Jaya	Indonesia	5,029	16,499
Puncak Trikora	Indonesia	4,750	15,584
Puncak Mandala	Indonesia	4,702	15,427
Mt Wilhelm	Papua New Guinea	4,508	14,790
Mauna Kea	USA (Hawaii)	4,205	13,796
Mauna Loa	USA (Hawaii)	4,170	13,681
Mt Cook (Aoraki)	New Zealand	3,753	12,313
Mt Balbi	Solomon Is.	2,439	8,002
Orohena	Tahiti	2,241	7,352
Mt Kosciuszko	Australia	2,237	7,339

North America		m	ft
Mt McKinley (Denali)	USA (Alaska)	6,194	20,321
Mt Logan	Canada	5,959	19,551
Citlaltepetl	Mexico	5,700	18,701
Mt St Elias	USA/Canada	5,489	18,008
Popocatepetl	Mexico	5,452	17,887
Mt Foraker	USA (Alaska)	5,304	17,401
Ixtaccihuatl	Mexico	5,286	17,342
Lucania	Canada	5,227	17,149
Mt Steele	Canada	5,073	16,644
Mt Bona	USA (Alaska)	5,005	16,420
Mt Blackburn	USA (Alaska)	4,996	16,391
Mt Sanford	USA (Alaska)	4,940	16,207
Mt Wood	Canada	4,848	15,905
Nevado de Toluca	Mexico	4,670	15,321
Mt Fairweather	USA (Alaska)	4,663	15,298
Mt Hunter	USA (Alaska)	4,442	14,573
Mt Whitney	USA	4,418	14,495
Mt Elbert	USA	4,399	14,432
Mt Harvard	USA	4,395	14,419
Mt Rainier	USA	4,392	14,409
Blanca Peak	USA	4,372	14,344
Longs Peak	USA	4,345	14,255
Tajumulco	Guatemala	4,220	13,845
Grand Teton	USA	4,197	13,770
Mt Waddington	Canada	3,994	13,104
Mt Robson	Canada	3,954	12,972
Chirripó Grande	Costa Rica	3,837	12,589
Mt Assiniboine	Canada	3,619	11,873
Pico Duarte	Dominican Rep.	3,175	10,417

South America		m	ft
Aconcagua	Argentina	6,960	22,834
Bonete	Argentina	6,872	22,546
Ojos del Salado	Argentina/Chile	6,863	22,516
Pissis	Argentina	6,779	22,241
Mercedario	Argentina/Chile	6,770	22,211
Huascaran	Peru	6,768	22,204
Llullaillaco	Argentina/Chile	6,723	22,057
Nudo de Cachi	Argentina	6,720	22,047
Yerupaja	Peru	6,632	21,758
N. de Tres Cruces	Argentina/Chile	6,620	21,719
Incahuasi	Argentina/Chile	6,601	21,654
Cerro Galan	Argentina	6,600	21,654
Tupungato	Argentina/Chile	6,570	21,555

South America (cont.)		m	ft
Sajama	Bolivia	6,542	21,463
Illimani	Bolivia	6,485	21,276
Coropuna	Peru	6,425	21,079
Ausangate	Peru	6,384	20,945
Cerro del Toro	Argentina	6,380	20,932
Siula Grande	Peru	6,356	20,853
Chimborazo	Ecuador	6,267	20,561
Cotapaxi	Ecuador	5,896	19,344
Pico Colon	Colombia	5,800	19,029
Pico Bolivar	Venezuela	5,007	16,427

Antarctica	m	ft
Vinson Massif	4,897	16,066
Mt Kirkpatrick	4,528	14,855
Mt Markham	4,349	14,268

Ocean Depths

Atlantic Ocean	m	ft
Puerto Rico (Milwaukee) Deep	9,220	30,249
Cayman Trench	7,680	25,197
Gulf of Mexico	5,203	17,070
Mediterranean Sea	5,121	16,801
Black Sea	2,211	7,254
North Sea	660	2,165
Baltic Sea	463	1,519

Indian Ocean	m	ft
Java Trench	7,450	24,442
Red Sea	2,635	8,454
Persian Gulf	73	239

Pacific Ocean	m	ft
Mariana Trench	11,022	36,161
Tonga Trench	10,882	35,702
Japan Trench	10,554	34,626
Kuril Trench	10,542	34,587
Mindanao Trench	10,497	34,439
Kermadec Trench	10,047	32,962
New Guinea Trench	9,140	29,987
Peru–Chile Trench	8,050	26,410

Antarctica	m	ft
Molloy Deep	5,608	18,399

Land Lows

		m	ft
Dead Sea	Asia	–403	–1,322
Lake Assal	Africa	–156	–512
Death Valley	North America	–86	–282
Valdés Peninsula	South America	–40	–131
Caspian Sea	Europe	–28	–92
Lake Eyre North	Oceania	–16	–52

Rivers

Europe		km	miles
Volga	Caspian Sea	3,700	2,300
Danube	Black Sea	2,850	1,770
Ural	Caspian Sea	2,535	1,575
Dnepr (Dnipro)	Black Sea	2,285	1,420
Kama	Volga	2,030	1,260
Don	Black Sea	1,990	1,240
Petchora	Arctic Ocean	1,790	1,110
Oka	Volga	1,480	920
Belaya	Kama	1,420	880

Europe (cont.)		km	miles
Dnister (Dniester)	Black Sea	1,400	870
Vyatka	Kama	1,370	850
Rhine	North Sea	1,320	820
North Dvina	Arctic Ocean	1,290	800
Desna	Dnepr (Dnipro)	1,190	740
Elbe	North Sea	1,145	710
Wisla	Baltic Sea	1,090	675
Loire	Atlantic Ocean	1,020	635
West Dvina	Baltic Sea	1,019	633

Asia		km	miles
Yangtze	Pacific Ocean	6,380	3,960
Yenisey–Angara	Arctic Ocean	5,550	3,445
Huang He	Pacific Ocean	5,464	3,395
Ob–Irtysh	Arctic Ocean	5,410	3,360
Mekong	Pacific Ocean	4,500	2,795
Amur	Pacific Ocean	4,400	2,730
Lena	Arctic Ocean	4,400	2,730
Irtysh	Ob	4,250	2,640
Yenisey	Arctic Ocean	4,090	2,540
Ob	Arctic Ocean	3,680	2,285
Indus	Indian Ocean	3,100	1,925
Brahmaputra	Indian Ocean	2,900	1,800
Syrdarya	Aral Sea	2,860	1,775
Salween	Indian Ocean	2,800	1,740
Euphrates	Indian Ocean	2,700	1,675
Vilyuy	Lena	2,650	1,645
Kolyma	Arctic Ocean	2,600	1,615
Amudarya	Aral Sea	2,540	1,575
Ural	Caspian Sea	2,535	1,575
Ganges	Indian Ocean	2,510	1,560
Si Kiang	Pacific Ocean	2,100	1,305
Irrawaddy	Indian Ocean	2,010	1,250
Tarim–Yarkand	Lop Nor	2,000	1,240
Tigris	Indian Ocean	1,900	1,180
Angara	Yenisey	1,830	1,135
Godavari	Indian Ocean	1,470	915
Sutlej	Indian Ocean	1,450	900
Yamuna	Indian Ocean	1,400	870

Africa		km	miles
Nile	Mediterranean	6,670	4,140
Congo	Atlantic Ocean	4,670	2,900
Niger	Atlantic Ocean	4,180	2,595
Zambezi	Indian Ocean	3,540	2,200
Oubangi/Uele	Congo (Zaïre)	2,250	1,400
Kasai	Congo (Zaïre)	1,950	1,210
Shaballe	Indian Ocean	1,930	1,200
Orange	Atlantic Ocean	1,860	1,155
Cubango	Okavango Swamps	1,800	1,120
Limpopo	Indian Ocean	1,600	995
Senegal	Atlantic Ocean	1,600	995
Volta	Atlantic Ocean	1,500	930
Benue	Niger	1,350	840

Australia		km	miles
Murray–Darling	Indian Ocean	3,750	2,330
Darling	Murray	3,070	1,905
Murray	Indian Ocean	2,575	1,600
Murrumbidgee	Murray	1,690	1,050

North America		km	miles
Mississippi–Missouri	Gulf of Mexico	6,020	3,740
Mackenzie	Arctic Ocean	4,240	2,630
Mississippi	Gulf of Mexico	3,780	2,350
Missouri	Mississippi	3,780	2,350
Yukon	Pacific Ocean	3,185	1,980
Rio Grande	Gulf of Mexico	3,030	1,880
Arkansas	Mississippi	2,340	1,450
Colorado	Pacific Ocean	2,330	1,445
Red	Mississippi	2,040	1,270

North America (cont.)		km	miles
Saskatchewan	Lake Winnipeg	1,940	1,205
Snake	Columbia	1,670	1,040
Churchill	Hudson Bay	1,600	990
Ohio	Mississippi	1,580	980
Brazos	Gulf of Mexico	1,400	870
St Lawrence	Atlantic Ocean	1,170	730

South America		km	miles
Amazon	Atlantic Ocean	6,450	4,010
Paraná–Plate	Atlantic Ocean	4,500	2,800
Purus	Amazon	3,350	2,080
Madeira	Amazon	3,200	1,990
São Francisco	Atlantic Ocean	2,900	1,800
Paraná	Plate	2,800	1,740
Tocantins	Atlantic Ocean	2,750	1,710
Paraguay	Paraná	2,550	1,580
Orinoco	Atlantic Ocean	2,500	1,550
Pilcomayo	Paraná	2,500	1,550
Araguaia	Tocantins	2,250	1,400
Juruá	Amazon	2,000	1,240
Xingu	Amazon	1,980	1,230
Ucayali	Amazon	1,900	1,180
Maranón	Amazon	1,600	990
Uruguay	Plate	1,600	990
Magdalena	Caribbean Sea	1,540	960

Lakes

Europe		km²	miles²
Lake Ladoga	Russia	17,700	6,800
Lake Onega	Russia	9,700	3,700
Saimaa system	Finland	8,000	3,100
Vänern	Sweden	5,500	2,100
Rybinskoye Reservoir	Russia	4,700	1,800

Asia		km²	miles²
Caspian Sea	Asia	371,800	143,550
Lake Baykal	Russia	30,500	11,780
Aral Sea	Kazak./Uzbek.	28,687	11,086
Tonlé Sap	Cambodia	20,000	7,700
Lake Balqash	Kazakstan	18,500	7,100
Lake Dongting	China	12,000	4,600
Lake Ysyk	Kyrgyzstan	6,200	2,400
Lake Orumiyeh	Iran	5,900	2,300
Lake Koko	China	5,700	2,200
Lake Poyang	China	5,000	1,900
Lake Khanka	China/Russia	4,400	1,700
Lake Van	Turkey	3,500	1,400
Lake Ubsa	China	3,400	1,300

Africa		km²	miles²
Lake Victoria	East Africa	68,000	26,000
Lake Tanganyika	Central Africa	33,000	13,000
Lake Malawi/Nyasa	East Africa	29,600	11,430
Lake Chad	Central Africa	25,000	9,700
Lake Turkana	Ethiopia/Kenya	8,500	3,300
Lake Volta	Ghana	8,500	3,300
Lake Bangweulu	Zambia	8,000	3,100
Lake Rukwa	Tanzania	7,000	2,700
Lake Mai-Ndombe	Congo (Zaïre)	6,500	2,500
Lake Kariba	Zambia/Zimbabwe	5,300	2,000
Lake Mobutu	Uganda/Congo (Zaïre)	5,300	2,000
Lake Nasser	Egypt/Sudan	5,200	2,000
Lake Mweru	Zambia/Congo (Zaïre)	4,900	1,900
Lake Cabora Bassa	Mozambique	4,500	1,700
Lake Kyoga	Uganda	4,400	1,700
Lake Tana	Ethiopia	3,630	1,400
Lake Kivu	Rwanda/Congo (Zaïre)	2,650	1,000
Lake Edward	Uganda/Congo (Zaïre)	2,200	850

Australia		km^2	$miles^2$
Lake Eyre	Australia	8,900	3,400
Lake Torrens	Australia	5,800	2,200
Lake Gairdner	Australia	4,800	1,900

North America		km^2	$miles^2$
Lake Superior	Canada/USA	82,350	31,800
Lake Huron	Canada/USA	59,600	23,010
Lake Michigan	USA	58,000	22,400
Great Bear Lake	Canada	31,800	12,280
Great Slave Lake	Canada	28,500	11,000
Lake Erie	Canada/USA	25,700	9,900
Lake Winnipeg	Canada	24,400	9,400
Lake Ontario	Canada/USA	19,500	7,500
Lake Nicaragua	Nicaragua	8,200	3,200
Lake Athabasca	Canada	8,100	3,100
Smallwood Reservoir	Canada	6,530	2,520
Reindeer Lake	Canada	6,400	2,500
Nettilling Lake	Canada	5,500	2,100
Lake Winnipegosis	Canada	5,400	2,100
Lake Nipigon	Canada	4,850	1,900
Lake Manitoba	Canada	4,700	1,800

South America		km^2	$miles^2$
Lake Titicaca	Bolivia/Peru	8,300	3,200
Lake Poopo	Peru	2,800	1,100

Islands

Europe		km^2	$miles^2$
Great Britain	UK	229,880	88,700
Iceland	Atlantic Ocean	103,000	39,800
Ireland	Ireland/UK	84,400	32,600
Novaya Zemlya (North)	Russia	48,200	18,600
West Spitzbergen	Norway	39,000	15,100
Novaya Zemlya (South)	Russia	33,200	12,800
Sicily	Italy	25,500	9,800
Sardinia	Italy	24,000	9,300
North-east Spitzbergen	Norway	15,000	5,600
Corsica	France	8,700	3,400
Crete	Greece	8,350	3,200
Zealand	Denmark	6,850	2,600

Asia		km^2	$miles^2$
Borneo	South-east Asia	744,360	287,400
Sumatra	Indonesia	473,600	182,860
Honshu	Japan	230,500	88,980
Sulawesi (Celebes)	Indonesia	189,000	73,000
Java	Indonesia	126,700	48,900
Luzon	Philippines	104,700	40,400
Mindanao	Philippines	101,500	39,200
Hokkaido	Japan	78,400	30,300
Sakhalin	Russia	74,060	28,600
Sri Lanka	Indian Ocean	65,600	25,300
Taiwan	Pacific Ocean	36,000	13,900
Kyushu	Japan	35,700	13,800
Hainan	China	34,000	13,100
Timor	Indonesia	33,600	13,000
Shikoku	Japan	18,800	7,300
Halmahera	Indonesia	18,000	6,900
Ceram	Indonesia	17,150	6,600
Sumbawa	Indonesia	15,450	6,000
Flores	Indonesia	15,200	5,900
Samar	Philippines	13,100	5,100
Negros	Philippines	12,700	4,900
Bangka	Indonesia	12,000	4,600
Palawan	Philippines	12,000	4,600
Panay	Philippines	11,500	4,400
Sumba	Indonesia	11,100	4,300
Mindoro	Philippines	9,750	3,800

Asia (cont.)		km^2	$miles^2$
Buru	Indonesia	9,500	3,700
Bali	Indonesia	5,600	2,200
Cyprus	Mediterranean	3,570	1,400

Africa		km^2	$miles^2$
Madagascar	Indian Ocean	587,040	226,660
Socotra	Indian Ocean	3,600	1,400
Réunion	Indian Ocean	2,500	965
Tenerife	Atlantic Ocean	2,350	900
Mauritius	Indian Ocean	1,865	720

Oceania		km^2	$miles^2$
New Guinea	Indon./Papua NG	821,030	317,000
New Zealand (South)	New Zealand	150,500	58,100
New Zealand (North)	New Zealand	114,700	44,300
Tasmania	Australia	67,800	26,200
New Britain	Papua NG	37,800	14,600
New Caledonia	Pacific Ocean	19,100	7,400
Viti Levu	Fiji	10,500	4,100
Hawaii	Pacific Ocean	10,450	4,000
Bougainville	Papua NG	9,600	3,700
Guadalcanal	Solomon Is.	6,500	2,500
Vanua Levu	Fiji	5,550	2,100
New Ireland	Papua NG	3,200	1,200

North America		km^2	$miles^2$
Greenland	Greenland	2,175,600	839,800
Baffin Is.	Canada	508,000	196,100
Victoria Is.	Canada	212,200	81,900
Ellesmere Is.	Canada	212,000	81,800
Cuba	Cuba	110,860	42,800
Newfoundland	Canada	110,680	42,700
Hispaniola	Atlantic Ocean	76,200	29,400
Banks Is.	Canada	67,000	25,900
Devon Is.	Canada	54,500	21,000
Melville Is.	Canada	42,400	16,400
Vancouver Is.	Canada	32,150	12,400
Somerset Is.	Canada	24,300	9,400
Jamaica	Caribbean Sea	11,400	4,400
Puerto Rico	Atlantic Ocean	8,900	3,400
Cape Breton Is.	Canada	4,000	1,500

South America		km^2	$miles^2$
Tierra del Fuego	Argentina/Chile	47,000	18,100
Falkland Is. (East)	Atlantic Ocean	6,800	2,600
South Georgia	Atlantic Ocean	4,200	1,600
Galapagos (Isabela)	Pacific Ocean	2,250	870

World Statistics – Climate

For each city, the top row of figures shows total rainfall in millimetres; the bottom row shows the average temperature in ° Celsius or centigrade. The total annual rainfall and average annual temperature are given at the end of the rows.

	Jan.	*Feb.*	*Mar.*	*Apr.*	*May*	*June*	*July*	*Aug.*	*Sept.*	*Oct.*	*Nov.*	*Dec.*	*Total*
Europe													
Berlin, Germany	46	40	33	42	49	65	73	69	68	49	46	43	603
Altitude 55 metres	1	0	4	9	14	17	19	18	15	9	5	1	9
London, UK	54	40	37	37	46	45	57	59	49	57	64	48	593
5 m	4	5	7	9	12	16	18	17	15	11	8	5	11
Málaga, Spain	61	51	62	46	26	5	1	3	29	64	64	62	474
33 m	12	13	16	17	19	29	25	26	23	20	16	13	18
Moscow, Russia	39	38	36	37	53	58	88	71	58	45	47	54	624
156 m	13	–10	–4	6	13	16	18	17	12	6	–1	–7	4
Paris, France	56	46	35	42	57	54	59	64	55	50	51	50	619
75 m	3	4	8	11	15	18	20	19	17	12	7	4	12
Rome, Italy	71	62	57	51	46	37	15	21	63	99	129	93	744
17 m	8	9	11	14	18	22	25	25	22	17	13	10	16
Asia													
Bangkok, Thailand	8	20	36	58	198	160	160	175	305	206	66	5	1,397
2 m	26	28	29	30	29	29	28	28	28	28	26	25	28
Bombay (Mumbai), India	3	3	3	<3	18	485	617	340	264	64	13	3	1,809
11 m	24	24	26	28	30	29	27	27	27	28	27	26	27
Ho Chi Minh, Vietnam	15	3	13	43	221	330	315	269	335	269	114	56	1,984
9 m	26	27	29	30	29	28	28	28	27	27	27	26	28
Hong Kong, China	33	46	74	137	292	394	381	361	257	114	43	31	2,162
33 m	16	15	18	22	26	28	28	28	27	25	21	18	23
Tokyo, Japan	48	74	107	135	147	165	142	152	234	208	97	56	1,565
6 m	3	4	7	13	17	21	25	26	23	17	11	6	14
Africa													
Cairo, Egypt	5	5	5	3	3	<3	0	0	<3	<3	3	5	28
116 m	13	15	18	21	25	28	28	28	26	24	20	15	22
Cape Town, South Africa	15	8	18	48	79	84	89	66	43	31	18	10	508
17 m	21	21	20	17	14	13	12	13	14	16	18	19	17
Lagos, Nigeria	28	46	102	150	269	460	279	64	140	206	69	25	1,836
3 m	27	28	29	28	28	26	26	25	26	26	28	28	27
Nairobi, Kenya	38	64	125	211	158	46	15	23	31	53	109	86	958
1,820 m	19	19	19	19	18	16	16	16	18	19	18	18	18
Australia, New Zealand & Antarctica													
Christchurch, New Zealand	56	43	48	48	66	66	69	48	46	43	48	56	638
10 m	16	16	14	12	9	6	6	7	9	12	14	16	11
Darwin, Australia	386	312	254	97	15	3	<3	3	13	51	119	239	1,491
30 m	29	29	29	29	28	26	25	26	28	29	30	29	28
Mawson, Antarctica	11	30	20	10	44	180	4	40	3	20	0	0	362
14 m	0	–5	–10	–14	–15	–16	–18	–18	–19	–13	–5	–1	–11
Sydney, Australia	89	102	127	135	127	117	117	76	73	71	73	73	1,181
42 m	22	22	21	18	15	13	12	13	15	18	19	21	17
North America													
Anchorage, Alaska, USA	20	18	15	10	13	18	41	66	66	56	25	23	371
40 m	–11	–8	–5	2	7	12	14	13	9	2	–5	–11	2
Kingston, Jamaica	23	15	23	31	102	89	38	91	99	180	74	36	800
34 m	25	25	25	26	26	28	28	28	27	27	26	26	26
Los Angeles, USA	79	76	71	25	10	3	<3	<3	5	15	31	66	381
95 m	13	14	14	16	17	19	21	22	21	18	16	14	17
Mexico City, Mexico	13	5	10	20	53	119	170	152	130	51	18	8	747
2,309 m	12	13	16	18	19	19	17	18	18	16	14	13	16
New York, USA	94	97	91	81	81	84	107	109	86	89	76	91	1,092
96 m	–1	–1	3	10	16	20	23	23	21	15	7	2	11
Vancouver, Canada	154	115	101	60	52	45	32	41	67	114	150	182	1,113
14 m	3	5	6	9	12	15	17	17	14	10	6	4	10
South America													
Antofagasta, Chile	0	0	0	<3	<3	3	5	3	<3	3	<3	0	13
94 m	21	21	20	18	16	15	14	14	15	16	18	19	17
Buenos Aires, Argentina	79	71	109	89	76	61	56	61	79	86	84	99	950
27 m	23	23	21	17	13	9	10	11	13	15	19	22	16
Lima, Peru	3	<3	<3	<3	5	5	8	8	8	3	3	<3	41
120 m	23	24	24	22	19	17	17	16	17	18	19	21	20
Rio de Janeiro, Brazil	125	122	130	107	79	53	41	43	66	79	104	137	1,082
61 m	26	26	25	24	22	21	21	21	21	22	23	25	23

The Earth in Focus

> Landsat image of the San Francisco Bay area. The narrow entrance to the bay (crossed by the Golden Gate Bridge) provides an excellent natural harbour. The San Andreas Fault runs parallel to the coastline.

The Universe & Solar System

BETWEEN 10 AND 20 billion (or 10,000 to 20,000 million) years ago, the Universe was created in a huge explosion known as the 'Big Bang'. In the first 10^{-24} of a second the Universe expanded rapidly and the basic forces of nature, radiation and subatomic particles, came into being. The Universe has been expanding ever since. Traces of the original 'fireball' of radiation can still be detected, and most scientists accept the Big Bang theory of the origin of the Universe.

The Nearest Stars ▾

The 20 nearest stars, excluding the Sun, with their distance from Earth in light-years.*

Proxima Centauri	4.25
Alpha Centauri A	4.3
Alpha Centauri B	4.3
Barnard's Star	6.0
Wolf 359	7.8
Lalande 21185	8.3
Sirius A	8.7
Sirius B	8.7
UV Ceti A	8.7
UV Ceti B	8.7
Ross 154	9.4
Ross 248	10.3
Epsilon Eridani	10.7
Ross 128	10.9
61 Cygni A	11.1
61 Cygni B	11.1
Epsilon Indi	11.2
Groombridge 34 A	11.2
Groombridge 34 B	11.2
L789-6	11.2

** A light-year equals approximately 9,500 billion km [5,900 billion miles].*

> The Lagoon Nebula is a huge cloud of dust and gas. Hot stars inside the nebula make the gas glow red.

GALAXIES

Almost a million years passed before the Universe cooled sufficiently for atoms to form. When a billion years had passed, the atoms had begun to form protogalaxies, which are masses of gas separated by empty space. Stars began to form within the protogalaxies, as particles were drawn together, producing the high temperatures necessary to bring about nuclear fusion. The formation of the first stars brought about the evolution of the protogalaxies into galaxies proper, each containing billions of stars.

Our Sun is a medium-sized star. It is

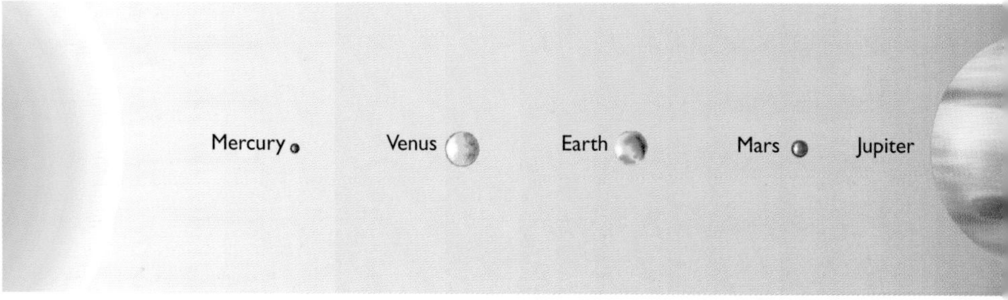
Mercury
Venus
Earth
Mars
Jupiter

PLANETARY DATA

	Mean distance from Sun *(million km)*	Mass *(Earth = 1)*	Period of orbit *(Earth years)*	Period of rotation *(Earth days)*	Equatorial diameter *(km)*	Escape velocity *(km/sec)*	Number of known satellites
Sun	–	332,946	–	25.38	1,392,000	617.5	–
Mercury	58.3	0.06	0.241	58.67	4,878	4.27	0
Venus	107.7	0.8	0.615	243.0	12,104	10.36	0
Earth	149.6	1.0	1.00	0.99	12,756	11.18	1
Mars	227.3	0.1	1.88	1.02	6,787	5.03	2
Jupiter	777.9	317.8	11.86	0.41	142,800	59.60	16
Saturn	1,427.1	95.2	29.46	0.42	120,000	35.50	20
Uranus	2,872.3	14.5	84.01	0.45	51,118	21.30	15
Neptune	4,502.7	17.2	164.79	0.67	49,528	23.3	8
Pluto	5,894.2	0.002	248.54	6.38	2,300	1.1	1

one of the billions of stars that make up the Milky Way galaxy, which is one of the millions of galaxies in the Universe.

THE SOLAR SYSTEM

The Solar System lies towards the edge of the Milky Way galaxy. It consists of the Sun and other bodies, including planets (together with their moons), asteroids, meteoroids, comets, dust and gas, which revolve around it.

The Earth moves through space in three distinct ways. First, with the rest of the Solar System, it moves around the centre of the Milky Way galaxy in an orbit that takes 200 million years.

As the Earth revolves around the Sun once every year, its axis is tilted by about 23.5 degrees. As a result, first the northern and then the southern hemisphere lean towards the Sun at different times of the year, causing the seasons experienced in the mid-latitudes.

The Earth also rotates on its axis every 24 hours, causing day and night. The movements of the Earth in the Solar System determine the calendar. The length of a year – one complete orbit of the Earth around the Sun – is 365 days, 5 hours, 48 minutes and 46 seconds. Leap years prevent the calendar from becoming out of step with the solar year.

> The diagram below shows the planets around the Sun. The sizes of the planets are relative but the distances are not to scale. Closest to the Sun are dense rocky bodies, known as the terrestrial planets. They are Mercury, Venus, Earth and Mars. Jupiter, Saturn, Uranus and Neptune are huge balls of gas. Pluto is a small, icy body.

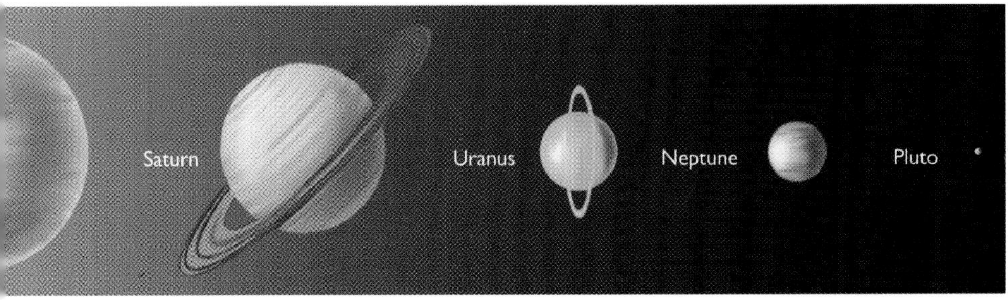
Saturn
Uranus
Neptune
Pluto

The Changing Earth

THE SOLAR SYSTEM was formed around 4.7 billion years ago, when the Sun, a glowing ball of gases, was created from a rotating disk of dust and gas. The planets were then formed from material left over after the creation of the Sun.

After the Earth formed, around 4.6 billion years ago, lighter elements rose to the hot surface, where they finally cooled to form a hard shell, or crust. Denser elements sank, forming the partly liquid mantle, the liquid outer core, and the solid inner core.

> Fold mountains, such as the Himalayan ranges which are shown above, were formed when two plates collided and the rock layers between them were squeezed upwards into loops or folds.

EARTH HISTORY

The oldest known rocks on Earth are around 4 billion years old. Natural processes have destroyed older rocks. Simple life forms first appeared on Earth around 3.5 billion years ago, though rocks formed in the first 4 billion years of Earth history contain little evidence of life. But rocks formed since the start of the Cambrian period (the first period in the Paleozoic era), about 590 million years ago, are rich in fossils. The study of fossils has enabled scientists to gradually piece together the long and complex story of life on Earth.

THE PLANET EARTH

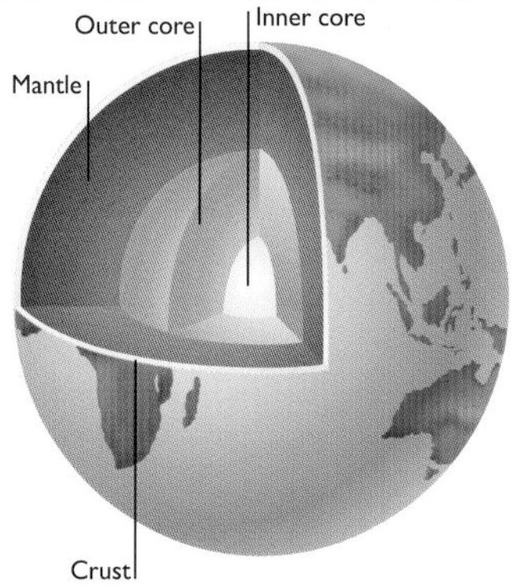

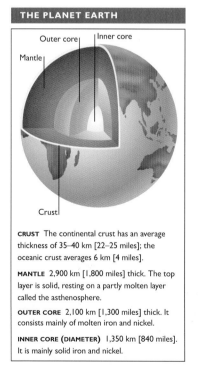

Outer core
Inner core
Mantle
Crust

CRUST The continental crust has an average thickness of 35–40 km [22–25 miles]; the oceanic crust averages 6 km [4 miles].

MANTLE 2,900 km [1,800 miles] thick. The top layer is solid, resting on a partly molten layer called the asthenosphere.

OUTER CORE 2,100 km [1,300 miles] thick. It consists mainly of molten iron and nickel.

INNER CORE (DIAMETER) 1,350 km [840 miles]. It is mainly solid iron and nickel.

ELEMENTS

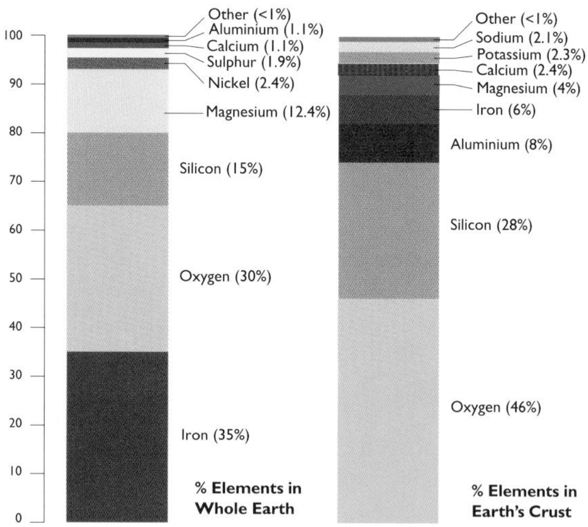

100
90
80
70
60
50
40
30
20
10
0
Other (<1%)
Aluminium (1.1%)
Calcium (1.1%)
Sulphur (1.9%)
Nickel (2.4%)
Magnesium (12.4%)
Silicon (15%)
Oxygen (30%)
Iron (35%)
% Elements in Whole Earth
Other (<1%)
Sodium (2.1%)
Potassium (2.3%)
Calcium (2.4%)
Magnesium (4%)
Iron (6%)
Aluminium (8%)
Silicon (28%)
Oxygen (46%)
% Elements in Earth's Crust

> The Earth contains about 100 elements, but eight of them account for 99% of the planet's mass. Iron makes up 35% of the Earth's mass, but most of it is in the core. The most common elements in the crust – oxygen and silicon – are often combined with one or more of the other common crustal elements, to form a group of minerals called silicates. The mineral quartz, which consists only of silicon and oxygen, occurs widely in such rocks as granites and sandstones.

PLATE BOUNDARIES

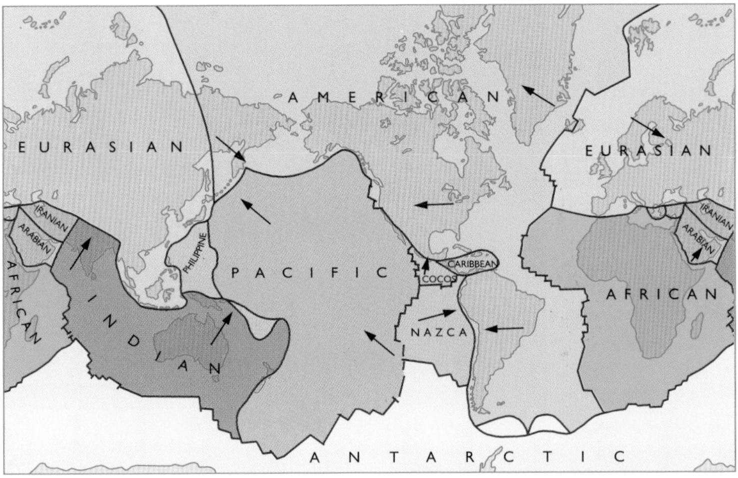

> The Earth's lithosphere is divided into six huge plates and several small ones. Ocean ridges, where plates are moving apart, are called constructive plate margins. Ocean trenches, where plates collide, are subduction zones. These are destructive plate margins. The map shows the main plates and the directions in which they are moving.

Plate boundaries

Direction of plate movements

PACIFIC Major plates

THE DYNAMIC EARTH

The Earth's surface is always changing because of a process called plate tectonics. Plates are blocks of the solid lithosphere (the crust and outer mantle), which are moved around by currents in the partly liquid mantle. Around 250 million years ago, the Earth contained one supercontinent called Pangaea. Around 180 million years ago, Pangaea split into a northern part, Laurasia, and a southern part, Gondwanaland. Later, these huge continents, in turn, also split apart and the continents drifted to their present positions. Ancient seas disappeared and mountain ranges, such as the Himalayas and Alps, were pushed upwards.

PLATE TECTONICS

In the early 1900s, two scientists suggested that the Americas were once joined to Europe and Africa. Together they proposed the theory of continental drift to explain the similarities between rock structures on both sides of the Atlantic. But no one could offer an explanation as to how the continents moved.

Evidence from the ocean floor in the 1950s and 1960s led to the theory of plate tectonics, which suggested that the lithosphere is divided into large blocks, or plates. The plates are solid, but they rest on the partly molten asthenosphere, within the mantle. Long ridges on the ocean floor were found to be the edges of plates which were moving apart, carried by currents in the asthenosphere. As the plates moved, molten material welled up from the mantle to fill the gaps. But at the ocean trenches, one plate is descending beneath another along what is called a subduction zone. The descending plate is melted and destroyed. This crustal destruction at subduction zones balances the creation of new crust along the ridges. Transform faults, where two plates are moving alongside each other, form another kind of plate edge.

GEOLOGICAL TIME SCALE

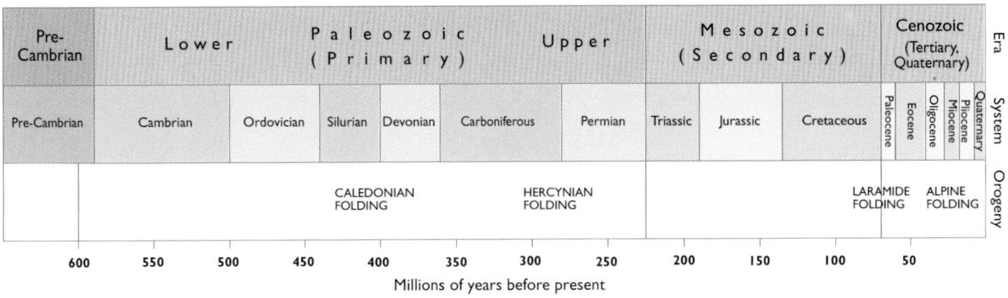

Earthquakes & Volcanoes

PLATE TECTONICS HELP us to understand such phenomena as earthquakes, volcanic eruptions, and mountain building.

EARTHQUAKES

Earthquakes can occur anywhere, but they are most common near the edges of plates. They occur when intense pressure breaks the rocks along plate edges, making the plates lurch forward.

Major Earthquakes since 1900 ▾

Year	Location	Mag.	Deaths
1906	San Francisco, *USA*	8.3	503
1906	Valparaiso, *Chile*	8.6	22,000
1908	Messina, *Italy*	7.5	83,000
1915	Avezzano, *Italy*	7.5	30,000
1920	Gansu, *China*	8.6	180,000
1923	Yokohama, *Japan*	8.3	143,000
1927	Nan Shan, *China*	8.3	200,000
1932	Gansu, *China*	7.6	70,000
1934	Bihar, *India/Nepal*	8.4	10,700
1935	Quetta, *Pakistan*	7.5	60,000
1939	Chillan, *Chile*	8.3	28,000
1939	Erzincan, *Turkey*	7.9	30,000
1960	Agadir, *Morocco*	5.8	12,000
1964	Anchorage, *Alaska*	8.4	131
1968	North-east Iran	7.4	12,000
1970	North Peru	7.7	66,794
1976	Guatemala	7.5	22,778
1976	Tangshan, *China*	8.2	255,000
1978	Tabas, *Iran*	7.7	25,000
1980	El Asnam, *Algeria*	7.3	20,000
1980	South Italy	7.2	4,800
1985	Mexico City, *Mexico*	8.1	4,200
1988	North-west Armenia	6.8	55,000
1990	North Iran	7.7	36,000
1993	Maharashtra, *India*	6.4	30,000
1994	Los Angeles, *USA*	6.6	51
1995	Kobe, *Japan*	7.2	5,000
1997	North-east Iran	7.1	2,400
1998	Takhar, *Afghanistan*	6.1	4,200
1998	Rostaq, *Afghanistan*	7.0	5,000

> The earthquake that struck Kobe in January 1995 was the worst one experienced in Japan since 1923. Japan lies alongside subduction zones.

Earthquakes are common along the mid-ocean ridges, but they are a long way from land and cause little damage. Other earthquakes occur near land in subduction zones, such as those that encircle much of the Pacific Ocean. These earthquakes often trigger off powerful sea waves, called tsunamis. Other earthquakes occur along transform faults, such as the San Andreas fault in California, a boundary between the North American and Pacific plates. Movements along this fault cause periodic disasters, such as the earthquakes in San Francisco (1906) and Los Angeles (1994).

VOLCANOES & MOUNTAINS

Volcanoes are fuelled by magma (molten rock) from the mantle. Some volcanoes, such as in Hawaii, lie above 'hot spots' (sources of heat in the mantle). But most volcanoes occur either along the ocean ridges or above subduction zones, where

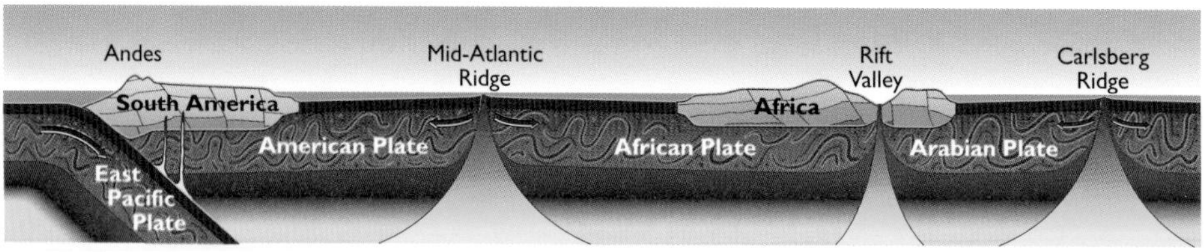

> The section between the Pacific and Indian oceans shows a subduction zone under the American plate, with spreading ocean ridges in the Atlantic and Indian oceans. East Africa may one day split away from the rest of Africa as plate movements pull the Rift Valley apart.

EARTHQUAKES

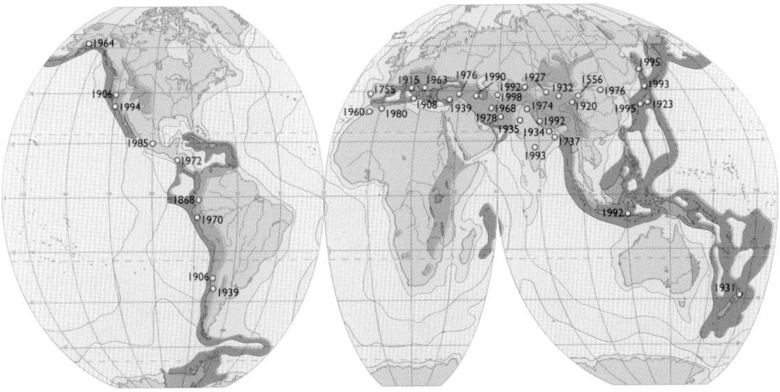

1976 ○ Selected major earthquakes & dates

Mobile land areas

Submarine zones of mobile land areas

Stable land platforms

Submarine extensions of land platforms

Mid-oceanic volcanic ridges

Oceanic platforms

VOLCANOES

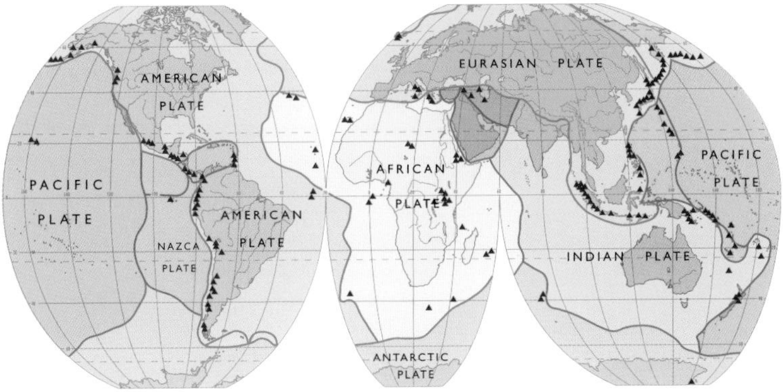

▲ Land volcanoes active since 1700

Boundaries of tectonic plates

The maps show that the main earthquake zones follow plate edges. Most volcanoes are also in these zones, whereas some lie over 'hot spots', far from plate edges.

magma is produced when the descending plate is melted.

Volcanic mountains are built up gradually by runny lava flows or by exploded volcanic ash. Fold mountains occur when two plates bearing land areas collide and the plate edges are buckled upwards into fold mountain ranges. Plate movements also fracture rocks and block mountains are formed when areas of land are pushed upwards along faults or between parallel faults. Blocks of land sometimes sink down between faults, creating deep, steep-sided rift valleys.

> Volcanoes occur when molten magma reaches the surface under pressure through long vents. 'Quiet' volcanoes emit runny lava (called pahoehoe). Explosive eruptions occur when the magma is sticky. Explosive gases shatter the magma into ash, which is hurled upwards into the air.

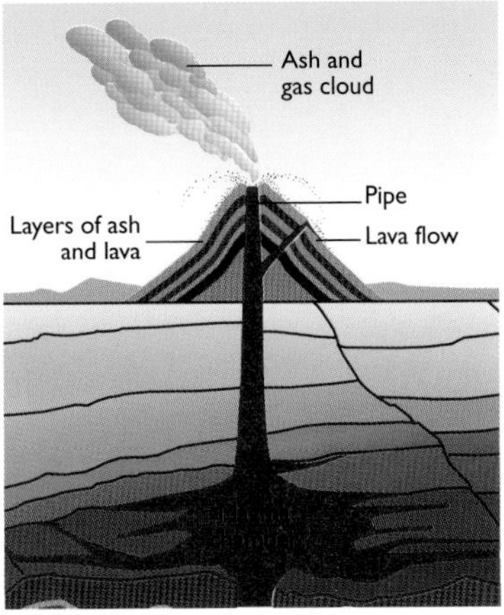

Water & Ice

A VISITOR FROM outer space might be forgiven for naming our planet 'Water' rather than 'Earth', because water covers more than 70% of its surface. Without water, our planet would be as lifeless as the Moon. Through the water cycle, fresh water is regularly supplied from the sea to the land. Most geographers divide the world's water into four main oceans: the Pacific, the Atlantic, the Indian and the Arctic. Together the oceans contain 97.2% of the world's water.

The water in the oceans is constantly on the move, even, albeit extremely slowly, in the deepest ocean trenches. The greatest movements of ocean water occur in the form of ocean currents. These are marked, mainly wind-blown

> Ice breaks away from the ice sheet of Antarctica, forming flat-topped icebergs. Researchers fear that warmer weather is melting Antarctica's ice sheets at a dangerous rate, after large chunks of the Larsen ice shelf and the Ronne ice shelf broke away in 1997 and 1998, respectively.

EXPLANATION OF TERMS

GLACIER A body of ice that flows down valleys in mountain areas. It is usually narrow and hence smaller than ice caps or ice sheets.

ICE AGE A period of Earth history when ice sheets spread over large areas. The most recent Ice Age began about 1.8 million years ago and ended 10,000 years ago.

ICEBERG A floating body of ice in the sea. About eight-ninths of the ice is hidden beneath the surface of the water.

ICE SHEET A large body of ice. During the last Ice Age, ice sheets covered large parts of the northern hemisphere.

OCEAN The four main oceans are the Pacific, the Atlantic, the Indian and the Arctic. Some people classify a fifth southern ocean, but others regard these waters as extensions of the Pacific, Atlantic and Indian oceans.

OCEAN CURRENTS Distinct currents of water in the oceans. Winds are the main causes of surface currents.

SEA An expanse of water, but smaller than an ocean.

JANUARY TEMPERATURE AND OCEAN CURRENTS

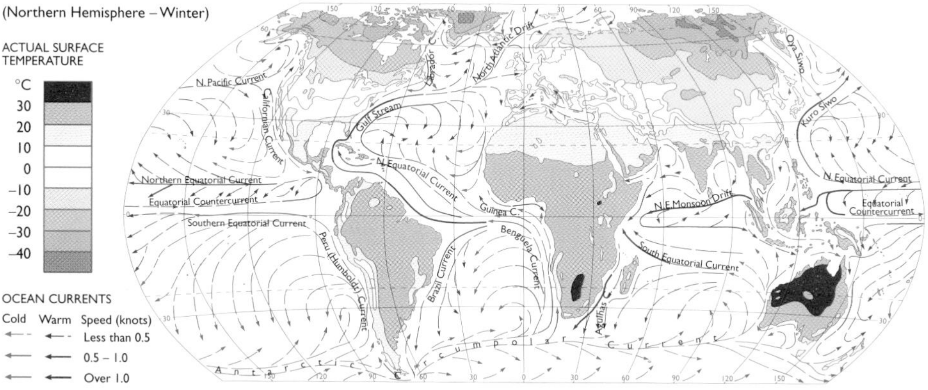

CROSS-SECTION OF ANTARCTICA

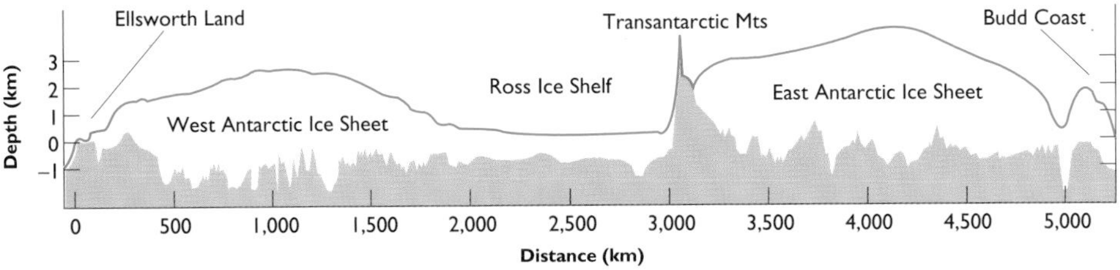

movements of water on or near the surface. Other dense, cold currents creep slowly across the ocean floor. Warm and cold ocean currents help to regulate the world's climate by transferring heat between the tropics and the poles.

ICE

About 2.15% of the world's water is locked in two large ice sheets, several smaller ice caps and glaciers. The world's largest ice sheet covers most of Antarctica. The ice is up to 4,800 m [15,750 ft] thick and it represents 70% of the world's fresh water. The volume of ice is about nine times greater than that contained in the world's other ice sheet in Greenland. Besides these two ice sheets, there are some smaller ice caps in northern Canada, Iceland, Norway and Spitzbergen, and many valley glaciers in high mountain regions throughout the world.

If global warming was to melt the world's ice, the sea level could rise by as much as 100 m [330 ft], flooding low-lying coastal regions. Many of the world's largest cities and most fertile plains would vanish beneath the waves.

> This section across Antarctica shows the concealed land areas in brown, with the top of the ice in blue. The section is divided into the West and East Antarctic Ice Sheets. The vertical scale has been exaggerated.

Composition of Seawater ▾

The principal components of seawater, by percentage, excluding the elements of water itself:

Chloride (Cl)	55.04%	Potassium (K)	1.10%
Sodium (Na)	30.61%	Bicarbonate (HCO_3)	0.41%
Sulphate (SO_4)	7.69%	Bromide (Br)	0.19%
Magnesium (Mg)	3.69%	Strontium (Sr)	0.04%
Calcium (Ca)	1.16%	Fluorine (F)	0.003%

The oceans contain virtually every other element, the more important ones being lithium, rubidium, phosphorus, iodine and barium.

JULY TEMPERATURE AND OCEAN CURRENTS

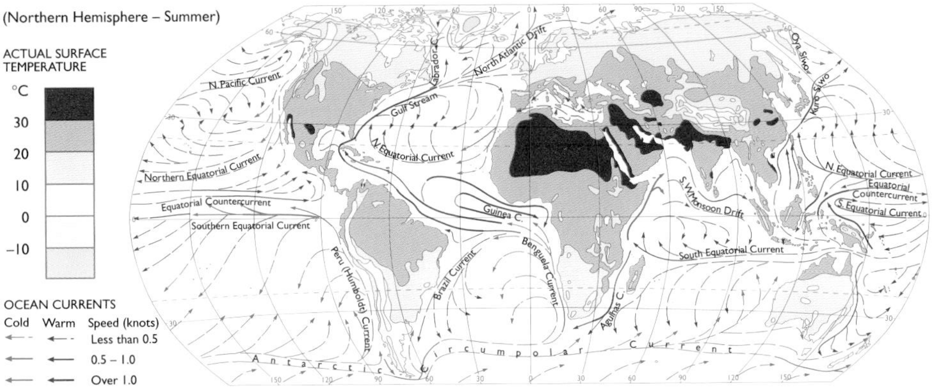

Weather & Climate

WEATHER IS A description of the day-to-day state of the atmosphere. Climate, on the other hand, is weather in the long term: the seasonal pattern of temperature and precipitation averaged over time.

In some areas, the weather is so stable and predictable that a description of the weather is much the same as a statement of the climate. But in parts of the mid-latitudes, the weather changes from hour to hour. Changeable weather is caused mainly by low air pressure systems, called cyclones or depressions, which form along the polar front where warm subtropical air meets cold polar air.

The main elements of weather and climate are temperature and rainfall. Temperatures vary because the Sun heats the Earth unequally, with the most intense heating around the Equator. Unequal heating is responsible for the general circulation of the atmosphere and the main wind belts.

Rainfall occurs when warm air containing invisible water vapour rises. As the rising air cools, the capacity of the air to hold water vapour decreases and so the water vapour condenses into droplets of water or ice crystals, which collect together to form raindrops or snowflakes.

> Lightning occurs in clouds and also between the base of clouds and the ground. Lightning that strikes the ground can kill people or start forest fires.

LIGHTNING

Lightning is a flash of light in the sky caused by a discharge of electricity in the atmosphere. Lightning occurs within cumulonimbus clouds during thunderstorms. Positive charges build up at the top of the cloud, while negative charges build up at the base. The charges are finally discharged as an electrical spark. Sheet lightning occurs inside clouds, while cloud to ground lightning is usually forked. Thunder occurs when molecules along the lightning channel expand and collide with cool molecules.

> The rainfall map shows areas affected by tropical storms, which are variously called hurricanes, tropical cyclones, willy willies and typhoons. Strong polar winds bring blizzards in winter.

ANNUAL RAINFALL

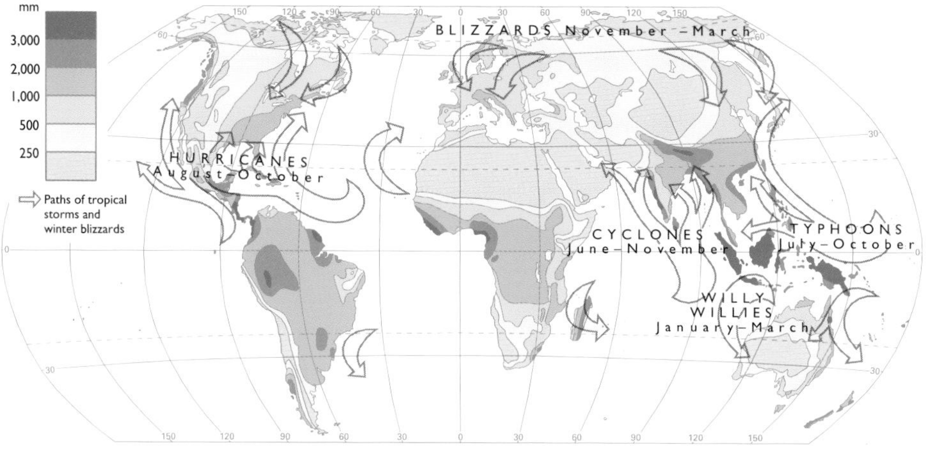
mm
3,000
2,000
1,000
500
250
Paths of tropical storms and winter blizzards
BLIZZARDS November – March
HURRICANES August – October
CYCLONES June – November
TYPHOONS July – October
WILLY WILLIES January – March

GLOBAL WARMING

The Earth's climates have changed many times during its history. Around 11,000 years ago, much of the northern hemisphere was buried by ice. Some scientists believe that the last Ice Age may not be over and that ice sheets may one day return. Other scientists are concerned that air

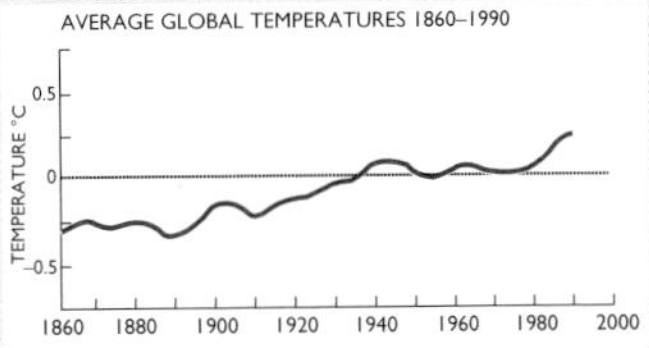
AVERAGE GLOBAL TEMPERATURES 1860–1990
TEMPERATURE °C
0.5
0
–0.5
1860
1880
1900
1920
1940
1960
1980
2000

pollution may be producing an opposite effect – a warming of the atmosphere. Since 1900, average world temperatures have risen by about 0.5°C [0.9°F] and increases are likely to continue. Global warming is the result of an increase in the amount of carbon dioxide in the atmosphere, caused by the burning of coal, oil and natural gas, together with deforestation. Short-wave radiation from the Sun passes easily through the atmosphere. But, as the carbon dioxide content rises, more of the long-wave radiation that returns from the Earth's surface is absorbed and trapped by the carbon dioxide. This creates a 'greenhouse effect', which will change the world's climates with, perhaps, disastrous environmental consequences.

CLIMATE

The world contains six main climatic types: hot and wet tropical climates; dry climates; warm temperate climates; cold temperate climates; polar climates; and mountain climates. These regions are further divided according to the character and amount of precipitation and special features of the temperature, notably seasonal variations. Regions with temperate climates include Mediterranean areas with hot, dry summers and mild, moist winters. The British Isles have a different type of temperate climate, with warm, rather than hot, summers and rain throughout the year.

CLIMATIC REGIONS

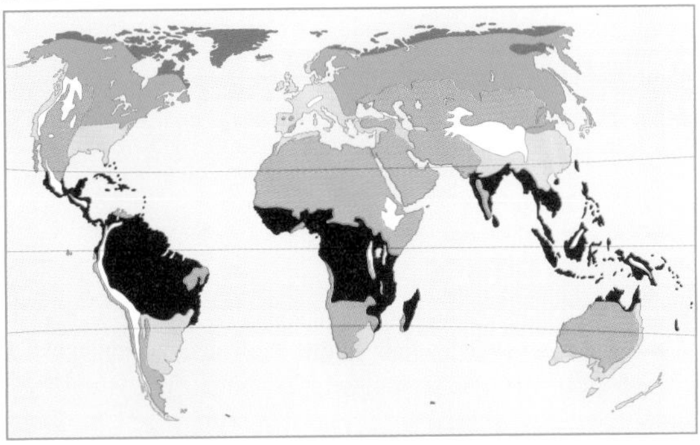

- Tropical Climate (hot & wet)
- Dry Climate (desert & steppe)
- Temperate Climate (warm & wet)
- Continental Climate (cold & wet)
- Polar Climate (very cold & wet)
- Mountainous Areas (where altitude affects climate types)

WORLD CLIMATIC RECORDS

Highest Recorded Temperature
Al Aziziyah, Libya: 58°C [136.4°F] on 13 September 1922

Highest Mean Annual Temperature
Dallol, Ethiopia: 34.4°C [94°F] from 1960–66

Lowest Mean Annual Temperature
Polus, Nedostupnosti, Pole of Cold, Antarctica: –57.8°C [–72°F]

Lowest Recorded Temperature (outside poles)
Verkhoyansk, Siberia, Russia: –68°C [–90°F] on 6 February 1933

Windiest Place
Commonwealth Bay, Antarctica: gales often exceed 320 km/h [200 mph]

Longest Heatwave
Marble Bar, Western Australia: 162 days over 38°C [94°F], 23 October 1923 to 7 April 1924

Driest Place
Calama, northern Chile: no recorded rainfall in 400 years to 1971

Wettest Place (average)
Tututendo, Colombia: mean annual rainfall 11,770 mm [463 in]

Wettest Place (24 hours)
Cilaos, Réunion, Indian Ocean: 1,870 mm [73.6 in] from 15–16 March 1952

Wettest Place (12 months)
Cherrapunji, Meghalaya, north-east India: 26,470 mm [1,040 in], August 1860 to1861. Cherrapunji also holds the record for rainfall in one month: 2,930 mm [115 in] in July 1861

Heaviest Hailstones
Gopalganj, central Bangladesh: up to 1.02 kg [2.25 lbs] in April 1986, which killed 92 people

Heaviest Snowfall (continuous)
Bessans, Savoie, France: 1,730 mm [68 in] in 19 hours over the period 5–6 April 1969

Heaviest Snowfall (season/year)
Paradise Ranger Station, Mt Rainier, Washington, USA: 31,102 mm [1,224 in] fell from 19 February 1971 to 18 February 1972

Landforms & Vegetation

THE CLIMATE LARGELY determines the nature of soils and vegetation types throughout the world. The studies of climate and plant and animal communities are closely linked. For example, tropical climates are divided into tropical forest and tropical grassland climates. The tropical forest climate, which is hot and rainy throughout the year, is ideal for the growth of forests that contain more than half of the world's known plant and animal species. But tropical grassland, or savanna, climates have a marked dry season. As a result, the forest gives way to grassland, with scattered trees.

CLIMATE & SCENERY

The climate also helps to shape the land. Frost action in cold areas splits boulders apart, while rapid temperature changes in hot deserts make rock surfaces peel away like the layers of an onion. These are examples of mechanical weathering.

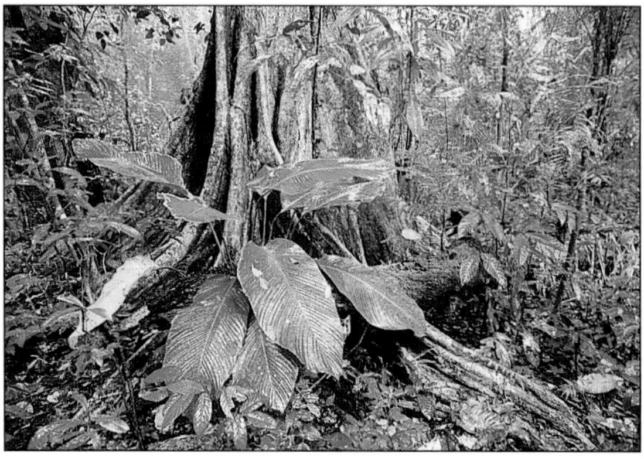

> The tropical broadleaf forests are rich in plant and animal species. The extinction of many species because of deforestation is one of the great natural disasters of our time.

Chemical weathering usually results from the action of water on rocks. For example, rainwater containing dissolved carbon dioxide is a weak acid, which reacts with limestone. This chemical process is responsible for the erosion of the world's most spectacular caves.

Running water and glaciers play a major part in creating scenery, while in

NATURAL VEGETATION

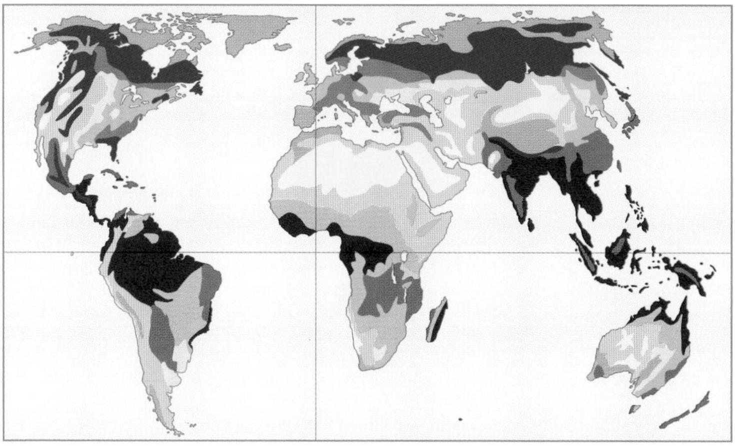

- Tundra & mountain vegetation
- Needleleaf evergreen forest
- Broadleaf deciduous forest
- Mixed needleleaf evergreen & broadleaf deciduous trees
- Mid-latitude grassland
- Semi-desert scrub land
- Evergreen broadleaf & deciduous trees & scrub
- Desert
- Tropical grassland (savanna)
- Tropical broadleaf & monsoon rainforest
- Subtropical broadleaf & needleleaf forest

> Human activities, especially agriculture, have greatly modified plant and animal communities throughout the world. As a result, world vegetation maps show the natural 'climax vegetation' of regions – that is, the kind of vegetation that would grow in a particular climatic area, had that area not been affected by human activities. For example, the climax vegetation of western Europe is broadleaf, deciduous forest, but most of the original forest, together with the animals which lived in it, was destroyed long ago.

DESERTIFICATION AND DEFORESTATION

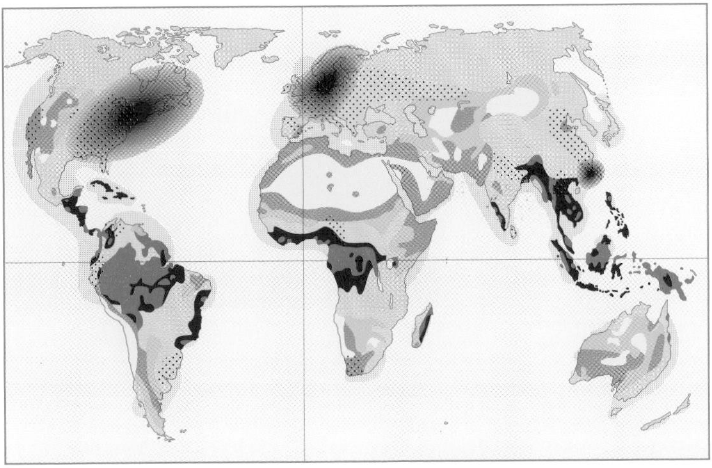

Pollution

Polluted seas

Main areas of sulphur & nitrogen emissions

Areas of acid rain

Desertification

Existing deserts

Areas with a high risk of desertification

Areas with a moderate risk of desertification

Deforestation

Former areas of rainforest

Existing rainforest

dry areas, wind-blown sand is a powerful agent of erosion. Most landforms seem to alter little in one person's lifetime. But geologists estimate that natural forces remove an average of 3.5 cm [1.4 in] from land areas every 1,000 years. Over millions of years, these forces reduce mountains to flat plains.

HUMAN INTERFERENCE

Climate also affects people, though air conditioning and central heating now make it possible for us live in comfort almost anywhere in the world.

However, human activities are damaging our planet. Pollution is poisoning rivers and seas, while acid rain, caused by air pollution, is killing trees and acidifying lakes. The land is also harmed by such things as nuclear accidents and the dumping of toxic wastes.

Some regions have been overgrazed or so intensively farmed that once fertile areas have been turned into barren deserts. The clearance of tropical forests means that some plant and animal species are disappearing before scientists have had a chance to study them.

MOULDING THE LAND

Powerful forces inside the Earth buckle rock layers to form fold mountain ranges. But even as they rise, the forces of erosion wear them away. On mountain slopes, water freezes in cracks in rocks. Because ice occupies more space than the equivalent amount of water, this 'frost action' shatters rocks, and the fragments tumble downhill. Some end up on or inside moving glaciers. Other rocks are carried away by running water. The glaciers and streams not only transport rock fragments, but they also wear out valleys and so add to their load. The eroded material breaks down into fragments of sand, silt and mud, much of which reaches the sea, where it piles up on the sea floor in layers. These layers eventually become compacted into sedimentary rocks, such as sandstones and shales. These rocks may eventually be squeezed up again by a plate collision to form new fold mountains, so completing a natural cycle of mountain building and destruction.

MAJOR FACTORS AFFECTING WEATHERING

WEATHERING RATE

	SLOW		FAST
Mineral solubility	low (*e.g. quartz*)	moderate (*e.g. feldspar*)	high (*e.g. calcite*)
Rainfall	low	moderate	heavy
Temperature	cold	temperate	hot
Vegetation	sparse	moderate	lush
Soil cover	bare rock	thin to moderate soil	thick soil

Weathering is the breakdown and decay of rocks in situ. It may be mechanical (physical), chemical or biological.

Population

THE ADVENT OF agriculture around 10,000 years ago had a great impact on human society. People abandoned their nomadic way of life and settled in farming villages. With plenty of food, some people were able to pursue jobs unconnected with farming. These developments eventually led to rapid social changes, including the growth of early cities and the emergence of civilization.

THE POPULATION EXPLOSION

The social changes had a major effect on the world's population, which rose from around 8 million in 8000 BC, to about 300 million by AD 1000. The rate of population increase then began to accelerate further, passing the 1 billion mark in the 19th century, the 2 billion mark in the 1920s, and the 4 billion mark in the 1970s.

Today the world has a population of more than 6 billion and experts forecast that it will reach around 11 billion by 2200. However, they then predict that it will stabilize at this level or even begin to decline. Most of the expected increase will occur in developing countries in Africa, Asia and Latin America.

> Many cities in India, such as Bombay (also known as Mumbai), have grown so quickly that they lack sufficient jobs and homes for their populations. As a result, slums now cover large areas.

POPULATION PYRAMIDS

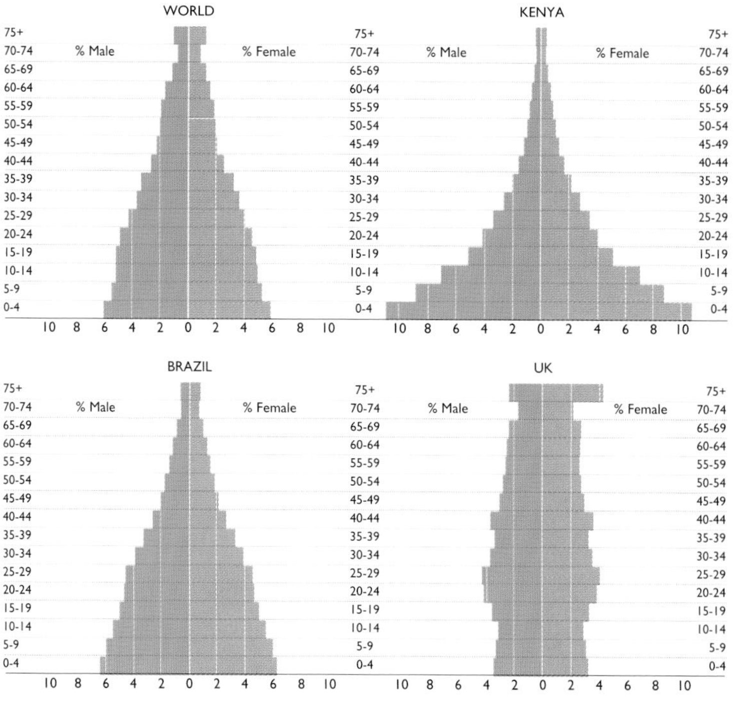

> The population pyramids compare the average age structures for the world with those of three countries at varying stages of development. Kenya, a developing country, had, until recently, one of the world's highest annual rates of population increase. As a result, a high proportion of Kenyans are aged under 15. Brazil has a much more balanced economy than Kenya's, and a lower rate of population increase. This is reflected in a higher proportion of people aged over 40. The UK is a developed country with a low rate of population growth, 0.3% per year between 1985–95, much lower than the world average of 1.6%. The UK has a far higher proportion of people over 60 years old.

The World's Largest Cities ▾

By early next century, for the first time ever, the majority of the world's population will live in cities. Below is a list of the 20 largest cities (in thousands) based on 1997 figures.

1	Tokyo, *Japan*	26,836
2	São Paulo, *Brazil*	16,417
3	New York, *USA*	16,329
4	Shanghai, *China*	15,082
5	Mexico City, *Mexico*	15,048
6	Bombay (Mumbai), *India*	12,572
7	Los Angeles, *USA*	12,410
8	Beijing, *China*	12,362
9	Seoul, *South Korea*	11,641
10	Jakarta, *Indonesia*	11,500
11	Buenos Aires, *Argentina*	11,256
12	Calcutta, *India*	10,916
13	Tianjin, *China*	10,687
14	Osaka, *Japan*	10,601
15	Lagos, *Nigeria*	10,287
16	Cairo, *Egypt*	9,900
17	Rio de Janeiro, *Brazil*	9,888
18	Karachi, *Pakistan*	9,863
19	Paris, *France*	9,319
20	Manila, *Philippines*	9,280

This population explosion has been caused partly by better medical care, which has reduced child mortality and increased the average life expectancy at birth throughout the world. But it has also created problems. In some developing countries, nearly half of the people are children. They make no contribution to the economy, but they require costly education and health services. In richer countries, the high proportion of retired people is also a strain on the economy.

As we enter the 21st century, for the first time in 10,000 years, the majority of people are no longer forced to rely on farming for their livelihood. Instead, nearly half of them live in cities where many of them enjoy a high standard of living. But rapid urbanization also creates problems, especially in the developing world, with the growth of slums and an increase in homelessness and crime.

POPULATION BY CONTINENT

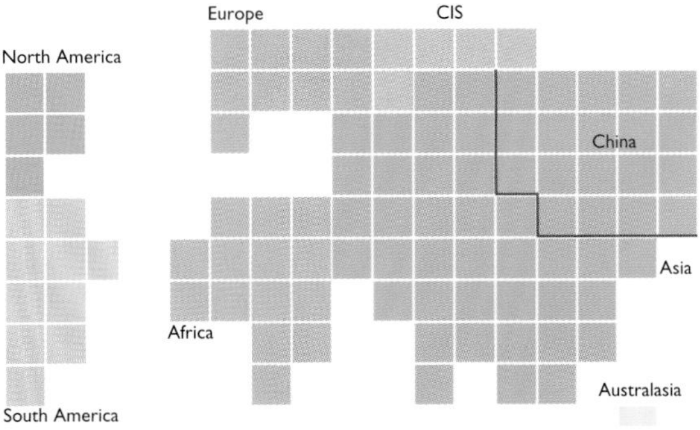

Europe
CIS
North America
China
Asia
Africa
Australasia
South America

> The cartogram shows the populations of the continents in a diagrammatic way, with each square representing 1% of the world's population. For example, North America is represented by five squares, which means that it contains about 5% of the world's population, while Asia, the most populous continent even excluding the Asian part of the former USSR, is represented by 56 squares (China accounting for 19 of these). By contrast, Australasia is represented by less than half of a square because it contains only 0.45% of the world's population.

WORLD DEMOGRAPHIC EXTREMES

Fastest growing population; average annual % growth (1992–2000)

1	Nigeria	5.09
2	Afghanistan	4.21
3	Ivory Coast	3.54
4	Oman	3.52
5	Syria	3.51

Slowest growing population; average annual % growth (1992–2000)

1	Kuwait	-1.39
2	Ireland	-0.24
3	St Kitts & Nevis	-0.22
4	Bulgaria	-0.13
5	Latvia	-0.10

Youngest populations; % aged under 15 years (1996)

1	West Bank/Gaza	51.7
2	Uganda	48.6
3	Benin	48.4
=	Niger	48.4
5	Zambia	48.2

Oldest populations; % aged over 65 years (1996)

1	Sweden	17.3
2	Italy	16.1
3	Greece	15.9
=	Norway	15.9
5	Belgium	15.8

Highest urban populations; % of population in urban areas (1996)

1	Singapore	100.0
=	Bermuda	100.0
3	Macau	99.0
4	Kuwait	97.0
5	Hong Kong	95.0

Lowest urban populations; % of population in urban areas (1996)

1	Bhutan	6.0
=	Rwanda	6.0
3	Burundi	8.0
4	Ethiopia	13.0
=	Uganda	13.0

Most male populations; number of men per 100 women (1997)

1	Qatar	193.3
2	United Arab Emirates	176.4
3	Bahrain	133.7
4	Saudi Arabia	125.1
5	Oman	113.4

Fewest male populations; number of men per 100 women (1997)

1	Latvia	84.3
2	Ukraine	86.8
3	Russia	88.0
5	Estonia	88.7
4	Belarus	88.8

Languages & Religions

ALL PEOPLE BELONG to one species, *Homo sapiens*, but within that species is a great diversity of cultures. Two of the main factors that give people an identity and sense of kinship with their neighbours are language and religion.

Definitions of languages vary and as a result estimates of the total number of languages in existence range from about 3,000 to 6,000. Many languages are spoken only by a small number of people. Papua New Guinea, for example, has only 4.2 million people but 869 languages.

The world's languages are grouped into families, of which the Indo-European is the largest. Indo-European languages are spoken in a zone stretching from

> Religion is a major force in South-east Asia. About 94% of the people in Thailand are Buddhists, and more than 40% of men over the age of 20 spend some time, if only a few weeks, serving as Buddhist monks. Confucianism, Islam, Hinduism, and Christianity are also practised in Thailand.

THE WORLD'S LANGUAGES

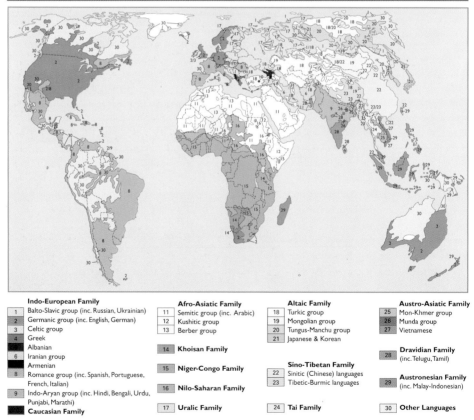

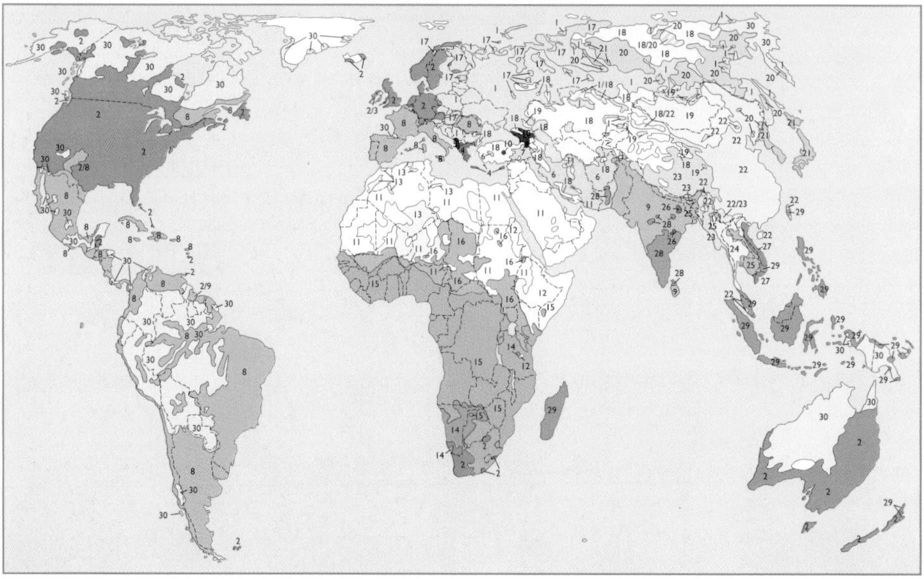

Indo-European Family
- 1 Balto-Slavic group (inc. Russian, Ukrainian)
- 2 Germanic group (inc. English, German)
- 3 Celtic group
- 4 Greek
- 5 Albanian
- 6 Iranian group
- 7 Armenian
- 8 Romance group (inc. Spanish, Portuguese, French, Italian)
- 9 Indo-Aryan group (inc. Hindi, Bengali, Urdu, Punjabi, Marathi)
- 10 **Caucasian Family**

Afro-Asiatic Family
- 11 Semitic group (inc. Arabic)
- 12 Kushitic group
- 13 Berber group
- 14 **Khoisan Family**
- 15 **Niger-Congo Family**
- 16 **Nilo-Saharan Family**
- 17 **Uralic Family**

Altaic Family
- 18 Turkic group
- 19 Mongolian group
- 20 Tungus-Manchu group
- 21 Japanese & Korean

Sino-Tibetan Family
- 22 Sinitic (Chinese) languages
- 23 Tibetic-Burmic languages
- 24 **Tai Family**

Austro-Asiatic Family
- 25 Mon-Khmer group
- 26 Munda group
- 27 Vietnamese
- 28 **Dravidian Family** (inc. Telugu, Tamil)
- 29 **Austronesian Family** (inc. Malay-Indonesian)
- 30 **Other Languages**

NATIVE SPEAKERS

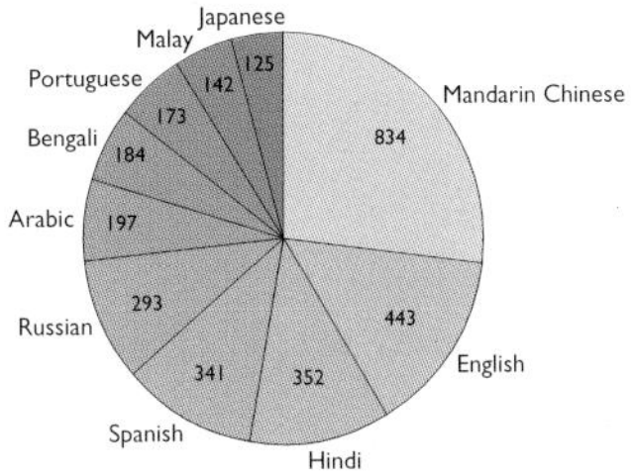

> The chart shows the native speakers of major languages in millions. Mandarin Chinese is the language of 834 million, as compared with English, which has 443 million speakers. However, many other people speak English as a second language.

Religious Adherents ▾

The world's major religions, with the number of adherents in millions (latest available year)

Christian	1,669
Roman Catholic	952
Protestant	337
Orthodox	162
Anglican	70
Other Christian	148
Muslim	945
Sunni	841
Shia	104
Hindu	663
Buddhist	312
Chinese folk	172
Ethnic/local	92
Jewish	18
Sikh	17

Europe, through south-western Asia into the Indian subcontinent. In addition, during the period of European colonization, they spread throughout North and South America and also to Australia and New Zealand. Today about two-fifths of the world's people speak an Indo-European language, as compared with one-fifth who speak a language belonging to the Sino-Tibetan language.

The Sino-Tibetan language family includes Chinese, which is spoken as a first language by more people than any other. English is the second most important first language, but it is more important than Chinese in international affairs and business, because so many people speak it as a second language.

> Most languages have alphabetic systems of writing. The Greek alphabet uses some letters from the Roman alphabet, such as the A and B. Russians use the Cyrillic alphabet, which is based partly on Roman and partly on Greek letters. The Cyrillic alphabet is also used for Bulgarian and some central Asian languages. Serbs use either the Cyrillic or the Roman alphabet to write Serbo-Croat.

RELIGIONS

Christianity is the religion of about a third of the world's population. Other major religions include Buddhism, Islam, Hinduism, Judaism, Chinese folk religions and traditional tribal religions.

Religion is a powerful force in human society, establishing the ethics by which people live. It has inspired great music, painting, architecture and literature, yet at the same time religion and language have contributed to conflict between people throughout history. Even today, the cause of many of the conflicts around the world are partly the result of linguistic and religious differences.

ALPHABETS

The Greek Alphabet

Α	Β	Γ	Δ	Ε	Ζ	Η	Θ	Ι	Κ	Λ	Μ	Ν	Ξ	Ο	Π	Ρ	Σ	Τ	Υ	Φ	Χ	Ψ	Ω
A	V/B	G	D	E	Z	E	TH	I	K	L	M	N	X	O	P	R	S	T	Y	F	CH	PS	O

The Cyrillic Alphabet

А	Б	В	Г	Д	Е	Ё	Ж	З	И	Й	К	Л	М	Н	О	П	Р	С	Т	У	Ф	Х	Ц	Ч	Ш	Щ	Ю	Я
A	B	V	G	D	E	YO	ZH	Z	I	Y	K	L	M	N	O	P	R	S	T	U	F	KH	TS	CH	SH	SHCH	YU	YA

Agriculture & Industry

BECAUSE IT SUPPLIES so many basic human needs, agriculture is the world's leading economic activity. But its relative importance varies from place to place. In most developing countries, agriculture employs more people than any other activity. For example, the diagram at the bottom of this page shows that more than 90% of the people of Nepal are employed in farming.

Many farmers in developing countries live at subsistence level, producing barely enough to supply the basic needs of their families. Alongside the subsistence sector, some developing countries produce one or two cash crops that they export. Dependence on cash crops is precarious: when world commodity prices fall, the country is plunged into financial crisis.

In developed countries, by contrast, the proportion of people engaged in agriculture has declined over the last 200 years. Yet, by using farm machinery and scientific methods, notably the selective breeding of crops and animals, the production of food has soared. For example, although agriculture employs only 3% of its workers, the United States is one of the world's top food producers.

> The cultivation of rice, one of the world's most important foods, is still carried out by hand in many areas. But the introduction of new strains of rice has greatly increased yields.

INDUSTRIALIZATION

The Industrial Revolution began in Britain in the late 18th century and soon spread to mainland Europe and other parts of the world. Industries first arose in areas with supplies of coal, iron ore and cheap water power. But later, after oil and gas came into use as industrial fuels, factories could be set up almost anywhere.

The growth of manufacturing led to an increase in the number of industrial cities. The flight from the land was accompanied by an increase in efficiency in agriculture. As a result, manufacturing replaced agriculture as the chief source of

EMPLOYMENT

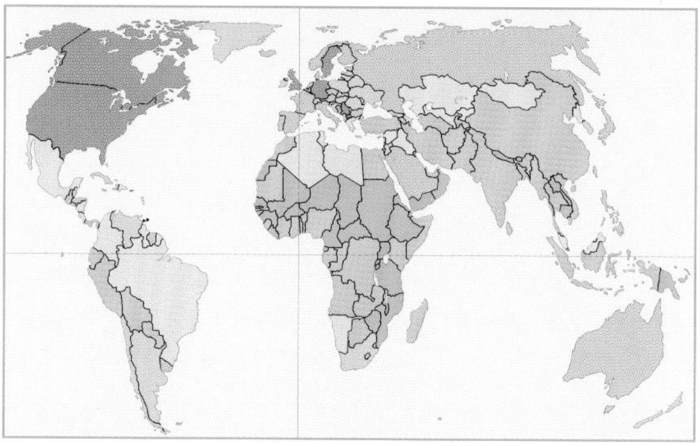

The number of workers employed in manufacturing for every 100 workers engaged in agriculture (latest available year)

- Under 10
- 10 – 50
- 50 – 100
- 100 – 200
- 200 – 500
- Over 500

DIVISION OF EMPLOYMENT

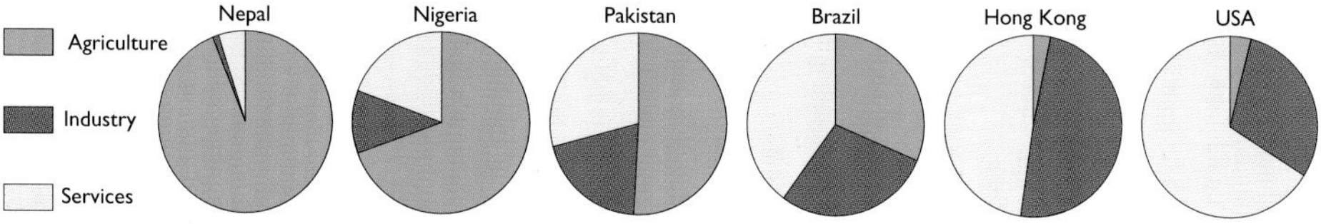
Agriculture
Industry
Services
Nepal
Nigeria
Pakistan
Brazil
Hong Kong
USA

PATTERNS OF PRODUCTION

> The table shows how the economy breaks down (in terms of the Gross Domestic Product for 1997) in a selection of industrialized countries. Agriculture remains important in some countries, though its percentage share has steadily declined since the start of the Industrial Revolution. Industry, especially manufacturing, accounts for a higher proportion, but service industries account for the greatest percentage of the GDP in most developed nations. The figures for Manufacturing are shown separately from Industry because of their importance in the economy.

Country	*Agriculture*	*Industry (excl. manufacturing)*	*Manufacturing*	*Services*
Australia	3%	24%	12%	61%
Austria	1%	24%	14%	61%
Brazil	10%	28%	18%	44%
Denmark	4%	7%	20%	69%
Finland	5%	3%	28%	64%
France	2%	20%	13%	65%
Germany	1%	8%	24%	67%
Greece	17%	13%	23%	47%
Hungary	4%	24%	14%	58%
Ireland	8%	7%	3%	82%
Italy	3%	8%	21%	68%
Japan	1%	28%	19%	52%
Kuwait	0%	46%	9%	45%
Mexico	4%	18%	17%	61%
Netherlands	3%	21%	12%	64%
Norway	2%	24%	10%	64%
Singapore	0%	29%	17%	54%
Sweden	3%	8%	28%	61%
UK	2%	8%	23%	67%
USA	3%	10%	20%	67%

income and employment in industrialized countries, and rapidly widened the wealth gap between them and the poorer non-industrialized countries whose economies continued to rely on agriculture.

SERVICE INDUSTRIES

Eventually, the manufacturing sector became so efficient that it could supply most of the things that people wanted to buy. Trade between industrialized countries also increased, so widening the choice for consumers in the developed world. These factors led to a further change in the economies of developed countries, namely a reduction in the relative importance of manufacturing and the growth of the service sector.

Service industries include such activities as government, transport, insurance, finance, and even the writing of computer software. In the United States, service industries now account for about two-thirds of the Gross National Product (GNP), while in Japan they account for just over half. But the wealth of both countries still rests on their massive industrial production.

AGRICULTURE

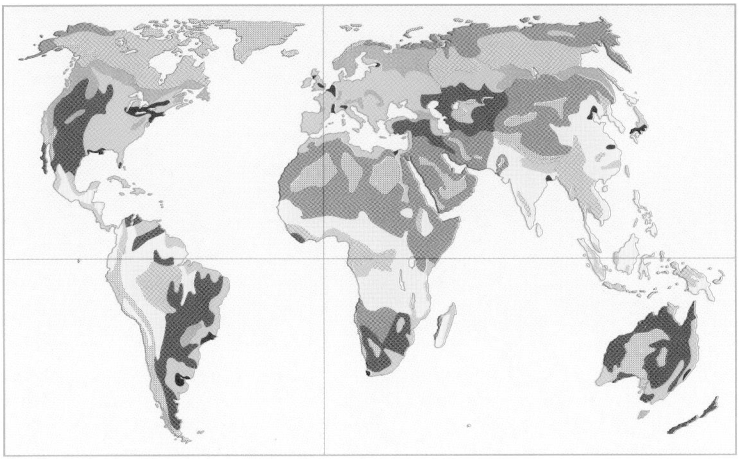

Predominant type of farming or land use

- Nomadic herding
- Hunting, fishing & gathering
- Subsistence agriculture
- Commercial ranching
- Commercial livestock & grain farming
- Urban areas
- Forestry
- Unproductive land

Trade & Commerce

TRADE HAS ALWAYS been an important human activity. It has widened the choice of goods available in any country, lowered prices and generally raised living standards. People regard any growth of world trade as a sign that the world economy is healthy, whereas a decline indicates a world recession.

Exports and imports are of two main kinds. Visible imports and exports include primary products, such as food and manufactures. Invisible imports and exports include services, such as banking, insurance, interest on loans, and money spent by tourists.

World trade, both visible and invisible, is dominated by the 29 members of the OECD (Organization for Economic Development), which includes the world's top trading nations, namely the United States, Japan, Germany, France, Italy and the United Kingdom, as well as Australia, New Zealand, Canada and Mexico. Hungary, Poland and South Korea joined in 1996.

> The new port of the historic Italian city of Ravenna is linked to the Adriatic Sea by a canal. The port has large oil refining and petrochemical industries.

CHANGING EXPORTS

From the late 19th century to the 1950s, primary products, including farm products, minerals, natural fibres, timber and, in the latter part of this period, oil

DEBT AND AID

International debtors and the development aid they receive (1996)

The provision of aid by rich countries to developing countries is part of international politics. But the grants made to developing countries are often dwarfed by the burden of debt which the countries are expected to repay. In 1990, the debts of Mozambique, one of the world's poorest countries, were estimated to be 75 times its entire earnings from exports.

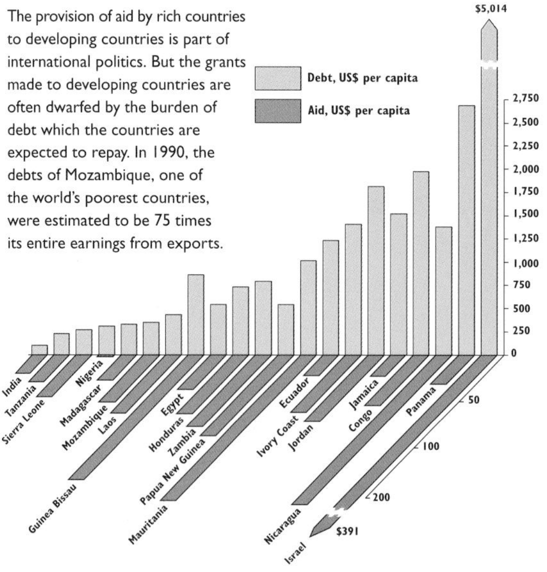

Debt, US$ per capita
Aid, US$ per capita
$5,014
2,750
2,500
2,250
2,000
1,750
1,500
1,250
1,000
750
500
250
0
50
100
200
$391
India
Tanzania
Sierra Leone
Nigeria
Madagascar
Mozambique
Laos
Guinea Bissau
Egypt
Honduras
Zambia
Papua New Guinea
Mauritania
Ecuador
Ivory Coast
Jordan
Nicaragua
Israel
Jamaica
Congo
Panama

The World's Largest Businesses ▼

The world's largest businesses in 1997 by sales, in billions of US$.

1	General Motors, *USA*	168.4
2	Ford Motor, *USA*	147.0
3	Mitsui, *Japan*	144.9
4	Mitsubishi, *Japan*	140.2
5	Itochu, *Japan*	135.5
6	Royal Dutch/Shell Group, *UK/Neths*	128.2
7	Marubeni, *Japan*	124.0
8	Exxon, *USA*	119.4
9	Summitomo, *Japan*	119.3
10	Toyota Motor, *Japan*	108.7
11	Wal-Mart Stores, *USA*	106.1
12	General Electric, *USA*	79.2
13	Nissho Iwai, *Japan*	78.9
14	Nippon Telegraph/Telephone, *Japan*	78.3
15	Intl. business Machines, *USA*	75.9
16	Hitachi, *Japan*	75.7
17	AT&T, *USA*	74.5
18	Nippon Life Insurance, *Japan*	72.6
19	Mobil, *USA*	72.3
20	Daimler-Benz, *Germany*	71.6

TRADED PRODUCTS

The character of world trade has greatly changed in the last 50 years. While primary products were once the leading commodities, world trade is now dominated by manufactured products. Cars are the single most valuable traded product, followed by vehicle parts and engines. The next most valuable goods are high-tech products such as data processing (computer) equipment, telecommunications equipment, and transistors. Other items include aircraft, paper and board, trucks, measuring and control instruments, and electrical machinery. Trade in most manufactured products is dominated by the OECD countries. For example, the leading vehicle exporter is Japan, which became the world's leading car manufacturer in the 1980s. The United States, Germany, the United Kingdom, France and Japan lead in the production of data processing equipment.

and natural gas, dominated world trade.

Many developing countries still remain dependent on exporting mineral ores, fossil fuels, or farm products such as cocoa or coffee whose prices fluctuate according to demand. But today, manufactured goods are the most important commodities in world trade. The OECD nations lead the world in exporting manufactured goods, though they are being challenged by a group of 'tiger economies' in eastern Asia, notably Singapore, Hong Kong and Taiwan. Other rapidly industrializing countries in Asia include Thailand, Malaysia and the Philippines. The generally cheap labour costs of these countries have enabled them to produce manufactured goods for export at prices lower than those charged for goods made in Western countries.

Private companies carry on most of the world's trade. The small proportion handled by governments decreased recently with the collapse of Communist regimes in eastern Europe and the former Soviet Union.

SHARE OF WORLD TRADE

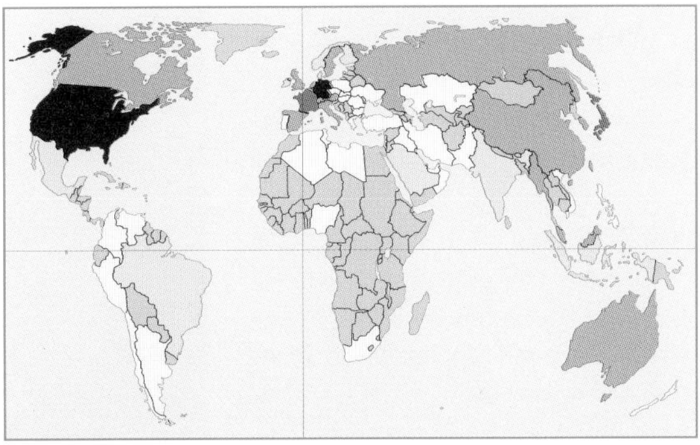

Percentage share of total world exports by value (1996)

- Over 10%
- 5 – 10%
- 1 – 5%
- 0.5 – 1%
- 0.1 – 0.5%
- Under 0.1%

DEPENDENCE ON TRADE

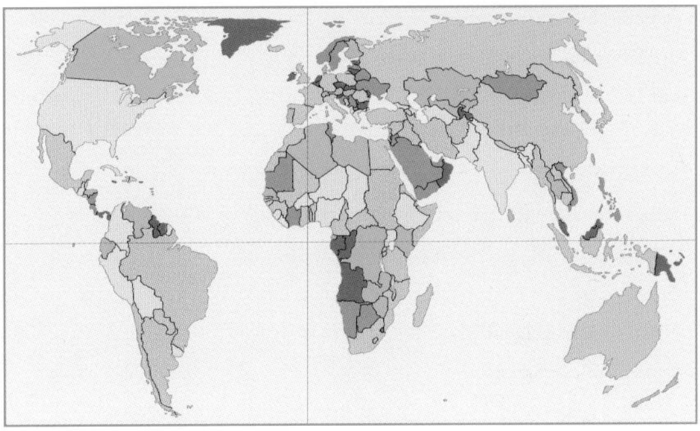

Value of exports as a percentage of Gross Domestic Product (1997)

- Over 50% GDP
- 40 – 50% GDP
- 30 – 40% GDP
- 20 – 30% GDP
- 10 – 20% GDP
- Under 10% GDP

Trade in Oil ▾

Major world trade in oil in millions of tonnes (1997)

Middle East to Asia (not Japan)	294.4
Middle East to Japan	218.1
Middle East to W. Europe	187.9
S. and C. America to USA	132.1
N. Africa to W. Europe	97.9
CIS to Western Europe	90.8
Middle East to USA	86.9
Canada to USA	72.7
West Africa to USA	68.3
Mexico to USA	68.0
W. Africa to W. Europe	40.1
Western Europe to USA	32.9
Middle East to Africa	32.0
Middle East to South and Central America	27.8
CIS to Central Europe	31.8
Middle East to Central Europe	19.3
Total world trade	1,978.9

Transport & Travel

ABOUT 200 YEARS ago, most people never travelled far from their birthplace. But adventurous travellers can now reach almost any part of the world.

Transport is concerned with moving goods and people around by land, water and air. Land transport was once laborious, and was dependent on pack animals or animal-drawn vehicles. But during the Industrial Revolution, railways played a vital role in moving bulky materials and equipment required by factories. They were also important in the opening up and development of remote areas around the world in North and South America, Africa, Asia and Australia.

Today, however, motor vehicles have taken over many of the functions once served by railways. Unlike railways, motor vehicles provide a door-to-door service and, through the invention of heavy trucks, they can also carry large loads. In the mid-1990s, about 90% of inland freight in Britain was carried by road, while car and van travel accounted for 86% of passenger travel, as compared with 6% by buses and coaches, 5% by rail and less than 1% by air.

> Traffic jams and vehicle pollution have affected cities throughout the world. Many of Bangkok's beautiful old canals have been filled in to provide extra roads to cope with the enormous volume of traffic in the city.

TRAVEL & TOURISM

Sea transport, which now employs huge bulk grain carriers, oil tankers and container ships, still carries most of the world's trade. But since the late 1950s, fewer passengers have travelled overseas by sea, because air travel is so much faster, though many former ocean liners now operate successfully as cruise ships.

Air travel has played a major part in the rapid growth of the tourist industry,

AIR TRAVEL

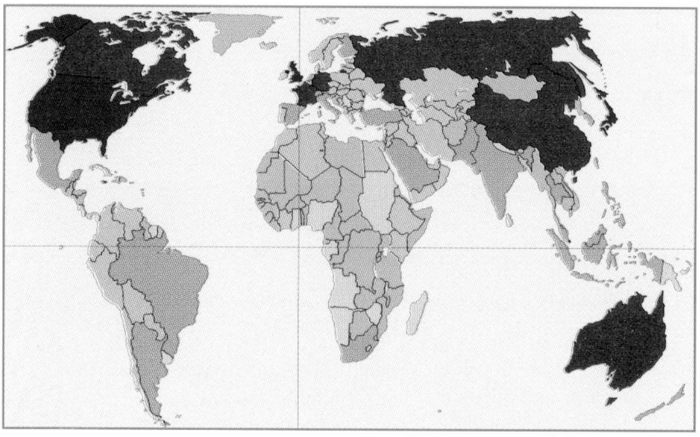

Number of passenger kilometres flown, in millions (1996). Passenger kilometres are the number of passengers (both international and domestic) multiplied by the distance flown by each passenger from airport of origin.

- Over 100,000
- 50,000 – 100,000
- 10,000 – 50,000
- 1,000 – 10,000
- 500 – 1,000
- Under 500

The World's Busiest Airports ▾

Total number of passengers, in thousands (1997)

1	O'Hare Intl., *Chicago*	70,295
2	Hartsfield Atlanta Int., *Atlanta*	68,206
3	Dallas/Fort Worth Int., *Dallas*	60,489
4	Los Angeles Intl., *Los Angeles*	60,143
5	Heathrow, *London*	57,975
6	Haneda, *Tokyo*	49,302
7	San Francisco Intl., *San Francisco*	40,500
8	Frankfurt/Main, *Frankfurt*	40,263
9	Kimpo Intl., *Seoul*	36,757
10	Charles de Gaulle, *Paris*	35,294
11	Denver Intl., *Denver*	34,973
12	Miami Intl., *Miami*	34,533
13	Schiphol, *Amsterdam*	31,570
14	Metro Wayne County, *Detroit*	31,521
15	John F. Kennedy Intl., *New York*	31,229

The Longest Rail Networks ▾

Extent of rail network, in thousands of kilometres (1996)

1	USA	243.3
2	Russia	87.1
3	India	62.9
4	China	56.7
5	Germany	40.8
6	Argentina	34.2
7	France	31.9
8	Mexico	26.5
9	South Africa	25.9
10	Poland	23.4

which accounted for 7.5% of world trade by the mid-1990s. Travel and tourism have greatly increased people's understanding and knowledge of the world, especially in the OECD countries, which account for about 8% of world tourism.

Some developing countries have large tourist industries which have provided employment and led to improvements in roads and other facilities. In some cases, tourism plays a vital role in the economy. For example, in Kenya, tourism provides more income than any other activity apart from the production and sale of coffee. However, too many tourists can damage fragile environments, such as the wildlife and scenery in national parks. Tourism can also harm local cultures.

THE IMPORTANCE OF TOURISM

Nations receiving the most from tourism, millions of US$ (1996)

1	USA	64,400
2	Spain	28,400
3	France	28,200
4	Italy	27,300
5	UK	20,400
6	Austria	15,100
7	Germany	13,200
8	Hong Kong	11,200
9	China	10,500
10	Switzerland	9,900

Fastest growing tourist destinations, % change in receipts (1994–95)

1	South Korea	49%
2	Czech Republic	27%
3	India	21%
4	Russia	19%
5	Philippines	18%
6	Turkey	17%
7	Thailand	15%
8	Poland	13%
9	China	12%
10	Israel	12%

Number of tourist arrivals, millions (1996)

1	France	66,800
2	USA	49,038
3	Spain	43,403
4	Italy	34,087
5	UK	25,960
6	China	23,770
7	Poland	19,514
8	Mexico	18,667
9	Canada	17,610
10	Czech Republic	17,400

Overseas travellers to the USA, thousands (1997)

1	Canada	13,900
2	Mexico	12,370
3	Japan	4,640
4	UK	3,350
5	Germany	1,990
6	France	1,030
7	Taiwan	885
8	Venezuela	860
9	South Korea	800
10	Brazil	785

THE WORLD'S VEHICLES

Proportion of the world's vehicles by region (1994)

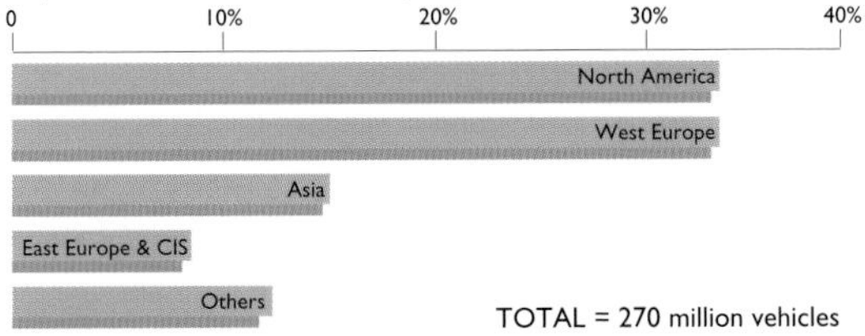
0
10%
20%
30%
40%
North America
West Europe
Asia
East Europe & CIS
Others
TOTAL = 270 million vehicles

CAR OWNERSHIP

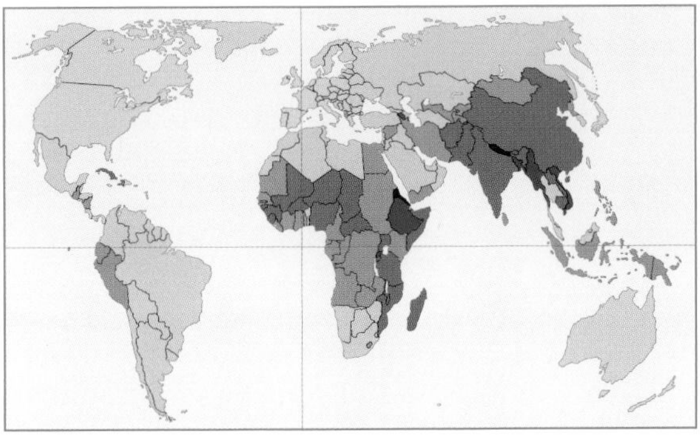

Number of people per car (1996)

- Over 1,000
- 500 – 1,000
- 100 – 500
- 25 – 100
- 5 – 25
- Under 5

Two-thirds of the world's vehicles are found in the developed countries of Europe and North America. Car ownership is also high in Australia and New Zealand, as well as in Japan, the world's leading car exporter. Car transport is the most convenient form of passenger travel, but air pollution caused by exhaust fumes is a serious problem in many large cities.

International Organizations

IN THE LATE 1980s, people rejoiced at the collapse of Communist regimes in eastern Europe and the former Soviet Union, because this brought to an end the Cold War, a long period of hostility between East and West. But hope of a new era of peace was shattered when ethnic and religious rivalries led to civil war in Yugoslavia and in parts of the former Soviet Union.

In order to help maintain peace, many governments have formed international organizations to increase co-operation. Some, such as NATO (North Atlantic Treaty Organization), are defence alliances, while others aim to encourage economic and social co-operation. Some organizations such as the Red Cross are non-governmental organizations, or NGOs.

> In the early 1990s, the United Nations peacekeeping mission worked to end the civil war in Bosnia-Herzegovina and also to bring aid to civilians affected by the fighting.

UN Contributions ▾

In 1996–97, the top ten contributing countries to the UN budget, which was US$2.6 billion, were as follows:

1	USA	25.0%
2	Japan	15.4%
3	Germany	9.0%
4	France	6.4%
5	UK	5.3%
6	Italy	5.2%
7	Russia	4.5%
8	Canada	3.1%
9	Spain	2.4%
10	Brazil	1.6%

UNITED NATIONS

The United Nations, the chief international organization, was formed in October 1945 and now has 185 member countries. The only independent nations that are not members are Kiribati, Nauru, Switzerland, Taiwan, Tonga, Tuvalu and the Vatican City.

THE UNITED NATIONS

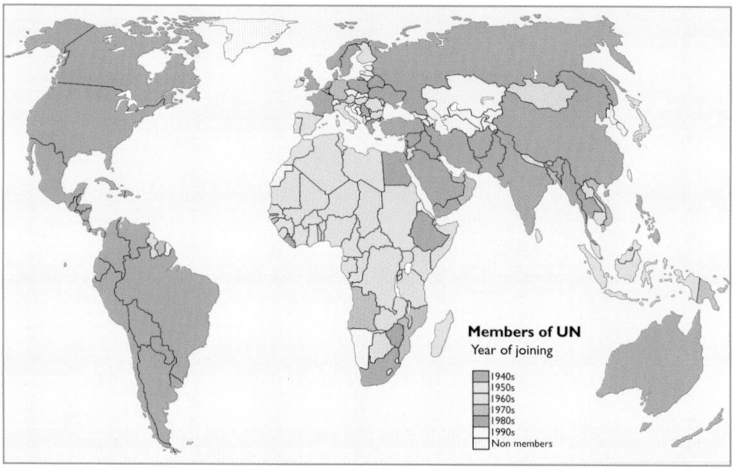
Members of UN
Year of joining
1940s
1950s
1960s
1970s
1980s
1990s
Non members

> The membership of the UN had risen from 51 in 1945 to 185 by the end of 1998. The first big period of expansion came in the 1960s when many former colonies achieved their independence. The membership again expanded rapidly in the 1990s when new countries were formed from the former Soviet Union and Yugoslavia. The most recent addition, Palau, is a former US trust territory in the Pacific Ocean and joined in 1994.

The United Nations was formed at the end of World War II to promote peace, international co-operation and security, and to help solve economic, social, cultural and humanitarian problems. It promotes human rights and freedom and is a forum for negotiations between nations.

The main organs of the UN are the General Assembly, the Security Council, the Economic and Social Council, the Trusteeship Council, the International Court of Justice and the Secretariat.

The UN also operates 14 specialized agencies concerned with particular issues, such as agriculture, education, working conditions, communications and health. For example, UNICEF (the United Nations International Children's Fund), established in 1946 to deliver post-war relief to children, now aims to provide basic health care to children and mothers worldwide. The ILO (International Labour Organization) seeks to improve working conditions, while the FAO (Food and Agricultural Organization) aims at improving the production and distribution of food. The WTO (World Trade Organization) was set up as recently as January 1995 to succeed GATT (General Agreements on Tariffs and Trade).

THE UNITED NATIONS

THE GENERAL ASSEMBLY is the meeting of all member nations every September under a newly-elected president to discuss issues affecting development, peace and security.

THE SECURITY COUNCIL has 15 members, of which five are permanent. It is responsible for maintaining international peace.

THE SECRETARIAT consists of the staff and employees of the UN, including the Secretary-General (appointed for a five-year term), who is the UN's chief administrator.

THE ECONOMIC & SOCIAL COUNCIL works with the specialized agencies to implement UN policies on improving living standards, health, cultural and educational co-operation.

THE TRUSTEESHIP COUNCIL was designed to bring several dependencies to independence. This work is now complete.

THE INTERNATIONAL COURT OF JUSTICE, or World Court, deals with legal problems and helps to settle disputes. Its headquarters are at The Hague, in the Netherlands.

UN DEPARTMENTS

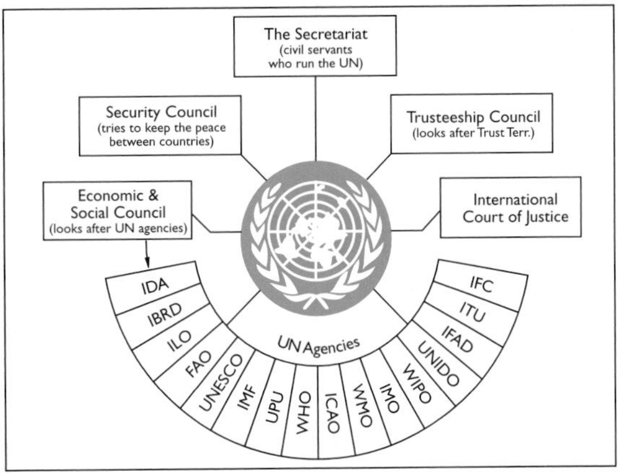

UN PEACEKEEPING MISSIONS

The United Nations tries to resolve international disputes in several ways. It sends unarmed observer missions to monitor cease-fires or supervise troop withdrawals, and the Security Council members also send peacekeeping forces.

The first of these forces was sent in 1948 to supervise the cease-fire between Arabs and Jews in disputed parts of Palestine and, since then, it has undertaken more than 30 other missions. The 'Blue Berets', as the 25,650 UN troops are called, must be impartial in any dispute and they can fire only in self-defence. Hence, they can operate only with the support of both sides, which leaves them open to criticism when they are unable to prevent violence by intervening.

By the mid-1990s, the UN was involved in 15 world conflicts, was policing the boundary in partitioned Cyprus, and was seeking to enforce a peace agreement in Angola after 20 years of civil war. Other UN missions were in Tajikistan, Georgia, the Israeli-occupied Golan Heights, Haiti, Kuwait, southern Lebanon, the India–Pakistan border, Liberia, Mozambique, Western Sahara and the former Yugoslavia. A force known as UNPROFOR (UN Protection Force) had been operating in Bosnia-Herzegovina and, by 1995, it accounted for 60% of the total UN peacekeeping budget. In February 1996, the Secretary-General of the UN approved the setting up of a new force, the United Nations Mission in Bosnia-Herzegovina (UNMIBH). Its main objective was to help create the right climate for the elections held in September 1996.

> The European Parliament, one of the branches of the EU, consists of 626 members. The number of members for each country is based mainly on population.

ECONOMIC ORGANIZATIONS

Over the last 40 years, many countries have joined common markets aimed at eliminating trade barriers and encouraging the free movement of workers and capital.

The best known of these is the European Union. Other organizations include ASEAN (the Association of South-east Asian Nations), which aims at reducing trade barriers between its nine members: Brunei, Burma, Indonesia, Laos, Malaysia, the Philippines, Singapore, Thailand and Vietnam.

APEC (the Asia-Pacific Co-operation Group) was founded in 1989 and includes the countries of East and South-east Asia, as well as North America, plus Australia, New Zealand and Chile. APEC aims to create a free trade zone by 2020.

Together the United States, Canada and Mexico form NAFTA (North American Free Trade Agreement), which aims at eliminating trade barriers within 15 years of its foundation on 1 January 1994. Other economic groupings link the countries of Latin America.

Another economic group with more limited aims is OPEC (Organization of Petroleum Exporting Countries). It works to unify policies concerned with the sale of petroleum on world markets.

The central aim of the Colombo Plan is to provide economic development assistance for South and South-east Asia.

OTHER ORGANIZATIONS

Some organizations exist for consultation on matters of common interest. The Commonwealth of Nations grew out of the links created by the British Empire, while the OAS (Organization of American States) works to increase understanding throughout the Western hemisphere. The OAU (Organization of

THE EUROPEAN UNION

At the end of World War II (1939–45), many Europeans wanted to end the ancient emnities that had caused such destruction and rebuild the shattered continent. It was in this mood that Belgium, France, West Germany, Italy, Luxembourg and the Netherlands signed the Treaty of Paris in 1951. This set up the European Coal and Steel Community (ECSC), the forerunner of the European Union.

In 1957, through the Treaty of Rome, the same six countries created the European Economic Community (EEC) and the European Atomic Community (EURATOM). In 1967, the ECSC, the EEC and EURATOM merged to form the single European Community (EC).

Another economic group, the European Free Trade Association (EFTA), was set up in 1960 by seven countries: Austria, Denmark, Norway, Portugal, Sweden, Switzerland, and the United Kingdom. However, Denmark, Ireland and the UK left to become members of the EC in 1973, followed by Greece in 1981, Spain and Portugal in 1986, and Austria, Finland and Sweden in 1995. The expansion of the EC to 15 members left EFTA with just four members: Iceland, Liechtenstein, Norway and Switzerland.

In 1993, following the signing of the Maastricht Treaty, the EC was reconstituted as the European Union (EU). The aims of the EU include economic and monetary union, a single currency for all 15 countries, and closer co-operation on foreign and security policies and also on home affairs. This step has led to a debate. Some people would like the EU to develop into a federal Europe, but others fear that this would lead to a loss of national identity. Another matter of importance is the future enlargement of the EU. By 1995, formal applications for membership had been received from Turkey, Malta, Cyprus, Poland, Hungary, Slovakia and Romania. Other possible members include the Czech Republic, Estonia, Latvia and Lithuania.

AUSTRALIA'S NEW ROLE

Most of the people who settled in Australia between 1788 and the mid-20th century came from the British Isles. However, the strong ties between Australia and Britain were weakened after Britain joined the European Community in 1973. Since 1973, many Australians have argued that their world position has changed and that they are part of a Pacific community of nations, rather than an extension of Europe. Some want closer integration with ASEAN, the increasingly powerful economic group formed by seven South-east Asian nations. But in 1995, the prime minister of Malaysia, Dr Mahathir Mohamad, argued that Australia could not be regarded as Asian until at least 70% of its people were of ethnic Asian origin.

African Unity) has a similar role in Africa, while the Arab League is made up of Arabic-speaking North African and Middle Eastern states. The recently formed CIS (Commonwealth of Independent States) aims to maintain links between 12 of the 15 republics which made up the Soviet Union.

NORTH–SOUTH DIVIDE

The deepest division in the world today is the divide between rich and poor nations. In international terms, this is called the North–South divide, because the North contains most of the world's developed countries, while the developing countries lie mainly in the South. The European Union recognizes this division and gives special trading terms to more than 60 former European dependencies, which form the ACP (African, Caribbean and Pacific) states. One organization containing a majority of developing countries is the Non-Aligned Movement. This Movement was created in 1961 during the Cold War as a political bloc allied neither to the East nor to the West. However, the aims of the 113 members who attended the movement's 11th gathering in 1995 were concerned mainly with economic matters. The 113 countries between them produce only about 7% of the world's gross output and they can speak for the poorer South.

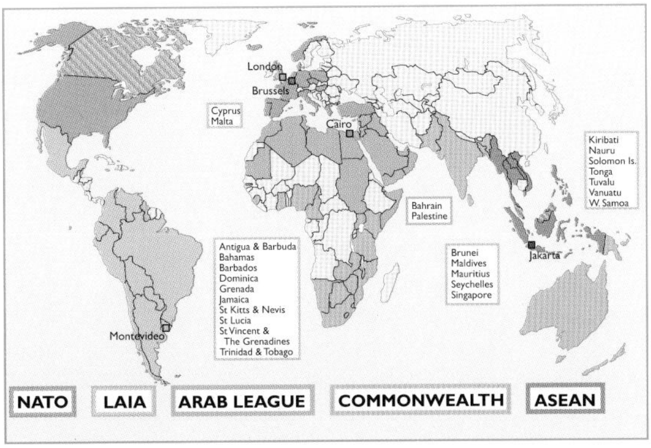

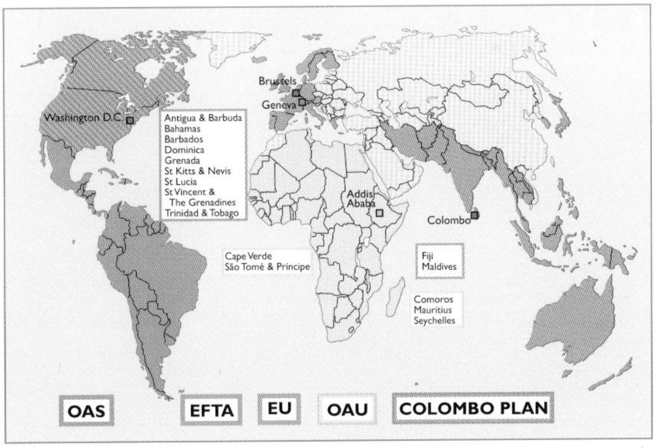

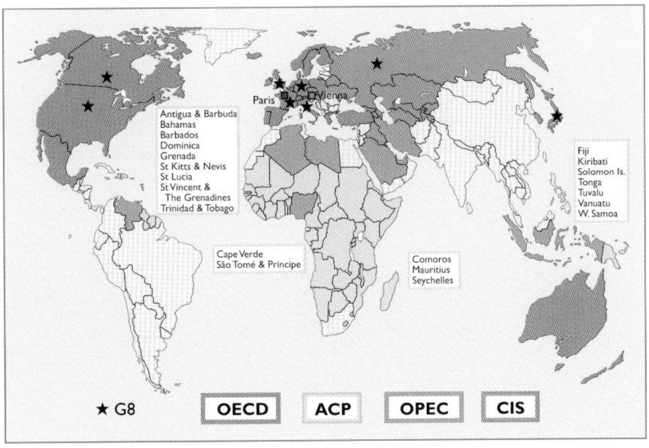

> The maps above show the membership of major international organizations. One important grouping shown on the bottom map is the Group of Eight (often called 'G8'). This group of eight leading industrial nations (comprising Canada, France, Germany, Italy, Japan, Russia, the United Kingdom and the United States) holds periodic meetings to discuss major problems, such as world recessions.

Regions in the News

THE BREAK-UP OF YUGOSLAVIA

> The former Yugoslavia, a federation of six republics, split apart in 1991–92. Fearing Serb domination, Croatia, Slovenia, Macedonia and Bosnia-Herzegovina declared themselves independent. This left two states, Serbia and Montenegro, to continue as Yugoslavia. The presence in Croatia and Bosnia-Herzegovina of Orthodox Christian Serbs, Roman Catholic Croats and Muslims led to civil war and 'ethnic cleansing'. In 1995, the war ended when the Dayton Peace Accord affirmed Bosnia-Herzegovina as a single state partitioned into a Muslim-Croat Federation and a Serbian Republic. But the status of Kosovo, a former autonomous Yugoslav region, remained unresolved. Kosovo's autonomy had been abolished in 1989 and the Albanian-speaking, Muslim Kosovars were forced to accept direct Serbian rule. After 1995, support grew for the rebel Kosovo Liberation Army, which took over large areas. The Serbs hit back and thousands of Kosovars were forced to flee their homes. In March 1999, NATO launched an aerial offensive against Serbia in an attempt to halt the 'ethnic cleansing'.

Population Breakdown ▾

Population totals and the proportion of ethnic groups (1995)

Yugoslavia	**10,881,000**
Serb 63%, Albanian 17%, Montenegrin 5%, Hungarian 3%, Muslim 3%	
Serbia	6,017,200
Kosovo	*2,045,600*
Vojvodina	*2,121,800*
Montenegro	696,400
Bosnia-Herzegovina	**4,400,000**
Muslim 49%, Serb 31%, Croat 17%	
Croatia	**4,900,000**
Croat 78%, Serb 12%	
Slovenia	**2,000,000**
Slovene 88%, Croat 3%, Serb 2%	
Macedonia (F.Y.R.O.M.)	**2,173,000**
Macedonian 64%, Albanian 22%, Turkish 5%, Romanian 3%, Serb 2%	

International borders

Republic boundaries

Province boundaries

Line of the Dayton Peace Accord

Muslim–Croat Federation

Serbian Republic

> Since its establishment in 1948, the State of Israel has seldom been out of the news. During wars with its Arab neighbours in 1948–49, 1956, 1967 and 1973, it occupied several areas. The largest of the occupied territories, the Sinai peninsula, was returned to Egypt in 1979 following the signing of an Egyptian–Israeli peace treaty. This left three Israeli-occupied territories: the Gaza Strip, the West Bank bordering Jordan, and the Golan Heights, a militarily strategic area overlooking south-western Syria.

Despite the peace agreement with Egypt, conflict continued in Israel with the PLO (Palestine Liberation Organization), which claimed to represent Arabs in Israel and Palestinians living in exile. Finally, on 13 September 1993 Israel officially recognized the PLO, and Yasser Arafat, leader of the PLO, renounced terrorism and recognized the State of Israel. This led to an agreement signed by both sides in Washington, DC. In May 1994, limited Palestinian self-rule was established in the Gaza Strip and in parts of the occupied West Bank. A Palestinian National Authority (PNA) was created and took over from the Israeli military administration when Israeli troops withdrew from the Gaza Strip and the city of Jericho. On 1 July 1994 the Palestinian leader, Yasser Arafat, stepped on to Palestinian land for the first time in 25 years.

Many people hoped that these developments would eventually lead to the creation of a Palestinian state, which would co-exist in peace with its neighbour Israel. But groups on both sides sought to undermine the peace process. In November 1995, a right-wing Jewish student assassinated the Israeli prime minister, Yitzhak Rabin, who was succeeded by Símon Peres.

In 1996, a right-wing coalition led by Binyamin Netanyahu was returned to power in a general election. The peace talks with the PLO were temporarily halted, but an agreement was reached in early 1997 over the withdrawal of Israeli troops from the town of Al Khalil (Hebron), on the West Bank. One-fifth of this town remained in the hands of about 400 Israeli settlers. Negotiations with Syria, however, over the Golan Heights were halted in 1996.

Population Breakdown ▾

Population totals and the proportion of ethnic groups (1995)

Israel **5,696,000**
Jewish 82%, Arab Muslim 14%, Arab Christian 3%, Druse 2%

West Bank *973,500*
Palestinian Arab 97% (Arab Muslim 85%, Christian 8%, Jewish 7%)

Gaza Strip *658,200*
Arab Muslim 98%

Jordan **5,547,000**
Arab 99% (Palestinian Arab 50%)

Syria **14,614,000**
Arab 89%, Kurdish 6%

THE NEAR EAST

—·—·— 1949 Armistice Line

- - - - - 1974 Cease-fire Lines (Golan Heights)

Efrata ● Main Jewish settlements in the West Bank and Gaza Strip

Halhul □ Main Palestinian Arab towns in the West Bank and Gaza Strip – under Palestinian control since May 1994 (Gaza and Jericho) and 28 September 1995 (West Bank)

World Flags

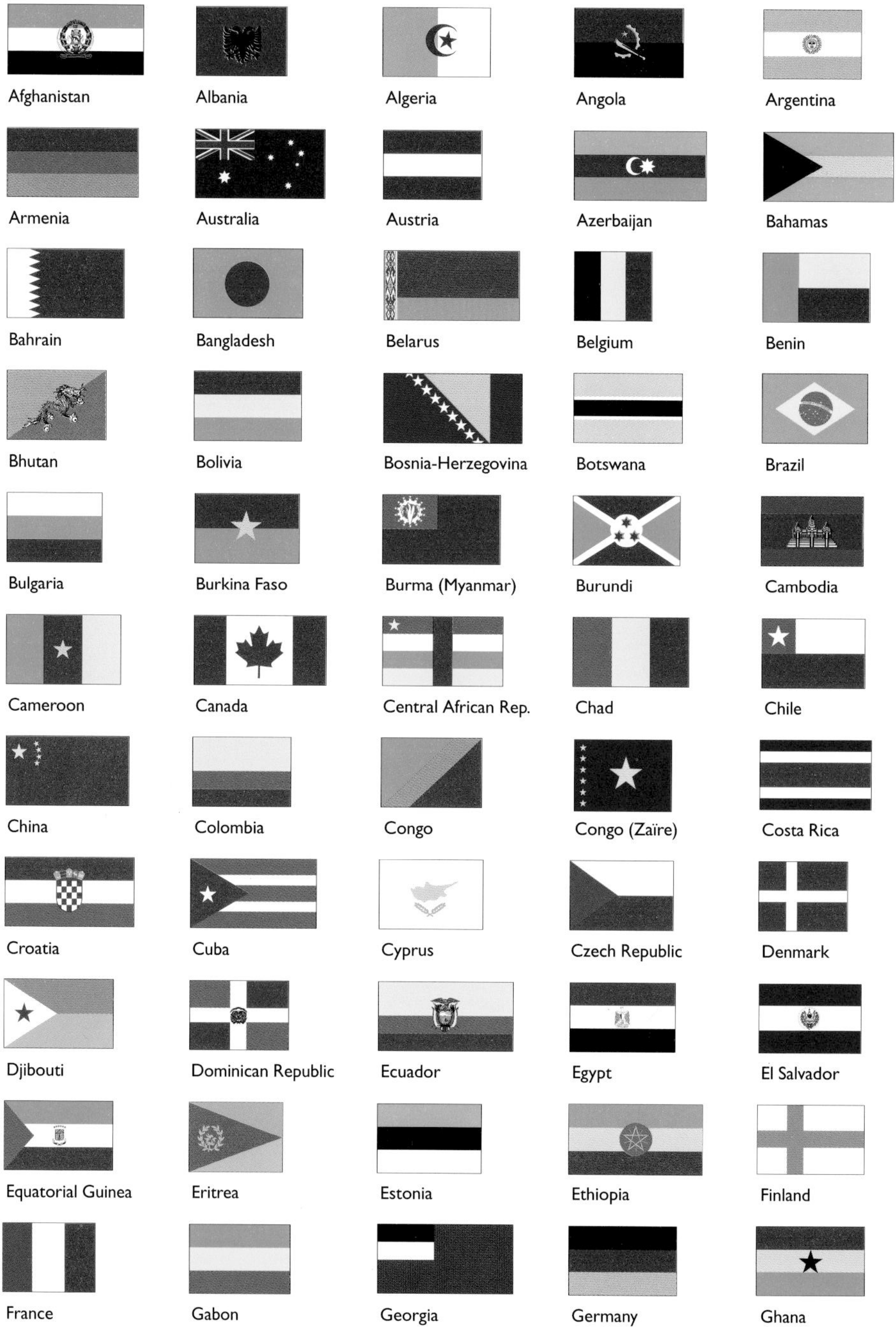
Afghanistan
Albania
Algeria
Angola
Argentina
Armenia
Australia
Austria
Azerbaijan
Bahamas
Bahrain
Bangladesh
Belarus
Belgium
Benin
Bhutan
Bolivia
Bosnia-Herzegovina
Botswana
Brazil
Bulgaria
Burkina Faso
Burma (Myanmar)
Burundi
Cambodia
Cameroon
Canada
Central African Rep.
Chad
Chile
China
Colombia
Congo
Congo (Zaïre)
Costa Rica
Croatia
Cuba
Cyprus
Czech Republic
Denmark
Djibouti
Dominican Republic
Ecuador
Egypt
El Salvador
Equatorial Guinea
Eritrea
Estonia
Ethiopia
Finland
France
Gabon
Georgia
Germany
Ghana

Greece | Guatemala | Guinea | Guinea–Bissau | Guyana

Haiti | Honduras | Hong Kong | Hungary | Iceland

India | Indonesia | Iran | Iraq | Ireland

Israel | Italy | Ivory Coast | Jamaica | Japan

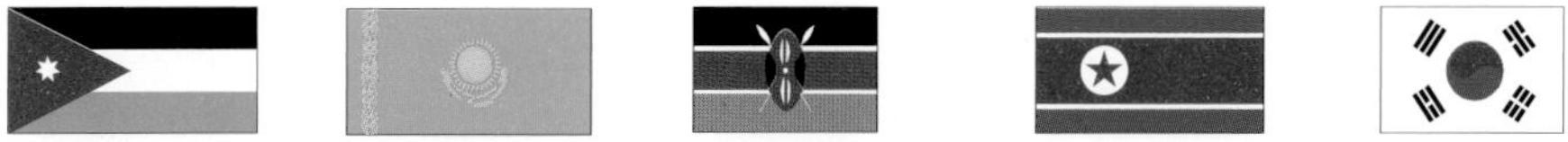

Jordan | Kazakstan | Kenya | Korea, North | Korea, South

Kuwait | Kyrgyzstan | Laos | Latvia | Lebanon

Lesotho | Liberia | Libya | Liechtenstein | Lithuania

Luxembourg | Macedonia | Madagascar | Malawi | Malaysia

Mali | Malta | Mauritania | Mexico | Moldova

Mongolia | Morocco | Mozambique | Namibia | Nepal

Netherlands | New Zealand | Nicaragua | Niger | Nigeria

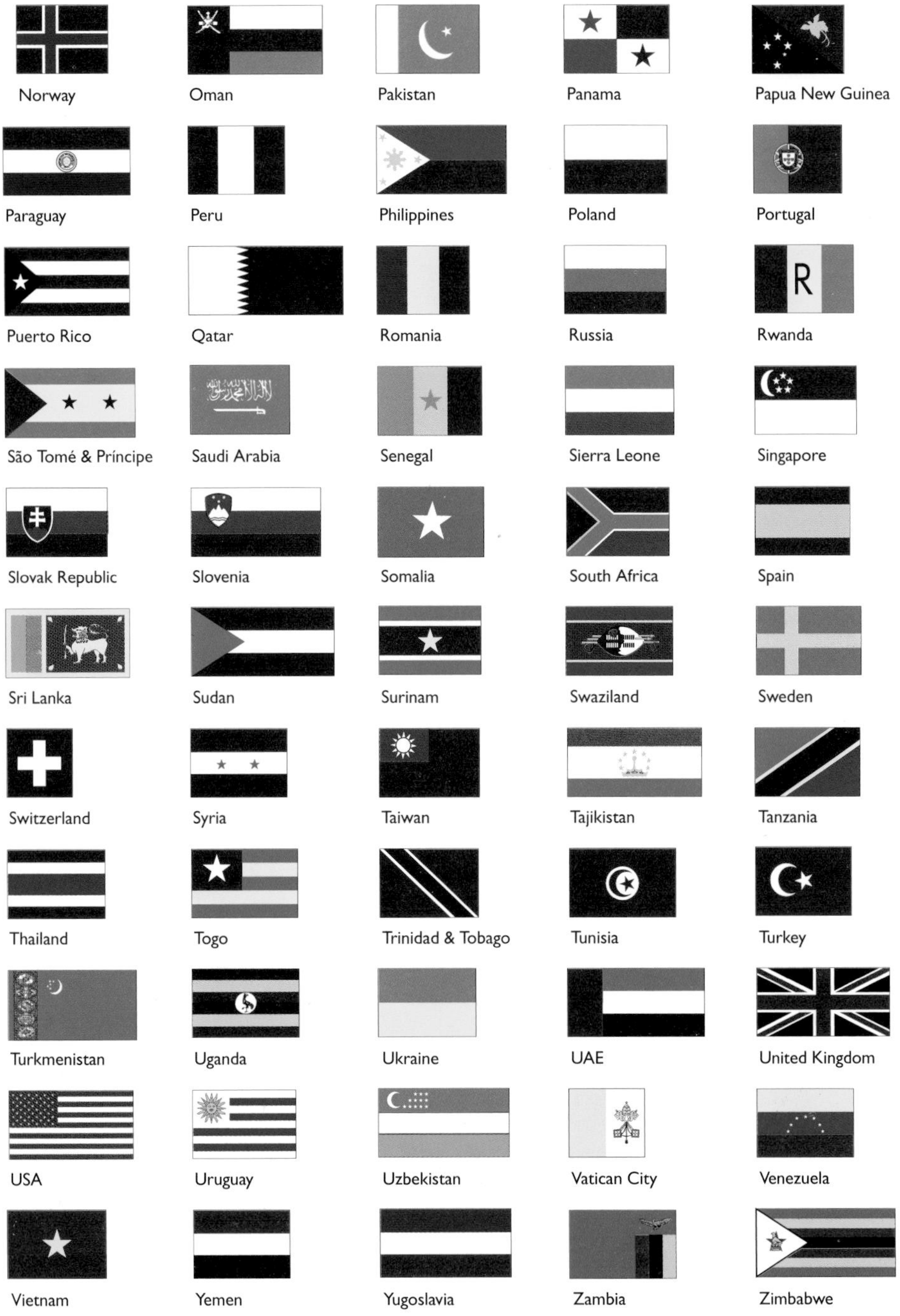
Norway
Oman
Pakistan
Panama
Papua New Guinea
Paraguay
Peru
Philippines
Poland
Portugal
Puerto Rico
Qatar
Romania
Russia
R
Rwanda
São Tomé & Príncipe
Saudi Arabia
Senegal
Sierra Leone
Singapore
Slovak Republic
Slovenia
Somalia
South Africa
Spain
Sri Lanka
Sudan
Surinam
Swaziland
Sweden
Switzerland
Syria
Taiwan
Tajikistan
Tanzania
Thailand
Togo
Trinidad & Tobago
Tunisia
Turkey
Turkmenistan
Uganda
Ukraine
UAE
United Kingdom
USA
Uruguay
Uzbekistan
Vatican City
Venezuela
Vietnam
Yemen
Yugoslavia
Zambia
Zimbabwe

World Maps — GENERAL REFERENCE

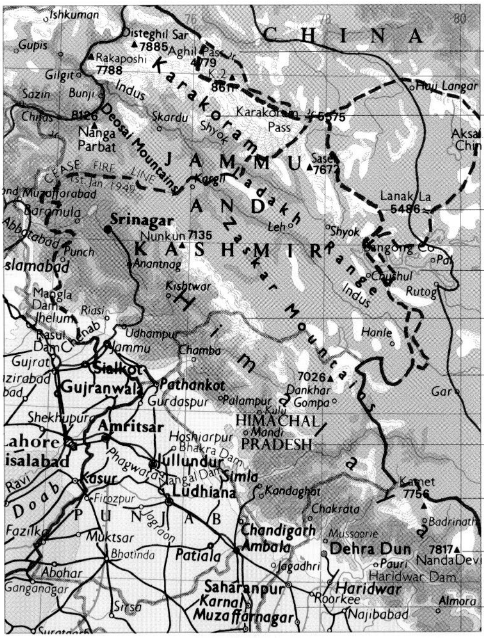

Pass

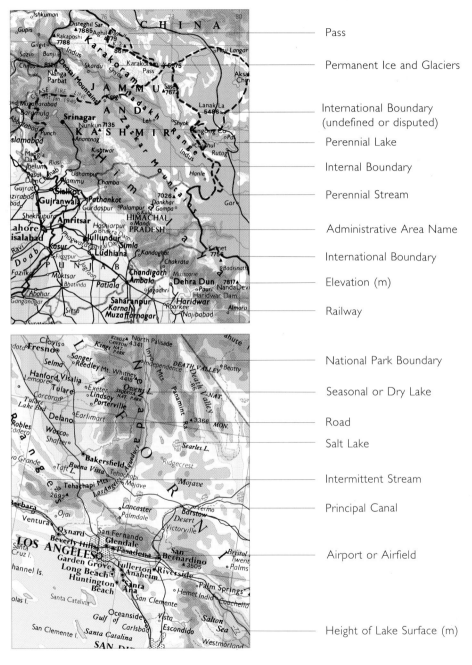

Permanent Ice and Glaciers

International Boundary (undefined or disputed)

Perennial Lake

Internal Boundary

Perennial Stream

Administrative Area Name

International Boundary

Elevation (m)

Railway

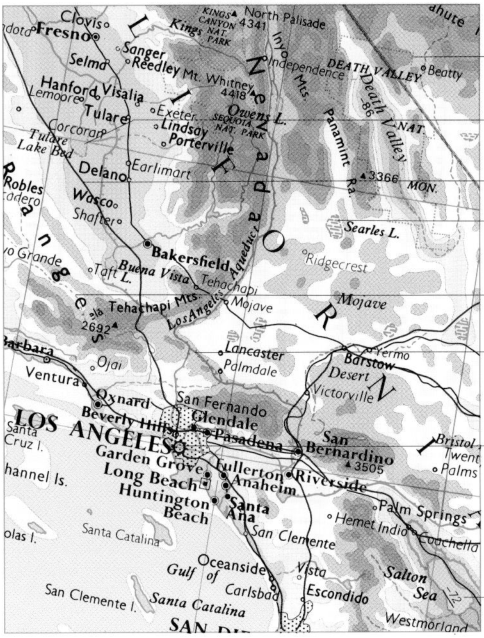

National Park Boundary

Seasonal or Dry Lake

Road

Salt Lake

Intermittent Stream

Principal Canal

Airport or Airfield

Height of Lake Surface (m)

Settlements

Settlement symbols and type styles vary according to the scale of each map and indicate the importance of towns rather than specific population figures.

NORTHERN HEMISPHERE

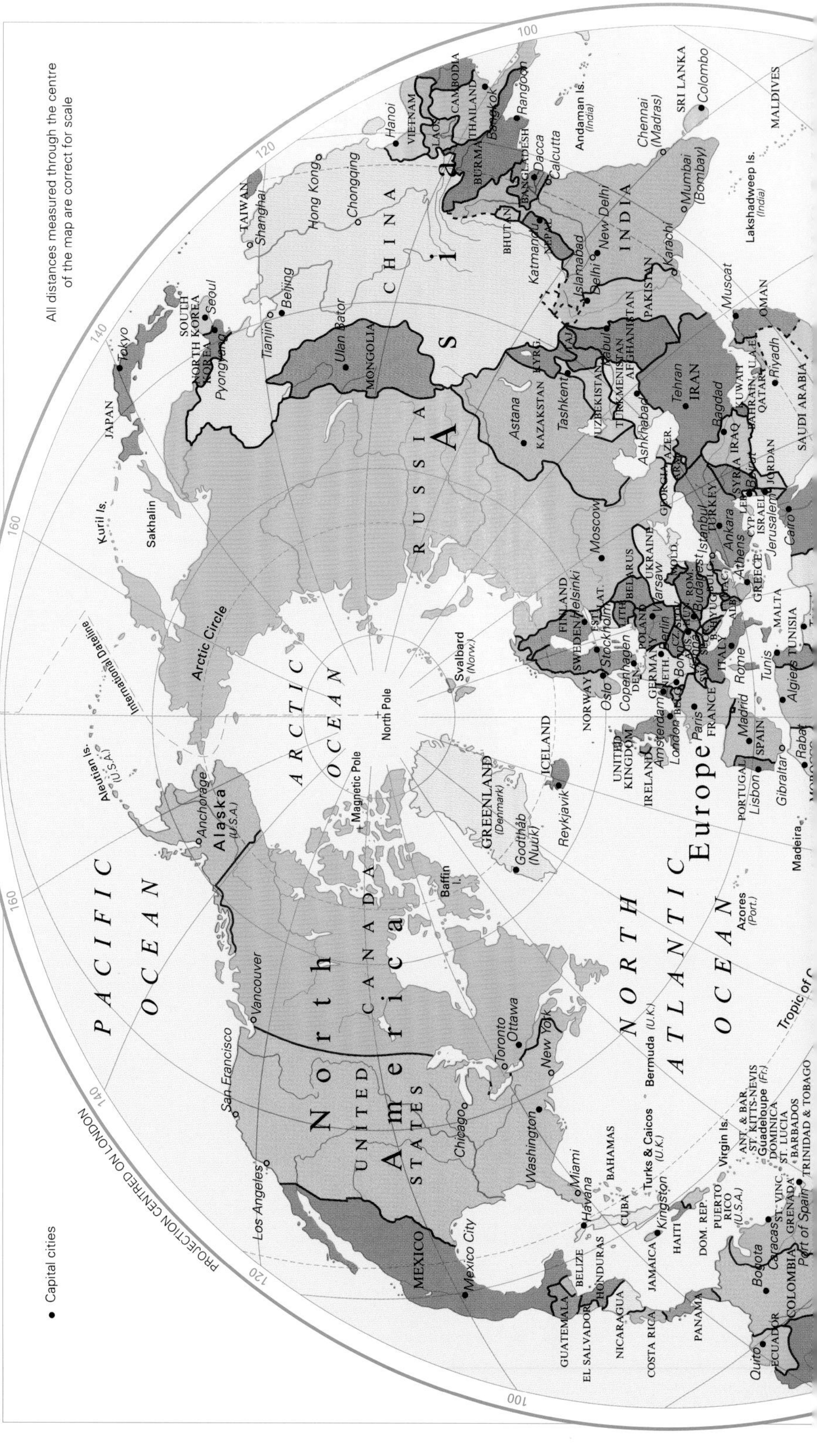
Capital cities
All distances measured through the centre of the map are correct for scale
PROJECTION CENTRED ON LONDON
PACIFIC OCEAN
ARCTIC OCEAN
NORTH ATLANTIC OCEAN
North America
Europe
Asia
North Pole
Magnetic Pole
Arctic Circle
International Dateline
Tropic of C
CANADA
UNITED STATES
MEXICO
Alaska (U.S.A.)
GREENLAND (Denmark)
ICELAND
RUSSIA
CHINA
INDIA
MONGOLIA
KAZAKSTAN
JAPAN
Aleutian Is. (U.S.A.)
Kuril Is.
Sakhalin
Svalbard (Norw.)
Baffin I.
Azores (Port.)
Madeira
Bermuda (U.K.)
Andaman Is. (India)
Lakshadweep Is. (India)
Anchorage
Vancouver
San Francisco
Los Angeles
Chicago
Toronto
Ottawa
New York
Washington
Miami
Havana
Mexico City
Godthåb (Nuuk)
Reykjavik
London
Paris
Madrid
Lisbon
Rome
Berlin
Moscow
Istanbul
Ankara
Tehran
Tashkent
Astana
Ulan Bator
Beijing
Tianjin
Seoul
Pyongyang
Tokyo
Shanghai
Hong Kong
Chongqing
Hanoi
Bangkok
Rangoon
Dacca
Calcutta
Katmandu
Delhi
New Delhi
Islamabad
Karachi
Mumbai (Bombay)
Chennai (Madras)
Colombo
Muscat
Riyadh
Cairo
Jerusalem
Athens
Algiers
Tunis
Rabat
Gibraltar
Caracas
Bogota
Quito
Port of Spain
Kingston

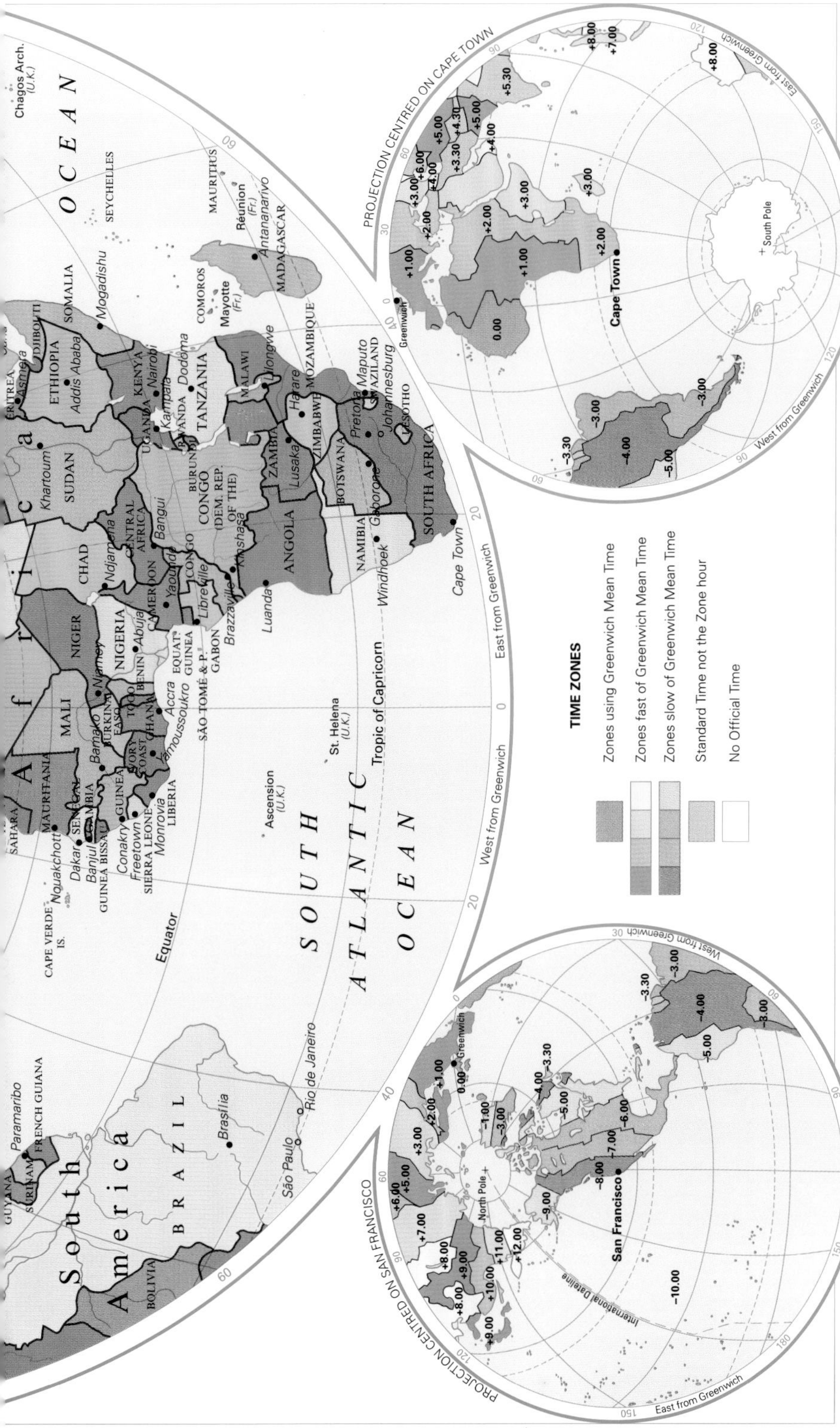

Projection: Oblique Azimuthal Equidistant

CARTOGRAPHY BY PHILIP'S.

COPYRIGHT GEORGE PHILIP LTD

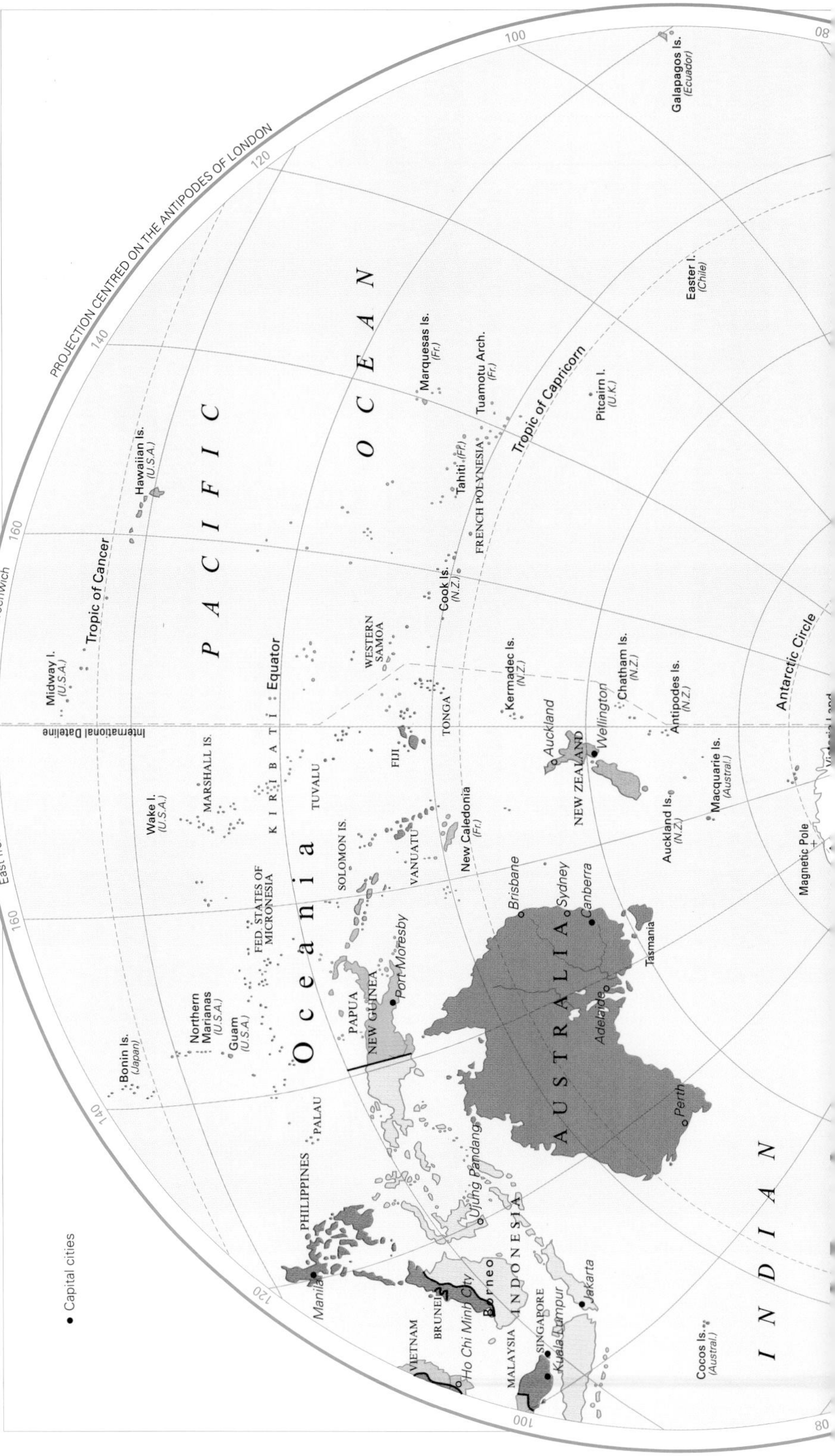
PROJECTION CENTRED ON THE ANTIPODES OF LONDON
West from Greenwich
East from Greenwich
International Dateline
Tropic of Cancer
Equator
Tropic of Capricorn
Antarctic Circle
P A C I F I C
O C E A N
I N D I A N
O c e a n i a
A U S T R A L I A
Capital cities
Midway I. (U.S.A.)
Hawaiian Is. (U.S.A.)
Wake I. (U.S.A.)
MARSHALL IS.
K I R I B A T I
TUVALU
WESTERN SAMOA
FIJI
TONGA
Cook Is. (N.Z.)
FRENCH POLYNESIA
Tahiti (Fr.)
Marquesas Is. (Fr.)
Tuamotu Arch. (Fr.)
Pitcairn I. (U.K.)
Easter I. (Chile)
Galapagos Is. (Ecuador)
Kermadec Is. (N.Z.)
Chatham Is. (N.Z.)
Antipodes Is. (N.Z.)
Auckland Is. (N.Z.)
Macquarie Is. (Austral.)
Magnetic Pole
Auckland
Wellington
NEW ZEALAND
New Caledonia (Fr.)
VANUATU
SOLOMON IS.
FED. STATES OF MICRONESIA
Northern Marianas (U.S.A.)
Guam (U.S.A.)
Bonin Is. (Japan)
PALAU
PAPUA NEW GUINEA
Port Moresby
Brisbane
Sydney
Canberra
Adelaide
Perth
Tasmania
PHILIPPINES
Manila
Ujung Pandang
INDONESIA
Borneo
Jakarta
BRUNEI
VIETNAM
Ho Chi Minh City
MALAYSIA
SINGAPORE
Kuala Lumpur
Cocos Is. (Austral.)
100
120
140
160
180
80

1:100 000 000

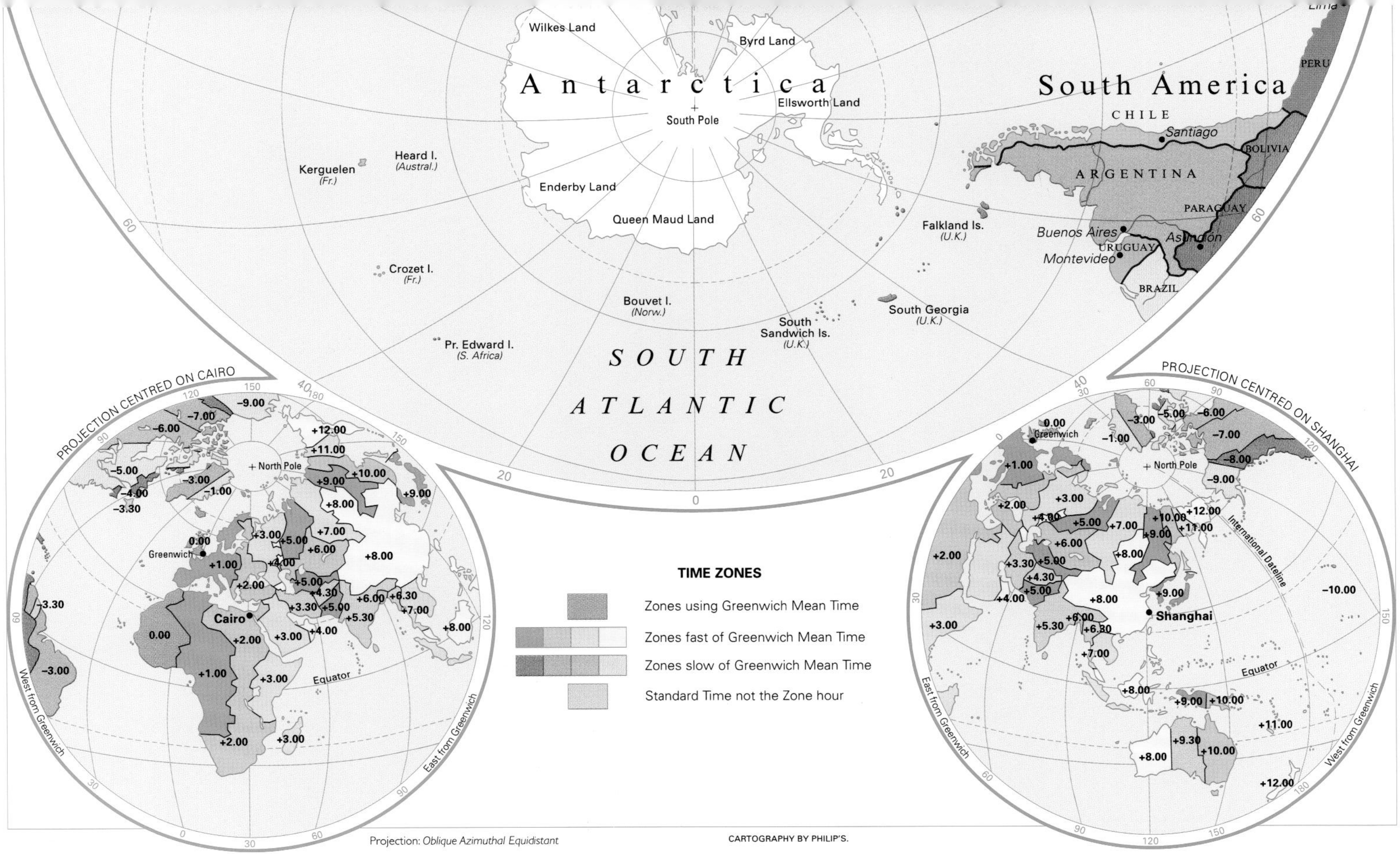

Antarctica
South Pole
Wilkes Land
Byrd Land
Ellsworth Land
Enderby Land
Queen Maud Land
Kerguelen (Fr.)
Heard I. (Austral.)
Crozet I. (Fr.)
Pr. Edward I. (S. Africa)
Bouvet I. (Norw.)
South Sandwich Is. (U.K.)
South Georgia (U.K.)
Falkland Is. (U.K.)
SOUTH ATLANTIC OCEAN
South America
CHILE
Santiago
ARGENTINA
BOLIVIA
PERU
PARAGUAY
Asunción
Buenos Aires
URUGUAY
Montevideo
BRAZIL
PROJECTION CENTRED ON CAIRO
Cairo
Greenwich
North Pole
Equator
West from Greenwich
East from Greenwich
PROJECTION CENTRED ON SHANGHAI
Shanghai
International Dateline
TIME ZONES
Zones using Greenwich Mean Time
Zones fast of Greenwich Mean Time
Zones slow of Greenwich Mean Time
Standard Time not the Zone hour

Projection: *Oblique Azimuthal Equidistant*

CARTOGRAPHY BY PHILIP'S.

ICELAND
Reykjavik
Arctic Circle
Norwegian Sea
Faroe Is. (Den.)
Shetland Is.
Orkney Is.
Hebrides
ATLANTIC OCEAN
UNITED KINGDOM
SCOTLAND
Aberdeen
Dundee
Glasgow
Edinburgh
N. IRELAND
Belfast
IRELAND
Dublin
Cork
Newcastle-upon-Tyne
Manchester
Leeds
Liverpool
Sheffield
Birmingham
WALES
ENGLAND
Cardiff
Bristol
LONDON
Plymouth
Southampton
English Channel
Channel Is. (U.K.)
North Sea
NORWAY
Bergen
Oslo
Stavanger
Trondheim
SWEDEN
Uppsala
Örebro
Vänern
Vättern
Jönköping
Gothenburg
Gävle
Skagerrak
Kattegatt
DENMARK
Ålborg
Århus
Copenhagen
Malmö
Gotland
Baltic
Tromsø
Kiel
Hamburg
Bremen
Elbe
Amsterdam
The Hague
Rotterdam
NETHERLANDS
Antwerp
BELGIUM
Brussels
Lille
GERMANY
Hannover
Berlin
Magdeburg
Essen
Dortmund
Halle
Cologne
Bonn
Leipzig
Chemnitz
Dresden
Wiesbaden
Frankfurt am Main
LUX.
Luxembourg
Meuse
Gdańsk
Szczecin
Bydgoszcz
POL
Oder
Poznań
Łódź
Wrocław
Katowice
Prague
CZECH REP.
Ostrava
Le Havre
Rouen
Seine
PARIS
Brest
FRANCE
Strasbourg
Rhine
Stuttgart
Nuremberg
Munich
Nantes
Loire
Dijon
Bay of Biscay
Limoges
Lyons
St.-Étienne
Bordeaux
Garonne
Toulouse
Rhône
Grenoble
Zürich
Bern
LIECH.
Vaduz
SWITZERLAND
Geneva
Innsbruck
Salzburg
Linz
Vienna
Bratislava
AUSTRIA
Graz
HUNG
SLO
SLOVENIA
Ljubljana
Zagreb
CROATIA
Trieste
Venice
Milan
Turin
Genoa
Bologna
BOSNIA-HERZ.
Sarajevo
Split
Nice
MONACO
Marseilles
Toulon
Corsica
Ajaccio
Florence
SAN MARINO
Tiber
Adriatic Sea
ITALY
Rome
Sardinia
Cagliari
Tyrrhenian Sea
Naples
Bari
Táranto
Tiran
ALB
La Coruña
Vigo
Porto
Douro
Bilbao
Valladolid
Ebro
Zaragoza
ANDORRA
Andorra-la-Vella
Barcelona
Lisbon
PORTUGAL
Tagus
SPAIN
Madrid
Guadiana
Valencia
Seville
Córdoba
Guadalquivir
Murcia
Alicante
Granada
Cádiz
Málaga
Gibraltar (U.K.)
Ceuta (Sp.)
Str. of Gibraltar
Tangier
Balearic Is.
Palma
Minorca
Majorca
Ibiza
Mediterranean Sea
Melilla (Sp.)
Africa
MOROCCO
Algiers
ALGERIA
Annaba
Constantine
Tunis
TUNISIA
Palermo
Messina
Sicily
Catánia
Pantelleria (Italy)
MALTA
Valletta
Ionian Sea
Projection: Bonne
West from Greenwich
East from Greenwich
LONDON Capital Cities

1: 20 000 000
100 0 100 200 300 400 500 miles
100 0 200 400 600 800 km
White Sea
Murmansk
Arkhangelsk
N. Dvina
Kotlas
Ob
Nizhniy Tagil
Perm
Yekaterinburg
Chelyabinsk
Kirov
L. Onega
L. Ladoga
Vyborg
ST. PETERBURG
Vologda
Rybinsk Res.
Kostroma
Yaroslavl
Ivanovo
Nizhniy Novgorod
Kazan
Ufa
Magnitogorsk
RUSSIA
MOSCOW
Simbirsk
Samara
Orenburg
Penza
Volga
Uralsk
Tula
Smolensk
Tambov
Saratov
Orel
Voronezh
Kursk
Ural
KAZAKSTAN
Atyrau
Volgograd
Don
Astrakhan
Caspian Sea
Hammerfest
Luleå
FINLAND
Vaasa
Turku
Helsinki
Tallinn
ESTONIA
L. Chudskoye
LATVIA
Riga
W. Dvina
LITHUANIA
Kaunas
Vilnius
Kaliningrad (Russia)
Vitebsk
Mogilev
Minsk
Gomel
BELARUS
Białystok
Brest
Pripet
Warsaw
Lublin
Vistula
Chernigov
Kiev
Dnieper
Kharkov
Zhitomir
UKRAINE
Lvov
Donetsk
Dnepropetrovsk
Dniester
Bug
Krivoy Rog
Zaporozhye
Taganrog
Rostov
Kherson
Nikolayev
Odessa
MOLDOVA
Kishinev
Miskolc
Debrecen
Cluj-Napoca
ROMANIA
Timişoara
Braşov
Galaţi
Ploieşti
Bucharest
Constanţa
Crimea
Sevastopol
Krasnodar
Stavropol
Makhachkala
Black Sea
GEORGIA
Tbilisi
AZERBAIJAN
Baku
ARMENIA
Yerevan
Araks
Belgrade
SERBIA
Niš
Danube
Varna
Sofia
BULGARIA
Plovdiv
Skopje
MACEDONIA
Bosporus
ISTANBUL
Samsun
Erzurum
Tabriz
Thessaloníki
Bursa
Ankara
TURKEY
Kayseri
Diyarbakır
IRAN
GREECE
Ægean Sea
İzmir
Konya
Adana
Asia
Aleppo
Euphrates
IRAQ
Tigris
Baghdād
Pátrai
Athens
Antalya
SYRIA
Rhodes
CYPRUS
Nicosia
Crete
CARTOGRAPHY BY PHILIPS.

8 SCANDINAVIA

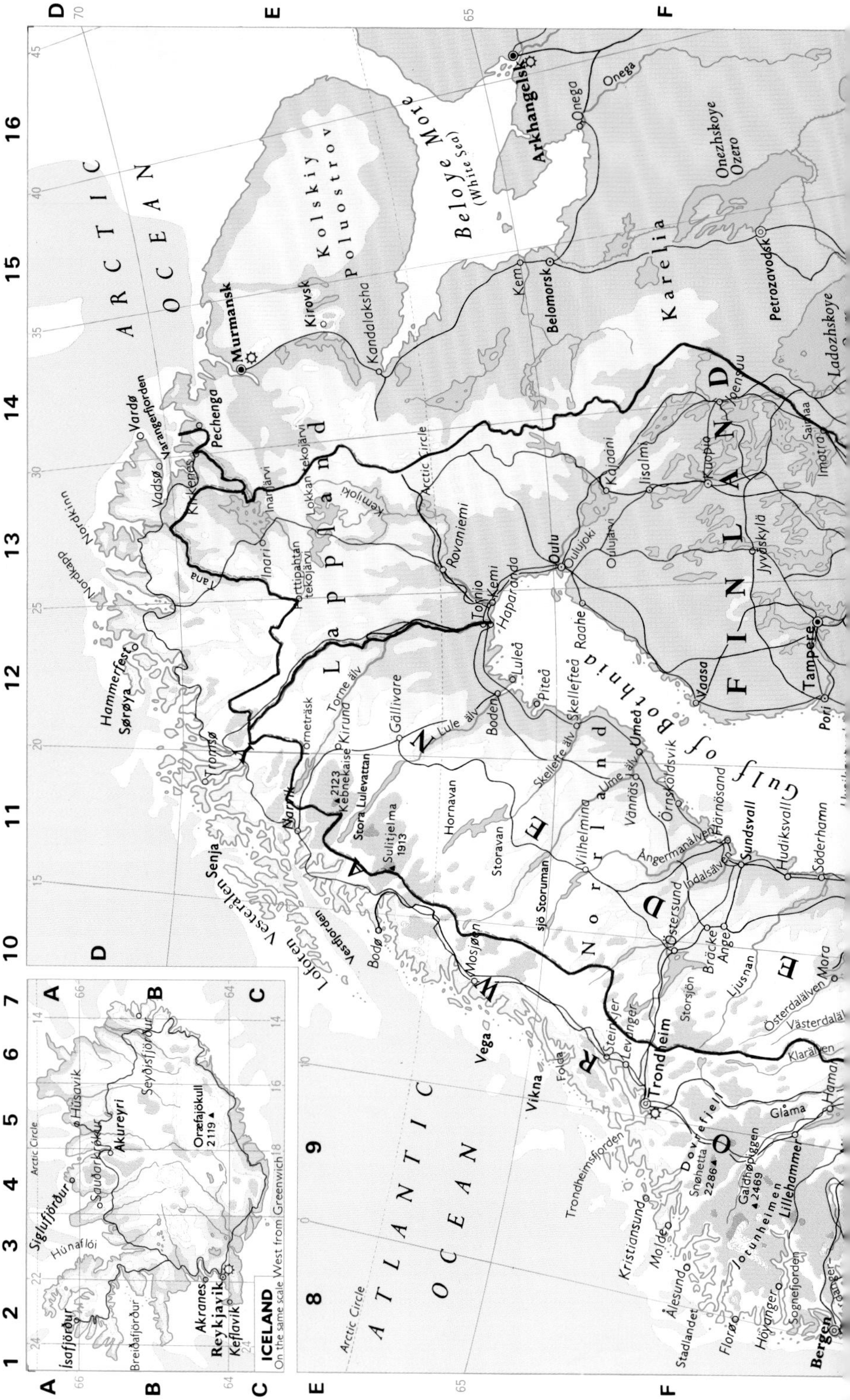
ARCTIC OCEAN
ATLANTIC OCEAN
Arctic Circle
Nordkapp
Nordkinn
Hammerfest
Sørøya
Tromsø
Senja
Vesterålen
Lofoten
Vestfjorden
Bodø
Narvik
Vadsø
Vardø
Varangerfjorden
Kirkenes
Pechenga
Murmansk
Kirovsk
Kandalaksha
Kolskiy Poluostrov
Beloye More
(White Sea)
Arkhangelsk
Onega
Onezhskoye Ozero
Belomorsk
Kem
Karelia
Petrozavodsk
Ladozhskoye
Lappland
Inari
Inarijärvi
Lokkan tekojärvi
Porttipahtan tekojärvi
Tana
Kemijoki
Rovaniemi
Arctic Circle
Tornio
Kemi
Haparanda
Oulu
Oulujoki
Oulujärvi
Kajaani
Iisalmi
Kuopio
Joensuu
Saimaa
Imatra
Jyväskylä
Raahe
Vaasa
Tampere
Pori
FINLAND
Gulf of Bothnia
Luleå
Piteå
Boden
Skellefteå
Umeå
Örnsköldsvik
Härnösand
Sundsvall
Hudiksvall
Söderhamn
Gällivare
Kiruna
Torneträsk
Torne älv
Lule älv
Kebnekaise
2123
Stora Lulevattan
Sulitjelma
1913
Hornavan
Storavan
Storuman
Vilhelmina
Vännäs
Skellefte älv
Ume älv
Ångermanälven
Indalsälven
Norrland
Östersund
Storsjön
Bräcke
Ånge
Ljusnan
Mora
Österdalälven
Västerdalälven
Klarälven
Mosjøen
Vega
Vikna
Folda
Steinkjer
Levanger
Trondheim
Trondheimsfjorden
Kristiansund
Molde
Ålesund
Stadlandet
Florø
Høyanger
Sognefjorden
Bergen
Dovrefjell
Snøhetta
2286
Galdhøpiggen
2469
Jotunheimen
Lillehammer
Glåma
Hamar
NORWAY
SWEDEN
ICELAND
On the same scale West from Greenwich
Ísafjörður
Breiðafjörður
Húnaflói
Siglufjörður
Sauðárkrókur
Akureyri
Húsavík
Seyðisfjörður
Öræfajökull
2119
Akranes
Reykjavík
Keflavík
Arctic Circle

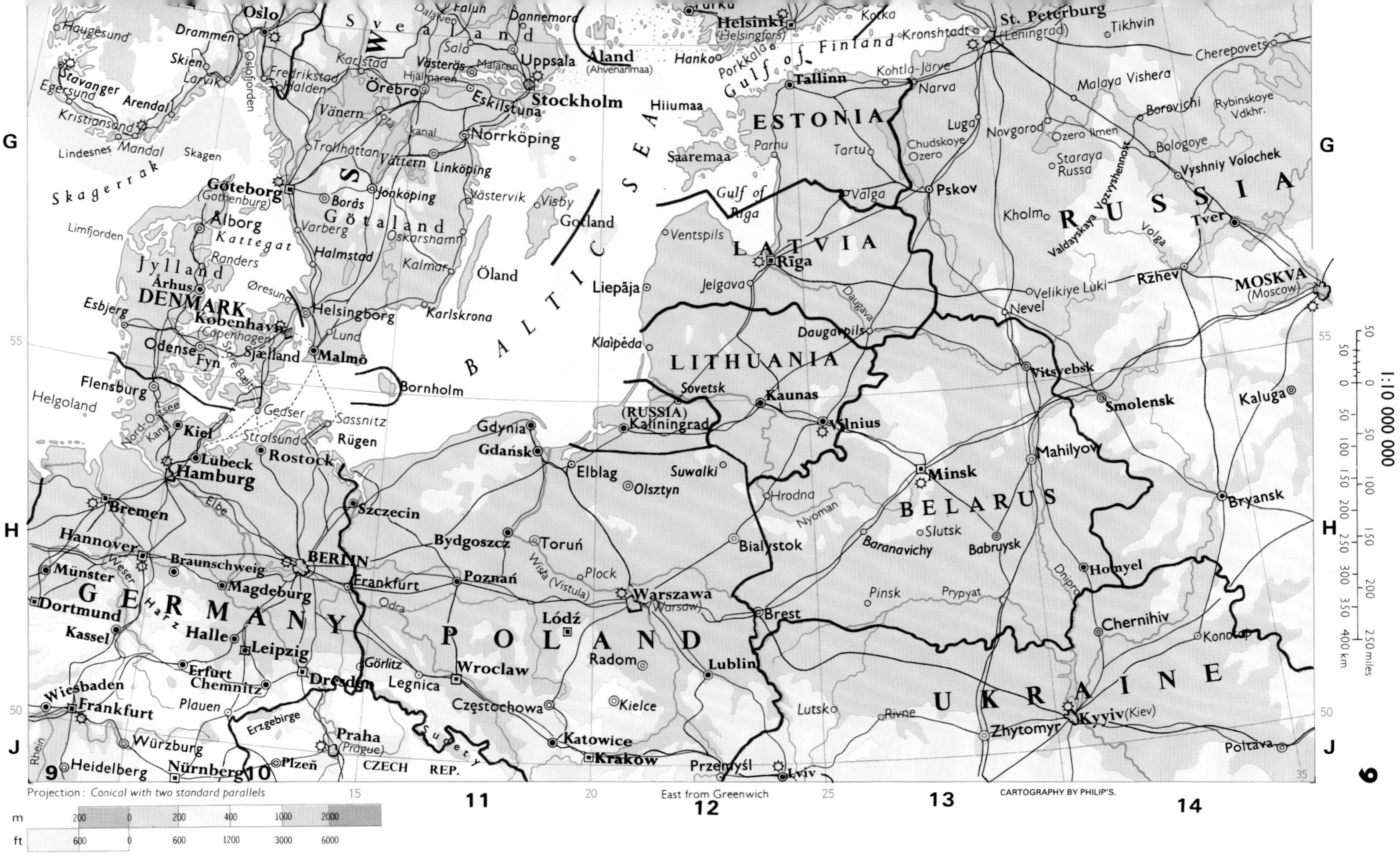

1:10 000 000
50 0 50 100 150 200 250 miles
50 0 50 100 150 200 250 300 350 400 km
G
H
J
11
12
13
14
55
50
15
20
25
35
East from Greenwich
CARTOGRAPHY BY PHILIP'S.
Projection: Conical with two standard parallels
m 200 0 200 400 1000 2000
ft 600 0 600 1200 3000 6000
B A L T I C S E A
Gulf of Finland
Gulf of Riga
Skagerrak
Kattegat
Øresund
Svealand
Götaland
Jylland
S W
ESTONIA
LATVIA
LITHUANIA
(RUSSIA)
RUSSIA
BELARUS
UKRAINE
POLAND
GERMANY
DENMARK
CZECH REP.
Sudety
Erzgebirge
Harz
Oslo
Drammen
Haugesund
Skien
Larvik
Stavanger
Egersund
Arendal
Kristiansand
Lindesnes
Mandal
Skagen
Oslofjorden
Fredrikstad
Halden
Karlstad
Vänern
Trollhättan
Vättern
Örebro
Västerås
Mälaren
Hjälmaren
Sala
Falun
Dannemora
Uppsala
Stockholm
Eskilstuna
Norrköping
Linköping
Jönköping
Västervik
Visby
Gotland
Göteborg
(Gothenburg)
Borås
Varberg
Halmstad
Oskarshamn
Kalmar
Öland
Karlskrona
Helsingborg
Lund
Malmö
Bornholm
Ålborg
Randers
Limfjorden
Århus
Esbjerg
København
(Copenhagen)
Sjælland
Odense
Fyn
Store Bælt
Flensburg
Helgoland
Nord-Ostsee Kanal
Kiel
Lübeck
Hamburg
Gedser
Sassnitz
Stralsund
Rügen
Rostock
Bremen
Elbe
Hannover
Weser
Münster
Dortmund
Braunschweig
Magdeburg
BERLIN
Frankfurt
Odra
Szczecin
Kassel
Halle
Leipzig
Erfurt
Chemnitz
Dresden
Görlitz
Legnica
Plauen
Wiesbaden
Frankfurt
Rhein
Würzburg
Heidelberg
Nürnberg
Praha
(Prague)
Plzeň
Åland
(Ahvenanmaa)
Turku
Helsinki
(Helsingfors)
Hanko
Porkkala
Kotka
Hiiumaa
Saaremaa
Tallinn
Parnu
Tartu
Valga
Kohtla-Järve
Narva
Ventspils
Riga
Jelgava
Liepāja
Daugava
Daugavpils
Klaipėda
Sovetsk
Kaunas
Vilnius
Kaliningrad
Gdynia
Gdańsk
Elblag
Suwalki
Olsztyn
Bydgoszcz
Toruń
Plock
Wisła (Vistula)
Poznań
Warszawa
(Warsaw)
Łódź
Radom
Lublin
Kielce
Wroclaw
Częstochowa
Katowice
Kraków
Przemyśl
Lviv
Hrodna
Nyoman
Bialystok
Brest
Lutsko
Rivne
Zhytomyr
Kyyiv (Kiev)
Poltava
Chernihiv
Konotop
Dnipro
Homyel
Pinsk
Prypyat
Baranavichy
Slutsk
Babruysk
Minsk
Mahilyow
Vitsyebsk
Smolensk
Kaluga
Bryansk
St. Petersburg
(Leningrad)
Kronshtadt
Tikhvin
Cherepovets
Malaya Vishera
Borovichi
Rybinskoye Vdkhr.
Luga
Chudskoye Ozero
Pskov
Novgorod
Ozero Ilmen
Staraya Russa
Bologoye
Vyshniy Volochek
Valdayskaya Vozvyshennost
Kholm
Volga
Tver
Velikiye Luki
Nevel
Rzhev
MOSKVA
(Moscow)

m 2000 1000 500 200 100 50 0 200 500 1000
ft 6000 3000 1500 600 300 150 0 600 1500 3000
ATLANTIC OCEAN
NORTH SEA
NORWAY
Askøy
Bergen
Osøyri
Stord
Bømlo
Leirvik
Haugesund
Kopervik
Åkrahamn
Boknafjorden
Stavanger
Sandnes
Bryne
Nærbø
Shetland Is.
Yell
Unst
Fetlar
Mainland
Lerwick
Foula
Fair Isle
Orkney Is.
Westray
Sanday
Stronsay
Mainland
Kirkwall
Hoy
South Ronaldsay
Pentland Firth
Thurso
Wick
Helmsdale
C. Wrath
Lairg
Golspie
Tain
Invergordon
Dingwall
Moray Firth
Buckie
Banff
Fraserburgh
Peterhead
Nairn
Elgin
Huntly
Inverness
Spey
Don
Inverurie
Aberdeen
Aviemore
Dee
Ballater
Stonehaven
1311
L. Ness
1182
North West Highlands
Ullapool
North Minch
Outer Hebrides
Lewis
Stornoway
789
Harris
St. Kilda
North Uist
Benbecula
South Uist
Barra
Inner Hebrides
Skye
Portree
Mallaig
Rhum
Eigg
Coll
Tiree
Fort William
Ben Nevis
1342
Tobermory
Mull
Oban
Colonsay
Jura
Islay
SCOTLAND
Grampian Mts.
1214
Tay
Perth
Forfar
Montrose
Arbroath
Dundee
St. Andrews
Glenrothes
Kirkcaldy
L. Lomond
973
Stirling
Dunfermline
Dunbar
Greenock
Clyde
Paisley
Glasgow
Edinburgh
East Kilbride
Hamilton
Uplands
Galashiels
Berwick-upon-Tweed
Irvine
Arran
Kilmarnock
Campbeltown
Ayr
840
Jedburgh
816
Alnwick
Malin Hd.
1224
316
238
1 2 3 4 5 6 7 8 9
A B C
60 58 56
10 8 6 4 2 0 2 4 6

1: 5 000 000

50 0 50 100 miles
50 0 50 100 150 km

Projection: Conical with two standard parallels

West from Greenwich

East from Greenwich

CARTOGRAPHY BY PHILIP'S

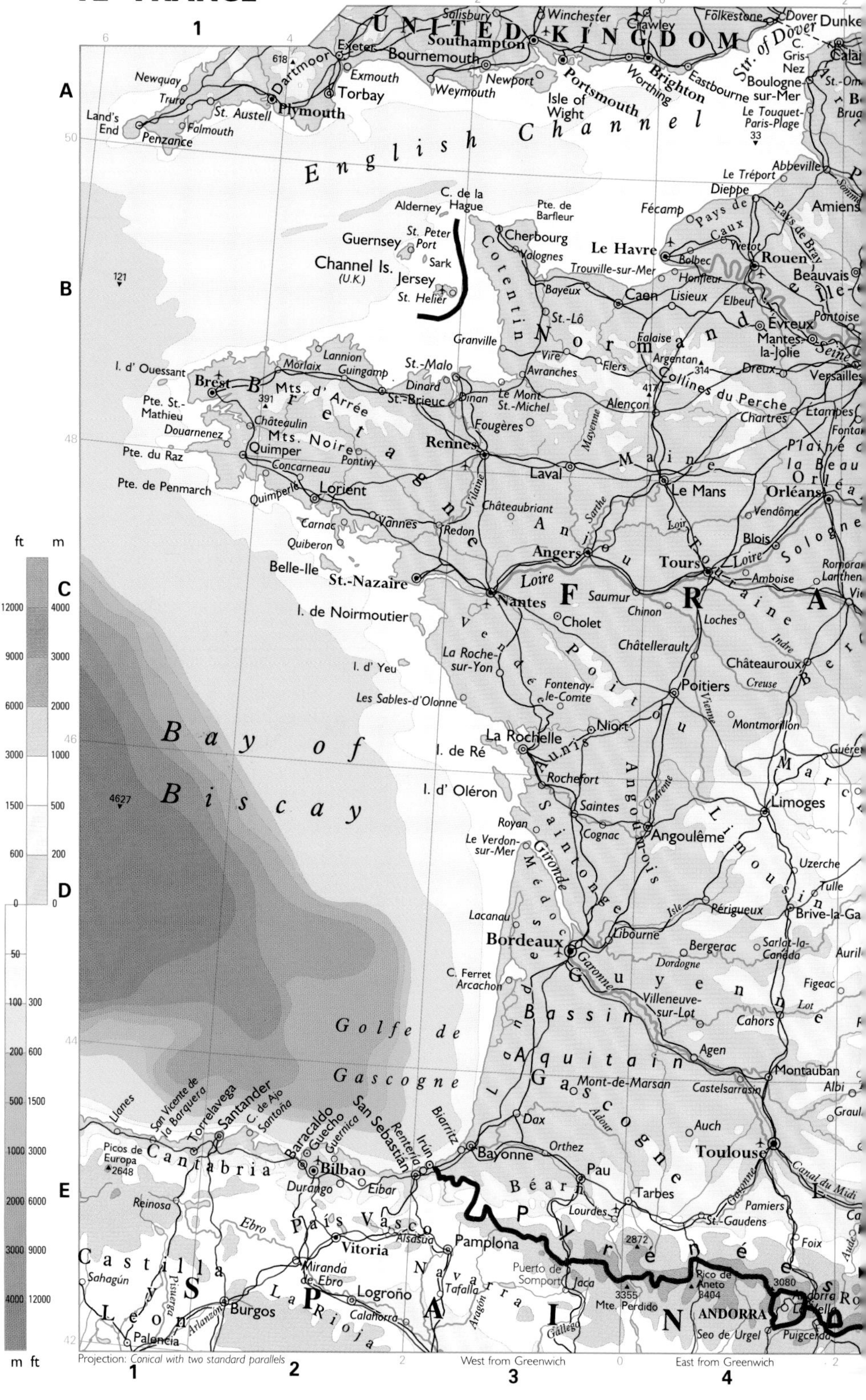

Projection: Conical with two standard parallels
West from Greenwich
East from Greenwich

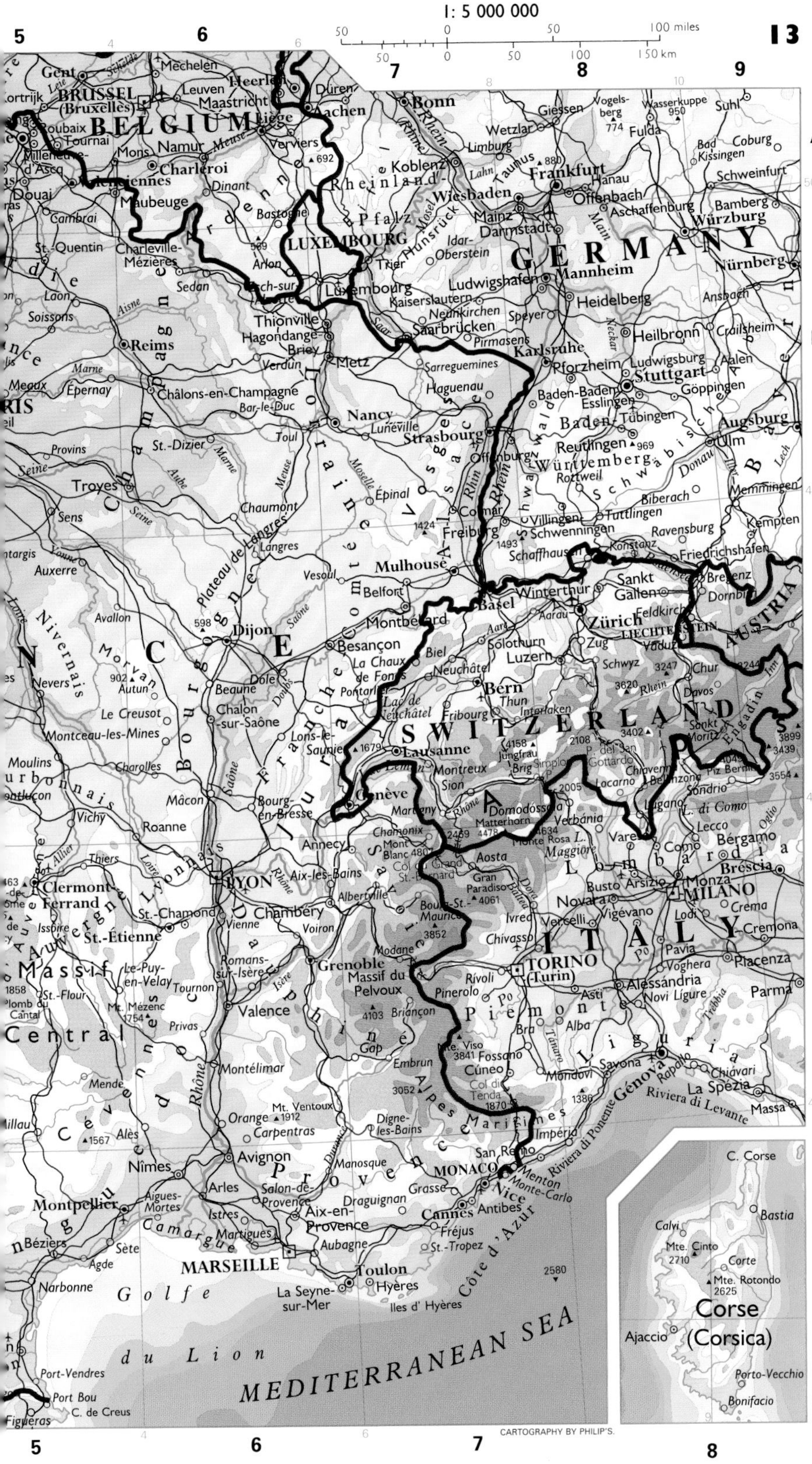
1: 5 000 000
50
0
50
100 miles
50
0
50
100
150 km
5
6
7
8
9
A
B
C
D
E
F
BELGIUM
LUXEMBOURG
GERMANY
SWITZERLAND
LIECHTENSTEIN
AUSTRIA
ITALY
MONACO
Gent
BRUSSEL
(Bruxelles)
Mechelen
Leuven
Maastricht
Heerlen
Düren
Aachen
Liège
Kortrijk
Roubaix
Tournai
Mons
Namur
Verviers
Charleroi
Villeneuve-d'Ascq
Valenciennes
Douai
Maubeuge
Dinant
Cambrai
Bastogne
St.-Quentin
Charleville-Mézières
Arlon
Sedan
Laon
Soissons
Reims
Thionville
Hagondange-Briey
Verdun
Metz
Marne
Épernay
Meaux
Châlons-en-Champagne
Bar-le-Duc
Nancy
Lunéville
Toul
St.-Dizier
Provins
Seine
Troyes
Sens
Aube
Chaumont
Plateau de Langres
Langres
Vesoul
Auxerre
Avallon
Nivernais
Morvan
Nevers
Autun
Dijon
Beaune
Dole
Le Creusot
Chalon-sur-Saône
Montceau-les-Mines
Moulins
Charolles
Mâcon
Vichy
Roanne
Bourg-en-Bresse
Thiers
Clermont-Ferrand
Issoire
St.-Étienne
St.-Chamond
LYON
Vienne
Massif Central
Le-Puy-en-Velay
Tournon
St.-Flour
Mt. Mézenc
1754
Privas
Valence
Romans-sur-Isère
Grenoble
Massif du Pelvoux
Montélimar
Mende
Cévennes
Alès
Nîmes
Orange
Carpentras
Mt. Ventoux
1912
Avignon
Arles
Montpellier
Aigues-Mortes
Camargue
Salon-de-Provence
Istres
Martigues
Sète
Agde
Béziers
Narbonne
MARSEILLE
Golfe du Lion
Aix-en-Provence
Aubagne
Toulon
La Seyne-sur-Mer
Hyères
Iles d' Hyères
Port-Vendres
Port Bou
C. de Creus
Figueras
MEDITERRANEAN SEA
Côte d'Azur
St.-Tropez
Fréjus
Cannes
Antibes
Nice
Monte-Carlo
Menton
Grasse
Draguignan
Manosque
Digne-les-Bains
Provence
Dauphiné
Alpes Maritimes
Gap
Embrun
Briançon
4103
Mte. Viso
3841
Savoie
Chambéry
Voiron
Albertville
Aix-les-Bains
Annecy
Chamonix
Mont Blanc 4807
Col du Grand St.-Bernard
Bourg-St.-Maurice
Modane
3852
Genève
Lausanne
Montreux
Sion
Martigny
Matterhorn
4478
Monte Rosa
4634
Domodóssola
Simplon
Brig
Jungfrau
4158
Interlaken
Thun
Fribourg
Bern
Neuchâtel
Lac de Neuchâtel
Biel
La Chaux de Fonds
Pontarlier
Lons-le-Saunier
1679
Besançon
Montbéliard
Belfort
Mulhouse
Basel
Aarau
Solothurn
Luzern
Zug
Zürich
Winterthur
Schaffhausen
Konstanz
Sankt Gallen
Feldkirch
Vaduz
Chur
Davos
Schwyz
3620
3247
3402
P. del San Gottardo
Lugano
Locarno
Bellinzona
Chiavenna
Sondrio
Sankt Moritz
Engadin
Piz Bernina
Inn
Dornbirn
Bregenz
Friedrichshafen
Ravensburg
Kempten
Memmingen
Biberach
Ulm
Augsburg
Lech
Donau
Schwäbische Alb
Tuttlingen
Villingen-Schwenningen
Rottweil
Reutlingen
969
Tübingen
Esslingen
Baden-Württemberg
Stuttgart
Göppingen
Ludwigsburg
Aalen
Crailsheim
Heilbronn
Pforzheim
Baden-Baden
Karlsruhe
Schwarzwald
Freiburg
Colmar
Épinal
1424
Vosges
Alsace
Strasbourg
Offenburg
Haguenau
Sarreguemines
Saarbrücken
Pirmasens
Speyer
Neunkirchen
Kaiserslautern
Ludwigshafen
Mannheim
Heidelberg
Ansbach
Nürnberg
Würzburg
Bamberg
Schweinfurt
Bad Kissingen
Coburg
Suhl
Wasserkuppe
950
Fulda
Vogelsberg
774
Giessen
Wetzlar
Limburg
Bonn
Koblenz
Rheinland-Pfalz
Hunsrück
Idar-Oberstein
Trier
Wiesbaden
Mainz
Darmstadt
Frankfurt
Hanau
Offenbach
Aschaffenburg
Taunus
880
Rhein
Mosel
Saar
Lorraine
Champagne
Bourgogne
Franche-Comté
Jura
Lyonnais
Auvergne
Bourbonnais
Rhône-Alpes
Lombardia
Piemonte
Liguria
Varese
Como
L. di Como
Lecco
Bergamo
Brescia
Monza
MILANO
Crema
Lodi
Cremona
Piacenza
Pavia
Voghera
Novara
Busto Arsizio
Vigévano
Vercelli
Ivrea
Chivasso
Aosta
Gran Paradiso
4061
Verbánia
L. Maggiore
TORINO
(Turin)
Rívoli
Pinerolo
Po
Asti
Alessándria
Novi Ligure
Alba
Bra
Fossano
Cúneo
Mondovì
Col di Tenda
1870
3052
Savona
Génova
Riviera di Ponente
Riviera di Levante
Chiávari
La Spezia
Massa
Parma
Impéria
San Remo
1386
2580
C. Corse
Bastia
Calvi
Mte. Cinto
2710
Corte
Mte. Rotondo
2625
Corse
(Corsica)
Ajaccio
Porto-Vecchio
Bonifacio
CARTOGRAPHY BY PHILIP'S.

NORTH SEA
UNITED KINGDOM
NETHERLANDS
BELGIUM
LUXEMBOURG
FRANCE
GERMANY
SWITZERLAND
LIECHTENSTEIN
Nordfriesische Inseln
Ostfriesische Inseln
Deutsche Bucht
Sylt
Föhr
Helgoland
Wangerooge
Norderney
Borkum
Schiermonnikoog
Ameland
Terschelling
Texel
IJsselmeer
Cromer
Norwich
Great Yarmouth
Lowestoft
Ipswich
Felixstowe
Harwich
Margate
Dover
Flensburg
Schleswig
Schleswig-Holstein
Rendsburg
Itzehoe
Elmshorn
Cuxhaven
Elbe
Stade
Buxtehude
Wilhelmshaven
Aurich
Emden
Leer
Oldenburg
Bremerhaven
Bremen
Delmenhorst
Lüneburg
Verden
Heide
Niedersachsen
Nienburg
Weser
Leine
Aller
Hannover
Hildesheim
Hameln
Goslar
Leeuwarden
Sneek
Groningen
Assen
Emmen
Meppel
Kampen
Zwolle
Den Helder
Hoorn
Alkmaar
Haarlem
AMSTERDAM
's-Gravenhage (Den Haag)
Hoek van Holland
Leiden
Gouda
Hilversum
Utrecht
ROTTERDAM
Dordrecht
Maas
Waal
Arnhem
Nijmegen
's-Hertogenbosch
Apeldoorn
Deventer
Almelo
Enschede
Lingen
Rheine
Osnabrück
Minden
Herford
Bielefeld
Detmold
Gütersloh
Münster
Teutoburger Wald
Nordrhein-Westfalen
Höxter
Paderborn
Lippe
Vlissingen
Breda
Tilburg
Eindhoven
Zeebrugge
Oostende
Dunkerque
Calais
Brugge
Gent
Antwerpen
Turnhout
Schelde
Mechelen
Kortrijk
Leie
BRUSSEL (Bruxelles)
Leuven
Heerlen
Maastricht
Mönchengladbach
Krefeld
Duisburg
Oberhausen
Gelsenkirchen
Essen
Bochum
Dortmund
Hamm
Hagen
Wuppertal
Düsseldorf
Ruhr
Arnsberg
Köln (Cologne)
Solingen
Sauerland
Bonn
Siegen
Düren
Aachen
Liège
Verviers
Namur
Meuse
Charleroi
Mons
Tournai
Roubaix
Tourcoing
Lille
Villeneuve-d'Ascq
Flandre
St.-Omer
Boulogne-sur-Mer
Béthune
Bruay-en-Artois
Lens
Douai
Arras
Valenciennes
Maubeuge
Dinant
Ardennes
Bastogne
Arlon
Esch-sur-Alzette
Luxembourg
Abbeville
Somme
Amiens
Picardie
Cambrai
St.-Quentin
Charleville-Mézières
Sedan
Beauvais
Noyon
Laon
Compiègne
Aisne
Soissons
Reims
Île-de-France
Oise
Senlis
St.-Denis
Meaux
Marne
Épernay
PARIS
Créteil
Évry
Melun
Provins
Seine
Fontainebleau
Troyes
Sens
Châlons-en-Champagne
Champagne
Bar-le-Duc
St.-Dizier
Aube
Chaumont
Auxerre
Yonne
Thionville
Hagondange-Briey
Verdun
Metz
Nancy
Toul
Lunéville
Lorraine
Moselle
Épinal
Vosges
Meuse
Koblenz
Rhein
Westerwald
Wetzlar
Limburg
Lahn
Giessen
Marburg
Hessen
Kassel
Göttingen
Fulda
Werra
Eisenach
Vogelsberg
Wasserkuppe
Rhön
Rheinland-Pfalz
Taunus
Wiesbaden
Frankfurt
Hanau
Offenbach
Aschaffenburg
Mainz
Main
Darmstadt
Würzburg
Hunsrück
Mosel
Trier
Idar-Oberstein
Worms
Ludwigshafen
Mannheim
Kaiserslautern
Neunkirchen
Saarbrücken
Saar
Speyer
Heidelberg
Pirmasens
Sarreguemines
Haguenau
Karlsruhe
Neckar
Heilbronn
Pforzheim
Ludwigsburg
Stuttgart
Baden-Baden
Esslingen
Göppingen
Aalen
Crailsheim
Strasbourg
Alsace
Offenburg
Baden-Württemberg
Schwarzwald
Tübingen
Reutlingen
Rottweil
Schwäbische Alb
Ulm
Augsburg
Biberach
Memmingen
Kempten
Ravensburg
Friedrichshafen
Konstanz
Tuttlingen
Villingen-Schwenningen
Schaffhausen
Freiburg
Colmar
Mulhouse
Belfort
Vesoul
Langres
Plateau de Langres
Bourgogne
Nivernais
Morvan
Avallon
Dijon
Saône
Montbéliard
Besançon
Doubs
Dole
Beaune
Autun
Nevers
Le Creusot
Montceau-les-Mines
Moulins
Charolles
Chalon-sur-Saône
Lons-le-Saunier
Mâcon
Bourg-en-Bresse
Allier
Vichy
Roanne
Thiers
Loire
Lyonnais
LYON
Rhône
St.-Étienne
St.-Chamond
Vienne
Chambéry
Voiron
Aix-les-Bains
Annecy
Albertville
Jura
Franche-Comté
Basel
Aarau
Aare
Winterthur
Zürich
Sankt Gallen
Bregenz
Dornbirn
Feldkirch
Arlberg P.
Landeck
Vaduz
Chur
Davos
Rhein
Schwyz
Zug
Luzern
Solothurn
Biel
La Chaux-de-Fonds
Pontarlier
Neuchâtel
Lac de Neuchâtel
Bern
Thun
Fribourg
Interlaken
Jungfrau
P. del San Gottardo
Lausanne
Lac Léman
Genève
Montreux
Sion
Brig
Simplon P.
Martigny
Rhône
Chamonix
Mont Blanc
Col du Grand St.-Bernard
Matterhorn
Monte Rosa
Domodossola
Aosta
Gran Paradiso
Locarno
Lugano
Bellinzona
Chiavenna
Sankt Moritz
Engadin
Inn
Piz Bernina
Sondrio
L. di Como
Lecco
Como
Varese
Verbania
L. Maggiore
Biella
Busto Arsizio
Bergamo
Mte. Adamello
Riva del Garda
Lago di Garda
Oglio
Wildspitze
Merano
Zugspitze
Projection: Conical with two standard parallels
ft m
12000 4000
9000 3000
6000 2000
3000 1000
1500 500
600 200
0 0
50 150
100 300
m ft

1: 5 000 000

BALTIC SEA
Zatoka Gdańska
Zalew Wiślany
Rügen
Sassnitz
Stralsund
Greifswald
Rostock
Wismar
Güstrow
Mecklenburg
Schwerin
Parchim
Neubrandenburg
Neustrelitz
Müritz-see
Usedom
Wolin
Świnoujście
Stettiner Haff
Police
Goleniów
Szczecin
Stargard Szczeciński
Choszczno
Gorzów Wielkopolski
Kołobrzeg
Koszalin
Białogard
Darłowo
Słupsk
Lębork
Wejherowo
Rumia
Gdynia
Sopot
Gdańsk
Tczew
Elbląg
Malbork
Kwidzyn
Iława
Bytów
Starogard Gdański
Pojezierze Pomorski
Szczecinek
Chojnice
Świecie
Grudziądz
Chełmno
Brodnica
Wałcz
Piła
Bydgoszcz
Toruń
Rypin
Wisła
(Vistula)
Noteć
Inowrocław
POLAND
Gniezno
Włocławek
Płock
Kutno
Warta
Poznań
Międzychód
Nowy Tomyśl
Września
Kolo
Łęczyca
Konin
Śrem
Kościan
Turek
Prosna
Łódź
Leszno
Kalisz
Zduńska Wola
Pabianice
Krotoszyn
Ostrów Wielkopolski
Sieradz
Piotrków Trybunalski
Wieluń
Oleśnica
Radomsko
Wrocław
Oława
Kluczbork
Częstochowa
Opole
Myszków
Zawiercie
Tarnowskie Góry
Bytom
Zabrze
Gliwice
Katowice
Sosnowiec
Tychy
Oświęcim
Racibórz
Bielsko-Biała
Żywiec
Frankfurt
Świebodzin
Zielona Góra
Nowa Sól
Żagań
(Odra)
Oder
Żary
Bóbr
Głogów
Lubin
Bolesławiec
Legnica
Śląsk
Zgorzelec
Forst
Neisse
Nysa
Wałbrzych
Świdnica
Dzierżoniów
Kłodzko
Nysa
Jelenia Góra
Śnieżka
1602
Sudety
Brandenburg
Wittenberge
Neuruppin
Schwedt
Eberswalde-Finow
Oranienburg
Rathenow
BERLIN
Fürstenwalde
Potsdam
Brandenburg
Spree
Havel
Salzwedel
Stendal
Wolfsburg
Magdeburg
Luckenwalde
Sachsen-Anhalt
Dessau
Wittenberg
Bernburg
Cottbus
Lauchhammer
Halle
Torgau
Saale
Leipzig
Merseburg
Naumburg
Riesa
Hoyerswerda
Bautzen
Elbe
Mulde
Meissen
Dresden
Görlitz
Zeitz
Weimar
Jena
Gera
Sachsen
Chemnitz
Zwickau
Greiz
Reichenbach
Plauen
Saalfeld
Hof
Erzgebirge
Teplice
Děčín
Ústí nad Labem
Liberec
Jablonec
Most
Chomutov
Litoměřice
Mladá Boleslav
Trutnov
Hradec Králové
Ohře
Labe
1244
Karlovy Vary
Kladno
Cheb
PRAHA (Prague)
Pardubice
Kolín
Beroun
Sázava
1425
1492
Šumperk
Plzeň
Příbram
CZECH REP.
Českomoravská Vrchovina
836
Olomouc
Opava
Ostrava
Havířov
Karviná
Frýdek-Místek
Cieszyn
1324
Havlíčkův Brod
Prostějov
Přerov
Klatovy
Vltava
Tábor
Jihlava
Vyškov
Zlín
Písek
Třebíč
Brno
Jihlava
Jindřichův Hradec
České Budějovice
Plöckenstein
1378
Znojmo
Hodonín
Bílé Karpaty
Považská Bystrica
Žilina
Martin
Trenčín
Prievidza
Banská Bystrica
2043
SLOVAK REP
Malé Karpaty
768
Morava
Váh
Nitra
Topoľčany
Zvolen
Trnava
Nitra
Levice
Hron
Bratislava
Nové Zámky
Komárno
(Dunaj)
Gmünd
Horn
Zwettl
Krems
Stockerau
Freistadt
Linz
(Donau)
Melk
Sankt Pölten
WIEN (Vienna)
Baden
Bruck an der Leitha
Neusiedler See
Mosonmagyaróvár
Győr
Esztergom
Vác
Dunakeszi
Wels
Steyr
Amstetten
Enns
Traun
Ried
Braunau
Inn
Passau
Wiener Neustadt
Semmering P.
985
Mürzzuschlag
Sopron
Tatabánya
Budapest
Bakony Hegység
704
Pápa
Rába
Szombathely
Ajka
Veszprém
Székesfehérvár
Dunaújváros
Siófok
Balaton
Zalaegerszeg
HUNGARY
Kalocsa
(Duna)
Nagykanizsa
Kaposvár
Szekszárd
Baja
681
Pécs
Mohács
Bayreuth
Naab
Weiden
652
Amberg
Böhmerwald
1042
Grosser Arber
1457
Regensburg
Straubing
Deggendorf
Ingolstadt
Isar
Bayern
Landshut
Freising
MÜNCHEN (Munich)
Rosenheim
Chiemsee
Salzburg
Gmunden
Bad Ischl
2514
2351
Kufstein
Innsbruck
2995
Eisenerz
Kapfenberg
Bruck an der Mur
Leoben
2449
Salzach
Hohe Tauern
AUSTRIA
3797
Gross Glockner
Badgastein
Steiermark
Graz
Mur
Lienz
2441
3435
Bressanone
Bolzano
Dolomiti
Karnische Alpen
Kärnten
Wolfsberg
Villach
Klagenfurt
Drava
Maribor
ITALY
2763
Triglav
2863
2558
Karawanken
Celje
Varaždin
Koprivnica
Belluno
Kobarid
Kranj
Vittorio Véneto
Tagliamento
Udine
Ljubljana
Sava
SLOVENIA
Gorizia
Pordenone
Conegliano
Kalce
1035
Zagreb
Bjelovar
Virovitica
Drava
Svendborg
Næstved
Møn
DENMARK
Nakskov
Falster
Lolland
Nykøbing
Rødbyhavn
Gedser
Fehmarn Bælt
Fehmarn
Mecklenburger Bucht
Travemünde
Elde
Stettiner
Warta
Nysa
Elbe
Regen
Donau
GERMANY
A
B
C
D
E
6
7
8
9
10
12
14
16
18
54
52
50
48
46
East from Greenwich
CARTOGRAPHY BY PHILIP'S.

16 CENTRAL EUROPE

Projection: *Conical with two standard parallels*

1: 5 000 000
50 0 50 100 miles
50 0 50 100 150 km
6
7
8
9
10
B
C
D
E
F
B E L A R U S
MINSK
Marijampolė
Alytus
Druskininkai
Lida
Hrodna
Navahrudak
Dzyarzhynsk
Hrodzyanka
Bykhaw
Slawharad
Drut
Sozh
(Nyoman)
Dzyatlava
Stowbtsy
Nyasvizh
Asipovichy
Babruysk
Ragachow
Zhlobin
Sokółka
Masty
Białystok
Vawkavysk
Slonim
Baranavichy
Klyetsk
Slutsk
Glusk
Ptsich
Byarezina
Aktsyabrski
Homyel
Svislach
Lyakhavichy
Salihorsk
Svyetlahorsk
Rechytsa
Hantsavichy
Ivatsevichy
Hajnówka
Bielsk Podlaski
Pruzhany
Bereza
Tsyelyakhany
Vasilevichi
Kalinkavichy
Luninyets
Pyetrikaw
Yaselda
(Pripyats)
Kobryn
Dragichyn
Zhabinka
Mazyr
Loyew
Khoyniki
Ivanava
Pinsk
(Pripet)
Haryn
Davyd Haradok
Biała Podlaska
Brest
Stolin
Ubort
Yelsk
Międzyrzec Podlaski
Malaryta
P r i p e t M a r s h e s
316
Ovruch
Prypyat
Chornobyl
Kamin-Kashyrskyy
Dubrovytsya
Uzh
Włodawa
Wieprz
Olevsk
Oster
Belokorovichi
Kyyivske Vdskh.
Korosten
Dymer
Lyuboml
Kovel
Staryy Chartoriysk
Sluch
Chełm
Malyn
Teterev
Irpin
Kostopil
Novohrad-Volynskyy
Rozhyshche
Kivertsi
Radomyshl
KYYIV (Kiev)
Novovolynsk
Volodymyr-Volynskyy
Oleksandriya
Korets
Lutsk
Rivne
Zdolbuniv
Korostyshev
Vasylkiv
Zamość
Horokhiv
Zhytomyr
Sokal
Chervonohrad
Dubno
341
Ostroh
Slavuta
Pershotravensk
Fastiv
Rava-Ruska
Radekhiv
Berestechko
Kremenets
Shepetivka
Polonne
Berdychiv
Bila Tserkva
390
Izyaslav
San
Kamyanka-Buzka
Brody
U K R A I N E
Skvyra
Tarashcha
Nesterov
Kozyatyn
Yavoriv
Starokonstyantyniv
Khemelnik
Mostyska
Lviv (Lvov)
Zolochiv
Zbarazh
Tetiyev
Przemyśl
Horodok
Ternopil
Khmelnytskyy
Lipovets
Zhashkiv
Sanok
P o d i l s k a V y s o c h y n a
Skalat
384
Vinnytsya
Sambir
Khodoriv
Berezhany
Hrymayliv
Bar
Drohobych
Rogatyn
Terebovlya
Kopychyntsi
Horodok
Zhmerynka
Haysyn
Boryslav
327
270
Uman
Truskavets
Stryy
Dnister
Buchach
Chortkiv
Tulchyn
1346
Skole
Kalush
Skala-Podilska
Kamyanets-Podilskyy
Vapnyarka
Hayvoron
Bolekhiv
Zalishchyky
(Dnester)
Bershad
Ivano-Frankivsk
Horodenka
Mohyliv-Podilskyy
Nadvirna
Kolomyya
Khotyn
Ocnița
Balta
Uzhhorod
Volovets
Pechenizhyn
Yaremcha
Snyatyn
Lipcani
Yampil
1881
Chernivtsi
Novoselytsya
Chop
Mukacheve
Drochia
Edineț
Soroca
Ananyiv
Berehove
Yasinya
Hlyboka
Storozhynets
Florești
Kotovsk
Khust
Rakhiv
Dorohoi
Bălți
Rîbnița
Vynohradiv
Tyachiv
Siret
M O L D O V A
Dubăsari Vdkhr.
Nyíregyháza
Sighetu-Marmatiei
Rădăuți
Fălești
Satu Mare
Botoșani
Dubăsari
Carei
Baia Mare
Borșa
1565
Suceava
Cornești
Orhei
2303 Pietrosul
Fălticeni
Chișinău
Tiraspol
Someș
Pașcani
Ungheni
Iași
Vatra Dornei
Bistrița
B e s s a r a b i a
2100 Pietrosul
1804
418
Tighina
Dnister (Nistru)
Bistrița
Roman
Zalău
Dej
Hușl
Cimișlia
Oradea
Piatra Neamț
Vaslui
Leova
Mureș
Reghin
Prut
Basarabeasca
Bilhorod-Dnistrovskyy
Cluj-Napoca
1777
Bacău
Turda
Tîrgu Mureș
Comrat
1836
Artsyz
Munții Bihor
1848
Odorheiu Secuiesc
Miercurea Ciuc
Siret
Bîrlad
Abrud
Onești
Ceadâr-Lunga
T r a n s i l v a n i a
Aiud
Tîrnăveni
Sighișoara
Cahul
Tatarbunary
Bîrlad
Sfîntu Gheorghe
Tecuci
Mediaș
Ozero Sasyk
Brad
Alba-Iulia
1783
Vulcănești
Bolhrad
Kiliya
Olt
Focșani
Vylkove
Deva
Făgăraș
Brașov
Reni
Izmayil
R O M A N I A
Sibiu
Sulina
Simeria
Săcele
Galați
1380
Rîmnicu Sărat
Lugoj
C a r p a ț i i M e r i d i o n a l i
2543 Moldoveana
Brăila
Tulcea
Hunedoara
P. Turnu Roșu
2507 Vf. Omul
Petroșani
Buzău
Cîmpulung
Cîmpina
Vf. Peleaga 2509
Dunărea (Danube)
Caransebeș
Vulcan
2518 Paringul Mare
Curtea de Argeș
Buzău
Babadag
1445
22
24
26
28
30
46
48
50
52
East from Greenwich
6
7
8
9
CARTOGRAPHY BY PHILIP'S.

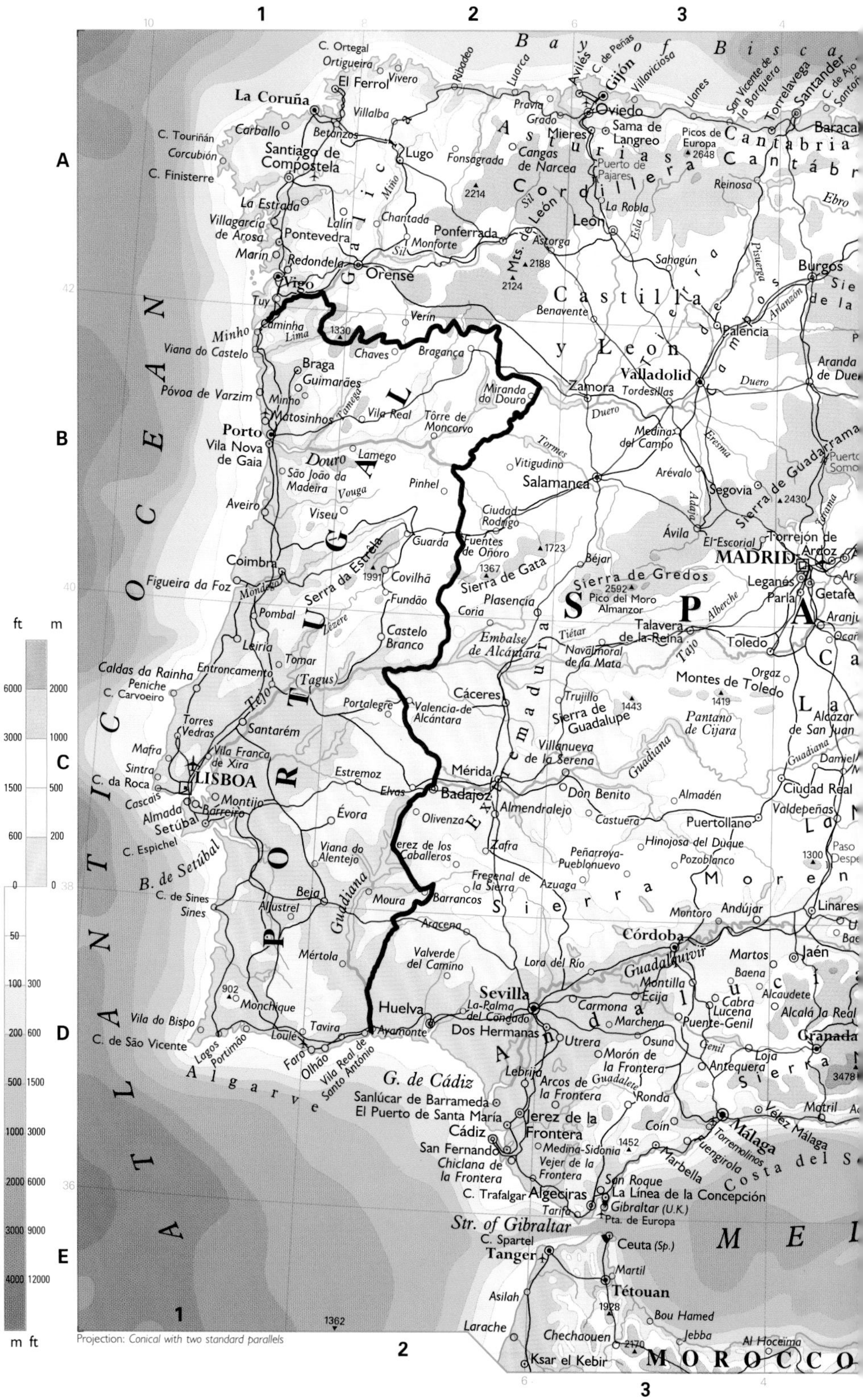

Projection: *Conical with two standard parallels*

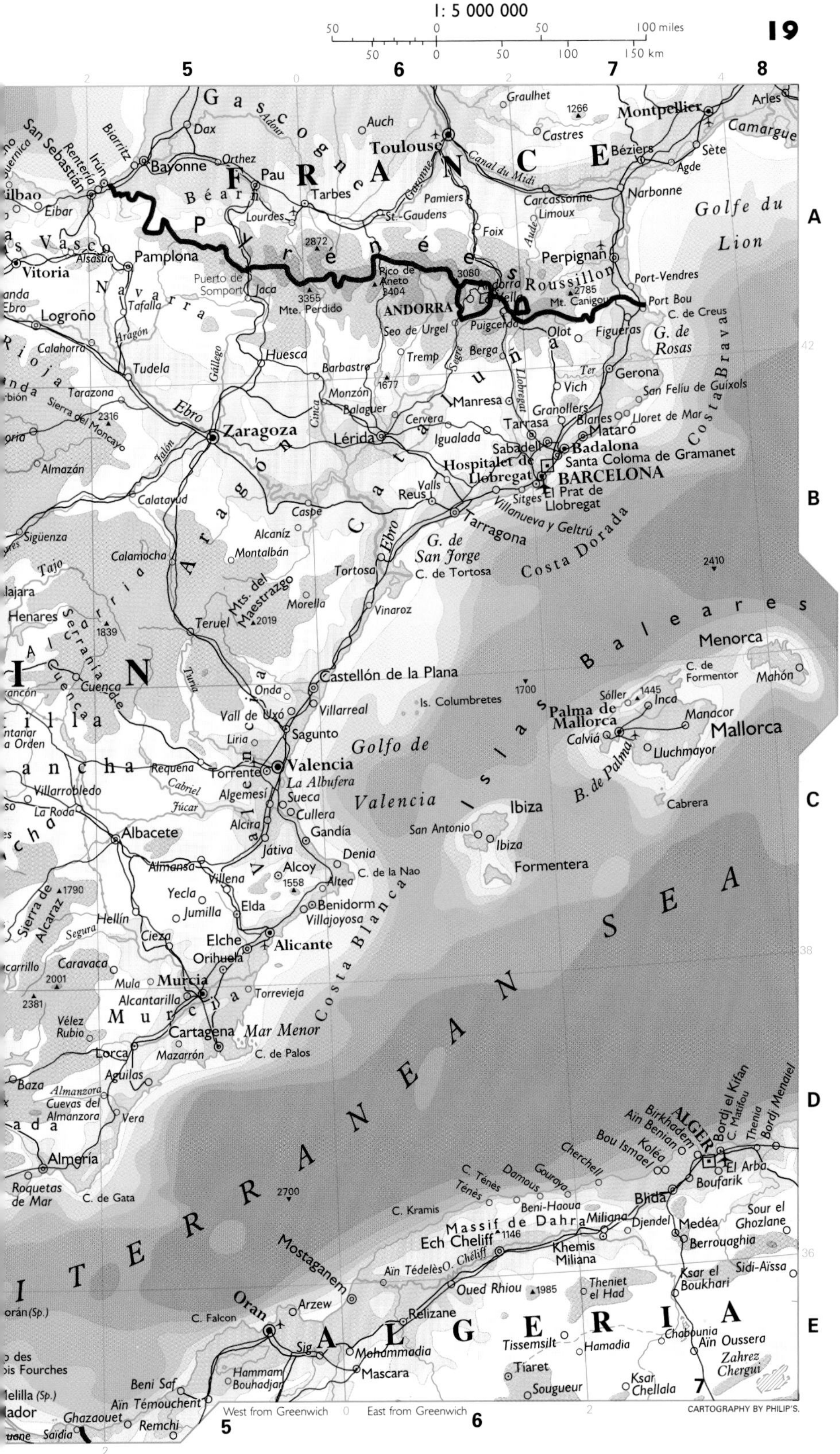
1: 5 000 000
50 0 50 100 miles
50 0 50 100 150 km
5 6 7 8
A B C D E
Gascogne
FRANCE
Pyrénées
Toulouse
Montpellier
Arles
Camargue
Béziers
Sète
Agde
Narbonne
Golfe du Lion
Carcassonne
Limoux
Perpignan
Roussillon
Port-Vendres
Port Bou
Mt. Canigou
C. de Creus
G. de Rosas
Figueras
Olot
Costa Brava
Gerona
San Felíu de Guíxols
Lloret de Mar
Blanes
Mataró
Badalona
Santa Coloma de Gramanet
BARCELONA
Hospitalet de Llobregat
El Prat de Llobregat
Sabadell
Tarrasa
Granollers
Vich
Manresa
Berga
Puigcerdà
ANDORRA
Seo de Urgel
Tremp
Cataluña
Lérida
Balaguer
Cervera
Igualada
Reus
Valls
Tarragona
Sitges
Villanueva y Geltrú
Costa Dorada
G. de San Jorge
C. de Tortosa
Tortosa
Vinaroz
Ebro
Zaragoza
Aragón
Huesca
Barbastro
Monzón
Jaca
Puerto de Somport
Mte. Perdido
Pico de Aneto
Pamplona
Navarra
Vitoria
Bilbao
Eibar
San Sebastián
Irún
Rentería
Biarritz
Bayonne
Dax
Orthez
Pau
Béarn
Tarbes
Lourdes
Auch
Pamiers
St.-Gaudens
Foix
Castres
Graulhet
Logroño
Calahorra
Tudela
Tafalla
Tarazona
Sierra del Moncayo
Almazán
Calatayud
Caspe
Alcañiz
Montalbán
Calamocha
Sigüenza
Tajo
Henares
Teruel
Mts. del Maestrazgo
Morella
Serranía de Cuenca
Cuenca
Castellón de la Plana
Villarreal
Onda
Vall de Uxó
Sagunto
Liria
Valencia
Torrente
La Albufera
Sueca
Cullera
Algemesí
Alcira
Gandía
Játiva
Requena
Golfo de Valencia
Is. Columbretes
Islas Baleares
Menorca
C. de Formentor
Mahón
Sóller
Inca
Palma de Mallorca
Manacor
Mallorca
Calviá
Lluchmayor
B. de Palma
Cabrera
Ibiza
San Antonio
Formentera
Villarrobledo
La Roda
Albacete
Almansa
Villena
Alcoy
Denia
C. de la Nao
Altea
Benidorm
Villajoyosa
Yecla
Jumilla
Elda
Hellín
Sierra de Alcaraz
Segura
Cieza
Elche
Alicante
Orihuela
Caravaca
Mula
Murcia
Alcantarilla
Torrevieja
Costa Blanca
Vélez Rubio
Cartagena
Mar Menor
C. de Palos
Mazarrón
Lorca
Aguilas
Baza
Almanzora
Cuevas del Almanzora
Vera
Almería
Roquetas de Mar
C. de Gata
MEDITERRANEAN SEA
ALGER
Bordj el Kifan
C. Matifou
Thenia
Bordj Menaiel
Birkhadem
Aïn Benian
Bou Ismaïel
Koléa
Cherchell
Gouraya
Damous
C. Ténès
Ténès
C. Kramis
Beni-Haoua
Massif de Dahra
Miliana
Blida
El Arba
Boufarik
Djendel
Medéa
Berrouaghia
Sour el Ghozlane
Ech Cheliff
Khemis Miliana
Sidi-Aïssa
Ksar el Boukhari
Theniet el Had
Oued Rhiou
Aïn Tédelès
Chéliff
Mostaganem
Oran
Arzew
C. Falcon
Relizane
ALGERIA
Sig
Mohammadia
Mascara
Hammam Bouhadjar
Beni Saf
Aïn Témouchent
Ghazaouet
Remchi
Saïdia
Tissemsilt
Hamadia
Chabounia
Aïn Oussera
Zahrez Chergui
Tiaret
Sougueur
Ksar Chellala
Melilla (Sp.)
Orán (Sp.)
West from Greenwich
East from Greenwich
CARTOGRAPHY BY PHILIP'S.

1
2
3
4
5
6
7
A
B
C
D
SWITZERLAND
AUSTRIA
FRANCE
HUNGARY
SLOVENIA
CROATIA
BOSNIA-HERZEGOVINA
MONACO
SAN MARINO
VATICAN CITY
ADRIATIC SEA
LIGURIAN SEA
Golfo di Venézia
Golfo di Génova
Golfo dell' Asinara
Kvarner
Kvarnerić
Piemonte
Lombárdia
Liguria
Toscana
Lazio
Dolomiti
Alpes Maritimes
Karnische Alpen
Karawanken
Steiermark
Kärnten
Dinara Planina
Velebit Planina
Velika Kapela
Istra
Dalmacija
Côte d'Azur
Riviera di Ponente
Riviera di Levante
Corse
Elba
TORINO (Turin)
MILANO
ROMA
Venézia (Venice)
Firenze (Florence)
Génova
Bologna
Trieste
Ljubljana
Zagreb
Sarajevo
Grenoble
Annecy
Chambéry
Nice
Cannes
Antibes
Monte-Carlo
Menton
Sanremo
Impéria
Savona
La Spezia
Livorno
Pisa
Lucca
Prato
Pistóia
Siena
Arezzo
Perúgia
Assisi
Terni
Rieti
L'Áquila
Pescara
Chieti
Ancona
Rímini
Pésaro
Ravenna
Ferrara
Pádova
Verona
Vicenza
Treviso
Bolzano
Trento
Udine
Bréscia
Bérgamo
Como
Novara
Alessándria
Asti
Cúneo
Piacenza
Parma
Reggio nell'Emília
Módena
Cremona
Mantova
Foggia
Campobasso
Latina
Frosinone
Viterbo
Grosseto
Ajaccio
Bastia
Rijeka
Pula
Zadar
Split
Šibenik
Dubrovnik
Mostar
Banja Luka
Tuzla
Osijek
Maribor
Graz
Klagenfurt
Villach
Pécs
Nikšić

1: 5 000 000

50 0 50 100 miles

50 0 50 100 150 km

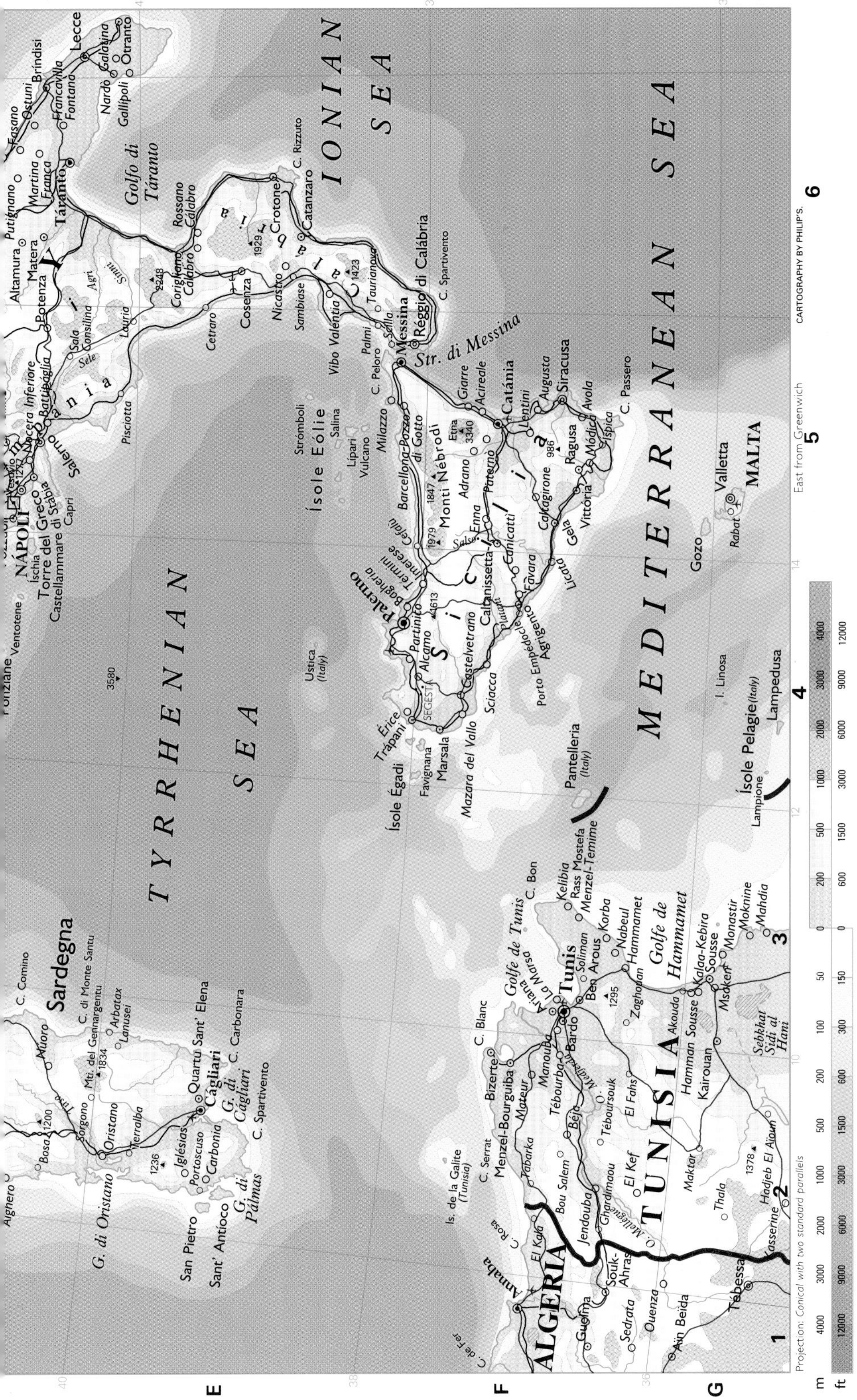

TYRRHENIAN SEA
IONIAN SEA
MEDITERRANEAN SEA
Sardegna
Sicilia
Calabria
MALTA
TUNISIA
ALGERIA
NÁPOLI
Palermo
Messina
Réggio di Calábria
Catánia
Siracusa
Táranto
Bríndisi
Lecce
Cágliari
Tunis
Valletta
Str. di Messina
Golfo di Táranto
Ísole Eólie
Ísole Égadi
Pantelleria (Italy)
Ísole Pelagie (Italy)
Lampedusa
Golfe de Tunis
Golfe de Hammamet
Etna 3340
Projection: Conical with two standard parallels
East from Greenwich
CARTOGRAPHY BY PHILIP'S.
m 4000 3000 2000 1000 500 200 100 50 0 200 500 1000 2000 3000 4000
ft 12000 9000 6000 3000 1500 600 300 150 0 600 1500 3000 6000 9000 12000

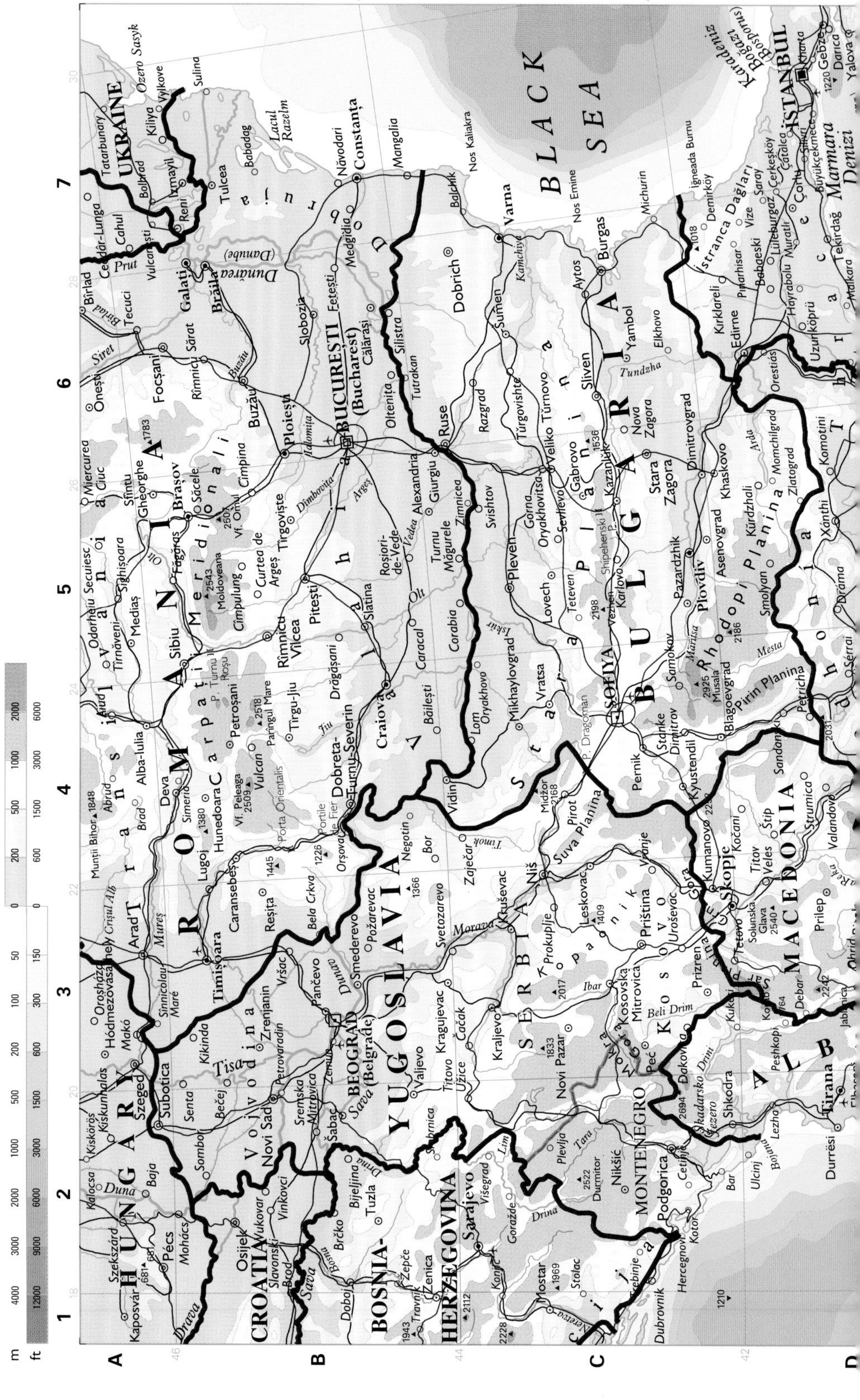
BLACK SEA
ROMANIA
BULGARIA
YUGOSLAVIA
MACEDONIA
MONTENEGRO
SERBIA
CROATIA
BOSNIA-HERZEGOVINA
HUNGARY
UKRAINE
ALB
BUCUREȘTI (Bucharest)
SOFIYA
BEOGRAD (Belgrade)
ISTANBUL
Sarajevo
Skopje
Tirana
Podgorica
Constanța
Varna
Burgas
Plovdiv
Ruse
Galați
Brăila
Brașov
Ploiești
Craiova
Timișoara
Novi Sad
Szeged
Pécs
Niš
Priština
Dubrovnik
Mostar
Tuzla
Osijek
Subotica
Dobrich
Pleven
Stara Zagora
Sliven
Yambol
Edirne
Kırklareli
Tekirdağ
Marmara Denizi
Dunărea (Danube)
Carpații Meridionali
Stara Planina
Rhodopi Planina
Pirin Planina
Vojvodina
Kosovo
Musala 2925
m
ft

1: 5 000 000

50 0 50 100 miles

50 0 50 100 150 km

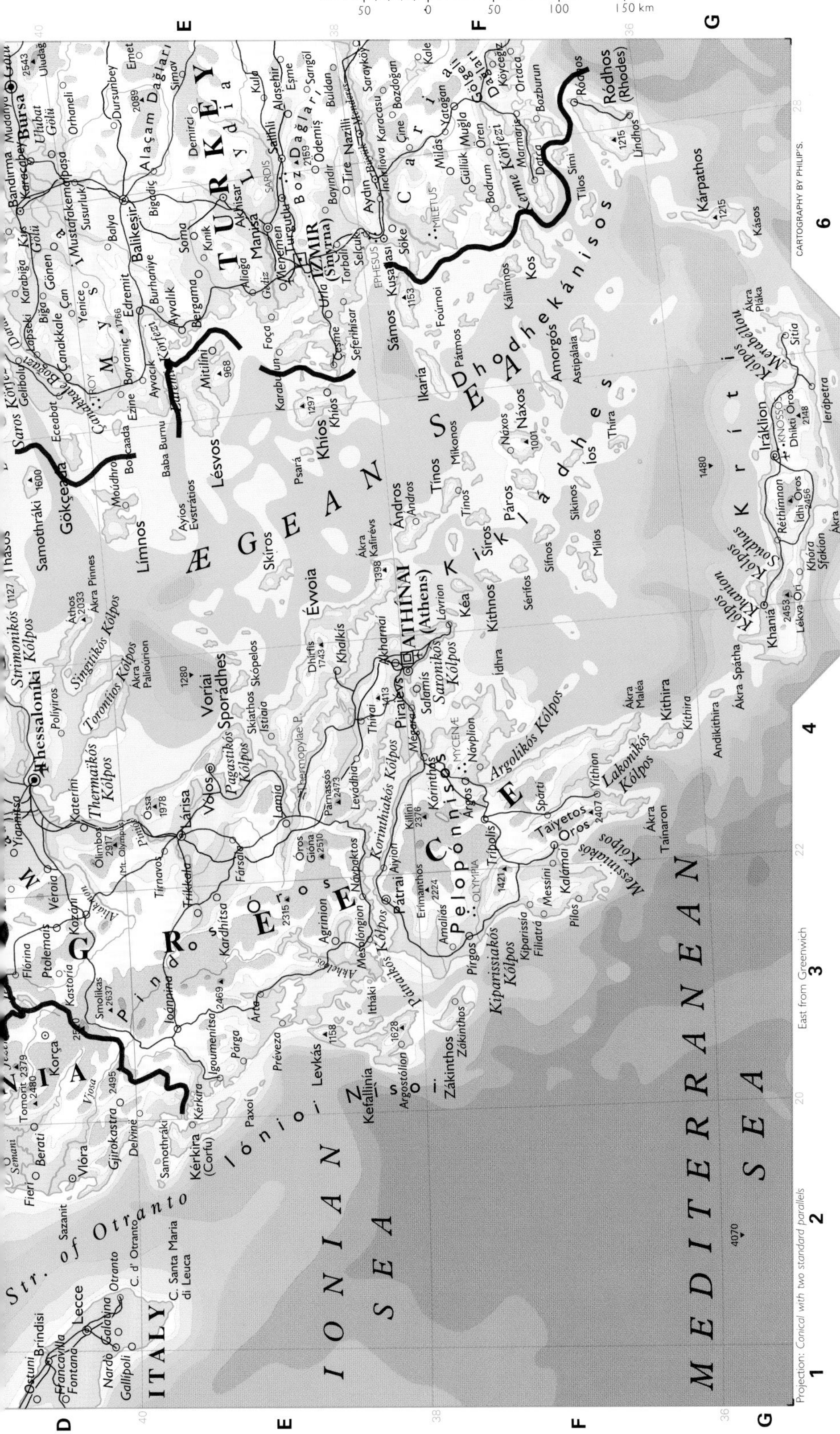

Projection: Conical with two standard parallels

East from Greenwich

CARTOGRAPHY BY PHILIP'S.

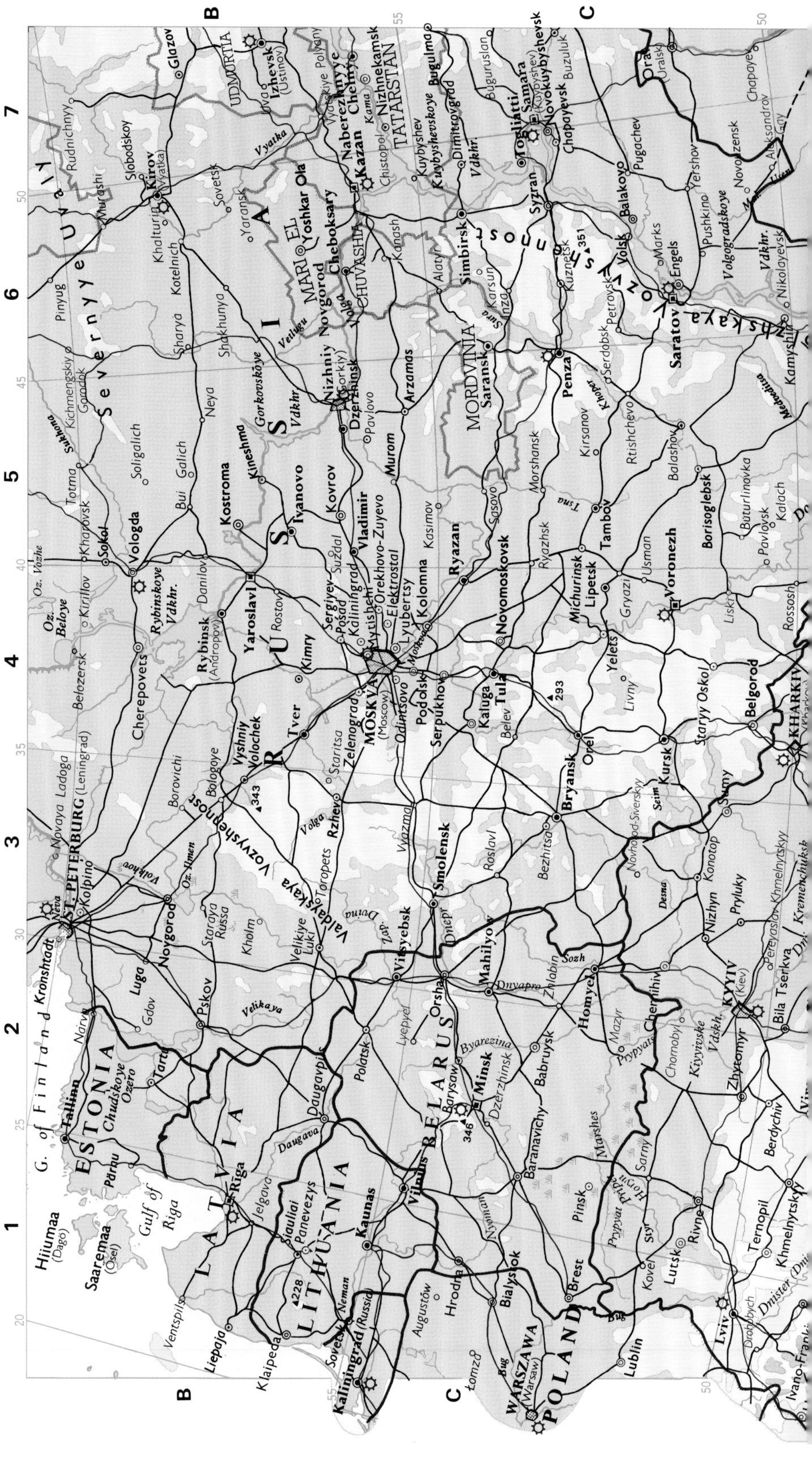

ESTONIA
LATVIA
LITHUANIA
BELARUS
POLAND
RUSSIA
MARI EL
CHUVASHIA
TATARSTAN
UDMURTIA
MORDVINIA
G. of Finland
Gulf of Riga
Severnyye Uvaly
Vozvyshennost
Valdayskaya
ST. PETERBURG (Leningrad)
MOSKVA (Moscow)
KYYIV (Kiev)
WARSZAWA (Warsaw)
Tallinn
Riga
Vilnius
Minsk
Kaunas
Kaliningrad (Russia)
Klaipeda
Liepaja
Ventspils
Pärnu
Tartu
Narva
Pskov
Novgorod
Luga
Kolpino
Kronshtadt
Vologda
Cherepovets
Rybinsk (Andropov)
Yaroslavl
Kostroma
Ivanovo
Vladimir
Tver
Kimry
Ryazan
Tula
Kaluga
Smolensk
Bryansk
Orel
Kursk
Belgorod
Voronezh
Lipetsk
Tambov
Penza
Saransk
Simbirsk
Samara
Togliatti
Syzran
Saratov
Engels
Volsk
Balakovo
Kazan
Cheboksary
Yoshkar Ola
Nizhniy Novgorod (Gorkiy)
Dzerzhinsk
Arzamas
Murom
Kovrov
Kirov (Vyatka)
Izhevsk (Ustinov)
Glazov
Naberezhnyye Chelny
Nizhnekamsk
Novokuybyshevsk
Chapayevsk
Mahilyov
Homyel
Vitsyebsk
Orsha
Babruysk
Baranavichy
Pinsk
Brest
Hrodna
Bialystok
Lublin
Lviv
Lutsk
Rivne
Zhytomyr
Chernihiv
Bila Tserkva
Ternopil
Khmelnytskyy
KHARKIV
Sumy
Konotop
Nizhyn
Pryluky
Vyaz'ma
Rzhev
Velikiye Luki
Daugavpils
Siauliai
Panevezys
Jelgava
Polatsk
Chudskoye Ozero
Oz. Ilmen
Oz. Beloye
Rybinskoye Vdkhr.
Gorkovskoye Vdkhr.
Kuybyshevskoye Vdkhr.
Volgogradskoye Vdkhr.
Volga
Dnyapro
Daugava
Neman
Pripyats
Desna
Sozh
Hiiumaa (Dagö)
Saaremaa (Ösel)

1: 10 000 000
100 50 0 50 100 150 200 miles
100 0 100 200 300 km
D
E
F
3
4
5
6
30
35 East from Greenwich
40
45
ROMANIA
MOLDOVA
BULGARIA
UKRAINE
KAZAKSTAN
Caspian Depression
KALMYKIA
CRIMEA
ADYGEA
ABKHAZIA
CHECHENIA
DAGESTAN
GEORGIA
AJARIA
South Ossetia
ARMENIA
AZERBAIJAN
NAXÇIVAN
Nagorno-Karabakh
TURKEY
IRAN
BLACK SEA
CASPIAN SEA
Sea of Azov
Caucasus Mountains
Kuzey Anadolu Dağlari
Anadolu
Krymskyy Piv.
Karkinitska Zatoka
BUCUREȘTI (Bucharest)
Chișinău (Kishinev)
Odesa
Kherson
Mykolayiv
Dnipropetrovsk
Zaporizhzhya
Donetsk
Luhansk
Rostov
Taganrog
Volgograd (Stalingrad)
Astrakhan
Krasnodar
Novorossiysk
Stavropol
Sochi
Sukhumi
Kutaisi
Tbilisi
Yerevan
Baki (Baku)
Grozny
Makhachkala
Vladikavkaz
Nalchik
Derbent
ISTANBUL
Ankara
Bursa
Eskişehir
Samsun
Trabzon
Erzurum
Kayseri
Sivas
Malatya
Sinop
Zonguldak
Varna
Burgas
Constanța
Galați
Brăila
Ploiești
Brașov
Iași
Sevastopol
Simferopol
Yalta
Feodosiya
Kerch
Batumi
Poti
Elbrus 5642
Kazbek 5047
Ağri Daği (Ararat) 5165
Erciyas Daği 3770
Kaçkar 3937
2211
Van Gölü
Tuz Gölü
Marmara Denizi
Volga
Don
Kuban
Terek
Dnipro (Dnieper)
Dunărea (Danube)
1. Karachey-Cherkessia
2. Kabardino-Balkaria
3. North Ossetia
4. Ingushetia
Projection: Conical with two standard parallels
m 4000 2000 1000 200 0 200 400 1000 2000 4000
ft 12 000 6000 3000 600 0 600 1200 3000 6000 12 000
CARTOGRAPHY BY PHILIP'S.

ATLANTIC OCEAN
GREENLAND
ICELAND
Arctic Circle
Svalbard
ARCTIC
Barents Sea
Novaya Zemlya
Kara Sea
UNITED KINGDOM
NORWAY
North Sea
LONDON
PARIS
FRANCE
SWEDEN
FINLAND
Murmansk
White Sea
Arkhangelsk
Vorkuta
Salekhard
Ob
GERMANY
Berlin
Europe
Prague
Warsaw
Vienna
ST. PETERSBURG
MOSCOW
Nizhniy Novgorod
Kazan
Perm
Yekaterinburg
Irtysh
Ufa
Chelyabinsk
Omsk
Volga
Samara
RU
ITALY
Rome
UKRAINE
Belgrade
Odessa
Danube
Black Sea
Don
Rostov
Volgograd
Astrakhan
Pavlodar
Astana
Karaganda
KAZAKSTAN
Athens
ISTANBUL
Bursa
Izmir
Ankara
TURKEY
Konya
GEORGIA
Tbilisi
Yerevan
ARMENIA
AZERBAIJAN
Baku
Caspian Sea
Aral Sea
Syrdarya
L. Balkhash
UZBEKISTAN
Alma Ata
Tashkent
Bishkek
KYRGYZSTAN
Samarkand
TURKMENISTAN
Ashkhabad
TAJIKISTAN
Dushanbe
Kashi
Mediterranean Sea
Nicosia
CYPRUS
Adana
Aleppo
Beirut
LEBANON
SYRIA
Euphrates
Mosul
Tabriz
ISRAEL
Damascus
Alexandria
CAIRO
'Ammān
Jerusalem
JORDAN
Suez
LIBYA
EGYPT
Nile
IRAQ
Baghdād
Tigris
TEHRĀN
IRAN
Esfahān
Mashhad
Herāt
Kābul
AFGHANISTAN
Qandahār
Islamabad
JAMMU & KASHMIR
Basra
KUWAIT
Kuwait
Shīrāz
Zāhedān
Faisalabad
Lahore
PAKISTAN
Aswân
Red Sea
SAUDI ARABIA
Medina
Riyadh
BAHRAIN
The Gulf
Al Manāmah
QATAR
Doha
UNITED ARAB EMIRATES
Abu Dhabi
G. of Oman
Muscat
KARACHI
Indus
DELHI
New Delhi
Jaipur
Lucknow
Kanpur
Jedda
Mecca
Port Sudan
SUDAN
Khartoum
ERITREA
Sana'
YEMEN
OMAN
INDIA
Ahmadabad
Vadodara
Bhopal
Indore
Surat
MUMBAI (Bombay)
Pune
DJIBOUTI
Aden
G. of Aden
Socotra (Yemen)
Arabian Sea
Africa
ETHIOPIA
Addis Ababa
SOMALI REP.
Bangalore
Lakshadweep Is. (India)
Madurai
UGANDA
L. Victoria
KENYA
Mogadishu
Equator
INDIAN OCEAN
Colombo
MALDIVES
Male
CONGO (DEM. REP. OF THE)
Nairobi
TANZANIA
Mombasa
Dar es Salaam
SEYCHELLES
Victoria
ZAMBIA
MALAWI
Aldabra Is. (Seychelles)
Amirante Is. (Seychelles)
Chagos Arch. (U.K.)
Projection: Bonne
East from Greenwich
Hanoi ● Capital Cities

1: 67 000 000
200 0 200 400 600 800 1000 1200 miles
200 0 400 800 1200 1600 2000 km
B
C
D
E
F
G
H
J
K
L
12
13
14
15
16
17
OCEAN
Laptev Sea
New Siberian Is.
Wrangel I.
ALASKA (U.S.A.)
Bering Sea
Aleutian Is. (U.S.A.)
Khatanga
Verkhoyansk
Gizhiga
Lena
Magadan
Okhotsk
Petropavlovsk-Kamchatskiy
Yakutsk
Sea of Okhotsk
S I A
Sakhalin
Kuril Is.
Angara
Komsomolsk
Krasnoyarsk
Bratsk
L. Baikal
Khabarovsk
Yuzhno-Sakhalinsk
Blagoveshchensk
Chita
Amur
Hokkaidō
Sapporo
Ulan Ude
Hailar
Qiqihar
Vladivostok
Irkutsk
Harbin
Changchun
Honshū
Ulan Bator
Jilin
Sea of Japan
TŌKYŌ
Yokohama
MONGOLIA
SHENYANG
Anshan
NORTH KOREA
JAPAN
Jinzhou
P'yongyang
Dalian
SOUTH KOREA
Kyōto
Nagoya
Ōsaka
Ürümqi
SEOUL
Hiroshima
Hami
Baotou
BEIJING
TIANJIN
Pusan
Kitakyūshū
Bonin Is. (Japan)
Yumen
Taiyuan
Jinan
Yellow Sea
Hwang-ho
SHANGHAI
Lanzhou
Nanjing
East China Sea
Volcano Is. (Japan)
Xi'an
Tropic of Cancer
CHINA
Wuhan
HANGZHOU
Ryukyu Is.
Nanchang
Chengdu
Fuzhou
Taipei
CHONGQING
Yangtze
Changsha
TAIWAN
Lhasa
PACIFIC
Thimphu
BHUTAN
GUANGZHOU
Brahmaputra
Kunming
Si Kiang
HONG KONG
GUAM (U.S.A.)
Macau
BANGLADESH
DACCA
BURMA
Hanoi
Haiphong
Chittagong
Hainan
Luzon
PHILIPPINES
(MYANMAR)
FED. STATES OF MICRONESIA
LAOS
MANILA
Vientiane
Mekong
Irrawaddy
Salween
VIETNAM
PALAU
Bay of Bengal
South China Sea
Cebu
Rangoon
THAILAND
BANGKOK
CAMBODIA
Mindanao
Phnom Penh
Ho Chi Minh City
Palawan
Sulu Sea
Davao
Andaman Is. (India)
Zamboanga
G. of Thailand
Bandar Seri Begawan
Halmahera
BRUNEI
SABAH
Celebes Sea
Manado
Nicobar Is. (India)
IRIAN JAYA
PEN. MALAYSIA
SARAWAK
Str. of Malacca
Kuala Lumpur
MALAYSIA
Ceram
Medan
SINGAPORE
Borneo
Celebes
Ambon
Banda Sea
Sumatra
Banjarmasin
INDONESIA
Ujung Pandang
Arafura Sea
Palembang
Java Sea
Flores
Timor
JAKARTA
Semarang
Surabaya
Bandung
Java
Sumba
Timor Sea
AUSTRALIA
CARTOGRAPHY BY PHILIP'S.

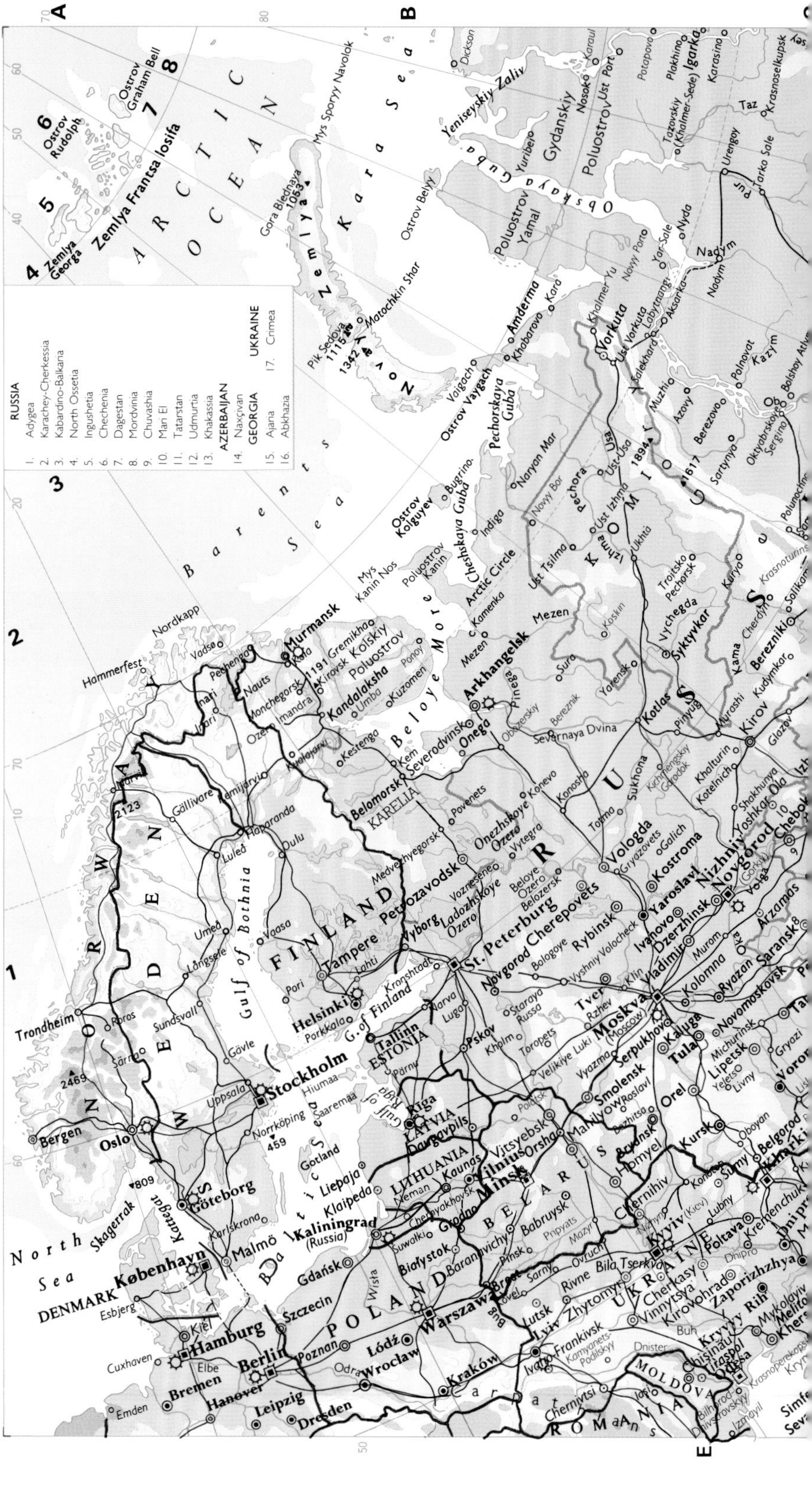
RUSSIA
1. Adygea
2. Karachey-Cherkessia
3. Kabardino-Balkaria
4. North Ossetia
5. Ingushetia
6. Chechenia
7. Dagestan
8. Mordvinia
9. Chuvashia
10. Mari El
11. Tatarstan
12. Udmurtia
13. Khakassia
AZERBAIJAN
14. Naxçıvan
GEORGIA
15. Ajaria
16. Abkhazia
UKRAINE
17. Crimea
ARCTIC OCEAN
Barents Sea
Kara Sea
Zemlya Frantsa Iosifa
Ostrov Rudolph
Zemlya Georga
Ostrov Graham Bell
Novaya Zemlya
Ostrov Kolguyev
Ostrov Vaygach
Ostrov Belyy
Poluostrov Yamal
Gydanskiy Poluostrov
Obskaya Guba
Yeniseyskiy Zaliv
Pechorskaya Guba
Cheshskaya Guba
Arctic Circle
Beloye More
Gulf of Bothnia
Gulf of Finland
Gulf of Riga
Baltic Sea
North Sea
Skagerrak
Kattegat
NORWAY
SWEDEN
FINLAND
ESTONIA
LATVIA
LITHUANIA
BELARUS
POLAND
UKRAINE
MOLDOVA
ROMANIA
DENMARK
RUSSIA
KOMI
KARELIA
Murmansk
Arkhangelsk
Severodvinsk
Onega
Belomorsk
Kandalaksha
Petrozavodsk
St. Peterburg
Novgorod
Cherepovets
Vologda
Yaroslavl
Kostroma
Rybinsk
Tver
Moskva
Nizhniy Novgorod
Kirov
Kotlas
Syktyvkar
Ukhta
Pechora
Vorkuta
Naryan Mar
Salekhard
Nadym
Urengoy
Smolensk
Kaluga
Tula
Orel
Kursk
Belgorod
Bryansk
Pskov
Vitsyebsk
Minsk
Homyel
Vilnius
Kaunas
Riga
Daugavpils
Tallinn
Helsinki
Tampere
Stockholm
Göteborg
Oslo
Bergen
Trondheim
København
Hamburg
Berlin
Bremen
Hanover
Leipzig
Dresden
Szczecin
Gdańsk
Kaliningrad (Russia)
Warszawa
Łódź
Wrocław
Kraków
Brest
Lviv
Kyyiv (Kiev)
Poltava
Chernihiv
Zaporizhzhya
Kryvyy Rih
Odesa
Chişinău

1: 20 000 000

100 0 100 200 300 400 500 miles

100 0 200 400 600 800 km

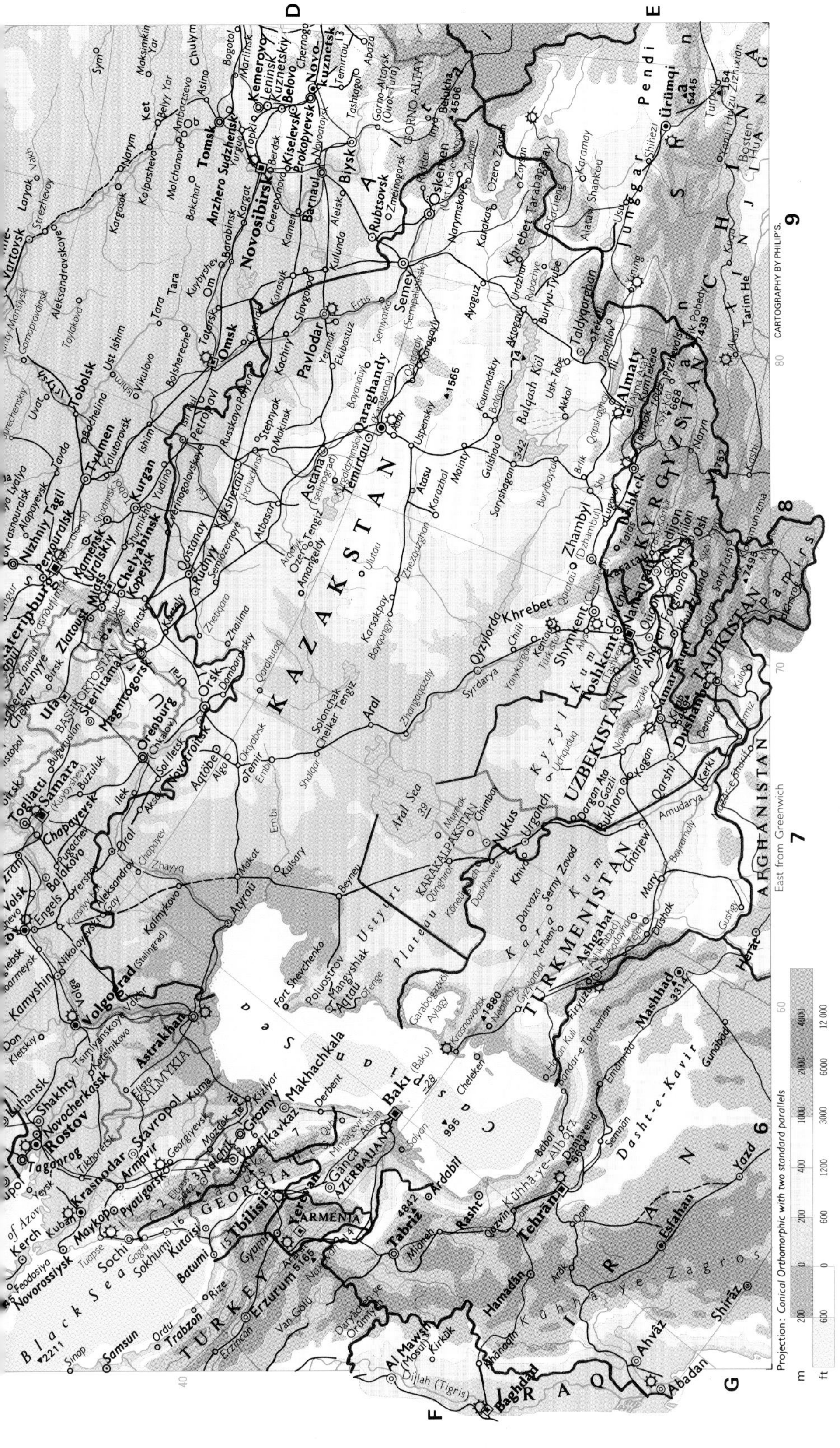

30 EASTERN SIBERIA

A

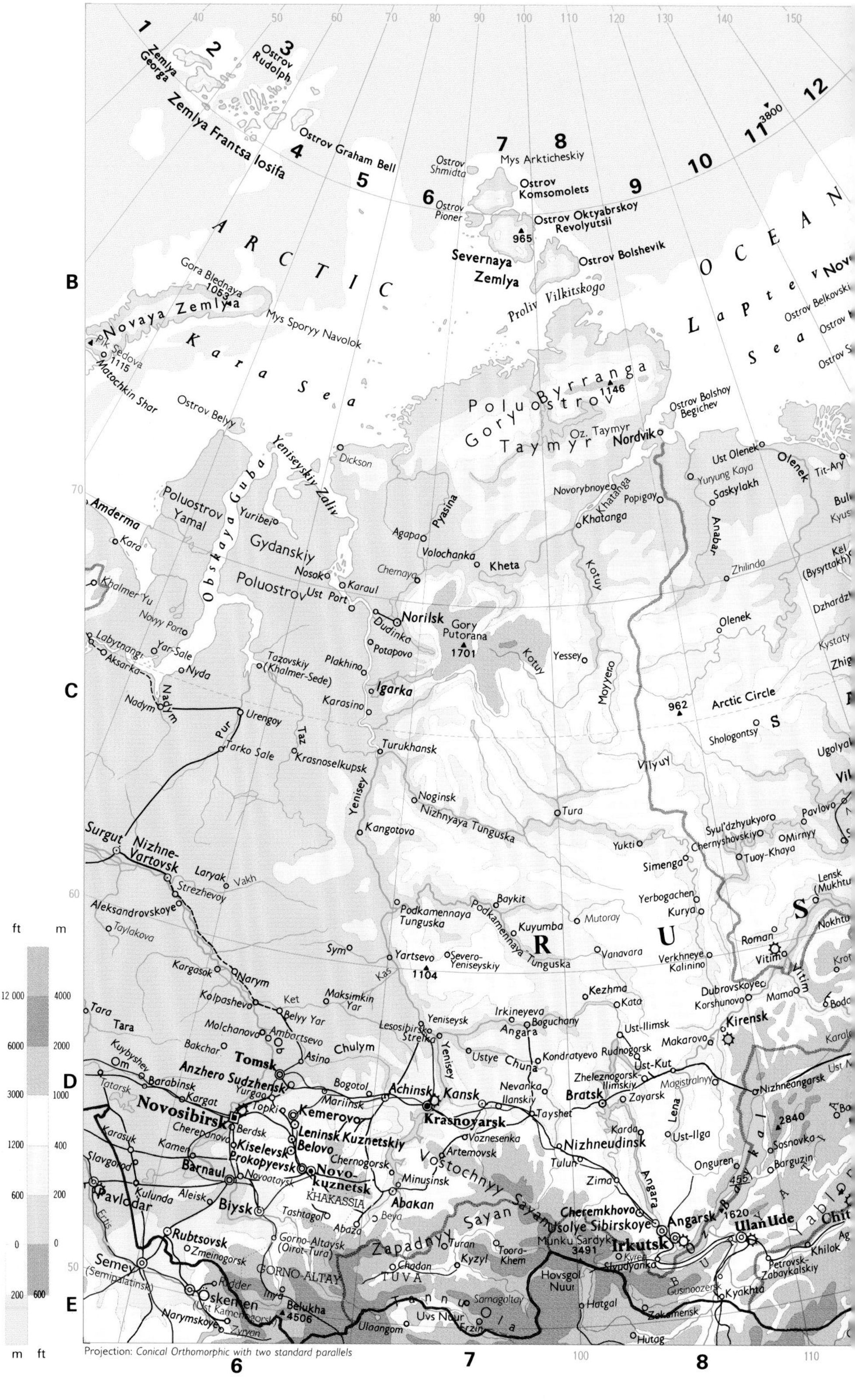

ARCTIC OCEAN
Kara Sea
Laptev Sea
Zemlya Georga
Ostrov Rudolph
Zemlya Frantsa Iosifa
Ostrov Graham Bell
Ostrov Shmidta
Mys Arkticheskiy
Ostrov Komsomolets
Ostrov Pioner
Ostrov Oktyabrskoy Revolyutsii
965
Severnaya Zemlya
Ostrov Bolshevik
Proliv Vilkitskogo
Gora Blednaya 1053
Novaya Zemlya
Mys Sporyy Navolok
Pik Sedova 1115
Matochkin Shar
Ostrov Belyy
Poluostrov Taymyr
Gory Byrranga
1146
Oz. Taymyr
Nordvik
Ostrov Bolshoy Begichev
Dickson
Yeniseyskiy Zaliv
Obskaya Guba
Poluostrov Yamal
Amderma
Kara
Yuribei
Gydanskiy Poluostrov
Agapa
Pyasina
Volochanka
Kheta
Khatanga
Novorybnoye
Popigay
Ust Olenek
Yuryung Kaya
Saskylakh
Olenek
Anabar
Zhilinda
Tit-Ary
Kotuy
Chernaya
Nosok
Karaul
Ust Port
Norilsk
Dudinka
Gory Putorana
1701
Potapovo
Plakhino
Igarka
Karasino
Yessey
Moyyero
Khalmer Yu
Novyy Port
Labytnangi
Aksarka
Yar-Sale
Nyda
Nadym
Tazovskiy (Khalmer-Sede)
Urengoy
Pur
Tarko Sale
Taz
Krasnoselkupsk
Turukhansk
Arctic Circle
962
Sholokontsy
Vilyuy
Yenisey
Noginsk
Nizhnyaya Tunguska
Tura
Kangotovo
Surgut
Nizhne-Vartovsk
Laryak
Vakh
Strezhevoy
Aleksandrovskoye
Taylakova
Yukti
Simenga
Chernyshovskiy
Syul'dzhyukyoro
Mirnyy
Tuoy-Khaya
Pavlovo
Lensk (Mukhtuya)
Yerbogachen
Kurya
Baykit
Podkamennaya Tunguska
Kuyumba
Mutoray
Vanavara
Sym
Yartsevo
Severo-Yeniseyskiy
1104
Kas
R U S
Verkhneye Kalinino
Roman
Vitim
Kargasok
Narym
Kolpashevo
Ket
Maksimkin Yar
Belyy Yar
Tara
Molchanovo
Ambartsevo
Ob
Bakchar
Asino
Chulym
Tomsk
Kuybyshev
Om
Tatarsk
Barabinsk
Kargat
Anzhero Sudzhensk
Yurga
Topki
Novosibirsk
Mariinsk
Bogotol
Achinsk
Kansk
Krasnoyarsk
Kemerovo
Leninsk Kuznetskiy
Belovo
Berdsk
Cherepanovo
Kiselevsk
Prokopyevsk
Novokuznetsk
Karasuk
Kamen
Slavgorod
Barnaul
Novoaltaysk
Pavlodar
Kulunda
Aleisk
Biysk
Yeniseysk
Lesosibirsk
Strelka
Irkineyeva
Angara
Boguchany
Kezhma
Kata
Ustye
Chuna
Kondratyevo
Rudnogorsk
Ust-Ilimsk
Zheleznogorsk-Ilimskiy
Ust-Kut
Magistralnyy
Makarovo
Kirensk
Dubrovskoye
Korshunovo
Mama
Nizhneangarsk
2840
Nevanka
Ilanskiy
Tayshet
Bratsk
Zayarsk
Lena
Karda
Ust-Ilga
Voznesenka
Artemovsk
Vostochnyy Sayan
Nizhneudinsk
Tulun
Zima
Chernogorsk
Minusinsk
Abakan
KHAKASSIA
Tashtagol
Abaza
Beya
Cheremkhovo
Usolye Sibirskoye
Angarsk
Irkutsk
Munku Sardyk 3491
Slyudyanka
Baikal
Onguren
Sosnovka
Barguzin
1620
Ulan Ude
Chita
Khilok
Petrovsk-Zabaykalskiy
Gusinoozersk
Kyakhta
Zakamensk
Hutag
Hatgal
Hovsgol Nuur
Kyzyl
Toora-Khem
Turan
Zapadnyy Sayan
Chadan
TUVA
Tannu Ola
Samagaltay
Uvs Nuur
Erzin
Ulaangom
Rubtsovsk
Zmeinogorsk
Gorno-Altaysk (Oirot-Tura)
GORNO-ALTAY
Semey (Semipalatinsk)
Ridder
Oskemen (Ust Kamenogorsk)
Belukha 4506
Inya
Narymskoye
Zyryan
Ertis
ft
m
12 000
6000
3000
1200
600
0
200
4000
2000
1000
400
200
0
600

Projection: *Conical Orthomorphic with two standard parallels*

6 7 8

1: 20 000 000
100 0 100 200 300 400 500 miles
100 0 200 400 600 800 km
B
C
D
E
14
15
16
9
10
11
170
60
50
40
120
130
East from Greenwich
Mys Dezhneva (East C.)
Uelen
Lavrentiya
Chukchi Sea
St. Lawrence I. (U.S.A.)
Provideniya
Anadyrskiy Zaliv
Vankarem
Amen
1843
Rene
Egvekinot
Chukotskoye Nagorye
Beringovskiy
Ostrov Henrietta
Ostrov Jeanette
Ostrova Delong
Ostrov Zhokhova
Ostrov Vrangelya
East Siberian Sea
Ostrov Bennett
Ostrova
Ostrov Faddeyevskiy
Ostrov Novaya Sibir
Ostrova Medvezhi
Pevek
Ust Chaun
Ostrov Ayon
Anadyr
Koryakskoye Nagorye
Khatyrka
Ambarchik
1853
Bilibino
Cherskiy
Ostrov Malyy Lyakhovskiy
Ostrov Bolshoy Lyakhovskiy
Proliv Dmitriya Lapteva
Nizhne Kolymsk
Bolshoy Anyuy
1742
Yeropol
Markovo
Penzhino
2562
Machevna
Kavacha
Bering Sea
Oloy
Kokuora
Kondakovo
Chokurdakh
Indigirka
Omolon
Kamenskoye
Tilichiki
Buorkhaya
Nizhneyansk
Shamanovo
Srednekolymsk
Kolmskoye Nagorye
Paren
Gizhiga
Penzhinskaya Guba
Rekinniki
Kichiga
Ostrov Karaginskiy
Kazachye
Uyandi
Druzhina
Stolbovaya
Abkit
Ossora
Ust Kuyga
Deputatskiy
Zyryanka
Kolyma
Balygychan
Evensk
Nayakhan
Palana
Komandorskiye Ostrova
Nikolskoye
Ust-Kamchatsk
Yana
Zashiversk
Khonuu
Pobeda 3147
Taskan
Seymchan
Omsukchan
Viliga
Gizhiginskaya Guba
Uka
Sredinnyy Khrebet
Verkhoyansk
Batagay
Gora-Chen 2682
Ust Nera
Orotukan
Yagodnoye
Zaliv Shelikhova
Tigil
4750
Klyuchevskaya
Poluostrov Kamchatka
Khrebet Cherskogo
Alyaskitovyy
Susuman
Atka
Iret
Palatka
Magadan
Ust Khayryuzovo
2389
Kyulyunken
Oymyakon
2959
Loshkalakh
Sanga-Tolon
Ust-Omchug
Icha
3621
Sobolevo
Pushchino
Zhupanovo
3456
Petropavlovsk-Kamchatskiy
Verkhoyanskiy Khrebet
Bilir
Staryy Kheydzhan
Vorovskoye
Kirovskiy
Kytal Ktakh
Lepikha
Aldan
Batamay
Khandyga
Okhotskiy Perevoz
Okhotsk
Sea of Okhotsk
Ust Bolsheretsk
Opala
Lena
Borogontsy
Allakh-Yun
Arka
Sangar
Srednevilyuysk
Bulus
Ytyk Kyuyel
Ynykchanskiy
Ulya
Namtsy
Yakutsk
Mayya
Amga
Yur
Severo-Kurilsk
Pokrovsk
Ust Maya
Ostrov Paramushir
Yelanskoye
Sinsk
Ust-Mil
1780
Aim
Maya
Nelkan
Ostrov Onekotan
Dzhugdzur
Olekminsk
Verkhnyaya Amga
Tommot
Chagda
Chasovnya-Uchurskaya
Ayon
Okha
Uchur
Ostrov Bolshoy Shantar
Sakhalinskiy Zaliv
Aldan
Dikimdya
Malyy Nimnyr
2246
Kankunskiy
Nemuy
Nikolayevsk-na-Amure
Sakhalin
Susanino
Bogorodskoye
Aleksandrovsk-Sakhalinskiy
G. Lopatina
Ostrov Simushir
Chulman
2482
Chumikan
Tugur
Katangli
1609
Kurilskiye Ostrova
Yenyuka
Olekma
imeni Poliny Osipenko
Amgun
Pobedino
Poronaysk
Ostrov Urup
Nagornyy
Stanovoy Khrebet
Chara
Ust-Nyukzha
Uda
Zeya
Ekimchan
Selemdzha
Sofiysk
Amur
Sredne Tambovskoye
Uglegorsk
Sovetskaya Gavan
Yuzhno-Sakhalinsk
Ust-Tungir
Tynda
Pavlovich
Skovorodino
Norsk
Bureya
2640
Komsomolsk
Amursk
Malamyzh
Khrebet Sikhote Alin
Ostrov Iturup
Kurilsk
Kalakan
Yerofey
Dzhalinda
Ushumun
Yermakovo
Kholmsk
Korsakov
Ostrov Kunashir
Tupik
2078
Khabarovsk
Nelma
Mogocha
Amur
Mohe
Shimanovsk
Chegdomyn
Birobidzhan
Smidevich
Wakkanai
Shilka
Kocheya
Svobodnyy
Belogorsk
Zavitinsk
Raychikhinsk
Obluchye
Volochayevka
Abashiri
2290
Sretensk
Nerchinsk
Argun
1054
Blagoveshchensk
Aihui
Poyarkovo
Leninskoye
Vyazemskiy
Bikin
Amgu
Rumoi
Obihiro
Kushiro
Nerchinskiy Zavod
Aleksandrovskiy Zavod
Nenjiang
Hegang
Amurzet
Jiamusi
Terney
Hokkaidō
Sapporo
Otaru
Muroran
Borzya
Zabaykalsk
Da Hinggan Ling
Qiqihar
CHINA
Songhua Jiang
Dalnerechensk
Lesozavodsk
Dalnegorsk
3669
Hakodate
Hailar
Manzhouli
Hulun Nur
Suihua
Spassk Dalniy
Olga
Okushiri-shima
Ang'angxi
Harbin
Ozero Khanka
Ussuriysk
Artem
Vladivostok
Nakhodka
JAPAN
Aomori
Hachinohe
Mudanjiang
Kraskino
Yanji
Unggi
CARTOGRAPHY BY PHILIP'S.

SOUTHERN HONSHU, KYUSHU AND SHIKOKU
SEA OF JAPAN
PACIFIC OCEAN
HONSHU
SHIKOKU
KYUSHU
TOKYO
YOKOHAMA
KAWASAKI
NAGOYA
KYOTO
OSAKA
KOBE
HIROSHIMA
KITAKYUSHU
Fukuoka
Kumamoto
Okayama
Sendai
Kagoshima
Miyazaki
Nagasaki
Sasebo
Shimonoseki
Matsue
Tottori
Himeji
Wakayama
Nara
Gifu
Shizuoka
Hamamatsu
Toyohashi
Kanazawa
Toyama
Nagano
Fukui
Niigata
Chiba
Utsunomiya
Mito
Takamatsu
Tokushima
Kochi
Matsuyama
Oita
Beppu
Kii-Suidō
Bungo-Suidō
Tosa-Wan
Ise-Wan
Suruga-Wan
Toyama-wan
Wakasa-Wan
Izu-Shotō
Oki-Shotō
HOKKAIDŌ
SAPPORO
Hakodate
Asahikawa
Kushiro
Obihiro
Otaru
Muroran
Nemuro
Sea of Okhotsk
Habomai, Shikotan, Kunashiri and Etorofu, occupied by Russia since 1945, are claimed by Japan pending a

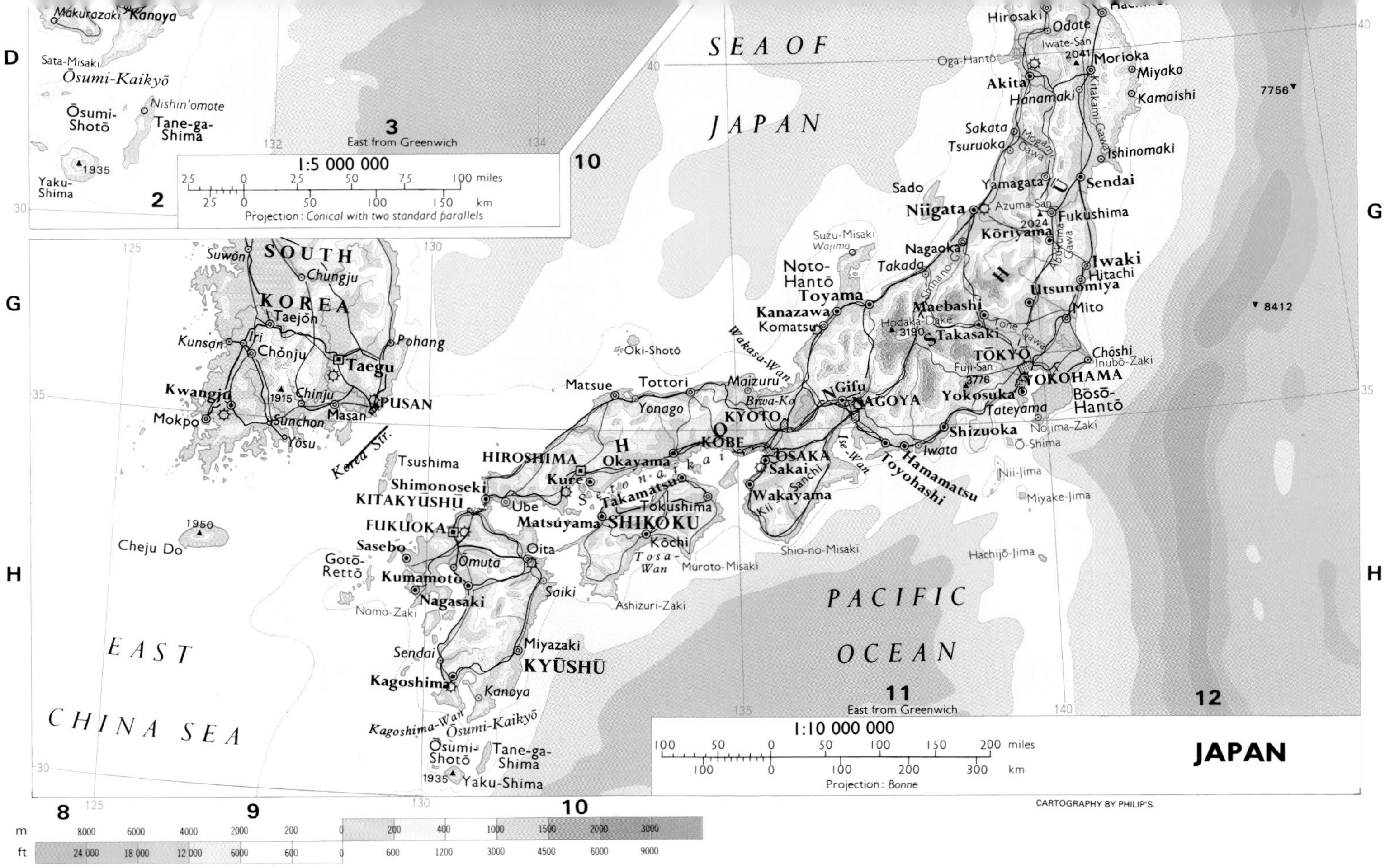
JAPAN
SEA OF JAPAN
PACIFIC OCEAN
EAST CHINA SEA
SOUTH KOREA
HONSHU
SHIKOKU
KYŪSHŪ
Tōkyō
Yokohama
Nagoya
Ōsaka
Kyoto
Kobe
Hiroshima
Fukuoka
Kitakyūshū
Sendai
Niigata
Pusan
Taegu
Kwangju
Cheju Do
Tsushima
Korea Str.
Seto naikai
1:10 000 000
East from Greenwich
Projection: Bonne
1:5 000 000
Projection: Conical with two standard parallels
CARTOGRAPHY BY PHILIP'S.

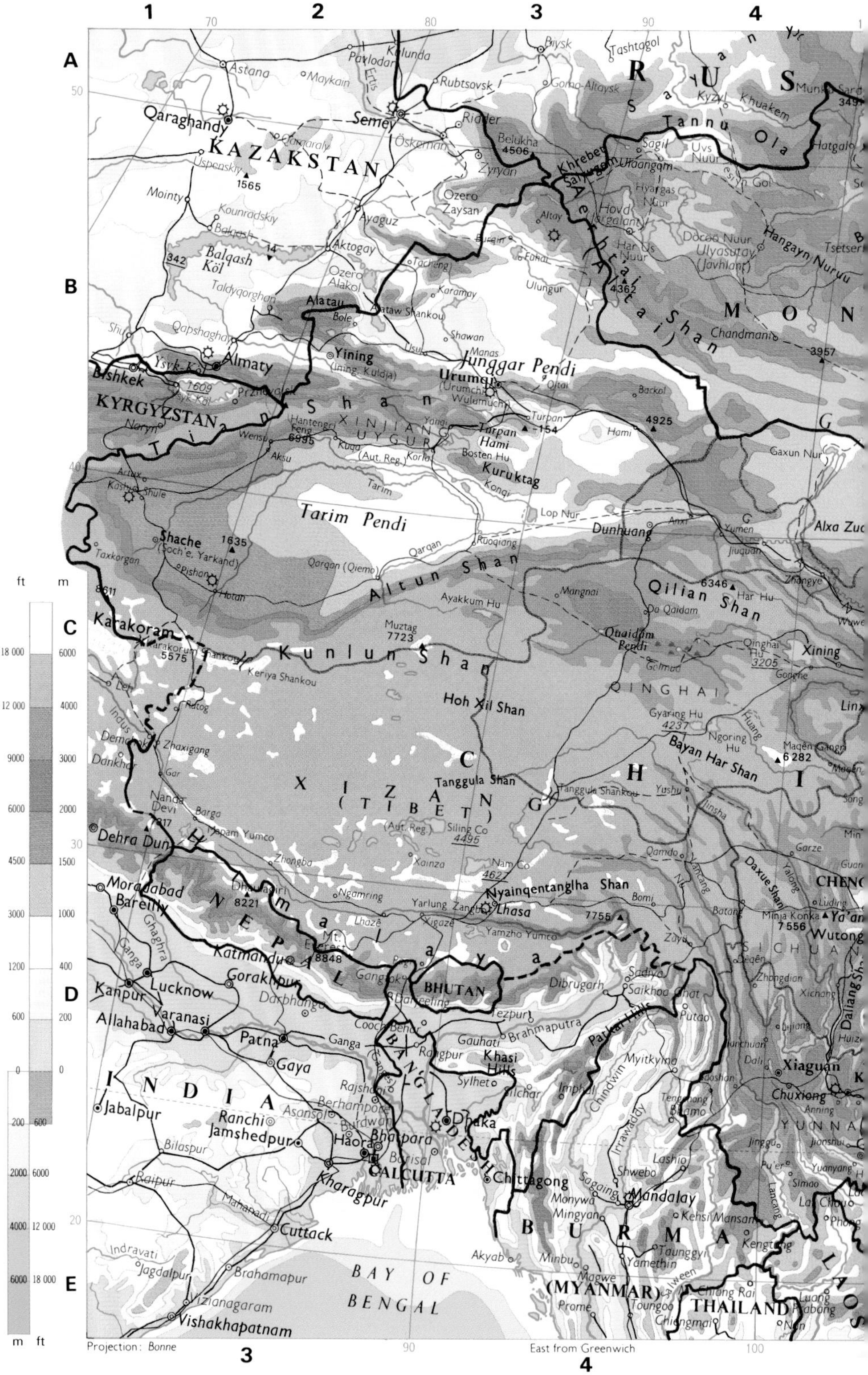

1
2
3
4
A
B
C
D
E
70
80
90
50
40
30
20
100
RUSSIA
Biysk
Tashtagol
Astana
Pavlodar
Kulunda
Maykain
Rubtsovsk
Gorno-Altaysk
Qaraghandy
Semey
Ridder
Kyzyl
Khuakem
Munku Sardyk
3491
Tannu Ola
Hatgal
KAZAKSTAN
Qarqaraly
Öskemen
Belukha
4506
Khrebet Saylyugem
Sagil
Uvs Nuur
Ulaangom
Uspenskiy
1565
Zyryan
Moiynty
Ozero Zaysan
Hyargas Nuur
Hovd
Kounradskiy
Ayaguz
Altay
Balqash
14
Aktogay
Burqin
Dorgon Nuur
Uliastay
(Javhlant)
Hangayn Nuruu
Tsetserleg
342
Balqash Köl
Fuhai
Har Us Nuur
Ozero Alakol
Tacheng
Ulungur
4362
Taldyqorghan
Karamay
Altai Shan
Alatau
Bole
Alataw Shankou
MONGOLIA
Shu
Qapshaghay
Shawan
Chandmani
Almaty
Usu
Manas
3957
Yining
(Ining, Kuldja)
Junggar Pendi
Bishkek
Ysyk-Köl
1609
Przhevalsk
Urumqi
(Urumchi, Wulumuchi)
Qitai
Barkol
KYRGYZSTAN
Tian Shan
Hantengri Feng
6995
XINJIANG UYGUR
(Aut. Reg.)
Yanqi
Turpan
Turpan Hami
-154
Hami
4925
Naryn
Wensu
Kuqa
Korla
Bosten Hu
Aksu
Kuruktag
Gaxun Nur
Artux
Kashi
Shule
Tarim
Konqi
Tarim Pendi
Lop Nur
Anxi
Yumen
Alxa Zuoqi
Shache
(Soch'e, Yarkand)
1635
Dunhuang
Ruoqiang
Jiuquan
Taxkorgan
Qarqan
Pishan
Qarqan (Qiemo)
Altun Shan
6346
Har Hu
Zhangye
Hotan
Mangnai
Qilian Shan
8611
Ayakkum Hu
Da Qaidam
Karakoram
Muztag
7723
Quaidam Pendi
Wuwei
Karakorum Shankou
5575
Kunlun Shan
Qinghai Hu
3205
Xining
Golmud
Gonghe
Keriya Shankou
Leh
Hoh Xil Shan
QINGHAI
Rutog
Linxia
Indus
Gyaring Hu
4237
Huang
Demchok
Zhaxigang
Ngoring Hu
Maqên Gangri
6 282
Bayan Har Shan
Dankhar
Gar
Tanggula Shan
XIZANG
(TIBET)
(Aut. Reg.)
CHINA
Nanda Devi
7817
Barga
Tanggula Shankou
Yushu
Siling Co
4495
Jinsha
Dehra Dun
Mapam Yumco
Qamdo
Garze
Zhongba
Xainza
Nam Co
4627
Yalong
Daxue Shan
Moradabad
Bareilly
Dhaulagiri
8221
Ngamring
Nyainqentanglha Shan
Bomi
CHENGDU
Yarlung Zangbo
Lhasa
Ludin
7755
Minya Konka
7 556
Ya'an
NEPAL
Lhazê
Xigazê
Yamzho Yumco
Batang
Wutongqiao
Ghaghra
Himalaya
Mt. Everest
8848
Zayü
SICHUAN
Ganga
Katmandu
Gangtok
BHUTAN
Sadiya
Dêqên
Kanpur
Lucknow
Gorakhpur
Darbhanga
Darjeeling
Dibrugarh
Saikhoa Ghat
Zhongdian
Xichang
Allahabad
Varanasi
Cooch Behar
Tezpur
Putao
Daliang Shan
Patna
Ganga
Gauhati
Brahmaputra
Patkai Hills
Lijiang
Gaya
Rangpur
Khasi Hills
Myitkyina
Dali
Xiaguan
INDIA
Rajshahi
Sylhet
Imphal
Chindwin
Tengchong
Baoshan
Chuxiong
Jabalpur
Berhampore
Silchar
Bhamo
Anning
Ranchi
Asansol
Burdwan
BANGLADESH
Dhaka
Irrawaddy
YUNNAN
Jamshedpur
Bhatpara
Haora
Barisal
Lashio
Jinggu
Jianshui
Bilaspur
CALCUTTA
Shwebo
Pu'er
Yuanyang
Raipur
Kharagpur
Chittagong
Sagaing
Mandalay
Simao
Mahanadi
Monywa
Kehsi Mansam
Lancang
Lai Chau
Mingyan
Phong Saly
Cuttack
BURMA
Kengtung
LAOS
Indravati
Akyab
Minbu
Taunggyi
Yamethin
Jagdalpur
Brahamapur
BAY OF BENGAL
Magwe
Salween
(MYANMAR)
Chiang Rai
Luang Prabang
Vizianagaram
Prome
Toungoo
THAILAND
Vishakhapatnam
Chiengmai
Nan
ft
m
18 000
12 000
9000
6000
4500
3000
1200
600
0
200
2000
4000
6000
4000
3000
2000
1500
1000
400
200
0
600
6000
12 000
18 000
Projection: Bonne
East from Greenwich

1: 20 000 000

100 0 100 200 300 400 500 miles

100 0 200 400 600 800 km

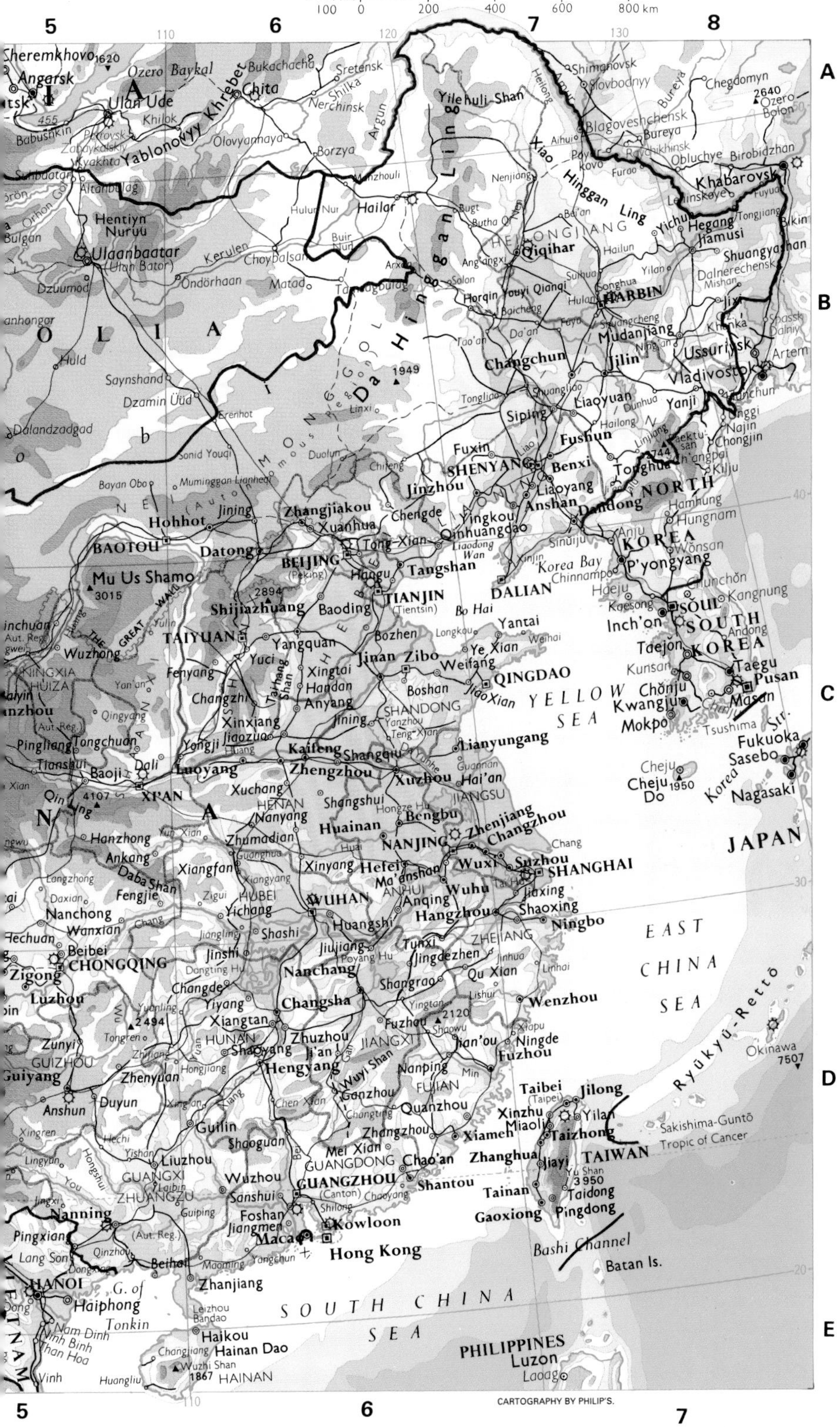

CARTOGRAPHY BY PHILIP'S.

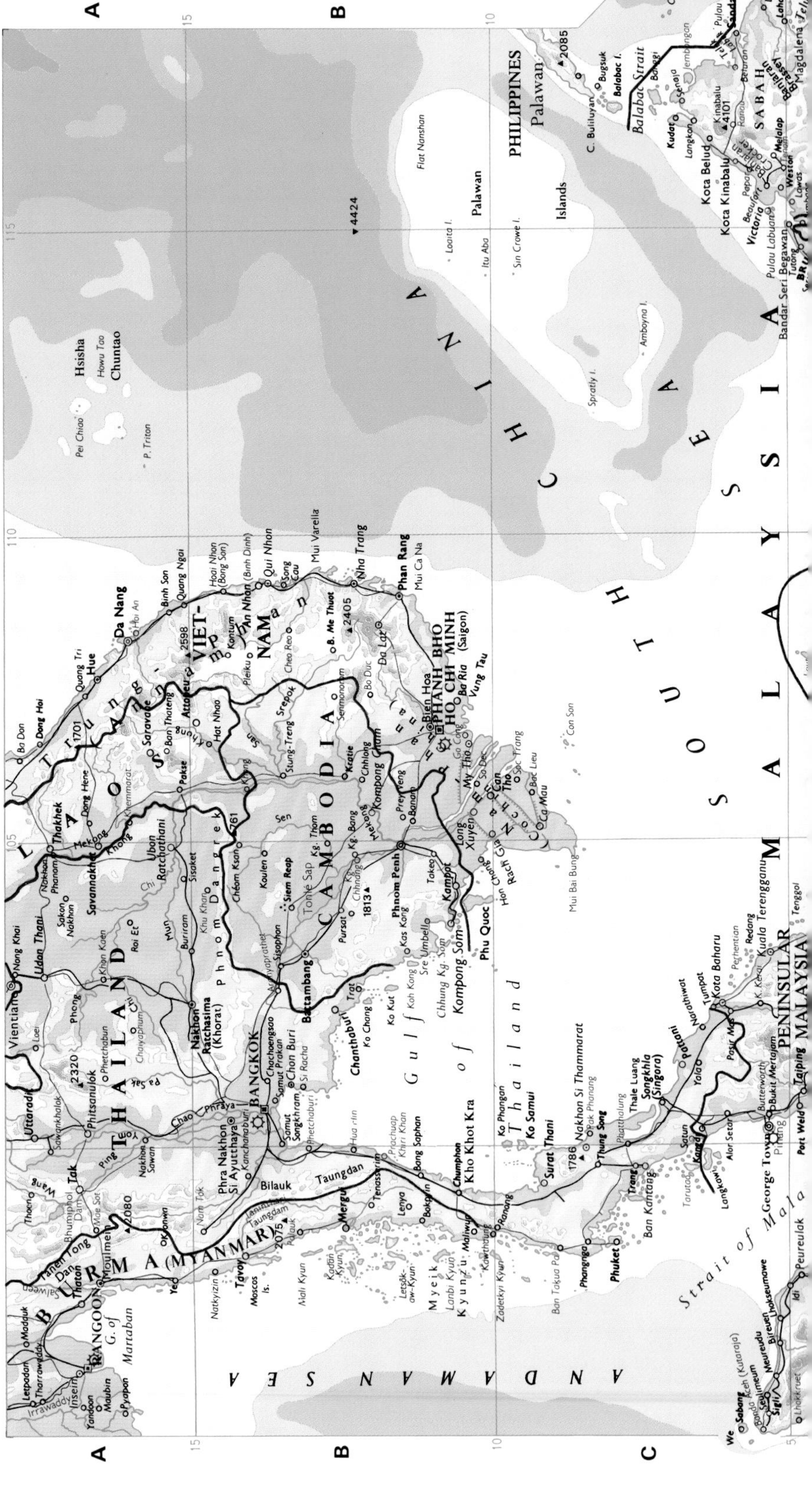
A
B
C
1
2
3
4
5
BURMA (MYANMAR)
RANGOON
G. of Martaban
Moulmein
Thaton
Pyapon
Maubin
Yandoon
Insein
Letpadan
Tharrawaddy
Irrawaddy
Salween
Ye
Tavoy
Moscos Is.
Natkyizin
Mergui
Myeik Kyunzu
Lenya
Bokpyin
Kawthaung
Zadetkyi Kyun
Mali Kyun
Tenasserim
Taungdan
Bilauk
ANDAMAN SEA
THAILAND
BANGKOK
Phra Nakhon Si Ayutthaya
Nakhon Ratchasima (Khorat)
Nakhon Sawan
Phitsanulok
Uttaradit
Tak
Chao Phraya
Udon Thani
Nong Khai
Khon Kaen
Ubon Ratchathani
Chanthaburi
Chumphon
Kho Khot Kra
Surat Thani
Ko Samui
Nakhon Si Thammarat
Phuket
Phangnga
Ranong
Trang
Songkhla (Singora)
Pattani
Hua Hin
Chon Buri
Samut Prakan
Chachoengsao
Gulf of Thailand
Strait of Malacca
LAOS
Vientiane
Thakhek
Savannakhet
Pakse
Saravane
Attopeu
Mekong
CAMBODIA
PHNOM PENH
Battambang
Siem Reap
Tonle Sap
Kompong Som
Kampot
Kratie
Stung Treng
Pursat
Phnom Dangrek
VIETNAM
Hue
Da Nang
Quang Ngai
Qui Nhon
Nha Trang
Phan Rang
Da Lat
HO CHI MINH (Saigon)
Vung Tau
My Tho
Can Tho
Ca Mau
Rach Gia
Phu Quoc
Long Xuyen
Kontum
Pleiku
B. Me Thuot
Dong Hoi
Con Son
Hsisha
Chuntao
SOUTH CHINA SEA
PHILIPPINES
Palawan
Spratly I.
Amboyna I.
Flat Nanshan
Balabac Strait
Kota Kinabalu
Kinabalu
SABAH
Sandakan
Labuan
Bandar Seri Begawan
MALAYSIA
PENINSULAR MALAYSIA
Kota Baharu
Kuala Terengganu
George Town
Butterworth
Taiping
Alor Setar
Langkawi
Peureulak
Banda Aceh (Kutaraja)
Sabang
Lhokseumawe

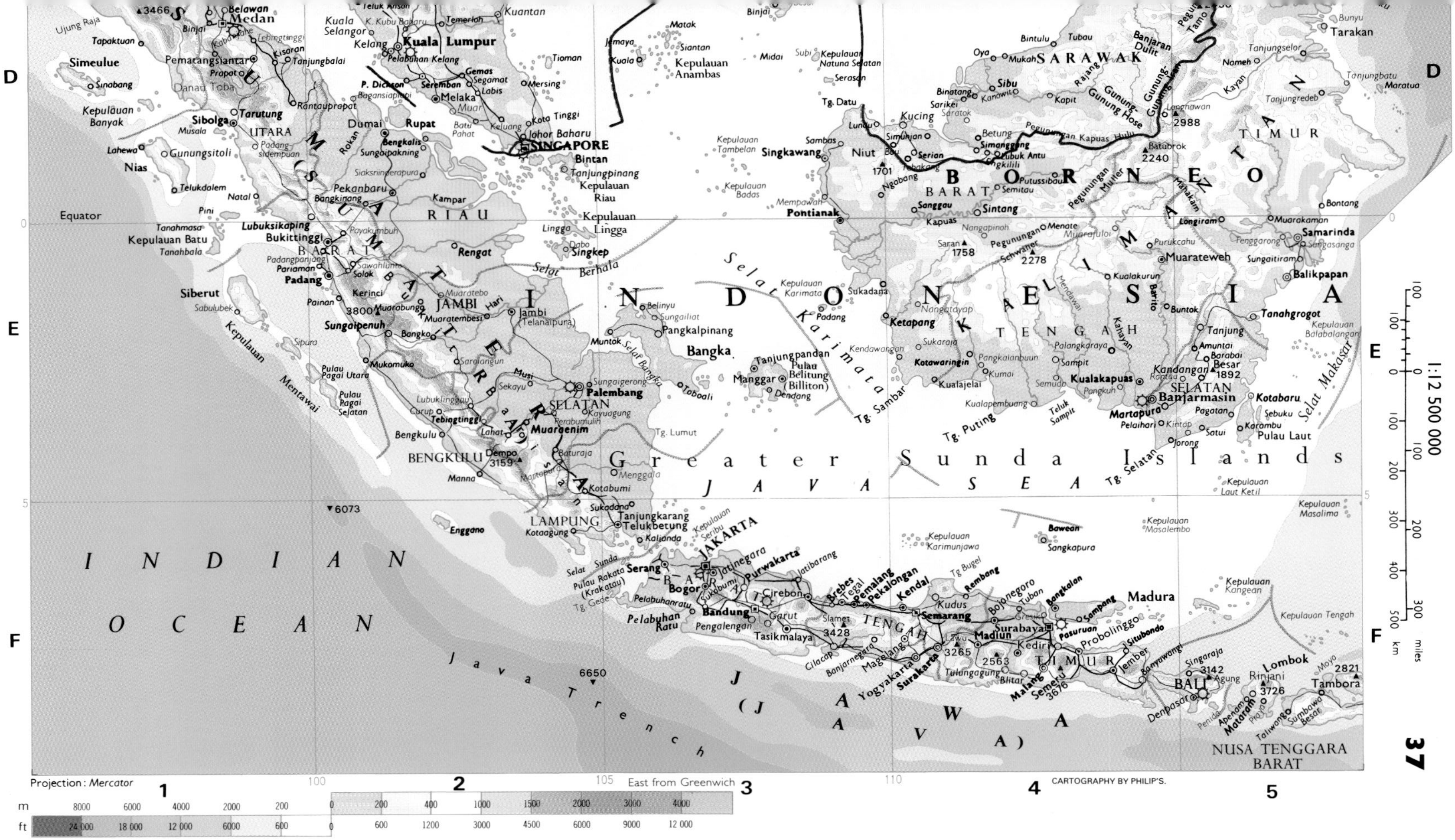
1:12 500 000
miles
km
INDIAN OCEAN
INDONESIA
Greater Sunda Islands
JAVA SEA
Java Trench
JAWA (JAVA)
Selat Karimata
Selat Makasar
Selat Sunda
SARAWAK
SUMATERA UTARA
SUMATERA BARAT
SUMATERA SELATAN
RIAU
JAMBI
BENGKULU
LAMPUNG
BORNEO
KALIMANTAN BARAT
KALIMANTAN TENGAH
KALIMANTAN SELATAN
KALIMANTAN TIMUR
JAWA BARAT
JAWA TENGAH
JAWA TIMUR
BALI
NUSA TENGGARA BARAT
JAKARTA
SINGAPORE
Kuala Lumpur
Medan
Padang
Palembang
Pontianak
Banjarmasin
Balikpapan
Samarinda
Surabaya
Semarang
Bandung
Yogyakarta
Surakarta
Malang
Denpasar
Mataram
Bangka
Belitung (Billiton)
Madura
Lombok
Nias
Siberut
Enggano
Kepulauan Mentawai
Kepulauan Riau
Kepulauan Lingga
Kepulauan Anambas
Kepulauan Natuna Selatan
Equator
East from Greenwich
Projection: Mercator
CARTOGRAPHY BY PHILIP'S

38 PHILIPPINES AND EASTERN INDONESIA

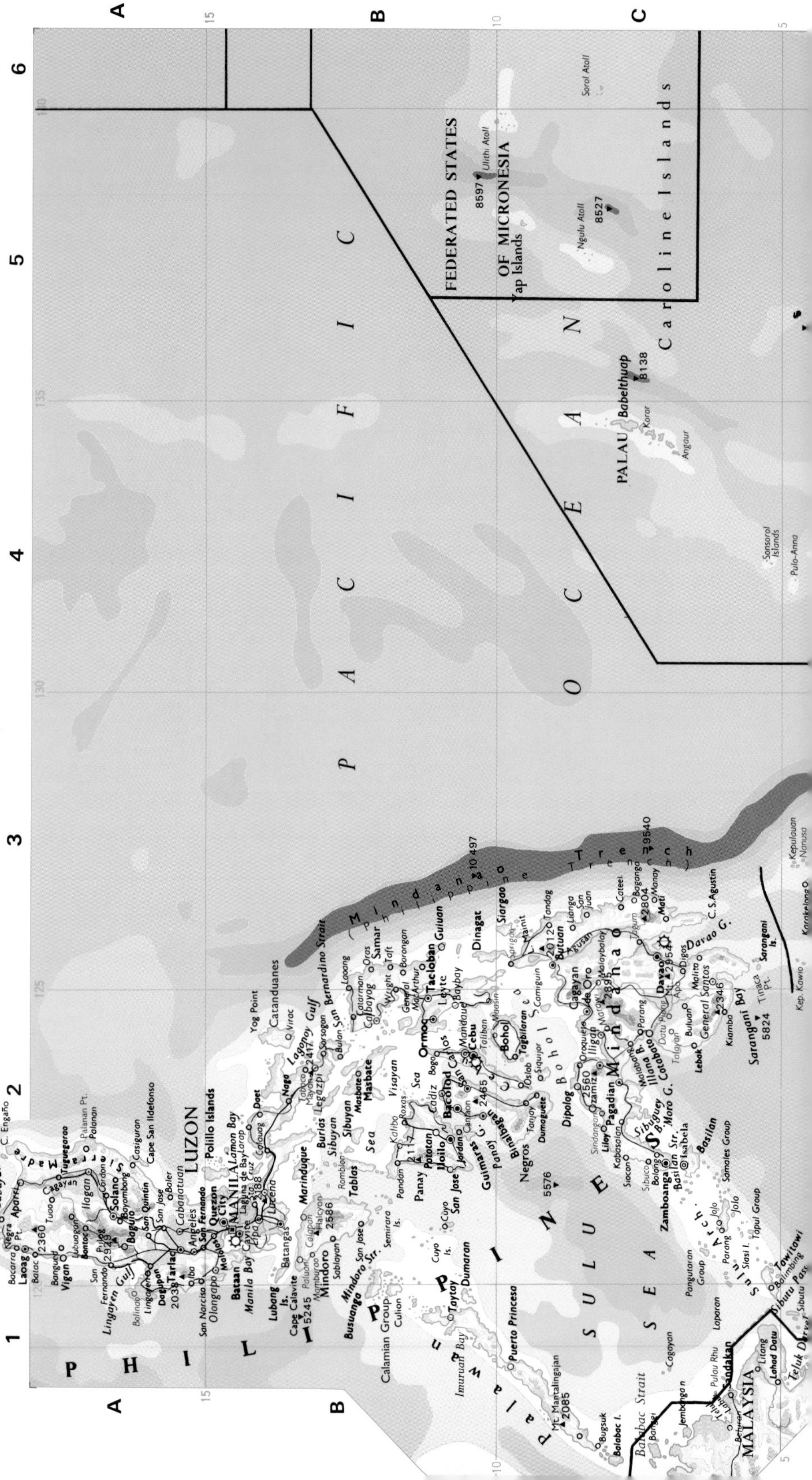

P A C I F I C
O C E A N
FEDERATED STATES
OF MICRONESIA
Yap Islands
Ulithi Atoll
Ngulu Atoll
Sorol Atoll
Caroline Islands
PALAU
Babelthuap
Koror
Angaur
Sonsorol Islands
Pulo-Anna
LUZON
MANILA
Quezon City
Polillo Islands
Lamon Bay
Manila Bay
Lingayen Gulf
Babuyan Chan.
C. Engaño
Sierra Madre
Catanduanes
San Bernardino Strait
Mindoro
Marinduque
Sibuyan Sea
Visayan Sea
Panay
Negros
Cebu
Bohol
Bohol Sea
Leyte
Samar
Masbate
Dinagat
Siargao
Mindanao
Davao
Davao G.
Zamboanga
Basilan
Sarangani Bay
Moro G.
Philippine Trench
Mindanao Trench
10 497
9540
SULU SEA
Sulu Arch.
Palawan
Puerto Princesa
Calamian Group
Balabac Strait
MALAYSIA
Sandakan

1:12 500 000

100 0 100 200 300 miles
100 0 100 200 300 400 500 km

PAPUA NEW GUINEA
IRIAN JAYA
INDONESIA
CELEBES SEA
MOLUCCA SEA
SERAM SEA
BANDA SEA
FLORES SEA
ARAFURA SEA
Sawu Sea
Equator
Halmahera
Morotai
Ternate
Tidore
Kep. Bacan
Obi
Kepulauan Sula
Buru
Seram (Ceram)
Ambon
Misool
Salawati
Waigeo
Jazirah Doberai
Teluk Cenderawasih
Biak
Yapen
Supiori
Pegunungan Sudirman
Pegunungan Jayawijaya
Puncak Jaya
Merauke
Kepulauan Aru
Kepulauan Kai
Kepulauan Tanimbar
Yamdena
MALUKU
Wetar
TIMUR
TIMOR
Dili
Kupang
Roti
Sumba
Flores
Sumbawa
Alor
Lesser Sunda Islands
NUSA TENGGARA TIMUR
SULAWESI (CELEBES)
UTARA
TENGAH
SELATAN
TENGGARA
Manado
Gorontalo
Palu
Poso
Ujung Pandang
Kendari
Buton
Muna
Kabaena
Teluk Tomini
Teluk Bone
Teluk Tolo
Selat Makasar
Kepulauan Banggai
Peleng
Salayar
Jayapura
Sorong
Manokwari
Fakfak
Kepulauan Sangihe
Helen Atoll
Tobi
East from Greenwich
Projection: Mercator
CARTOGRAPHY BY PHILIP'S
m 8000 6000 4000 2000 200 0 200 400 1000 1500 2000 3000 4000
ft 24 000 18 000 12 000 6000 600 0 600 1200 3000 4500 6000 9000 12 000

EASTERN INDIA, BANGLADESH AND BURMA

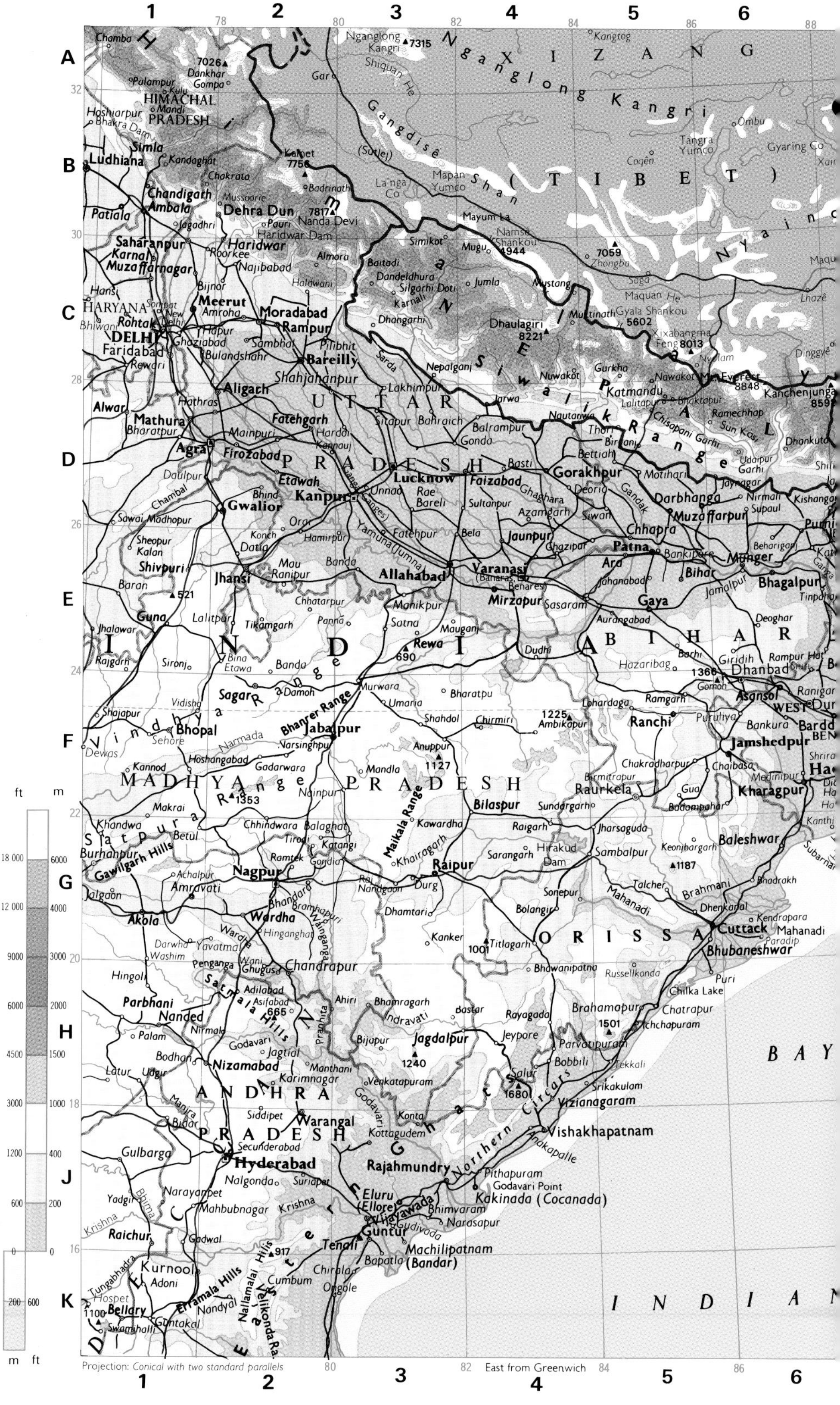

X I Z A N G (TIBET)
Nganglong Kangri
Gangdisê Shan
HIMACHAL PRADESH
HARYANA
UTTAR PRADESH
NEPAL
Siwalik Range
BIHAR
MADHYA PRADESH
ORISSA
ANDHRA PRADESH
Vindhya Range
Satpura Range
Eastern Ghats
INDIA
BAY
INDIAN
Delhi
Lucknow
Kanpur
Allahabad
Varanasi
Patna
Agra
Gwalior
Jhansi
Bhopal
Jabalpur
Nagpur
Raipur
Ranchi
Jamshedpur
Cuttack
Bhubaneshwar
Hyderabad
Secunderabad
Warangal
Vishakhapatnam
Rajahmundry
Vijayawada
Guntur
Kakinada (Cocanada)
Machilipatnam (Bandar)
Kurnool
Bellary
Katmandu
Everest 8848
Kanchenjunga
Dhaulagiri 8221
Nanda Devi 7817
Kamet 7756
Ludhiana
Chandigarh
Ambala
Dehra Dun
Haridwar
Meerut
Moradabad
Bareilly
Aligarh
Mathura
Gorakhpur
Darbhanga
Muzaffarpur
Gaya
Dhanbad
Asansol
Bhagalpur
Munger
Kharagpur
Baleshwar
Sambalpur
Bilaspur
Amravati
Akola
Wardha
Chandrapur
Nizamabad
Nanded
Parbhani
Jagdalpur
Brahmapur
Chilka Lake
Godavari
Krishna
Narmada
Mahanadi
Yamuna (Jumna)
Ganga (Ganges)
Projection: Conical with two standard parallels
East from Greenwich
ft m
18 000 6000
12 000 4000
9000 3000
6000 2000
4500 1500
3000 1000
1200 400
600 200
0 0
200 600
m ft

1: 10 000 000

50 0 50 100 150 200 250 miles

50 0 50 100 150 200 250 300 350 400 km

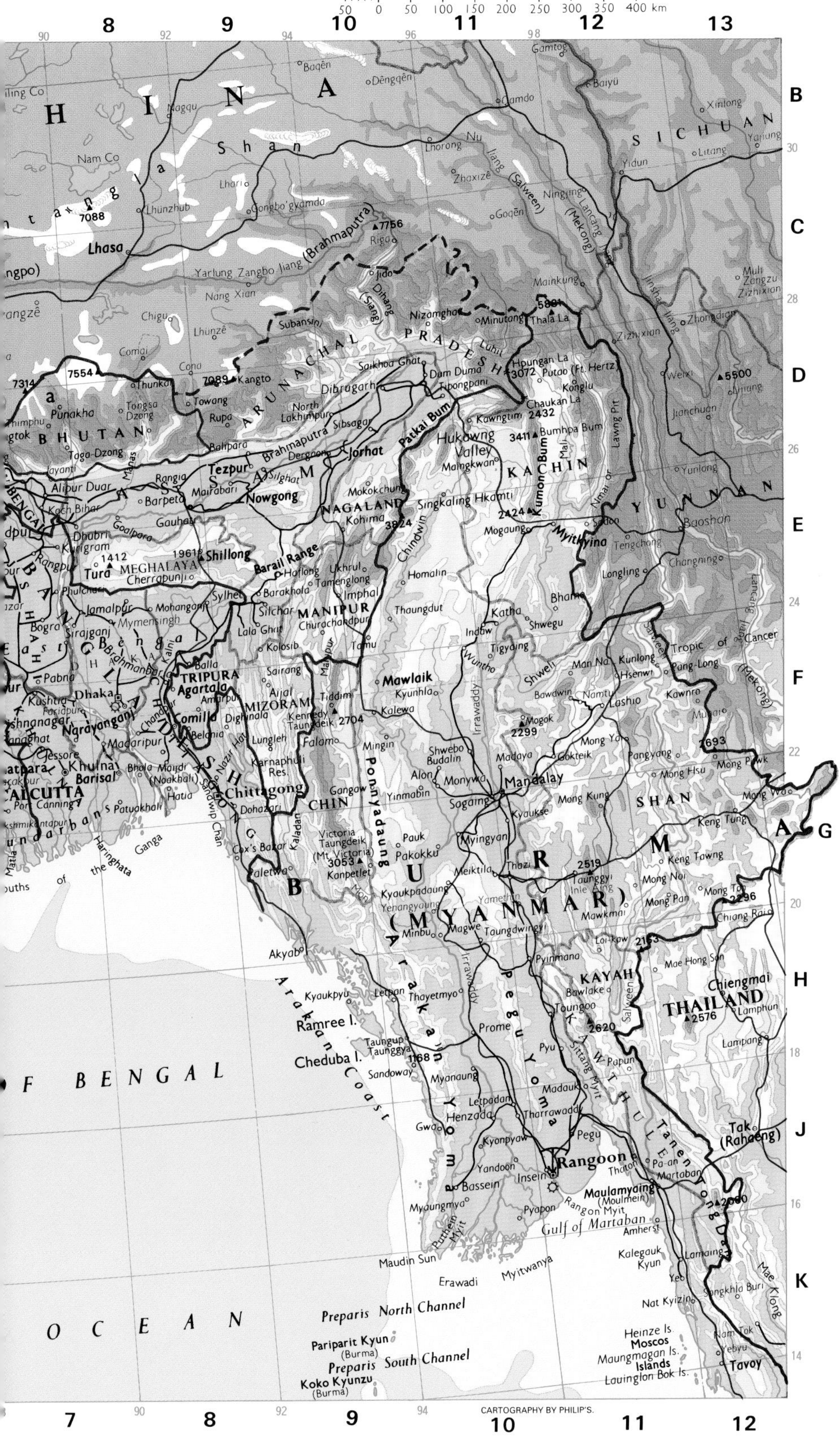

CARTOGRAPHY BY PHILIP'S.

42 WESTERN INDIA AND PAKISTAN

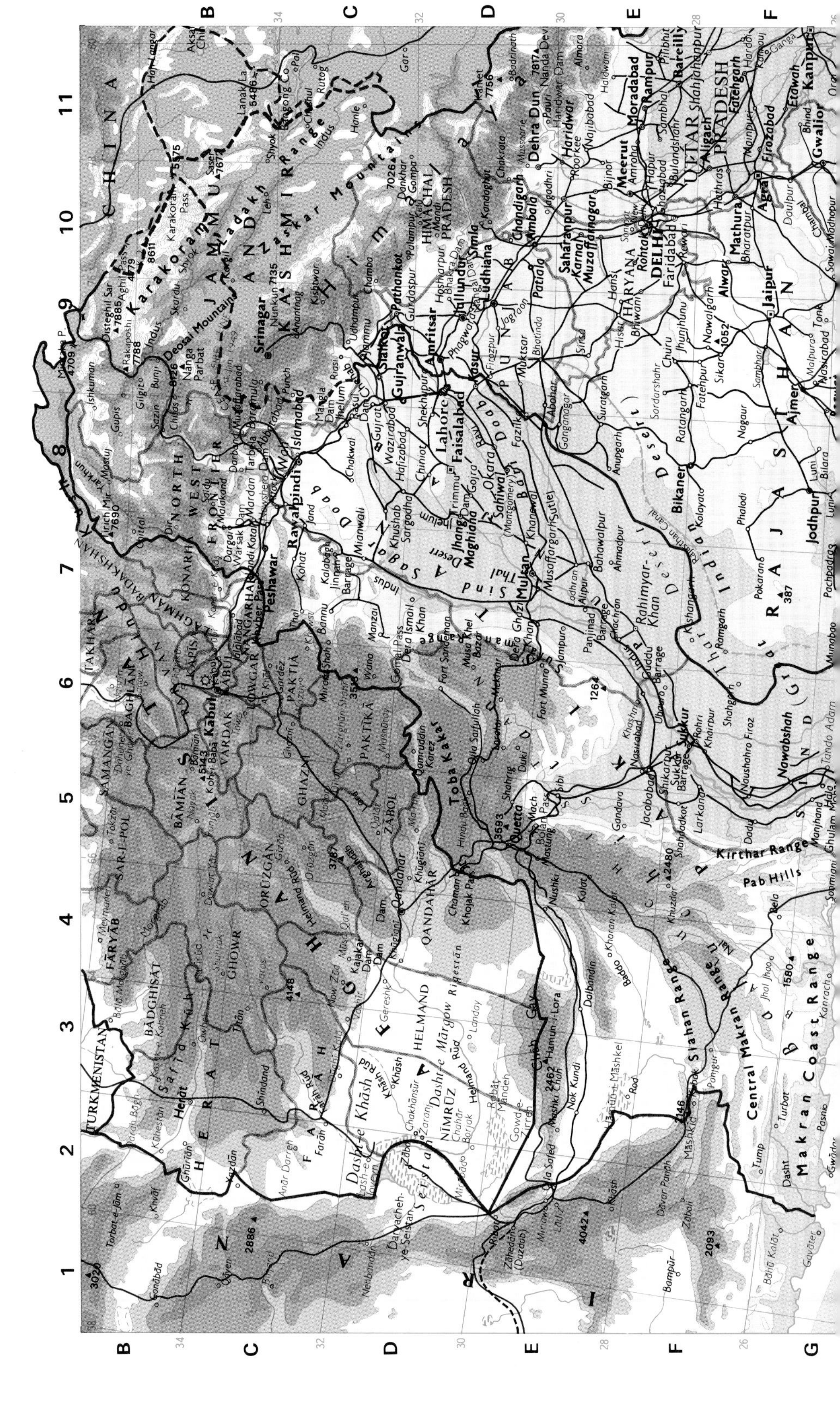

CHINA
Aksai Chin
Karakoram Pass
Karakoram
JAMMU AND KASHMIR
Ladakh Range
Zaskar Mountains
HIMACHAL PRADESH
Srinagar
Leh
Nanga Parbat
Deosai Mountains
Gilgit
NORTH WEST FRONTIER
Peshawar
Rawalpindi
Islamabad
Kabul
Lahore
Amritsar
Faisalabad
Multan
Jullundur
Ludhiana
Chandigarh
Simla
Dehra Dun
Saharanpur
Meerut
Moradabad
Bareilly
Rampur
DELHI
Faridabad
Rohtak
HARYANA
UTTAR PRADESH
Aligarh
Agra
Mathura
Firozabad
Gwalior
Kanpur
Etawah
Jaipur
Ajmer
Jodhpur
Bikaner
Alwar
PUNJAB
RAJASTHAN
Thar Desert
Indian Desert
Sind Sagar Doab
Thal Desert
Bahawalpur
Rahimyar-Khan
Sukkur
Jacobabad
Larkana
Nawabshah
Dera Ghazi Khan
Dera Ismail Khan
Quetta
Toba Kakar
Kirthar Range
Pab Hills
Central Makran Range
Makran Coast Range
Siahan Range
Qandahar
QANDAHAR
HELMAND
ZABOL
GHAZNI
PAKTIA
PAKTIKA
ORUZGAN
GHOWR
BAMIAN
SAMANGAN
BAGHLAN
FARYAB
BADGHISAT
SAR-E-POL
HERAT
NIMRUZ
FARAH
VARDAK
LOWGAR
KONARHA
NANGARHAR
LAGHMAN
KAPISA
TAKHAR
BADAKHSHAN
TURKMENISTAN
Herat
Farah
Shindand
Safid Kuh
Dasht-e Margow
Dasht-e Khash
Registan
Zahedan (Duzdab)
Chah Gay
Hamun-i-Lora
Nushki
Kalat
Khuzdar
Dalbandin
Kharan Kalat
Panjgur
Turbat
Seistan
Mashkid

1:10 000 000

50 0 50 100 150 200 250 miles

50 0 50 100 150 200 250 300 350 400 km

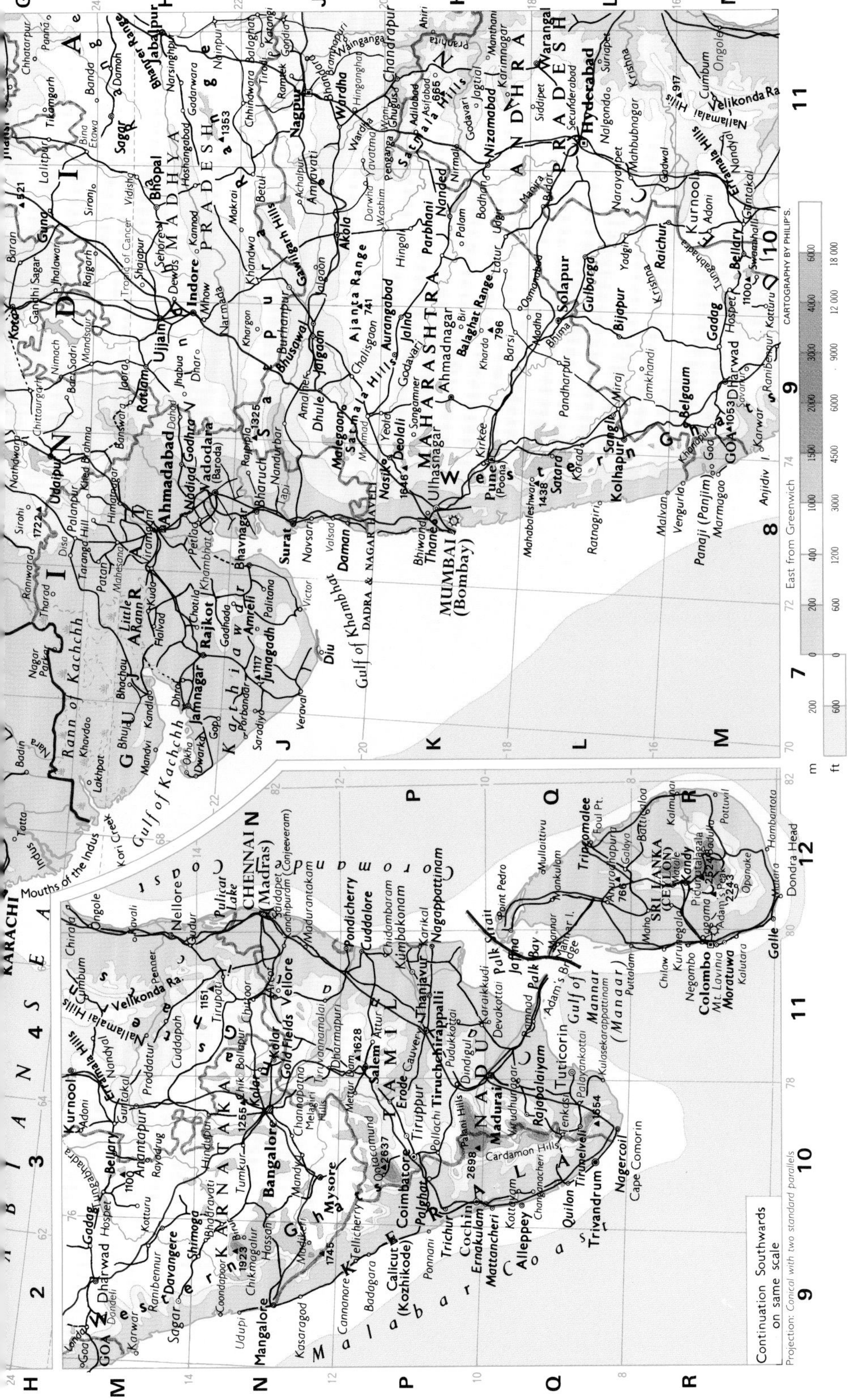

44 IRAN, THE GULF AND AFGHANISTAN

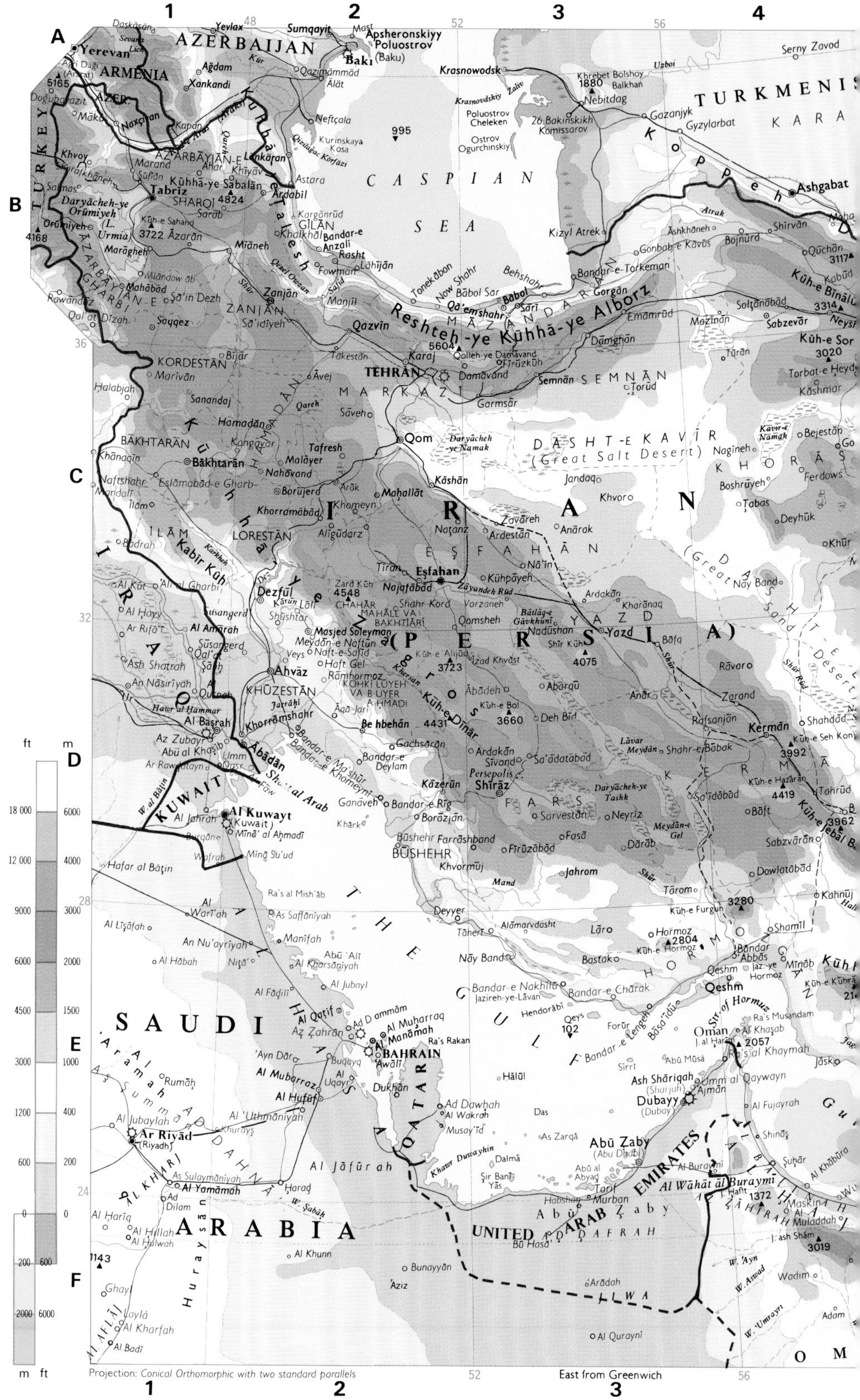
1
2
3
4
A
B
C
D
E
F
48
52
56
36
32
28
24
AZERBAIJAN
ARMENIA
Yerevan
Baki (Baku)
Sumqayit
Yevlax
Apsheronskiyy Poluostrov
Krasnowodsk
TURKMENISTAN
Ashgabat
CASPIAN SEA
995
TURKEY
Tabriz
Urmia
Daryacheh-ye Orumiyeh (L. Urmia)
Kuhha-ye Sabalan
4824
3722
4168
5165
Ardabil
Astara
Lankaran
Rasht
Bandar-e Anzali
Zanjan
Qazvin
Reshteh-ye Kuhha-ye Alborz
TEHRAN
Damavand
5604
Qolleh-ye Damavand
Semnan
Qom
Kashan
Hamadan
Bakhtaran
KORDESTAN
Sanandaj
Arak
Borujerd
Khorramabad
LORESTAN
Dezful
Ahvaz
KHUZESTAN
Abadan
Khorramshahr
Esfahan
Najafabad
Zard Kuh
4548
Yazd
4075
DASHT-E KAVIR (Great Salt Desert)
DASHT-E LUT (Great Sand Desert)
IRAN (PERSIA)
Zagros
Kuh-e Dinar
4431
3723
3660
Shiraz
Persepolis
FARS
Kerman
3992
4419
3962
Bandar-e Bushehr
Kazerun
Jahrom
Lar
Bandar Abbas
Qeshm
Str. of Hormuz
Ras Musandam
2057
2804
3280
Kopet Dag
KHORASAN
Mashhad
Sabzevar
Neyshabur
Torbat-e Heydariyeh
Tabas
IRAQ
Al Basrah
Al Amarah
Al Kut
An Nasiriyah
Hawr al Hammar
Shatt al Arab
KUWAIT
Al Kuwayt (Kuwait)
Mina' al Ahmadi
Hafar al Batin
THE GULF
SAUDI ARABIA
Ad Dammam
Al Qatif
Az Zahran
Al Mubarraz
Al Hufuf
Ar Riyad (Riyadh)
Al Kharj
BAHRAIN
Al Manamah
QATAR
Ad Dawhah
UNITED ARAB EMIRATES
Abu Zaby (Abu Dhabi)
Dubayy (Dubai)
Ash Shariqah (Sharjah)
Ras al Khaymah
Al Fujayrah
Al Jafurah
Ad Dahna'
Al Khunn
Liwa
Oman
OMAN
3019
1372
1143
Projection: Conical Orthomorphic with two standard parallels
East from Greenwich
ft
m
18 000
6000
12 000
4000
9000
3000
6000
2000
4500
1500
3000
1000
1200
400
600
200
0
0
200
600
2000
6000

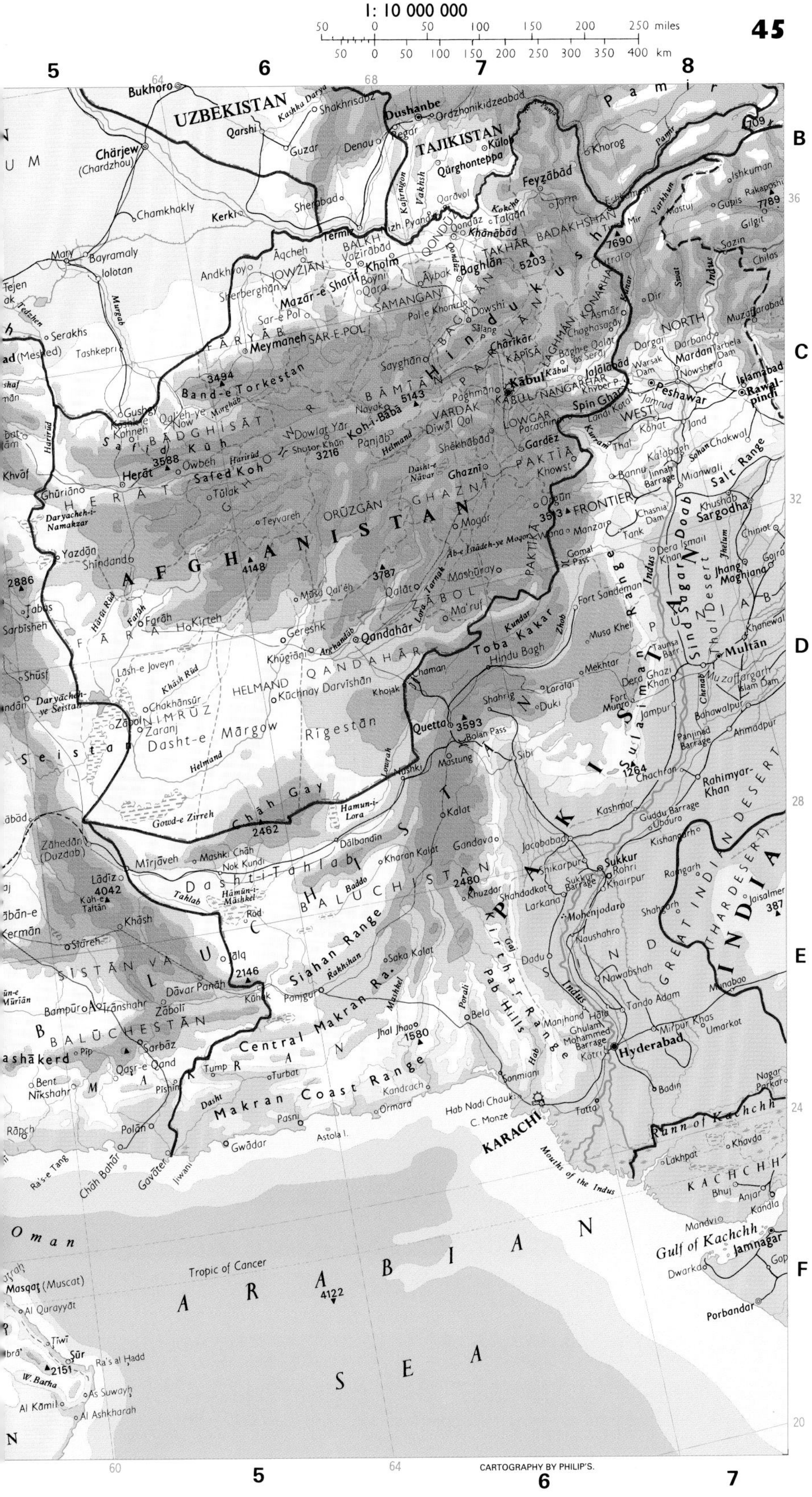

CARTOGRAPHY BY PHILIP'S.

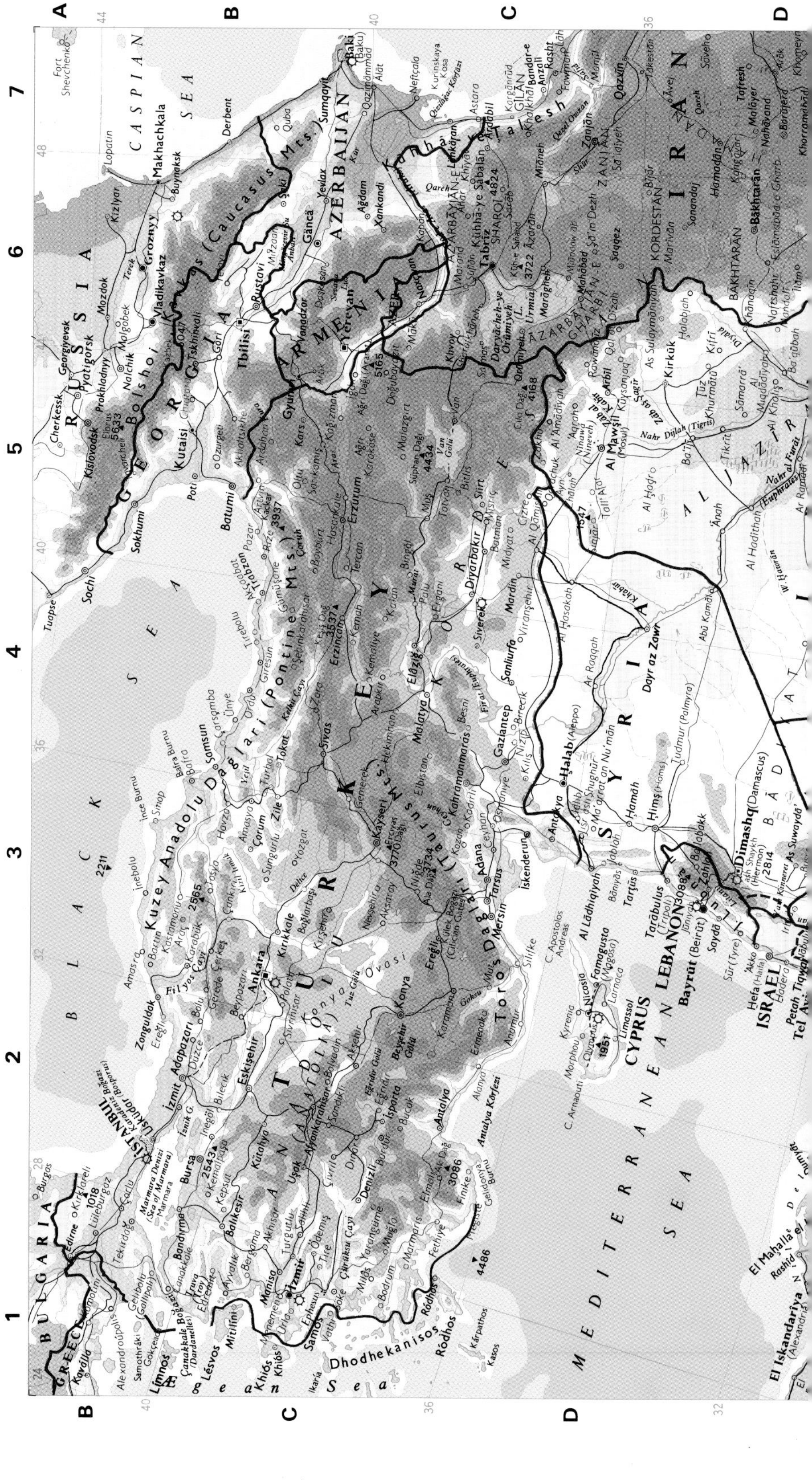
BLACK SEA
CASPIAN SEA
MEDITERRANEAN SEA
RUSSIA
GEORGIA
ARMENIA
AZERBAIJAN
TURKEY
SYRIA
IRAN
CYPRUS
LEBANON
ISRAEL
BULGARIA
GREECE
ANATOLIA
Bolshoi Kavkas (Caucasus Mts.)
Kuzey Anadolu Dağlari (Pontine Mts.)
Toros Dağlari (Taurus Mts.)
İSTANBUL
Ankara
Tbilisi
Yerevan
Baki (Baku)
Tabriz
Halab (Aleppo)
Dimashq (Damascus)
Bayrūt (Beirūt)
Nicosia
Dhodhekanisos
Rodhos
Lésvos
Limnos
Samos
Kriti
Batumi
Sochi
Trabzon
Erzurum
Samsun
Sivas
Kayseri
Konya
Adana
Mersin
Antalya
İzmir
Bursa
Eskişehir
Diyarbakir
Malatya
Elâzığ
Van Gölü
Tuz Gölü
Ağri Daği 5165
Al Mawşil (Mosul)
Kirkūk
Dayr az Zawr
Ḥimş (Homs)
Ḥamāh
Grozny
Makhachkala
Vladikavkaz

1:10 000 000

50 0 50 100 150 200 250 miles

50 0 50 100 150 200 250 300 350 400 km

--- Division between Greeks and Turks in Cyprus; Turks to the North.

CARTOGRAPHY BY PHILIP'S.

Projection: Conical Orthomorphic with two standard parallels

m	200	0	200	400	1000	1500	2000	3000	4000
ft	600	0	600	1200	3000	4500	6000	9000	12 000

m 2000, ft 6000

48 ARABIA AND THE HORN OF AFRICA

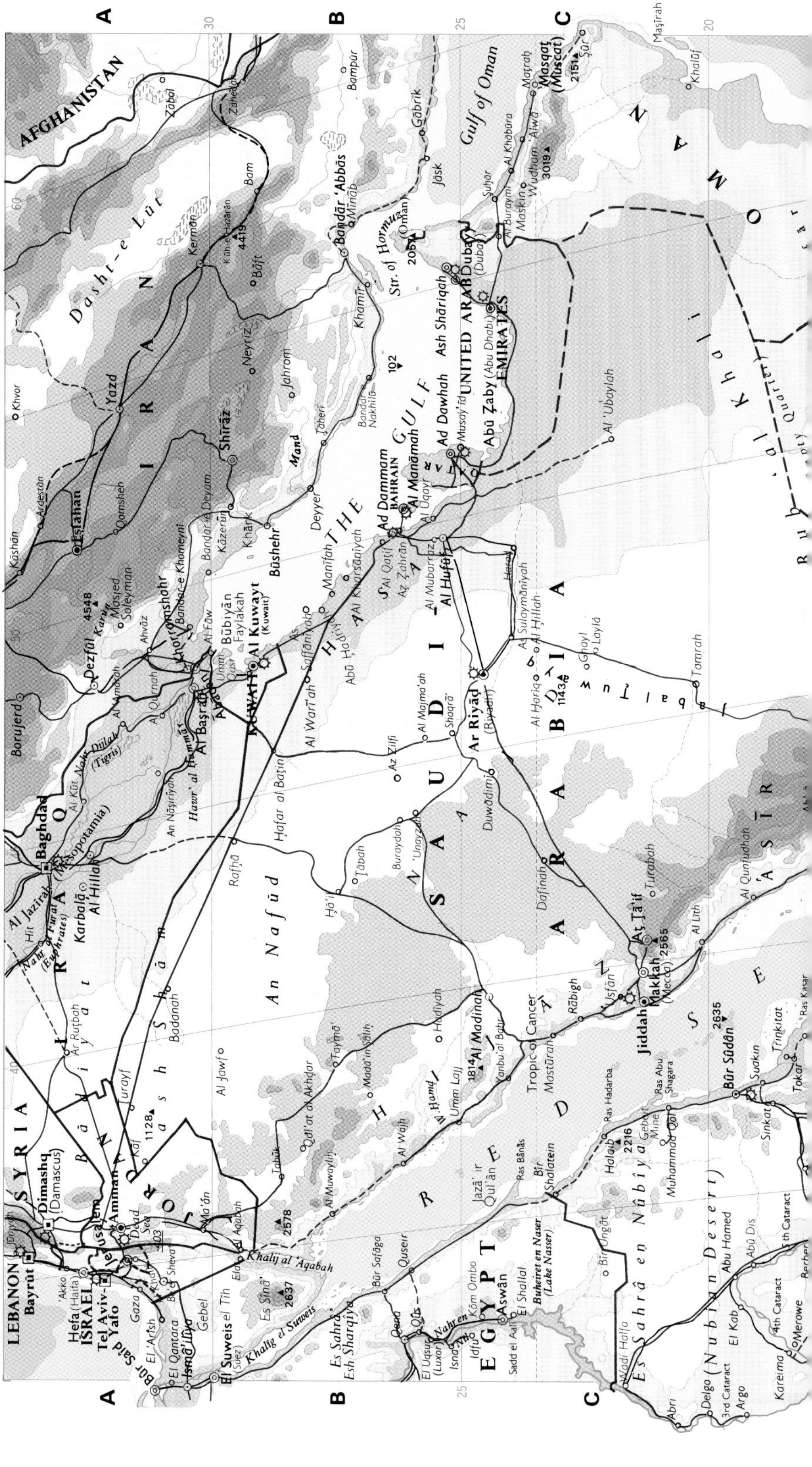

AFGHANISTAN
IRAN
IRAQ
SYRIA
LEBANON
ISRAEL
JORDAN
KUWAIT
BAHRAIN
SAUDI ARABIA
UNITED ARAB EMIRATES
OMAN
EGYPT
THE GULF
Gulf of Oman
Str. of Hormuz
Dasht-e Lūt
An Nafūd
Rub' al Khali
Tropic of Cancer
Baghdād
Al Başrah
Al Kuwayt (Kuwait)
Ar Riyāḍ (Riyadh)
Ad Dammām
Al Manāmah
Ad Dawḥah
Abū Ẓaby (Abu Dhabi)
Dubayy (Dubai)
Ash Shāriqah
Masqaṭ (Muscat)
Bandar 'Abbās
Shīrāz
Eşfahān
Yazd
Kermān
Būshehr
Dimashq (Damascus)
'Ammān
Jerusalem
Tel Aviv-Yafo
Bayrūt
Jiddah
Makkah (Mecca)
Al Madīnah
Aţ Ţā'if
Bûr Sûdân
El Suweis (Suez)
Aswân
Khalīj al 'Aqabah
Khalîg el Suweis
Nahr al Furāt (Euphrates)
Nahr Dijlah (Tigris)
Es Sahrâ en Nûbîya (Nubian Desert)
Buheiret en Naser (Lake Nasser)

1: 15 000 000

100 0 100 200 300 400 miles

100 0 100 200 300 400 500 600 km

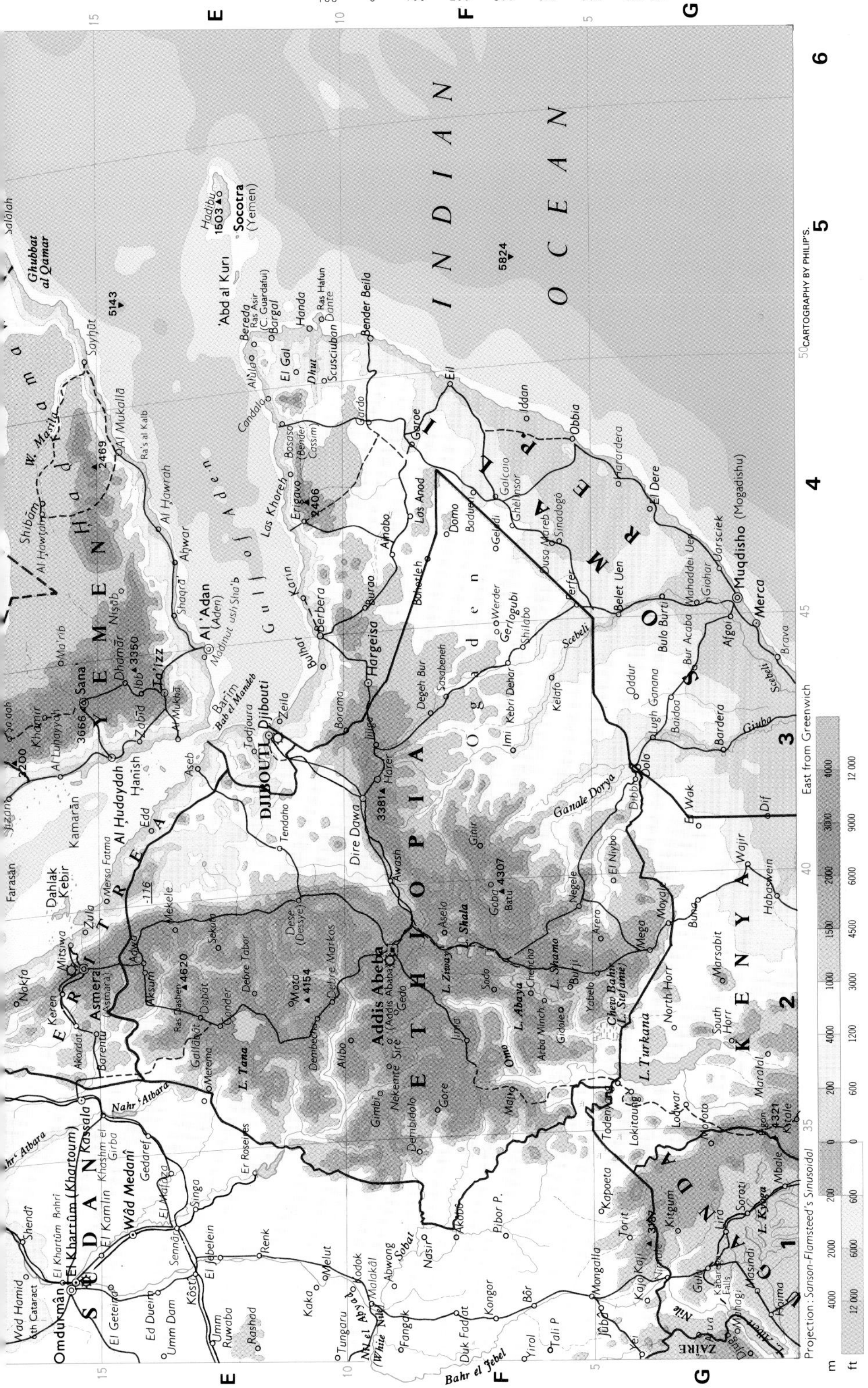

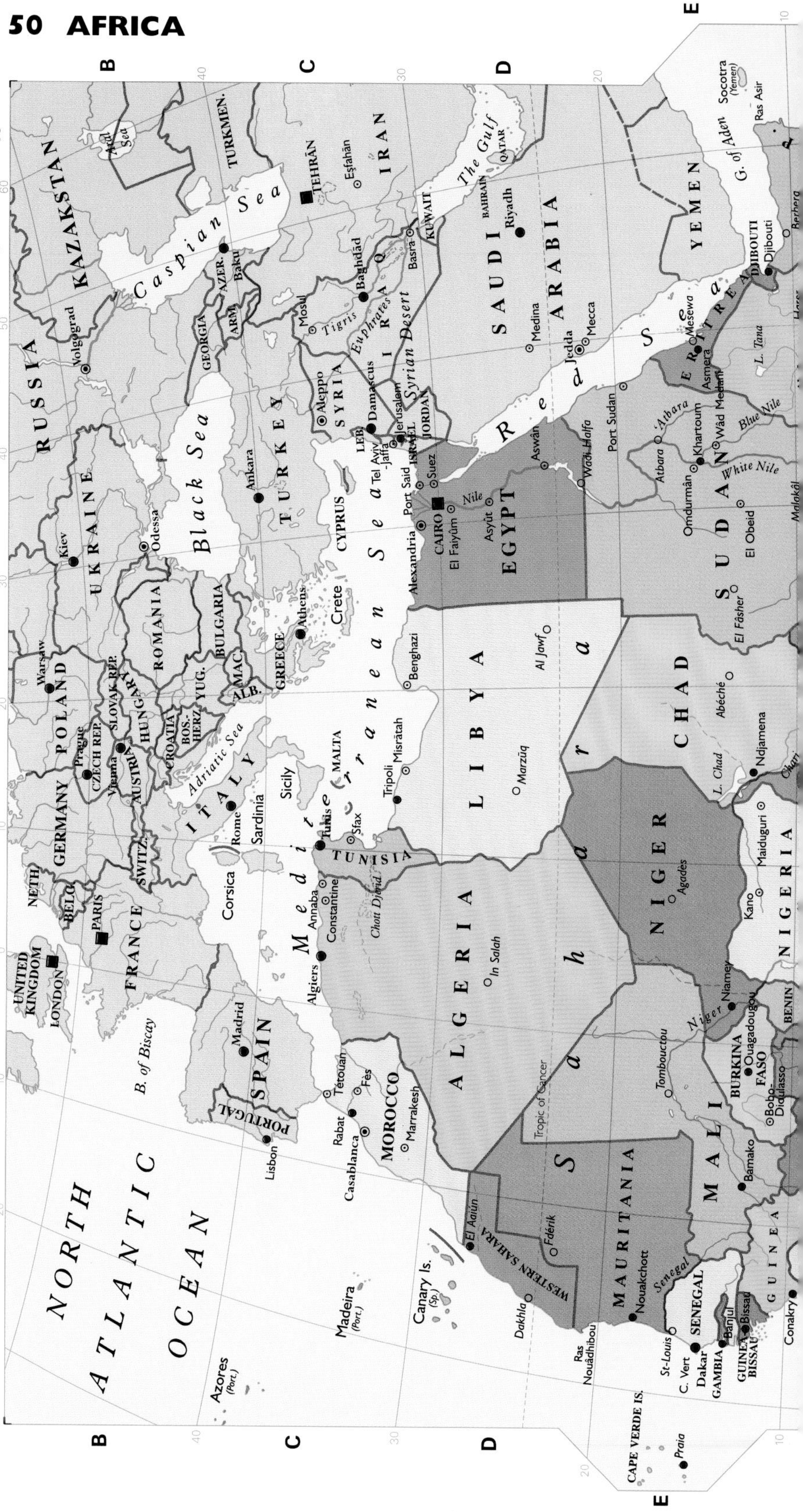
NORTH ATLANTIC OCEAN
Azores (Port.)
Madeira (Port.)
Canary Is. (Sp.)
CAPE VERDE IS.
Praia
B. of Biscay
UNITED KINGDOM
LONDON
NETH.
BELG.
PARIS
FRANCE
GERMANY
POLAND
Warsaw
CZECH REP.
Prague
SLOVAK REP.
Vienna
AUSTRIA
HUNGARY
SWITZ.
ITALY
Rome
Corsica
Sardinia
Sicily
MALTA
Adriatic Sea
CROATIA
BOS.-HERZ.
YUG.
ROMANIA
BULGARIA
MAC.
ALB.
GREECE
Athens
Crete
SPAIN
Madrid
PORTUGAL
Lisbon
RUSSIA
Volgograd
KAZAKSTAN
Aral Sea
UKRAINE
Kiev
Odessa
Black Sea
Caspian Sea
GEORGIA
ARM.
AZER.
Baku
TURKMEN.
TURKEY
Ankara
CYPRUS
SYRIA
Aleppo
Damascus
LEB.
ISRAEL
Tel Aviv-Jaffa
Jerusalem
JORDAN
Mosul
Tigris
Euphrates
Baghdad
IRAQ
Syrian Desert
Basra
KUWAIT
IRAN
TEHRĀN
Eşfahān
The Gulf
BAHRAIN
QATAR
SAUDI ARABIA
Riyadh
Medina
Mecca
Jedda
YEMEN
G. of Aden
Socotra (Yemen)
Ras Asir
DJIBOUTI
Djibouti
Berbera
ERITREA
Asmera
Mesewa
Red Sea
Mediterranean Sea
MOROCCO
Tétouan
Fès
Rabat
Casablanca
Marrakesh
ALGERIA
Algiers
Annaba
Constantine
Chott Djerid
In Salah
TUNISIA
Tunis
Sfax
LIBYA
Tripoli
Misrātah
Benghazi
Marzūq
Al Jawf
EGYPT
Alexandria
Port Said
Suez
CAIRO
El Faiyûm
Asyût
Nile
Aswân
Wadi Halfa
Sahara
Tropic of Cancer
WESTERN SAHARA
El Aaiún
Dakhla
Ras Nouâdhibou
MAURITANIA
Fdérik
Nouakchott
Senegal
SENEGAL
St-Louis
Dakar
C. Vert
GAMBIA
Banjul
GUINEA-BISSAU
Bissau
GUINEA
Conakry
MALI
Bamako
Tombouctou
BURKINA FASO
Ouagadougou
Bobo-Dioulasso
Niger
Niamey
BENIN
NIGER
Agadès
NIGERIA
Kano
Maiduguri
CHAD
Ndjamena
L. Chad
Chari
Abéché
SUDAN
El Fâsher
El Obeid
Omdurmân
Khartoum
Wad Medani
Atbara
White Nile
Blue Nile
Port Sudan
L. Tana
Malakâl

1:56 000 000
200 0 200 400 600 800 1000 1200 miles
200 0 200 400 600 800 1000 1200 1400 1600 1800 km
Projection: Azimuthal Equidistant
West from Greenwich
East from Greenwich
Dakar Capital Cities
CARTOGRAPHY BY PHILIP'S.
Equator
Tropic of Capricorn
SOUTH ATLANTIC OCEAN
INDIAN OCEAN
Gulf of Guinea
Bight of Benin
Mozambique Channel
Monrovia
Abidjan
Sekondi-Takoradi
Accra
Porto Novo
Lagos
Port Harcourt
CAMEROON
Douala
Malabo
Yaoundé
EQUATORIAL GUINEA
SÃO TOMÉ & PRINCIPE
Annobón
C. Lopez
Libreville
GABON
CONGO
Bangui
Oubangi
Congo
Mbandaka
CONGO (DEM. REP. OF THE)
Kisangani
Kasai
Lualaba
Brazzaville
Kinshasa
Pointe Noire
Matadi
CABINDA (Angola)
Kananga
Cuango
L. Albert
L. Edward
L. Kivu
RWANDA
Kigali
BURUNDI
Bujumbura
UGANDA
Kampala
L. Turkana
KENYA
Kisumu
L. Victoria
Nairobi
Tana
Juba
Mogadishu
Kismayu
Mombasa
TANZANIA
Dodoma
Zanzibar
Dar es Salaam
L. Tanganyika
SEYCHELLES
Aldabra Is.
C. Delgado
COMOROS
Mayotte (Fr.)
Antsiranana
Mahajanga
Toamasina
Antananarivo
MADAGASCAR
Fianarantsoa
MAURITIUS
Réunion (Fr.)
Ascension I. (U.K.)
St. Helena (U.K.)
Tristan da Cunha (U.K.)
Luanda
Lobito
Huambo
ANGOLA
Namibe
Cubango
Cunene
C. Fria
L. Mweru
Likasi
Lubumbashi
L. Malawi
Ndola
ZAMBIA
Lusaka
Lilongwe
MALAWI
Zambezi
Blantyre
MOZAMBIQUE
Moçambique
Livingstone
Harare
ZIMBABWE
Bulawayo
Beira
NAMIBIA
Windhoek
BOTSWANA
Limpopo
Gaborone
Pretoria
Johannesburg
Vaal
Mbabane
SWAZ.
Maputo
Orange
Kimberley
Maseru
LESOTHO
Durban
SOUTH AFRICA
East London
Port Elizabeth
Cape Town
C. of Good Hope
C. Agulhas

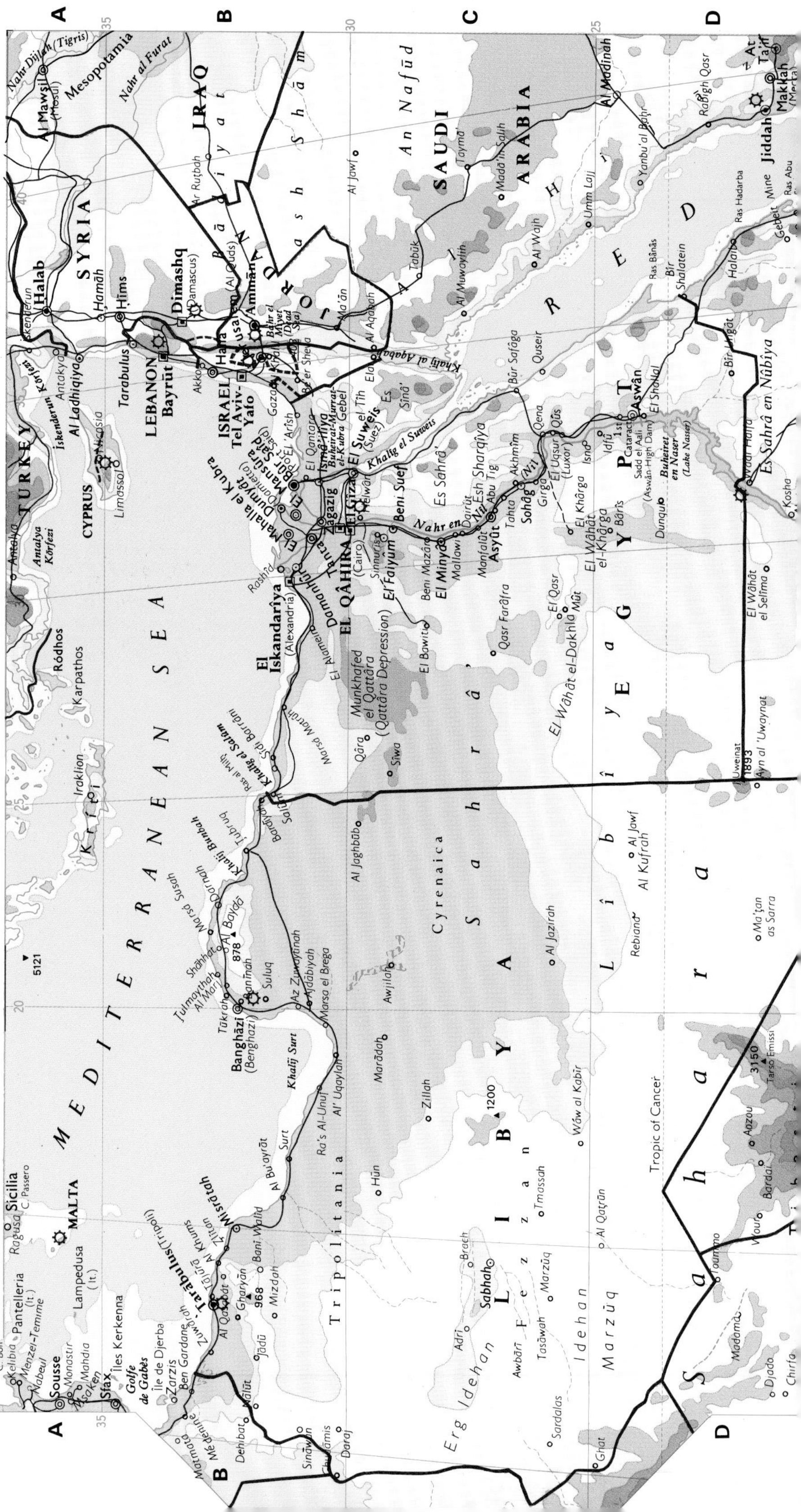

MEDITERRANEAN SEA
TURKEY
SYRIA
IRAQ
LEBANON
ISRAEL
JORDAN
CYPRUS
MALTA
SAUDI ARABIA
EGYPT
LIBYA
Mesopotamia
Nahr Dijlah (Tigris)
Nahr al Furat
Halab
Hamāh
Hims
Dimashq (Damascus)
Bayrūt
Tarabulus
Al Ladhiqiya
Antakya
Iskenderun
Tel Aviv-Yafo
Haifa
Jerusalem (Al Quds)
Ammān
Al Aqabah
Khalīj al Aqaba
Rodhos
Karpathos
Iraklion
Kríti
Sicilia
Lampedusa (It.)
Pantelleria (It.)
Sousse
Sfax
Golfe de Gabès
Île de Djerba
Tarābulus (Tripoli)
Misrātah
Khalīj Surt
Banghāzī (Benghazi)
Tobruq
Cyrenaica
Tripolitania
El Iskandarîya (Alexandria)
EL QÂHIRA (Cairo)
Bûr Sa'îd (Port Said)
El Suweis (Suez)
Khalîg el Suweis
El Faiyûm
Beni Suef
El Minya
Asyût
Sohâg
Qena
El Uqsur (Luxor)
Aswân
Sadd el Aali (Aswân High Dam)
Buheiret en Naser (Lake Nasser)
Wadi Halfa
Es Sahrâ en Nûbîya
Munkhafed el Qattâra (Qattâra Depression)
Sîwa
El Wâhât el-Khârga
El Wâhât el-Dakhla
Sahrâ Lîbîya
Al Kufrah
Sabhah
Marzūq
Tropic of Cancer
Tarso Emissi 3150
Jiddah
Makkah
Al Madīnah
An Nafūd
Sinai

1: 15 000 000

100 0 100 200 300 400 miles
100 0 100 200 300 400 500 600 km

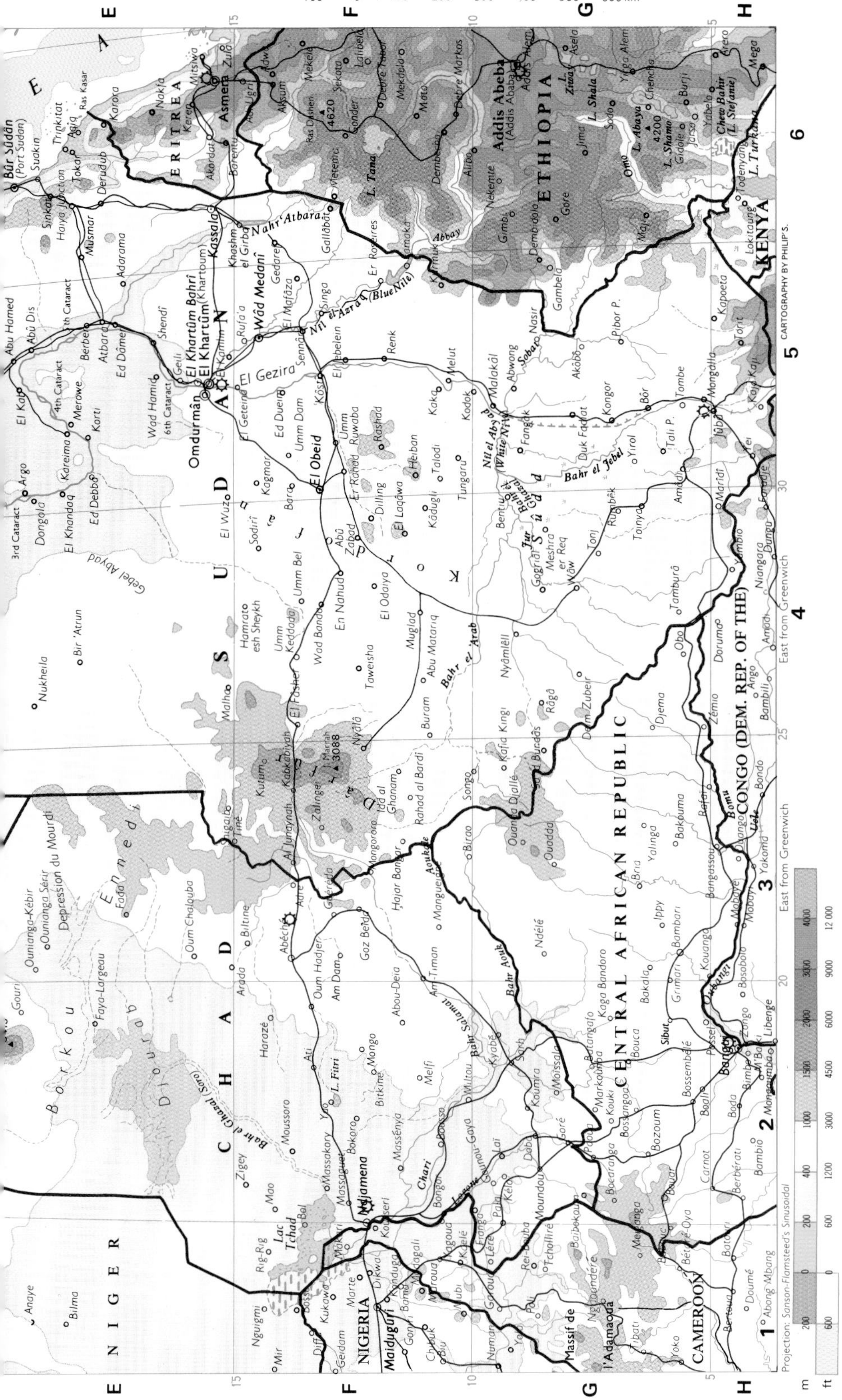

54 NORTH-WEST AFRICA

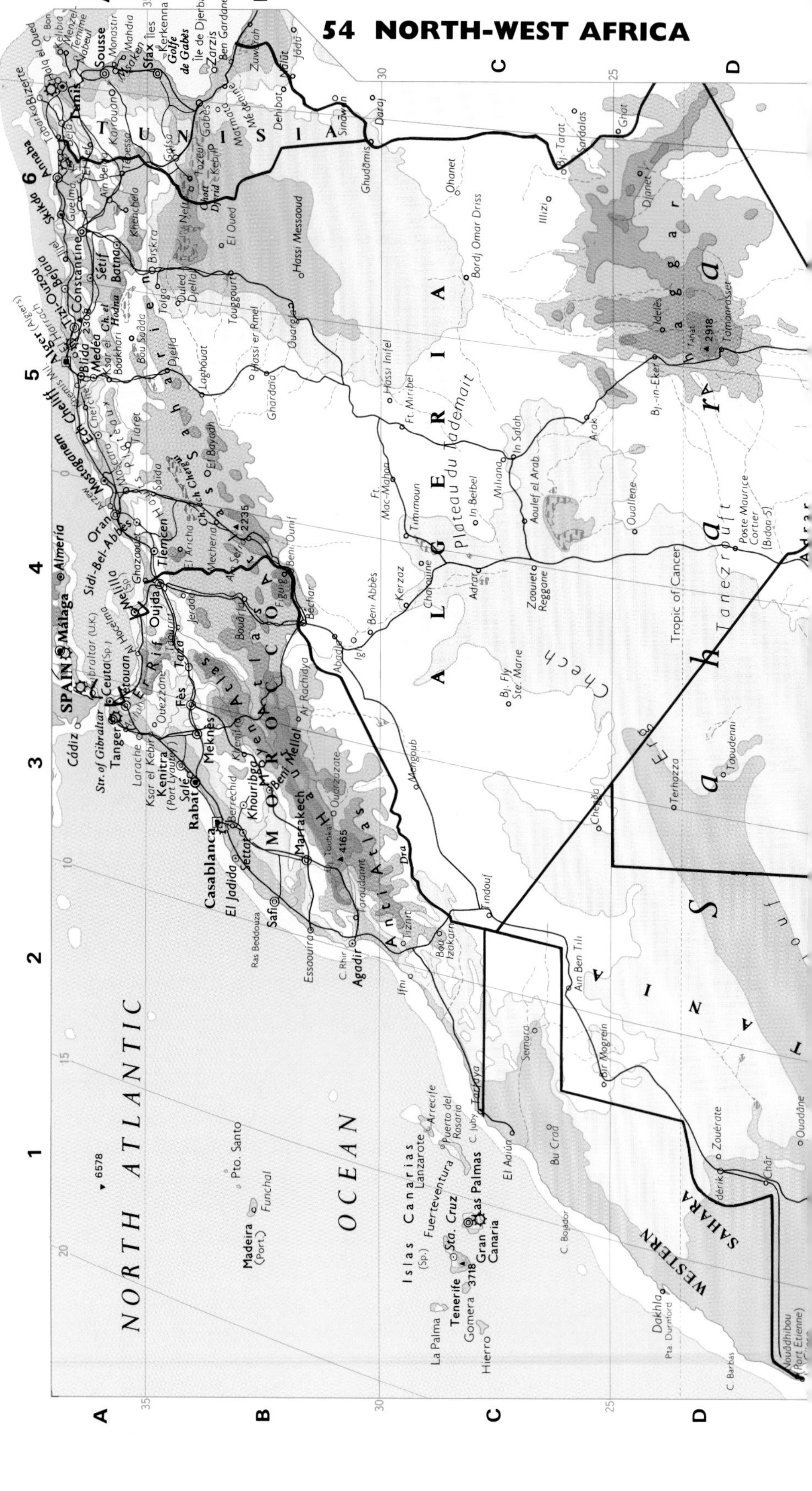

NORTH ATLANTIC
OCEAN
SPAIN
Cádiz
Málaga
Almería
Str. of Gibraltar
Gibraltar (U.K.)
Ceuta (Sp.)
Melilla (Sp.)
Tanger
Tetouan
Larache
Ksar el Kebir
Kenitra (Port Lyautey)
Salé
Rabat
Casablanca
El Jadida
Settat
Khouribga
Meknes
Fès
Taza
Oujda
Marrakech
Safi
Essaouira
Agadir
Ifni
Tiznit
Tarfaya
El Aaiún
Semara
Bir Mogrein
Tindouf
Ouarzazate
Beni Mellal
Ar Rachidiya
Figuig
Bechar
Beni Abbès
Adrar
In Salah
Timimoun
Tamanrasset
Ouargla
Ghardaia
Laghouat
Djelfa
Biskra
Touggourt
El Oued
Hassi Messaoud
Tlemcen
Sidi-Bel-Abbès
Oran
Mostaganem
Ech Chelif
Alger (Algiers)
Blida
Médéa
Sétif
Constantine
Batna
Skikda
Annaba
Bizerte
Tunis
Sousse
Sfax
Kairouan
Gafsa
Gabès
Zarzis
Ghudāmis
Ghat
Djanet
Illizi
Taoudenni
Zouérate
Nouâdhibou (Port Etienne)
Dakhla
C. Bojador
C. Juby
C. Barbas
Madeira (Port.)
Funchal
Pto. Santo
Islas Canarias (Sp.)
Lanzarote
Fuerteventura
Gran Canaria
Las Palmas
Tenerife
Sta. Cruz
La Palma
Gomera
Hierro
MOROCCO
ALGERIA
TUNISIA
WESTERN SAHARA
Tropic of Cancer

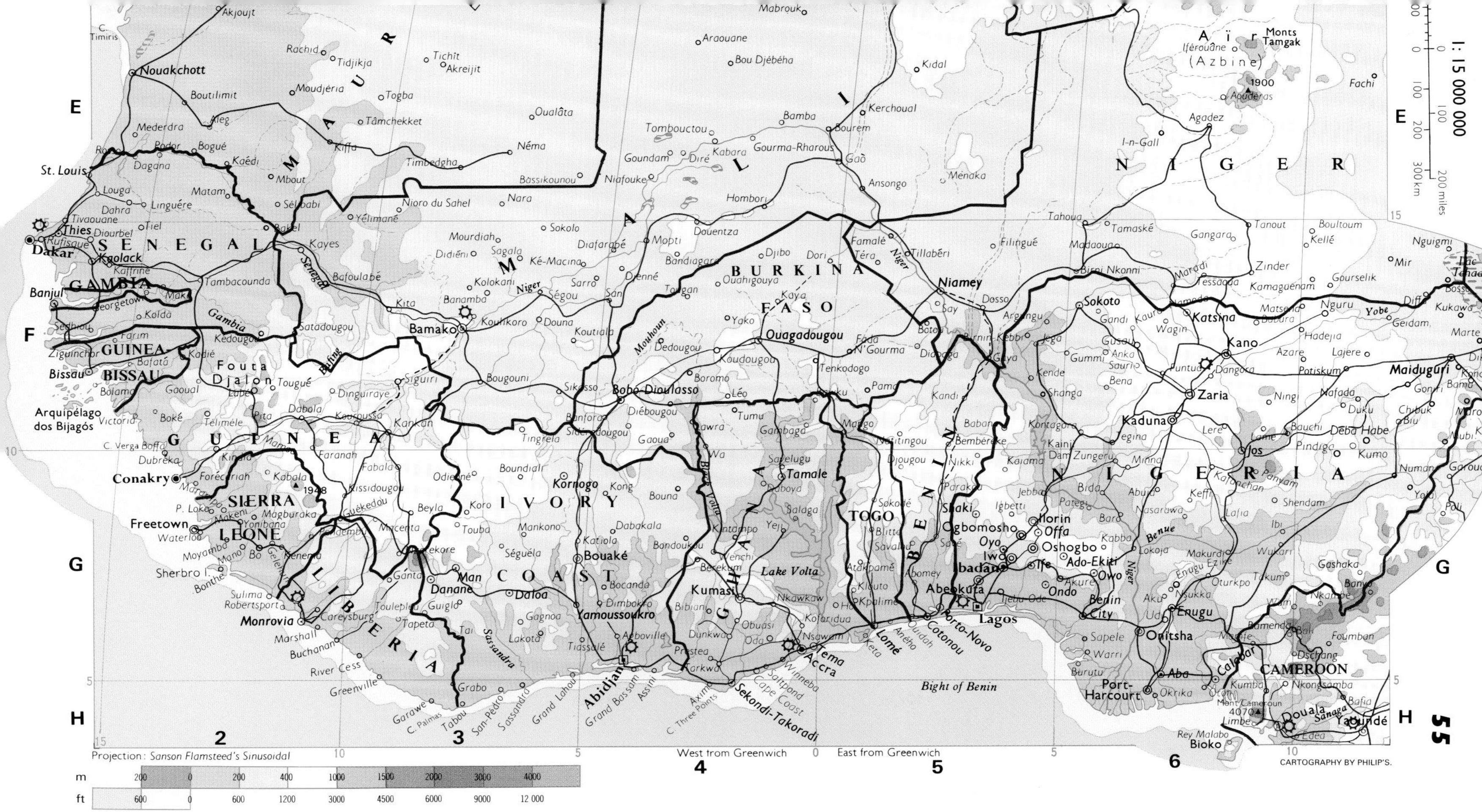
1: 15 000 000
0 100 200 miles
0 100 200 300 km
MAURITANIA
MALI
NIGER
SENEGAL
GAMBIA
GUINEA-BISSAU
GUINEA
SIERRA LEONE
LIBERIA
IVORY COAST
BURKINA FASO
GHANA
TOGO
BENIN
NIGERIA
CAMEROON
Aïr (Azbine)
Monts Tamgak
Fouta Djalon
Arquipélago dos Bijagós
Nouakchott
Dakar
St. Louis
Thies
Kaolack
Banjul
Bissau
Conakry
Freetown
Monrovia
Bamako
Tombouctou
Gao
Niamey
Agadez
Zinder
Ouagadougou
Bobo-Dioulasso
Tamale
Kumasi
Accra
Tema
Sekondi-Takoradi
Abidjan
Yamoussoukro
Bouaké
Lomé
Cotonou
Porto-Novo
Lagos
Ibadan
Abeokuta
Ogbomosho
Oshogbo
Ilorin
Benin City
Onitsha
Enugu
Port-Harcourt
Kaduna
Zaria
Kano
Katsina
Sokoto
Maiduguri
Jos
Calabar
Douala
Yaoundé
Bioko
Niger
Senegal
Gambia
Benue
Black Volta
Lake Volta
Bight of Benin
Lac Tchad
West from Greenwich
East from Greenwich
Projection: Sanson Flamsteed's Sinusoidal
m 200 0 200 400 1000 1500 2000 3000 4000
ft 600 0 600 1200 3000 4500 6000 9000 12 000
CARTOGRAPHY BY PHILIP'S.

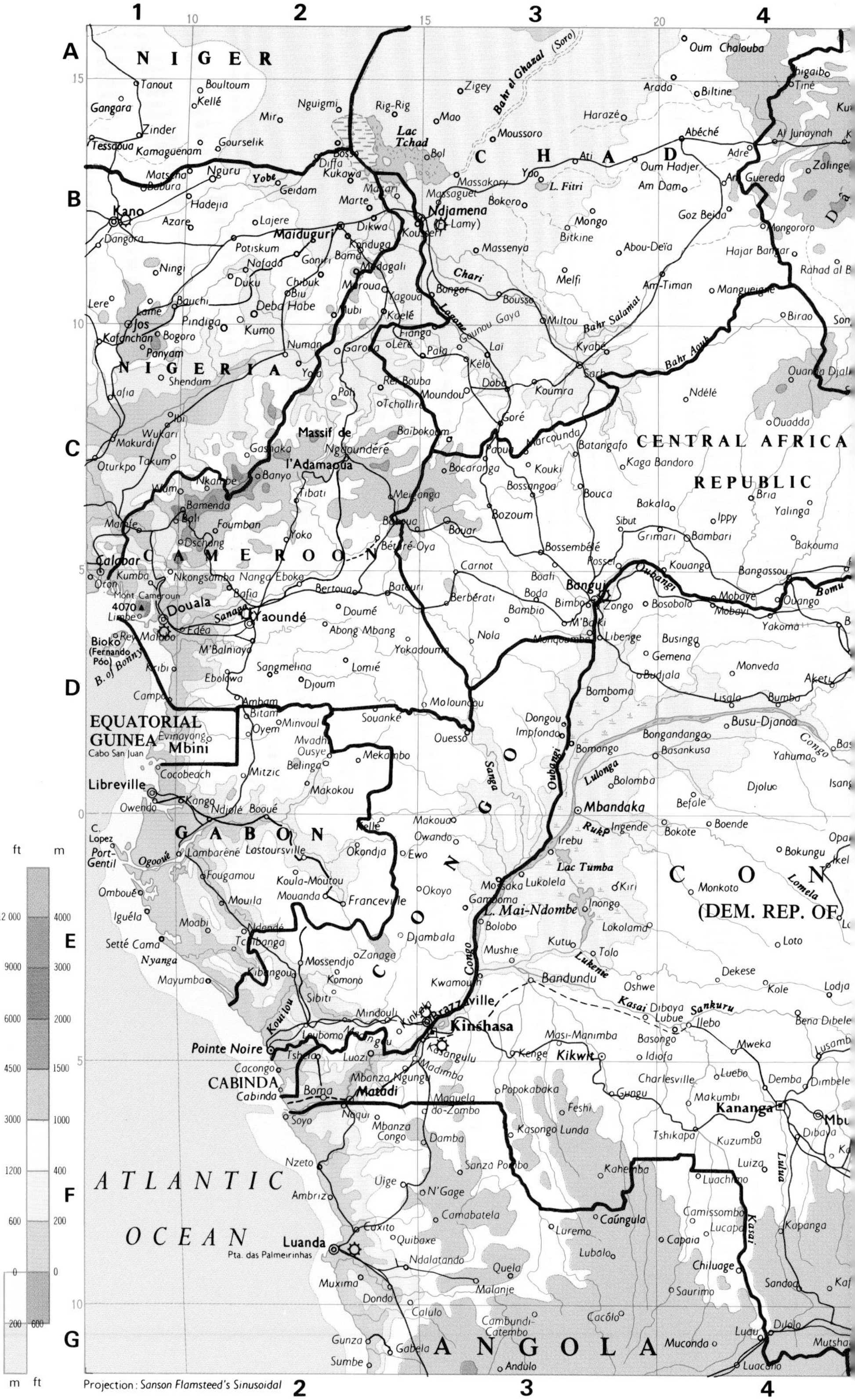

Projection: Sanson Flamsteed's Sinusoidal

1: 15 000 000

100 0 100 200 300 400 miles
100 0 100 200 300 400 500 600 km

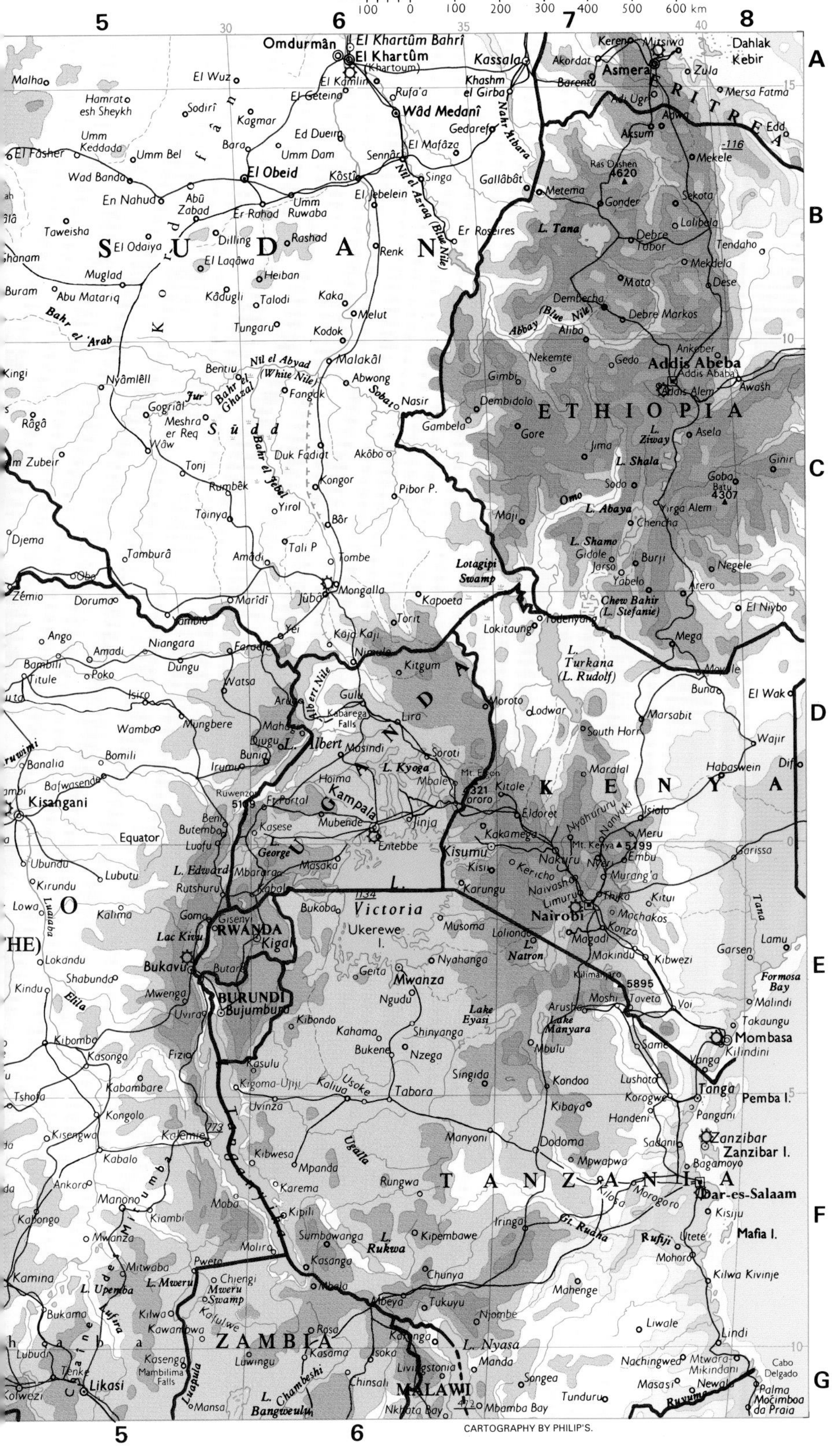
5
6
7
8
A
B
C
D
E
F
G
Omdurmân
El Khartûm Bahrî
El Khartûm
(Khartoum)
Kassala
Keren
Mitsiwa
Dahlak Kebir
Akordat
Asmera
Zula
Barentu
ERITREA
Mersa Fatma
Adi Ugri
Adwa
Aksum
Edd
Mekele
Ras Dashen 4620
Gonder
Sekota
Lalibela
Malha
El Wuz
El Kamlin
Rufa'a
Khashm el Girba
Hamrat esh Sheykh
Sodirî
Kagmar
El Geteina
Wâd Medanî
Nahr Atbara
Gedaref
Umm Keddada
El Fasher
Umm Bel
Bara
Umm Dam
Ed Dueim
El Mafâza
Sennâr
Wad Banda
El Obeid
Kôstî
Singa
Gallâbât
Metema
En Nahud
Abû Zabad
Er Rahad
Umm Ruwaba
El Jebelein
Nîl el Azraq (Blue Nile)
Taweisha
El Odaiya
SUDAN
KORDOFAN
Dilling
Rashad
Renk
Er Roseires
L. Tana
Debre Tabor
Tendaho
El Laqâwa
Heiban
Mekdela
Muglad
Kâdugli
Talodi
Mota
Dese
Buram
Abu Matariq
Kaka
Melut
Dembecha
Debre Markos
Bahr el 'Arab
Tungaru
Kodok
Abbay (Blue Nile)
Alibo
Malakâl
Ankober
Bentiu
Nîl el Abyad (White Nile)
Nekemte
Gedo
Addis Abeba
Kingi
Nyâmlêll
Abwong
Gimbi
Addis Alem
Awash
Bahr el Ghazal
Jur
Fangak
Sobat
Nasir
Dembidolo
ETHIOPIA
Gogriâl
Meshra er Req
Sûdd
Bahr el Jebel
Gambela
Gore
L. Ziway
Asela
Râgâ
Wâw
Duk Fadiat
Akôbo
Jima
L. Shala
Ginir
Zubeir
Tonj
Kongor
Pibor P.
Sodo
Goba
Batu 4307
Rumbêk
Omo
L. Abaya
Yirga Alem
Toinya
Yirol
Bôr
Maji
Chencha
Djema
Tali P
L. Shamo
Gidole
Burji
Tamburâ
Amâdi
Tombe
Jarso
Negele
Lotagipi Swamp
Yabelo
Arero
Obo
Zémio
Doruma
Marîdî
Jûba
Mongalla
Kapoeta
Chew Bahir (L. Stefanie)
El Niybo
Yambio
Torit
Todenyang
Lokitaung
Ango
Niangara
Yei
Kajo Kaji
Mega
Amadi
Faradje
Nimule
L. Turkana (L. Rudolf)
Moyale
Bambili
Poko
Dungu
Kitgum
Titule
Watsa
UGANDA
Buna
El Wak
Isiro
Aru
Albert Nile
Gulu
Moroto
Lodwar
Marsabit
Wamba
Mungbere
Kabarega Falls
Lira
Mahagi
Djugu
L. Albert
Masindi
South Horr
Wajir
Aruwimi
Banalia
Bomili
Bunia
Soroti
Maralal
Irumu
L. Kyoga
Habaswein
Dif
Bafwasende
Hoima
Mbale
Mt. Elgon 4321
Kitale
KENYA
Ruwenzori 5109
Ft. Portal
Tororo
Kisangani
Kampala
Isiolo
Beni
Mubende
Jinja
Eldoret
Nyahururu
Nanyuki
Equator
Butembo
Kasese
Kakamega
Meru
Luofu
Entebbe
Mt. Kenya 5199
Embu
Garissa
Ubundu
L. George
Kisumu
Nakuru
Nyeri
Lubutu
L. Edward
Masaka
Kisii
Kericho
Murang'a
Kirundu
Mbarara
Naivasha
Rutshuru
Kabale
1134
Karungu
Thika
Kitui
Tana
Lowa
Lualaba
Kalima
Goma
Bukoba
Victoria
Musoma
Limuru
Nairobi
Machakos
O
Lac Kivu
Gisenyi
RWANDA
Kigali
Ukerewe I.
Lolionda
Konza
Lamu
HE)
Lokandu
Bukavu
Butare
L. Natron
Magadi
Garsen
Shabunda
Geita
Mwanza
Nyahanga
Makindu
Kibwezi
Kindu
Elila
Mwenga
BURUNDI
Bujumbura
Ngudu
Kilimanjaro
5895
Formosa Bay
Uvira
Moshi
Taveta
Voi
Malindi
Kibondo
Lake Eyasi
Arusha
Lake Manyara
Takaungu
Kibombo
Kahama
Shinyanga
Mombasa
Kilindini
Fizi
Bukene
Nzega
Mbulu
Same
Kasongo
Kasulu
Vanga
Singida
Tshofa
Kabambare
Kigoma-Ujiji
Kaliua
Usoke
Tabora
Kondoa
Lushoto
Tanga
Pemba I.
Uvinza
Korogwe
Kongolo
Tanganyika
Kibaya
Pangani
Handeni
Kisengwa
773
Kalemie
Manyoni
Dodoma
Zanzibar
Zanzibar I.
Kibwesa
Ugalla
Saadani
Kabalo
Mpanda
Mpwapwa
Bagamoyo
Ankoro
Karema
Rungwa
TANZANIA
Manono
Kilosa
Morogoro
Dar-es-Salaam
Mitumba
Moba
Kipili
Kabongo
Kiambi
Iringa
Kisiju
Mwanza
Sumbawanga
L. Rukwa
Kipembawe
Gt. Ruaha
Rufiji
Utete
Mafia I.
Moliro
Mohoro
Pweto
Kasanga
Kamina
Mitwaba
L. Mweru
Chiengi
Mweru Swamp
Chunya
Kilwa Kivinje
L. Upemba
Mbala
Mahenge
Lufira
Kalulwe
Tukuyu
Bukama
Kilwa
Kawambwa
Abeya
Njombe
Rosa
Liwale
ZAMBIA
Karonga
L. Nyasa
Lindi
Lubudi
Kasenga
Mambilima Falls
Kasama
Isoka
Manda
Nachingwea
Mtwara-Mikindani
Cabo Delgado
Tenke
Likasi
Luwingu
Livingstonia
Songea
Masasi
Newala
Kolwezi
Luapula
Chambeshi
Chinsali
MALAWI
Ruvuma
Palma
Mocimboa da Praia
Mansa
L. Bangweulu
Nkhata Bay
Mbamba Bay
Tunduru
30
35
40
15
10
0
-116
472

CARTOGRAPHY BY PHILIP'S.

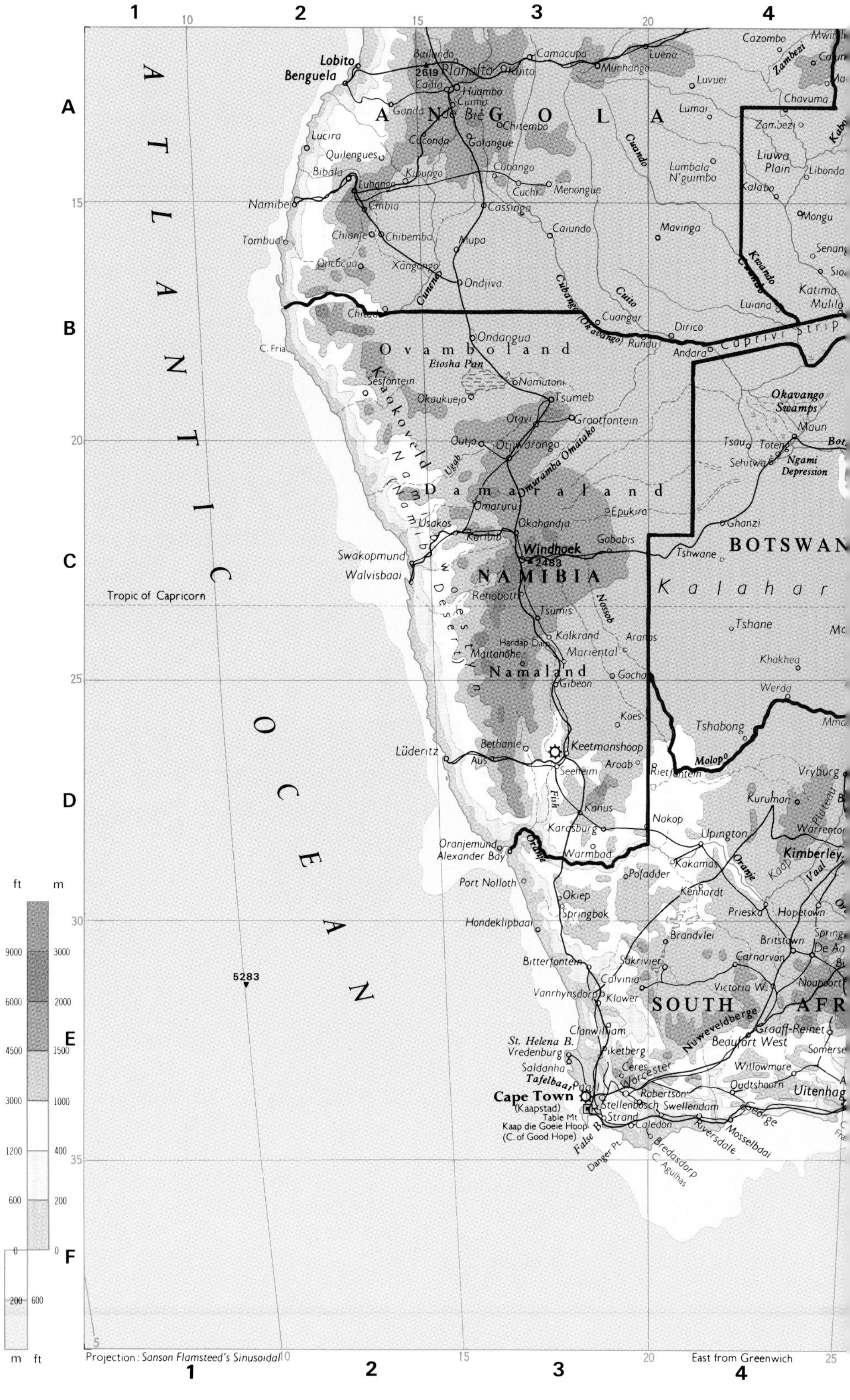

1
2
3
4
A
B
C
D
E
F
10
15
20
25
30
35
ATLANTIC OCEAN
ANGOLA
NAMIBIA
BOTSWANA
SOUTH AFRICA
Lobito
Benguela
Bailundo
2619
Planalto
Caála
Huambo
Cuima
Ganda
Bié
Chitembo
Camacupa
Kuito
Munhango
Luena
Luvuei
Cazombo
Zambezi
Chavuma
Zambezi
Liuwa Plain
Libonda
Kalabo
Mongu
Lumai
Cuando
Lumbala N'guimbo
Mavinga
Lucira
Quilengues
Caconda
Galangue
Bibala
Kipungo
Cubango
Lubango
Cuchi
Menongue
Namibe
Chibia
Cassinga
Caiundo
Tombua
Chianje
Chibemba
Mupa
Oncocua
Xangongo
Ondjiva
Cunene
Cubango (Okavango)
Cuito
Cuangar
Kwando
Cuando
Luiana
Katima Mulilo
Chitado
Ondangua
Rundu
Dirico
Andara
Caprivi Strip
C. Fria
Ovamboland
Etosha Pan
Sesfontein
Namutoni
Okaukuejo
Tsumeb
Kaokoveld
Otavi
Grootfontein
Okavango Swamps
Maun
Tsau
Toteng
Sehitwa
Ngami Depression
Outjo
Otjiwarongo
Omuramba Omatako
Ugab
Damaraland
Omaruru
Epukiro
Namib Desert
Okahandja
Ghanzi
Usakos
Karibib
Windhoek
2483
Gobabis
Tshwane
Swakopmund
Walvisbaai
Kalahari
Tropic of Capricorn
Rehoboth
Nossob
Tsumis
Tshane
Hardap Dam
Kalkrand
Maltahöhe
Mariental
Aranos
Khakhea
Namaland
Gochas
Gibeon
Werda
Koes
Tshabong
Bethanie
Keetmanshoop
Lüderitz
Aus
Aroab
Molopo
Seeheim
Rietfontein
Vryburg
Fish
Kanus
Kuruman
Nakop
Karasburg
Upington
Warrenton
Oranjemund
Alexander Bay
Oranje
Warmbad
Kakamas
Oranje
Kimberley
Vaal
Pofadder
Port Nolloth
Kenhardt
Okiep
Springbok
Prieska
Hopetown
Hondeklipbaai
Brandvlei
Britstown
De Aar
5283
Bitterfontein
Sakrivier
Carnarvon
Calvinia
Victoria W.
Vanrhynsdorp
Klawer
Nuweveldberge
Graaff-Reinet
Clanwilliam
Beaufort West
St. Helena B.
Vredenburg
Piketberg
Saldanha
Ceres
Willowmore
Tafelbaai
Worcester
Paarl
Oudtshoorn
Uitenhage
Cape Town
(Kaapstad)
Robertson
Stellenbosch
Swellendam
George
Table Mt.
Strand
Kaap die Goeie Hoop
(C. of Good Hope)
Caledon
Riversdale
Mosselbaai
False B.
Bredasdorp
Danger Pt.
C. Agulhas
ft
m
9000
3000
6000
2000
4500
1500
3000
1000
1200
400
600
200
0
200
600
m
ft

Projection: Sanson Flamsteed's Sinusoidal

East from Greenwich

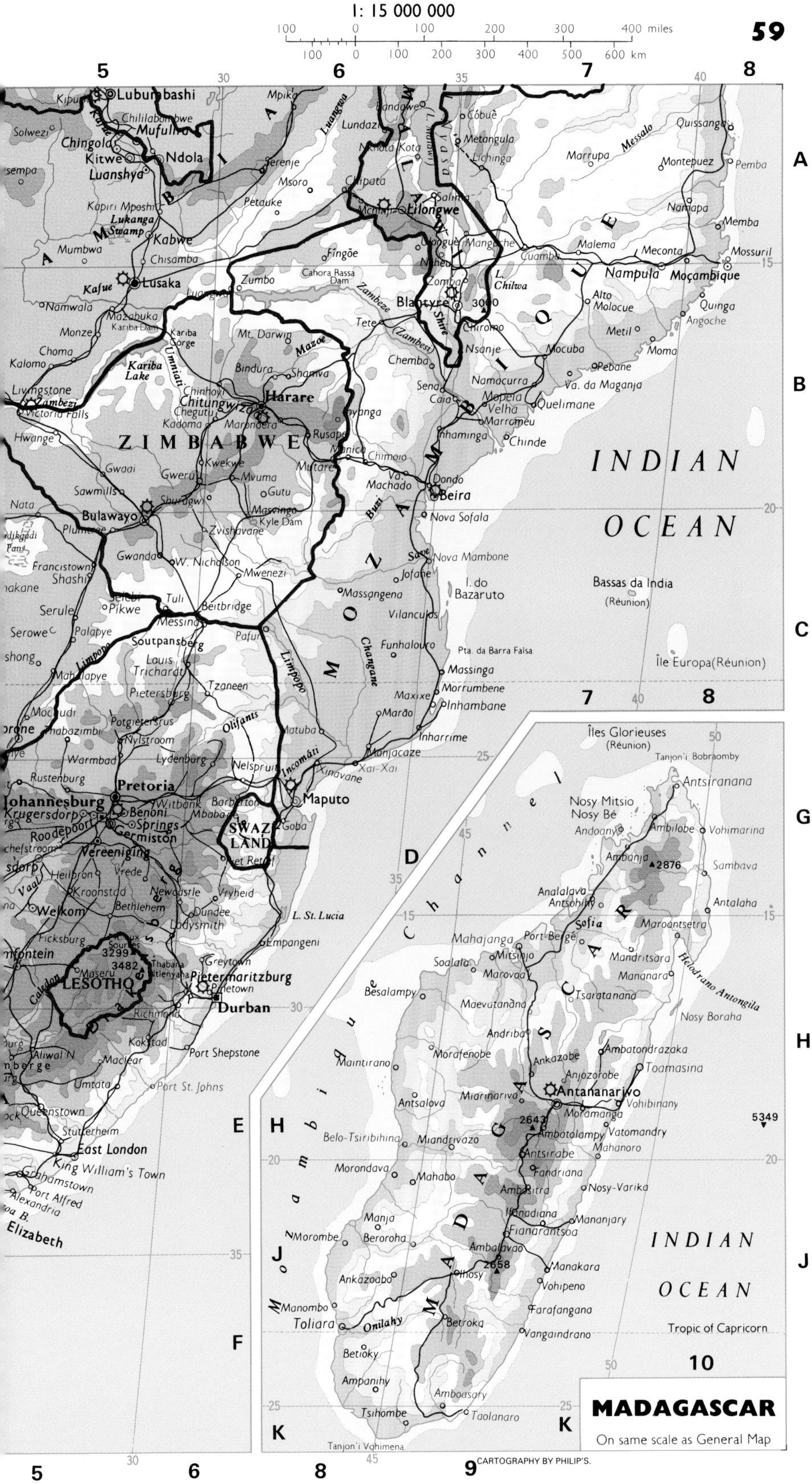
1: 15 000 000
miles
km
Lubumbashi
Chililabombwe
Mufulira
Solwezi
Chingola
Kitwe
Ndola
Luanshya
Kapiri Mposhi
Lukanga Swamp
Kabwe
Mumbwa
Chisamba
Kafue
Lusaka
Namwala
Mazabuka
Kariba Dam
Monze
Choma
Kalomo
Kariba Gorge
Kariba Lake
Livingstone
Victoria Falls
Zambezi
Hwange
Mpika
Luangwa
Serenje
Msoro
Petauke
Lundazi
Nkhota Kota
Chipata
Lilongwe
Salima
Mchinji
Cóbuè
Metangula
Lichinga
Marrupa
Messalo
Quissanga
Montepuez
Pemba
Namapa
Memba
Mossuril
Moçambique
Nampula
Meconta
Malema
Cuamba
Mangoche
Fíngoè
Cahora Bassa Dam
Zumbo
Zambeze
Tete
Zomba
Blantyre
L. Chilwa
Shire
3000
Chiromo
Nsanje
Alto Molocue
Quinga
Angoche
Metil
Moma
Mocuba
Pebane
Va. da Maganja
Quelimane
Chemba
Sena
Caia
Namacurra
Mopeia Velha
Marromeu
Chinde
Inhaminga
Mt. Darwin
Mazoe
Bindura
Shamva
Chinhoyi
Harare
Chitungwiza
Chegutu
Kadoma
Marondera
Rusape
Nyanga
ZIMBABWE
Gwaai
Kwekwe
Gweru
Mvuma
Gutu
Sawmills
Shurugwi
Masvingo
Kyle Dam
Bulawayo
Plumtree
Zvishavane
Mutare
Manica
Chimoio
Va. Machado
Dondo
Beira
Busi
Nova Sofala
Save
Nova Mambone
Jofane
I. do Bazaruto
Massangena
Vilanculos
Funhalouro
Changane
MOZAMBIQUE
Pta. da Barra Falsa
Massinga
Morrumbene
Maxixe
Inhambane
Mardo
Inharrime
Manjacaze
Xai-Xai
Xinavane
Maputo
Incomáti
Limpopo
INDIAN OCEAN
Bassas da India (Réunion)
Île Europa (Réunion)
Nata
Francistown
Shashi
Gwanda
W. Nicholson
Mwenezi
Selebi Pikwe
Tuli
Beitbridge
Messina
Serule
Serowe
Palapye
Mahalapye
Soutpansberg
Louis Trichardt
Pafuri
Pietersburg
Tzaneen
Mochudi
Potgietersrus
Olifants
Nylstroom
Warmbad
Lydenburg
Matuba
Nelspruit
Rustenburg
Pretoria
Witbank
Barberton
Mbabane
Johannesburg
Benoni
Krugersdorp
Springs
Roodepoort
Germiston
SWAZILAND
Goba
Vereeniging
Piet Retief
Heilbron
Vrede
Vaal
Kroonstad
Newcastle
Vryheid
Welkom
Bethlehem
Dundee
L. St. Lucia
Ladysmith
Ficksburg
Empangeni
Sources
3299
3482
Thabana Ntlenyana
Maseru
LESOTHO
Caledon
Greytown
Pietermaritzburg
Pinetown
Durban
Richmond
Kokstad
Aliwal N
Maclear
Port Shepstone
Umtata
Port St. Johns
Queenstown
Stutterheim
East London
King William's Town
Grahamstown
Port Alfred
Alexandria
Elizabeth
Mozambique Channel
Îles Glorieuses (Réunion)
Tanjon'i Bobraomby
Antsiranana
Nosy Mitsio
Nosy Bé
Andoany
Ambilobe
Vohimarina
Ambanja
2876
Sambava
Analalava
Antsohihy
Antalaha
Sofia
Maroantsetra
Mahajanga
Port Bergé
Mitsinjo
Mandritsara
Soalala
Marovoay
Mananara
Besalampy
Tsaratanana
Maevatanana
Helodrano Antongila
Nosy Boraha
Andriba
Morafenobe
Ambatondrazaka
Maintirano
Ankazobe
Toamasina
Anjozorobe
Antananarivo
Miarinarivo
Antsalova
Vohibinany
Moramanga
2643
Ambatolampy
Vatomandry
5349
Belo-Tsiribihina
Miandrivazo
Mahanoro
Antsirabe
Fandriana
Morondava
Mahabo
Ambositra
Nosy-Varika
Ifanadiana
Mananjary
Manja
Fianarantsoa
MADAGASCAR
Morombe
Beroroha
Ambalavao
2658
Ihosy
Manakara
Ankazoabo
Vohipeno
Manombo
Farafangana
Toliara
Onilahy
Betroka
Vangaindrano
Tropic of Capricorn
Betioky
Ampanihy
Amboasary
Tsihombe
Taolanaro
Tanjon'i Vohimena
MADAGASCAR
On same scale as General Map
CARTOGRAPHY BY PHILIP'S.

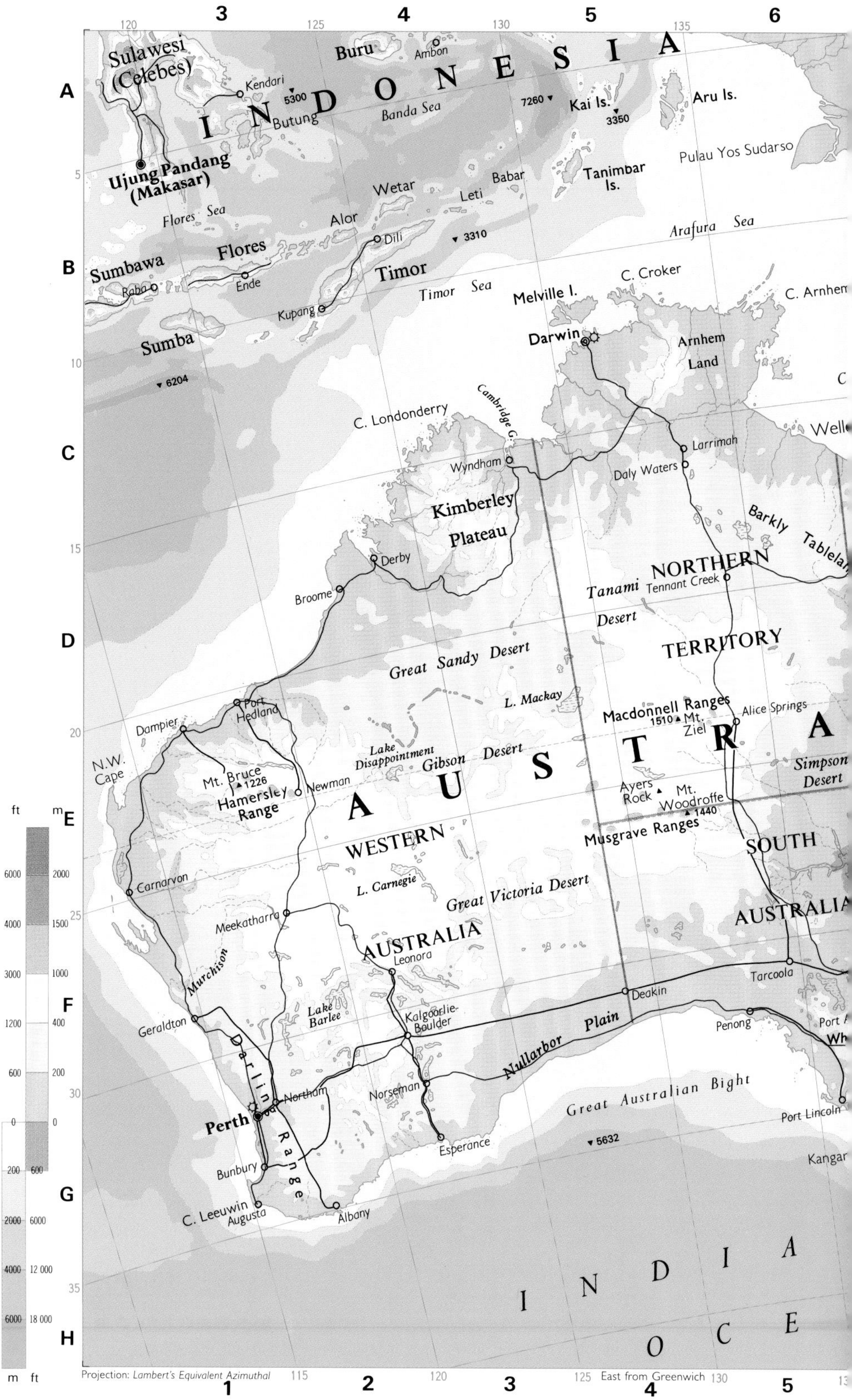
3
4
5
6
A
B
C
D
E
F
G
H
1
2
3
4
5
120
125
130
135
115
120
125
130
5
10
15
20
25
30
35
INDONESIA
Sulawesi (Celebes)
Kendari
Buru
Ambon
5300
Butung
Banda Sea
7260
Kai Is.
3350
Aru Is.
Ujung Pandang (Makasar)
Pulau Yos Sudarso
Tanimbar Is.
Wetar
Babar
Leti
Flores Sea
Alor
Dili
3310
Arafura Sea
Sumbawa
Flores
Timor
Raba
Ende
C. Croker
Timor Sea
Melville I.
C. Arnhem
Kupang
Sumba
Darwin
Arnhem Land
6204
Cambridge G.
C. Londonderry
Larrimah
Wyndham
Daly Waters
Kimberley Plateau
Barkly Tableland
Derby
NORTHERN
Tennant Creek
Broome
Tanami Desert
TERRITORY
Great Sandy Desert
L. Mackay
Port Hedland
Macdonnell Ranges
1510 Mt. Ziel
Alice Springs
Dampier
Lake Disappointment
Gibson Desert
N.W. Cape
Mt. Bruce
1226
Hamersley Range
Newman
AUSTRALIA
Simpson Desert
Ayers Rock
Mt. Woodroffe
1440
Musgrave Ranges
WESTERN
SOUTH
L. Carnegie
Carnarvon
Great Victoria Desert
AUSTRALIA
Meekatharra
AUSTRALIA
Leonora
Tarcoola
Murchison
Deakin
Lake Barlee
Kalgoorlie-Boulder
Nullarbor Plain
Penong
Geraldton
Darling Range
Northam
Norseman
Great Australian Bight
Port Lincoln
Perth
5632
Esperance
Bunbury
C. Leeuwin
Augusta
Albany
INDIAN OCEAN
ft
m
6000
4000
3000
1200
600
0
200
2000
4000
6000
2000
1500
1000
400
200
0
600
6000
12 000
18 000
m
ft

Projection: *Lambert's Equivalent Azimuthal*

East from Greenwich

1:20 000 000
100 0 100 200 300 400 500 miles
100 0 200 400 600 800 km
PAPUA NEW GUINEA
Mount Hagen
4508 Mt. Wilhelm
Lae
New Britain
9140
Mt. Balbi
Bougainville
SOLOMON ISLANDS
Choiseul
Santa Isabel
New Georgia
Malaita
Honiara
2331
Guadalcanal
San Cristobal
Rennell
Solomon Sea
Fly
Gulf of Papua
Owen Stanley Range
Port Moresby
D'Entrecasteaux Arch.
Louisiade Archipelago
Torres Strait
C. York
Weipa
Cape York Peninsula
Great Barrier Reef
Coral Sea
Cooktown
Mitchell
Cairns
1611 Bartle Frere
Normanton
Forsayth
Flinders
Townsville
Charters Towers
Coral Sea Islands Territory
Chesterfield Is.
PACIFIC OCEAN
Mount Isa
Hughenden
Mackay
Winton
QUEENSLAND
Great Dividing Range
Rockhampton
Gladstone
Tropic of Capricorn
Longreach
Diamantina
Bundaberg
Yaraka
Maryborough
Gympie
Grey Range
Charleville
Roma
BRISBANE
Quilpie
Toowoomba
Ipswich
Gold Coast
Cunnamulla
Thargomindah
Dirranbandi
Lismore
Creek
Eyre
Warrego
Walgett
Bourke
1615 Round Mt.
Tamworth
Flinders Range
NEW SOUTH WALES
Cobar
Taree
Lord Howe (Austr.)
734
Broken Hill
Darling
Dubbo
Newcastle
Orange
Bathurst
SYDNEY
Port Pirie
Murray
Mildura
Wollongong
Shellharbour
Goulburn
Canberra
CAPITAL TERRITORY
Tasman Sea
Adelaide
Wagga Wagga
Mt. Kosciuszko
2237
Shepparton
Albury
Australian Alps
Horsham
Bendigo
Bombala
VICTORIA
C. Howe
Ballarat
MELBOURNE
Geelong
Mount Gambier
Warrnambool
Bass Strait
King I.
Furneaux Group
5267
Burnie
Launceston
1617 Mt. Ossa
TASMANIA
Hobart
S.E. Cape
CARTOGRAPHY BY PHILIP'S.

SOUTH AUSTRALIA
TASMANIA
Lake Eyre (North)
L. Eyre (South)
Lake Torrens
Lake Gairdner
Lake Frome
Flinders Ranges
Stuart Range
Barrier Range
Spencer Gulf
G. St. Vincent
Investigator Str.
Kangaroo I.
Eyre Peninsula
Yorke Pen.
Encounter Bay
L. Alexandrina
Younghusband Peninsula
Lacepede Bay
Bass Strait
Banks Strait
King Island
Flinders Island
Furneaux Group
Cape Barren I.
ADELAIDE
Port Adelaide
Elizabeth
Glenelg
Brighton
Port Augusta
Whyalla
Port Pirie
Port Lincoln
Broken Hill
Mildura
Murray Bridge
Mount Gambier
Millicent
Naracoorte
Hamilton
Portland
Warrnambool
Horsham
Ararat
Ballarat
Stawell
Maryborough
Hobart
Glenorchy
Launceston
Devonport
Burnie
Wynyard
Ulverstone
Woomera
Coober Pedy
Oodnadatta
Marree
Leigh Creek South
Ceduna
Quorn
Victor Harbor
Kingscote
Kingston South East
Mt. Ossa 1617
Ben Lomond 1527
St. Mary Pk. 1165
Mt. Remarkable 969
Mt. Bryan 934
Nukey Bluff 472
Benbonyathe Hill 1058
Projection: Bonne
East from Greenwich

1:8 000 000

50 0 50 100 150 200 miles
50 0 50 100 150 200 250 300 km

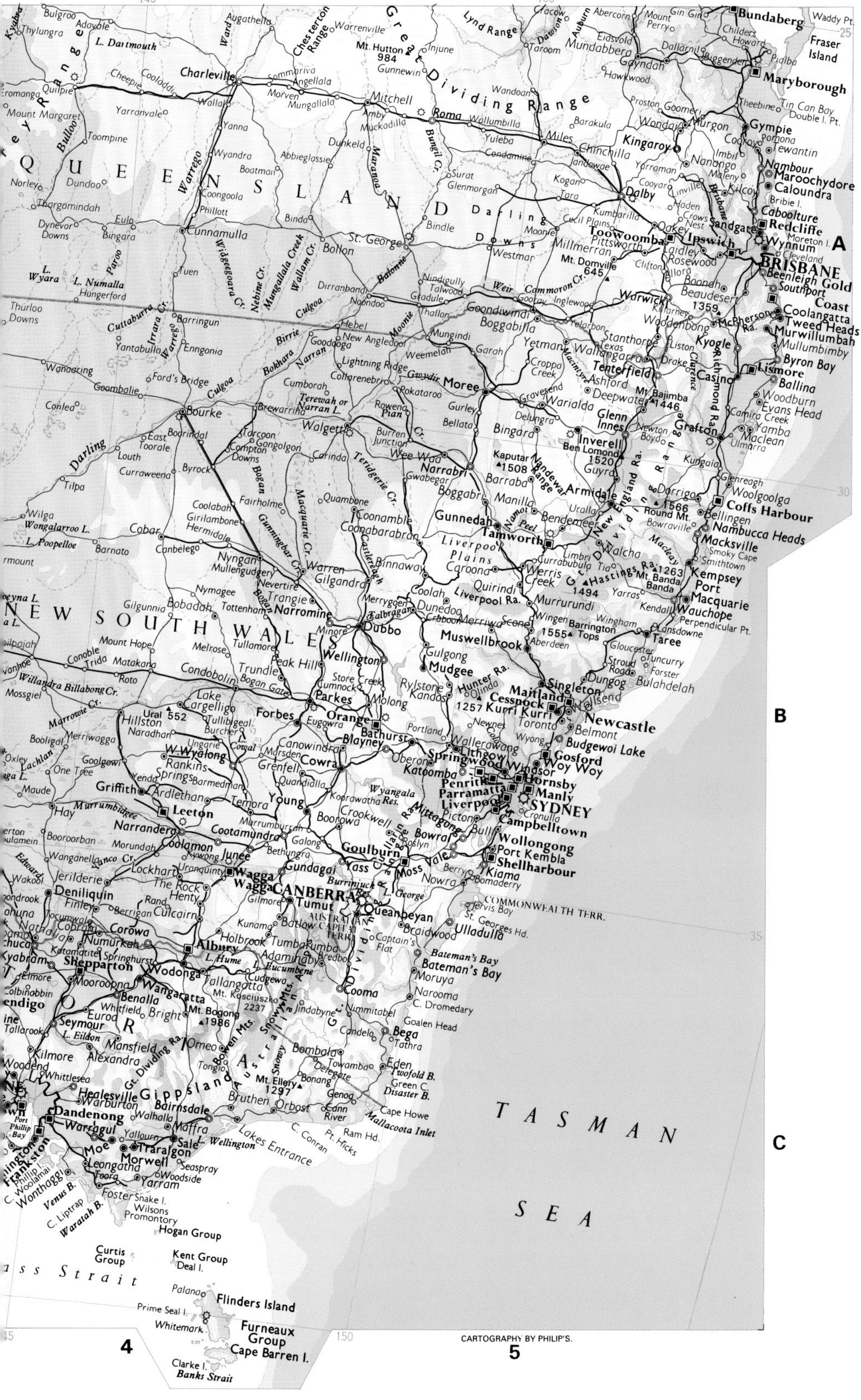

NEW ZEALAND, CENTRAL AND SOUTH-WEST PACIFIC

SOUTH-WEST PACIFIC
1: 54 000 000
500 miles
1000 km
NORTHERN MARIANAS (U.S.)
Saipan
Mariana Trench
GUAM (U.S.)
Micronesia
Melanesia
FEDERATED STATES OF MICRONESIA
Truk
Pohnpei
Caroline Islands
MARSHALL IS.
Bikini Atoll
Enewetak Atoll
Jaluit
International Date Line
Butaritari
Gilbert Is.
Baker I. (U.S.)
Equator
NAURU
Banaba
KIRIBATI
Admiralty Is.
Bismarck Arch.
New Ireland
Rabaul
9103
New Britain
PAPUA NEW GUINEA
Lae
Port Moresby
SOLOMON IS.
Guadalcanal
Honiara
TUVALU
Sta. Cruz I.
9165
Louisiade Arch.
Rotuma
Wallis & Futuna (Fr.)
FIJI
Vanua Levu
Viti Levu
Suva
VANUATU
Coral Sea
Is. Chesterfield
7570
NEW CALEDONIA (Fr.)
Is. Loyauté
Nouméa
Tropic of Capricorn
Cairns
Townsville
Rockhampton
Great Divide
AUSTRALIA
Brisbane
Norfolk I. (Aust.)
Kermadec Is. (N.Z.)
NEW ZEALAND
10,047
NORTH ISLAND
Three Kings Is.
C. Reinga
C. Maria van Diemen
North C.
Rangaunu Bay
Doubtless Bay
Mangonui
Whangaroa Bay
Houhora
Ahipara B.
Kaitaia
Tauroa Pt.
B. of Islands
C. Brett
Opua
Rawene
Kaikohe
Hikurangi
Hokianga Harb.
Donnelly's Crossing
Whangarei
Whangarei Harb.
Bream Hd.
Bream Bay
Dargaville
Waipu
Lit. Barrier I.
Gt. Barrier I.
C. Rodney
C.Colville
Hauraki Gulf
Cuvier I.
Kaipara Harb.
Warkworth
Helensville
Takapuna
Devonport
Coromandel
Whitianga
AUCKLAND
Onehunga
Manukau
Papakura
Thames
Pukekohe
Waiuku
Waikato
Mercer
Paeroa
Waihi
Mayor I.
Tauranga Harb.
Huntly
Te Aroha
Morrinsville
Mt. Maunganui
Te Puke
Bay of Plenty
White I.
C. Runaway
East C.
Raglan
Hamilton
Cambridge
Tauranga
Whakatane
Opotiki
Raukumara Ra.
Hikurangi 1753
Kawhia Harb.
Te Awamutu
Otorohanga
Putaruru
Rotorua
L. Rotorua
Kawerau
L. Tarawera
Waipiro
Kinleith
Te Kuiti
Kaingaroa Forest
Murupara
Motu
Tolaga Bay
Mokau
Mokai
Wairakei
L. Taupo
Taupo
Ongarue
Ormond
Gisborne
North Taranaki Bight
Waitara
Taumarunui
Kaimanawa Mts.
Tarawera
L. Waikaremoana
Nuhaka
Poverty Bay
Waikokopu
New Plymouth
Inglewood
Whangamomona
Turungi
Mt. Egmont (Taranaki) 2518
C. Egmont
Stratford
Ruapehu 2797
Wairoa
Mahia Peninsula
Opunake
Kaponga
Eltham
Raetihi
Ohakune
Waiouru
Bay View
Hawke Bay
Napier
Hawera
South Taranaki Bight
Patea
Waverley
Taihape
Mangaweka
Ruahine Ra.
C. Kidnappers
Hastings
Wanganui
Hunterville
Waipawa
Marton
Bulls
Halcombe
Feilding
Waipukurau
Palmerston N.
Dannevirke
Foxton
Shannon
Woodville
Pahiatua
C. Farewell

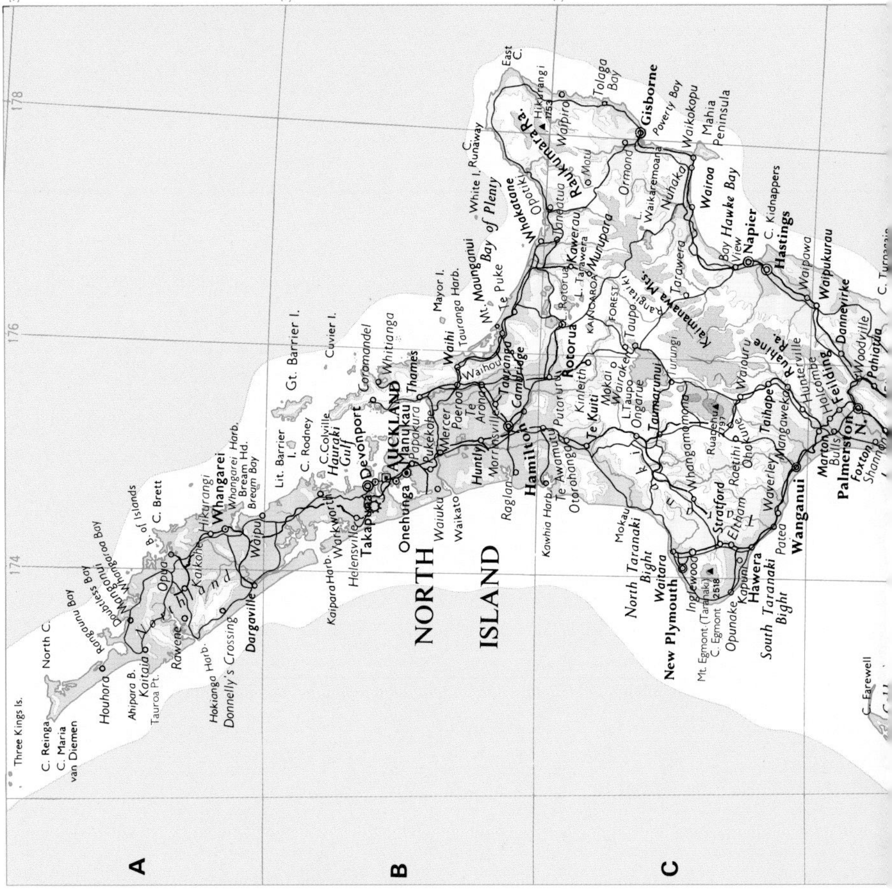

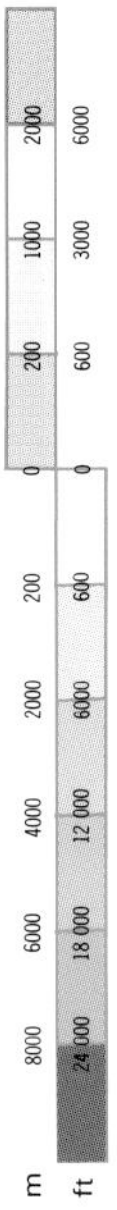

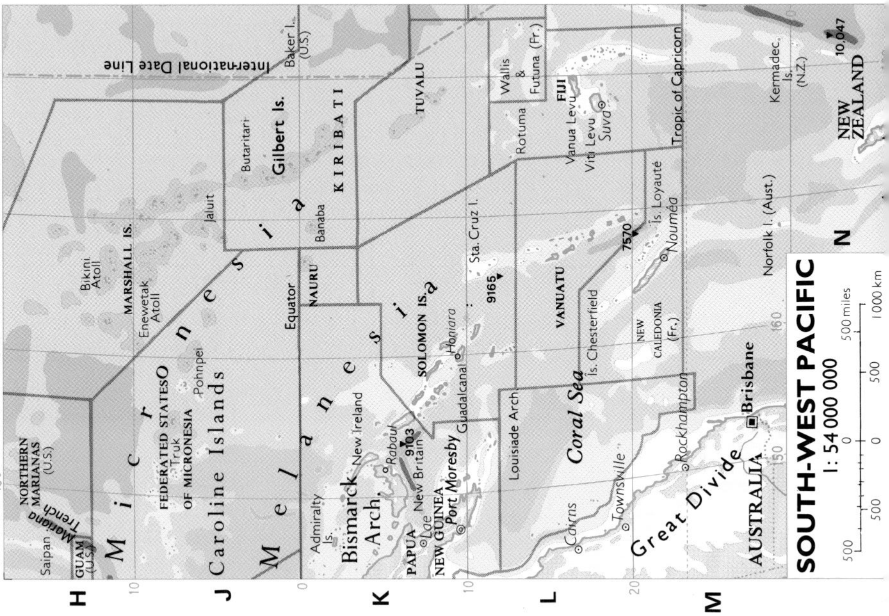

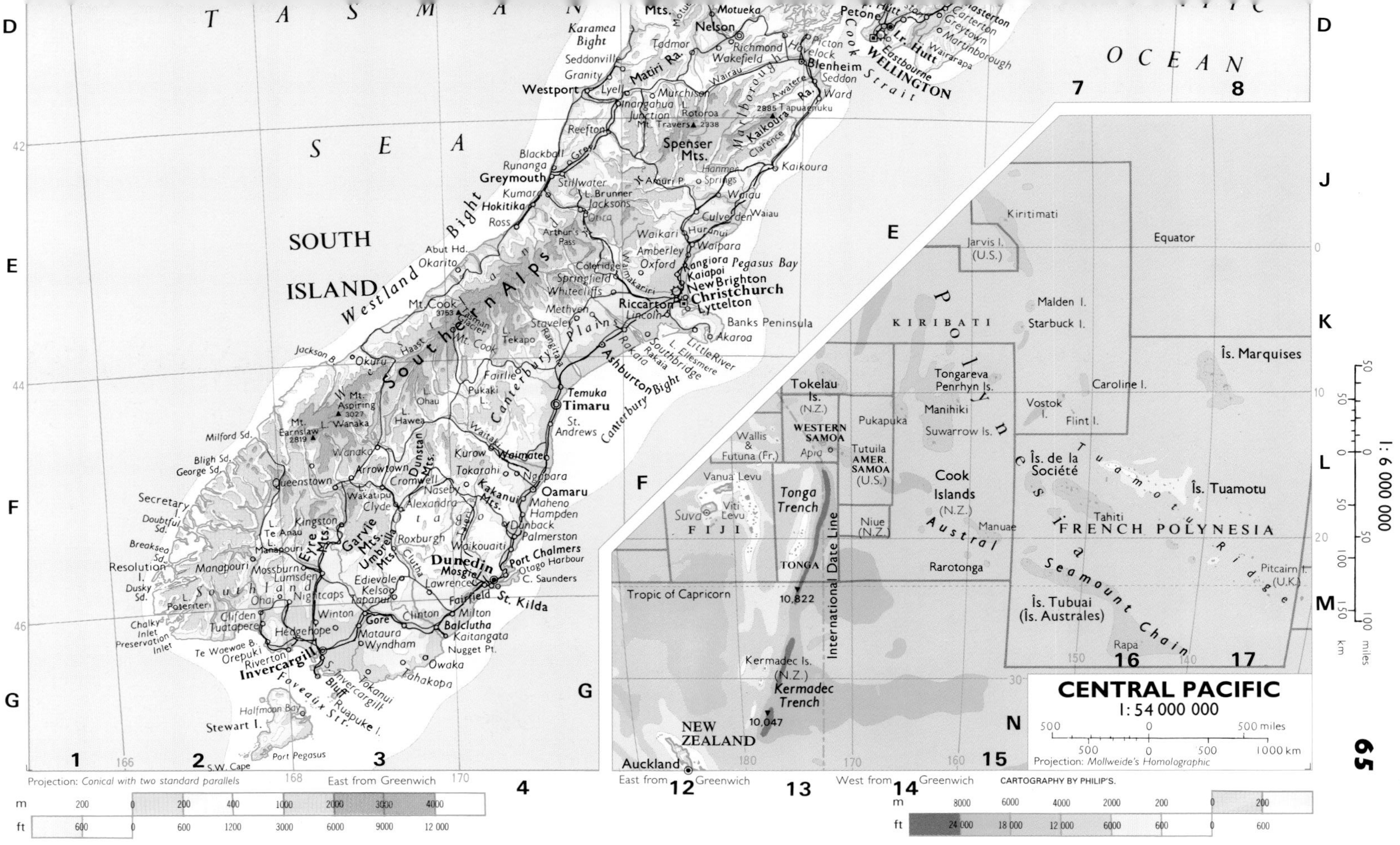

1: 6 000 000
TASMAN SEA
SOUTH ISLAND
Southern Alps
Westland Bight
Canterbury Plains
Canterbury Bight
Pegasus Bay
Banks Peninsula
Cook Strait
WELLINGTON
Lr. Hutt
Nelson
Blenheim
Westport
Greymouth
Hokitika
Christchurch
Lyttelton
Ashburton
Timaru
Oamaru
Dunedin
Invercargill
Foveaux Str.
Stewart I.
Mt. Cook 3753
Mt. Aspiring 3027
Kaikoura
Southland
Otago
Projection: Conical with two standard parallels
East from Greenwich
CENTRAL PACIFIC
1: 54 000 000
Projection: Mollweide's Homolographic
KIRIBATI
Kiritimati
Equator
Îs. Marquises
Îs. Tuamotu
FRENCH POLYNESIA
Tahiti
Îs. de la Société
Îs. Tubuai (Îs. Australes)
Cook Islands (N.Z.)
Rarotonga
Niue (N.Z.)
Tokelau Is. (N.Z.)
WESTERN SAMOA
AMER. SAMOA (U.S.)
Wallis & Futuna (Fr.)
FIJI
TONGA
Tonga Trench
Kermadec Trench
Kermadec Is. (N.Z.)
International Date Line
Tropic of Capricorn
NEW ZEALAND
Auckland
Pitcairn I. (U.K.)
Austral Seamount Chain
West from Greenwich
CARTOGRAPHY BY PHILIP'S.

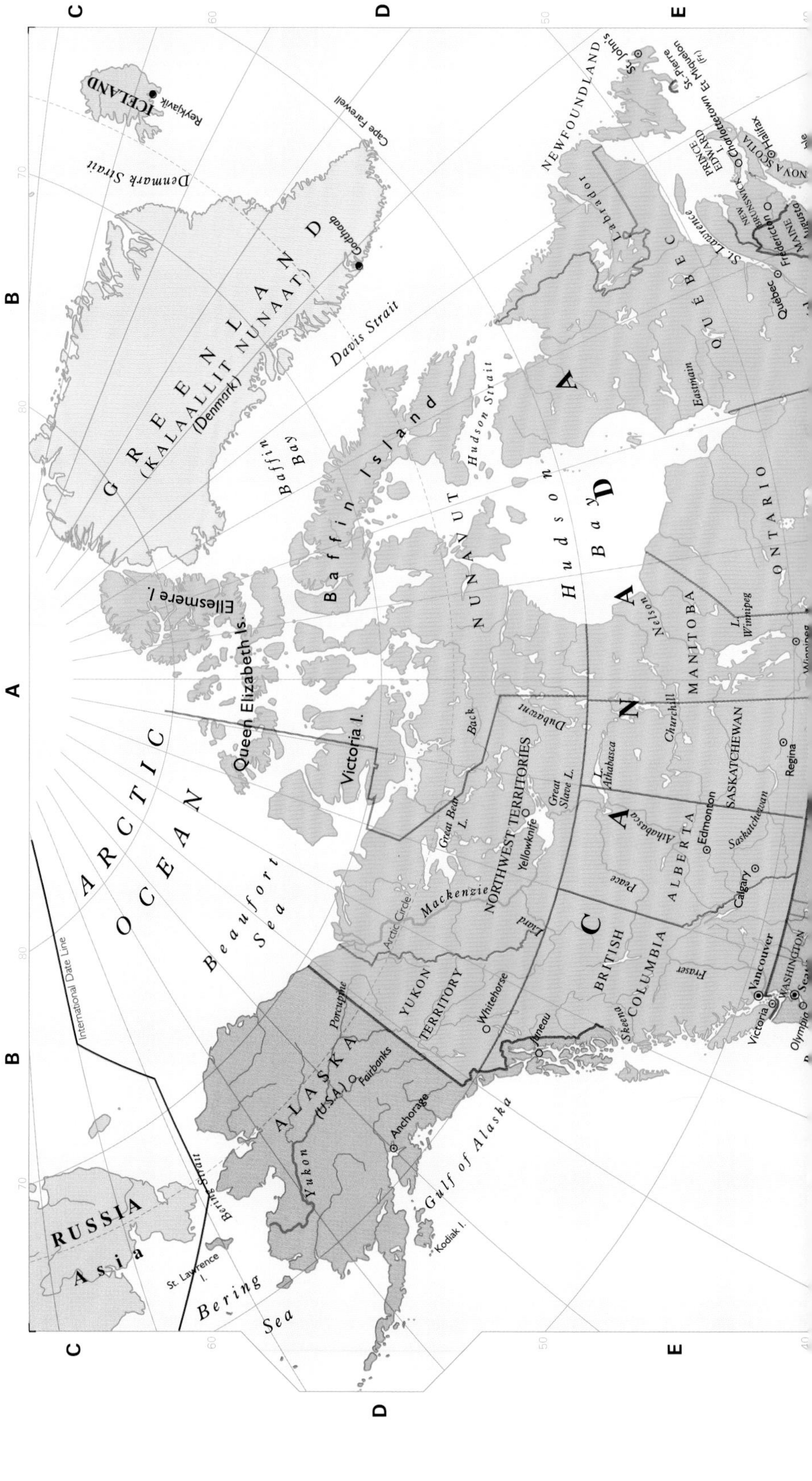

ARCTIC OCEAN
GREENLAND (KALAALLIT NUNAAT) (Denmark)
ICELAND
Reykjavik
Denmark Strait
Cape Farewell
Godthaab
Davis Strait
Baffin Bay
Baffin Island
Hudson Strait
Hudson Bay
Ellesmere I.
Queen Elizabeth Is.
Victoria I.
Beaufort Sea
International Date Line
Arctic Circle
NUNAVUT
NORTHWEST TERRITORIES
YUKON TERRITORY
ALASKA (USA)
CANADA
BRITISH COLUMBIA
ALBERTA
SASKATCHEWAN
MANITOBA
ONTARIO
QUEBEC
NEWFOUNDLAND
Labrador
NOVA SCOTIA
NEW BRUNSWICK
PRINCE EDWARD I.
St.-Pierre Et-Miquelon (Fr.)
MAINE
WASHINGTON
St. John's
Halifax
Charlottetown
Fredericton
Quebec
St. Lawrence
Eastmain
Nelson
Churchill
L. Winnipeg
Winnipeg
Regina
Edmonton
Calgary
Vancouver
Victoria
Olympia
Seattle
Whitehorse
Juneau
Yellowknife
Fairbanks
Anchorage
Great Bear L.
Great Slave L.
L. Athabasca
Athabasca
Saskatchewan
Peace
Liard
Mackenzie
Back
Dubawnt
Fraser
Skeena
Porcupine
Yukon
Gulf of Alaska
Kodiak I.
Bering Strait
Bering Sea
St. Lawrence I.
RUSSIA
Asia
A
B
C
D
E
50
60
70
80

1: 35 000 000
200 0 200 400 600 800 miles
400 0 400 800 1200 km
F
G
H
J
7
8
9
10
11
12
NORTH ATLANTIC OCEAN
PACIFIC OCEAN
Gulf of Mexico
Caribbean Sea
UNITED STATES
MEXICO
South America
OREGON
IDAHO
Boise
Snake
Helena
WYOMING
Cheyenne
DAKOTA
SOUTH DAKOTA
Minneapolis
NEBRASKA
Lincoln
IOWA
WISCONSIN
Madison
Milwaukee
CHICAGO
ILLINOIS
Springfield
L. Michigan
MICHIGAN
Lansing
Huron
Toronto
L. Ontario
Buffalo
NEW YORK
Hartford
MASS.
CT.
R.I.
NEW YORK CITY
PHILADELPHIA
N.J.
DE.
MD.
Detroit
Toledo
Cleveland
PA.
Pittsburgh
Baltimore
Washington D.C.
Richmond
W.V.
VIRGINIA
OHIO
Columbus
INDIANA
Indianapolis
Cincinnati
St. Louis
KENTUCKY
Nashville
NORTH CAROLINA
Raleigh
Charlotte
SOUTH CAROLINA
Columbia
Charleston
TENNESSEE
Memphis
GEORGIA
Atlanta
ALABAMA
Montgomery
Birmingham
MISSISSIPPI
Jackson
Mississippi
Tallahassee
Jacksonville
FLORIDA
Tampa
Miami
LOUISIANA
Baton Rouge
New Orleans
ARKANSAS
Little Rock
MISSOURI
Kansas City
Topeka
KANSAS
OKLAHOMA
Oklahoma City
TEXAS
Dallas
Austin
Houston
El Paso
Rio Grande
NEW MEXICO
Santa Fe
Albuquerque
COLORADO
Denver
UTAH
Salt Lake City
NEVADA
Carson City
Las Vegas
CALIFORNIA
Sacramento
SAN FRANCISCO
San Jose
LOS ANGELES
San Diego
Colorado
ARIZONA
Phoenix
Tucson
Hermosillo
Culiacan
Monterrey
Guadalajara
MÉXICO
Puebla
Acapulco
Mérida
Guadalupe (Mex.)
Revilla Gigedo Is. (Mex.)
Tropic of Cancer
Bermuda (U.K.)
Nassau
BAHAMAS
Turks & Caicos Is. (U.K.)
Florida Str.
Havana
CUBA
Cayman Is. (U.K.)
JAMAICA
Kingston
HAITI
Port-au-Prince
DOMINICAN REP.
Santo Domingo
San Juan
PUERTO RICO (U.S.A.)
BELIZE
Belmopan
GUATEMALA
Guatemala
HONDURAS
Tegucigalpa
San Salvador
EL SALVADOR
NICARAGUA
L. Nicaragua
Managua
COSTA RICA
San José
PANAMA
Panamá
COLOMBIA
Barranquilla
Medellín
Maracaibo
VENEZUELA
Projection: Bonne
West from Greenwich
■ MÉXICO Capital Cities
CARTOGRAPHY BY PHILIP'S.

A
B
C
1
2
3
4
5
6
7
GREENLAND
(KALAALLIT NUNAAT)
(Den.)
ATLANTIC OCEAN
Angmagssalik
Kong Frederik VI's Kyst
Kap Farvel
Nanortalik
Julianehåb
Ivigtut
Frederikshåb
Fiskenæsset
Godthåb
(Nuuk)
Sukkertoppen
Søndre Strømfjord
Holsteinsborg
Christianshåb
Disko
Disko B.
Svartenhuk
Halvø
2850
3809
Baffin Bay
2136
Davis Strait
C. Dyer
Cape Dyer
Broughton Island
Qikiqtarjuaq
Cumberland Peninsula
Pangnirtung
Hoare B.
C. Mercy
Cumberland Sd.
Home B.
2591
C. Hewett
Clyde
Scott I.
Pond Inlet
Bylot I.
1890
Milne Inlet
Arctic Bay
Devon Island
Lancaster Sound
Brodeur Peninsula
Gulf of Boothia
Somerset Island
Prince of Wales Island
Franklin Str.
Boothia Peninsula
573
Spence Bay
Pelly Bay
King William I.
Gjoa Haven
Chantrey Inlet
Adelaide Pen.
Committee B.
Rae Isthmus
Repulse Bay
Wager B.
Wager Bay
Arctic Circle
NUNAVUT
Melville Peninsula
Igloolik Island
Fury & Hecla Str.
Sanirajak
Baffin Island
Prince Charles I.
Foxe Basin
Foxe Channel
C. Dorchester
Netilling L.
Amadjuak L.
Amadjuak
Foxe Penin.
Cape Dorset
Iqaluit
Frobisher Bay
Lake Harbour
Resolution I.
C. Chidley
Hudson Strait
Akpatok I.
Ungava Bay
Quaqtaq
Kangirsuk
Kangiqsujuaq
Salluit
Ivujivik
Digges Is.
Mansel I.
Coats I.
Southampton I.
Salliq
Bell Pen.
Roes Welcome Sd.
Ottawa Is.
Hudson Bay
257
Ungava Peninsula
Arnaud
Feuilles
Portland Promontory
Inukjuak
Kuujjuaq
Koksoak
Kaniapi
Mélèzes
Whale
George
Kangiqsualujjuaq
1676
Hebron
Nutak
Nain
Hopedale
NEWFOUNDLAND
C. Harrison
Indian Harbour
Chesterfield Inlet
Baker L.
Baker Lake
Rankin Inlet
Igluligaarjuk
Whale Cove
Arviat
C. Churchill
Churchill
30
40
50
60
70
80
100

1: 20 000 000
100 0 100 200 300 400 miles
100 0 100 200 300 400 500 600 km
Projection: Bonne
CARTOGRAPHY BY PHILIP'S.
West from Greenwich
C A N A D A
O N T A R I O
Q U E B E C
MANITOBA
NEW BRUNSWICK
NOVA SCOTIA
PR. EDWARD I.
Newfoundland
UNITED STATES
NEW YORK
PENNSYLVANIA
OHIO
INDIANA
ILLINOIS
WISCONSIN
MINNESOTA
IOWA
VERMONT
NEW HAMPSHIRE
MAINE
MASS.
NEW JERSEY
James Bay
Hudson Bay
Gulf of St. Lawrence
Lake Superior
L. Michigan
Lake Huron
Georgian Bay
L. Ontario
Lake Erie
L. of the Woods
Rainy L.
L. Nipigon
L. St. Joseph
Str. of Belle Isle
Cabot Str.
B. of Fundy
Sable I. (Nova Scotia)
St.-Pierre et Miquelon (Fr.)
Is. la Madeleine
Anticosti I.
MONTREAL
TORONTO
Québec
Ottawa
Boston
NEW YORK
DETROIT
CHICAGO
Milwaukee
Cleveland
Buffalo
Halifax
St. John's
Minneapolis
St. Paul
Duluth
Thunder Bay
Sault Ste. Marie
Sudbury
Timmins
Moosonee
Providence
Portland
Hamilton
London
Windsor
Toledo
Akron
Rochester
Syracuse
Albany
Sherbrooke
Trois-Rivières
Chicoutimi
Saint John
Moncton
Charlottetown
Sydney
Dartmouth
C. Race
C. Sable
C. Cod
C. Henrietta Maria
C. Tatnam
1 2 3 4
C D
40 50 70 80 90
m ft
200 600 1000 1500 2000 6000

A
B
C
10
9
8
7
6
5
4
Hudson Bay
Somerset Island
Prince of Wales Island
Boothia Peninsula
King William I.
Chantrey Inlet
Chesterfield Inlet
Baker L.
Baker Lake
Rankin Inlet
Whale Cove
Arviat
Churchill
Viscount Melville Sound
M'Clintock Channel
Queen Maud Gulf
Victoria Island
Prince Albert Pen.
Wollaston Pen.
Coronation Gulf
Bathurst Inlet
Kent Pen.
Banks Island
Amundsen Gulf
Dolphin & Union Str.
Coppermine
Kugluktuk
N U N A V U T
Arctic Circle
L. Garry
Back
Burnside
Clinton Colden L.
Dubawnt L.
Yathkyed L.
Thlewiaza
Nueltin L.
Kasba L.
Wholdaia L.
Lake Athabasca
Uranium City
Fort Chipewyan
Wollaston L.
N O R T H W E S T T E R R I T O R I E S
Great Slave L.
Yellowknife
Fort Reliance
Snowdrift
Fort Resolution
Fort Providence
Gt. Bear Lake
Franklin Mts.
Horton
C. Bathurst
Anderson
Tuktoyaktuk
Inuvik
Aklavik
Mackenzie
Ft. Good Hope
Norman Wells
Ft. Norman
Wrigley
Ft. Simpson
Liard
Fort Liard
Ft. Nelson
Peace
Wabiskaw
Ft. Vermilion
Caribou Mts.
Mackenzie Mountains
S. Nahanni
YUKON TERRITORY
Dawson
Klondike
Keno Hill
Mayo
Pelly
Yukon
Forty Mile
Old Crow
Ft. McPherson
Eagle
Stewart River
Ft. Selkirk
Carmacks
Big Salmon
Teslin
Watson Lake
Whitehorse
Kluane
Carcross
Atlin
Cassiar Mountains
Rocky Mountains
Churchill Pk. 3200
Dease L.
Telegraph Creek
Stikine
Skeena
Stewart
Hazelton
Babine L.
Prince Rupert
Kitimat
Queen Charlotte Is.
Dixon Entrance
Pr. of Wales I.
Ketchikan
Wrangell
Juneau
Skagway
St. Elias Mts.
Mt. Logan 6050
Mt. St. Elias 5489
Mt. Lucania 5226
Mt. Fairweather 4663
Yakutat
Chichagof I.
Baranof I.
Sitka
ALASKA
Fairbanks
Tanana
Big Delta
Mt. Sanford 4940
Wrangell Mts.
Talkeetna
Valdez
Cordova
Anchorage
Seward
Mt Gerdine 3840
PACIFIC OCEAN
3959

1: 15 000 000

100 0 100 200 300 400 miles

100 0 100 200 300 400 500 600 km

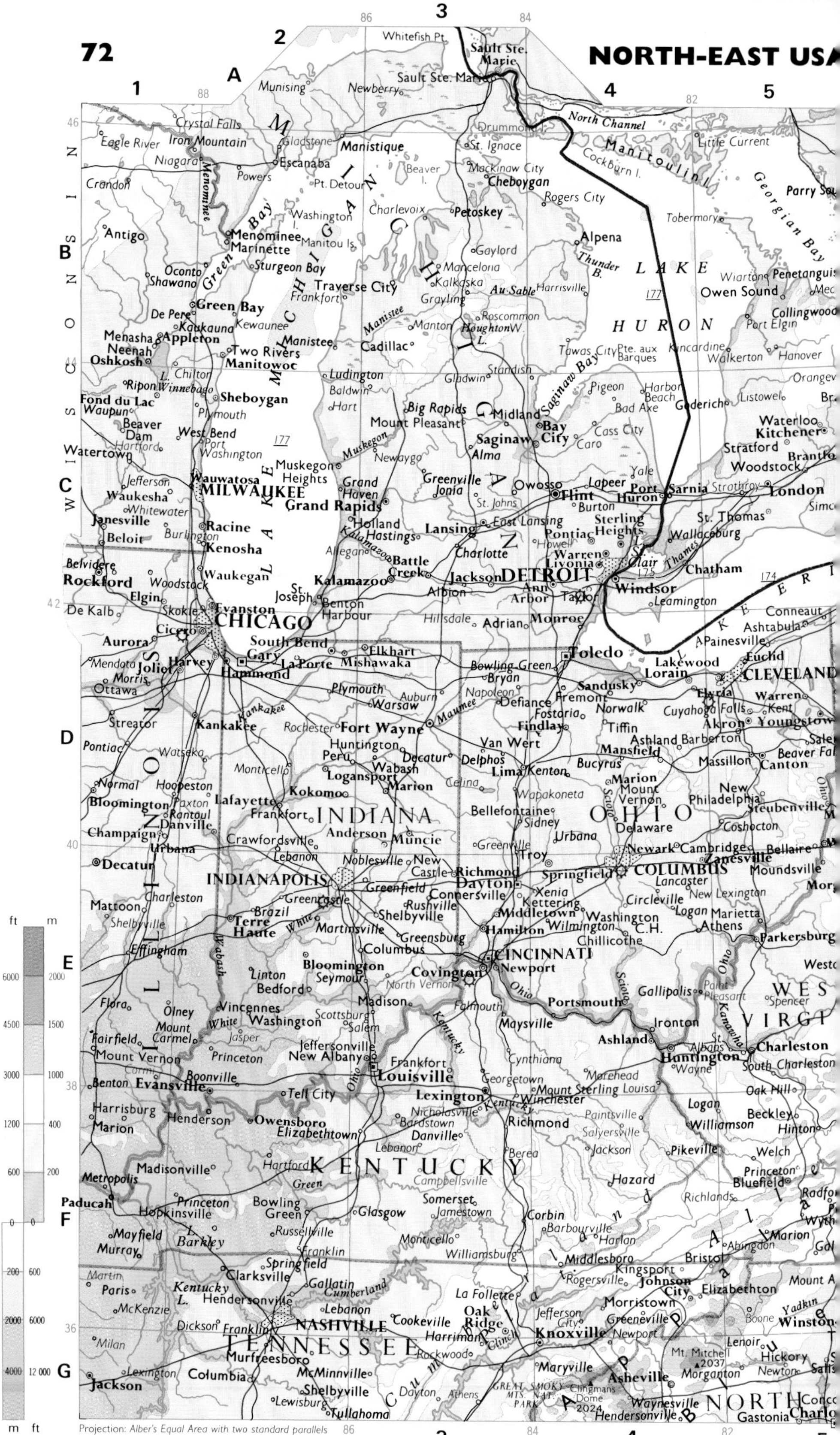

Projection: *Alber's Equal Area with two standard parallels*

1: 6 000 000

50 0 50 100 miles

50 0 50 100 150 km

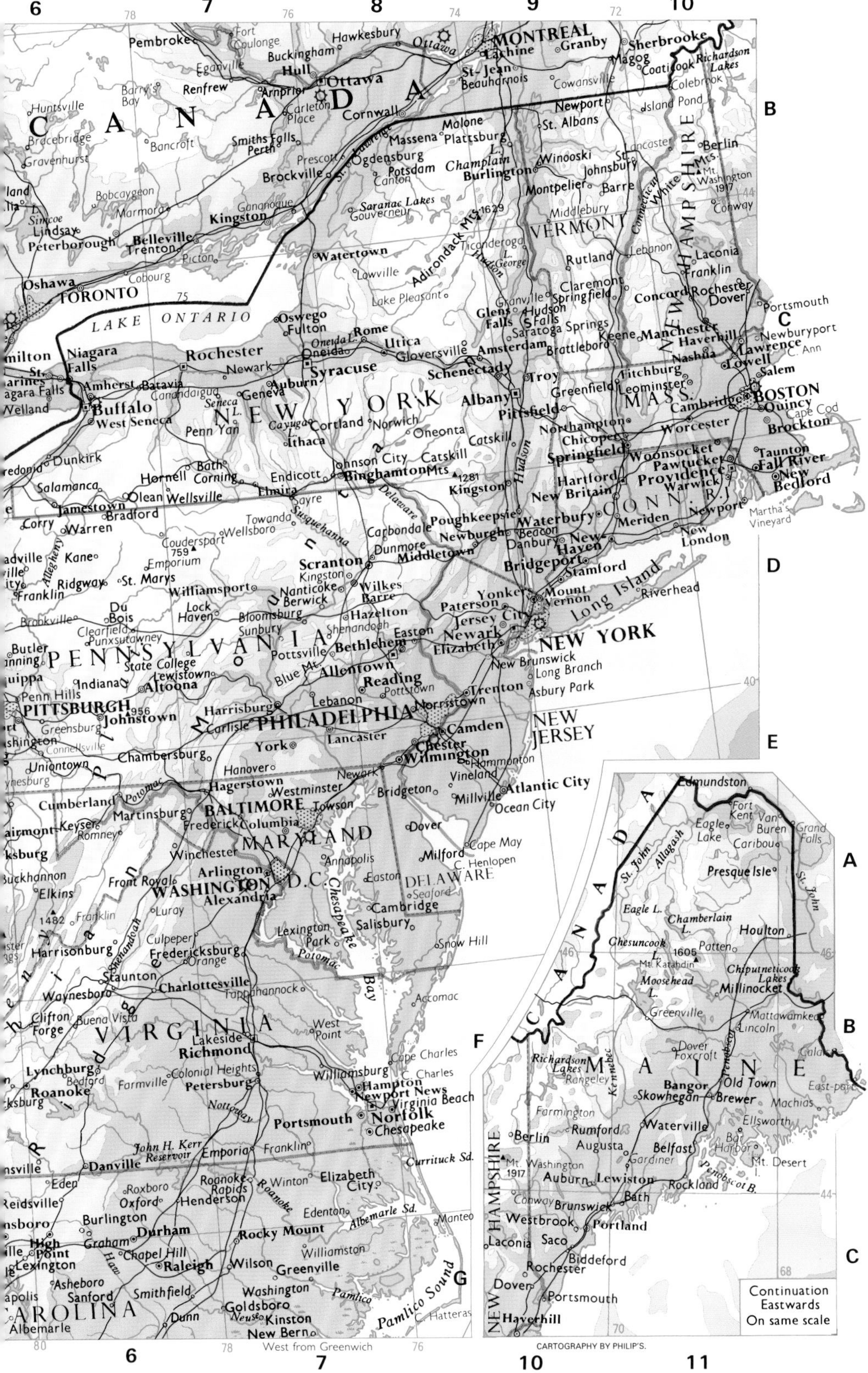

West from Greenwich

CARTOGRAPHY BY PHILIP'S.

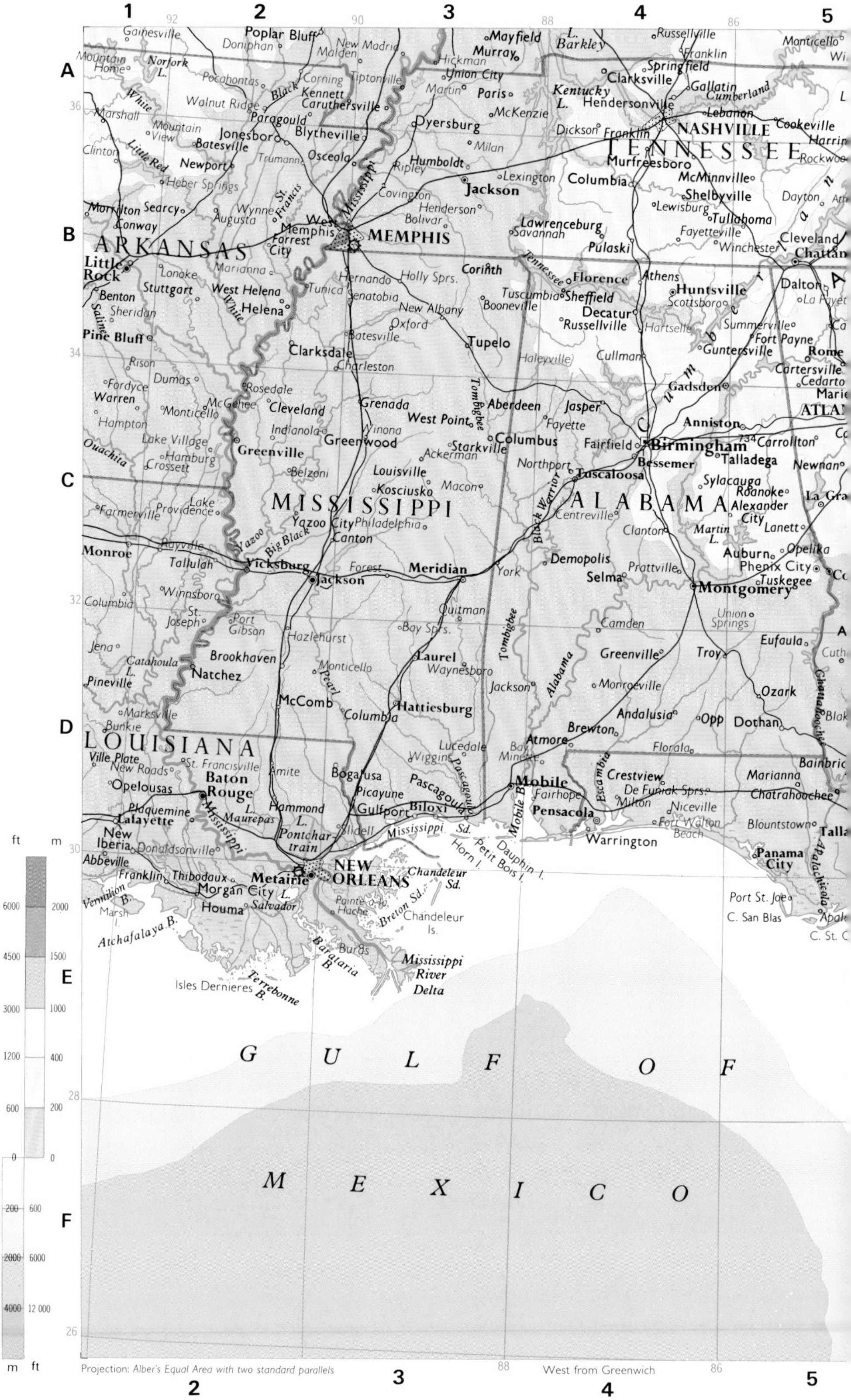
1
2
3
4
5
A
B
C
D
E
F
92
90
88
86
36
34
32
30
28
26
Gainesville
Poplar Bluff
Doniphan
New Madrid
Malden
Mayfield
Murray
L. Barkley
Russellville
Franklin
Monticello
Mountain Home
Norfork L.
Pocahontas
Corning
Tiptonville
Hickman
Union City
Kentucky L.
Clarksville
Springfield
Gallatin
Cumberland
Walnut Ridge
Black
Kennett
Caruthersville
Martin
Paris
Hendersonville
Lebanon
White
Marshall
Paragould
Dyersburg
McKenzie
Dickson
Franklin
NASHVILLE
Cookeville
Mountain View
Jonesboro
Blytheville
Batesville
TENNESSEE
Murfreesboro
Clinton
Little Red
Trumann
Osceola
Milan
Newport
Humboldt
Ripley
Lexington
Columbia
McMinnville
Rockwood
Heber Springs
Jackson
Shelbyville
St. Francis
Covington
Mississippi
Dayton
Morrilton
Searcy
Wynne
Henderson
Lewisburg
Tullahoma
Augusta
West Memphis
Bolivar
Conway
Forrest City
MEMPHIS
Lawrenceburg
Savannah
Fayetteville
Pulaski
Winchester
Cleveland
ARKANSAS
Little Rock
Lonoke
Marianna
Hernando
Holly Sprs.
Corinth
Tennessee
Florence
Athens
Dalton
Stuttgart
Tunica
Tuscumbia
Sheffield
Huntsville
Benton
West Helena
Helena
Senatobia
Booneville
Decatur
Scottsboro
Saline
Sheridan
New Albany
Russellville
Hartselle
Summerville
Oxford
Fort Payne
Pine Bluff
Batesville
Tupelo
Guntersville
Rome
Clarksdale
Haleyville
Cullman
Cartersville
Rison
Charleston
Dumas
Rosedale
Gadsden
Fordyce
Tombigbee
Warren
McGehee
Cleveland
Grenada
Aberdeen
Jasper
Monticello
Hampton
West Point
Fayette
Anniston
Winona
Indianola
Lake Village
Greenwood
Columbus
Fairfield
Birmingham
Carrollton
Ouachita
Starkville
Hamburg
Greenville
Ackerman
Talladega
Crossett
Bessemer
Belzoni
Northport
Tuscaloosa
Louisville
Newnan
Sylacauga
Kosciusko
Macon
Roanoke
MISSISSIPPI
ALABAMA
Farmerville
Providence
Lake
Black Warrior
Centreville
Alexander City
Yazoo City
Philadelphia
Martin L.
Lanett
Big Black
Clanton
Yazoo
Canton
Opelika
Monroe
Rayville
Auburn
Tallulah
Forest
Meridian
Demopolis
Phenix City
York
Prattville
Vicksburg
Jackson
Selma
Tuskegee
Winnsboro
Montgomery
Columbia
Quitman
St. Joseph
Port Gibson
Union Springs
Camden
Bay Sprs.
Hazlehurst
Eufaula
Jena
Tombigbee
Catahoula L.
Brookhaven
Laurel
Greenville
Troy
Natchez
Monticello
Waynesboro
Alabama
Pineville
Pearl
Jackson
Monroeville
Ozark
McComb
Hattiesburg
Marksville
Columbia
Andalusia
Opp
Dothan
Bunkie
Brewton
LOUISIANA
Lucedale
Atmore
Bay Minette
Florala
Ville Platte
St. Francisville
Wiggins
Pascagoula
Escambia
Crestview
Marianna
New Roads
Amite
Bogalusa
Opelousas
Baton Rouge
Picayune
Mobile
Fairhope
De Funiak Sprs.
Chattahoochee
Pascagoula
Milton
Niceville
Plaquemine
Hammond
Gulfport
Biloxi
Pensacola
Lafayette
L. Maurepas
Mississippi Sd.
Fort Walton Beach
Blountstown
New Iberia
Mississippi
L. Pontchartrain
Slidell
Mobile B.
Warrington
Donaldsonville
Horn I.
Petit Bois I.
Dauphin I.
Panama City
Abbeville
Apalachicola
Franklin
Thibodaux
Metairie
NEW ORLEANS
Chandeleur Sd.
Vermilion B.
Morgan City
Port St. Joe
Marsh I.
Houma
Salvador
Pointe à la Hache
Breton Sd.
C. San Blas
Chandeleur Is.
Atchafalaya B.
Burås
Barataria B.
Mississippi River Delta
Isles Dernieres
Terrebonne B.
GULF OF MEXICO
ft
m
6000
4500
3000
1200
600
0
2000
1500
1000
400
200
0
200
2000
4000
600
6000
12 000
m
ft
Projection: Alber's Equal Area with two standard parallels
West from Greenwich
2
3
4
5
88
86

1: 6 000 000

50 0 50 100 miles
50 0 50 100 150 km
6
7
8
9
10
84
82
80
78
76
A
B
C
D
E
F
G
36
34
32
30
28
26
Harlan
Middlesboro
Kingsport
Bristol
Abingdon
Marion
Galax
Martinsville
Danville
Emporia
Currituck Sd.
Rogersville
Johnson City
Elizabethton
Mount Airy
Reidsville
Eden
Roxboro
Oxford
Roanoke Rapids
Henderson
Roanoke
Winton
Elizabeth City
Edenton
Albemarle Sd.
Manteo
Roanoke I.
Morristown
Greeneville
Jefferson City
Knoxville
Newport
Boone
Yadkin
Winston-Salem
Greensboro
High Point
Burlington
Graham
Haw
Durham
Chapel Hill
Raleigh
Rocky Mount
Wilson
Williamston
Greenville
Pamlico Sound
Thomasville
Lexington
Lenoir
Mt. Mitchell
2037
Hickory
Statesville
Salisbury
Morganton
Newton
Asheboro
Sanford
Smithfield
Washington
Pamlico
Maryville
Asheville
Clingmans Dome
2024
SMOKY NAT. PARK
Waynesville
Hendersonville
Brevard
Kannapolis
Concord
Gastonia
Shelby
Charlotte
Albemarle
NORTH CAROLINA
Goldsboro
Neuse
Kinston
New Bern
C. Hatteras
Southern Pines
Dunn
Fayetteville
Clinton
Jacksonville
Raleigh B.
Murphy
Spartanburg
Gaffney
Rock Hill
Monroe
Beaufort
C. Lookout
Greenville
Easley
Brasstown Bald
1458
Seneca
Union
Chester
Lancaster
Laurinburg
Cape Fear
Lumberton
Onslow B.
Toccoa
Anderson
Belton
Laurens
Bennettsville
Hartsville
Dillon
Darlington
Whiteville
Wilmington
Hartwell
Gainesville
Greenwood
Saluda
Newberry
Broad
Camden
Florence
Mullins
Marion
Elberton
Abbeville
L. Murray
Columbia
Sumter
Lake City
Conway
Southport
C. Fear
Buford
Athens
Clark Hill L.
Lawrenceville
SOUTH CAROLINA
Myrtle Beach
Kingstree
Manning
Covington
Orangeburg
Augusta
Aiken
L. Marion
Bamberg
L. Moultrie
Georgetown
Griffin
Sparta
Savannah
GEORGIA
Milledgeville
Waynesboro
Summerville
Cooper
North Charleston
Walterboro
Charleston
Mt. Pleasant
Hampton
Millen
Macon
Warner Robins
Swainsboro
Ogeechee
Ridgeland
Combahee
Dublin
Beaufort
Perry
Cochran
Oconee
Statesboro
Parris I.
Vidalia
Eastman
Ocmulgee
Savannah
Cordele
Hinesville
Hazlehurst
Altamaha
Ossabaw I.
Fitzgerald
Baxley
St. Catherines I.
Jesup
Sylvester
Tifton
Sapelo I.
Douglas
Brunswick
Waycross
Adel
Satilla
Cairo
Valdosta
Okefenokee Swamp
Folkston
Cumberland I.
Quitman
Fernandina Beach
ATLANTIC
Monticello
Madison
Jasper
St. Johns
Jacksonville Beach
Live Oak
JACKSONVILLE
Lake City
Suwannee
Perry
Starke
Green Cove Springs
St. Augustine
High Springs
Palatka
Gainesville
FLORIDA
Cross City
Bunnell
L. George
Ormond Beach
Ocala
Daytona Beach
New Smyrna Beach
OCEAN
De Land
Eustis
Crystal River
Sanford
Inverness
Leesburg
Titusville
Winter Park
Orlando
C. Canaveral
Brooksville
Cocoa
Merritt Island
Dade City
Kissimmee
Melbourne
Tarpon Springs
Lakeland
Haines City
Winter Haven
Indian River
Clearwater
TAMPA
Largo
Bartow
St. Petersburg
Tampa Bay
Vero Beach
Kissimmee
Fort Pierce
Bradenton
Sebring
L. Istokpoga
Grand Cays
Sarasota
Okeechobee
Stuart
Arcadia
L. Okeechobee
Little Abaco I.
Gt. Guana Cay
Punta Gorda
Pahokee
Settlement Pt.
Hope Town
La Belle
Belle Glade
West Palm Beach
Charlotte Harb.
Fort Myers
Cape Coral
Grand Bahama I.
Freeport
Great Abaco I.
Delray Beach
Immokalee
Boca Raton
Pompano Beach
BAHAMAS
Naples
Big Cypress Swamp
Fort Lauderdale
Hollywood
Everglades
Carol City
Miami Beach
Hialeah
MIAMI
EVERGLADES NAT. PARK
Biscayne B.
Homestead
CARTOGRAPHY BY PHILIP'S.

Projection: Alber's Equal Area with two standard parallels

West from Greenwich

1: 6 000 000
50 0 50 100 miles
50 0 50 100 150 km
7 8 9 10 11
96 94 92 90 88
A
B
C
D
E
F
CANADA
Lake of the Woods
Roseau
Warroad
Rainy River
Baudette
Rainy
International Falls
Rainy Lake
Fort Frances
Atikokan
Lac la Croix
Thunder Bay
183
48
Isle Royale
Big Fork
Little Fork
Thief River Falls
Upper Red L.
Lower Red L.
Red Lake Falls
Crookston
Vermilion L.
Grand Marais
LAKE SUPERIOR
Copper Harbor
Keweenaw Pt.
Keweenaw Pen.
Keweenaw B.
Hancock
Houghton
Fosston
Bagley
Bemidji
Mahnomen
L. Winnibigoshish
Cass Lake
Leech L.
Walker
Hibbing
Virginia
Eveleth
Grand Rapids
St. Louis
Two Harbors
Apostle Is.
Ontonagon
604
L'Anse
Ishpeming
Marquette
Negaunee
Hawley
Moorhead
Detroit Lakes
Park Rapids
Cloquet
Duluth
Superior
Washburn
Ashland
Bessemer
Hurley
Ironwood
MINNESOTA
MICHIGAN
Perham
Wadena
Staples
Aitkin
Brainerd
Mille Lacs L.
Moose Lake
Crystal Falls
Fergus Falls
Little Falls
Hayward
Park Falls
Eagle River
Iron Mountain
Niagara
Powers
Alexandria
Mora
Milaca
Pine City
Grantsburg
Spooner
Phillips
Rhinelander
Crandon
Menominee
Sauk Rapids
Cumberland
Rice Lake
Ladysmith
Tomahawk
Wisconsin
Glenwood
Morris
St. Cloud
Mississippi
Cambridge
Paynesville
St. Croix
Cornell
Medford
Merrill
Antigo
Menominee
Green Bay
Marinette
Anoka
Wausau
Oconto
Sturgeon Bay
Litchfield
Willmar
Montevideo
MINNEAPOLIS
St. Paul
Stillwater
Hudson
Chippewa Falls
Menomonie
WISCONSIN
Shawano
Green Bay
Granite Falls
Hutchinson
Glencoe
Bloomington
Hastings
Chippewa
Eau Claire
Marshfield
Stevens Point
De Pere
Kaukauna
Kewaunee
Canby
Redwood Falls
Red Wing
Lake City
Alma
Whitehall
Wisconsin Rapids
Waupaca
Menasha
Neenah
Appleton
Two Rivers
Manitowoc
Marshall
New Ulm
Northfield
St. Peter
Faribault
Black River Falls
Wautoma
Oshkosh
L. Chilton
Mankato
Owatonna
Winona
Black
Sparta
Tomah
Ripon
Winnebago
Sheboygan
Waseca
Rochester
Onalaska
Montello
Mauston
Fond du Lac
Waupun
Plymouth
Pipestone
Windom
St. James
La Crosse
Preston
Viroqua
Reedsburg
Baraboo
Portage
Beaver Dam
West Bend
Port Washington
LAKE MICHIGAN
Worthington
Jackson
Fairmont
Albert Lea
Austin
Richland Center
Hartford
Estherville
Northwood
Decorah
Waukon
Wisconsin
Watertown
Wauwatosa
MILWAUKEE
Sibley
Forest City
Osage
Charles City
Prairie du Chien
Madison
Jefferson
Spencer
Emmetsburg
Mason City
New Hampton
Waukesha
Whitewater
Racine
Sheldon
Algona
Garner
Dodgeville
Lancaster
Darlington
Janesville
Burlington
Kenosha
Le Mars
Cherokee
Pocahontas
Clarion
Hampton
Waverly
Oelwein
Monroe
Beloit
Waukegan
Storm Lake
Sioux City
Fort Dodge
Webster City
Iowa Falls
Cedar Falls
Independence
Dubuque
Freeport
Rockford
Woodstock
Belvidere
Elgin
Skokie
Evanston
CHICAGO
Little Sioux
Sac City
Ida Grove
IOWA
Waterloo
Wapsipinicon
Vinton
Marion
Maquoketa
De Kalb
Dixon
Cicero
Carroll
Boone
Marshalltown
Cedar Rapids
Clinton
Denison
Jefferson
Ames
Cedar
Tipton
Sterling
Aurora
Harvey
Grinnell
Marengo
Mendota
Joliet
Audubon
Perry
Newton
Iowa City
Davenport
Moline
Princeton
Morris
Harlan
W. Des Moines
Des Moines
L. Red Rock
Montezuma
Muscatine
Rock Island
Ottawa
Fremont
Omaha
Atlantic
Winterset
Indianola
Pella
Washington
Kewanee
Peru
Streator
Kankakee
Council Bluffs
Greenfield
Knoxville
Des Moines
Oskaloosa
Ottumwa
Aledo
Galesburg
Chillicothe
Pontiac
Plattsmouth
Glenwood
Red Oak
Creston
Osceola
Albia
Fairfield
Mt. Pleasant
Monmouth
Illinois
Corning
Burlington
Peoria
Pekin
Normal
Paxton
Lincoln
Shenandoah
Bloomfield
Nebraska City
Clarinda
Bedford
Leon
Centerville
Fort Madison
Canton
Bloomington
Macomb
Keokuk
Rantoul
Auburn
Beatrice
Rockport
Grant City
Bethany
Thompson
Princeton
Unionville
Kahoka
ILLINOIS
Champaign
Missouri
Milan
Kirksville
Chariton
Edina
Rushville
Lincoln
Pawnee City
Falls City
Trenton
Beardstown
Decatur
Hiawatha
Savannah
Palmyra
Quincy
Springfield
Marysville
Troy
Chillicothe
Brookfield
Hannibal
Jacksonville
Grand
Macon
Taylorville
Pana
Mattoon
Shelbyville
St. Joseph
Illinois
Carrollton
Holton
Atchison
Excelsior Sprs.
Carrollton
Moberly
Carlinville
Litchfield
Effingham
Leavenworth
Richmond
Fayette
Jerseyville
Kansas City
Lexington
Independence
Marshall
Mexico
Vandalia
Kansas
Topeka
Kansas City
Boonville
Columbia
Fulton
Troy
St. Charles
Alton
Granite City
Greenville
Lawrence
Olathe
Missouri
ST. LOUIS
E. St. Louis
Flora
Centralia
Council Grove
Ottawa
Warrensburg
Sedalia
Jefferson City
Hermann
Belleville
Fairfield
Harrisonville
Union
Waterloo
Mount Vernon
Paola
MISSOURI
Emporia
Clinton
Lake of the Ozarks
Osage
Sullivan
De Soto
Ste. Genevieve
Pinckneyville
Du Quoin
Benton
Burlington
Garnett
Butler
96 94 92
CARTOGRAPHY BY PHILIP'S.

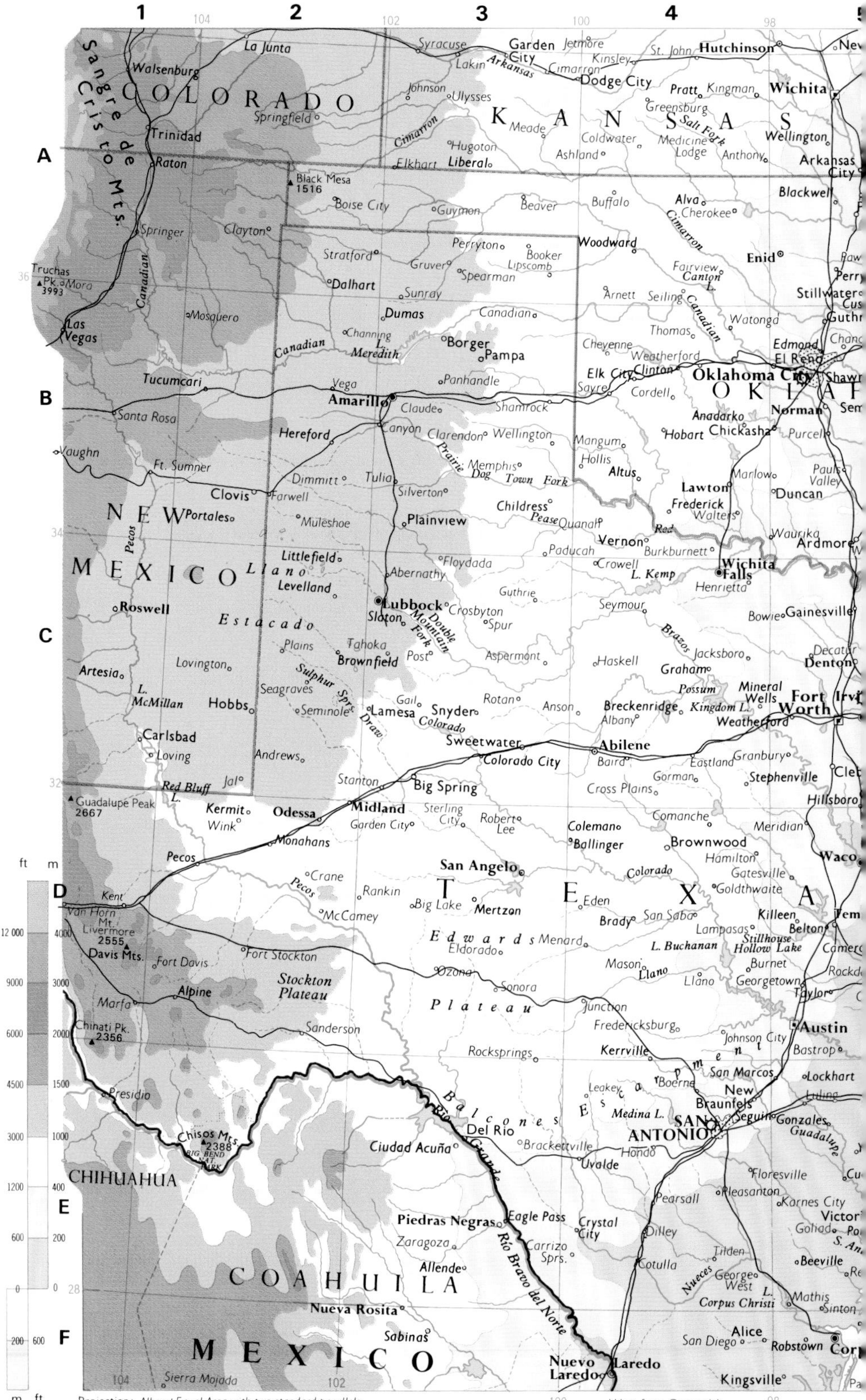

Projection: *Albers' Equal Area with two standard parallels*
100 West from Greenwich 98

2 3 4

1: 6 000 000

CARTOGRAPHY BY PHILIP'S.

miles
km
MISSOURI
ARKANSAS
LOUISIANA
MISSISSIPPI
TENNESSEE
MEMPHIS
NEW ORLEANS
HOUSTON
DALLAS
GULF OF MEXICO
MEXICO
Little Rock
Springfield
Shreveport
Jackson
Baton Rouge
Continuation Southwards on same scale

Projection: Alber's Equal Area with two standard parallels

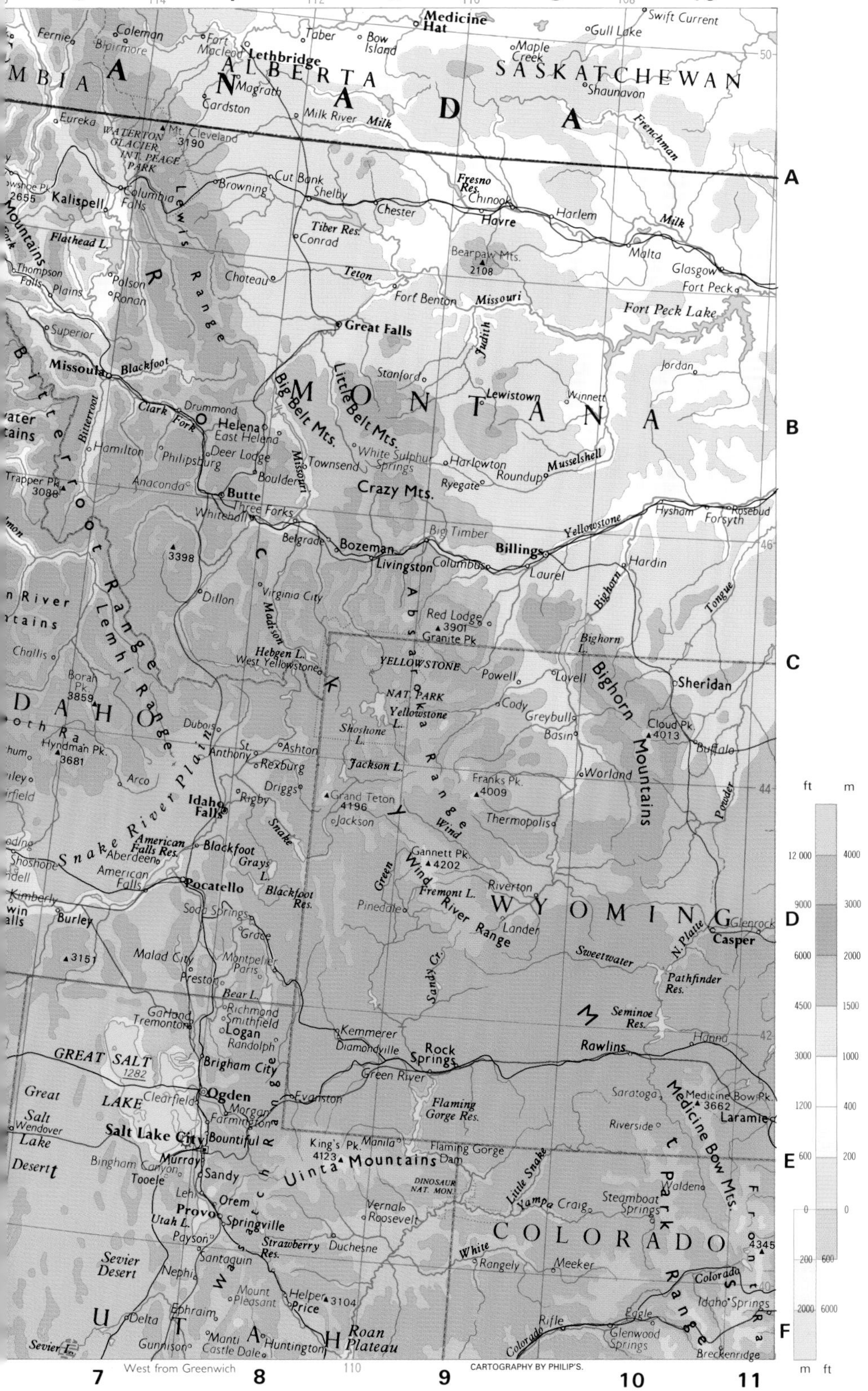
1: 6 000 000
50 0 50 100 miles
50 0 50 100 150 km
6 7 8 9 10
114 112 110 108
A B C D E F
7 8 9 10 11
CANADA
ALBERTA
SASKATCHEWAN
MONTANA
IDAHO
WYOMING
UTAH
COLORADO
ROCKY MOUNTAINS
Medicine Hat
Swift Current
Gull Lake
Maple Creek
Shaunavon
Lethbridge
Taber
Bow Island
Fort Macleod
Magrath
Cardston
Milk River
Milk
Frenchman
Fernie
Coleman
Blairmore
Eureka
WATERTON GLACIER INT. PEACE PARK
Mt. Cleveland 3190
Cut Bank
Shelby
Browning
Columbia Falls
Kalispell
Lewis Range
Fresno Res.
Chinook
Havre
Harlem
Chester
Tiber Res.
Conrad
Bearpaw Mts.
2108
Malta
Glasgow
Fort Peck
Fort Peck Lake
Flathead L.
Thompson Falls
Plains
Polson
Ronan
Chateau
Teton
Fort Benton
Missouri
Superior
Great Falls
Judith
Jordan
Missoula
Blackfoot
Stanford
Lewistown
Winnett
Bitterroot Range
Bitterroot
Clark Fork
Drummond
Helena
East Helena
Big Belt Mts.
Little Belt Mts.
Hamilton
Philipsburg
Deer Lodge
Townsend
White Sulphur Springs
Harlowton
Roundup
Musselshell
Trapper Pk. 3096
Anaconda
Boulder
Butte
Crazy Mts.
Ryegate
Three Forks
Whitehall
Belgrade
Bozeman
Livingston
Big Timber
Columbus
Billings
Laurel
Yellowstone
Hysham
Forsyth
Rosebud
Hardin
3398
Dillon
Virginia City
Madison
Absaroka Range
Red Lodge
Granite Pk 3901
Bighorn
Tongue
Lemhi Range
Challis
Hebgen L.
West Yellowstone
YELLOWSTONE NAT. PARK
Yellowstone L.
Shoshone L.
Powell
Lovell
Bighorn L.
Sheridan
Borah Pk. 3859
Cody
Greybull
Basin
Bighorn Mountains
Cloud Pk. 4013
Buffalo
Dubois
St. Anthony
Ashton
Rexburg
Hyndman Pk. 3681
Arco
Jackson L.
Driggs
Rigby
Idaho Falls
Snake River Plain
Franks Pk. 4009
Worland
Grand Teton 4196
Jackson
Thermopolis
Powder
Snake
American Falls Res.
Aberdeen
Blackfoot
American Falls
Shoshone
Grays L.
Gannett Pk. 4202
Wind River Range
Green
Pocatello
Blackfoot Res.
Fremont L.
Riverton
Kimberly
Burley
Soda Springs
Pinedale
Lander
Grace
N. Platte
Glenrock
Casper
3151
Malad City
Montpelier
Paris
Preston
Sandy Cr.
Sweetwater
Pathfinder Res.
Bear L.
Seminoe Res.
Garland
Tremonton
Richmond
Smithfield
Logan
Randolph
Kemmerer
Diamondville
Rock Springs
Rawlins
Hanna
GREAT SALT LAKE
1282
Brigham City
Green River
Great Salt Lake Desert
Clearfield
Ogden
Evanston
Flaming Gorge Res.
Saratoga
Medicine Bow Pk. 3662
Medicine Bow Mts.
Laramie
Wendover
Morgan
Farmington
Salt Lake City
Bountiful
Riverside
Wasatch Range
King's Pk. 4123
Manila
Flaming Gorge Dam
Uinta Mountains
Murray
Bingham Canyon
Sandy
Tooele
Lehi
DINOSAUR NAT. MON.
Little Snake
Walden
Orem
Provo
Utah L.
Springville
Vernal
Roosevelt
Yampa
Craig
Steamboat Springs
Park Range
Front Range
4345
Payson
Strawberry Res.
Duchesne
White
Rangely
Meeker
Sevier Desert
Santaquin
Nephi
Colorado
Mount Pleasant
Helper
3104
Price
Idaho Springs
Ephraim
Delta
Eagle
Rifle
Glenwood Springs
Sevier L.
Manti
Gunnison
Castle Dale
Huntington
Roan Plateau
Breckenridge
West from Greenwich
110
ft m
12 000 4000
9000 3000
6000 2000
4500 1500
3000 1000
1200 400
600 200
0 0
200 600
2000 6000
m ft

CARTOGRAPHY BY PHILIP'S.

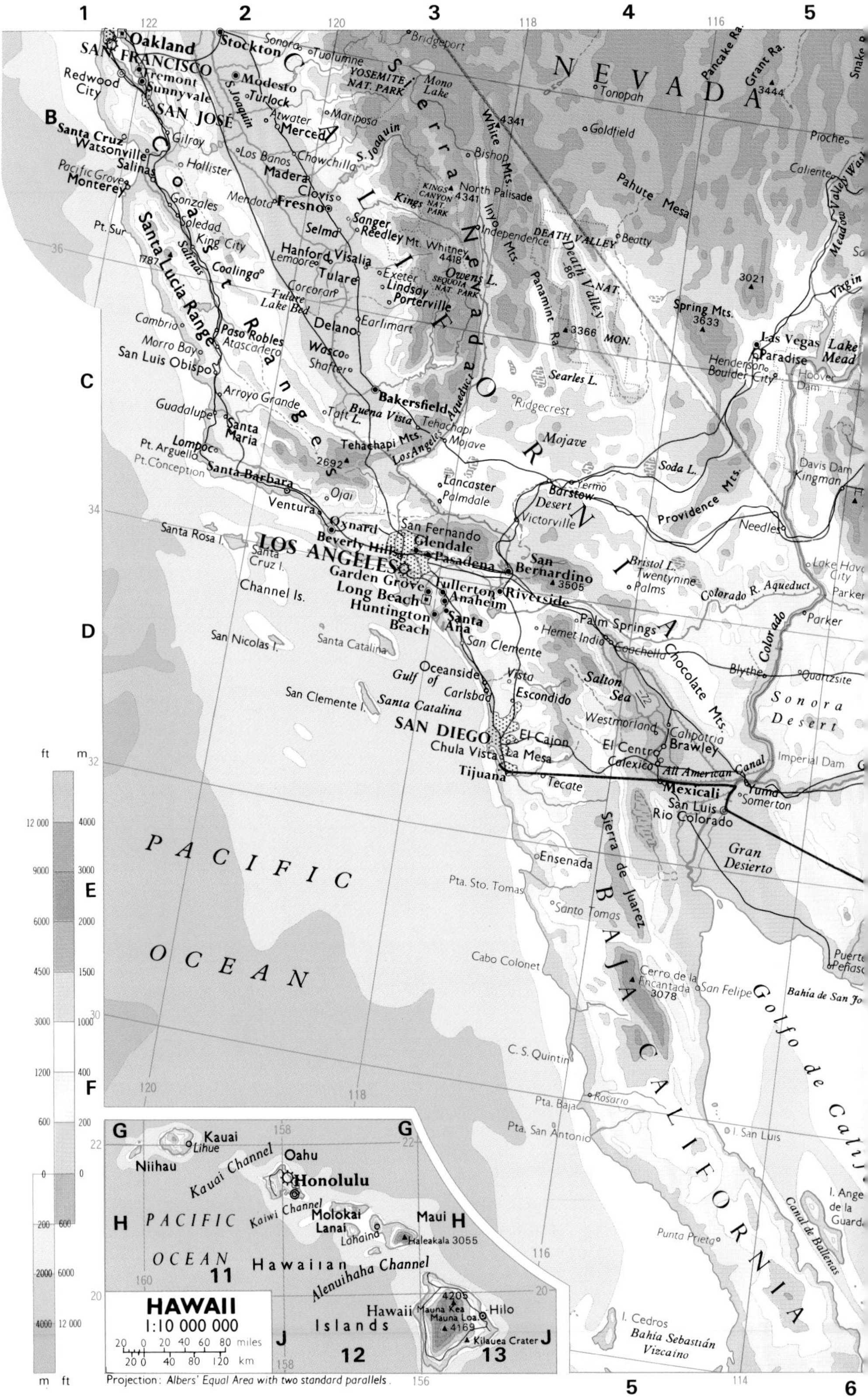
1
2
3
4
5
NEVADA
CALIFORNIA
Sierra Nevada
Coast Ranges
Santa Lucia Range
Oakland
SAN FRANCISCO
Redwood City
Fremont
Sunnyvale
SAN JOSÉ
Stockton
Sonora
Tuolumne
Modesto
Turlock
Atwater
Merced
Mariposa
YOSEMITE NAT. PARK
Mono Lake
Bridgeport
Tonopah
Goldfield
Pancake Ra.
Grant Ra.
3444
Santa Cruz
Watsonville
Gilroy
Hollister
Salinas
Pacific Grove
Monterey
Los Banos
Chowchilla
Madera
Clovis
Fresno
Mendota
S. Joaquin
White Mts.
4341
Bishop
North Palisade
KINGS CANYON NAT. PARK
Inyo Mts.
Independence
Pahute Mesa
Pioche
Caliente
Meadow Valley Wash
DEATH VALLEY
Death Valley
Beatty
Gonzales
Soledad
King City
Pt. Sur
Salinas
Coalinga
Sanger
Reedley
Selma
Hanford
Lemoore
Visalia
Tulare
Mt. Whitney 4418
Exeter
Lindsay
Porterville
SEQUOIA NAT. PARK
Owens L.
Panamint Ra.
-86
NAT. MON.
3366
Spring Mts. 3633
3021
Virgin
1787
Corcoran
Tulare Lake Bed
Delano
Earlimart
Cambria
Paso Robles
Atascadero
Morro Bay
San Luis Obispo
Wasco
Shafter
Las Vegas
Paradise
Lake Mead
Henderson
Boulder City
Hoover Dam
Searles L.
Arroyo Grande
Bakersfield
Buena Vista
Taft
Ridgecrest
Guadalupe
Santa Maria
Tehachapi
Tehachapi Mts.
Mojave
Los Angeles Aqueduct
Lompoc
Pt. Arguello
Pt. Conception
2692
Santa Barbara
Lancaster
Palmdale
Soda L.
Providence Mts.
Yermo
Barstow
Davis Dam
Kingman
Ojai
Ventura
Oxnard
Desert
Victorville
Needles
Santa Rosa I.
Santa Cruz I.
San Fernando
Glendale
Beverly Hills
LOS ANGELES
Pasadena
San Bernardino
3505
Bristol L.
Twentynine Palms
Lake Havasu City
Parker
Channel Is.
Garden Grove
Long Beach
Fullerton
Anaheim
Riverside
Colorado R. Aqueduct
Huntington Beach
Santa Ana
Palm Springs
Hemet
Indio
Coachella
San Nicolas I.
Santa Catalina
San Clemente
Chocolate Mts.
Colorado
Blythe
Quartzsite
Oceanside
Gulf of Santa Catalina
Vista
Carlsbad
Escondido
Salton Sea
Sonora Desert
San Clemente I.
-72
Westmorland
SAN DIEGO
El Cajon
Chula Vista
La Mesa
Calipatria
Brawley
El Centro
Calexico
All American Canal
Imperial Dam
Tijuana
Tecate
Mexicali
Yuma
Somerton
San Luis Rio Colorado
Gran Desierto
PACIFIC OCEAN
Ensenada
Pta. Sto. Tomas
Santo Tomas
Sierra de Juárez
BAJA CALIFORNIA
Cabo Colonet
Cerro de la Encantada 3078
San Felipe
Golfo de California
Puerto Peñasco
Bahía de San Jorge
C. S. Quintin
Pta. Baja
Rosario
Pta. San Antonio
I. San Luis
I. Angel de la Guarda
Canal de Ballenas
Punta Prieta
I. Cedros
Bahía Sebastián Vizcaino
122
120
118
116
114
36
34
32
30
ft
m
12 000
4000
9000
3000
6000
2000
4500
1500
3000
1000
1200
400
600
200
0
0
200
600
2000
6000
4000
12 000
m
ft
B
C
D
E
F
G
H
J
5
6
Kauai
Lihue
Niihau
Kauai Channel
Oahu
Honolulu
PACIFIC OCEAN
Kaiwi Channel
Molokai
Lanai
Maui
Lahaina
Haleakala 3055
Hawaiian Islands
Alenuihaha Channel
Hawaii
Mauna Kea 4205
Mauna Loa 4169
Hilo
Kilauea Crater
11
12
13
158
156
160
22
20
HAWAII
1:10 000 000
0 20 40 60 80 miles
0 20 40 80 120 km

Projection: Albers' Equal Area with two standard parallels.

1: 6 000 000

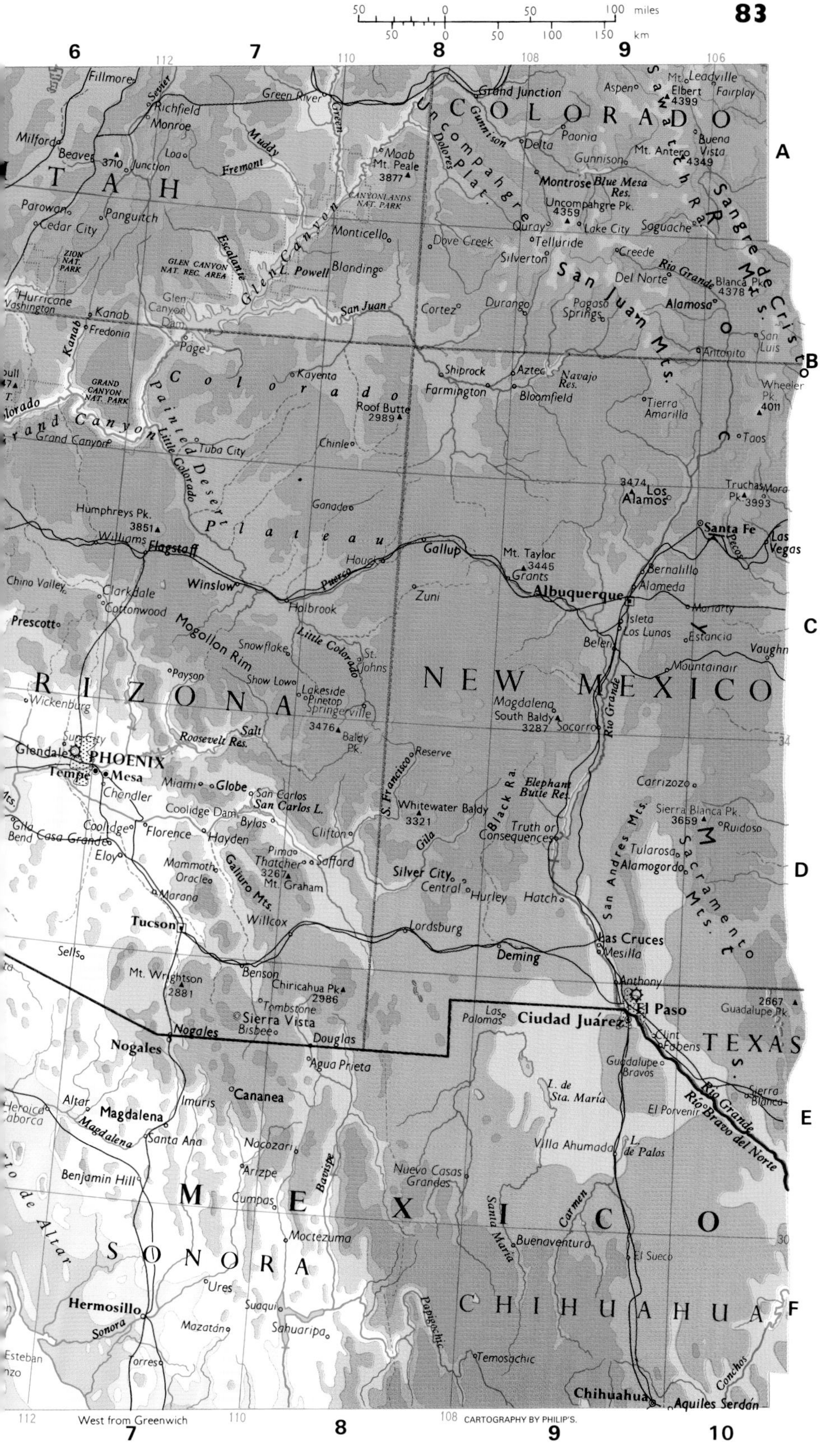

50 0 50 100 miles
50 0 50 100 150 km
6 7 8 9
112 110 108 106
A B C D E F
UTAH
COLORADO
ARIZONA
NEW MEXICO
TEXAS
MEXICO
SONORA
CHIHUAHUA
Fillmore
Richfield
Monroe
Milford
Beaver
3710
Junction
Loa
Fremont
Muddy
Green River
Green
Grand Junction
Gunnison
Uncompahgre Plat.
Dolores
Moab
Mt. Peale
3877
CANYONLANDS NAT. PARK
Parowan
Panguitch
Cedar City
ZION NAT. PARK
GLEN CANYON NAT. REC. AREA
Escalante
Glen Canyon
L. Powell
Monticello
Blanding
Dove Creek
Hurricane
Washington
Kanab
Fredonia
Glen Canyon Dam
Page
San Juan
Cortez
Durango
Aspen
Mt. Elbert
4399
Leadville
Fairplay
Paonia
Delta
Gunnison
Mt. Antero
4349
Buena Vista
Montrose
Blue Mesa Res.
Uncompahgre Pk.
4359
Ouray
Lake City
Saguache
Telluride
Silverton
Creede
Rio Grande
Del Norte
San Juan Mts.
Pagosa Springs
Alamosa
Blanca Pk.
4378
Sawatch Ra.
Sangre de Cristo Mts.
San Luis
Antonito
GRAND CANYON NAT. PARK
Grand Canyon
Colorado Plateau
Painted Desert
Little Colorado
Kayenta
Shiprock
Farmington
Aztec
Bloomfield
Navajo Res.
Roof Butte
2989
Tuba City
Chinle
Wheeler Pk.
4011
Tierra Amarilla
Taos
3474
Los Alamos
Truchas Pk.
3993
Mora
Humphreys Pk.
3851
Williams
Flagstaff
Ganado
Houck
Gallup
Puerco
Mt. Taylor
3445
Grants
Santa Fe
Pecos
Las Vegas
Bernalillo
Alameda
Albuquerque
Chino Valley
Clarkdale
Cottonwood
Winslow
Holbrook
Zuni
Prescott
Mogollon Rim
Snowflake
Little Colorado
St. Johns
Isleta
Los Lunas
Belen
Moriarty
Estancia
Vaughn
Mountainair
Payson
Show Low
Lakeside
Pinetop
Springerville
Wickenburg
3476
Baldy Pk.
Magdalena
South Baldy
3287
Socorro
Rio Grande
Salt
Roosevelt Res.
Sun City
Glendale
PHOENIX
Tempe
Mesa
Chandler
Reserve
S. Francisco
Miami
Globe
San Carlos
San Carlos L.
Coolidge Dam
Black Ra.
Elephant Butte Res.
Carrizozo
Sierra Blanca Pk.
3659
Ruidoso
Gila Bend
Casa Grande
Coolidge
Florence
Hayden
Bylas
Clifton
Whitewater Baldy
3321
Gila
Truth or Consequences
San Andres Mts.
Tularosa
Alamogordo
Sacramento Mts.
Eloy
Mammoth
Oracle
Galiuro Mts.
Pima
Thatcher
Safford
3267
Mt. Graham
Silver City
Central
Hurley
Hatch
Marana
Tucson
Willcox
Lordsburg
Las Cruces
Mesilla
Deming
Sells
Benson
Mt. Wrightson
2881
Chiricahua Pk.
2986
Tombstone
Sierra Vista
Bisbee
Douglas
Nogales
Anthony
El Paso
Las Palomas
Ciudad Juárez
2667
Guadalupe Pk.
Clint
Fabens
Guadalupe Bravos
Agua Prieta
Cananea
Altar
Heroica Caborca
Magdalena
Imuris
Santa Ana
Nacozari
Arizpe
Bavispe
L. de Sta. María
El Porvenir
Sierra Blanca
Rio Grande
Río Bravo del Norte
Villa Ahumada
L. de Palos
Benjamin Hill
Nuevo Casas Grandes
Cumpas
Santa María
Carmen
Moctezuma
Buenaventura
El Sueco
Ures
Hermosillo
Sonora
Suaqui
Mazatán
Sahuaripa
Papigochic
Temosachic
Torres
Esteban
Chihuahua
Aquiles Serdán
Conchos
Río de Altar
112 West from Greenwich 110 108
CARTOGRAPHY BY PHILIP'S.
7 8 9 10

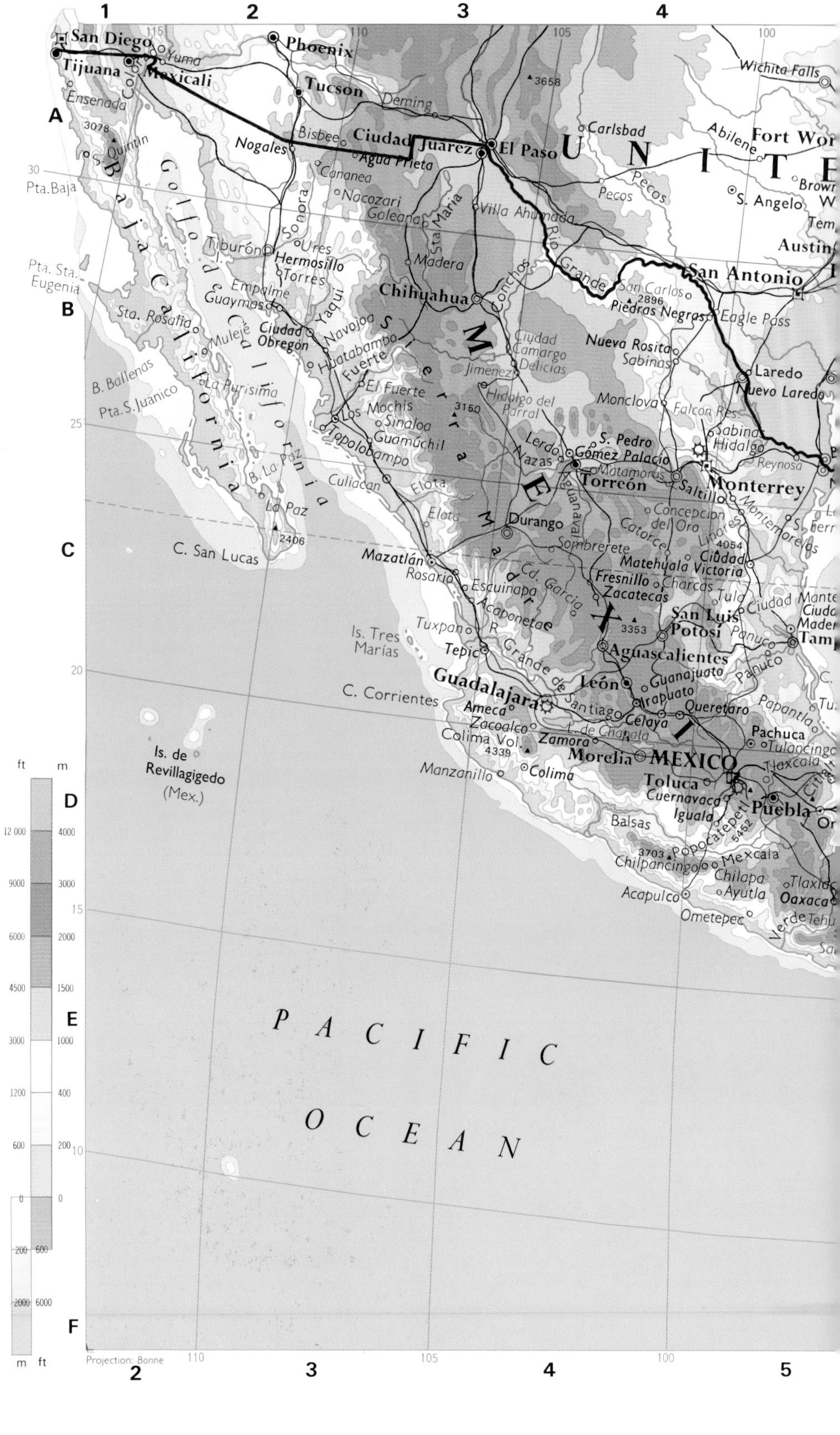
1
2
3
4
A
B
C
D
E
F
5
San Diego
Tijuana
Ensenada
Mexicali
Yuma
Phoenix
Tucson
Deming
Nogales
Bisbee
Ciudad Juarez
Agua Prieta
El Paso
Carlsbad
Wichita Falls
Abilene
Fort Wor
Pecos
S. Angelo
Austin
San Antonio
U N I T E
3658
3078
S. Quintin
Pta. Baja
Pta. Sta. Eugenia
Baja California
Golfo de California
Cananea
Nacozari
Galeana
Villa Ahumada
Sta Maria
Madera
Tiburón
Ures
Hermosillo
Torres
Sonora
Empalme
Guaymas
Yaqui
Chihuahua
Conchos
Rio Grande
San Carlos
2896
Piedras Negras
Eagle Pass
Sta. Rosalia
Mulejé
Ciudad Obregón
Navojoa
Huatabampo
Fuerte
Ciudad Camargo
Delicias
Jimenez
Nueva Rosita
Sabinas
Laredo
Nuevo Laredo
B. Ballenas
Pta. S. Juanico
La Purisima
El Fuerte
Los Mochis
Sinaloa
3150
Hidalgo del Parral
Monclova
Falcon Res.
Sabinas Hidalgo
Guamúchil
Topolobampo
Lerdo
Nazas
S. Pedro
Gómez Palacio
Torreón
Matamoros
Saltillo
Monterrey
Reynosa
Sierra Madre
B. La Paz
Culiacán
Elota
Aguanaval
Concepción del Oro
Montemorelos
La Paz
2406
Durango
Catorce
Linares
C. San Lucas
Mazatlán
Sombrerete
4054
Ciudad Victoria
Matehuala
Rosario
Escuinapa
Fresnillo
Charcas
Cd. Garcia
Zacatecas
Tula
Ciudad Mante
Acaponeta
Tuxpan
Is. Tres Marías
San Luis Potosí
3353
Panuco
Tepic
Aguascalientes
R. Grande de Santiago
Guadalajara
León
Guanajuato
Irapuato
C. Corrientes
Ameca
Celaya
Queretaro
Papantla
Zacoalco
L. de Chapala
Pachuca
Colima Vol.
4339
Zamora
Tulancingo
Is. de Revillagigedo (Mex.)
Morelia
MEXICO
Tlaxcala
Manzanillo
Colima
Toluca
Cuernavaca
Puebla
Iguala
Balsas
Popocatepetl
5452
3703
Chilpancingo
Mexcala
Chilapa
Acapulco
Ayutla
Oaxaca
Ometepec
Verde
PACIFIC OCEAN
ft
m
12 000
9000
6000
4500
3000
1200
600
0
200
2000
4000
3000
2000
1500
1000
400
200
0
600
6000
110
105
100
30
25
20
15
10
115
Projection: Bonne

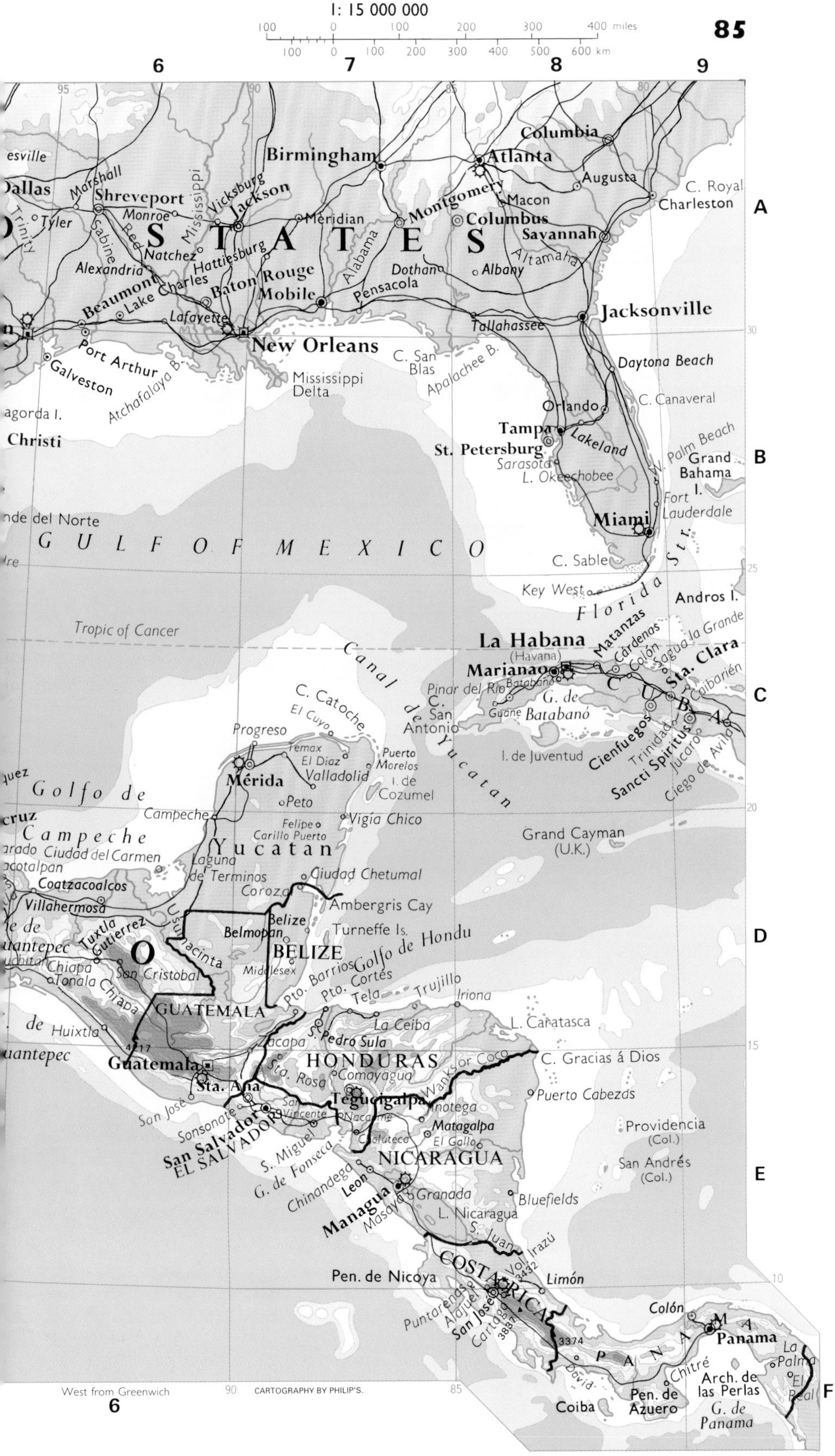
1: 15 000 000
100 0 100 200 300 400 miles
100 0 100 200 300 400 500 600 km
6 7 8 9
A B C D E F
Columbia
Birmingham
Atlanta
Augusta
C. Royal
Charleston
Dallas
Marshall
Shreveport
Vicksburg
Jackson
Montgomery
Macon
Tyler
Monroe
Meridian
Columbus
Savannah
Trinity
Sabine
Red
Mississippi
STATES
Natchez
Hattiesburg
Alabama
Altamaha
Alexandria
Baton Rouge
Dothan
Albany
Beaumont
Lake Charles
Mobile
Pensacola
Jacksonville
Lafayette
Tallahassee
Port Arthur
New Orleans
Galveston
C. San Blas
Apalachee B.
Daytona Beach
Atchafalaya B.
Mississippi Delta
C. Canaveral
agorda I.
Orlando
Christi
Tampa
Lakeland
St. Petersburg
W. Palm Beach
Sarasota
Grand Bahama I.
L. Okeechobee
Fort Lauderdale
nde del Norte
Miami
GULF OF MEXICO
C. Sable
Key West
Florida Str.
Andros I.
Tropic of Cancer
La Habana
(Havana)
Matanzas
Cárdenas
Colón
Sagua la Grande
Marianao
Sta. Clara
Canal de Yucatan
Caibarién
Pinar del Rio
Batabanó
G. de Batabanó
CUBA
C. Catoche
C. San Antonio
Guane
El Cuyo
Cienfuegos
Trinidad
Progreso
Temax
I. de Juventud
Sancti Spiritus
Jucaro
Ciego de Avila
El Diaz
Puerto Morelos
Mérida
Valladolid
I. de Cozumel
Golfo de Campeche
Peto
Campeche
Felipe Carillo Puerto
Vigía Chico
Grand Cayman (U.K.)
Yucatan
Ciudad del Carmen
Laguna de Terminos
Ciudad Chetumal
Coatzacoalcos
Corozal
Ambergris Cay
Villahermosa
Usumacinta
Belize
Belmopan
Turneffe Is.
Tuxtla Gutierrez
BELIZE
Golfo de Hondu
Chiapa
Middlesex
Pto. Barrios
Pto. Cortés
Tonala
San Cristobal
Tela
Trujillo
Iriona
GUATEMALA
La Ceiba
L. Caratasca
Huixtla
S. Pedro Sula
Zacapa
4217
HONDURAS
C. Gracias á Dios
Guatemala
Wanks or Coco
Sta. Rosa
Comayagua
Sta. Ana
Puerto Cabezas
San José
Tegucigalpa
San Vicente
Jinotega
Sonsonate
Nacaome
Providencia (Col.)
San Salvador
Matagalpa
EL SALVADOR
Choluteca
El Gallo
S. Miguel
NICARAGUA
San Andrés (Col.)
G. de Fonseca
Chinandega
Leon
Managua
Masaya
Granada
Bluefields
L. Nicaragua
S. Juan
Vol. Irazú
COSTA RICA
3432
Pen. de Nicoya
Limón
Puntarenas
Alajuela
San José
Cartago
3837
Colón
PANAMA
Panama
3374
David
Chitré
La Palma
El Real
Arch. de las Perlas
Pen. de Azuero
Coiba
G. de Panama
West from Greenwich
CARTOGRAPHY BY PHILIP'S.

1
2
3
4
90
85
80
75
A
B
C
D
E
F
25
20
15
10
5
Orlando
C. Canaveral
UNITED STATES
Tampa
St. Petersburg
Sarasota
L. Okeechobee
Grand Bahama I.
Freeport
Gt. Abaco I.
Fort Lauderdale
Miami
New Providence I.
Eleuthera I.
Nassau
C. Sable
Key West
Florida Str.
Andros I.
Cat I.
BAHAMAS
Long I.
G U L F O F
M E X I C O
Canal de Yucatan
La Habana
(Havana)
Marianao
Matanzas
Cárdenas
Colón
Sagua la Grande
Sta. Clara
Caibarién
Batabanó
Pinar del Rio
C. San Antonio
Guane
G. de Batabanó
I. de Juventud
Cienfuegos
Trinidad
Sancti Spiritus
Jucaro
Ciego de Avila
Morón
Camaguey
Nuevitas
Marti
Holguin
Antilla
Manzanillo
Campechuela
Bayamo
2000
Santiago de Cuba
Guantánamo
CUBA
G R E A T E R
C. Catoche
El Cuyo
Progreso
Temax
El Diaz
Mérida
Valladolid
Puerto Morelos
I. de Cozumel
Vigía Chico
MEXICO
Yucatan
Grand Cayman
(U.K.)
Montego Bay
St. Ann's Bay
P. Antonio
Savanna la Mar
JAMAICA
Kingston
Spanish Town
Paso de los Vientos
Jérémie
Les Cayes
Ciudad Chetumal
Corozal
Ambergris Cay
Belize
Belmopan
Turneffe Is.
BELIZE
Middlesex
Golfo de Honduras
Pto. Barrios
Pto. Cortés
Tela
Trujillo
Iriona
La Ceiba
L. Caratasca
GUATEMALA
S. Pedro Sula
HONDURAS
Sta. Rosa
Comayagua
Wanks or Coco
C. Gracias á Dios
Guatemala
Tegucigalpa
Puerto Cabezas
C A R I B
Sta. Ana
San Salvador
EL SALVADOR
San Vicente
Nacaome
Jinotega
Matagalpa
Choluteca
El Gallo
Providencia
(Col.)
San Andrés
(Col.)
S. Miguel
G. de Fonseca
NICARAGUA
Chinandega
Leon
Managua
Masaya
Granada
Bluefields
L. Nicaragua
San Juan
Santa Marta
Barranquilla
Soledad
Cartagena
Sincelejo
Corozal
G. del Darién
Pen. de Nicoya
COSTA RICA
Vol. Irazú
3432
Limón
Puntarenas
Alajuela
San José
Cartago
3837
3374
Colón
PANAMA
Panama
David
Chitré
Coiba
Pen. de Azuero
Arch. de las Perlas
G. de Panama
La Palma
El Real
Turbo
Atrato
Antioquia
Yarumal
3960
Pto. Wilches
Medellín
G. de Cupica
Quibdó
Riosucio
P A C I F I C
O C E A N
Manizales
Pereira
Ibague
5215
Cartago
Armenia
Girardot
Pta. Charambirá
Buga
Buenaventura
Palmira
Cali
5750
Neiva
Magdalena
Popayán
4646
ft
m
12 000
4000
9000
3000
6000
2000
4500
1500
3000
1000
1200
400
600
200
0
0
200
600
2000
6000
m
ft
Projection: Bonne
West from Greenwich

1: 15 000 000
100 0 100 200 300 400 miles
100 0 100 200 300 400 500 600 km
ATLANTIC
OCEAN
Tropic of Cancer
Mayaguana
Caicos I. (U.K.)
Turks Is. (U.K.)
Port de Paix
Cap Haïtien
Monte Cristi
Valverde
Pto. Plata
Santiago
S. Francisco de Macoris
Sanchez
La Vega
3175
DOMINICAN REP.
La Romana
Canal de la Mona
Aguadilla
Arecibo
PUERTO RICO (U.S.A.)
San Juan
1338
Caguas
Guayama
Mayagüez
Ponce
Christiansted
St. Croix (U.S.A.)
St. Thomas (U.S.A.)
Charlotte Amalie
Virgin Is. (U.K.)
Sombrero (U.K.)
Anguilla (U.K.)
St. Martin (Fr. & Neth.)
ST. KITTS-NEVIS
ANTIGUA & BARBUDA
Basseterre
Charlestown
St. John's
Plymouth
Montserrat (U.K.)
Guadeloupe (Fr.)
Pointe à Pitre
Leeward Islands
LESSER
DOMINICA
Roseau
Martinique (Fr.)
Fort de France
Castries
ST. LUCIA
BARBADOS
Bridgetown
ANTILLES
Windward
ST. VINCENT & THE GRENADINES
Kingstown
Islands
GRENADA
St. George's
La Blanquilla (Ven.)
Tobago
Port of Spain
TRINIDAD & TOBAGO
San Fernando
G. de Paria
Margarita
La Asunción
Carúpano
La Tortuga (Ven.)
Cumaná
Cariplto
2596
Maturín
Tucupita
Ciudad Guayana
Orinoco
Ciudad Bolívar
El Tigre
Barcelona
Las Mercedes
Santo Domingo
S. Pedro de Macoris
Bani
Azua
Barahona
Duverge
2680
Prince
Hispaniola
ANTILLES
CARIBBEAN SEA
Pta. Gallinas
Pen. de la Guajira
Golfo de Venezuela
Aruba (Neth.)
Curaçao
Willemstad
Bonaire
NETH. ANTILLES
Coro
Pto. Cabello
Maiquetía
Caracas
Dabajuro
Maracaibo
Cabimas
Sa. Nevada de S. Marta
L. de Maracaibo
Trujillo
Valera
Maracay
Valencia
San Felipe
Barquisimeto
Calabozo
Portuguesa
Cord. de Mérida
Guanare
5007
San Fernando de Apure
Apure
Ocaña
Cúcuta
Rubio
San Cristóbal
Pamplona
Bucaramanga
Barrancabermeja
Tunja
Arauca
Caicara
VENEZUELA
Pto. Páez
Meta
Pto. Carreño
2285
Pto. Ayacucho
COLOMBIA
Bogotá
Caura
Caroni
2560
Roraima
2810
El Callao
Tumeremo
Cuyuni
GUYANA
Georgetown
Bartica
New Amsterdam
Wismar
Essequibo
Corentyne
SURINAM
1280
Sierra Pacaraima
Sa. Parima
Casiquiare
Guaviare
BRAZIL
CARTOGRAPHY BY PHILIP'S.

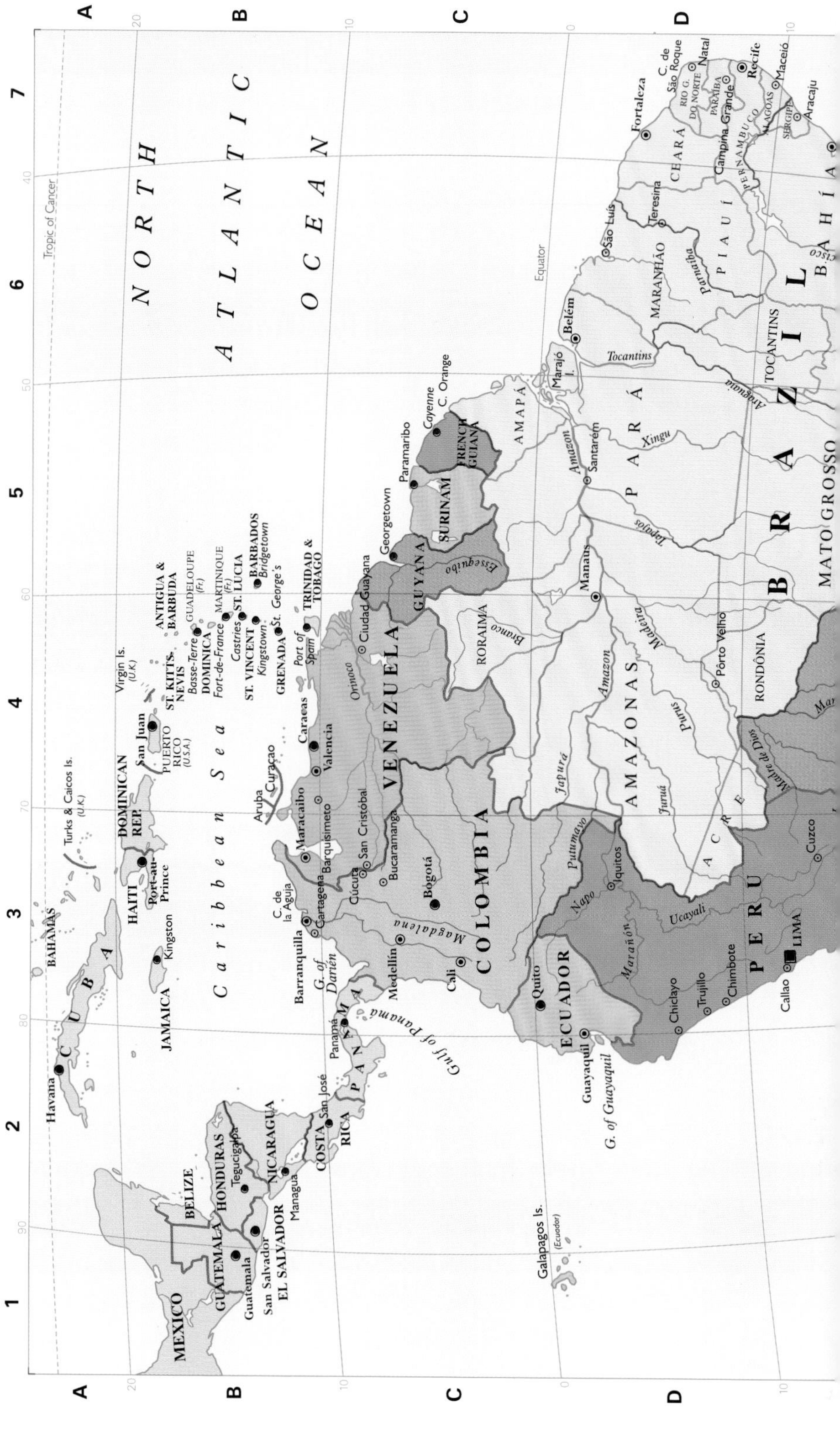

NORTH ATLANTIC OCEAN
Caribbean Sea
Tropic of Cancer
Equator
MEXICO
GUATEMALA
Guatemala
BELIZE
HONDURAS
Tegucigalpa
EL SALVADOR
San Salvador
NICARAGUA
Managua
COSTA RICA
San José
PANAMA
Panamá
Gulf of Panamá
G. of Darién
CUBA
Havana
BAHAMAS
Turks & Caicos Is.
(U.K.)
JAMAICA
Kingston
HAITI
Port-au-Prince
DOMINICAN REP.
PUERTO RICO
(U.S.A.)
San Juan
Virgin Is.
(U.K.)
ST. KITTS-NEVIS
ANTIGUA & BARBUDA
GUADELOUPE
(Fr.)
Basse-Terre
DOMINICA
MARTINIQUE
(Fr.)
Fort-de-France
ST. LUCIA
Castries
ST. VINCENT
Kingstown
BARBADOS
Bridgetown
GRENADA
St. George's
TRINIDAD & TOBAGO
Port of Spain
Aruba
Curaçao
VENEZUELA
Caracas
Valencia
Maracaibo
Barquisimeto
San Cristóbal
Ciudad Guayana
Orinoco
COLOMBIA
Bogotá
Medellín
Cali
Cúcuta
Bucaramanga
Barranquilla
Cartagena
C. de la Aguja
Magdalena
GUYANA
Georgetown
Essequibo
SURINAM
Paramaribo
FRENCH GUIANA
Cayenne
C. Orange
ECUADOR
Quito
Guayaquil
G. of Guayaquil
Galapagos Is.
(Ecuador)
PERU
LIMA
Callao
Chiclayo
Trujillo
Chimbote
Cuzco
Iquitos
Ucayali
Marañón
Napo
Putumayo
BRAZIL
AMAPÁ
PARÁ
AMAZONAS
RORAIMA
RONDÔNIA
ACRE
TOCANTINS
MARANHÃO
PIAUÍ
CEARÁ
RIO G. DO NORTE
PARAÍBA
PERNAMBUCO
ALAGOAS
SERGIPE
BAHIA
MATO GROSSO
Belém
Marajó I.
Santarém
Manaus
Pôrto Velho
São Luís
Teresina
Fortaleza
Natal
C. de São Roque
Campina Grande
Recife
Maceió
Aracaju
Amazon
Xingu
Tapajós
Tocantins
Araguaia
Parnaíba
Madeira
Purus
Juruá
Japurá
Branco
Madre de Dios

1: 35 000 000

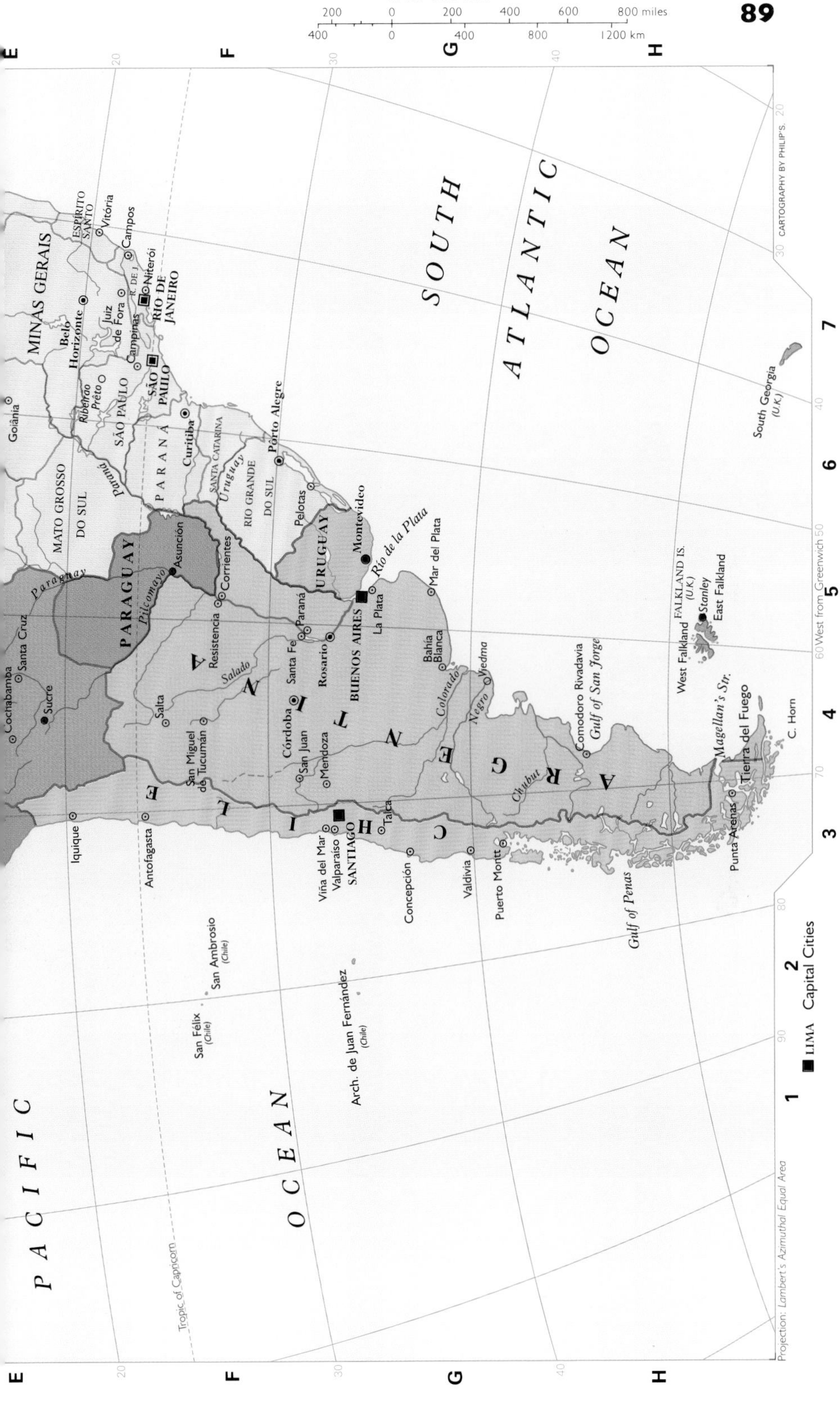
200 0 200 400 600 800 miles
400 0 400 800 1200 km
E F G H
1 2 3 4 5 6 7
PACIFIC OCEAN
SOUTH ATLANTIC OCEAN
MINAS GERAIS
ESPIRITO SANTO
Vitória
Campos
Niterói
RIO DE JANEIRO
Belo Horizonte
Juiz de Fora
Campinas
SÃO PAULO
Ribeirão Prêto
Goiânia
MATO GROSSO DO SUL
Paraná
PARANÁ
Curitiba
SANTA CATARINA
Uruguay
RIO GRANDE DO SUL
Porto Alegre
Pelotas
URUGUAY
Montevideo
Río de la Plata
Mar del Plata
PARAGUAY
Asunción
Paraguay
Pilcomayo
Corrientes
Resistencia
Cochabamba
Santa Cruz
Sucre
Salta
San Miguel de Tucumán
Salado
Santa Fe
Paraná
Rosario
BUENOS AIRES
La Plata
Córdoba
San Juan
Mendoza
Bahía Blanca
Colorado
Viedma
Negro
Chubut
Comodoro Rivadavia
Gulf of San Jorge
ARGENTINA
CHILE
Iquique
Antofagasta
Viña del Mar
Valparaíso
SANTIAGO
Talca
Concepción
Valdivia
Puerto Montt
Gulf of Penas
Magellan's Str.
Tierra del Fuego
Punta Arenas
C. Horn
FALKLAND IS. (U.K.)
West Falkland
East Falkland
Stanley
South Georgia (U.K.)
San Ambrosio (Chile)
San Félix (Chile)
Arch. de Juan Fernández (Chile)
Tropic of Capricorn
60 West from Greenwich 50
CARTOGRAPHY BY PHILIP'S.
Projection: Lambert's Azimuthal Equal Area
■ LIMA Capital Cities

SOUTH AMERICA-NORTH-WEST

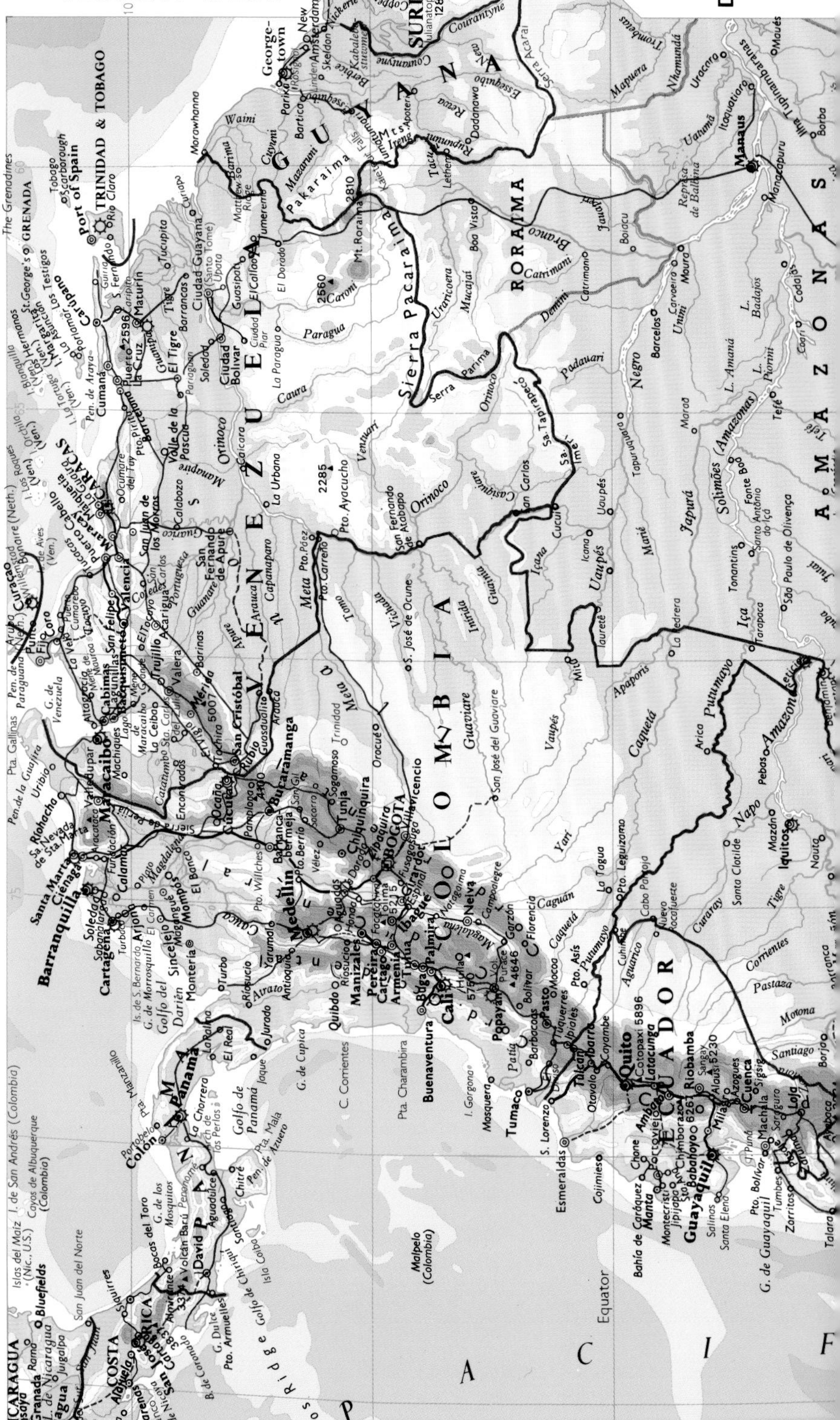

NICARAGUA
COSTA RICA
PANAMA
TRINIDAD & TOBAGO
Port of Spain
GRENADA
CARACAS
Maracaibo
Barranquilla
Cartagena
Medellín
BOGOTA
Cali
Quito
Guayaquil
Manaus
George-town
SURINAM
GUYANA
RORAIMA
VENEZUELA
COLOMBIA
ECUADOR
AMAZONAS
Orinoco
Equator
P A C I F
Cocos Ridge
Sierra Pacaraima
Mt. Roraima 2810
Cotopaxi 5896

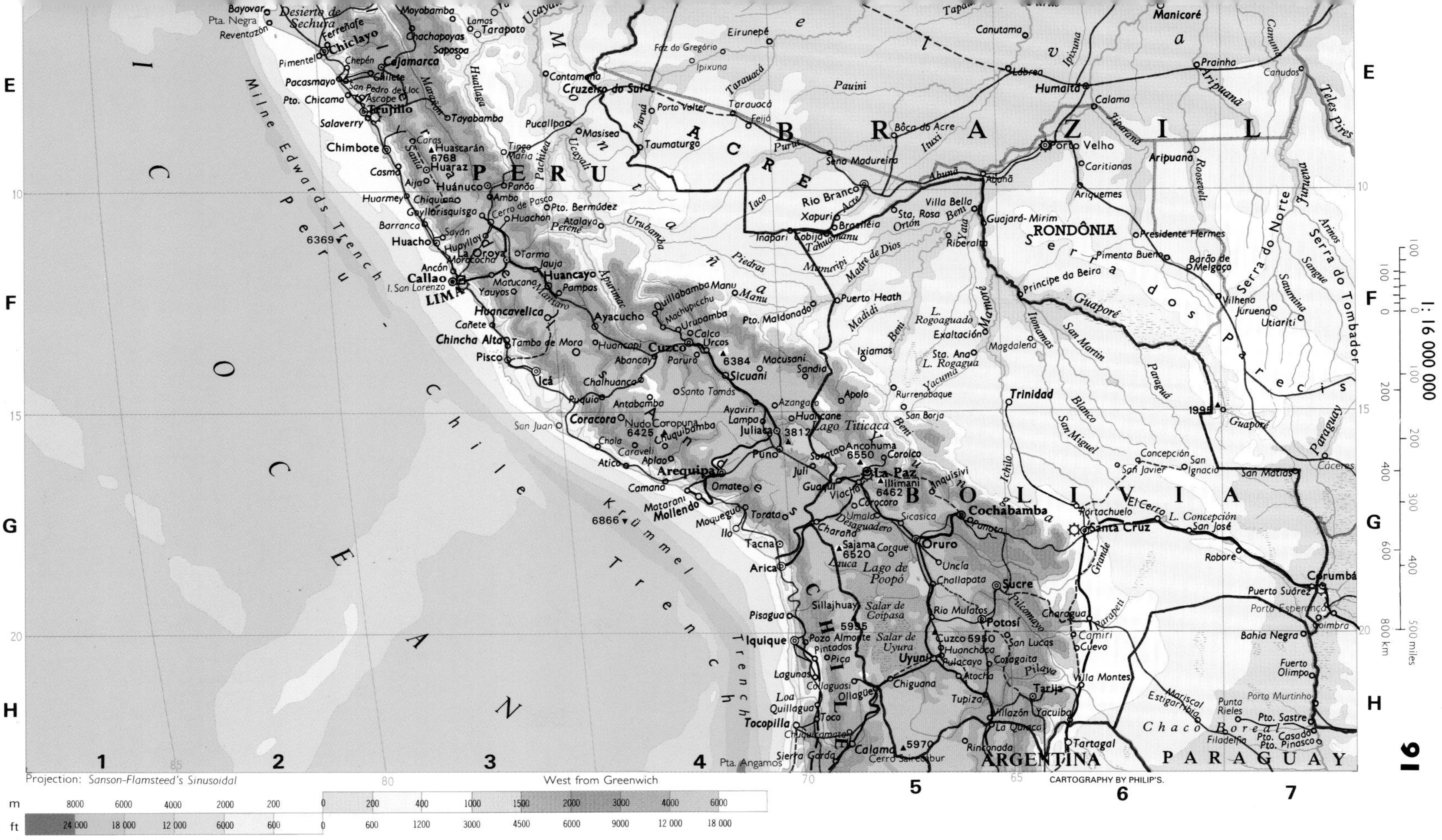
1: 16 000 000
100 0 100 200 300 400 500 miles
100 0 200 400 600 800 km
PERU
BRAZIL
ACRE
RONDÔNIA
BOLIVIA
CHILE
ARGENTINA
PARAGUAY
PACIFIC OCEAN
Milne Edwards Trench
Peru - Chile Trench
Krümmel Trench
6369
6866
Lima
Callao
I. San Lorenzo
Ancón
Huacho
Barranca
Huarmey
Casma
Chimbote
Salaverry
Trujillo
Pto. Chicama
Pacasmayo
Pimentel
Chiclayo
Ferreñafe
Desierto de Sechura
Bayovar
Pta. Negra
Reventazón
Chepén
Cajamarca
Chilete
San Pedro de Lloc
Ascope
Moyobamba
Chachapoyas
Lamas
Tarapoto
Saposoa
Huallaga
Marañón
Tayabamba
Caras
Huascarán
6768
Huaraz
Santa
Aija
Huánuco
Panão
Ambo
Cerro de Pasco
Huachon
Chiquián
Gayllorisquisgo
Sayán
Huayllay
La Oroya
Morococha
Tarma
Jauja
Huancayo
Pampas
Matucana
Yauyos
Mantaro
Huancavelica
Cañete
Chincha Alta
Tambo de Mora
Pisco
Icá
Ayacucho
Huancapi
Abancay
Apurimac
Chalhuanca
Puquio
Antabamba
Coracora
Nudo Coropuna
6425
Chuquibamba
Chala
Caraveli
Aplao
Atico
Camaná
San Juan
Arequipa
Matarani
Mollendo
Omate
Moquegua
Ilo
Torata
Tacna
Arica
Cuzco
Urcos
Paruro
Calca
Urubamba
Machupicchu
Quillabamba
Santo Tomás
Sicuani
6384
Macusani
Sandia
Azangaro
Ayaviri
Lampa
Juliaca
Huancane
3812
Lago Titicaca
Puno
Juli
Pucallpa
Masisea
Ucayali
Pachitea
Tingo María
Pto. Bermúdez
Atalaya
Perené
Urubamba
Contamana
Cruzeiro do Sul
Juruá
Porto Valter
Taumaturgo
Tarauacá
Feijó
Eirunepé
Ipixuna
Faz do Gregório
Pauini
Purus
Sena Madureira
Bôca do Acre
Ituxi
Iaco
Rio Branco
Xapuri
Acre
Brasiléia
Cobija
Tahuamanu
Inapari
Piedras
Manuripi
Madre de Dios
Manu
Pto. Maldonado
Puerto Heath
Madidi
Ixiamas
Apolo
Rurrenabaque
San Borja
Beni
Sta. Rosa
Ortón
Riberalta
Villa Bella
Yata
Abunã
Porto Velho
Humaitá
Lábrea
Canutama
Ipixuna
Manicoré
Calama
Jiparaná
Prainha
Aripuanã
Canumã
Canudos
Teles Pires
Caritianas
Ariquemes
Roosevelt
Presidente Hermes
Pimenta Bueno
Barão de Melgaço
Vilhena
Juruena
Utiariti
Saturnina
Sangue
Arinos
Serra do Tombador
Serra do Norte
Serra dos Parecis
Guajará-Mirim
Principe da Beira
Guaporé
Mamoré
L. Rogoaguado
Exaltación
Sta. Ana
L. Rogagua
Yacuma
Magdalena
Itonamas
San Martin
Paraguá
Trinidad
Blanco
San Miguel
Ichilo
Concepción
San Javier
San Ignacio
San Matías
1995
Cáceres
Paraguay
Cochabamba
Punata
Santa Cruz
Portachuelo
El Cerro
L. Concepción
San José
Roboré
Corumbá
Puerto Suárez
Porto Esperança
Coimbra
Grande
La Paz
Illimani
6462
Ancohuma
6550
Coroico
Sorata
Inquisivi
Viacha
Corocoro
Umala
Desaguadero
Guaqui
Charaña
Sajama
6520
Lauca
Corque
Sicasica
Oruro
Uncía
Challapata
Lago de Poopó
Sillajhuay
Salar de Coipasa
5995
Salar de Uyuni
Pozo Almonte
Pintados
Pica
Pisagua
Iquique
Lagunas
Collaguasi
Ollagüe
Loa
Quillagua
Toco
Tocopilla
Chuquicamata
Calama
5970
Sierra Gorda
Pta. Angamos
Cerro Sairecabur
Chiguana
Uyuni
Cuzco 5950
Huanchaca
Pulacayo
Atocha
Tupiza
Rio Mulatos
Potosí
Sucre
Pilcomayo
San Lucas
Cotagaita
Pilaya
Tarija
Villazón
Yacuiba
La Quiaca
Rinconada
Tartagal
Villa Montes
Charagua
Camiri
Cuevo
Parapeti
Chaco Boreal
Mariscal Estigarribia
Punta Rieles
Filadelfia
Pto. Casado
Pto. Pinasco
Pto. Sastre
Porto Murtinho
Fuerto Olimpo
Bahia Negra
E
F
G
H
1
2
3
4
5
6
7
10
15
20
65
70
80
85
Projection: Sanson-Flamsteed's Sinusoidal
West from Greenwich
CARTOGRAPHY BY PHILIP'S.
m 8000 6000 4000 2000 200 0 200 400 1000 1500 2000 3000 4000 6000
ft 24 000 18 000 12 000 6000 600 0 600 1200 3000 4500 6000 9000 12 000 18 000

SOUTH AMERICA-NORTH-EAST

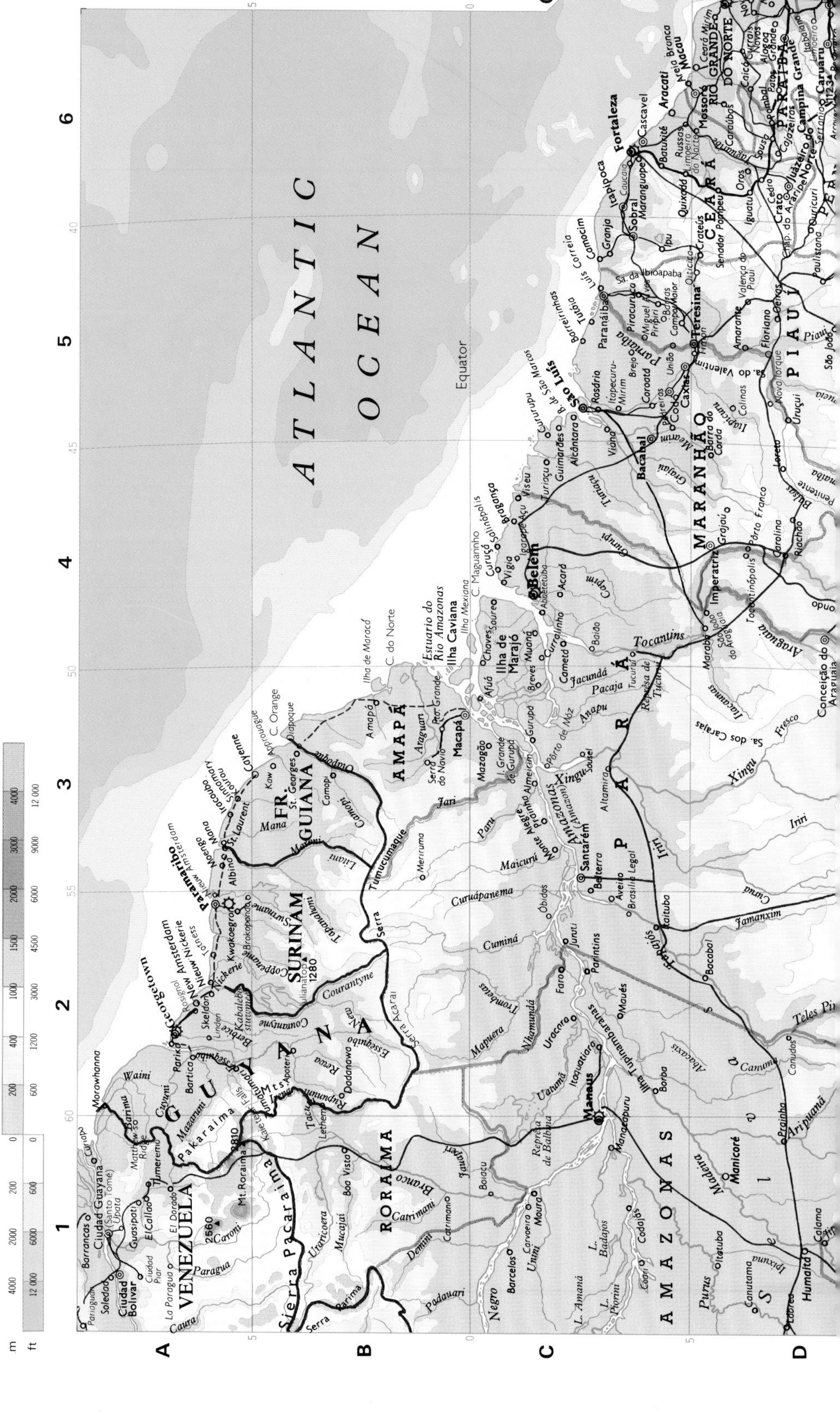
ATLANTIC OCEAN
Equator
VENEZUELA
GUYANA
SURINAM
FR. GUIANA
AMAPÁ
RORAIMA
AMAZONAS
PARÁ
MARANHÃO
PIAUÍ
CEARÁ
RIO GRANDE DO NORTE
PARAÍBA
Georgetown
Paramaribo
Cayenne
Ciudad Guayana
Ciudad Bolívar
Macapá
Belém
São Luís
Fortaleza
Teresina
Natal
João Pessoa
RECIFE
Olinda
Manaus
Santarém
Humaitá
Ilha de Marajó
Estuario do Rio Amazonas
Sierra Pacaraima
Mt. Roraima 2810
Pakaraima Mts.
Amazonas (Amazon)
Tocantins
Xingu
Negro
Madeira
Purus
A
B
C
D
1
2
3
4
5
6
m
ft
4000
2000
200
0
200
400
1000
1500
2000
3000
4000
12 000
6000
600
0
600
1200
3000
4500
6000
9000
12 000

1 : 16 000 000
100 0 100 200 300 400 500 miles
100 0 200 400 600 800 km
Tropic of Capricorn
West from Greenwich
CARTOGRAPHY BY PHILIP'S.
Projection: Sanson-Flamsteed's Sinusoidal
B R A Z I L
BAHIA
TOCANTINS
MATO GROSSO
MATO GROSSO DO SUL
GOIÁS
MINAS GERAIS
ESPÍRITO SANTO
RIO DE JANEIRO
SÃO PAULO
PARANÁ
RONDÔNIA
BOLIVIA
PARAGUAY
ARGENTINA
DIST. FED.
Brasília
Salvador
Rio de Janeiro
São Paulo
Belo Horizonte
Goiânia
Cuiabá
Campo Grande
Curitiba
Asunción
Santa Cruz
Aracaju
Maceió
Vitória
Santos
Corumbá
Planalto do Mato Grosso
Serra do Roncador
Chaco Boreal
Chaco Central
Ilha do Bananal

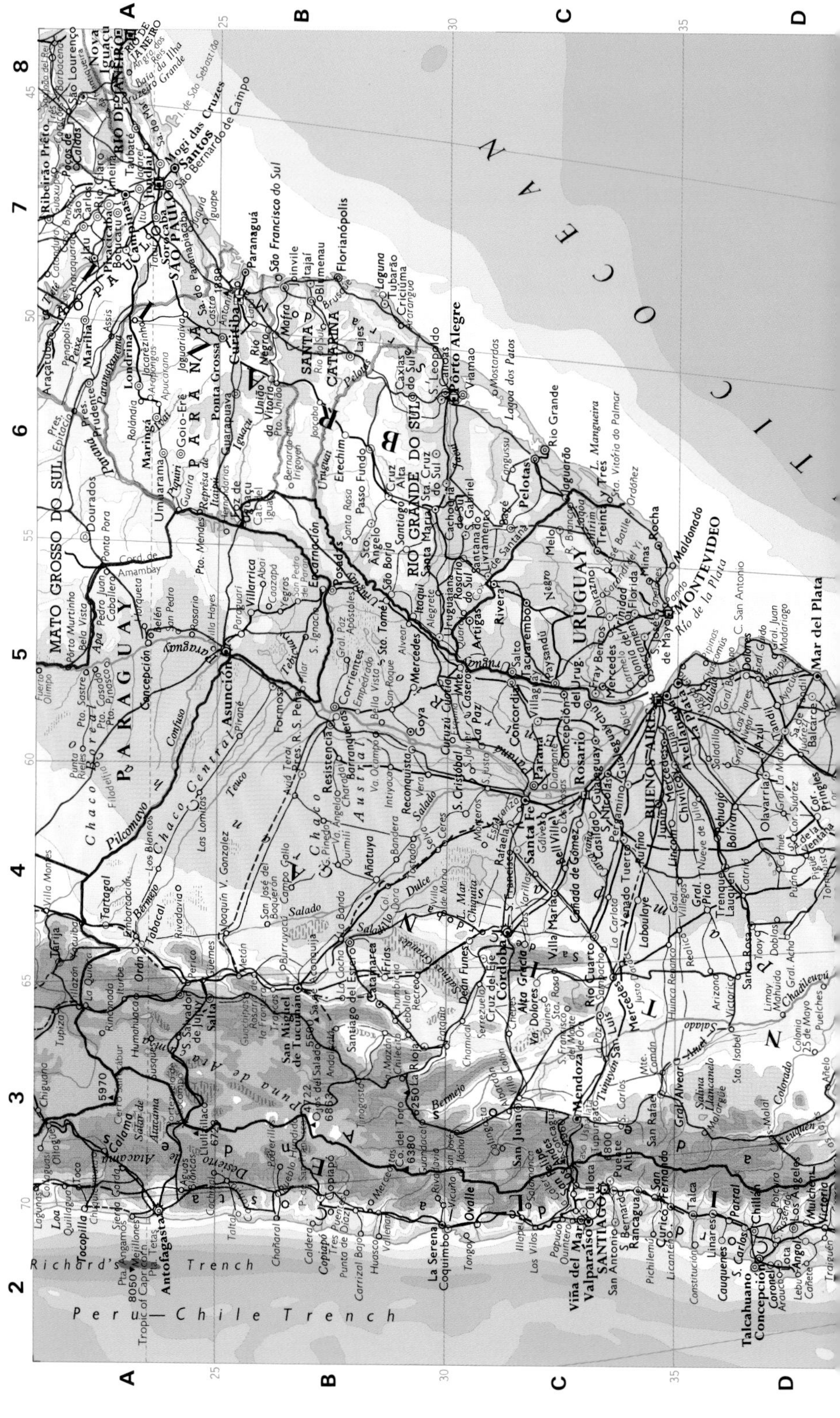

A
B
C
D
2
3
4
5
6
7
8
25
30
35
45
50
55
60
65
70
MATO GROSSO DO SUL
PARAGUAY
PARANÁ
SANTA CATARINA
RIO GRANDE DO SUL
URUGUAY
BRAZIL
SÃO PAULO
RIO DE JANEIRO
Asunción
Concepción
Curitiba
Paranaguá
Florianópolis
Porto Alegre
Pelotas
Rio Grande
Santos
Campinas
Londrina
Maringá
Ponta Grossa
Foz do Iguaçu
Encarnación
Posadas
Corrientes
Resistencia
Formosa
Santa Fe
Paraná
Rosario
Córdoba
BUENOS AIRES
La Plata
Mar del Plata
MONTEVIDEO
Maldonado
Salto
Paysandú
Tacuarembó
Rivera
Artigas
Mendoza
San Juan
San Luis
Río Cuarto
Santiago del Estero
San Miguel de Tucumán
Salta
Jujuy
Catamarca
La Rioja
Antofagasta
Calama
Tocopilla
Copiapó
La Serena
Coquimbo
Valparaíso
Viña del Mar
SANTIAGO
Rancagua
Talca
Chillán
Concepción
Talcahuano
Los Angeles
Gran Chaco
Chaco Boreal
Chaco Central
Chaco Austral
Pampa
Puna de Atacama
Desierto de Atacama
Salar de Atacama
Río de la Plata
Lagoa dos Patos
L. Mirim
Tropic of Capricorn
Richard's Trench
Peru – Chile Trench
ATLANTIC OCEAN
Pilcomayo
Bermejo
Salado
Paraná
Uruguay
Iguaçu

1: 16 000 000

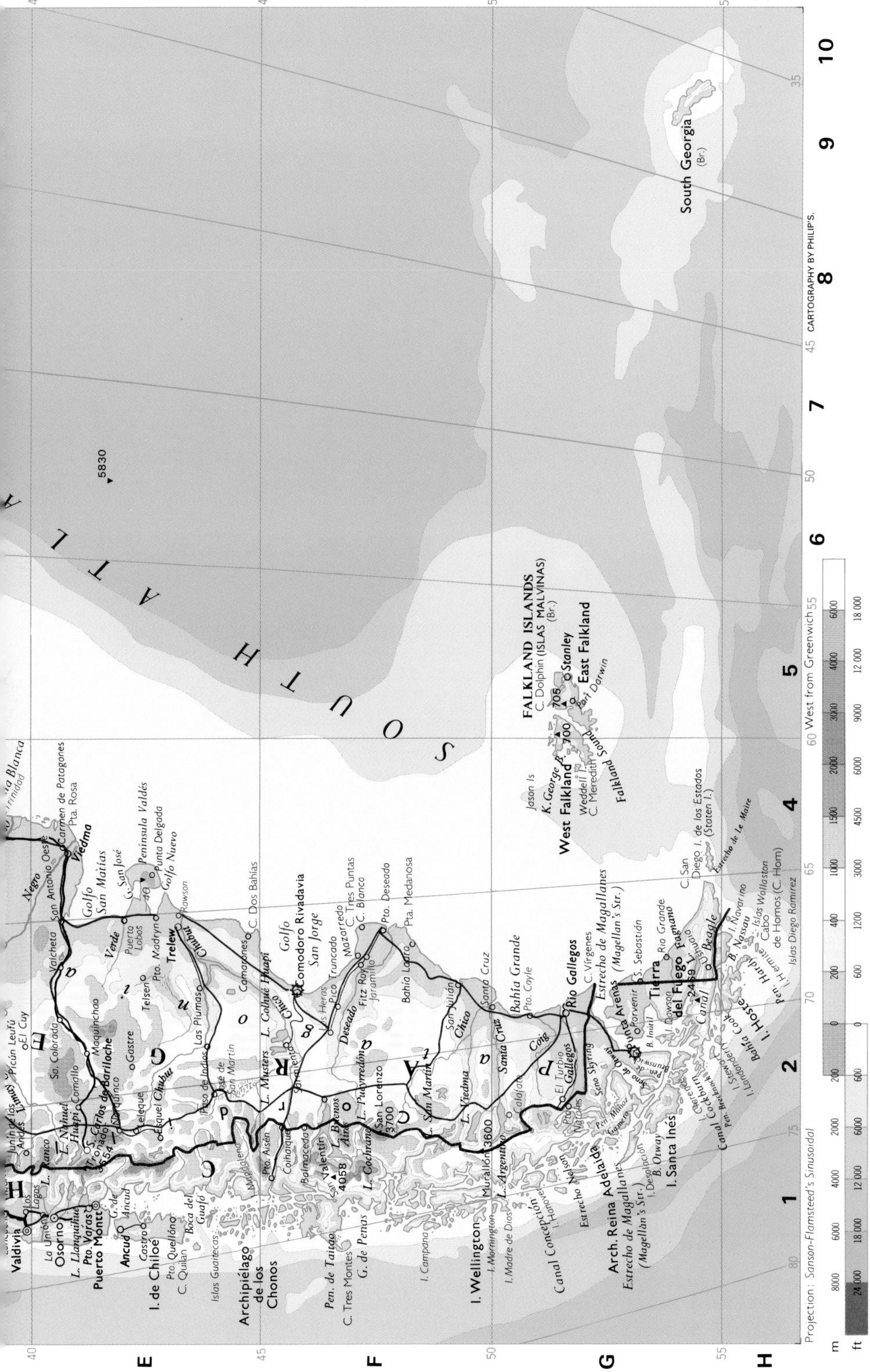
SOUTH ATLANTIC
FALKLAND ISLANDS (ISLAS MALVINAS) (Br.)
West Falkland
East Falkland
Stanley
Falkland Sound
South Georgia (Br.)
Valdivia
Osorno
Puerto Montt
I. de Chiloé
Archipiélago de los Chonos
Comodoro Rivadavia
Golfo San Jorge
Golfo San Matías
Península Valdés
Trelew
Viedma
Río Gallegos
Punta Arenas
Estrecho de Magallanes (Magellan's Str.)
Tierra del Fuego
Ushuaia
Canal Beagle
I. Hoste
Cabo de Hornos (C. Horn)
I. de los Estados (Staten I.)
Estrecho de Le Maire
I. Santa Inés
Arch. Reina Adelaida
Canal Concepción
I. Wellington
Pen. de Taitao
G. de Penas
Bahía Grande
Puerto Deseado
San Carlos de Bariloche
5830
West from Greenwich
Projection: Sanson-Flamsteed's Sinusoidal
CARTOGRAPHY BY PHILIP'S.

1: 35 000 000

200 0 200 400 600 800 miles

400 0 400 800 1200 km

CARTOGRAPHY BY PHILIP'S.
Projection: Zenithal Equidistant

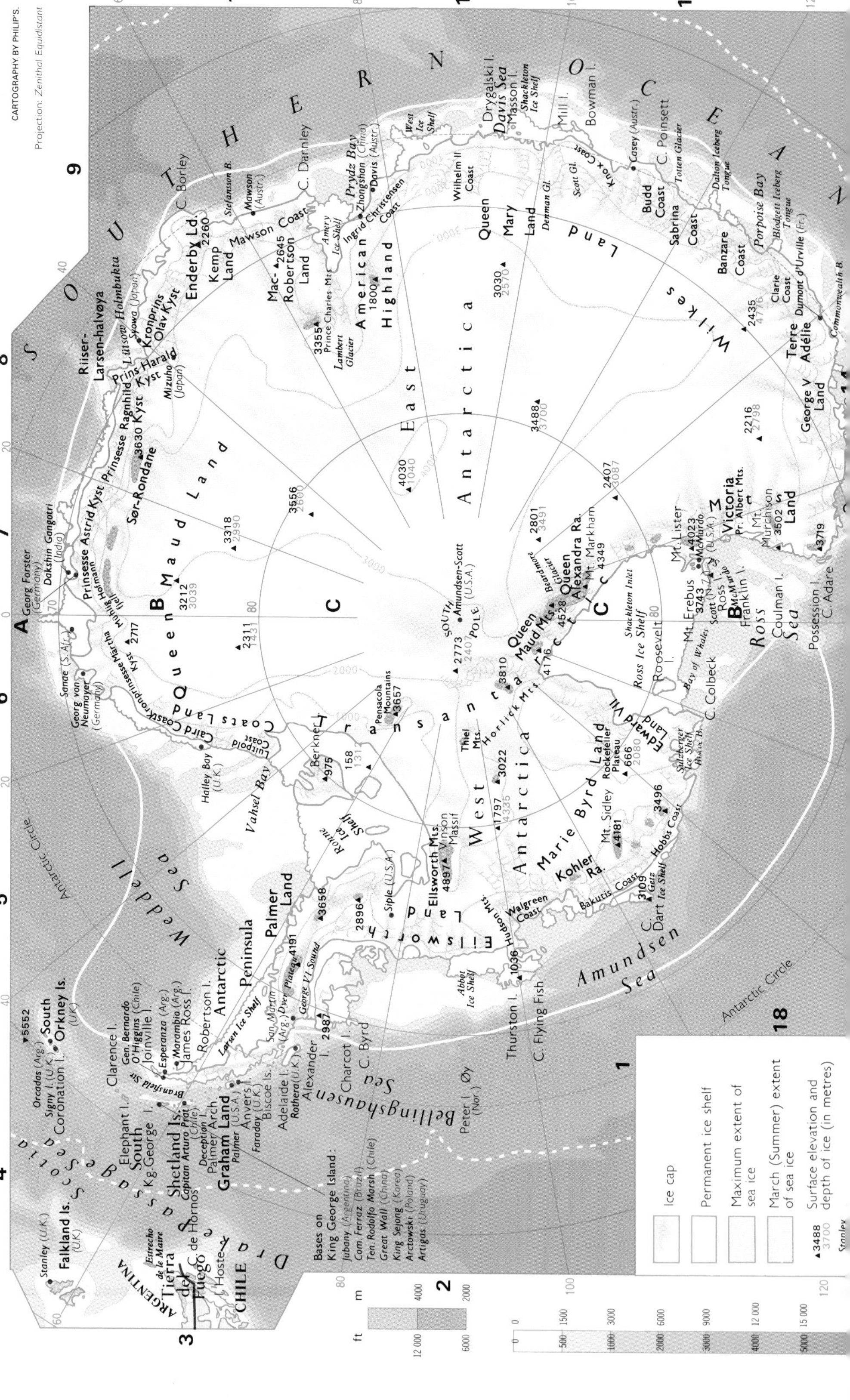

Index to Map Pages

The index contains the names of all principal places and features shown on the maps. Physical features composed of a proper name (Erie) and a description (Lake) are positioned alphabetically by the proper name. The description is positioned after the proper name and is usually abbreviated:

Erie, L. **72 C5**

Where a description forms part of a settlement or administrative name however, it is always written in full and put in its true alphabetical position:

Lake Charles **79 D7**

Names beginning St. are alphabetized under Saint, but Sankt, Sint, Sant, Santa and San are all spelt in full and are alphabetized accordingly.

The number in bold type which follows each name in the index refers to the number of the map page where that feature or place will be found. This is usually the largest scale at which the place or feature appears.

The letter and figure which are in bold type immediately after the page number give the grid square on the map page, within which the feature is situated.

Rivers carry the symbol → after their names. A solid square ■ follows the name of a country while an open square □ refers to a first order administrative area.

A

A Coruña = La Coruña **18 A1**
Aachen **14 C4**
Aalborg = Ålborg **9 G9**
Aalen **14 D6**
Aarau **13 C8**
Aare → **13 C8**
Aarhus = Århus **9 G10**
Aba **55 G6**
Ābādān **47 E7**
Ābādeh **44 D3**
Abadla **54 B4**
Abaetetuba ... **92 C4**
Abakan **30 D7**
Abancay **91 F4**
Abarqū **44 D3**
Abashiri **32 F12**
Abay **29 E8**
Abaya, L. **53 G6**
Abbay = Nîl el Azraq → ... **53 E5**
Abbeville **12 A4**
Abbieglassie .. **63 A4**
Abbot Ice Shelf **96 B2**
Abbottabad ... **42 B8**
Abd al Kūrī ... **49 E5**
Abéché **53 F3**
Abeokuta **55 G5**
Abercorn = Mbala **57 F6**
Abercorn **63 A5**
Aberdeen, *Australia* **63 B5**
Aberdeen, *U.K.* **10 C5**
Aberdeen, *S. Dak., U.S.A.* **76 C5**
Aberdeen, *Wash., U.S.A.* **80 B2**
Aberystwyth .. **11 E4**
Abidjan **55 G4**
Abilene **78 C4**
Abitibi L. **69 D3**
Abkhaz Republic □ = Abkhazia □ . **25 E5**
Abkhazia □ ... **25 E5**
Abminga **62 A1**
Åbo = Turku .. **9 F12**
Abohar **42 D9**
Aboméy **55 G5**
Abong-Mbang . **56 D2**
Abou-Deïa **53 F2**
Abri **52 D5**
Abrolhos, Banka **93 F6**
Abrud **17 E6**
Absaroka Range **81 C9**
Abū al Khaşīb . **47 E6**
Abū 'Alī **47 F7**
Abu 'Arīsh **49 D3**
Abu Dhabi = Abū Ẓāby ... **44 E3**
Abû Dis **53 E5**
Abu Hamed ... **53 E5**
Abū Kamāl **46 D5**
Abū Madd, Ra's **47 F4**
Abu Matariq .. **53 F4**
Abu Rudeis ... **47 E3**
Abu Tig **52 C5**
Abû Zabad **53 F4**
Abū Ẓāby **44 E3**
Abuja **55 G6**
Abukuma-Gawa → ... **33 G12**
Abunã **91 E5**
Abunã → **91 E5**
Abut Hd. **65 E4**
Abwong **53 G5**
Acaponeta **84 C3**
Acapulco **84 D5**
Acarigua **90 B5**
Accra **55 G4**
Aceh □ **36 D1**
Achalpur **43 J10**
Achill I. **11 E1**
Achinsk **30 D7**
Acireale **21 F5**
Acklins I. **86 B5**
Aconcagua, Cerro **94 C3**
Aconquija, Mt. . **94 B3**
Açores, Is. dos = Azores ... **50 C1**
Acraman, L. ... **62 B2**
Acre = 'Akko .. **46 D3**
Acre □ **91 E4**
Acre → **91 E5**
Ad Dahnā **47 F7**
Ad Dammām .. **47 F7**
Ad Dawhah ... **44 E2**
Ad Dilam **47 G6**
Ad Dīwānīyah . **47 E6**
Ada **79 B5**
Adaja → **18 B3**
Adam **44 F4**
Adamaoua, Massif de l' . **53 G1**
Adamawa Highlands = Adamaoua, Massif de l' . **53 G1**
Adamello, Mte. **20 A3**
Adaminaby ... **63 C4**
Adam's Bridge **43 Q11**
Adams Mt. **80 B3**
Adana **46 C3**
Adapazarı **46 B2**
Adarama **53 E5**
Adare, C. **96 B15**
Adaut **39 F4**
Adavale **63 A3**
Adda → **20 B2**
Addis Ababa = Addis Abeba **53 G6**
Addis Abeba .. **53 G6**
Addis Alem ... **53 G6**
Adelaide **62 B2**
Adelaide I. **96 A3**
Adelaide Pen. . **70 B10**
Adélie, Terre .. **96 A14**
Adélie Land = Adélie, Terre **96 A14**
Aden = Al 'Adan **49 E4**
Aden, G. of ... **49 E4**
Adi **39 E4**
Adi Ugri **53 F6**
Adige → **20 B4**
Adilabad **43 K11**
Adirondack Mts. **73 C8**
Admer **54 D6**
Admiralty I. ... **71 C6**
Admiralty Is. .. **64 K9**
Ado-Ekiti **55 G6**
Adonara **39 F2**
Adoni **43 M10**
Adour → **12 E3**
Adra **18 D4**
Adrano **21 F5**
Adrar **54 C4**
Adré **53 F3**
Adrī **52 C1**
Adriatic Sea ... **20 C5**
Adua **39 E3**

Adwa 53 F6
Adzhar Republic □ = Ajaria □ 25 E5
Ægean Sea 23 E5
Aerhtai Shan 34 B4
Afghanistan ■ 45 C6
Afgoi 49 G3
'Afif 47 G5
Afognak I. 71 C4
Afuá 92 C3
Afyonkarahisar 46 C2
Agadès = Agadez 55 E6
Agadez 55 E6
Agadir 54 B3
Agapa 30 B6
Agartala 41 F8
Agats 39 F5
Agboville 55 G4
Agde 13 E5
Agen 12 D4
Agra 42 F10
Agri → 21 D6
Ağrı Dağı 46 C6
Ağrı Karakose 46 C5
Agrigento 21 F4
Agrinion 23 E3
Água Clara 93 G3
Agua Prieta 84 A3
Aguadas 90 B3
Aguadilla 87 C6
Aguarico → 90 D3
Aguas Blancas 94 A3
Aguascalientes 84 C4
Aguilas 19 D5
Agulhas, C. 58 E4
Agung 37 F5
Agusan → 38 C3
Ahaggar 54 D6
Ahar 46 C6
Ahipara B. 64 A5
Ahiri 43 K12
Ahmadabad 43 H8
Ahmadnagar 43 K9
Ahmadpur 42 E7
Ahmedabad = Ahmadabad 43 H8
Ahmednagar = Ahmadnagar 43 K9
Ahvāz 47 E7
Ahvenanmaa = Åland 9 F11
Aḩwar 49 E4
Aigues-Mortes 13 E6
Aihui 35 A7
Aija 91 E3
Aiken 75 C7
Aimere 39 F2
Aimorés 93 F5
Ain Banaiyan 44 F2
Aïn Beïda 54 A6
Aïn Ben Tili 54 C3
Aïn-Sefra 54 B4
Ainabo 49 F4
Aïr 55 E6
Aisne → 13 B5
Aiud 17 E6
Aix-en-Provence 13 E6
Aix-la-Chapelle = Aachen 14 C4
Aix-les-Bains 13 D6
Aiyion 23 E4
Aizawl 41 F9
Ajaccio 13 F8
Ajanta Ra. 43 J9
Ajari Rep. = Ajaria □ 25 E5
Ajaria □ 25 E5
Ajdâbiyah 52 B3
Ajka 16 E3
'Ajmān 44 E3
Ajmer 42 F9
Ajo, C. de 18 A4
Akaroa 65 E5
Akashi 32 B4
Akelamo 39 D3
Aketi 56 D4
Akharnaí 23 E4
Akhelóös → 23 E3
Akhisar 23 E6
Akhmîm 52 C5
Akimiski I. 69 C2
Akita 33 G12
Akjoujt 55 E2
'Akko 46 D3
Akkol 29 E8
Aklavik 70 B6
Akmolinsk = Astana 29 D8
Akobo → 53 G5
Akola 43 J10
Akordat 53 E6
Akpatok I. 68 B4
Akreïjit 55 E3
Akron 72 D5
Aksai Chin 42 B11
Aksaray 46 C3
Aksarka 28 C7
Akşehir 46 C2
Aksu 34 B3
Aksum 53 F6
Aktogay 29 E8
Aktsyabrski 17 B9
Aktyubinsk = Aqtöbe 29 D6
Aku 55 G6
Akure 55 G6
Akyab = Sittwe 41 G9
Al 'Adan 49 E4
Al Aḩsā 47 F7
Al Amādīyah 46 C5
Al Amārah 47 E6
Al 'Aqabah 47 E3
Al 'Aramah 47 F6
Al Ashkhara 45 F4
Al Badī' 47 G6
Al Başrah 47 E6
Al Bayḑā 52 B3
Al Bu'ayrāt al Ḩasūn 52 B2
Al Fallūjah 46 D5
Al Fāw 47 E7
Al Fujayrah 44 E4
Al Hābah 47 F6
Al Haddār 47 G6
Al Hāmad 47 E4
Al Ḩamar 47 G6
Al Ḩamrā' 47 F4
Al Ḩarīq 47 G6
Al Ḩasakah 46 C5
Al Ḩawrah 49 E4
Al Ḩayy 47 D6
Al Ḩijāz 47 F4
Al Ḩillah, *Iraq* 47 D6
Al Ḩillah, *Si. Arabia* 47 G6
Al Hindīyah 47 D6
Al Hoceïma 54 A4
Al Ḩudaydah 49 E3
Al Hufūf 47 F7
Al Ḩulwah 47 G6
Al Ittihad = Madīnat ash Sha'b 49 E3
Al Jāfūrah 47 F7
Al Jaghbūb 52 C3
Al Jahrah 47 E6
Al Jalāmīd 47 E4
Al Jawf, *Libya* 52 D3
Al Jawf, *Si. Arabia* 47 E4
Al Jazirah, *Iraq* 46 D5
Al Jazirah, *Libya* 52 C3
Al Jubayl 47 F7
Al Jubaylah 47 F6
Al Junaynah 53 F3
Al Khābūra 44 F4
Al Khalīl 47 E3
Al Kharfah 47 G6
Al Kharj 47 F6
Al Khasab 44 E4
Al Kufrah 52 D3
Al Kūt 47 D6
Al Kuwayt 47 E7
Al Lādhiqīyah 46 D3
Al Luḩayyah 49 D3
Al Madīnah 47 F4
Al Majma'ah 47 F6
Al Manāmah 44 E2
Al Marj 52 B3
Al Mawşil 46 C5
Al Midhnab 47 F6
Al Mish'āb 47 E7
Al Mubarraz 47 F7
Al Muḩarraq 44 E2
Al Mukallā 49 E4
Al Mukhā 49 E3
Al Musayyib 47 D6
Al Muwayliḩ 47 F3
Al Qaḑīmah 47 G4
Al Qā'iyah 47 F5
Al Qāmishli 46 C5
Al Qaşabát 52 B1
Al Qaşīm 47 F5
Al Qaţīf 47 F7
Al Qaţrūn 52 D2
Al Qayşūmah 47 E6
Al Quaisūmah 47 E6
Al Quds = Jerusalem 47 E3
Al Qurayyāt 45 F4
Al Qurnah 47 E6
Al 'Ulā 47 F4
Al Uqaylah ash Sharqīgah 52 B2
Al Uqayr 47 F7
Al 'Uthmānīyah 47 F7
Al 'Uwaynid 47 F6
Al 'Uwayqīlah 47 E5
Al 'Uyūn 47 F5
Al Wakrah 44 E2
Al Wari'āh 47 F6
Al Yamāmah 47 F6
Alabama □ 74 C4
Alabama → 74 D4
Alaçam Dağları 23 E7
Alagoa Grande 92 D6
Alagoas □ 93 D6
Alagoinhas 93 E6
Alajuela 86 D3
Alamosa 83 B10
Åland 9 F11
Alania = North Ossetia □ 25 E5
Alanya 46 C2
Alapayevsk 29 D7
Alaşehir 23 E7
Alaska □ 71 B4
Alaska, G. of 71 C5
Alaska Peninsula 71 C4
Alaska Range 71 B4
Alataw Shankou 34 B3
Alatyr 24 C6
Alausi 90 D3
Alawoona 62 B3
Alba 20 B2
Alba-Iulia 17 E6
Albacete 19 C5
Albacutya, L. 62 C3
Albania ■ 23 D3
Albany, *Australia* 60 H2
Albany, *Ga., U.S.A.* 75 D5
Albany, *N.Y., U.S.A.* 73 C9
Albany, *Oreg., U.S.A.* 80 C2
Albany → 69 C2
Albardón 94 C3
Albemarle 75 B7
Alberche → 18 C3
Albert, L. 62 C2
Albert L. 57 D6
Albert Nile → 57 D6
Albertville 13 D7
Albi 12 E5
Albina 92 A3
Alborán 18 E4
Ålborg 9 G9
Alborz, Reshteh-ye Kūhhā-ye 44 B3
Albuquerque 83 C9
Albury 63 C4
Alcalá de Henares 18 B4
Alcalá la Real 18 D4
Alcamo 21 F4
Alcaníz 19 B5
Alcântara 92 C5
Alcántara, Embalse de 18 C2
Alcantarilla 19 D5
Alcaraz, Sierra de 19 C4
Alcaudete 18 D3
Alcázar de San Juan 18 C4
Alchevsk 25 D4
Alcira 19 C5
Alcoy 19 C5
Aldabra Is. 51 G8
Aldan → 31 C10
Alderney 11 G5
Aleg 55 E2
Alegrete 94 B5
Aleisk 29 D9
Aleksandriya = Oleksandriya 17 C8
Aleksandrovskoye 29 C8
Alemania 94 B3
Alençon 12 B4
Aleppo = Ḩalab 46 C4
Alès 13 D6
Alessándria 20 B2
Ålesund 8 F9
Aleutian Is. 71 C2
Alexander Arch. 71 C6
Alexander I. 96 A3
Alexandra, *Australia* 63 C4
Alexandra, *N.Z.* 65 F3
Alexandria = El Iskandarîya 52 B4
Alexandria, *Canada* 71 C7
Alexandria, *Romania* 22 C5
Alexandria, *S. Africa* 59 E5
Alexandria, *La., U.S.A.* 79 D7
Alexandria, *Va., U.S.A.* 73 E7

Alexandrina, L. 62 C2
Alexandroúpolis 22 D5
Alga 29 E6
Algarve 18 D1
Algeciras 18 D3
Algemesí 19 C5
Alger 54 A5
Algeria ■ 54 C5
Alghero 21 D2
Algiers = Alger 54 A5
Algoa B. 59 E5
Alhucemas = Al Hoceïma 54 A4
'Alī al Gharbī 47 D6
'Alī Khēl 42 C6
Aliağa 23 E6
Alibo 53 G6
Alicante 19 C5
Alice Springs 60 E5
Aligarh 42 F11
Alīgūdarz 46 D7
Alipur 42 E7
Alipur Duar 41 D7
Aliwal North 59 E5
Aljustrel 18 D1
Alkmaar 14 B3
All American Canal 82 D5
Allahabad 40 E3
Allanmyo 41 H10
Allegheny → 73 D5
Allegheny Plateau 73 F5
Allentown 73 D8
Alleppey 43 Q10
Aller → 14 B5
Allier → 13 C5
Allora 63 A5
Alma Ata = Almaty 29 E8
Almada 18 C1
Almadén 18 C3
Almansa 19 C5
Almanzor, Pico del Moro 18 B3
Almanzora → 19 D5
Almaty 29 E8
Almazán 19 B4
Almeirim 92 C3
Almelo 14 B4
Almendralejo 18 C2
Almería 19 D4
Almora 42 E11
Alnwick 10 D6
Alon 41 F10
Alor 39 F2
Alor Setar 36 C2
Alps 14 E5
Alsace 13 B7
Alsask 71 C9
Alsásua 19 A4
Alta Gracia 94 C4
Altagracia 90 A4
Altai = Aerhtai Shan 34 B4
Altamira 92 C3
Altamura 21 D6
Altanbulag 35 A5
Altay 34 B3
Altea 19 C5
Alto Araguaia 93 F3
Alto Molocue 59 B7
Alton 77 F9
Alton Downs 62 A2
Altoona 73 D6
Altun Shan 34 C3
Alùla 49 E5
Alusi 39 F4
Alvarado 85 D5
Alvear 94 B5
Alvie 62 C3
Alwar 42 F10
Alxa Zuoqi 35 C5
Am Dam 53 F3
Am-Timan 53 F3
Amâdi, *Sudan* 53 G5
Amadi, *Dem. Rep. of the Congo* 57 D5
Amadjuak 68 B3
Amadjuak L. 68 B3
Amagasaki 32 B4
Amakusa-Shotō 32 C2
Amaliás 23 F3
Amalner 43 J9
Amambay, Cordillera de 94 A5
Amangeldy 29 D7
Amapá 92 B3
Amapá □ 92 B3
Amarante 92 D5
Amargosa 93 E6
Amarillo 78 B3
Amaro, Mte. 20 C5
Amasra 46 B3
Amasya 46 B3
Amazon = Amazonas → 92 C3
Amazonas □ 90 D6
Amazonas → 92 C3
Ambala 42 D10
Ambalavao 59 J9
Ambam 56 D2
Ambanja 59 G9
Ambartsevo 29 D9
Ambato 90 D3
Ambatolampy 59 H9
Ambatondrazaka 59 H9
Amberg 15 D6
Ambergris Cay 85 D7
Amberley 65 E5
Ambikapur 40 F4
Ambilobé 59 G9
Ambo 91 F3
Amboise 12 C4
Ambon 39 E3
Ambositra 59 J9
Amboyna I. 36 C4
Ambriz 56 F2
Amby 63 A4
Amchitka I. 71 C1
Amderma 28 C7
Ameca 84 C4
Ameland 14 B3
American Highland 96 B10
American Samoa ■ 65 L13
Americus 75 C5
Amery 71 C10
Amery Ice Shelf 96 A10
Ames 77 D8
Amherst, *Burma* 41 J11
Amherst, *Canada* 69 D4
Amiata, Mte. 20 C3
Amiens 12 B5
Amirante Is. 26 K9
'Ammān 47 E3
Amorgós 23 F5
Amoy = Xiamen 35 D6
Ampanihy 59 J8
Ampenan 37 F5
Amper → 15 D6
Amravati 43 J10
Amreli 43 J7
Amritsar 42 D9
Amroha 42 E11
Amsterdam 14 B3
Amstetten 15 D8
Amudarya → 29 E6
Amundsen Gulf 70 A7
Amundsen Sea 96 B1
Amuntai 37 E5
Amur → 31 D12
Amurang 39 D2
Amuri Pass 65 E5
Amyderya = Amudarya → 29 E6
An Nafūd 47 E5
An Najaf 47 D6
An Nhon 36 B3
An Nu'ayrīyah 47 F7
Anabar → 30 B9
Anaconda 81 B7
Anadolu 46 C2
'Ānah 46 D5
Anaheim 82 D4
Anakapalle 40 J4
Analalava 59 G9
Anambas, Kepulauan 37 D3
Anambas Is. = Anambas, Kepulauan 37 D3
Anamur 46 C3
Anan 32 C4
Anantnag 42 C9
Ananyiv 17 E9
Anápolis 93 F4
Anār 44 D3
Anārak 44 C3
Anatolia = Anadolu 46 C2
Añatuya 94 B4
Anaye 53 E1
Anchorage 71 B5
Ancohuma, Nevada 91 G5
Ancón 91 F3
Ancona 20 C4
Ancud 95 E2
Ancud, G. de 95 E2
Andalgalá 94 B3
Andalucía □ 18 D3
Andalusia 74 D4
Andalusia □ = Andalucía □ 18 D3
Andaman Is. 27 H13
Andaman Sea 36 B1
Andara 58 B4
Anderson 72 D3
Anderson → 70 B7
Andes = Andes, Cord. de los 91 G4
Andes, Cord. de los 91 G4
Andhra Pradesh □ 43 L11
Andijon 29 E8
Andikíthira 23 G4
Andizhan = Andijon 29 E8
Andkhvoy 45 B6
Andoany 59 G9
Andorra ■ 19 A6
Andorra La Vella 19 A6
Andreanof Is. 71 C2
Andrewilla 62 A2
Ándria 20 D6
Andriba 59 H9
Andropov = Rybinsk 24 B4
Ándros 23 F5
Andros I. 86 B4
Andújar 18 C3
Andulo 56 G3
Aného 55 G5
Aneto, Pico de 19 A6
Angamos, Punta 94 A2
Ang'angxi 35 B7
Angara → 30 D7
Angarsk 30 D8
Angaston 62 B2
Ånge 8 F11
Angeles 38 A2
Angellala 63 A4
Ångermanälven → 8 F11
Angers 12 C3
Anglesey 11 E4
Ango 57 D5
Angola ■ 58 A3
Angoulême 12 D4
Angoumois 12 D4
Angra dos Reis 94 A8
Angren 29 E8
Anguilla ■ 87 C7
Anhui □ 35 C6
Anhwei □ = Anhui □ 35 C6
Anjidiv I. 43 M9
Anjou 12 C3
Anjozorobe 59 H9
Anju 35 C7
Anka 55 F6
Ankang 35 C5
Ankara 46 C3
Ankazoabo 59 J8
Ankazobe 59 H9
Ankoro 57 F5
Ann Arbor 72 C4
Annaba 54 A6
Annan 11 D5
Annapolis 73 E7
Annecy 13 D7
Anning 34 D5
Anniston 74 C5
Annobón 51 G4
Annuello 62 B3
Anqing 35 C6
Ansbach 14 D6
Anshan 35 B7
Anshun 35 D5
Ansirabe 59 H9
Ansongo 55 E5
Ansudu 39 E5
Antabamba 91 F4
Antakya 46 C4
Antalaha 59 G10
Antalya 46 C2
Antalya Körfezi 46 C2
Antananarivo 59 H9
Antarctic Pen. 96 A4
Antarctica 96 C
Antequera 18 D3
Anti Atlas 54 C3
Antibes 13 E7
Anticosti, I. d' 69 D4
Antigua & Barbuda ■ 87 C7
Antilla 86 B4
Antioquia 90 B3
Antofagasta 94 A2
Antofagasta de la Sierra 94 B3
Antongila, Helodrano 59 H9
Antonina 94 B7
Antrim 11 D3
Antsalova 59 H8
Antsiranana 59 G9
Antsohihy 59 G9
Antwerp = Antwerpen 14 C3
Antwerpen 14 C3

Anupgarh 42 E8
Anvers = Antwerpen . . 14 C3
Anvers I. 96 A3
Anxi 34 B4
Anxious B. 62 B1
Anyang 35 C6
Anzhero-Sudzhensk . . 29 D9
Ánzio 20 D4
Aomori 33 F12
Aosta 20 B1
Aoudéras 55 E6
Aoulef el Arab . 54 C5
Apalachicola → 74 E5
Apaporis → . . 90 D5
Aparri 38 A2
Apeldoorn 14 B3
Apennines = Appennini . . 20 B3
Apia 65 L13
Apiacás, Serra dos 91 E7
Aplao 91 G4
Apo, Mt. 38 C3
Apollonia = Marsá Susah 52 B3
Apolo 91 F5
Apoteri 90 C7
Appalachian Mts. 73 F5
Appennini 20 B3
Appleton 72 B1
Approuague . . 92 B3
Aprília 20 D4
Apucarana 94 A6
Apure → 90 B5
Apurimac → . . 91 F4
Aqabah = Al 'Aqabah 47 E3
'Aqabah, Khalīj al 47 E3
Āqcheh 45 B6
Aqîq 53 E6
Aqmola = Astana 29 D8
Aqrah 46 C5
Aqtöbe 29 D6
Aquidauana . . . 93 G2
Aquitain, Bassin 12 D3
Ar Rachidiya . . 54 B4
Ar Ramādī 46 D5
Ar Raqqah 46 D4
Ar Rass 47 F5
Ar Rifā'ī 47 E6
Ar Riyāḍ 47 F6
Ar Ruṭbah 46 D5
Ar Ruwayḍah . 47 G6
Ara 40 E5
'Arab, Bahr el → 53 G4
Arab, Shatt al → 47 E7
Arabian Desert = Es Sahrâ' Esh Sharqîya 52 C5
Arabian Gulf = Gulf, The . . . 44 E2
Arabian Sea . . . 26 H10
Araç 46 B3
Aracaju 93 E6
Aracataca 90 A4
Aracati 92 C6
Araçatuba 93 G3
Aracena 18 D2
Araçuaí 93 F5
Arad 16 E5
Arada 53 F3
Arafura Sea . . . 39 F4
Aragón □ 19 B5
Aragón → 19 A5
Araguacema . . 92 D4
Araguaia → . . 92 D4
Araguari 93 F4
Araguari → . . 92 B4
Arak 54 C5
Arakan Coast . . 41 H9
Arakan Yoma . 41 H10
Araks = Aras, Rūd-e → . . . 46 B7
Aral 29 E7
Aral Sea 29 E6
Aral Tengizi = Aral Sea 29 E6
Aralsk = Aral . . 29 E7
Aralskoye More = Aral Sea . . 29 E6
Aran I. 10 D2
Aran Is. 11 E2
Aranda de Duero 18 B4
Aranjuez 18 B4
Aranos 58 C3
Araouane 55 E4
Arapgir 46 C4
Arapiraca 93 D6
Arapongas 94 A6
Araranguá 94 B7
Araraquara . . . 93 G4
Ararat 62 C3
Ararat, Mt. = Ağrı Dağı . . . 46 C6
Araripe, Chapada do . 92 D6
Aras, Rūd-e → 46 B7
Arauca 90 B4
Arauca → 90 B5
Arauco 94 D2
Araxá 93 F4
Araya, Pen. de . 90 A6
Arbatax 21 E2
Arbīl 46 C6
Arbroath 10 C5
Arcachon 12 D3
Archangel = Arkhangelsk . 28 C5
Arcila = Asilah 54 A3
Arckaringa 62 A1
Arckaringa Cr. → 62 A2
Arcos de la Frontera 18 D3
Arcot 43 N11
Arcoverde 92 D6
Arctic Bay 68 A2
Arctic Red River 70 B6
Arda → 22 D6
Ardabīl 46 C7
Ardahan 46 B5
Ardakān = Sepīdān 44 D3
Ardenne 14 D3
Ardennes = Ardenne 14 D3
Ardestān 44 C3
Ardlethan 63 B4
Ardmore 78 B5
Ardrossan 62 B2
Arecibo 87 C6
Areia Branca . . 92 C6
Arendal 9 G9
Arequipa 91 G4
Arero 53 H6
Arévalo 18 B3
Arezzo 20 C3
Argamakmur . . 37 E2
Arganda 18 B4
Argentan 12 B3
Argentário, Mte. 20 C3
Argentina ■ . . . 94 D3
Argentina Is. . . 96 A3
Argentino, L. . . 95 G2
Argeş → 22 B6
Arghandab → 42 D4
Argo 53 E5
Argolikós Kólpos 23 F4
Árgos 23 F4
Argostólion . . . 23 E3
Argungu 55 F5
Århus 9 G10
Arica, *Chile* . . . 91 G4
Arica, *Colombia* 90 D4
Aridh 47 F6
Arinos → 91 F7
Aripuanã 91 E6
Aripuanã → . . 90 E6
Ariquemes 91 E6
Arizona 94 D3
Arizona □ 83 C7
Arjona 90 A3
Arkalyk = Arqalyk 29 D7
Arkansas □ . . . 79 B7
Arkansas → . . 79 C8
Arkansas City . 78 A5
Arkhangelsk . . . 28 C5
Arklow 11 E3
Arkticheskiy, Mys 30 A7
Arlanzón → . . 18 A3
Arlberg P. 14 E6
Arles 13 E6
Arlington, *Va., U.S.A.* 73 E7
Arlington, *Wash., U.S.A.* 80 A2
Arlon 14 D3
Armagh 11 D3
Armavir 25 D5
Armenia 90 C3
Armenia ■ 25 E5
Armidale 63 B5
Armstrong 69 C2
Arnaud → 68 B3
Arnauti, C. 46 D3
Arnhem 14 C3
Arnhem, C. . . . 60 C6
Arnhem Land . 60 C5
Arno → 20 C3
Arno Bay 62 B2
Arnsberg 14 C5
Aroab 58 D3
Arqalyk 29 D7
Arrabury 62 A3
Arrah = Ara . . . 40 E5
Arran 10 D4
Arras 13 A5
Arrecife 54 C2
Arrée, Mts. d' . 12 B2
Arrowtown . . . 65 F3
Árta 23 E3
Arthur → 62 D3
Arthur's Pass . . 65 E4
Artigas 94 C5
Artois 12 A5
Artsyz 17 E9
Artvin 46 B5
Aru, Kepulauan 39 F4
Aru Is. = Aru, Kepulauan . . 39 F4
Arua 57 D6
Aruanã 93 E3
Aruba ■ 87 D6
Arumpo 62 B3
Arunachal Pradesh □ . . 41 C10
Arusha 57 E7
Aruwimi → . . . 56 D4
Arviat 70 B10
Arxan 35 B6
Arys 29 E7
Arzamas 24 B5
Arzew 54 A4
'As Saffānīyah . 47 E7
As Samāwah . . 47 E6
As Sulaymānīyah, *Iraq* 46 D6
As Sulaymānīyah, *Si. Arabia* . . . 47 F6
As Summān . . 47 F6
As Sūq 47 G5
As Suwaydā' . . 46 D4
As Suwayh . . . 45 F4
As Ṣuwayrah . . 47 D6
Asahigawa 32 F12
Asansol 40 F6
Ascension I. . . . 51 G2
Aschaffenburg . 14 D5
Aschersleben . . 15 C6
Áscoli Piceno . . 20 C4
Ascope 91 E3
Aseb 49 E3
Asela 53 G6
Asenovgrad . . . 22 C5
Ash Shām, Bādiyat 47 D4
Ash Shāmīyah . 47 E6
Ash Shāriqah . 44 E3
Ash Shaṭrah . . 47 E6
Ash Shaykh, J. 46 D3
Ash Shu'aybah 47 F6
Ash Shu'bah . . 47 E6
Ashburton 65 E4
Ashcroft 71 C7
Asheville 75 B6
Ashford, *Australia* 63 A5
Ashford, *U.K.* . . 11 F7
Ashgabat 29 F6
Ashikaga 32 A6
Ashizuri-Zaki . . 32 C3
Ashkhabad = Ashgabat . . . 29 F6
Ashmyany 17 A7
Ashqelon 47 E3
Ashtabula 72 D5
Ashuanipi, L. . . 69 C4
Asia, Kepulauan 39 D4
Asifabad 43 K11
Asike 39 F6
Asilah 54 A3
Asinara 20 D2
Asinara, G. dell' 20 D2
Asino 29 D9
Asipovichy 17 B9
'Asīr □ 48 D3
Asir, Ras 49 E5
Asmara = Asmera 53 E6
Asmera 53 E6
Aspiring, Mt. . . 65 F3
Assam □ 41 D9
Assen 14 B4
Assini 55 G4
Assiniboia 71 D9
Assiniboine → 71 D10
Assis 94 A6
Assisi 20 C4
Astana 29 D8
Asti 20 B2
Astipálaia 23 F6
Astorga 18 A2
Astoria 80 B2
Astrakhan 25 D6
Astrakhan-Bazàr 25 F6

Asturias □ 18 A3
Asunción 94 B5
Aswân 52 D5
Aswân High Dam = Sadd el Aali 52 D5
Asyût 52 C5
At Ţafīlah 47 E3
At Tā'if 48 C3
Atacama, Desierto de 94 A3
Atacama, Salar de 94 A3
Atakpamé 55 G5
Atalaya 91 F4
Atami 32 B6
Atapupu 39 F2
Atâr 54 D2
Atasu 29 E8
Atauro 39 F3
Atbara 53 E5
'Atbara → 53 E5
Atbasar 29 D7
Athabasca 71 C8
Athabasca → 70 C8
Athabasca, L. 70 C8
Athens = Athínai 23 F4
Athens, *Ala., U.S.A.* 74 B4
Athens, *Ga., U.S.A.* 75 C6
Athínai 23 F4
Athlone 11 E3
Áthos 23 D5
Athy 11 E3
Ati 53 F2
Atico 91 G4
Atlanta 75 C5
Atlantic City 73 E8
Atlas Mts. = Haut Atlas 54 B3
Atrak = Atrek → 44 B3
Atrek → 44 B3
Attawapiskat → 69 C2
Attock 42 C8
Attopeu 36 B3
Attur 43 P11
Atuel → 94 D3
Atyraū 29 E6
Aubagne 13 E6
Aube → 13 B5
Auburn 74 C5
Auburn Ra. 63 A5
Aubusson 12 D5
Auch 12 E4
Auckland 64 B6
Aude → 13 E5
Augathella 63 A4
Augsburg 14 D6
Augusta, *Italy* 21 F5
Augusta, *Ga., U.S.A.* 75 C7
Augusta, *Maine, U.S.A.* 73 B11
Aunis 12 C3
Auponhia 39 E3
Aurangabad, *Bihar, India* 40 E5
Aurangabad, *Maharashtra, India* 43 K9
Aurich 14 B4
Aurillac 12 D5
Aurora, *Colo., U.S.A.* 76 F2
Aurora, *Ill., U.S.A.* 72 D1
Aus 58 D3
Auschwitz = Oświęcim 16 C4
Austin, *Minn., U.S.A.* 77 D8
Austin, *Tex., U.S.A.* 78 D5
Austral Is. = Tubuai Is. 65 M16
Austral Seamount Chain 65 M16
Australia ■ 60 E6
Australian Alps 63 C4
Australian Capital Territory □ 63 C4
Austria ■ 15 E8
Autun 13 C6
Auvergne 13 D5
Auvergne, Mts. d' 13 D5
Auxerre 13 C5
Avallon 13 C5
Aveiro, *Brazil* 92 C2
Aveiro, *Portugal* 18 B1
Āvej 46 D7
Avellaneda 94 C5
Avellino 21 D5
Aversa 21 D5
Avezzano 20 C4
Aviá Terai 94 B4
Aviemore 10 C5
Avignon 13 E6
Ávila 18 B3
Avilés 18 A3
Avoca → 62 C3
Avola 21 F5
Avranches 12 B3
'Awālī 44 E2
Awash 49 F3
Awatere → 65 D6
Awbārī 52 C1
Awjilah 52 C3
Axim 55 H4
Axiós → 23 D4
Ayabaca 90 D3
Ayabe 32 B4
Ayacucho, *Argentina* 94 D5
Ayacucho, *Peru* 91 F4
Ayaguz 29 E9
Ayamonte 18 D2
Ayaviri 91 F4
Āybak 45 B7
Aydın 23 F6
Ayers Rock 60 F5
Áyios Evstrátios 23 E5
Aylmer, L. 70 B8
Ayn Dār 47 F7
Ayn Zālah 46 C5
Ayr 10 D4
Aytos 22 C6
Ayu, Kepulauan 39 D4
Ayutla 84 D5
Ayvacık 23 E6
Ayvalık 23 E6
Aẓ Ẓahrān 47 F7
Az Zarqā 46 D4
Az-Zilfī 47 F6
Az Zubayr 47 E6
Az Zuwaytīnah 52 B3
Azamgarh 40 D4
Azärbayjan = Azerbaijan ■ 25 E6
Āzarbāyjān-e Gharbī □ 46 C6
Āzarbāyjān-e Sharqī □ 46 C6
Azare 55 F7
Azbine = Aïr 55 E6
Azerbaijan ■ 25 E6
Azerbaijchan = Azerbaijan ■ 25 E6
Azogues 90 D3
Azores 50 C1
Azov 25 D4
Azov, Sea of 25 D4
Azovskoye More = Azov, Sea of 25 D4
Azovy 28 C7
Azúa 87 C5
Azuaga 18 C3
Azuero, Pen. de 86 E3
Azul 94 D5

B

Ba Don 36 A3
Ba Ria 36 B3
Bab el Mandeb 49 E3
Baba Burnu 23 E6
Babadag 22 B7
Babadayhan 29 F7
Babaeski 22 D6
Babahoyo 90 D3
Babana 55 F5
Babar 39 F3
Babo 39 E4
Bābol 44 B3
Bābol Sar 44 B3
Baboua 56 C2
Babruysk 17 B9
Babura 55 F6
Babuyan Chan. 38 A2
Babylon 47 D6
Bacabal 92 C5
Bacan, Kepulauan 39 E3
Bacan, Pulau 39 E3
Bacarra 38 A2
Bacău 17 E8
Bachelina 29 D7
Back → 70 B9
Backstairs Passage 62 C2
Bacolod 38 B2
Bad Ischl 15 E7
Bad Kissingen 14 C6
Bad Lands 76 D3
Badagara 43 P9
Badajoz 18 C2
Badalona 19 B7
Badalzai 42 E4
Badampahar 40 F6
Badanah 47 E5
Badarinath 42 D11
Badas 36 D4
Badas, Kepulauan 37 D3
Baddo → 42 E4
Bade 39 F5
Baden 15 D9
Baden-Baden 14 D5
Baden-Württemberg □ 14 D5
Badgastein 15 E7
Bādghīsāt □ 42 B3
Badin 43 G6
Baduen 49 F4
Baena 18 D3
Baeza 18 D4
Bafatá 55 F2
Baffin B. 68 A4
Baffin I. 68 B3
Bafia 56 D2
Bafing → 55 F2
Bafoulabé 55 F2
Bāfq 44 D3
Bafra 46 B3
Bāft 44 D4
Bafwasende 57 D5
Bagamoyo 57 F7
Baganga 38 C3
Bagansiapiapi 37 D2
Bagdarin 30 D9
Bagé 94 C6
Baghdād 46 D6
Bagheria 21 E4
Baghlān 42 A6
Baghlān □ 45 C7
Baguio 38 A2
Bahamas ■ 86 A4
Baharampur 40 E7
Bahawalpur 42 E7
Bahía = Salvador 93 E6
Bahía □ 93 E5
Bahía Blanca 94 D4
Bahía de Caráquez 90 D2
Bahía Laura 95 F3
Bahía Negra 91 H7
Bahr Aouk → 56 C3
Bahr Salamat → 53 G2
Bahraich 40 D3
Bahrain ■ 44 E2
Baia Mare 17 E6
Baïbokoum 53 G2
Baidoa 49 G3
Baie Comeau 69 D4
Ba'ījī 46 D5
Baikal, L. = Baykal, Oz. 30 D8
Baile Atha Cliath = Dublin 11 E3
Băileşti 22 B4
Bailundo 58 A3
Bā'ir 47 E4
Baird Mts. 71 B3
Bairnsdale 63 C4
Baitadi 40 C3
Baiyin 35 C5
Baja 16 E4
Baja, Pta. 84 B1
Baja California 84 A1
Bajimba, Mt. 63 A5
Bakala 56 C4
Bakchar 29 D9
Bakel 55 F2
Baker, L. 70 B10
Baker I. 64 J13
Baker Lake 70 B10
Baker Mt. 80 A3
Baker's Dozen Is. 69 C3
Bakersfield 82 C3
Bākhtarān 46 D6
Bakı 25 E6
Bakony Forest = Bakony Hegyseg 16 E3
Bakony Hegyseg 16 E3
Bakouma 56 C4
Baku = Bakı 25 E6
Bakutis Coast 96 B1
Baky = Bakı 25 E6
Balabac I. 36 C5
Balabac Str. 36 C5
Balabalangan, Kepulauan 37 E5

Balaghat Ra. 43 K10
Balaguer 19 B6
Balaklava, *Australia* 62 B2
Balaklava, *Ukraine* 25 E3
Balakovo 24 C6
Balashov 24 C5
Balasore = Baleshwar 40 G6
Balaton 16 E3
Balbina, Reprêsa de 90 D7
Balchik 22 C7
Balclutha 65 G3
Baleares, Is. 19 C7
Balearic Is. = Baleares, Is. 19 C7
Baler 38 A2
Baleshwar 40 G6
Bali, *Cameroon* 55 G7
Bali, *Indonesia* 37 F5
Bali □ 37 F5
Balikeşir 23 E6
Balikpapan 37 E5
Balimbing 38 C1
Balipara 41 D9
Baliza 93 F3
Balkan Mts. = Stara Planina 22 C4
Balkh 45 B6
Balkhash = Balqash 29 E8
Balkhash, Ozero = Balqash Köl 29 E8
Balla 41 E8
Ballarat 62 C3
Ballater 10 C5
Ballina, *Australia* 63 A5
Ballina, *Ireland* 11 D2
Ballinasloe 11 E2
Ballymena 11 D3
Balmaceda 95 F2
Balmoral 62 C3
Balonne → 63 A4
Balqash 29 E8
Balqash Köl 29 E8
Balrampur 40 D4
Balranald 62 B3
Balsas → 84 D4
Balta 17 D9
Bălţi 17 E8
Baltic Sea 9 G11
Baltimore 73 E7
Baluchistan □ 42 F4
Balya 23 E6
Bam 44 D4
Bama 53 F1
Bamako 55 F3
Bamba 55 E4
Bambari 56 C4
Bamberg 14 D6
Bambili 57 D5
Bamenda 55 G7
Bāmīān □ 42 B5
Bampūr 45 E5
Ban Don = Surat Thani 36 C1
Ban Mê Thuôt = Buon Me Thuot 36 B3
Banaba 64 K11
Banalia 57 D5
Banam 36 B3
Banamba 55 F3
Bananal, I. do 93 E3
Banaras = Varanasi 40 E4
Band-e Torkestān 45 C6
Banda, Kepulauan 39 E3
Banda Aceh 36 C1
Banda Banda, Mt. 63 B5
Banda Elat 39 F4
Banda Is. = Banda, Kepulauan 39 E3
Banda Sea 39 F3
Bandanaira 39 E3
Bandar = Machilipatnam 40 J3
Bandār 'Abbās 44 E4
Bandar-e Anzalī 46 C7
Bandar-e Bushehr = Būshehr 44 D2
Bandar-e Chārak 44 E3
Bandar-e Deylam 47 E7
Bandar-e Khomeynı 47 E7
Bandar-e Lengeh 44 E3
Bandar-e Ma'shur 47 E7
Bandar-e Nakhīlū 44 E3
Bandar-e Rīg 44 D2
Bandar-e Torkeman 44 B3
Bandar Maharani = Muar 37 D2
Bandar Penggaram = Batu Pahat 37 D2
Bandar Seri Begawan 36 D5
Bandawe 59 A6
Bandeira, Pico da 93 G5
Bandera 94 B4
Bandiagara 55 F4
Bandırma 23 D7
Bandon 11 F2
Bandundu 56 E3
Bandung 37 F3
Banff, *Canada* 71 C8
Banff, *U.K.* 10 C5
Banfora 55 F4
Bang Saphan 36 B1
Bangalore 43 N10
Bangassou 56 D4
Banggai, Kepulauan 39 E2
Banggi, P. 36 C5
Banghāzī 52 B3
Bangka, P., *Sulawesi, Indonesia* 39 D3
Bangka, P., *Sumatera, Indonesia* 37 E3
Bangka, Selat 37 E3
Bangkinang 37 D2
Bangko 37 E2
Bangkok 36 B2
Bangladesh ■ 41 E7
Bangong Co 42 B11
Bangor, *Down, U.K.* 11 D4
Bangor, *Gwynedd, U.K.* 11 E4
Bangor, *U.S.A.* 73 B11
Bangued 38 A2
Bangui 56 D3
Bangweulu, L. 57 G6
Bani 87 C5
Banī Walīd 52 B1
Banīnah 52 B3
Bāniyās 46 D3
Banja Luka 20 B6
Banjarmasin 37 E4
Banjul 55 F1
Bankipore 40 E5
Banks I. 70 A7
Banks Pen. 65 E5
Banks Str. 62 D4
Bankura 40 F6
Banningville = Bandundu 56 E3
Bannu 42 C7
Banská Bystrica 16 D4
Banswara 43 H9
Bantry 11 F2
Banu 42 B6
Banyak, Kepulauan 37 D1
Banyo 55 G7
Banzare Coast 96 A13
Banzyville = Mobayi 56 D4
Baoding 35 C6
Baoji 35 C5
Baoshan 34 D4
Baotou 35 B6
Bapatla 40 K3
Ba'qūbah 46 D6
Bar, *Montenegro, Yug.* 22 C2
Bar, *Ukraine* 17 D8
Bar-le-Duc 13 B6
Barabai 37 E5
Barabinsk 29 D8
Baracaldo 19 A4
Baracoa 86 B5
Barahona 87 C5
Barail Range 41 E9
Barakhola 41 E9
Barakpur 41 F7
Barakula 63 A5
Baramula 42 B9
Baran 43 G10
Baranavichy 17 B8
Baranof I. 71 C6
Barão de Melgaço 91 F6
Barapasi 39 E5
Barat Daya, Kepulauan 39 F3
Barbacena 93 G5
Barbacoas 90 C3
Barbados ■ 87 D8
Barbastro 19 A6
Barberton 59 D6
Barcellona Pozzo di Gotto 21 E5
Barcelona, *Spain* 19 B7
Barcelona, *Venezuela* 90 A6
Barcelos 90 D6
Bardai 52 D2
Barddhaman 40 F6
Bardejov 16 D5
Bardera 49 G3
Bardi, Ra's 47 F4
Bardīyah 52 B4
Bareilly 42 E11
Barentu 53 E6
Barfleur, Pte. de 12 B3
Barga 34 C3
Bargal 49 E5
Barhi 40 E5
Bari 20 D6
Bari Doab 42 D8
Barīm 49 E3
Barinas 90 B4
Baring, C. 70 B8
Bârîs 52 D5
Barisal 41 F8
Barisan, Bukit 37 E2
Barito → 37 E4
Barkly Tableland 60 D6
Barlee, L. 60 F2
Barletta 20 D6
Barmedman 63 B4
Barmer 42 G7
Barmera 62 B3
Barnato 63 B4
Barnaul 29 D9
Barnsley 11 E6
Barnstaple 11 F4
Baro 55 G6
Baroda = Vadodara 43 H8
Barpeta 41 D8
Barquísimeto 90 A5
Barra, *Brazil* 93 E5
Barra, *U.K.* 10 C3
Barra do Corda 92 D4
Barra do Piraí 93 G5
Barra Falsa, Pta. da 59 C7
Barraba 63 B5
Barrackpur = Barakpur 41 F7
Barraigh = Barra 10 C3
Barranca, *Lima, Peru* 91 F3
Barranca, *Loreto, Peru* 90 D3
Barrancabermeja 90 B4
Barrancas 90 B6
Barrancos 18 C2
Barranqueras 94 B5
Barranquilla 90 A4
Barras 92 C5
Barreiras 93 E5
Barreirinhas 92 C5
Barreiro 18 C1
Barreiros 92 D6
Barretos 93 G4
Barrier Ra. 62 B3
Barrington Tops 63 B5
Barringun 63 A4
Barrow 71 A4
Barrow-in-Furness 11 D5
Barry 11 F5
Barsi 43 K9
Barsoi 40 E6
Barstow 82 C4
Bartica 90 B7
Bartin 46 B3
Bartle Frere 61 D8
Bartlesville 79 A6
Barysaw 17 A9
Bāsa'idū 44 E3
Basankusa 56 D3
Basarabeasca 17 E9
Basel 13 C7
Bashi Channel 35 D7
Bashkir Republic = Bashkortostan □ 29 D6
Bashkortostan □ 29 D6
Basilan 38 C2
Basilan Str. 38 C2
Basildon 11 F7
Basim = Washim 43 J10

Basingstoke	11	F6
Basle = Basel	13	C7
Basoka	56	D4
Basongo	56	E4
Basque Provinces = País Vasco □	19	A4
Basra = Al Başrah	47	E6
Bass Str.	61	H8
Bassano	71	C8
Bassano del Grappa	20	B3
Bassas da India	59	C7
Bassein	41	J10
Basseterre	87	C7
Bassikounou	55	E3
Bastak	44	E3
Bastar	40	H3
Basti	40	D4
Bastia	13	E8
Bastogne	14	C3
Bata	56	D1
Bataan	38	B2
Batabanó	86	B3
Batabanó, G. de	86	B3
Batac	38	A2
Batagoy	31	C11
Batamay	31	C10
Batang	34	C4
Batangafo	56	C3
Batangas	38	B2
Batanta	39	E4
Bateman's B.	63	C5
Batemans Bay	63	C5
Bath	11	F5
Bathurst, *Australia*	63	B4
Bathurst, *Canada*	69	D4
Bathurst, C.	70	A7
Bathurst Harb.	62	D4
Bathurst Inlet	70	B9
Batinah	44	F4
Batlow	63	C4
Batman	46	C5
Batna	54	A6
Baton Rouge	79	D8
Batouri	56	D2
Battambang	36	B2
Battipáglia	21	D5
Battle Creek	72	C3
Battle Harbour	69	C5
Battleford	71	C9
Batu	49	F2
Batu, Kepulauan	37	E1
Batu Is. = Batu, Kepulauan	37	E1
Batu Pahat	37	D2
Batuata	39	F2
Batumi	25	E5
Baturaja	37	E2
Baturité	92	C6
Bau	37	D4
Baubau	39	F2
Bauchi	55	F6
Bauer, C.	62	B1
Baukau	39	F3
Bauru	93	G4
Baús	93	F3
Bautzen	15	C8
Bavaria = Bayern □	15	D6
Bawdwin	41	F11
Bawean	37	F4
Bawku	55	F4
Bawlake	41	H11
Bay, L. de	38	B2
Bay City	72	C4
Bay View	64	C7
Bayamo	86	B4
Bayan Har Shan	34	C4
Bayan Hot = Alxa Zuoqi	35	C5
Bayanaūyl	29	D8
Bayanhongor	35	B5
Bayázeh	44	C3
Baybay	38	B2
Bayburt	46	B5
Bayern □	15	D6
Bayeux	12	B3
Bayındır	23	E6
Baykal, Oz.	30	D8
Baykit	30	C7
Baykonur = Bayqongyr	29	E7
Bayombong	38	A2
Bayonne	12	E3
Bayovar	91	E2
Bayqongyr	29	E7
Bayram-Ali = Bayramaly	29	F7
Bayramaly	29	F7
Bayramiç	23	E6
Bayreuth	15	D6
Bayrūt	46	D3
Baytown	79	E6
Baza	19	D4
Bazaruto, I. do	59	C7
Beachport	62	C2
Beagle, Canal	95	G3
Beardmore Glacier	96	C14
Béarn	12	E3
Beauce, Plaine de la	12	B4
Beaudesert	63	A5
Beaufort	36	C5
Beaufort Sea	66	B6
Beaufort West	58	E4
Beaumont	79	D6
Beaune	13	C6
Beauvais	12	B5
Beauval	71	C9
Beaver	71	B5
Beaver →	71	C9
Beawar	42	F9
Bečej	22	B3
Béchar	54	B4
Bedford	11	E6
Beenleigh	63	A5
Be'er Sheva	47	E3
Beersheba = Be'er Sheva	47	E3
Befale	56	D4
Bega	63	C4
Behbehān	47	E7
Behshahr	44	B3
Bei Jiang →	35	D6
Bei'an	35	B7
Beibei	35	D5
Beihai	35	D5
Beijing	35	C6
Beilpajah	63	B3
Beinn na Faoghla = Benbecula	10	C3
Beira	59	B6
Beirut = Bayrūt	46	D3
Beitbridge	59	C6
Beja, *Portugal*	18	C2
Béja, *Tunisia*	54	A6
Bejaia	54	A6
Béjar	18	B3
Bejestān	44	C4
Békéscsaba	16	E5
Bela, *India*	40	E4
Bela, *Pakistan*	42	F5
Bela Crkva	22	B3
Bela Vista	94	A5
Belarus ■	24	C2
Belau = Palau ■	38	C4
Belawan	37	D1
Belaya Tserkov = Bila Tserkva	17	D10
Belcher Is.	69	C3
Belém	92	C4
Belén	94	A5
Belet Uen	49	G4
Belev	24	C4
Belfast	11	D4
Belfort	13	C7
Belgaum	43	M9
Belgium ■	14	C3
Belgorod	24	C4
Belgorod-Dnestrovskiy = Bilhorod-Dnistrovskyy	25	D3
Belgrade = Beograd	22	B3
Beli Drim →	22	C3
Belinga	56	D2
Belinyu	37	E3
Beliton Is. = Belitung	37	E3
Belitung	37	E3
Belize ■	85	D7
Belize City	85	D7
Belkovskiy, Ostrov	30	B11
Bell Bay	62	D4
Bell Peninsula	68	B2
Bell Ville	94	C4
Bella Unión	94	C5
Bella Vista	94	B5
Bellary	43	M10
Bellata	63	A4
Belle-Ile	12	C2
Belle Isle	69	C5
Belle Isle, Str. of	69	C5
Belleville, *Canada*	69	D3
Belleville, *U.S.A.*	77	F10
Bellin = Kangirsuk	68	C4
Bellingen	63	B5
Bellingham	80	A2
Bellingshausen Sea	96	A2
Bellinzona	13	C8
Belluno	20	A4
Belmont	63	B5
Belmonte	93	F6
Belmopan	85	D7
Belo Horizonte	93	F5
Belo-Tsiribihina	59	H8
Beloit	77	D10
Belokorovichi	17	C9
Belomorsk	28	C4
Belonia	41	F8
Belorussia ■ = Belarus ■	24	C2
Belovo	29	D9
Beloye, Ozero	24	A4
Beloye More	28	C4
Belozersk	24	A4
Beltana	62	B2
Belterra	92	C3
Beltsy = Bălţi	17	E8
Belukha	29	E9
Beluran	36	C5
Belyy, Ostrov	28	B8
Belyy Yar	29	D9
Bembéréke	55	F5
Bemidji	77	B7
Ben Gardane	52	B1
Ben Lomond, *N.S.W., Australia*	63	B5
Ben Lomond, *Tas., Australia*	62	D4
Ben Nevis	10	C4
Bena	55	F6
Bena Dibele	56	E4
Benagerie	62	B3
Benalla	63	C4
Benambra, Mt.	63	C4
Benares = Varanasi	40	E4
Benavente	18	A3
Benbecula	10	C3
Benbonyathe	62	B2
Bend	80	C3
Bender Beila	49	F5
Bendery = Tighina	17	E9
Bendigo	63	C3
Benevento	20	D5
Bengal, Bay of	41	J7
Bengbu	35	C6
Benghazi = Banghāzī	52	B3
Bengkalis	37	D2
Bengkulu	37	E2
Bengkulu □	37	E2
Benguela	58	A2
Beni	57	D5
Beni →	91	F5
Beni Abbès	54	B4
Beni Mazâr	52	C5
Beni Mellal	54	B3
Beni Ounif	54	B4
Beni Suef	52	C5
Benidorm	19	C5
Benin ■	55	G5
Benin, Bight of	55	H5
Benin City	55	G6
Benjamin Constant	90	D4
Benoni	59	D5
Bent	44	E4
Benteng	39	F2
Benton Harbor	72	C2
Benue →	55	G6
Benxi	35	B7
Beo	38	D3
Beograd	22	B3
Beppu	32	C2
Berati	23	D2
Berau, Teluk	39	E4
Berber	53	E5
Berbera	49	E4
Berbérati	56	D3
Berbice →	90	B7
Berdichev = Berdychiv	17	D9
Berdsk	29	D9
Berdyansk	25	D4
Berdychiv	17	D9
Berebere	39	D3
Bereda	49	E5
Berehove	17	D6
Berekum	55	G4
Berestechko	17	C7
Bereza	17	B7
Berezhany	17	D7
Berezina = Byarezina →	17	B10
Berezniki	28	D6
Berezovo	28	C7
Berga	19	A6
Bergama	23	E6
Bérgamo	20	B2
Bergen	8	F9
Bergerac	12	D4

Berhala, Selat 37 E2
Berhampore = Baharampur 40 E7
Berhampur = Brahamapur 40 H5
Bering Sea 71 C1
Bering Strait 71 B3
Berja 19 D4
Berkeley 80 G2
Berkner I. 96 B4
Berlin 15 B7
Bermejo →, *Formosa, Argentina* 94 B5
Bermejo →, *San Juan, Argentina* 94 C3
Bermuda ■ 67 F13
Bern 13 C7
Bernardo de Irigoyen 94 B6
Bernburg 15 C6
Berne = Bern 13 C7
Bernina, Piz 13 C8
Beroroha 59 J9
Beroun 16 D2
Berrechid 54 B3
Berri 62 B3
Berry, *Australia* 63 B5
Berry, *France* 12 C5
Bershad 17 D9
Bertoua 56 D2
Berwick-upon-Tweed 10 D6
Besalampy 59 H8
Besançon 13 C7
Besar 37 E5
Besni 46 C4
Bessarabiya 17 E9
Bessarabka = Basarabeasca 17 E9
Bessemer 74 C4
Betanzos 18 A1
Bétaré Oya 56 C2
Bethanien 58 D3
Bethel 71 B3
Bethlehem, *S. Africa* 59 D5
Bethlehem, *U.S.A.* 73 D8
Béthune 13 A5
Bethungra 63 B4
Betioky 59 J8
Betroka 59 J9
Betsiamites 69 D4
Bettiah 40 D5
Betul 43 J10
Betung 37 D4
Beverley 11 E6
Beverly Hills 82 C3
Beyla 55 G3
Beyneu 29 E6
Beypazarı 46 B2
Beyşehir Gölü 46 C2
Bezhitsa 24 C3
Béziers 13 E5
Bezwada = Vijayawada 40 J3
Bhachau 43 H7
Bhadrakh 40 G6
Bhadravati 43 N9
Bhagalpur 40 E6
Bhakra Dam 42 D10
Bhamo 41 E11
Bhandara 43 J11
Bhanrer Ra. 43 H11
Bharat = India ■ 43 J10
Bharatpur 42 F10
Bhatpara 41 F7
Bhaunagar = Bhavnagar 43 J8
Bhavnagar 43 J8
Bhawanipatna 40 H3
Bhilsa = Vidisha 43 H10
Bhilwara 43 G9
Bhima → 43 L10
Bhimavaram 40 J3
Bhind 42 F11
Bhiwandi 43 K8
Bhiwani 42 E10
Bhola 41 F8
Bhopal 43 H10
Bhubaneshwar 40 G5
Bhuj 43 H6
Bhumiphol Dam = Phumiphon, Khuan 36 A1
Bhusaval 43 J9
Bhutan ■ 41 D8
Biafra, B. of = Bonny, Bight of 56 D1
Biak 39 E5
Biała Podlaska 17 B6
Białogard 16 A2
Białystok 17 B6
Biaro 39 D3
Biarritz 12 E3
Bibala 58 A2
Biberach 14 D5
Bibiani 55 G4
Bida 55 G6
Bidar 43 L10
Biddeford 73 C10
Bidon 5 = Poste Maurice Cortier 54 D5
Bié, Planalto de 58 A3
Biel 13 C7
Bielefeld 14 B5
Biella 20 B2
Bielsk Podlaski 17 B6
Bielsko-Biała 16 D4
Bien Hoa 36 B3
Bienne = Biel 13 C7
Bienville, L. 69 C3
Big Horn Mts. = Bighorn Mts. 81 C10
Big Spring 78 C3
Big Trout L. 69 C2
Biğa 23 D6
Bigadiç 23 E7
Biggar 71 C9
Biggenden 63 A5
Bighorn → 81 B10
Bighorn Mts. 81 C10
Bihać 20 B5
Bihar 40 E5
Bihar □ 40 E5
Bihor, Munţii 17 E6
Bijagós, Arquipélago dos 55 F1
Bijapur, *Karnataka, India* 43 L9
Bijapur, *Mad. P., India* 40 H3
Bījār 46 D6
Bijeljina 20 B7
Bijnor 42 E11
Bikaner 42 E8
Bikini Atoll 64 H11
Bila Tserkva 17 D10
Bilara 42 F8
Bilaspur 40 F4
Bilauk Taungdan 36 B1
Bilbao 19 A4
Bilbo = Bilbao 19 A4
Bilecik 46 B2
Bilhorod-Dnistrovskyy 25 D3
Bilir 31 C11
Billings 81 C9
Billiton Is. = Belitung 37 E3
Bilma 53 E1
Biloxi 79 D9
Biltine 53 F3
Bima 39 F1
Bimbo 56 D3
Bina-Etawah 43 G11
Binalbagan 38 B2
Binalong 63 B4
Bīnālūd, Kūh-e 44 B4
Binatang 37 D4
Binda 63 A4
Bindle 63 A4
Bindura 59 B6
Bingara, *N.S.W., Australia* 63 A5
Bingara, *Queens., Australia* 63 A3
Bingham Canyon 81 E7
Binghamton 73 C8
Bingöl 46 C5
Binh Dinh = An Nhon 36 B3
Binh Son 36 A3
Binjai 37 D1
Binnaway 63 B4
Binongko 39 F2
Bintan 37 D2
Bintulu 37 D4
Bintuni 39 E4
Binzert = Bizerte 54 A6
Bioko 56 D1
Bir 43 K9
Bir Autrun 53 E4
Bir Mogrein 54 C2
Bîr Ungât 52 D5
Bira 39 E4
Birao 53 F3
Birchip 62 C3
Birecik 46 C4
Bireuen 36 C1
Bîrlad 17 E8
Bîrlad → 17 F8
Birmingham, *U.K.* 11 E6
Birmingham, *U.S.A.* 74 C4
Birmitrapur 40 F5
Birni Nkonni 55 F6
Birnin Kebbi 55 F5
Birr 11 E3
Birrie → 63 A4
Birsk 29 D6
Birur 43 N9
Bisa 39 E3
Biscay, B. of 12 D2
Biscoe Bay 96 B17
Biscoe Is. 96 A3
Bishkek 29 E8
Biskra 54 B6
Bislig 38 C3
Bismarck 76 B4
Bismarck Arch. 64 K9
Bissagos = Bijagós, Arquipélago dos 55 F1
Bissau 55 F1
Bistriţa 17 E7
Bistriţa → 17 E8
Bitam 56 D2
Bitkine 53 F2
Bitlis 46 C5
Bitola 22 D3
Bitolj = Bitola 22 D3
Bitter L. = Buheirat-Murrat-el-Kubra 52 B5
Bitterfontein 58 E3
Bitterroot Range 81 B6
Biu 53 F1
Biwa-Ko 32 B5
Biysk 29 D9
Bizerte 54 A6
Bjelovar 20 B6
Black Forest = Schwarzwald 14 D5
Black Hills 76 D3
Black Sea 25 E3
Black Volta → 55 G4
Blackball 65 E4
Blackburn 11 E5
Blackpool 11 E5
Blackwater → 11 E2
Blagodarnoye = Blagodarnyy 25 D5
Blagodarnyy 25 D5
Blagoevgrad 22 C4
Blagoveshchensk 31 D10
Blairmore 71 D8
Blanc, Mont 13 D7
Blanca, B. 95 D4
Blanca Peak 83 B10
Blanche, C. 62 B1
Blanche, L. 62 A2
Blanes 19 B7
Blantyre 59 B6
Blayney 63 B4
Blednaya, Gora 28 B7
Blenheim 65 D5
Blida 54 A5
Bligh Sound 65 F2
Blitta 55 G5
Blodgett Iceberg Tongue 96 A13
Bloemfontein 59 D5
Bloemhof 59 D5
Blois 12 C4
Bloomington, *Ill., U.S.A.* 77 E10
Bloomington, *Ind., U.S.A.* 72 E2
Blue Mts., *Oreg., U.S.A.* 80 C4
Blue Mts., *Pa., U.S.A.* 73 D7
Blue Nile = Nîl el Azraq → 53 E5
Blue Ridge Mts. 75 A7
Bluefields 86 D3
Bluff 65 G3
Blumenau 94 B7
Bo 55 G2
Bo Duc 36 B3
Bo Hai 35 C6
Boa Vista 90 C6
Boatman 63 A4
Bobadah 63 B4
Bobbili 40 H4
Bobo-Dioulasso 55 F4
Bóbr → 16 B2
Bobraomby, Tanjon' i 59 G9
Bobruysk = Babruysk 17 B9
Bôca do Acre 91 E5

Boca Raton 75 F7
Bocaiúva 93 F5
Bocanda 55 G4
Bocaranga 56 C3
Bochnia 16 D5
Bochum 14 C4
Boda 56 D3
Bodaybo 30 D9
Boden 8 E12
Bodensee 13 C8
Bodhan 43 K10
Bodø 8 E10
Bodrog → 16 D5
Bodrum 23 F6
Boende 56 E4
Boffa 55 F2
Bogalusa 79 D9
Bogan Gate 63 B4
Boggabilla 63 A5
Boggabri 63 B5
Bogo 38 B2
Bogong, Mt. 63 C4
Bogotá 90 C4
Bogotol 29 D9
Bogra 41 E7
Bogué 55 E2
Bohemian Forest = Böhmerwald 15 D7
Bohena Cr. → 63 B4
Böhmerwald 15 D7
Bohol 38 C2
Bohol Sea 38 C2
Bohotleh 49 F4
Boise 80 D5
Boise City 78 A2
Bojador C. 54 C2
Bojana → 22 D2
Bojnūrd 44 B4
Boké 55 F2
Bokhara → 63 A4
Bokoro 53 F2
Bokote 56 E4
Bokungu 56 E4
Bol 53 F1
Bolama 55 F1
Bolan Pass 42 E5
Bolbec 12 B4
Bole 34 B3
Bolekhiv 17 D6
Bolekhov = Bolekhiv 17 D6
Bolesławiec 16 C2
Bolgrad = Bolhrad 17 F9
Bolhrad 17 F9
Bolinao C. 38 A1
Bolívar, *Argentina* 94 D4
Bolívar, *Colombia* 90 C3
Bolivia ■ 91 G6
Bollon 63 A4
Bolobo 56 E3
Bologna 20 B3
Bologoye 24 B3
Bolomba 56 D3
Bolong 38 C2
Bolsena, L. di 20 C3
Bolshereche 29 D8
Bolshevik, Ostrov 30 B8
Bolshoi Kavkas = Caucasus Mountains 25 E5
Bolshoy Atlym 28 C7
Bolshoy Begichev, Ostrov 30 B9
Bolshoy Lyakhovskiy, Ostrov 31 B12
Bolton 11 E5
Bolu 46 B2
Bolvadin 46 C2
Bolzano 20 A3
Bom Despacho 93 F4
Bom Jesus da Lapa 93 E5
Boma 56 F2
Bomaderry 63 B5
Bombala 63 C4
Bombay 43 K8
Bomboma 56 D3
Bomili 57 D5
Bomongo 56 D3
Bomu → 56 D4
Bon, C. 52 A1
Bonaire 87 D6
Bonang 63 C4
Bonavista 69 D5
Bondo 56 D4
Bondoukou 55 G4
Bone, Teluk 39 E2
Bonerate 39 F2
Bonerate, Kepulauan 39 F2
Bong Son = Hoai Nhon 36 B3
Bongandanga 56 D4
Bongor 53 F2
Bonifacio 13 F8
Bonn 14 C4
Bonney, L. 62 C3
Bonny, Bight of 56 D1
Bonoi 39 E5
Bontang 37 D5
Bonthain 39 F1
Bonthe 55 G2
Bontoc 38 A2
Boolaboolka L. 62 B3
Booligal 63 B3
Boonah 63 A5
Boorindal 63 B4
Boorowa 63 B4
Boothia, Gulf of 68 A2
Boothia Pen. 70 A10
Booué 56 E2
Bor, *Serbia, Yug.* 22 B4
Bôr, *Sudan* 53 G5
Borama 49 F3
Borås 9 G10
Borāzjān 44 D2
Borba 90 D7
Borda, C. 62 C2
Bordeaux 12 D3
Bordertown 62 C3
Bordj Fly Ste. Marie 54 C4
Bordj-in-Eker 54 D6
Bordj Omar Driss 54 C6
Bordj-Tarat 54 C6
Borger 78 B3
Borisoglebsk 24 C5
Borisov = Barysaw 17 A9
Borja 90 D3
Borkou 53 E2
Borkum 14 B4
Borley, C. 96 A9
Borneo 37 D4
Bornholm 9 G11
Boromo 55 F4
Borongan 38 B3
Borovichi 24 B3
Borşa 17 E7
Borūjerd 46 D7
Boryslav 17 D6
Bosa 21 D2
Bosanska Gradiška 20 B6
Bosaso 49 E4
Boshan 35 C6
Boshrūyeh 44 C4
Bosna → 20 B7
Bosna i Hercegovina = Bosnia-Herzegovina ■ 20 B6
Bosnia-Herzegovina ■ 20 B6
Bosnik 39 E5
Bosobolo 56 D3
Bosporus = Karadeniz Boğazı 22 D7
Bossangoa 56 C3
Bossembélé 53 G2
Bosso 53 F1
Bosten Hu 34 B3
Boston, *U.K.* 11 E6
Boston, *U.S.A.* 73 C10
Botany B. 63 B5
Bothnia, G. of 8 F12
Bothwell 62 D4
Botletle → 58 C4
Botoşani 17 E8
Botswana ■ 58 C4
Botucatu 94 A7
Bou Djébéha 55 E4
Bou Izakarn 54 C3
Bouaké 55 G3
Bouar 56 C3
Bouârfa 54 B4
Bouca 56 C3
Bougie = Bejaia 54 A6
Bougouni 55 F3
Boulder 76 E2
Boulder Dam = Hoover Dam 82 B5
Boulogne-sur-Mer 12 A4
Boultoum 55 F7
Bouna 55 G4
Boundiali 55 G3
Bourbonnais 13 C5
Bourem 55 E4
Bourg-en-Bresse 13 C6
Bourg-St.-Maurice 13 D7
Bourges 12 C5
Bourgogne 13 C6
Bourke 63 B4
Bournemouth 11 F6
Bousso 53 F2
Boutilimit 55 E2
Bowen Mts. 63 C4
Bowman I. 96 A12
Bowmans 62 B2
Bowral 63 B5
Bowraville 63 B5
Boyne → 11 E3
Boyni Qara 45 B6
Boz Dağları 23 E7
Bozburun 23 F7
Bozcaada 23 E6
Bozdoğan 23 F7
Bozeman 81 C8
Bozen = Bolzano 20 A3
Bozoum 56 C3
Bra 20 B1
Brač 20 C6
Bracciano, L. di 20 C4
Brach 52 C1
Bräcke 8 F11
Brad 17 E6
Bradenton 75 F6
Bradford 11 E6
Braemar 62 B2
Braga 18 B1
Bragança, *Brazil* 92 C4
Bragança, *Portugal* 18 B2
Brahamapur 40 H5
Brahmanbaria 41 F8
Brahmani → 40 G6
Brahmaputra → 41 F7
Braidwood 63 C4
Brăila 17 F8
Branco → 90 D6
Brandenburg = Neubrandenburg 15 B7
Brandenburg 15 B7
Brandenburg □ 15 B7
Brandon 71 D10
Brandvlei 58 E4
Braniewo 16 A4
Bransfield Str. 96 A4
Brantford 69 D2
Branxholme 62 C3
Brasiléia 91 F5
Brasília 93 F4
Braşov 17 F7
Brassey, Banjaran 36 D5
Bratislava 16 D3
Bratsk 30 D8
Braunau 15 D7
Braunschweig 14 B6
Brava 49 G3
Bravo del Norte, R. → = Grande, Rio → 79 F5
Brawley 82 D5
Bray 11 E3
Bray, Pays de 12 B4
Brazil ■ 93 E4
Brazos → 79 E6
Brazzaville 56 E3
Brčko 20 B7
Breaksea Sd. 65 F2
Bream B. 64 A6
Bream Hd. 64 A6
Brecon 11 F5
Breda 14 C3
Bredasdorp 58 E4
Bredbo 63 C4
Bregenz 14 E5
Brejo 92 C5
Bremen 14 B5
Bremerhaven 14 B5
Bremerton 80 B2
Brenner P. 15 E6
Bréscia 20 B3
Breslau = Wrocław 16 C3
Bressanone 20 A3
Brest, *Belarus* 17 B6
Brest, *France* 12 B1
Brest-Litovsk = Brest 17 B6
Bretagne 12 B2
Brett, C. 64 A6
Brewarrina 63 A4
Brezhnev = Naberezhnyye Chelny 29 D6
Bria 56 C4
Briançon 13 D7
Bribie I. 63 A5
Bridgeport 73 D9

Bridgetown 87 D8
Bridgewater 69 D4
Bridgewater, C. 62 C3
Bridlington 11 D6
Bridport 62 D4
Brig 13 C7
Brigham City 81 E7
Bright 63 C4
Brighton, *Australia* 62 C2
Brighton, *U.K.* 11 F6
Bríndisi 21 D6
Brinkworth 62 B2
Brisbane 63 A5
Brisbane → 63 A5
Bristol, *U.K.* 11 F5
Bristol, *U.S.A.* 75 A6
Bristol B. 71 C3
Bristol Channel 11 F4
Britstown 58 E4
Brittany = Bretagne 12 B2
Brive-la-Gaillarde 12 D4
Brixen = Bressanone 20 A3
Brlik 29 E8
Brno 16 D3
Brocken 14 C6
Brodeur Pen. 68 A2
Brodnica 16 B4
Brody 17 C7
Broken Hill = Kabwe 59 A5
Broken Hill 62 B3
Bronte Park 62 D4
Brooks Ra. 71 B5
Brooloo 63 A5
Broome 60 D3
Broughton Island 68 B4
Brown, Pt. 62 B1
Brownsville 78
Brownwood 78 D4
Bruay-en-Artois 13 A5
Bruce, Mt. 60 E2
Bruck an der Mur 15 E8
Bruges = Brugge 14 C2
Brugge 14 C2
Brumado 93 E5
Brunei = Bandar Seri Begawan 36 D5
Brunei ■ 36 D4
Brunner, L. 65 E4
Brunswick = Braunschweig 14 B6
Brunswick 75 D7
Brunswick, Pen. de 95 G2
Brusque 94 B7
Brussel 14 C3
Brussels = Brussel 14 C3
Bruthen 63 C4
Bruxelles = Brussel 14 C3
Bryan 79 D5
Bryan, Mt. 62 B2
Bryansk 24 C3
Bu Craa 54 C2
Buapinang 39 E2
Buayan 38 C3
Bucak 46 C2
Bucaramanga 90 B4
Buchach 17 D7
Buchanan 55 G2
Buchans 69 D5
Bucharest = Bucureşti 22 B6
Buckie 10 C5
Buckleboo 62 B2
Bucureşti 22 B6
Budalin 41 F10
Budapest 16 E4
Budd Coast 96 A12
Bude 11 F4
Budennovsk 25 E5
Budgewoi 63 B5
Budjala 56 D3
Buenaventura 90 C3
Buenos Aires 94 C5
Buenos Aires, L. 95 F2
Buffalo 73 C6
Bug → = Buh → 25 D3
Bug → 16 B5
Buga 90 C3
Bugel, Tanjung 37 F4
Bugsuk 36 C5
Bugun Shara 35 B5
Buguruslan 29 D6
Buh → 25 D3
Buheirat-Murrat-el-Kubra 52 B5
Buir Nur 35 B6
Bujumbura 57 E5
Bukama 57 F5
Bukavu 57 E5
Bukene 57 E6
Bukhara = Bukhoro 29 F7
Bukhoro 29 F7
Bukittinggi 37 E2
Bukoba 57 E6
Bula 39 E4
Bulahdelah 63 B5
Bulan 38 B2
Bulandshahr 42 E10
Bulawayo 59 C5
Buldan 23 E7
Bulgan 35 B5
Bulgaria ■ 22 C5
Bulgroo 63 A3
Bulgunnia 62 B1
Bulhar 49 E3
Buli, Teluk 39 D3
Buliluyan, C. 36 C5
Bulli 63 B5
Bulloo → 63 A3
Bulloo Downs 62 A3
Bulloo L. 62 A3
Bulls 64 D6
Bulo Burti 49 G4
Bulsar = Valsad 43 J8
Bulukumba 39 F2
Bulun 30 B10
Bumba 56 D4
Bumhpa Bum 41 D11
Buna 57 D7
Bunbah, Khalīj 52 B3
Bunbury 60 G2
Buncrana 11 D3
Bundaberg 63
Bundi 43 G9
Bundoran 11 D2
Bungo-Suidō 32 C3
Bunia 57 D6
Bunji 42 B9
Buntok 37 E4
Bunyu 37 D5
Buol 39 D2
Buon Me Thuot 36 B3
Buorkhaya, Mys 31 B11
Buqayq 47 F7
Bur Acaba 49 G3
Bûr Safâga 52 C5
Bûr Sa'îd 52 B5
Bûr Sûdân 53 E6
Burao 49 F4
Buraydah 47 F6
Buraymī, Al Wāhāt al 44 E3
Burcher 63 B4
Burdur 46 C2
Burdwan = Barddhaman 40 F6
Burgas 22 C6
Burgersdorp 59 E5
Burgos 18 A4
Burgundy = Bourgogne 13 C6
Burhaniye 23 E6
Burhanpur 43 J10
Burias 38 B2
Buriram 36 A2
Burji 53 G6
Burkina Faso ■ 55 F4
Burlington, *Iowa, U.S.A.* 77 E9
Burlington, *N.C., U.S.A.* 75 A8
Burlington, *Vt., U.S.A.* 73 B9
Burlyu-Tyube 29 E8
Burma ■ 41 G11
Burnie 62 D4
Burnley 11 E5
Burnside → 70 B9
Burqān 47 E6
Burqin 34 B3
Burra 62 B2
Burren Junction 63 B4
Burrendong Dam 63 B4
Burrinjuck Res. 63 C4
Burruyacú 94 B4
Bursa 23 D7
Burtundy 62 B3
Buru 39 E3
Burundi ■ 57 E6
Burutu 55 G6
Bury St. Edmunds 11 E7
Buşayyah 47 E6
Būshehr 44 D2
Būshehr □ 44 D2
Bushire = Būshehr 44 D2
Businga 56 D4
Busra ash Shām 46 D4
Busto Arsízio 20 B2
Busu-Djanoa 56 D4
Busuanga 38 B1
Buta 57 D4
Butare 57 E5
Butaritari 64 J12
Butembo 57 D5
Butha Qi 35 B7
Buton 39 E2
Butte 81 B7
Butterworth 36 C2
Butuan 38 C3
Butung = Buton 39 E2
Buturlinovka 24 C5
Buxtehude 14 B5
Buy 24 B5
Büyük Menderes → 23 F6
Büyükçekmece 22 D7
Buzău 17 F8
Buzău → 17 F8
Buzen 32 C2
Buzi → 59 B6
Buzuluk 29 D6
Byarezina → 17 B10
Bydgoszcz 16 B3
Byelarus = Belarus ■ 24 C2
Byelorussia = Belarus ■ 24 C2
Bykhaw 17 B10
Bykhov = Bykhaw 17 B10
Bylot I. 68 A3
Byrd, C. 96 A3
Byrock 63 B4
Byron Bay 63 A5
Byrranga, Gory 30 B8
Byrranga Mts. = Byrranga, Gory 30 B8
Bytom 16 C4
Bytów 16 A3

C

Ca Mau = Quan Long 36 C3
Caála 58 A3
Cabanatuan 38 A2
Cabedelo 92 D7
Cabimas 90 A4
Cabinda 56 F2
Cabinda □ 56 F2
Cabinet Mts. 81 B6
Cabo Blanco 95 F3
Cabo Frio 93 G5
Cabo Pantoja 90 D3
Cabonga, Réservoir 69 D3
Caboolture 63 A5
Cabora Bassa Dam = Cahora Bassa Dam 59 B6
Cabot Str. 69 D5
Cabra 18 D3
Cabrera 19 C7
Cabriel → 19 C5
Čačak 22 C3
Cáceres, *Brazil* 91 G7
Cáceres, *Spain* 18 C2
Cachimbo, Serra do 93 D2
Cachoeira 93 E6
Cachoeira de Itapemirim 93 G5
Cachoeira do Sul 94 C6
Cacólo 56 G3
Caconda 58 A3
Cacongo 56 F2
Cadibarrawirracanna, L. 62 A2
Cadiz, *Phil.* 38 B2
Cádiz, *Spain* 18 D2
Cádiz, G. de 18 D2
Cadney Park 62 A1
Caen 12 B3
Caeté 93 F5
Caetité 93 E5
Cagayan → 38 A2
Cagayan de Oro 38 C2
Cágliari 21 E2
Cágliari, G. di 21 E2
Caguas 87 C6
Cahora Bassa Dam 59 B6
Cahors 12 D4
Cahuapanas 91 E3
Cahul 17 F9

Caia 59 B7
Caibarién 86 B4
Caicara 90 B5
Caicó 92 D6
Caicos Is. 87 B5
Caird Coast 96 B5
Cairns 61 D8
Cairo = El Qâhira 52 B5
Cairo 79 A9
Caiundo 58 B3
Caiza 91 H5
Cajamarca 91 E3
Cajàzeiras 92 D6
Calabar 55 H6
Calábria □ 21 E6
Calafate 95 G2
Calahorra 19 A5
Calais 12 A4
Calama, *Brazil* 91 E6
Calama, *Chile* 94 A3
Calamar, *Bolívar, Colombia* 90 A4
Calamar, *Vaupés, Colombia* 90 C4
Calamian Group 38 B1
Calamocha 19 B5
Calang 36 D1
Calapan 38 B2
Călăraşi 22 B6
Calatayud 19 B5
Calauag 38 B2
Calavite, C. 38 B2
Calbayog 38 B2
Calca 91 F4
Calcutta 41 F7
Caldas da Rainha 18 C1
Caldera 94 B2
Caldwell 80 D5
Caledon 58 E3
Caledon → 59 E5
Calgary 71 C8
Cali 90 C3
Calicut 43 P9
California □ 82 B3
California, G. de 84 B2
Calingasta 94 C3
Callabonna, L. 62 A3
Callao 91 F3
Caloundra 63 A5
Caltagirone 21 F5
Caltanissetta 21 F5
Calulo 56 G2
Calunda 58 A4
Calvi 13 E8
Calviá 19 C7
Calvinia 58 E3
Camabatela 56 F3
Camacupa 58 A3
Camagüey 86 B4
Camaná 91 G4
Camargo 91 H5
Camargue 13 E6
Camarones 95 E3
Cambay = Khambhat 43 H8
Cambay, G. of = Khambat, G. of 43 J8
Cambodia ■ 36 B3
Cambrai 13 A5
Cambrian Mts. 11 E5
Cambridge, *N.Z.* 64 B6
Cambridge, *U.K.* 11 E7
Cambridge, *U.S.A.* 73 C10
Cambridge Bay = Ikaluktutiak 70 B9
Cambridge G. 60 C4
Cambundi-Catembo 56 G3
Camden, *Ark., U.S.A.* 79 C7
Camden, *N.J., U.S.A.* 73 E8
Cameroon ■ 56 C2
Cameroun, Mt. 56 D1
Cametá 92 C4
Caminha 18 B1
Camira Creek 63 A5
Camissombo 56 F4
Camocim 92 C5
Camopi → 92 B3
Campana, I. 95 F1
Campánia □ 21 D5
Campbell Town 62 D4
Campbellton 69 D4
Campbelltown 63 B5
Campbeltown 10 D4
Campeche 85 D6
Campeche, B. de 85 D6
Camperdown 62 C3
Campina Grande 92 D6
Campinas 94 A7
Campo 56 D1
Campo Belo 93 G4
Campo Formoso 93 E5
Campo Grande 93 G3
Campo Maíor 92 C5
Campo Mourão 93 G3
Campoalegre 90 C3
Campobasso 20 D5
Campos 93 G5
Campos Belos 93 E4
Campuya → 90 D4
Camrose 71 C8
Çan 23 D6
Can Tho 36 B3
Canada ■ 70 C8
Cañada de Gómez 94 C4
Çanakkale 23 D6
Çanakkale Boğazı 23 D6
Cananea 84 A2
Canarias, Is. 54 C1
Canary Is. = Canarias, Is. 54 C1
Canavieiras 93 F6
Canbelego 63 B4
Canberra 63 C4
Candala 49 E4
Candelo 63 C4
Candia = Iráklion 23 G5
Canea = Khaniá 23 G5
Canelones 94 C5
Cañete, *Chile* 94 D2
Cañete, *Peru* 91 F3
Cangas de Narcea 18 A2
Canguaretama 92 D6
Canguçu 94 C6
Canicattì 21 F4
Canigou, Mt. 12 E5
Canipaan 36 C5
Çankırı 46 B3
Cann River 63 C4
Cannanore 43 P9
Cannes 13 E7
Canoas 94 B6
Canora 71 C9
Canowindra 63 B4
Cantabria □ 18 A4
Cantabrian Mts. = Cantábrica, Cordillera 18 A3
Cantábrica, Cordillera 18 A3
Cantal, Plomb du 13 D5
Canterbury 11 F7
Canterbury □ 65 E4
Canterbury Bight 65 F4
Canterbury Plains 65 E4
Canton = Guangzhou 35 D6
Canton 72 D5
Canudos 91 E7
Canutama 91 E6
Cap-Haïtien 87 C5
Cap St.-Jacques = Vung Tau 36 B3
Capaia 56 F4
Capanaparo → 90 B5
Cape Barren I. 62 D4
Cape Breton I. 69 D4
Cape Coast 55 G4
Cape Dorset 68 B3
Cape Dyer 68 B4
Cape Girardeau 79 A9
Cape Jervis 62 C2
Cape Town 58 E3
Cape Verde Is. ■ 50 E1
Cape York Peninsula 61 C7
Capela 93 E6
Capim → 92 C4
Capraia 20 C2
Capri 21 D5
Caprivi Strip 58 B4
Captain's Flat 63 C4
Caquetá → 90 D5
Caracal 22 B5
Caracas 90 A5
Caracol 93 D5
Caradoc 62 B3
Carajás, Serra dos 92 D3
Carangola 93 G5
Caransebeş 17 F6
Caratasca, L. 86 C3
Caratinga 93 F5
Caraúbas 92 D6
Caravaca 19 C5
Caravelas 93 F6
Caraveli 91 G4
Carballo 18 A1
Carbonara, C. 21 E2
Carbondale 79 A9
Carbonear 69 D5
Carbonia 21 E2
Carcassonne 12 E5
Carcross 70 B6
Cardamon Hills 43 Q10
Cárdenas 86 B3
Cardiff 11 F5
Cardigan B. 11 E4
Cardston 71 D8
Carei 17 E6
Careysburg 55 G2
Carhué 94 D4
Caria 23 F7
Cariacica 93 G5
Caribbean Sea 86 D5
Cariboo Mts. 71 C7
Carinda 63 B4
Carinhanha 93 E5
Carinthia □ = Kärnten □ 15 E7
Caripito 90 A6
Caritianas 91 E6
Carlisle 11 D5
Carlow 11 E3
Carlsbad 78 C1
Carmacks 70 B6
Carman 71 D10
Carmarthen 11 F4
Carmaux 12 D5
Carmelo 94 C5
Carmen 90 B3
Carmen de Patagones 95 E4
Carmona 18 D3
Carnac 12 C2
Carnarvon, *Australia* 60 E1
Carnarvon, *S. Africa* 58 E4
Carnegie, L. 60 F3
Carnic Alps = Karnische Alpen 20 A4
Carniche Alpi = Karnische Alpen 20 A4
Carnot 56 D3
Carnot, C. 62 B2
Carolina 92 D4
Caroline I. 65 K15
Caroline Is. 64 J10
Caroni → 90 B6
Caroníe = Nébrodi, Monti 21 F5
Caroona 63 B5
Carpathians 16 D5
Carpaţii Meridionali 17 F7
Carpentaria, G. of 60 C6
Carpentras 13 D6
Carpi 20 B3
Carpolac = Morea 62 C3
Carrara 20 B3
Carrauntoohill 11 E2
Carrick-on-Suir 11 E3
Carrieton 62 B2
Carrizal Bajo 94 B2
Çarşamba 46 B4
Carson City 80 F4
Cartagena, *Colombia* 90 A3
Cartagena, *Spain* 19 D5
Cartago, *Colombia* 90 C3
Cartago, *Costa Rica* 86 E3
Carterton 65 D6
Carthage 79 A6
Cartwright 68 C5
Caruaru 92 D6
Carúpano 90 A6
Carvoeiro 90 D6
Carvoeiro, C. 18 C1
Casablanca 54 B3
Cascade Ra. 80 B3
Cascais 18 C1
Cascavel 94 A6
Cáscina 20 C3
Caserta 20 D5
Casiguran 38 A2
Casilda 94 C4
Casino 63 A5
Casiquiare → 90 C5
Casma 91 E3
Caspe 19 B5
Casper 81 D10

Caspian Sea 29 E6
Cassinga 58 B3
Castellammare di Stábia 21 D5
Castellón de la Plana 19 C5
Castelo Branco 18 C2
Castelsarrasin 12 D4
Castelvetrano 21 F4
Casterton 62 C3
Castilla La Mancha □ 18 C4
Castilla y Leon □ 18 A3
Castlebar 11 E2
Castleblaney 11 D3
Castlemaine 63 C3
Castlereagh → 63 B4
Castres 12 E5
Castries 87 D7
Castro 95 E2
Castro Alves 93 E6
Castuera 18 C3
Cat I. 86 B4
Catacáos 91 E2
Catalão 93 F4
Çatalca 22 D7
Catalonia = Cataluña □ 19 B6
Cataluña □ 19 B6
Catamarca 94 B3
Catanduanes 38 B2
Catanduva 93 G4
Catánia 21 F5
Catanzaro 21 E6
Catarman 38 B2
Cateel 38 C3
Catoche, C. 85 C7
Catrimani 90 C6
Catskill Mts. 73 C8
Cauca → 90 B4
Caucaia 92 C6
Caucasus Mountains 25 E5
Caúngula 56 F3
Cauquenes 94 D2
Caura → 90 B6
Cauvery → 43 P11
Caux, Pays de 12 B4
Cavan 11 D3
Cavendish 62 C3
Caviana, I. 92 B3
Cavite 38 B2
Cawndilla L. 62 B3
Cawnpore = Kanpur 40 D3
Caxias 92 C5
Caxias do Sul 94 B6
Caxito 56 F2
Cayambe 90 C3
Cayenne 92 A3
Cayman Is. ■ 67 H11
Cazombo 58 A4
Ceadâr-Lunga 17 E9
Ceanannus Mor 11 E3
Ceará = Fortaleza 92 C6
Ceará □ 92 D6
Ceará Mirim 92 D6
Cebollar 94 B3
Cebu 38 B2
Cecil Plains 63 A5
Cedar L. 71 C10
Cedar Rapids 77 E9
Cedro 92 D6
Ceduna 62 B1
Cefalù 21 E5
Cegléd 16 E4
Celaya 84 C4
Celebes = Sulawesi □ 39 E2
Celebes Sea 39 D2
Celje 20 A5
Celle 14 B6
Celtic Sea 11 F2
Central, Cordillera 90 C3
Central African Rep. ■ 56 C4
Central Makran Range 42 F4
Cephalonia = Kefallinía 23 E3
Ceram = Seram 39 E3
Ceram Sea = Seram Sea 39 E3
Ceres, *Argentina* 94 B4
Ceres, *S. Africa* 58 E3
Cerignola 20 D5
Cerigo = Kíthira 23 F4
Çerkeş 46 B3
Çerkeşköy 22 D6
Cervera 19 B6
Cesena 20 B4
Česka Republika = Czech Rep. ■ 16 D2
České Budějovice 16 D2
Ceskomoravská Vrchovina 16 D2
Çeşme 23 E6
Cessnock 63 B5
Cetinje 22 C2
Cetraro 21 E5
Ceuta 18 E3
Cévennes 13 D5
Ceyhan 46 C3
Ceylon = Sri Lanka ■ 43 R12
Chachapoyas 91 E3
Chachran 42 E7
Chad ■ 53 E2
Chad, L. = Tchad, L. 53 F1
Chadileuvú → 94 D3
Chadyr-Lunga = Ceadâr-Lunga 17 E9
Chagai Hills 42 E3
Chagos Arch. 27 K11
Chāh Bahār 45 E5
Chāh Gay Hills 45 D6
Chahar Burjak 42 D3
Chaibasa 40 F5
Chakhānsūr 42 D3
Chakradharpur 40 F5
Chakwal 42 C8
Chala 91 G4
Chalcis = Khalkís 23 E4
Chalhuanca 91 F4
Chalisgaon 43 J9
Chalky Inlet 65 G2
Challapata 91 G5
Chalon-sur-Saône 13 C6
Châlons-en-Champagne 13 B6
Chaman 42 D5
Chamba, *India* 42 C10
Chamba, *Tanzania* 59 A7
Chambal → 42 F11
Chambéry 13 D6
Chamical 94 C3
Chamonix-Mont Blanc 13 D7
Champagne 13 B6
Champaign 72 D1
Champlain, L. 73 B9
Chañaral 94 B2
Chandigarh 42 D10
Chandler 62 A1
Chandmani 34 B4
Chandpur 41 F8
Chandrapur 43 K11
Chang Jiang → 35 C7
Changanacheri 43 Q10
Changane → 59 C6
Changchiak'ou = Zhangjiakou 35 B6
Ch'angchou = Changzhou 35 C6
Changchun 35 B7
Changde 35 D6
Changhai = Shanghai 35 C7
Changjiang 35 E5
Changsha 35 D6
Changting 35 D6
Changzhi 35 C6
Changzhou 35 C6
Channapatna 43 N10
Channel Is. 11 G5
Chantada 18 A2
Chanthaburi 36 B2
Chantrey Inlet 70 B10
Chanute 79 A6
Chao Phraya → 36 B2
Chao'an 35 D6
Chaoyang 35 D6
Chapala, L. de 84 C4
Chapayevsk 24 C6
Chapra = Chhapra 40 E5
Châr 54 D2
Chara 31 D9
Charadai 94 B5
Charagua 91 G6
Charaña 91 G5
Chardara 29 E7
Chardzhou = Chärjew 29 F7
Charente → 12 D3
Chari → 53 F1
Chārīkār 42 B6
Chärjew 29 F7
Charleroi 14 C3
Charles, C. 73 F8
Charleston, *S.C., U.S.A.* 75 C8
Charleston, *W. Va., U.S.A.* 72 E5
Charlesville 56 F4
Charleville 63 A4
Charleville-Mézières 13 B6
Charlotte 75 B7
Charlotte Amalie 87 C7
Charlottesville 73 E6
Charlottetown 69 D4
Charlton 62 C3
Charolles 13 C6
Charouine 54 C4
Charters Towers 61 E8
Chartres 12 B4
Chascomús 94 D5
Châteaubriant 12 C3
Châteaulin 12 B1
Châteauroux 12 C4
Châtellerault 12 C4
Chatham, *N.B., Canada* 69 D4
Chatham, *Ont., Canada* 69 D2
Chatham, *U.K.* 11 F7
Chatrapur 40 H5
Chattahoochee → 74 D5
Chattanooga 74 B5
Chauk 41 G10
Chaukan La 41 D11
Chaumont 13 B6
Chaves, *Brazil* 92 C4
Chaves, *Portugal* 18 B2
Chavuma 58 A4
Cheb 16 C1
Cheboksary 24 B6
Chech, Erg 54 D4
Chechenia □ 25 E6
Checheno-Ingush Republic = Chechenia □ 25 E6
Chechnya = Chechenia □ 25 E6
Cheduba I. 41 H9
Cheepie 63 A4
Chegga 54 C3
Chegutu 59 B6
Chehalis 80 B2
Cheju Do 35 C7
Chekiang = Zhejiang □ 35 D7
Cheleken 29 F6
Chelforó 95 D3
Chelkar = Shalqar 29 E6
Chelkar Tengiz, Solonchak 29 E7
Chełm 17 C6
Chełmno 16 B4
Chelmsford 11 F7
Cheltenham 11 F5
Chelyabinsk 29 D7
Chemnitz 15 C7
Chen Xian 35 D6
Chenab → 42 D7
Chencha 53 G6
Chenchiang = Zhenjiang 35 C6
Chengde 35 B6
Chengdu 35 C5
Chengjiang 34 D5
Ch'engtu = Chengdu 35 C5
Chennai = Madras 43 N12
Cheo Reo 36 B3
Cheom Ksan 36 B2
Chepén 91 E3
Chepes 94 C3
Cher → 12 C4
Cherbourg 12 B3
Cherchell 54 A5
Cherdyn 28 C6
Cherepanovo 29 D9
Cherepovets 24 B4
Chergui, Chott ech 54 B5
Cherikov = Cherykaw 17 B10
Cherkasy 24 D3
Cherlak 29 D8
Chernaya 30 B6
Chernigov = Chernihiv 24 C3
Chernihiv 24 C3
Chernivtsi 17 D7
Chernobyl = Chornobyl 17 C10
Chernovtsy = Chernivtsi 17 D7
Chernyakhovsk 28 D3
Cherquenco 94 D2
Cherrapunji 41 E8

Cherven 17 B9
Chervonohrad 17 C7
Cherykaw 17 B10
Chesapeake 73 F7
Chesapeake B. 73 E7
Cheshskaya Guba 28 C5
Chester, *U.K.* 11 E5
Chester, *U.S.A.* 73 E8
Chesterfield 11 E6
Chesterfield, Is. 64 L10
Chesterfield Inlet 70 B10
Chesterton Ra. 63 A4
Cheviot Hills 10 D5
Chew Bahir 53 H6
Cheyenne 76 E2
Cheyenne → 76 C4
Chhapra 40 E5
Chhatarpur 43 G11
Chhindwara 43 H11
Chhlong 36 B3
Chi → 36 A2
Chiamussu = Jiamusi 35 B8
Chiange 58 B2
Chiapa → 85 D6
Chiávari 20 B2
Chiavenna 20 A2
Chiba 32 B7
Chibemba 58 B2
Chibia 58 B2
Chibougamau 69 D3
Chibuk 53 F1
Chicacole = Srikakulam 40 H4
Chicago 72 D2
Chichagof I. 71 C6
Chichibu 32 A6
Ch'ich'ihaerh = Qiqihar 35 B7
Chickasha 78 B5
Chiclana de la Frontera 18 D2
Chiclayo 91 E3
Chico 80 F3
Chico →, *Chubut, Argentina* 95 E3
Chico →, *Santa Cruz, Argentina* 95 F3
Chicoutimi 69 D3
Chidambaram 43 P11
Chidley, C. 68 B4
Chiemsee 15 E7
Chiengi 57 F5
Chiese → 20 B3
Chieti 20 C5
Chiguana 91 H5
Chihli, G. of = Bo Hai 35 C6
Chihuahua 84 B3
Chiili 29 E7
Chik Bollapur 43 N10
Chikmagalur 43 N9
Chilapa 84 D5
Chilas 42 B9
Chilaw 43 R11
Childers 63 A5
Chile ■ 94 D2
Chilete 91 E3
Chililabombwe 59 A5
Chilin = Jilin 35 B7
Chilka L. 40 H5
Chillán 94 D2
Chiloé, I. de 95 E2
Chilpancingo 84 D5
Chiluage 56 F4
Chilwa, L. 59 B7
Chimbay 29 E6
Chimborazo 90 D3
Chimbote 91 E3
Chimkent = Shymkent 29 E7
Chimoio 59 B6
Chin □ 41 F9
China ■ 35 C5
Chinan = Jinan 35 C6
Chinandega 85 E7
Chincha Alta 91 F3
Chinchilla 63 A5
Chinchou = Jinzhou 35 B7
Chinde 59 B7
Chindwin → 41 G10
Chingola 59 A5
Ch'ingtao = Qingdao 35 C7
Chinguetti 54 D2
Chinhoyi 59 B6
Chiniot 42 D8
Chinju 35 C7
Chinnampo 35 C7
Chinon 12 C4
Chinsali 57 G6
Chióggia 20 B4
Chíos = Khíos 23 E6
Chipata 59 A6
Chiquián 91 F3
Chiquinquira 90 B4
Chirchiq 29 E7
Chirmiri 40 F4
Chiromo 59 B7
Chisamba 59 A5
Chisapani Garhi 40 D5
Chişinău 17 E9
Chistopol 24 B7
Chita 30 D9
Chitado 58 B2
Chitembo 58 A3
Chitral 42 B7
Chitré 86 E3
Chittagong 41 F8
Chittagong □ 41 E8
Chittaurgarh 43 G9
Chittoor 43 N11
Chiusi 20 C3
Chivasso 20 B1
Chivilcoy 94 B4
Chkalov = Orenburg 29 D6
Choele Choel 95 D3
Chojnice 16 B3
Cholet 12 C3
Choluteca 85 E7
Choma 59 B5
Chomutov 16 C1
Chon Buri 36 B2
Chone 90 D3
Chŏngjin 35 B7
Chŏngju 35 C7
Chongqing 35 D5
Chŏnju 35 C7
Chonos, Arch. de los 95 F2
Chop 17 D6
Chornobyl 17 C10
Chortkiv 17 D7
Chorzów 16 C4
Chos-Malal 94 D2
Chōshi 32 B7
Choszczno 16 B2
Chotila 43 H7
Choybalsan 35 B6
Christchurch 65 E5
Christiana 59 D5
Christmas I. = Kiritimati 65 J15
Chu = Shu 29 E8
Ch'uanchou = Quanzhou 35 D6
Chubut → 95 E3
Chudskoye, Oz. 24 B2
Chūgoku-Sanchi 32 B3
Chula Vista 82 D4
Chulucanas 90 E2
Chulym → 29 D9
Chumbicha 94 B3
Chumphon 36 B1
Chuna → 30 D7
Chunchŏn 35 C7
Chungking = Chongqing 35 D5
Chunya 57 F6
Chuquibamba 91 G4
Chuquicamata 94 A3
Chur 13 C8
Churachandpur 41 E9
Churchill 70 C10
Churchill →, *Man., Canada* 70 C10
Churchill →, *Nfld., Canada* 69 C4
Churchill, C. 70 C10
Churchill Falls 69 C4
Churchill L. 71 C9
Churu 42 E9
Chushal 42 C11
Chusovoy 28 D6
Chuvash Republic □ = Chuvashia □ 24 B6
Chuvashia □ 24 B6
Cicero 72 D2
Ciechanów 16 B5
Ciego de Avila 86 B4
Ciénaga 90 A4
Cienfuegos 86 B3
Cieszyn 16 D4
Cieza 19 C5
Cijara, Pantano de 18 C3
Cilician Gates P. 46 C3
Cill Chainnigh = Kilkenny 11 E3
Cimişlia 17 E9
Cimone, Mte. 20 B3
Cîmpina 17 F7
Cîmpulung 17 F7
Cinca → 19 B6
Cincar 20 C6
Cincinnati 72 E3
Çine 23 F7
Cinto, Mte. 13 E8
Circle 71 B5
Cirebon 37 F3
Citlaltépetl 84 D5
Città di Castello 20 C4
Ciudad Bolívar 90 B6
Ciudad Chetumal 85 D7
Ciudad del Carmen 85 D6
Ciudad Delicias = Delicias 84 B3
Ciudad Guayana 90 B6
Ciudad Juárez 84 A3
Ciudad Madero 84 C5
Ciudad Mante 84 C5
Ciudad Obregón 84 B3
Ciudad Real 18 C4
Ciudad Rodrigo 18 B2
Ciudad Trujillo = Santo Domingo 87 C6
Ciudad Victoria 84 C5
Civitanova Marche 20 C4
Civitavécchia 20 C3
Cizre 46 C5
Clanwilliam 58 E3
Clare 62 B2
Clarence →, *Australia* 63 A5
Clarence →, *N.Z.* 65 E5
Clarence, I. 95 G2
Clarence I. 96 A4
Clarie Coast 96 A13
Clarke I. 62 D4
Clarksdale 79 B8
Clarksville 74 A4
Claveria 38 A2
Clear, C. 11 F2
Clearwater 75 F6
Clearwater Mts. 81 B6
Clermont-Ferrand 13 D5
Cleveland, *Australia* 63 A5
Cleveland, *U.S.A.* 72 D5
Clifden 65 G2
Clifton 63 A5
Clifton Hills 62 A2
Clinton, *Canada* 71 C7
Clinton, *N.Z.* 65 G3
Clinton, *U.S.A.* 77 E9
Clinton Colden L. 70 B9
Clones 11 D3
Clonmel 11 E3
Clovis 78 B2
Cluj-Napoca 17 E6
Clunes 62 C3
Clutha → 65 G3
Clyde 65 F3
Clyde → 10 D4
Clyde, Firth of 10 D4
Clyde River 68 A4
Coari 90 D6
Coast Mts. 70 C7
Coast Ranges 80 F2
Coats I. 68 B2
Coats Land 96 B5
Coatzacoalcos 85 D6
Cobalt 69 D3
Cobar 63 B4
Cóbh 11 F2
Cobham 62 B3
Cobija 91 F5
Cobourg 69 D3
Cobram 63 C4
Cóbué 59 A6
Coburg 15 C6
Cocanada = Kakinada 40 J4
Cochabamba 91 G5
Cochin 43 Q10
Cochin China = Nam-Phan 36 B3
Cochrane 69 D2
Cochrane, L. 95 F2
Cockburn 62 B3
Cockburn, Canal 95 G2
Coco → 86 D3
Cocobeach 56 D1
Cod, C. 73 C10
Codajás 90 D6
Codó 92 C5
Cœur d'Alene 80 B5
Coffeyville 79 A6
Coffin B. 62 B2
Coffin Bay Peninsula 62 B2
Coffs Harbour 63 B5
Cognac 12 D3

Cohuna 63 C3
Coiba, I. 86 E3
Coig → 95 G3
Coihaique 95 F2
Coimbatore 43 P10
Coimbra, *Brazil* 91 G7
Coimbra, *Portugal* 18 B1
Coín 18 D3
Cojimies 90 C3
Colac 62 C3
Colatina 93 F5
Colbeck, C. 96 B17
Colbinabbin 63 C3
Colchester 11 F7
Colebrook 62 D4
Coleman 71 D8
Coleraine, *Australia* 62 C3
Coleraine, *U.K.* 11 D3
Coleridge, L. 65 E4
Colesberg 59 E5
Colhué Huapi, L. 95 F3
Colima 84 D4
Colinas 92 D5
Coll 10 C3
Collaguasi 91 H5
Collarenebri 63 A4
Collingwood 64 D5
Colmar 13 B7
Colo → 63 B5
Cologne = Köln 14 C4
Colomb-Béchar = Béchar 54 B4
Colômbia 93 G4
Colombia ■ 90 C4
Colombo 43 R11
Colón, *Cuba* 86 B3
Colón, *Panama* 85 F9
Colonia 94 C5
Colonia Dora 94 B4
Colonsay 10 C3
Colorado □ 83 A10
Colorado →, *Argentina* 95 D4
Colorado →, *N. Amer.* 82 E5
Colorado Plateau 83 B7
Colorado Springs 76 F2
Columbia, *Mo., U.S.A.* 77 F8
Columbia, *S.C., U.S.A.* 75 B7
Columbia, *Tenn., U.S.A.* 74 B4
Columbia → 80 B1
Columbia, District of □ 73 E7
Columbia Basin 80 B4
Columbretes, Is. 19 C6
Columbus, *Ga., U.S.A.* 74 C5
Columbus, *Miss., U.S.A.* 74 C3
Columbus, *Ohio, U.S.A.* 72 E4
Colville → 71 A4
Colville, C. 64 B6
Colwyn Bay 11 E5
Comácchio 20 B4
Comallo 95 E2
Comilla 41 F8
Comino, C. 21 D2
Committee B. 68 B2
Commonwealth B. 96 A14
Commoron Cr. → 63 A5
Communism Pk. = Kommunizma, Pik 29 F8
Como 20 B2
Como, L. di 20 B2
Comodoro Rivadavia 95 F3
Comorin, C. 43 Q10
Comoro Is. = Comoros ■ 51 H8
Comoros ■ 51 H8
Comox 71 D7
Compiègne 13 B5
Compton Downs 63 B4
Comrat 17 E9
Conakry 55 G2
Conara Junction 62 D4
Concarneau 12 C2
Conceição da Barra 93 F6
Concepción, *Bolivia* 91 G6
Concepción, *Chile* 94 D2
Concepción, *Paraguay* 94 A5
Concepción, L. 91 G6
Concepción del Oro 84 C4
Concepción del Uruguay 94 C5
Conchos → 84 B3
Concord, *N.C., U.S.A.* 75 B7
Concord, *N.H., U.S.A.* 73 C10
Concordia, *Argentina* 94 C5
Concórdia, *Brazil* 90 D5
Condamine 63 A5
Condeúba 93 E5
Condobolin 63 B4
Conegliano 20 B4
Confuso → 94 B5
Congo ■ 56 E3
Congo → 56 F2
Congo, Dem. Rep. of the ■ 56 E4
Conjeeveram = Kanchipuram 43 N11
Conlea 63 B3
Conn, L. 11 D2
Connacht □ 11 E2
Connecticut □ 73 D9
Connecticut → 73 D9
Connemara 11 E2
Conoble 63 B3
Cononaco → 90 D3
Conran, C. 63 C4
Conselheiro Lafaiete 93 G5
Constance = Konstanz 14 E5
Constance, L. = Bodensee 13 C8
Constanța 22 B7
Constantine 54 A6
Constitución 94 D2
Contai 40 G6
Contamana 91 E4
Contas → 93 E6
Conway, L. 62 A2
Coober Pedy 62 A1
Cooch Behar = Koch Bihar 41 D7
Cook, B. 95 H2
Cook, Mt. 65 E4
Cook Inlet 71 C4
Cook Is. 65 L14
Cook Strait 65 D6
Cooktown 61 D8
Coolabah 63 B4
Cooladdi 63 A4
Coolah 63 B4
Coolamon 63 B4
Coolangatta 63 A5
Cooma 63 C4
Coonabarabran 63 B4
Coonamble 63 B4
Coondapoor 43 N9
Coongie 62 A3
Coongoola 63 A4
Cooninie, L. 62 A2
Cooper Cr. →, *N. Terr., Australia* 60 C5
Cooper Cr. →, *S. Austral., Australia* 62 A2
Cooroy 63 A5
Cootamundra 63 B4
Cooyar 63 A5
Copenhagen = København 9 G10
Copiapó 94 B2
Copiapó → 94 B2
Copley 62 B2
Copper Center 71 B5
Copper Cliff 69 D2
Coppermine = Kugluktuk 70 B8
Coppermine → 70 B8
Coquimbo 94 C2
Corabia 22 C5
Coracora 91 G4
Coral Harbour = Salliq 68 B2
Coral Sea 64 L10
Corato 21 D6
Corby 11 E6
Corcaigh = Cork 11 F2
Corcubión 18 A1
Córdoba, *Argentina* 94 C4
Córdoba, *Spain* 18 D3
Córdoba, Sierra de 94 C4
Cordon 38 A2
Cordova 71 B5
Corfu = Kérkira 23 E2
Coria 18 C2
Corigliano Cálabro 21 E6
Corinna 62 D4
Corinth = Kórinthos 23 F4
Corinth, G. of = Korinthiakós Kólpos 23 E4
Corinto 93 F5
Cork 11 F2
Çorlu 22 D6
Corner Brook 69 D5
Cornești 17 E9
Cornwall 69 D3
Corny Pt. 62 B2
Coro 90 A5
Coroatá 92 C5
Corocoro 91 G5
Coroico 91 G5
Coromandel 64 B6
Corona 62 B3
Coronation Gulf 70 B8
Coronation I. 96 A4
Coronel 94 D2
Coronel Dorrego 94 D4
Coronel Suárez 94 D4
Corowa 63 C4
Corpus Christi 78 F5
Corque 91 G5
Corrib, L. 11 E2
Corrientes 94 B5
Corrientes → 90 D4
Corrientes, C., *Colombia* 90 B3
Corrientes, C., *Mexico* 84 C3
Corse 13 E8
Corse, C. 13 E8
Corsica = Corse 13 E8
Corsicana 79 C5
Corte 13 E8
Çorum 46 B3
Corumbá 91 G7
Corumbá de Goiás 93 F4
Corunna = La Coruña 18 A1
Corvallis 80 C2
Cosenza 21 E6
Costa Blanca 19 C5
Costa Brava 19 B7
Costa del Sol 18 D3
Costa Dorada 19 B6
Costa Rica ■ 86 E3
Cotabato 38 C2
Cotagaita 91 H5
Côte d'Azur 13 E7
Côte-d'Ivoire ■ = Ivory Coast ■ 55 G3
Cotentin 12 B3
Cotonou 55 G5
Cotopaxi 90 D3
Cotswold Hills 11 F5
Cottbus 15 C8
Couedic, C. du 62 C2
Coulman I. 96 B15
Council 71 B3
Council Bluffs 77 E7
Courantyne → 90 B7
Courtrai = Kortrijk 14 C2
Coventry 11 E6
Covilhã 18 B2
Covington 72 E3
Cowal, L. 63 B4
Cowangie 62 C3
Cowarie 62 A2
Cowell 62 B2
Cowra 63 B4
Coxim 93 F3
Cox's Bazar 41 G8
Cozumel, I. de 85 C7
Craboon 63 B4
Cracow = Kraków 16 C4
Cracow 63 A5
Cradock 59 E5
Craigavon 11 D3
Crailsheim 14 D6
Craiova 22 B4
Cranbrook, *Australia* 62 D4
Cranbrook, *Canada* 71 D8
Crateús 92 D5
Crato 92 D6
Crawley 11 F6
Crazy Mts. 81 B8
Crema 20 B2
Cremona 20 B3
Cres 20 B5
Cressy 62 C3
Crete = Kríti 23 G5
Créteil 12 B5

Creus, C. de . . . 19 A7
Creuse → 12 C4
Crewe 11 E5
Criciúma 94 B7
Crimean Pen. = Krymskyy Pivostriv 25 D3
Crişul Alb → . 16 E5
Crişul Negru → 16 E5
Crna Gora = Montenegro □ 22 C2
Crna Gora 22 C3
Crna Reka → . 22 D3
Croatia ■ 20 B6
Crocker, Banjaran 36 C5
Croker, C. 60 C5
Cromer 11 E7
Cromwell 65 F3
Cronulla 63 B5
Crookwell 63 B4
Cross Sound . . 71 C6
Crotone 21 E6
Crows Nest . . . 63 A5
Crowsnest Pass 71 D8
Cruz Alta 94 B6
Cruz del Eje . . . 94 C4
Cruzeiro 93 G5
Cruzeiro do Sul 91 E4
Crystal Brook . . 62 B2
Csongrád 16 E5
Cuamba 59 A7
Cuando → . . . 58 B4
Cuarto → 94 C4
Cuba ■ 86 B4
Cubango → . . 58 B4
Cuchi 58 A3
Cúcuta 90 B4
Cuddalore 43 P11
Cuddapah 43 M11
Cudgewa 63 C4
Cuenca, *Ecuador* 90 D3
Cuenca, *Spain* . 19 B4
Cuenca, Serranía de . 19 C5
Cuernavaca . . . 84 D5
Cuevas del Almanzora . . 19 D5
Cuevo 91 H6
Cuiabá 93 F2
Cuiabá → 93 F2
Cuima 58 A3
Cuito → 58 B4
Cukai 36 D2
Culcairn 63 C4
Culgoa → 63 A4
Culiacán 84 C3
Culion 38 B2
Cullarin Ra. . . . 63 B4
Cullera 19 C5
Culuene → . . . 93 E3
Culverden 65 E5
Cumaná 90 A6
Cumberland, *Canada* 71 D7
Cumberland, *U.S.A.* 73 E6
Cumberland Pen. 68 B4
Cumberland Plateau 72 F3
Cumberland Sd. 68 B4
Cumborah 63 A4
Cumbum 43 M11
Cummins 62 B2
Cumnock 63 B4
Cunene → . . . 58 B2
Cúneo 20 B1
Cunnamulla . . . 63 A4
Cupica, G. de . . 90 B3
Curaçao 87 D6
Curaray → . . . 90 D4
Curiapo 90 B6
Curicó 94 C2
Curitiba 94 B7
Currabubula . . 63 B5
Currais Novos . 92 D6
Curralinho 92 C4
Curraweena . . . 63 B4
Currie 62 C3
Curtea de Argeş 17 F7
Curtis Group . . 62 C4
Curuápanema → 92 C2
Curuçá 92 C4
Curup 37 E2
Cururupu 92 C5
Curuzú Cuatiá . 94 B5
Cuttaburra → . 63 A3
Cuttack 40 G5
Cuvier I. 64 B6
Cuxhaven 14 B5
Cuyo 38 B2
Cuzco, *Bolivia* . 91 H5
Cuzco, *Peru* . . . 91 F4
Cwmbran 11 F5
Cyclades = Kikládhes . . . 23 F5
Cygnet 62 D4
Cyprus ■ 46 D3
Cyrenaica 52 C3
Cyrene = Shaḩḩāt 52 B3
Czech Rep. ■ . . 16 D2
Częstochowa . . 16 C4

D

Da Hinggan Ling 35 B7
Da Lat 36 B3
Da Nang 36 A3
Da Qaidam . . . 34 C4
Da Yunhe → . 35 C7
Daba Shan 35 C5
Dabakala 55 G4
Dabo 37 E2
Dabola 55 F2
Daboya 55 G4
Dacca = Dhaka 41 F8
Dacca = Dhaka □ 41 E8
Dachau 15 D6
Dadanawa 90 C7
Dadra and Nagar Haveli □ 43 J8
Dadu 42 F5
Daet 38 B2
Dagana 55 E1
Dagestan □ . . . 25 E6
Daghestan Republic = Dagestan □ . 25 E6
Dagö = Hiiumaa 24 B1
Dagupan 38 A2
Dahlak Kebir . . 49 D3
Dahod 43 H9
Dahomey = Benin ■ 55 G5
Dahra 55 E1
Daiō-Misaki . . . 32 B5
Dairût 52 C5
Dakar 55 F1
Dakhla 54 D1
Dakhla, El Wâhât el- . . . 52 C4
Dakhovskaya . . 25 E5
Đakovica 22 C3
Dalaman → . . 23 F7
Dalandzadgad . 35 B5
Dālbandīn 42 E4
Dalby 63 A5
Dalhousie 69 D4
Dali 34 D5
Dalian 35 C7
Daliang Shan . . 34 D5
Dallarnil 63 A5
Dallas 79 C5
Dalmacija 20 C6
Dalmatia = Dalmacija . . . 20 C6
Daloa 55 G3
Dalton 74 B5
Dalton Iceberg Tongue 96 A13
Daly Waters . . . 60 D5
Daman 43 J8
Damanhûr 52 B5
Damar 39 F3
Damaraland . . . 58 C3
Damascus = Dimashq 46 D4
Damāvand 44 C3
Damāvand, Qolleh-ye . . . 44 C3
Damba 56 F3
Dāmghān 44 B3
Damiel 18 C4
Damietta = Dumyât 52 B5
Dammam = Ad Dammām . . . 47 F7
Damoh 43 H11
Dampier 60 E2
Dampier, Selat 39 E4
Danbury 73 D9
Dandeldhura . . 40 C3
Dandeli 43 M9
Dandenong . . . 63 C4
Dandong 35 B7
Danger Is. = Pukapuka . . . 65 L14
Danger Pt. 58 E3
Dangora 55 F6
Danilov 24 B5
Dankhar Gompa 42 C11
Dannemora . . . 9 F11
Dannevirke . . . 64 D7
Dante 49 E5
Danube = Dunărea → . 17 F9
Danville 75 A8
Danzig = Gdańsk 16 A4
Dao 38 B2
Daoud = Aïn Beïda 54 A6
Dar el Beida = Casablanca . . 54 B3
Dar es Salaam . 57 F7
Dārāb 44 D3
Daraj 54 B7
Darband 42 B8
Darbhanga 40 D5
Dardanelles = Çanakkale Boğazı 23 D6
Dârfûr 53 F3
Dargai 42 B7
Dargan Ata . . . 29 E7
Dargaville 64 A5
Darıca 22 D7
Darién, G. del . 90 B3
Darjeeling = Darjiling 40 D7
Darjiling 40 D7
Darling → 62 B3
Darling Downs 63 A5
Darling Ra. 60 G2
Darlington 11 D6
Darłowo 16 A3
Darmstadt 14 D5
Darnah 52 B3
Darnley, C. 96 A10
Darnley B. 70 B7
Dart, C. 96 B18
Dartmoor 11 F5
Dartmouth 69 D4
Dartmouth, L. . 63 A4
Darvaza 29 E6
Darvel, Teluk . . 38 D1
Darwha 43 J10
Darwin 60 C5
Daryoi Amu = Amudarya → 29 E6
Dās 44 E3
Dashhowuz . . . 29 E6
Dasht → 42 G2
Dasht-e Kavīr . . 44 C3
Dasht-e Mārgow 42 D3
Datça 23 F6
Datia 43 G11
Datong 35 B6
Datu, Tanjung . 37 D3
Datu Piang 38 C2
Daugava → . . 24 B1
Daugavpils 24 B2
Daulpur 42 F10
Dauphin 71 C9
Dauphiné 13 D6
Davangere 43 M9
Davao 38 C3
Davao, G. of . . 38 C3
Dāvar Panāh . . 45 E5
Davenport 77 E9
David 86 E3
David Gorodok = Davyd Haradok 17 B8
Davis Sea 96 A11
Davis Str. 68 B5
Davos 13 C8
Davyd Haradok 17 B8
Dawson 70 B6
Dawson, I. 95 G2
Dax 12 E3
Daxian 35 C5
Daxue Shan . . . 34 C5
Daylesford 62 C3
Dayr az Zawr . . 46 D5
Dayton 72 E3
Daytona Beach 75 E7
Dead Sea 47 E3
Deakin 60 G4
Deal I. 62 C4
Deán Funes . . . 94 C4
Death Valley . . 82 B4
Deba Habe 55 F7
Debar 22 D3
Dębica 16 C5
Debre Markos . 53 F6
Debre Tabor . . 53 F6
Debrecen 16 E5
Decatur, *Ala., U.S.A.* 74 B4
Decatur, *Ill., U.S.A.* 77 F10
Deccan 43 L11
Děčín 16 C2
Dedéagach = Alexandroúpolis 22 D5

Dédougou 55 F4
Dee → 10 C5
Deepwater 63 A5
Degeh Bur 49 F3
Deggendorf 15 D7
Deh Bīd 44 D3
Dehi Titan 42 C3
Dehibat 54 B7
Dehkareqan 46 C6
Dehra Dun 42 D11
Dej 17 E6
Dekese 56 E4
Delano 82 C3
Delaware □ 73 E8
Delaware → 73 E8
Delegate 63 C4
Delgado, C. 57 G8
Delgo 53 D5
Delhi 42 E10
Delice → 46 C3
Delicias 84 B3
Delmenhorst 14 B5
Delmiro Gouveia 93 D6
Deloraine 62 D4
Delungra 63 A5
Delvinë 23 E3
Demanda, Sierra de la 18 A4
Demavand = Damāvand 44 C3
Demba 56 F4
Dembecha 53 F6
Dembidolo 53 G5
Demini → 90 D6
Demirci 23 E7
Demirköy 22 D6
Dempo 37 E2
Den Haag = 's-Gravenhage 14 B3
Den Helder 14 B3
Denau 29 F7
Dendang 37 E3
Denia 19 C6
Denial B. 62 B1
Deniliquin 63 C3
Denman Glacier 96 A11
Denmark ■ 9 G9
Denmark Str. 66 C17
Denpasar 37 F5
Denton 78 C5
D'Entrecasteaux Is. 61 B9
Denver 76 F2
Deoghar 40 E6
Deolali 43 K8
Deoria 40 D4
Deosai Mts. 42 B9
Dêqên 34 D4
Dera Ghazi Khan 42 D7
Dera Ismail Khan 42 D7
Derbent 25 E6
Derby, *Australia* 60 D3
Derby, *U.K.* 11 E6
Derg, L. 11 E2
Dergaon 41 D9
Derry = Londonderry 11 D3
Derudub 53 E6
Des Moines 77 E8
Des Moines → 77 E9
Desaguadero → 91 G5
Dese 49 E2
Desna → 17 C10
Desolación, I. 95 G2
Despeñaperros, Paso 18 C4
Dessau 15 C7
Dessye = Dese 49 E2
D'Estrees B. 62 C2
Detmold 14 C5
Detroit 72 C4
Deutsche Bucht 14 A5
Deva 17 F6
Devakottai 43 Q11
Deventer 14 B4
Devonport, *Australia* 62 D4
Devonport, *N.Z.* 64 B6
Dewas 43 H10
Deyhūk 44 C4
Deyyer 44 E2
Dezfūl 47 D7
Dezhneva, Mys 31 C16
Dhafra 44 F3
Dhahira 44 F4
Dhahran = Az̧ Z̧ahrān 47 F7
Dhaka 41 F8
Dhaka □ 41 E8
Dhamar 49 E3
Dhamtari 40 G3
Dhanbad 40 F6
Dhangarhi 40 C3
Dhankuta 40 D6
Dhar 43 H9
Dharmapuri 43 N11
Dharwad 43 M9
Dhaulagiri 40 C4
Dhenkanal 40 G5
Dhíkti Óros 23 G5
Dhírfis 23 E4
Dhodhekánisos 23 F6
Dhrol 43 H7
Dhubaibah 44 F3
Dhuburi 41 D7
Dhule 43 J9
Dhut → 49 E5
Diafarabé 55 F4
Diamantina 93 F5
Diamantina → 62 A2
Diamantino 93 E2
Diamond Harbour 40 F7
Diapaga 55 F5
Dībā 44 E4
Dibaya 56 F4
Dibaya-Lubue 56 E3
Dibbi 49 G3
Dibrugarh 41 D10
Dickson 28 B9
Didiéni 55 F3
Diébougou 55 F4
Diefenbaker L. 71 C9
Dieppe 12 B4
Digby 69 D4
Digges Is. 68 B3
Dighinala 41 F9
Digne-les-Bains 13 D7
Digos 38 C3
Digul → 39 F5
Dihang → 41 D10
Dijlah, Nahr → 47 E6
Dijon 13 C6
Dikimdya 31 D10
Dikson = Dickson 28 B9
Dikwa 53 F1
Dili 39 F3
Dilling 53 F4
Dillingham 71 C4
Dilolo 56 G4
Dilston 62 D4
Dimashq 46 D4
Dimbokro 55 G4
Dimboola 62 C3
Dîmboviţa → 22 B6
Dimitrovgrad, *Bulgaria* 22 C5
Dimitrovgrad, *Russia* 24 C6
Dimitrovo = Pernik 22 C4
Dinagat 38 B3
Dinajpur 41 E7
Dinan 12 B2
Dinant 14 C3
Dinar 46 C2
Dīnār, Kūh-e 44 D2
Dinara Planina 20 B6
Dinard 12 B2
Dinaric Alps = Dinara Planina 20 B6
Dindigul 43 P11
Dingle 11 E1
Dinguiraye 55 F2
Dingwall 10 C4
Dinosaur National Monument 81 E9
Diourbel 55 F1
Dipolog 38 C2
Dir 42 B7
Diré 55 E4
Dire Dawa 49 F3
Dirico 58 B4
Dirranbandi 63 A4
Disa 43 G8
Disappointment, L. 60 E3
Disaster B. 63 C4
Discovery B. 62 C3
Disteghil Sar 42 A9
Distrito Federal □ 93 F4
Diu 43 J7
Divinópolis 93 G5
Divnoye 25 D5
Dīwāl Kol 42 B5
Diyarbakır 46 C5
Diz Chah 44 C3
Djado 52 D1
Djakarta = Jakarta 37 F3
Djambala 56 E2
Djanet 54 D6
Djawa = Jawa 37 F3
Djelfa 54 B5
Djema 57 C5
Djenné 55 F4
Djerba, I. de 52 B1
Djerid, Chott 54 B6
Djibo 55 F4
Djibouti 49 E3
Djibouti ■ 49 E3
Djolu 56 D4
Djougou 55 G5
Djoum 56 D2
Djourab 53 E2
Djugu 57 D6
Dmitriya Lapteva, Proliv 31 B12
Dnepr → = Dnipro → 25 D3
Dneprodzerzhinsk = Dniprodzerzhynsk 25 D3
Dnepropetrovsk = Dnipropetrovsk 25 D4
Dnestr → = Dnister → 17 E10
Dnestrovski = Belgorod 24 C4
Dnieper = Dnipro → 25 D3
Dniester = Dnister → 17 E10
Dnipro → 25 D3
Dniprodzerzhynsk 25 D3
Dnipropetrovsk 25 D4
Dnister → 17 E10
Dnistrovskyy Lyman 17 E10
Dnyapro = Dnipro → 25 D3
Doba 53 G2
Doberai, Jazirah 39 E4
Doblas 94 D4
Dobo 39 F4
Doboj 20 B7
Dobreta-Turnu-Severin 22 B4
Dobrich 22 C6
Dobruja 22 B7
Dobrush 17 B10
Dodecanese = Dhodhekánisos 23 F6
Dodge City 78 A3
Dodoma 57 F7
Dogi 42 C3
Doha = Ad Dawhah 44 E2
Dohazari 41 F9
Doi 39 D3
Dois Irmãos, Sa. 93 D5
Dolbeau 69 D3
Dole 13 C6
Dolomites = Dolomiti 20 A3
Dolomiti 20 A3
Dolores 94 D5
Dolphin, C. 95 G5
Dolphin and Union Str. 70 B8
Dombarovskiy 29 D6
Dominica ■ 87 C7
Dominican Rep. ■ 87 C5
Domo 49 F4
Domodóssola 20 A2
Domville, Mt. 63 A5
Don →, *Russia* 25 D4
Don →, *U.K.* 10 C5
Don Benito 18 C3
Donald 62 C3
Donau = Dunărea → 17 F9
Donauwörth 14 D6
Doncaster 11 E6
Dondo, *Angola* 56 F2
Dondo, *Mozam.* 59 B6
Dondo, Teluk 39 D2
Donegal 11 D2
Donets → 25 D5
Donetsk 25 D4
Donggala 39 E1
Dongola 53 E5
Dongou 56 D3
Dongting Hu 35 D6
Dongxing 35 D5
Donington, C. 62 B2
Donnelly's Crossing 64 A5
Donostia = San Sebastián 19 A5
Dora Báltea → 20 B2
Dorchester, C. 68 B3
Dordogne → 12 D3
Dordrecht 14 C3
Dori 55 F4
Dornbirn 14 E5
Dorohoi 17 E8

Döröö Nuur 34 B4
Dorrigo 63 B5
Dortmund 14 C4
Doruma 57 D5
Dos Bahías, C. 95 E3
Dos Hermanas 18 D3
Dosso 55 F5
Dothan 74 D5
Douai 13 A5
Douala 56 D1
Douarnenez 12 B1
Double Island Pt. 63 A5
Doubs → 13 C6
Doubtful Sd. 65 F2
Doubtless B. 64 A5
Douentza 55 F4
Douglas, *U.K.* 11 D4
Douglas, *U.S.A.* 83 E8
Doumé 56 D2
Dourados 94 A6
Douro → 18 B1
Dover, *Australia* 62 D4
Dover, *U.K.* 11 F7
Dover, Str. of 11 F7
Dovrefjell 8 F9
Dowlat Yār 45 C6
Dowlatābād 44 D4
Dowshī 45 C7
Draa, Oued → 54 C2
Drăgăşani 22 B5
Dragichyn 17 B7
Dragoman, Prokhod 22 C4
Draguignan 13 E7
Drake 63 A5
Drakensberg 59 E5
Dráma 22 D5
Drammen 9 G10
Drau = Drava → 20 B7
Drava → 20 B7
Dresden 15 C7
Dreux 12 B4
Drina → 20 B7
Drini → 22 C2
Drochia 17 D8
Drogheda 11 E3
Drogichin = Dragichyn 17 B7
Drogobych = Drohobych 17 D6
Drohobych 17 D6
Droichead Atha = Drogheda 11 E3
Dromedary, C. 63 C5
Drumheller 71 C8
Drummond Pt. 62 B2
Drut → 17 B10
Drygalski I. 96 A11
Dschang 55 G7
Ḑubā 47 F3
Dubai = Dubayy 44 E3
Dubăsari 17 E9
Dubăsari Vdkhr. 17 E9
Dubawnt → 70 B9
Dubawnt, L. 70 B9
Dubayy 44 E3
Dubbo 63 B4
Dublin, *Ireland* 11 E3
Dublin, *U.S.A.* 75 C6
Dubno 17 C7
Dubossary = Dubăsari 17 E9
Dubossary Vdkhr. = Dubăsari Vdkhr. 17 E9
Dubovka 24 D5
Dubréka 55 G2
Dubrovitsa = Dubrovytsya 17 C8
Dubrovnik 20 C7
Dubrovytsya 17 C8
Dudhi 40 E4
Dudinka 30 C6
Duero = Douro → 18 B1
Dugi Otok 20 B5
Duisburg 14 C4
Dukelský Průsmyk 16 D5
Dukhān 44 E2
Duki 42 D6
Duku 55 F7
Dulce → 94 C4
Dulit, Banjaran 37 D4
Duluth 77 B8
Dum Duma 41 D10
Dum Hadjer 53 F2
Dumaguete 38 C2
Dumai 37 D2
Dumaran 38 B1
Dumfries 11 D5
Dumyât 52 B5
Dún Dealgan = Dundalk 11 D3
Dun Laoghaire 11 E3
Duna = Dunărea → 17 F9
Dunaj = Dunărea → 17 F9
Dunakeszi 16 E4
Dunărea → 17 F9
Dunaújváros 16 E4
Dunav = Dunărea → 17 F9
Dunback 65 F4
Dunbar 10 D5
Duncan 78 B5
Dundalk 11 D3
Dundee, *S. Africa* 59 D6
Dundee, *U.K.* 10 C5
Dundoo 63 A3
Dunedin 65 F4
Dunfermline 10 C5
Dungarvan 11 E3
Dungog 63 B5
Dungu 57 D5
Dunhuang 34 B4
Dunkerque 12 A5
Dunkirk = Dunkerque 12 A5
Dunkwa 55 G4
Dúnleary = Dun Laoghaire 11 E3
Dunolly 62 C3
Dunqul 52 D5
Dunstan Mts. 65 F3
Durance → 13 E6
Durango, *Mexico* 84 C4
Durango, *Spain* 19 A4
Durazno 94 C5
Durazzo = Durrësi 22 D2
Durban 59 D6
Düren 14 C4
Durg 40 G3
Durgapur 40 F6
Durham, *U.K.* 11 D6
Durham, *U.S.A.* 75 B8
Durham Downs 63 A4
Durmitor 22 C2
Durrësi 22 D2
Dursunbey 23 E7
D'Urville, Tanjung 39 E5
D'Urville I. 65 D5
Dusa Mareb 49 F4
Dushak 29 F7
Dushanbe 29 F7
Dusky Sd. 65 F2
Düsseldorf 14 C4
Dutch Harbor 71 C3
Duwādimi 47 F6
Duyun 35 D5
Düzce 46 B2
Duzdab = Zāhedān 45 D5
Dvina, Severnaya → 28 C5
Dvinsk = Daugavpils 24 B2
Dwarka 43 H6
Dyatlovo = Dzyatlava 17 B7
Dyer, C. 68 B4
Dyer Plateau 96 B3
Dyersburg 79 A9
Dymer 17 C10
Dynevor Downs 63 A3
Dzamin Üüd 35 B6
Dzerzhinsk 24 B5
Dzhambul = Zhambyl 29 E8
Dzhankoy 25 D3
Dzhardzhan 30 C10
Dzhezkazgan = Zhezqazghan 29 E7
Dzhizak = Jizzakh 29 E7
Działdowa 16 B5
Dzierzoniów 16 C3
Dzungaria = Junggar Pendi 34 B3
Dzungarian Gate = Alataw Shankou 34 B3
Dzuumod 35 B5
Dzyarzhynsk 17 B8
Dzyatlava 17 B7

E

Earnslaw, Mt. 65 F3
East Bengal 41 E7
East Beskids = Vychodné Beskydy 17 D5
East C. 64 B8
East China Sea 35 C7
East Falkland 95 G5
East Kilbride 10 D4
East London 59 E5
East Main = Eastmain 69 C3
East Orange 73 D8
East St. Louis 77 F9
East Toorale 63 B4
Eastbourne, *N.Z.* 65 D6
Eastbourne, *U.K.* 11 F7
Eastern Ghats 43 N11
Eastmain 69 C3
Eastmain → 69 C3
Eau Claire 77 C9
Eberswalde-Finow 15 B7
Ebolowa 56 D2
Ebro → 19 B6
Eceabat 23 D6
Ech Cheliff 54 A5
Echo Bay 70 B8
Echuca 63 C3
Ecija 18 D3
Ecuador ■ 90 D3
Ed Dâmer 53 E5
Ed Debba 53 E5
Ed Dueim 53 F5
Edd 49 E3
Eddystone Pt. 62 D4
Édea 56 D2
Eden 63 C4
Eder → 14 C5
Édhessa 23 D4
Edievale 65 F3
Edinburg 78 F4
Edinburgh 10 D5
Edinţa 17 D8
Edirne 22 D6
Edithburgh 62 C2
Edmonton 71 C8
Edmundston 69 D4
Edremit 23 E6
Edremit Körfezi 23 E6
Edson 71 C8
Edward → 62 C3
Edward, L. 57 E5
Edward VII Land 96 C17
Edwards Plateau 78 D3
Égadi, Ísole 21 F4
Eger = Cheb 16 C1
Eger 16 E5
Egersund 9 G9
Egmont, C. 64 C5
Egmont, Mt. 64 C6
Eğridir 46 C2
Eğridir Gölü 46 C2
Egypt ■ 52 C5
Eibar 19 A4
Eidsvold 63 A5
Eifel 14 C4
Eigg 10 C3
Eil 49 F4
Eildon, L. 63 C4
Eindhoven 14 C3
Eire = Ireland ■ 11 E3
Eirunepé 91 E5
Eisenach 14 C6
Eisenerz 15 E8
Eivissa = Ibiza 19 C6
Eketahuna 64 D6
Ekibastuz 29 D8
El Aaiún 54 C2
El Alamein 52 B4
El Aricha 54 B4
El 'Arîsh 52 B5
El Asnam = Ech Cheliff 54 A5
El Bawiti 52 C4
El Bayadh 54 B5
El Callao 90 B6
El Centro 82 D5
El Cerro 91 G6
El Cuy 95 D3
El Cuyo 85 C7
El Dere 49 G4
El Diviso 90 C3
El Djouf 55 D3
El Dorado, *Ark., U.S.A.* 79 C7
El Dorado, *Kans., U.S.A.* 78 A5
El Dorado, *Venezuela* 90 B6
El Escorial 18 B3
El Faiyûm 52 C5
El Fâsher 53 F4
El Ferrol 18 A1
El Fuerte 84 B3
El Gal 49 E5

El Geneina = Al Junaynah **53 F3**
El Geteina **53 F5**
El Gîza **52 C5**
El Iskandarîya **52 B4**
El Jadida **54 B3**
El Jebelein **53 F5**
El Kab **53 E5**
El Kala **54 A6**
El Kamlin **53 E5**
El Kef **54 A6**
El Khandaq **53 E5**
El Khârga **52 C5**
El Khartûm **53 E5**
El Khartûm Bahrî **53 E5**
El Laqâwa **53 F4**
El Mafâza **53 F5**
El Mahalla el Kubra **52 B5**
El Mansûra **52 B5**
El Minyâ **52 C5**
El Obeid **53 F5**
El Odaiya **53 F4**
El Oued **54 B6**
El Paso **83 E9**
El Prat de Llobregat **19 B7**
El Puerto de Santa María **18 D2**
El Qâhira **52 B5**
El Qantara **52 B5**
El Qasr **52 C4**
El Reno **78 B5**
El Salvador ■ **85 E7**
El Shallal **52 D5**
El Suweis **52 C5**
El Tigre **90 B6**
El Tocuyo **90 B5**
El Turbio **95 G2**
El Uqsur **52 C5**
El Vigía **90 B4**
El Wak **57 D8**
El Wuz **53 E5**
Elat **47 E3**
Elâzığ **46 C4**
Elba **20 C3**
Elbasani **22 D3**
Elbe → **14 B5**
Elbert, Mt. **83 A9**
Elbeuf **12 B4**
Elbidtan **46 C4**
Elbing = Elbląg **16 A4**
Elbląg **16 A4**
Elbrus **25 E5**
Elburz Mts. = Alborz, Reshteh-ye Kūhhā-ye **44 B3**
Elche **19 C5**
Elda **19 C5**
Elde → **15 B6**
Eldoret **57 D7**
Elektrostal **24 B4**
Elephant I. **96 A4**
Eleuthera **86 A4**
Elgin, *U.K.* **10 C5**
Elgin, *U.S.A.* **72 C1**
Elgon, Mt. **57 D6**
Eliase **39 F4**
Elisabethville = Lubumbashi **59 A5**
Elista **25 D5**
Elizabeth, *Australia* **62 B2**
Elizabeth, *U.S.A.* **73 D8**
Elizabeth City **75 A9**
Elizabethton **75 A6**
Ełk **16 B6**
Elkhart **72 D3**
Elkhovo **22 C6**
Elko **80 E6**
Ellery, Mt. **63 C4**
Ellesmere, L. **65 G5**
Ellice Is. = Tuvalu ■ **64 K12**
Elliston **62 B1**
Ellore = Eluru **40 J3**
Ellsworth Land **96 B2**
Ellsworth Mts. **96 B2**
Elmore **63 C3**
Elmshorn **14 B5**
Eltham **64 C6**
Eluru **40 J3**
Elvas **18 C2**
Elx = Elche **19 C5**
Ely **11 E7**
Emāmrūd **44 B3**
Emba = Embi **29 E6**
Emba → = Embi → **29 E6**
Embarcación **94 A4**
Embi **29 E6**
Embi → **29 E6**
Embrun **13 D7**
Embu **57 E7**
Emden **14 B4**
Emerson **71 D10**
Emet **23 E7**
Emi Koussi **53 E2**
Emine, Nos **22 C6**
Emmen **14 B4**
Empalme **84 B2**
Empangeni **59 D6**
Empedrado **94 B5**
Empty Quarter = Rub' al Khali **48 D4**
Ems → **14 B4**
En Nahud **53 F4**
Enaratoli **39 E5**
Enare = Inarijärvi **8 E13**
Encanto, C. **38 A2**
Encarnación **94 B5**
Encounter B. **62 C2**
Ende **39 F2**
Enderby Land **96 A9**
Enewetak Atoll **64 H11**
Enez **23 D6**
Engadin **13 C9**
Engaño, C. **38 A2**
Engels **24 C6**
Enggano **37 F2**
Engkilili **37 D4**
England □ **11 E6**
Englewood **76 F2**
English Bazar = Ingraj Bazar **40 E7**
English Channel **11 F5**
Enid **78 A5**
Enna **21 F5**
Ennedi **53 E3**
Enngonia **63 A4**
Ennis **11 E2**
Enniskillen **11 D3**
Enns → **15 D8**
Enschede **14 B4**
Ensenada **84 A1**
Entebbe **57 D6**
Entroncamento **18 C1**
Enugu **55 G6**
Enugu Ezike **55 G6**
Eólie, Ís. **21 E5**
Épernay **13 B5**
Ephesus **23 F6**
Épinal **13 B7**
Epukiro **58 C3**
Equatorial Guinea ■ **56 D1**
Er Rahad **53 F5**
Er Rif **54 A4**
Er Roseires **53 F5**
Erāwadī Myit = Irrawaddy → **41 K10**
Erbil = Arbīl **46 C6**
Erciyaş Dağı **46 C3**
Érd **16 E4**
Erdek **23 D6**
Erebus, Mt. **96 B15**
Erechim **94 B6**
Ereğli, *Konya, Turkey* **46 C3**
Ereğli, *Zonguldak, Turkey* **46 B2**
Eresma → **18 B3**
Erewadi Myitwanya **41 K10**
Erfurt **15 C6**
Ergani **46 C4**
Érice **21 E4**
Erie **73 C5**
Erie, L. **72 C5**
Erigavo **49 E4**
Erímanthos **23 F3**
Erimo-misaki **32 F12**
Eritrea ■ **49 E2**
Erlangen **15 D6**
Ermenak **46 C3**
Ermoúpolis = Síros **23 F5**
Ernakulam = Cochin **43 Q10**
Erne, Lower L. **11 D3**
Erode **43 P10**
Eromanga **63 A3**
Erramala Hills **43 M11**
Ertis → = Irtysh → **28 C7**
Erzgebirge **15 C7**
Erzincan **46 C4**
Erzurum **46 C5**
Es Sahrâ' Esh Sharqîya **52 C5**
Es Sînâ' **52 C5**
Esbjerg **9 G9**
Esch-sur-Alzette **13 B6**
Escuinapa **84 C3**
Eşfahān **44 C2**
Esh Sham = Dimashq **46 D4**
Esil → = Ishim → **29 D8**
Eskilstuna **9 G11**
Eskimo Pt. = Arviat **70 B10**
Eskişehir **46 C2**
Esla → **18 B2**
Eslāmābād-e Gharb **46 D6**
Eşme **23 E7**
Esmeraldas **90 C3**
Esperance **60 G3**
Esperanza **94 C4**
Espichel, C. **18 C1**
Espinal **90 C4**
Espinazo, Sierra del = Espinhaço, Serra do **93 F5**
Espinhaço, Serra do **93 F5**
Espírito Santo □ **93 G5**
Esquel **95 E2**
Esquina **94 C5**
Essaouira **54 B3**
Essen **14 C4**
Essequibo → **90 B7**
Esslingen **14 D5**
Estados, I. de Los **95 G4**
Estância **93 E6**
Estevan **71 D9**
Estonia ■ **24 B2**
Estrêla, Serra da **18 B2**
Estremoz **18 C2**
Estrondo, Serra do **92 D4**
Esztergom **16 E4**
Etadunna **62 A2**
Étampes **12 B5**
Etawah **42 F11**
Ethiopia ■ **49 F2**
Etna **21 F5**
Etosha Pan **58 B3**
Euboea = Évvoia **23 E5**
Eucumbene, L. **63 C4**
Eufaula **74 D5**
Eugene **80 C2**
Eugowra **63 B4**
Eulo **63 A4**
Euphrates = Furāt, Nahr al → **47 E6**
Eureka **80 E1**
Euroa **63 C4**
Europa, I. **59 J8**
Europa, Picos de **18 A3**
Europa, Pta. de **18 D3**
Europa Pt. = Europa, Pta. de **18 D3**
Evans Head **63 A5**
Evanston **72 C2**
Evansville **72 F2**
Everard, L. **62 B1**
Everest, Mt. **40 C6**
Everett **80 B2**
Everglades National Park **75 G7**
Evinayong **56 D2**
Évora **18 C2**
Évreux **12 B4**
Évros → **22 D6**
Evry **12 B5**
Évvoia **23 E5**
Ewo **56 E2**
Exaltación **91 F5**
Exeter **11 F5**
Exmoor **11 F5**
Exmouth **11 F5**
Extremadura □ **18 C2**
Eyasi, L. **57 E6**
Eyre (North), L. **62 A2**
Eyre (South), L. **62 A2**
Eyre, L. **60 F6**
Eyre Cr. → **62 A2**
Eyre Mts. **65 F3**
Eyre Pen. **62 B2**
Ezine **23 E6**

F

F.Y.R.O.M. = Macedonia ■ **22 D3**
Fabriano **20 C4**
Facatativá **90 C4**
Fachi **55 E7**
Fada **53 E3**
Fada-n-Gourma **55 F5**
Faddeyevskiy, Ostrov **31 B12**

Fāḑilī 47 F7
Faenza 20 B3
Færoe Is. = Føroyar 6 C4
Făgăras 17 F7
Fagnano, L. 95 G3
Fahraj 45 D4
Fahūd 44 F4
Fair Isle 10 B6
Fairbanks 71 B5
Fairfield, *Ala., U.S.A.* 74 C4
Fairfield, *Calif., U.S.A.* 80 F2
Fairlie 65 F4
Fairweather, Mt. 71 C6
Faisalabad 42 D8
Faizabad 40 D4
Fakfak 39 E4
Falaise 12 B3
Falam 41 F9
Falconara Maríttima 20 C4
Falcone, C. 20 D2
Faleshty = Făleşti 17 E8
Făleşti 17 E8
Falkland Is. □ 95 G5
Falkland Sd. 95 G5
Fall River 73 D10
Falmouth 11 F4
False B. 58 E3
Fălticeni 17 E8
Falun 9 F11
Famagusta 46 D3
Fandriana 59 J9
Fano 20 C4
Fao = Al Fāw 47 E7
Faradje 57 D5
Farafangana 59 J9
Farāh 42 C3
Farāh □ 42 C3
Faranah 55 F2
Farasān, Jazā'ir 49 D3
Farasan Is. = Farasān, Jazā'ir 49 D3
Fareham 11 F6
Farewell, C. 64 D5
Farewell C. = Farvel, Kap 68 C6
Farghona 29 E8
Fargo 76 B6
Farim 55 F1
Farīmān 45 C4
Farina 62 B2
Faro, *Brazil* 92 C2
Faro, *Portugal* 18 D2
Farrāshband 44 D3
Farrell Flat 62 B2
Farrukhabad-cum-Fatehgarh 42 F11
Fārs □ 44 D3
Fársala 23 E4
Fartak, Râs 47 E3
Farvel, Kap 68 C6
Fāryāb □ 45 B6
Fasā 44 D3
Fasano 21 D6
Fastiv 17 C9
Fastov = Fastiv 17 C9
Fatagar, Tanjung 39 E4
Fatehgarh 42 F11
Fatehpur, *Raj., India* 42 F9
Fatehpur, *Ut. P., India* 40 E3
Favara 21 F4
Favignana 21 F4
Faya-Largeau 53 E2
Fayd 47 F5
Fayetteville, *Ark., U.S.A.* 79 A6
Fayetteville, *N.C., U.S.A.* 75 B8
Fazilka 42 D9
Fdérik 54 D2
Feather → 80 F3
Featherston 65 D6
Fécamp 12 B4
Fehmarn 15 A6
Feilding 64 D6
Feira de Santana 93 E6
Feldkirch 14 E5
Felipe Carrillo Puerto 85 D7
Felixstowe 11 F7
Fengjie 35 C5
Fenyang 35 C6
Feodosiya 25 D4
Ferdows 44 C4
Ferfer 49 F4
Fergana = Farghona 29 E8
Fermo 20 C4
Fernando de Noronha 92 C7
Fernando Póo = Bioko 56 D1
Ferozepore = Firozpur 42 D9
Ferrara 20 B3
Ferreñafe 91 E3
Ferret, C. 12 D3
Ferrol = El Ferrol 18 A1
Fès 54 B4
Feshi 56 F3
Feteşti 22 B6
Fetlar 10 A6
Feuilles → 68 C3
Fezzan 52 C2
Fianarantsoa 59 J9
Fianga 53 G2
Ficksburg 59 D5
Fieri 23 D2
Figeac 12 D5
Figueira da Foz 18 B1
Figueras 19 A7
Figuig 54 B4
Fiji ■ 64 L12
Filiatrá 23 F3
Filyos → 46 B3
Fíngõe 59 A6
Finike 46 C2
Finisterre, C. 18 A1
Finke → 62 A2
Finland ■ 8 F13
Finland, G. of 9 G13
Finlay → 70 C7
Finley 63 C4
Finniss, C. 62 B1
Fiora → 20 C3
Firat = Furāt, Nahr al → 47 E6
Firenze 20 C3
Firozabad 42 F11
Firozpur 42 D9
Fīrūzābād 44 D3
Fīrūzkūh 44 C3
Fish → 58 D3
Fishguard 11 E4
Fitri, L. 53 F2
Fitz Roy 95 F3
Fiume = Rijeka 20 B5
Fizi 57 E5
Flagstaff 83 C7
Flaming Gorge Reservoir 81 E9
Flamingo, Teluk 39 F5
Flandre 14 C2
Flathead L. 81 B6
Flattery, C. 80 A1
Flensburg 14 A5
Flers 12 B3
Flesko, Tanjung 39 D2
Flin Flon 71 C9
Flinders → 61 D7
Flinders I. 62 C4
Flinders Ras. 62 B2
Flint 72 C4
Flint I. 65 L15
Flinton 63 A4
Florence = Firenze 20 C3
Florence, *Ala., U.S.A.* 74 B4
Florence, *S.C., U.S.A.* 75 B8
Florence, L. 62 A2
Flores 39 F2
Flores Sea 39 F2
Floreşti 17 E9
Floriano 92 D5
Florianópolis 94 B7
Florida 94 C5
Florida □ 75 F6
Florida, Straits of 86 B3
Flórina 23 D3
Florø 8 F9
Fluk 39 E3
Flushing = Vlissingen 14 C2
Fly → 61 B7
Flying Fish, C. 96 B1
Foça 23 E6
Focşani 17 F8
Fóggia 20 D5
Föhr 14 A5
Foix 12 E4
Foligno 20 C4
Folkestone 11 F7
Fond du Lac 77 D10
Fondi 20 D4
Fonsagrada 18 A2
Fonseca, G. de 85 E7
Fontainebleau 13 B5
Fonte Boa 90 D5
Fontenay-le-Comte 12 C3
Foochow = Fuzhou 35 D6
Forbes 63 B4
Ford's Bridge 63 A4
Forécariah 55 G2
Forestier Pen. 62 D4
Forfar 10 C5
Forlì 20 B4
Formentera 19 C6
Formentor, C. de 19 C7
Former Yugoslav Republic of Macedonia = Macedonia ■ 22 D3
Fórmia 20 D4
Formosa = Taiwan ■ 35 D7
Formosa 94 B5
Formosa, Serra 93 E3
Formosa Bay 57 E8
Føroyar = Føroyar 6 C4
Føroyar 6 C4
Forrest 62 C3
Forsayth 61 D7
Forst 15 C8
Forster 63 B5
Fort Albany 69 C2
Fort Collins 76 E2
Fort-de-France 87 D7
Fort de Possel = Possel 56 C3
Fort Dodge 77 D7
Fort Franklin 70 B7
Fort Good-Hope 70 B7
Fort Hertz = Putao 41 D11
Fort Lauderdale 75 F7
Fort Liard 70 B7
Fort Macleod 71 D8
Fort MacMahon 54 C5
Fort McPherson 70 B6
Fort Miribel 54 C5
Fort Myers 75 F7
Fort Norman 70 B7
Fort Peck L. 81 B10
Fort Pierce 75 F7
Fort Portal 57 D6
Fort Providence 70 B8
Fort Resolution 70 B8
Fort Rosebery = Mansa 57 G5
Fort Rupert = Waskaganish 69 C3
Fort Sandeman 42 D6
Fort Scott 79 A6
Fort Severn 69 C2
Fort Shevchenko 29 E6
Fort Simpson 70 B7
Fort Smith, *Canada* 70 B8
Fort Smith, *U.S.A.* 79 B6
Fort Trinquet = Bir Mogrein 54 C2
Fort Walton Beach 74 D4
Fort Wayne 72 D3
Fort William 10 C4
Fort Worth 78 C5
Fort Yukon 71 B5
Fortaleza 92 C6
Forūr 44 E3
Foshan 35 D6
Fossano 20 B1
Fougamou 56 E2
Fougères 12 B3
Foula 10 A5
Foumban 55 G7
Foúrnoi 23 F6
Fouta Djalon 55 F2
Foveaux Str. 65 G3
Foxe Basin 68 B3
Foxe Chan. 68 B2
Foxe Pen. 68 B3
Foxton 64 D6
Foz do Gregório 91 E4
Foz do Iguaçu 94 B6
Franca 93 G4
Francavilla Fontana 21 D6
France ■ 13 C5
Frances 62 C3
Franceville 56 E2
Franche-Comté 13 C6
Francistown 59 C5
Frankfurt, *Brandenburg, Germany* 15 B8
Frankfurt, *Hessen, Germany* 14 C5
Fränkische Alb 15 D6

Franklin B. 70 B7
Franklin I. 96 B15
Franklin Mts. . . 70 B7
Franklin Str. . . . 70 A10
Frankston 63 C4
Frantsa Iosifa, Zemlya 28 A6
Franz 69 D2
Franz Josef Land = Frantsa Iosifa, Zemlya 28 A6
Fraser → 71 D7
Fraser I. 63 A5
Fraserburgh . . . 10 C5
Fray Bentos . . . 94 C5
Fredericksburg 73 E7
Fredericton . . . 69 D4
Fredrikstad 9 G10
Freeport, *Bahamas* . . . 86 A4
Freeport, *U.S.A.* 77 D10
Freetown 55 G2
Fregenal de la Sierra 18 C2
Freibourg = Fribourg 13 C7
Freiburg 14 E4
Freire 95 D2
Freising 15 D6
Freistadt 15 D8
Fréjus 13 E7
Fremont 82 B2
French Guiana ■ . . . 92 B3
French Polynesia ■ . 65 M16
Fresco → 92 D3
Freshfield, C. . . 96 A14
Fresnillo 84 C4
Fresno 82 B3
Freycinet Pen. . 62 D4
Fria, C. 58 B2
Frías 94 B3
Fribourg 13 C7
Friedrichshafen 14 E5
Friendly Is. = Tonga ■ 65 L13
Frobisher B. . . . 68 B4
Frobisher Bay = Iqaluit 68 B4
Frome, L. 62 B2
Frome Downs . 62 B2
Front Range . . . 81 E11
Frosinone 20 D4
Frunze = Bishkek 29 E8
Frutal 93 F4
Frýdek-Místek . 16 D4
Fuchou = Fuzhou 35 D6
Fuengirola 18 D3
Fuentes de Oñoro 18 B2
Fuerte → 84 B3
Fuerte Olimpo . 91 H7
Fuerteventura . 54 C2
Fuhai 34 B3
Fuji-San 32 B6
Fujian □ 35 D6
Fujinomiya 32 B6
Fujisawa 32 B6
Fukien = Fujian □ 35 D6
Fukuchiyama . . 32 B4
Fukui 32 A5
Fukuoka 32 C2
Fukushima 33 G12
Fukuyama 32 B3
Fulda 14 C5
Fulda → 14 C5
Fullerton 82 D4
Funabashi 32 B7
Funchal 54 B1
Fundación 90 A4
Fundão 18 B2
Fundy, B. of . . . 69 D4
Funtua 55 F6
Furāt, Nahr al → 47 E6
Furneaux Group 62 D4
Fürstenwalde . . 15 B8
Fürth 14 D6
Fury and Hecla Str. 68 B2
Fusagasuga . . . 90 C4
Fushun 35 B7
Futuna 64 L12
Fuxin 35 B7
Fuyuan 35 B8
Fuzhou 35 D6
Fyn 9 G10

G

Gabela 56 G2
Gabès 54 B7
Gabès, G. de . . 52 B1
Gabon ■ 56 E2
Gaborone 59 C5
Gabrovo 22 C5
Gachsārān 44 D2
Gadag 43 M9
Gadarwara 43 H11
Gadhada 43 J7
Gadsden 74 B4
Gadwal 43 L10
Gafsa 54 B6
Gagnoa 55 G3
Gagnon 69 C4
Gaillimh = Galway 11 E2
Gainesville, *Fla., U.S.A.* 75 E6
Gainesville, *Ga., U.S.A.* 75 B6
Gainesville, *Tex., U.S.A.* . 78 C5
Gairdner, L. . . . 62 B2
Galangue 58 A3
Galashiels 10 D5
Galaţi 17 F9
Galatina 21 D7
Galcaio 49 F4
Galdhøpiggen . 8 F9
Galela 39 D3
Galesburg 77 E9
Galich 24 B5
Galicia □ 18 A2
Galilee, Sea of = Yam Kinneret 46 D3
Gallabat 53 F6
Gállego → . . . 19 B5
Gallegos → . . 95 G3
Gallinas, Pta. . . 90 A4
Gallipoli = Gelibolu 23 D6
Gallípoli 21 D6
Gällivare 8 E12
Galloway, Mull of 11 D4
Galong 63 B4
Galveston 79 E6
Gálvez 94 C4
Galway 11 E2
Galway B. 11 E2
Gambaga 55 F4
Gambela 53 G5
Gambia ■ 55 F1
Gambia → . . . 55 F1
Gambier Is. . . . 62 C2
Gamboma 56 E3
Gan Jiang → . 35 D6
Ganāveh 44 D2
Gäncä 25 E6
Gand = Gent . . 14 C2
Ganda 58 A2
Gandak → . . . 40 E5
Gandava 42 E5
Gander 69 D5
Gandhi Sagar . 43 G9
Gandi 55 F6
Gandía 19 C5
Ganedidalem = Gani 39 E3
Ganga → 41 F8
Ganganagar . . . 42 E8
Gangara 55 F6
Gangaw 41 F10
Gangdisê Shan 40 B3
Ganges = Ganga → . . 41 F8
Gangtok 41 D7
Gani 39 E3
Gansu □ 34 C5
Ganta 55 G3
Gantheaume, C. 62 C2
Gantsevichi = Hantsavichy . 17 B8
Ganyem 39 E6
Ganzhou 35 D6
Gaoua 55 F4
Gaoual 55 F2
Gaoxiong 35 D7
Gap 13 D7
Gar 34 C2
Garabogazköl Aylagy 29 E6
Garanhuns 92 D6
Garawe 55 H3
Gard 49 F4
Garda, L. di . . . 20 B3
Garden City . . . 78 A3
Garden Grove . 82 D4
Gardēz 42 C6
Gargano, Mte. . 20 D5
Garigliano → . 20 D4
Garland 81 E7
Garm 29 F8
Garmisch-Partenkirchen 14 E6
Garmsār 44 C3
Garoe 49 F4
Garonne → . . 12 D3
Garoua 53 G1
Garrison Res. = Sakakawea, L. 76 B4
Garry, L. 70 B9
Garsen 57 E8
Garvie Mts. . . . 65 F3
Garwa = Garoua 53 G1
Gary 72 D2
Garzê 34 C5
Garzón 90 C3
Gasan Kuli = Hasan Kuli . . 29 F6
Gascogne 12 E4
Gascogne, G. de 12 D2
Gascony = Gascogne . . . 12 E4
Gashaka 55 G7
Gaspé 69 D4
Gaspé, C. de . . 69 D4
Gaspé, Pén. de 69 D4
Gasteiz = Vitoria 19 A4
Gastonia 75 B7
Gastre 95 E3
Gata, C. de 19 D4
Gata, Sierra de 18 B2
Gateshead 11 D6
Gauhati 41 D8
Gavāter 45 E5
Gávdhos 23 G5
Gävle 8 F11
Gawilgarh Hills 43 J10
Gawler 62 B2
Gaxun Nur 34 B5
Gaya, *India* . . . 40 E5
Gaya, *Niger* . . . 55 F5
Gayndah 63 A5
Gaysin = Haysyn 17 D9
Gayvoron = Hayvoron . . . 17 D9
Gaza 47 E3
Gaziantep 46 C4
Gazli 29 E7
Gdańsk 16 A4
Gdańska, Zatoka 16 A4
Gdov 24 B2
Gdynia 16 A4
Gebe 39 D3
Gebeit Mine . . . 52 D6
Gebze 22 D7
Gedaref 53 F6
Gede, Tanjung 37 F3
Gediz → 23 E6
Gedser 9 H10
Geelong 63 C3
Geesthacht . . . 14 B6
Geidam 53 F1
Geili 53 E5
Geita 57 E6
Gejiu 34 D5
Gela 21 F5
Geladi 49 F4
Gelehun 55 G2
Gelibolu 23 D6
Gelsenkirchen . 14 C4
Gemas 37 D2
Gemena 56 D3
Gemerek 46 C4
Gemlik 23 D7
General Acha . 94 D4
General Alvear, *Buenos Aires, Argentina* . . . 94 D5
General Alvear, *Mendoza, Argentina* . . . 94 D3
General Artigas 94 B5
General Belgrano 94 D5
General Guido . 94 D5
General Juan Madariaga . . 94 D5
General La Madrid 94 D4
General MacArthur . . 38 B3
General Martin Miguel de Güemes 94 A4
General Paz . . . 94 B5
General Pico . . 94 D4
General Pinedo 94 B4
General Santos 38 C3
General Villegas 94 D4
Geneva = Genève 13 C7

Geneva, L. = Léman, L. 13 C7
Genève 13 C7
Genil → 18 D3
Gennargentu, Mti. del 21 D2
Genoa = Génova 20 B2
Genoa 63 C4
Génova 20 B2
Génova, G. di 20 C2
Gent 14 C2
Georga, Zemlya 28 A5
George 58 E4
George → 68 C4
George, L., *N.S.W., Australia* 63 C4
George, L., *S. Austral., Australia* 62 C3
George, L., *Uganda* 57 D6
George River = Kangiqsualujjuaq 68 C4
George Sound 65 F2
George Town 36 C2
George V Land 96 A14
George VI Sound 96 B3
Georgetown, *Gambia* 55 F2
Georgetown, *Guyana* 90 B7
Georgia □ 75 C6
Georgia ■ 25 E5
Georgian B. 69 D2
Georgiu-Dezh = Liski 24 C4
Georgiyevsk 25 E5
Gera 15 C7
Geral de Goiás, Serra 93 E4
Geraldton 60 F1
Gerede 46 B3
Gereshk 42 D4
Gerlogubi 49 F4
Germany ■ 14 C6
Germiston 59 D5
Gerona 19 B7
Geser 39 E4
Getafe 18 B4
Gettysburg 73 E7
Getz Ice Shelf 96 B18
Ghaghara → 40 E5
Ghana ■ 55 G4
Ghanzi 58 C4
Ghardaïa 54 B5
Gharyān 52 B1
Ghat 54 D7
Ghawdex = Gozo 21 F5
Ghayl 47 G6
Ghazal, Bahr el →, *Chad* 53 F2
Ghazâl, Bahr el →, *Sudan* 57 C6
Ghazaouet 54 A4
Ghaziabad 42 E10
Ghazipur 40 E4
Ghaznī 42 C6
Ghaznī □ 42 C6
Ghèlinsor 49 F4
Ghent = Gent 14 C2
Ghizao 42 C4
Ghowr □ 42 C4
Ghugus 43 K11
Ghūrīān 42 B2
Gia Lai = Pleiku 36 B3
Gian 38 C3
Giarabub = Al Jaghbūb 52 C3
Giarre 21 F5
Gibraltar ■ 18 D3
Gibraltar, Str. of 18 E3
Gibson Desert 60 E4
Gidole 53 G6
Giessen 14 C5
Gifu 32 B5
Giglio 20 C3
Gijón 18 A3
Gila → 82 D5
Gīlān □ 46 C7
Gilbert Is. 64 J12
Gilgandra 63 B4
Gilgit 42 B9
Gilles, L. 62 B2
Gilmore 63 C4
Gimbi 53 G6
Gin Gin 63 A5
Ginir 49 F3
Giohar 49 G4
Gióna, Óros 23 E4
Girardot 90 C4
Giresun 46 B4
Girga 52 C5
Giridih 40 E6
Girilambone 63 B4
Girne = Kyrenia 46 D3
Girona = Gerona 19 B7
Gironde → 12 D3
Girvan 10 D4
Gisborne 64 C8
Gisenyi 57 E5
Gitega 57 E5
Giuba → 49 G3
Giurgiu 22 C5
Giza = El Gîza 52 C5
Giżycko 16 A5
Gjirokastra 23 D3
Gjoa Haven 70 B10
Glace Bay 69 D5
Gladstone, *Queens., Australia* 61 E9
Gladstone, *S. Austral., Australia* 62 B2
Glåma = Glomma → 9 G10
Glasgow 10 D4
Glazov 28 D6
Gleiwitz = Gliwice 16 C4
Glen Canyon National Recreation Area 83 B7
Glen Innes 63 A5
Glendale 82 C3
Glenelg 62 B2
Glenelg → 62 C3
Glenmorgan 63 A4
Glenorchy 62 D4
Glenreagh 63 B5
Glenrothes 10 C5
Glens Falls 73 C9
Gliwice 16 C4
Głogów 16 C3
Glomma → 9 G10
Glorieuses, Is. 59 G9
Gloucester, *Australia* 63 B5
Gloucester, *U.K.* 11 F5
Glusk 17 B9
Gmünd 15 D8
Gmunden 15 E7
Gniezno 16 B3
Go Cong 36 B3
Goa 43 M8
Goa □ 43 M8
Goalen Hd. 63 C5
Goalpara 41 D8
Goba, *Ethiopia* 49 F2
Goba, *Mozam.* 59 D6
Gobabis 58 C3
Gobi 35 B6
Gochas 58 C3
Godavari → 40 J4
Godavari Point 40 J4
Godhra 43 H8
Gods → 71 C10
Gods L. 71 C10
Godthåb 68 B5
Godwin Austen = K2 42 B10
Goeie Hoop, Kaap die = Good Hope, C. of 58 E3
Gogra = Ghaghara → 40 E5
Goiânia 93 F4
Goiás 93 F3
Goiás □ 93 E4
Goio-Ere 94 A6
Gojra 42 D8
Gökçeada 23 D5
Gokteik 41 F11
Gold Coast 63 A5
Golden Gate 80 G2
Goldsboro 75 B9
Goleniów 16 B2
Golfo Aranci 20 D2
Golspie 10 C5
Goma 57 E5
Gomel = Homyel 17 B10
Gomera 54 C1
Gómez Palacio 84 B4
Gomogomo 39 F4
Gomoh 40 F6
Gompa = Ganta 55 G3
Gonābād 44 C4
Gonaïves 87 C5
Gonbab-e Kāvūs 44 B3
Gonda 40 D3
Gonder 53 F6
Gönen 23 D6
Gonghe 34 C5
Gongolgon 63 B4
Goniri 53 F1
Good Hope, C. of 58 E3
Goodooga 63 A4
Goolgowi 63 B4
Goombalie 63 A4
Goondiwindi 63 A5
Gooray 63 A5
Gop 43 H6
Göppingen 14 D5
Gorakhpur 40 D4
Goražde 20 C7
Gordon → 62 D4
Gore, *Australia* 63 A5
Goré, *Chad* 53 G2
Gore, *Ethiopia* 53 G6
Gore, *N.Z.* 65 G3
Gorgān 44 B3
Gorgona, I. 90 C3
Gorízia 20 B4
Gorki = Nizhniy Novgorod 24 B5
Gorkiy = Nizhniy Novgorod 24 B5
Gorkovskoye Vdkhr. 24 B5
Görlitz 15 C8
Gorlovka = Horlivka 25 D4
Gorna Dzhumayo = Blagoevgrad 22 C4
Gorna Oryakhovitsa 22 C5
Gorno-Altay □ 29 D9
Gorno-Altaysk 29 D9
Gorno Slinkino = Gornopravdinsk 29 C8
Gornopravdinsk 29 C8
Gorodenka = Horodenka 17 D7
Gorodok = Horodok 17 D6
Gorokhov = Horokhiv 17 C7
Gorontalo 39 D2
Gorzów Wielkopolski 16 B2
Gosford 63 B5
Goslar 14 C6
Gospič 20 B5
Göta kanal 9 G11
Göteborg 9 G10
Gotha 14 C6
Gothenburg = Göteborg 9 G10
Gotland 9 G11
Göttingen 14 C5
Gottwaldov = Zlin 16 D3
Gouda 14 B3
Gouin, Rés. 69 D3
Goulburn 63 B4
Gounou-Gaya 53 G2
Gouri 53 E2
Gourma Rharous 55 E4
Gourock Ra. 63 C4
Governador Valadares 93 F5
Gowd-e Zirreh 42 E3
Goya 94 B5
Goyder Lagoon 62 A2
Goyllarisquisga 91 F3
Goz Beîda 53 F3
Gozo 21 F5
Graaff-Reinet 58 E4
Gračac 20 B5
Gracias a Dios, C. 86 D3
Grado 18 A2
Gradule 63 A4
Grafton 63 A5
Graham Bell, Os. 28 A7
Graham Land 96 A3
Grahamstown 59 E5
Grajaú 92 D4
Grajaú → 92 C5
Grampian Highlands = Grampian Mts. 10 C4
Grampian Mts. 10 C4
Gran Canaria 54 C1
Gran Chaco 94 B4
Gran Paradiso 20 B1
Gran Sasso d'Italia 20 C4
Granada, *Nic.* 85 E7
Granada, *Spain* 18 D4

Granby 69 D3
Grand Bahama 86 A4
Grand Bassam 55 G4
Grand Canyon 83 B6
Grand Cayman 86 C3
Grand Coulee Dam 80 B4
Grand Forks, *Canada* 71 D8
Grand Forks, *U.S.A.* 76 B6
Grand Island 76 E5
Grand Lahou 55 G3
Grand Rapids, *Canada* 71 C10
Grand Rapids, *U.S.A.* 72 C3
Grand St.-Bernard, Col du 13 D7
Grand Teton 81 D8
Grande →, *Argentina* 94 A3
Grande →, *Bolivia* 91 G6
Grande →, *Bahia, Brazil* 93 E5
Grande →, *Minas Gerais, Brazil* 93 G3
Grande, B. 95 G3
Grande, Rio → 79 F5
Grande Baleine, R. de la → 69 C3
Grande de Santiago → 84 C3
Granite City 77 F9
Granity 65 D4
Granja 92 C5
Granollers 19 B7
Grantham 11 E6
Granville 12 B3
Gras, L. de 70 B8
Grasse 13 E7
Grassmere 62 B3
Graulhet 12 E4
's-Gravenhage 14 B3
Gravesend 63 A5
Graz 15 E8
Great Abaco I. 86 A4
Great Australian Bight 60 G4
Great Barrier I. 64 B6
Great Barrier Reef 61 D8
Great Basin 80 F5
Great Bear → 70 B7
Great Bear L. 70 B7
Great Belt = Store Bælt 9 G10
Great Dividing Ra. 61 E8
Great Falls 81 B8
Great Inagua I. 86 B5
Great Indian Desert = Thar Desert 42 F7
Great Karoo 58 E4
Great Lake 62 D4
Great Ouse → 11 E7
Great Ruaha → 57 F7
Great Saint Bernard P. = Grand St.-Bernard, Col du 13 D7
Great Salt L. 81 E7
Great Salt Lake Desert 81 E7
Great Sandy Desert 60 E3
Great Sangi = Sangihe, P. 39 D3
Great Slave L. 70 B8
Great Smoky Mts. Nat. Pk. 75 B6
Great Victoria Desert 60 F4
Great Wall 35 C5
Great Yarmouth 11 E7
Greater Antilles 86 C5
Greater Sunda Is. 37 F4
Gredos, Sierra de 18 B3
Greece ■ 23 E4
Greeley 76 E2
Green → 83 A8
Green Bay 72 B2
Green C. 63 C5
Greenland ■ 66 C9
Greenock 10 D4
Greensboro 75 A8
Greenville, *Liberia* 55 G3
Greenville, *Ala., U.S.A.* 74 D4
Greenville, *Miss., U.S.A.* 79 C8
Greenville, *N.C., U.S.A.* 75 B9
Greenville, *S.C., U.S.A.* 75 B6
Greenwood, *Miss., U.S.A.* 79 C8
Greenwood, *S.C., U.S.A.* 75 B6
Gregory, L. 62 A2
Greifswald 15 A7
Greiz 15 C7
Gremikha 28 C4
Grenada ■ 87 D7
Grenfell 63 B4
Grenoble 13 D6
Grey → 65 E4
Grey Ra. 63 A3
Greymouth 65 E4
Greytown, *N.Z.* 65 D6
Greytown, *S. Africa* 59 D6
Griffin 75 C5
Griffith 63 B4
Grimari 56 C4
Grimaylov = Hrymayliv 17 D8
Grimsby 11 E6
Gris-Nez, C. 12 A4
Grodno = Hrodna 17 B6
Grodzyanka = Hrodzyanka 17 B9
Grójec 16 C5
Groningen 14 B4
Grootfontein 58 B3
Gross Glockner 15 E7
Grosser Arber 15 D7
Grosseto 20 C3
Groznyy 25 E6
Grudziądz 16 B4
Gryazi 24 C4
Gryazovets 28 D5
Gua 40 F5
Guadalajara, *Mexico* 84 C4
Guadalajara, *Spain* 18 B4
Guadalcanal 64 K11
Guadalete → 18 D2
Guadalquivir → 18 D2
Guadalupe = Guadeloupe ■ 87 C7
Guadalupe, Sierra de 18 C3
Guadarrama, Sierra de 18 B4
Guadeloupe ■ 87 C7
Guadiana → 18 D2
Guadix 18 D4
Guafo, Boca del 95 E2
Guaíra 94 A6
Guaitecas, Is. 95 E2
Guajará-Mirim 91 F5
Guajira, Pen. de la 90 A4
Gualeguay 94 C5
Gualeguaychú 94 C5
Guam ■ 64 H9
Guamúchil 84 B3
Guan Xian 34 C5
Guanahani = San Salvador 86 B5
Guanajuato 84 C4
Guandacol 94 B3
Guane 86 B3
Guangdong □ 35 D6
Guanghua 35 C6
Guangxi Zhuangzu Zizhiqu □ 35 D5
Guangzhou 35 D6
Guanipa → 90 B6
Guantánamo 86 B4
Guaporé → 91 F5
Guaqui 91 G5
Guarapuava 94 B6
Guarda 18 B2
Guardafui, C. = Asir, Ras 49 E5
Guasdualito 90 B4
Guasipati 90 B6
Guatemala 85 E6
Guatemala ■ 85 D6
Guatire 90 A5
Guaviare □ 90 C4
Guaviare → 90 C5
Guaxupé 93 G4
Guayama 87 C6
Guayaquil 90 D3
Guayaquil, G. de 90 D2
Guaymas 84 B2
Guddu Barrage 42 E6
Gudivada 40 J3
Gudur 43 M11
Guecho 19 A4
Guékédou 55 G2
Guelma 54 A6
Guelph 69 D2
Guéréda 53 F3
Guéret 12 C4
Guernica 19 A4
Guernsey 11 G5
Guidónia-Montecélio 20 C4
Guiglo 55 G3
Guildford 11 F6
Guilin 35 D6
Guimarães, *Brazil* 92 C5
Guimarães, *Portugal* 18 B1
Guimaras 38 B2
Guinea ■ 55 F2
Guinea, Gulf of 51 F3
Guinea-Bissau ■ 55 F1
Guingamp 12 B2
Guiping 35 D6
Güiria 90 A6
Guiuan 38 B3
Guiyang 35 D5
Guizhou □ 35 D5
Gujarat □ 43 H7
Gujranwala 42 C9
Gujrat 42 C9
Gulbarga 43 L10
Gulf, The 44 E2
Gulgong 63 B4
Güllük 23 F6
Gulshad 29 E8
Gulu 57 D6
Gum Lake 62 B3
Gummi 55 F6
Gümüşhane 46 B4
Gumzai 39 F4
Guna 43 G10
Gundagai 63 C4
Gungu 56 F3
Gunnedah 63 B5
Gunningbar Cr. → 63 B4
Guntakal 43 M10
Guntur 40 J3
Gunungapi 39 F3
Gunungsitoli 37 D1
Gunza 56 G2
Gupis 42 A8
Gūrchān 46 D7
Gurdaspur 42 C9
Gurgaon 42 E10
Gurkha 40 C5
Gurley 63 A4
Gurupá 92 C3
Gurupá, I. Grande de 92 C3
Gurupi → 92 C4
Guryev = Atyraū 29 E6
Gusau 55 F6
Güstrow 15 B7
Gütersloh 14 C5
Guthrie 78 B5
Guyana ■ 90 B7
Guyane française ■ = French Guiana ■ 92 B3
Guyenne 12 D4
Guyra 63 B5
Gwa 41 J10
Gwaai 59 B5
Gwabegar 63 B4
Gwādar 42 G3
Gwalior 42 F11
Gwanda 59 C5
Gweru 59 B5
Gwydir → 63 A4
Gyandzha = Gäncä 25 E6
Gyaring Hu 34 C4
Gydanskiy P-ov. 28 B8
Gympie 63 A5
Gyöngyös 16 E4
Györ 16 E3
Gypsumville 71 C10
Gyula 16 E5
Gyumri 25 E5
Gyzylarbat 29 F6

H

Ha 'Arava → 47 E3
Haarlem 14 B3
Haast → 65 E3
Habaswein 57 D7
Hachinohe 33 F12
Hadarba, Ras 52 D6

Hadd, R'as al 45 F4
Hadejia 55 F7
Haden 63 A5
Hadera 46 D3
Hadhramaut = Haḑramawt 49 D4
Haḑramawt 49 D4
Haeju 35 C7
Haerhpin = Harbin 35 B7
Hafar al Bāţin 47 E6
Hafizabad 42 C8
Haflong 41 E9
Haft Gel 47 E7
Hafun, Ras 49 E5
Hagen 14 C4
Hagerstown 73 E7
Hagi 32 B2
Hagondange-Briey 13 B7
Hague, C. de la 12 B3
Hague, The = 's-Gravenhage 14 B3
Haguenau 13 B7
Hai'an 35 C7
Haifa = Hefa 46 D3
Haikou 35 D6
Ḩā'il 47 F5
Hailar 35 B6
Haileybury 69 D3
Hailun 35 B7
Hainan □ 35 E5
Haiphong 35 D5
Haiti ■ 87 C5
Haiya Junction 53 E6
Hajar Bangar 53 F3
Hajdúböszörmény 16 E5
Hajnówka 17 B6
Hakken-Zan 32 B4
Hakodate 32 F12
Hala 42 G6
Ḩalab 46 C4
Ḩalabjah 46 D6
Halaib 52 D6
Halberstadt 15 C6
Halcombe 64 D6
Halcon, Mt. 38 B2
Halden 9 G10
Haldia 40 F7
Haldwani 42 E11
Halifax, *Canada* 69 D4
Halifax, *U.K.* 11 E6
Halīl → 44 E4
Hall Beach = Sanirajak 68 B2
Halle 15 C6
Hallett 62 B2
Halmahera 39 D3
Halmstad 9 G10
Halq el Oued 52 A1
Hälsingborg = Helsingborg 9 G10
Halul 44 E3
Hamada 32 B3
Hamadān 46 D7
Hamadān □ 46 D7
Hamāh 46 D4
Hamamatsu 32 B5
Hamar 8 F10
Hamburg 14 B5
Hameln 14 B5
Hamersley Ra. 60 E2
Hamhung 35 C7
Hami 34 B4
Hamilton, *Australia* 62 C3
Hamilton, *Canada* 69 D3
Hamilton, *N.Z.* 64 B6
Hamilton, *U.K.* 10 D4
Hamley Bridge 62 B2
Hamlin = Hameln 14 B5
Hamm 14 C4
Hammerfest 8 D12
Hammond 72 D2
Hampden 65 F4
Hampton 73 F7
Hamrat esh Sheykh 53 F4
Han Pijesak 20 B7
Hanamaki 33 G12
Hanau 14 C5
Hancock 77 C7
Handa 49 E5
Handan 35 C6
Handeni 57 F7
Hangayn Nuruu 34 B4
Hangchou = Hangzhou 35 C7
Hangu 35 C6
Hangzhou 35 C7
Hangzhou Wan 35 C7
Ḩanīsh 49 E3
Hanle 42 C11
Hanmer Springs 65 E5
Hanna 71 C8
Hannibal 77 F9
Hannover 14 B5
Hanoi 35 D5
Hanover = Hannover 14 B5
Hanover, I. 95 G2
Hansi 42 E9
Hanson, L. 62 B2
Hantsavichy 17 B8
Hanzhong 35 C5
Haora 40 F7
Haparanda 8 E12
Happy Valley-Goose Bay 69 C4
Hapur 42 E10
Ḩaql 47 E3
Har 39 F4
Har Hu 34 C4
Har Us Nuur 34 B4
Ḩaraḑ 47 F7
Haraisan Plateau = Huraysān 47 G6
Harardera 49 G4
Harare 59 B6
Harazé 53 F2
Harbin 35 B7
Harbour Grace 69 D5
Hardangerfjorden 8 F9
Hardap Dam 58 C3
Hardwar = Haridwar 42 E11
Hardy, Pen. 95 H3
Harer 49 F3
Hargeisa 49 F3
Hari → 37 E2
Haridwar 42 E11
Haringhata → 41 G7
Harīrūd 45 C5
Harīrūd → 42 A2
Harlingen 78 F5
Harlow 11 F7
Harney Basin 80 D4
Härnösand 8 F11
Ḩarrat al Kishb 47 G5
Ḩarrat al 'Uwairidh 47 F4
Harris 10 C3
Harris L. 62 B2
Harrisburg 73 D7
Harrison, C. 68 C5
Harrison Bay 71 A4
Harrogate 11 D6
Hart, L. 62 B2
Hartford 73 D9
Hartlepool 11 D6
Harvey 72 D2
Harwich 11 F7
Haryana □ 42 E10
Haryn → 17 B8
Harz 14 C6
Hasa 47 F7
Hasan Kuli 29 F6
Hassi Inifel 54 C5
Hassi Messaoud 54 B6
Hastings, *N.Z.* 64 C7
Hastings, *U.K.* 11 F7
Hastings, *U.S.A.* 76 E5
Hastings Ra. 63 B5
Hatay = Antalya 46 C2
Hatfield P.O. 62 B3
Hatgal 34 A5
Hathras 42 F11
Hatia 41 F8
Hattah 62 B3
Hatteras, C. 75 B10
Hattiesburg 79 D9
Hatvan 16 E4
Hau Bon = Cheo Reo 36 B3
Haugesund 9 G9
Hauraki G. 64 B6
Haut Atlas 54 B3
Hautah, Wahāt al 47 G6
Hauts Plateaux 54 B4
Havana = La Habana 86 B3
Havant 11 F6
Havel → 15 B7
Havelock 65 D5
Haverfordwest 11 F4
Havlíčkův Brod 16 D2
Havre 81 A9
Havza 46 B3
Hawaii □ 82 J12
Hawaiian Is. 82 H12
Hawea, L. 65 F3
Hawera 64 C6
Hawick 10 D5
Hawke B. 64 C7
Hawker 62 B2
Hawkwood 63 A5
Hay 63 B3
Hay River 70 B8
Haya 39 E3
Hayes → 71 C10
Hayrabolu 22 D6
Haysyn 17 D9
Hayvoron 17 D9
Hazaribag 40 F5
Healesville 63 C4
Hearst 69 D2
Hebei □ 35 C6
Hebel 63 A4
Hebron = Al Khalīl 47 E3
Hebron 68 C4
Hechi 35 D5
Hechuan 35 C5
Heerlen 13 A6
Hefa 46 D3
Hefei 35 C6
Hegang 35 B8
Heidelberg 14 D5
Heilbron 59 D5
Heilbronn 14 D5
Heilongjiang □ 35 B7
Heilunkiang = Heilongjiang □ 35 B7
Heinze Is. 41 K11
Hejaz = Al Ḩijāz 47 F4
Hekımhan 46 C4
Hekou 34 D5
Helena, *Ark., U.S.A.* 79 B8
Helena, *Mont., U.S.A.* 81 B7
Helensville 64 B6
Helgoland 14 A4
Heligoland = Helgoland 14 A4
Heligoland B. = Deutsche Bucht 14 A5
Hellín 19 C5
Helmand □ 42 D3
Helmand → 42 D2
Helmand, Hamun 45 D5
Helmsdale 10 B5
Helsingborg 9 G10
Helsingfors = Helsinki 9 F13
Helsinki 9 F13
Helwân 52 C5
Hemel Hempstead 11 F6
Henan □ 35 C6
Henares → 18 B4
Henderson 75 A8
Hendon 63 A5
Hengyang 35 D6
Henrietta Maria, C. 69 C2
Hentiyn Nuruu 35 B5
Henty 63 C4
Henzada 41 J10
Herāt 42 B3
Herāt □ 42 B3
Hercegnovi 22 C2
Hereford 11 E5
Herford 14 B5
Hermidale 63 B4
Hermitage 65 E4
Hermite, I. 95 H3
Hermon, Mt. = Ash Shaykh, J. 46 D3
Hermosillo 84 B2
Hernád → 16 E5
Hernandarias 94 B6
Heroica Nogales = Nogales 84 A2
Heron Bay 69 D2
Herrick 62 D4
's-Hertogenbosch 14 C3
Hesse = Hessen □ 14 C5
Hessen □ 14 C5
Hewett, C. 68 A4
Hexham 11 D5
Heyfield 63 C4
Heywood 62 C3
Hibbing 77 B8
Hibbs B. 62 D4
Hickory 75 B7
Hicks, Pt. 63 C4
Hida-Sammyaku 32 A5
Hidalgo del Parral 84 B3
Higashiōsaka 32 B4
High Atlas = Haut Atlas 54 B3

High Point 75 B8
High River 71 C8
High Tatra = Tatry 16 D4
High Wycombe 11 F6
Hiiumaa 24 B1
Ḥijārah, Ṣaḥrā' al 47 E6
Ḥijāz □ 48 C2
Hijo = Tagum 38 C3
Hikone 32 B5
Hikurangi 64 A6
Hikurangi, Mt. 64 C7
Hildesheim 14 B5
Hillston 63 B4
Hilo 82 J13
Hilversum 14 B3
Himachal Pradesh □ 42 D10
Himalaya 40 C5
Himatnagar 43 H8
Himeji 32 B4
Himi 32 A5
Ḥimş 46 D4
Hindmarsh, L. 62 C3
Hindu Kush 42 B7
Hindubagh 42 D5
Hindupur 43 N10
Hinganghat 43 J11
Hingoli 43 K10
Hinna = Imi 49 F3
Hinojosa del Duque 18 C3
Hirakud Dam 40 G4
Hiratsuka 32 B6
Hirosaki 33 F12
Hiroshima 32 B3
Hisar 42 E9
Hispaniola 87 C5
Hita 32 C2
Hitachi 32 A7
Hjälmaren 9 G11
Hlyboka 17 D7
Ho 55 G5
Ho Chi Minh City = Phanh Bho Ho Chi Minh 36 B3
Hoai Nhon 36 B3
Hoare B. 68 B4
Hobart 62 D4
Hobbs Coast 96 B18
Hodgson 71 C10
Hódmezövásárhely 16 E5
Hodna, Chott el 54 A5
Hodonín 16 D3
Hoek van Holland 14 B3
Hof 15 C6
Hōfu 32 B2
Hogan Group 62 C4
Hoggar = Ahaggar 54 D6
Hoh Xil Shan 34 C3
Hohe Rhön 14 C5
Hohhot 35 B6
Hoi An 36 A3
Hokianga Harbour 64 A5
Hokitika 65 E4
Hokkaidō □ 32 F12
Holbrook 63 C4
Holguín 86 B4
Hollandia = Jayapura 39 E6
Holman Island 70 A8
Holy Cross 71 B4
Holyhead 11 E4
Homalin 41 E10
Hombori 55 E4
Home B. 68 B4
Homer 71 C4
Homs = Ḥimş 46 D4
Homyel 17 B10
Hon Chong 36 B2
Honan = Henan □ 35 C6
Honda 90 B4
Hondeklipbaai 58 E3
Honduras ■ 85 E7
Honduras, G. de 85 D7
Honfleur 12 B4
Hong Kong 35 D6
Hongjiang 35 D5
Hongshui He → 35 D5
Hongze Hu 35 C6
Honiara 64 K10
Honolulu 82 H12
Honshū 32 G11
Hood, Mt. 80 C3
Hooghly → = Hughli → 40 G7
Hook of Holland = Hoek van Holland 14 B3
Hoorn 14 B3
Hoover Dam 82 B5
Hope, L. 62 A2
Hope, Pt. 71 B3
Hopedale 68 C4
Hopei = Hebei □ 35 C6
Hopetoun 62 C3
Hopetown 58 D4
Hoquiam 80 B2
Horlick Mts. 96 C1
Horlivka 25 D4
Hormoz 44 E3
Hormoz, Jaz. ye 44 E4
Hormozgān □ 44 E3
Hormuz, Str. of 44 E4
Horn 15 D8
Horn, Cape = Hornos, C. de 95 H3
Hornavan 8 E11
Hornos, C. de 95 H3
Hornsby 63 B5
Horodenka 17 D7
Horodok, *Khmelnytskyy, Ukraine* 17 D8
Horodok, *Lviv, Ukraine* 17 D6
Horokhiv 17 C7
Horqin Youyi Qianqi 35 B7
Horqueta 94 A5
Horsham 62 C3
Horton → 70 B7
Hose, Gunung-Gunung 37 D4
Hoshangabad 43 H10
Hoshiarpur 42 D9
Hospet 43 M10
Hospitalet de Llobregat 19 B7
Hoste, I. 95 H3
Hot Springs 79 B7
Hotan 34 C2
Houhora Heads 64 A5
Houlton 73 A12
Houma 79 E8
Houston 79 E6
Hovd 34 B4
Hövsgöl Nuur 34 A5
Howard 63 A5
Howe, C. 63 C5
Howitt, L. 62 A2
Howrah = Haora 40 F7
Höxter 14 C5
Hoy 10 B5
Høyanger 8 F9
Hoyerswerda 15 C8
Hpungan Pass 41 D11
Hradec Králové 16 C2
Hrodna 17 B6
Hrodzyanka 17 B9
Hron → 16 E4
Hrvatska = Croatia ■ 20 B6
Hrymayliv 17 D8
Hsenwi 41 F11
Hsiamen = Xiamen 35 D6
Hsian = Xi'an 35 C5
Hsinhailien = Lianyungang 35 C6
Hsisha Chuntao 36 A4
Hsüchou = Xuzhou 35 C6
Hua Hin 36 B1
Huacho 91 F3
Huachón 91 F3
Huai He → 35 C6
Huainan 35 C6
Huallaga → 90 E3
Huambo 58 A3
Huancabamba 91 E3
Huancane 91 G5
Huancapi 91 F4
Huancavelica 91 F3
Huancayo 91 F3
Huang Hai = Yellow Sea 35 C7
Huang He → 35 C6
Huangliu 35 E5
Huangshi 35 C6
Huánuco 91 E3
Huaraz 91 E3
Huarmey 91 F3
Huascarán 91 E3
Huasco 94 B2
Huatabampo 84 B3
Huayllay 91 F3
Hubei □ 35 C6
Hubli-Dharwad = Dharwad 43 M9
Huddersfield 11 E6
Hudiksvall 8 F11
Hudson → 73 D8
Hudson Bay 68 B2
Hudson Mts. 96 B2
Hudson Str. 68 B4
Hue 36 A3
Huelva 18 D2
Huesca 19 A5
Hughenden 61 E7
Hughli → 40 G7
Huila, Nevado del 90 C3
Huinca Renancó 94 C4
Huize 34 D5
Hukawng Valley 41 D11
Hulan 35 B7
Ḥulayfā' 47 F5
Huld 35 B5
Hull = Kingston upon Hull 11 E6
Hull 69 D3
Hulun Nur 35 B6
Humahuaca 94 A3
Humaitá, *Brazil* 91 E6
Humaitá, *Paraguay* 94 B5
Humber → 11 E6
Humboldt 71 C9
Humboldt → 80 F4
Hume, L. 63 C4
Humenné 16 D5
Hūn 52 C2
Hunan □ 35 D6
Hunedoara 17 F6
Hungary ■ 16 E4
Hungerford 63 A3
Hŭngnam 35 C7
Hunsrück 14 D4
Hunter I. 62 D3
Hunter Ra. 63 B5
Hunterville 64 C6
Huntington 72 E4
Huntington Beach 82 D3
Huntly, *N.Z.* 64 B6
Huntly, *U.K.* 10 C5
Huntsville 74 B4
Huonville 62 D4
Hupeh = Hubei □ 35 C6
Huraysān 47 G6
Huron, L. 72 B4
Hurunui → 65 E5
Huşi 17 E9
Hutchinson 78
Hutton, Mt. 63 A4
Hvar 20 C6
Hwang Ho = Huang He → 35 C6
Hwange 59 B5
Hyargas Nuur 34 B4
Hyderabad, *India* 43 L11
Hyderabad, *Pakistan* 42 G6
Hyères 13 E7
Hyères, Is. d' 13 E7

I

I-n-Gall 55 E6
Iaco → 91 E5
Ialomiţa → 22 B6
Iaşi 17 E8
Iba 38 A2
Ibadan 55 G5
Ibagué 90 C3
Ibar → 22 C3
Ibarra 90 C3
Ibi 55 G6
Ibiá 93 F4
Ibicuy 94 C5
Ibioapaba, Sa. da 92 C5
Ibiza 19 C6
Ibonma 39 E4
Ibotirama 93 E5
Ibu 39 D3
Icá 91 F3
Iça → 90 D5
Içana 90 C5
Içel = Mersin 46 C3
Iceland ■ 8 B4
Ich'ang = Yichang 35 C6
Ichchapuram 40 H5
Ichihara 32 B7
Ichikawa 32 B6
Ichilo → 91 G6
Ichinomiya 32 B5
Idaho □ 81 C6
Idaho Falls 81 D7
Idar-Oberstein 14 D4
Idd el Ghanam 53 F3

Iddan 49 F4
Idehan 52 C1
Idehan Marzūq 52 D1
Idelès 54 D6
Idfû 52 D5
Ídhi Óros 23 G5
Ídhra 23 F4
Idi 36 C1
Idiofa 56 E3
Idlip 46 D4
Ierápetra 23 G5
Iesi 20 C4
Ifanadiana 59 J9
Ife 55 G5
Ifni 54 C2
Iforas, Adrar des 54 G4
Igarapava 93 G4
Igarapé Açu 92 C4
Igarka 28 C9
Igbetti 55 G5
Iglésias 21 E2
Igli 54 B4
Igloolik 68 B2
Igluligaarjuk 68 B1
İğneada Burnu 22 D7
Igoumenítsa 23 E3
Iguaçu → 94 B6
Iguaçu, Cat. del 94 B6
Iguaçu Falls = Iguaçu, Cat. del 94 B6
Iguala 84 D5
Igualada 19 B6
Iguassu = Iguaçu → 94 B6
Iguatu 92 D6
Iguéla 56 E1
Ihosy 59 J9
Iida 32 B5
Iisalmi 8 F13
Iizuka 32 C2
Ijebu-Ode 55 G5
IJsselmeer 14 B3
Ikaluktutiak 70 B9
Ikaría 23 F6
Ikela 56 E4
Iki 32 C1
Ilagan 38 A2
Īlām 46 D6
Iława 16 B4
Île-de-France 12 B5
Ilebo 56 E4
Ilhéus 93 E6
Ili → 29 E8
Ilich 29 E7
Iligan 38 C2
Illampu = Ancohuma, Nevada 91 G5
Illana B. 38 C2
Illapel 94 C2
Iller → 14 D5
Illimani 91 G5
Illium = Troy 23 E6
Ilmen, Ozero 24 B3
Ilo 91 G4
Iloilo 38 B2
Ilorin 55 G5
Ilwaki 39 F3
Imabari 32 B3
Imandra, Ozero 28 C4
Imari 32 C1
imeni 26 Bakinskikh Komissarov = Neftçala 46 C7
Imeri, Serra 90 C5
Imi 49 F3
Imola 20 B3
Imperatriz 92 D4
Impéria 20 C2
Imperial Dam 82 D5
Impfondo 56 D3
Imphal 41 E9
İmroz = Gökçeada 23 D5
Imuruan B. 38 B1
In Belbel 54 C5
In Salah 54 C5
Ina 32 B5
Inangahua Junction 65 D4
Inanwatan 39 E4
Iñapari 91 F5
Inarijärvi 8 E13
Inca 19 C7
İnce-Burnu 46 B3
Inchon 35 C7
İncirliova 23 F6
Incomáti → 59 D6
Indalsälven → 8 F11
Indaw 41 E11
Independence, *Kans., U.S.A.* 79 A6
Independence, *Mo., U.S.A.* 77 F7
India ■ 43 J10
Indian → 75 F7
Indian Harbour 68 C5
Indian Head 71 C9
Indiana □ 72 D3
Indianapolis 72 E2
Indiga 28 C5
Indigirka → 31 B12
Indonesia ■ 37 E4
Indore 43 H9
Indravati → 40 H3
Indre → 12 C4
Indus → 43 G5
İnebolu 46 B3
Ingende 56 E3
Inglewood, *Queens., Australia* 63 A5
Inglewood, *Vic., Australia* 62 C3
Inglewood, *N.Z.* 64 C6
Ingolstadt 15 D6
Ingraj Bazar 40 E7
Ingrid Christensen Coast 96 A10
Ingulec = Inhulec 25 D3
Inhambane 59 C7
Inhaminga 59 B7
Inharrime 59 C7
Inhulec 25 D3
Ining = Yining 34 B3
Inírida → 90 C5
Injune 63 A4
Inle L. 41 G11
Inn → 15 D7
Innamincka 62 A3
Inner Hebrides 10 C3
Inner Mongolia = Nei Monggol Zizhiqu □ 35 B6
Innisfail 71 C8
Innsbruck 15 E6
Inongo 56 E3
Inoucdjouac = Inukjuak 68 C3
Inowrocław 16 B4
Inquisivi 91 G5
Insein 41 J11
Interlaken 13 C7
International Falls 77 A8
Intiyaco 94 B4
Inukjuak 68 C3
Inútil, B. 95 G2
Inuvik 70 B6
Invercargill 65 G3
Inverell 63 A5
Invergordon 10 C4
Inverness 10 C4
Inverurie 10 C5
Investigator Group 62 B1
Investigator Str. 62 C2
Inya 29 D9
Inza 24 C6
Ioánnina 23 E3
Ionian Is. = Iónioi Nísoi 23 E3
Ionian Sea 21 F6
Iónioi Nísoi 23 E3
Íos 23 F5
Iowa □ 77 D8
Iowa City 77 E9
Ipameri 93 F4
Ipatinga 93 F5
Ipiales 90 C3
Ipin = Yibin 35 D5
Ipixuna 91 E4
Ipoh 36 D2
Ippy 56 C4
İpsala 22 D6
Ipswich, *Australia* 63 A5
Ipswich, *U.K.* 11 E7
Ipu 92 C5
Iqaluit 68 B4
Iquique 91 H4
Iquitos 90 D4
Iracoubo 92 A3
Iráklion 23 G5
Iran ■ 44 C3
Iran, Gunung-Gunung 37 D4
Iran Ra. = Iran, Gunung-Gunung 37 D4
Īrānshahr 45 E5
Irapuato 84 C4
Iraq ■ 46 D5
Irbid 46 D3
Irebu 56 E3
Ireland ■ 11 E3
Irian Jaya □ 39 E5
Iringa 57 F7
Iriri → 92 C3
Irish Sea 11 E4
Irkineyeva 30 D7
Irkutsk 30 D8
Iron Baron 62 B2
Iron Gate = Portile de Fier 22 B4
Iron Knob 62 B2
Ironwood 77 B9
Irpin 17 C10
Irrara Cr. → 63 A4
Irrawaddy □ 41 J10
Irrawaddy → 41 K10
Irtysh → 28 C7
Irumu 57 D5
Irún 19 A5
Irunea = Pamplona 19 A5
Irvine 10 D4
Irymple 62 B3
Isabella 38 C2
Isangi 56 D4
Isar → 15 D7
Íschia 21 D4
Ise 32 B5
Ise-Wan 32 B5
Isère → 13 D6
Isérnia 20 D5
Ishikari-Wan 32 F12
Ishim → 29 D8
Ishinomaki 33 G12
Ishkuman 42 A8
Isil Kul 29 D8
Isiolo 57 D7
Isiro 57 D5
İskenderun 46 C4
Iskŭr → 22 C5
Islamabad 42 C8
Island L. 71 C10
Island Lagoon 62 B2
Islay 10 D3
Isle → 12 D3
Isle of Wight □ 11 F6
Ismail = Izmayil 17 F9
Ismâ'ilîya 47 E3
Isna 52 C5
İsparta 46 C2
Íspica 21 F5
Israel ■ 46 E3
Issoire 13 D5
Issyk-Kul, Ozero = Ysyk-Köl, Ozero 29 E8
İstanbul 22 D7
Istiaía 23 E4
Istra 20 B4
İstranca Dağları 22 D6
Istres 13 E6
Istria = Istra 20 B4
Itabaiana 92 D6
Itaberaba 93 E5
Itabira 93 F5
Itabuna 93 E6
Itaipú, Représa de 94 B6
Itaituba 92 C2
Itajaí 94 B7
Italy ■ 20 C4
Itapecuru-Mirim 92 C5
Itaperuna 93 G5
Itapicuru →, *Bahia, Brazil* 93 E6
Itapicuru →, *Maranhão, Brazil* 92 C5
Itapipoca 92 C6
Itaquatiara 90 D7
Itaquí 94 B5
Itatuba 91 E6
Ithaca = Itháki 23 E3
Itháki 23 E3
Ito 32 B6
Itonamas → 91 F6
Ituaçu 93 E5
Ituiutaba 93 F4
Itumbiara 93 F4
Iturbe 94 A3
Itzehoe 14 B5
Ivanava 17 B7
Ivanhoe 63 B3
Ivano-Frankivsk 17 D7
Ivano-Frankovsk = Ivano-Frankivsk 17 D7
Ivanovo = Ivanava 17 B7
Ivanovo 24 B5
Ivatsevichy 17 B7
Ivory Coast ■ 55 G3
Ivrea 20 B1
Ivujivik 68 B3
Iwahig 36 C5
Iwaki 33 G12

Iwakuni 32 B3
Iwata 33 H11
Iwate-San 33 G12
Iwo 55 G5
Ixiamas 91 F5
Izhevsk 28 D6
Izmayil 17 F9
İzmir 23 E6
İzmit 25 E2
İznik Gölü 23 D7
Izumi-sano 32 B4
Izumo 32 B3
Izyaslav 17 C8

J

Jabalpur 43 H11
Jablah 46 D4
Jablanica 22 D3
Jablonec 16 C2
Jaboatão 92 D6
Jaca 19 A5
Jacareí 94 A7
Jacarèzinho 94 A7
Jackson, *Australia* 63 A4
Jackson, *Mich., U.S.A.* 72 C3
Jackson, *Miss., U.S.A.* 79 C8
Jackson, *Tenn., U.S.A.* 74 B3
Jackson B. 65 E3
Jacksons 65 E4
Jacksonville, *Fla., U.S.A.* 75 D7
Jacksonville, *Ill., U.S.A.* 77 F9
Jacksonville, *N.C., U.S.A.* 75 B9
Jacmel 87 C5
Jacobabad 42 E6
Jacobina 93 E5
Jacundá → 92 C3
Jadotville = Likasi 57 G5
Jādū 52 B1
Jaén, *Peru* 91 E3
Jaén, *Spain* 18 D4
Jaffa = Tel Aviv-Yafo 46 D3
Jaffa, C. 62 C2
Jaffna 43 Q12
Jagadhri 42 D10
Jagdalpur 40 H3
Jagraon 42 D9
Jagtial 43 K11
Jaguariaíva 94 A7
Jaguaribe → 92 C6
Jahrom 44 D3
Jailolo 39 D3
Jailolo, Selat 39 D3
Jaipur 42 F9
Jakarta 37 F3
Jalalabad 42 B7
Jalapa Enríquez 84 D5
Jalas, Jabal al 47 F4
Jalgaon, *Maharashtra, India* 43 J10
Jalgaon, *Maharashtra, India* 43 J9
Jalna 43 K9
Jalón → 19 B5
Jalpaiguri 41 D7
Jalq 45 E5
Jaluit I. 64 J11
Jamaica ■ 86 C4
Jamalpur, *Bangla.* 41 E7
Jamalpur, *India* 40 E6
Jamanxim → 92 C2
Jambe 39 E4
Jambi 37 E2
Jambi □ 37 E2
James → 76 D6
James B. 69 C2
James Ross I. 96 A4
Jamestown, *Australia* 62 B2
Jamestown, *N. Dak., U.S.A.* 76 B5
Jamestown, *N.Y., U.S.A.* 73 C6
Jamkhandi 43 L9
Jammu 42 C9
Jammu & Kashmir □ 42 B10
Jamnagar 43 H7
Jamrud 42 C7
Jamshedpur 40 F6
Jand 42 C8
Jandaq 44 C3
Jandowae 63 A5
Janesville 77 D10
Januária 93 F5
Jaora 43 H9
Japan ■ 33 G11
Japan, Sea of 33 G11
Japen = Yapen 39 E5
Japurá → 90 D5
Jaque 90 B3
Jarama → 18 B4
Jargalant = Hovd 34 B4
Jarosław 17 C6
Jarso 53 G6
Jarvis I. 65 K15
Jarwa 40 D4
Jāsk 44 E4
Jasło 16 D5
Jasper 74 C4
Jászberény 16 E4
Jataí 93 F3
Játiva 19 C5
Jaú 93 G4
Jauja 91 F3
Jaunpur 40 E4
Java = Jawa 37 F3
Java Sea 37 E3
Javhlant = Ulyasutay 34 B4
Jawa 37 F3
Jaya, Puncak 39 E5
Jayanti 41 D7
Jayapura 39 E6
Jayawijaya, Pegunungan 39 E5
Jaynagar 40 D6
Jean Marie River 70 B7
Jebba 55 G5
Jebel, Bahr el → 53 G5
Jedburgh 10 D5
Jedda = Jiddah 47 G4
Jędrzejów 16 C5
Jefferson City 77 F8
Jega 55 F5
Jelenia Góra 16 C2
Jelgava 24 B1
Jemaja 37 D3
Jembongan 36 C5
Jena 15 C6
Jeparit 62 C3
Jequié 93 E5
Jequitinhonha 93 F5
Jequitinhonha → 93 F6
Jerada 54 B4
Jerantut 37 D2
Jérémie 86 C5
Jerez de la Frontera 18 D2
Jerez de los Caballeros 18 C2
Jerilderie 63 C4
Jersey 11 G5
Jersey City 73 D8
Jerusalem 47 E3
Jervis B. 63 C5
Jesselton = Kota Kinabalu 36 C5
Jessore 41 F7
Jeypore 40 H4
Jhal Jhao 42 F4
Jhalawar 43 G10
Jhang Maghiana 42 D8
Jhansi 43 G11
Jharsaguda 40 G5
Jhelum 42 C8
Jhelum → 42 D8
Jhunjhunu 42 E9
Jiamusi 35 B8
Ji'an 35 D6
Jianchuan 34 D4
Jiangling 35 C6
Jiangmen 35 D6
Jiangsu □ 35 C6
Jiangxi □ 35 D6
Jian'ou 35 D6
Jianshui 34 D5
Jiao Xian 35 C7
Jiaozuo 35 C6
Jiaxing 35 C7
Jiayi 35 D7
Jibuti = Djibouti ■ 49 E3
Jiddah 47 G4
Jido 41 C10
Jihlava 16 D2
Jihlava → 16 D3
Jijel 54 A6
Jijiga 49 F3
Jilin 35 B7
Jilong 35 D7
Jima 53 G6
Jiménez 84 B4
Jinan 35 C6
Jindabyne 63 C4
Jindrichuv Hradeç 16 D2
Jingdezhen 35 D6
Jinggu 34 D5
Jingxi 35 D5
Jinhua 35 D6
Jining, *Nei Mongol Zizhiqu, China* 35 B6
Jining, *Shandong, China* 35 C6
Jinja 57 D6
Jinnah Barrage 42 C7
Jinotega 85 E7
Jinshi 35 D6
Jinzhou 35 B7
Jiparaná → 91 E6
Jipijapa 90 D2
Jisr ash Shughūr 46 D4
Jiu → 22 C4
Jiujiang 35 D6
Jiuquan 34 C4
Jixi 35 B8
Jizzakh 29 E7
Joaçaba 94 B6
João Pessoa 92 D7
Joaquín V. González 94 B4
Jodhpur 42 F8
Jofane 59 C6
Jogjakarta = Yogyakarta 37 F4
Johannesburg 59 D5
Johnson City 75 A6
Johnston Falls = Mambilima Falls 57 G5
Johnstown 73 D6
Johor Baharu 37 D2
Joinvile 94 B7
Joinville I. 96 A4
Joliet 72 D1
Joliette 69 D3
Jolo 38 C2
Jome 39 E3
Jonesboro 79 B8
Jönköping 9 G10
Jonquière 69 D3
Joplin 79 A6
Jordan ■ 47 E4
Jorhat 41 D10
Jorong 37 E4
Jos 55 G6
Jowzjān □ 45 B6
Juan de Fuca Str. 80 A1
Juan de Nova 59 H8
Juan Fernández, Arch. de 89 G3
Juárez 94 D5
Juàzeiro 93 D5
Juàzeiro do Norte 92 D6
Jubbulpore = Jabalpur 43 H11
Juby, C. 54 C2
Júcar → 19 C5
Juchitán 85 D5
Jugoslavia = Yugoslavia ■ 22 B3
Juiz de Fora 93 G5
Juli 91 G5
Juliaca 91 G4
Jullundur 42 D9
Jumilla 19 C5
Jumla 40 C4
Jumna = Yamuna → 40 E3
Junagadh 43 J7
Jundiaí 94 A7
Juneau 71 C6
Junee 63 B4
Jungfrau 13 C7
Junggar Pendi 34 B3
Junín 94 C4
Junín de los Andes 95 D2
Jūniyah 46 D3
Jur, Nahr el → 53 G4
Jura = Jura, Mts. du 13 C7
Jura = Schwäbische Alb 14 D5
Jura 10 D4
Jura, Mts. du 13 C7
Jurado 90 B3
Juruá → 90 D5
Juruena → 91 E7
Juruti 92 C2

Justo Daract 94 C3
Jutland = Jylland 9 G9
Juventud, I. de la 86 B3
Juwain 42 D2
Jylland 9 G9
Jyväskylä 8 F13

K

K2 42 B10
Kaapkruis 58 C2
Kaapstad = Cape Town 58 E3
Kabaena 39 F2
Kabala 55 G2
Kabale 57 E6
Kabalo 57 F5
Kabambare 57 E5
Kabanjahe 37 D1
Kabara 55 E4
Kabardino-Balkar Republic = Kabardino Balkaria □ 25 E5
Kabardino Balkaria □ 25 E5
Kabare 39 E4
Kabarega Falls 57 D6
Kabasalan 38 C2
Kabba 55 G6
Kabīr, Zab al → 46 C5
Kabīr Kūh 47 D6
Kabkabīyah 53 F3
Kabompo → 58 A4
Kabongo 57 F5
Kabūd Gonbad 44 B4
Kābul 42 B6
Kābul □ 42 B6
Kabul → 42 C8
Kaburuang 39 D3
Kabwe 59 A5
Kachchh, Gulf of 43 H6
Kachchh, Rann of 43 G6
Kachin □ 41 D11
Kachiry 29 D8
Kaçkar 46 B5
Kadan Kyun 36 B1
Kadina 62 B2
Kadirli 46 C4
Kadiyevka = Stakhanov 25 D4
Kadoma 59 B5
Kâdugli 53 F4
Kaduna 55 F6
Kaédi 55 E2
Kaelé 53 F1
Kaesŏng 35 C7
Kāf 47 E4
Kafakumba 56 F4
Kafan = Kapan 25 F6
Kafanchan 55 G6
Kaffrine 55 F1
Kafia Kingi 53 G3
Kafirévs, Ákra 23 E5
Kafue → 59 B5
Kafulwe 57 F5
Kaga Bandoro 56 C3
Kagan 29 F7
Kağizman 46 B5
Kagoshima 33 D2
Kagoshima-Wan 33 D2
Kagul = Cahul 17 F9
Kahama 57 E6
Kahayan → 37 E4
Kahemba 56 F3
Kahnūj 44 E4
Kahoolawe 82 H12
Kahramanmaraş 46 C4
Kai, Kepulauan 39 F4
Kai Besar 39 F4
Kai Is. = Kai, Kepulauan 39 F4
Kai Kecil 39 F4
Kaiama 55 G5
Kaiapoi 65 E5
Kaieteur Falls 90 B7
Kaifeng 35 C6
Kaikohe 64 A5
Kaikoura 65 E5
Kaikoura Ra. 65 D5
Kaimana 39 E4
Kaimanawa Mts. 64 C6
Kaingaroa Forest 64 C7
Kainji Res. 55 F5
Kaipara Harbour 64 B6
Kaironi 39 E4
Kairouan 54 A7
Kaiserslautern 14 D4
Kaitaia 64 A5
Kaitangata 65 G3
Kajaani 8 F13
Kajabbi 61 D6
Kajana = Kajaani 8 F13
Kajo Kaji 53 H5
Kaka 53 F5
Kakamas 58 D4
Kakamega 57 D6
Kakanui Mts. 65 F4
Kakhovka 25 D3
Kakhovske Vdskh. 25 D3
Kakinada 40 J4
Kalaallit Nunaat = Greenland ■ 66 C9
Kalabagh 42 C7
Kalabahi 39 F2
Kalabo 58 A4
Kalach 24 C5
Kaladan → 41 G9
Kalahari 58 C4
Kalakan 31 D9
Kalámai 23 F4
Kalamata = Kalámai 23 F4
Kalamazoo 72 C3
Kalan 46 C4
Kalao 39 F2
Kalaotoa 39 F2
Kalat 42 E5
Kalce 20 B5
Kale 23 F7
Kalegauk Kyun 41 K11
Kalemie 57 F5
Kalewa 41 F10
Kalgan = Zhangjiakou 35 B6
Kalgoorlie-Boulder 60 G3
Kaliakra, Nos 22 C7
Kalianda 37 F3
Kalibo 38 B2
Kalima 57 E5
Kalimantan 37 E4
Kalimantan Barat □ 37 D4
Kalimantan Selatan □ 37 E5
Kalimantan Tengah □ 37 E4
Kalimantan Timur □ 37 D5
Kálimnos 23 F6
Kalinin = Tver 24 B4
Kaliningrad, *Kaliningd., Russia* 24 C1
Kaliningrad, *Moskva, Russia* 24 B4
Kalinkavichy 17 B9
Kalinkovichi = Kalinkavichy 17 B9
Kalispell 81 A6
Kalisz 16 C4
Kaliua 57 F6
Kalkrand 58 C3
Kalmar 9 G11
Kalmyk Republic = Kalmykia □ 25 D6
Kalmykia □ 25 D6
Kalocsa 16 E4
Kalomo 59 B5
Kaluga 24 C4
Kalush 17 D7
Kalutara 43 R11
Kama → 29 D6
Kamaishi 33 G12
Kamaran 49 D3
Kamchatka, P-ov. 31 D13
Kamchatka Pen. = Kamchatka, P-ov. 31 D13
Kamchiya → 22 C6
Kamen 29 D9
Kamenjak, Rt. 20 B4
Kamenka Bugskaya = Kamyanka-Buzka 17 C7
Kamensk Uralskiy 29 D7
Kamin-Kashyrskyy 17 C7
Kamina 57 F5
Kamloops 71 C7
Kampala 57 D6
Kampar → 37 D2
Kampen 14 B3
Kampot 36 B2
Kampuchea = Cambodia ■ 36 B3
Kampung → 39 F5
Kampungbaru = Tolitoli 39 D2
Kamrau, Teluk 39 E4
Kamsack 71 C9
Kamyanets-Podilskyy 17 D8
Kamyanka-Buzka 17 C7
Kamyshin 24 C6
Kanaaupscow 69 C3
Kananga 56 F4
Kanash 24 B6
Kanastraíon, Ákra = Palioúrion, Ákra 23 E4
Kanazawa 32 A5
Kanchanaburi 36 B1
Kanchenjunga 40 D7
Kanchipuram 43 N11
Kanda Kanda 56 F4
Kandahar = Qandahār 42 D4
Kandalaksha 28 C4
Kandalu 42 E3
Kandangan 37 E5
Kandi 55 F5
Kandla 43 H7
Kandos 63 B4
Kandy 43 R12
Kangaroo I. 62 C2
Kangāvar 46 D7
Kangean, Kepulauan 37 F5
Kangean Is. = Kangean, Kepulauan 37 F5
Kangiqsualujjuaq 68 C4
Kangiqsujuaq 68 B3
Kangirsuk 68 C4
Kangnŭng 35 C7
Kango 56 D2
Kangto 41 D9
Kaniapiskau → 68 C4
Kaniapiskau L. 69 C4
Kanin, Poluostrov 28 C5
Kanin Nos, Mys 28 C5
Kanin Pen. = Kanin, Poluostrov 28 C5
Kaniva 62 C3
Kankakee 72 D2
Kankan 55 F3
Kankendy = Xankändi 25 F6
Kanker 40 G3
Kannapolis 75 B7
Kannauj 42 F11
Kannod 43 H10
Kano 55 F6
Kanowit 37 D4
Kanoya 33 D2
Kanpetlet 41 G9
Kanpur 40 D3
Kansas □ 76 F5
Kansas City, *Kans., U.S.A.* 77 F7
Kansas City, *Mo., U.S.A.* 77 F7
Kansk 30 D7
Kansu = Gansu □ 34 C5
Kantang 36 C1
Kanuma 32 A6
Kanye 59 C5
Kaohsiung = Gaoxiong 35 D7
Kaokoveld 58 B2
Kaolack 55 F1
Kapan 25 F6
Kapanga 56 F4
Kapchagai = Qapshaghay 29 E8
Kapfenberg 15 E8
Kapiri Mposhi 59 A5
Kāpīsā □ 45 C7
Kapit 37 D4
Kapoeta 53 H5
Kaposvár 16 E3
Kapuas → 37 E3
Kapuas Hulu, Pegunungan 37 D4
Kapuas Hulu Ra. = Kapuas Hulu, Pegunungan 37 D4
Kapunda 62 B2
Kapuni 64 C6
Kaputar 63 B5
Kara 28 C7

Kara Bogaz Gol, Zaliv = Garabogazköl Aylagy 29 E6
Kara Kalpak Republic □ = Karakalpakstan □ 29 E6
Kara Kum 29 F6
Kara Sea 28 B8
Karabiğa 23 D6
Karabük 46 B3
Karaburun 23 E6
Karabutak = Qarabutaq 29 E7
Karacabey 23 D7
Karacasu 23 F7
Karachi 43 G5
Karad 43 L9
Karadeniz Boğazı 22 D7
Karaganda = Qaraghandy 29 E8
Karagayly 29 E8
Karaikal 43 P11
Karaikkudi 43 P11
Karaj 44 C2
Karakalpakstan □ 29 E6
Karakas 29 E9
Karakelong 38 D3
Karakitang 39 D3
Karaklis = Vanadzor 25 E5
Karakoram Pass 42 B10
Karakoram Ra. 42 B10
Karalon 30 D9
Karaman 46 C3
Karamay 34 B3
Karambu 37 E5
Karamea Bight 65 D4
Karasburg 58 D3
Karasino 28 C9
Karasuk 29 D8
Karatau = Qarataū 29 E8
Karatau, Khrebet 29 E7
Karawanken 20 A5
Karazhal 29 E8
Karbalā 47 D6
Karcag 16 E5
Kardhítsa 23 E3
Karelia □ 28 C4
Karelian Republic □ = Karelia □ 28 C4
Kargānrūd 46 C7
Kargasok 29 D9
Kargat 29 D9
Kargil 42 B10
Kariba, L. 59 B5
Kariba Dam 59 B5
Kariba Gorge 59 B5
Karibib 58 C3
Karimata, Kepulauan 37 E3
Karimata, Selat 37 E3
Karimata Is. = Karimata, Kepulauan 37 E3
Karimnagar 43 K11
Karimunjawa, Kepulauan 37 F4
Karin 49 E4
Karkaralinsk = Qarqaraly 29 E8
Karkinitska Zatoka 25 D3
Karkinitskiy Zaliv = Karkinitska Zatoka 25 D3
Karl-Marx-Stadt = Chemnitz 15 C7
Karlovac 20 B5
Karlovo 22 C5
Karlovy Vary 16 C1
Karlsbad = Karlovy Vary 16 C1
Karlskrona 9 G11
Karlsruhe 14 D5
Karlstad 9 G10
Karnal 42 E10
Karnali → 40 C3
Karnaphuli Res. 41 F9
Karnataka □ 43 N10
Karnische Alpen 20 A4
Kärnten □ 15 E7
Karonga 57 F6
Karoonda 62 C2
Karora 53 E6
Kárpathos 23 G6
Kars 46 B5
Karsakpay 29 E7
Karshi = Qarshi 29 F7
Karsun 24 C6
Karufa 39 E4
Karungu 57 E6
Karviná 16 D4
Karwar 43 M9
Kasai → 56 E3
Kasama 57 G6
Kasanga 57 F6
Kasangulu 56 E3
Kasaragod 43 N9
Kasba L. 70 B9
Kasempa 59 A5
Kasenga 57 G5
Kāshān 44 C2
Kashi 34 C2
Kashk-e Kohneh 42 B3
Kāshmar 44 C4
Kashun Noerh = Gaxun Nur 34 B5
Kasimov 24 C5
Kasiruta 39 E3
Kasongo 57 E5
Kasongo Lunda 56 F3
Kásos 23 G6
Kassalâ 53 E6
Kassel 14 C5
Kassue 39 F5
Kastamonu 46 B3
Kasulu 57 E6
Kasur 42 D9
Katako Kombe 56 E4
Katamatite 63 C4
Katanga = Shaba □ 57 F4
Katangi 43 J11
Kateríni 23 D4
Katha 41 E11
Kathiawar 43 H7
Katihar 40 E6
Katima Mulilo 58 B4
Katingan = Mendawai → 37 E4
Katiola 55 G3
Katmandu 40 D5
Katoomba 63 B5
Katowice 16 C4
Katsina 55 F6
Kattegat 9 G10
Kauai 82 G11
Kaunas 24 C1
Kaura Namoda 55 F6
Kaválla 22 D5
Kaw 92 B3
Kawagoe 32 B6
Kawaguchi 32 B6
Kawambwa 57 F5
Kawardha 40 G3
Kawasaki 32 B6
Kawerau 64 C7
Kawhia Harbour 64 C6
Kawio, Kepulauan 38 D3
Kawnro 41 F12
Kawthoolei = Kawthule □ 41 H11
Kawthule □ 41 H11
Kaya 55 F4
Kayah □ 41 H11
Kayan → 37 D5
Kayeli 39 E3
Kayes 55 F2
Kayoa 39 D3
Kayrunnera 62 B3
Kayseri 46 C3
Kayuagung 37 E2
Kazachye 31 B11
Kazakstan ■ 29 E7
Kazan 24 B6
Kazanlŭk 22 C5
Kazatin = Kozyatyn 17 D9
Kāzerūn 44 D2
Kazumba 56 F4
Kazym → 28 C7
Ké-Macina 55 F3
Kéa 23 F5
Kebnekaise 8 E11
Kebri Dehar 49 F3
Kecskemét 16 E4
Kediri 37 F4
Kédougou 55 F2
Keetmanshoop 58 D3
Kefallinía 23 E3
Kefamenanu 39 F2
Keffi 55 G6
Keighley 11 E6
Keith 62 C3
Keith Arm 70 B7
Kekri 42 G9
Kël 30 C10
Kelang 37 D2
Kelibia 52 A1
Kellé 56 E2
Kells = Ceanannus Mor 11 E3
Kélo 53 G2
Kelowna 71 D8
Kelso 65 F3
Keluang 37 D2
Kem 28 C4
Kema 39 D3
Kemah 46 C4
Kemerovo 29 D9
Kemi 8 E12
Kemi älv = Kemijoki → 8 E12
Kemijoki → 8 E12
Kemp Land 96 A9
Kempsey 63 B5
Kempten 14 E6
Kendal 37 F4
Kendall 63 B5
Kendari 39 E2
Kendawangan 37 E4
Kende 55 F5
Kendrapara 40 G6
Kenema 55 G2
Keng Tawng 41 G12
Keng Tung 41 G12
Kenge 56 E3
Kenhardt 58 D4
Kenitra 54 B3
Kennedy Taungdeik 41 F9
Kennewick 80 B4
Kenogami → 69 C2
Kenosha 72 C2
Kent Group 62 C4
Kent Pen. 70 B9
Kentau 29 E7
Kentucky □ 72 F3
Kentville 69 D4
Kenya ■ 57 D7
Kenya, Mt. 57 E7
Kepi 39 F5
Kerala □ 43 P10
Kerang 62 C3
Kerch 25 D4
Kerchoual 55 E5
Keren 53 E6
Kericho 57 E7
Kerinci 37 E2
Kerki 29 F7
Kérkira 23 E2
Kermadec Is. 64 M13
Kermadec Trench 65 N13
Kermān 44 D4
Kermān □ 44 D4
Kermānshāh = Bākhtarān 46 D6
Kerme Körfezi 23 F6
Kerrobert 71 C9
Kerulen → 35 B6
Kerzaz 54 C4
Keşan 22 D6
Kestenga 28 C4
Ket → 29 D9
Keta 55 G5
Ketapang 37 E4
Ketchikan 71 C6
Kętrzyn 16 A5
Keweenaw B. 69 D2
Key West 86 B3
Khabarovo 28 C7
Khabarovsk 31 E11
Khābūr → 46 D5
Khairpur 42 F6
Khakassia □ 30 D6
Khakhea 58 C4
Khalkhāl 46 C7
Khalkís 23 E4
Khalmer-Sede = Tazovskiy 28 C8
Khalmer Yu 28 C7
Khalturin 24 B6
Khalūf 48 C6
Khambat, G. of 43 J8
Khambhat 43 H8
Khamir 49 D3
Khānābād 45 B7
Khānaqīn 46 D6
Khandwa 43 J10
Khanewal 42 D7
Khaniá 23 G5
Khaníon, Kólpos 23 G4
Khankendy = Xankändi 25 F6
Khanty-Mansiysk 29 C7
Khapcheranga 30 E9
Kharagpur 40 F6
Kharan Kalat 42 E4
Kharānaq 44 C3
Kharda 43 K9
Khârga, El Wâhât el 52 C5
Khargon 43 J9
Khārk, Jazireh 47 E7
Kharkiv 24 D4

Kharkov = Kharkiv 24 D4
Kharovsk 24 B5
Kharsānīya 47 F7
Kharta 22 D7
Khartoum = El Khartûm 53 E5
Khāsh 42 E2
Khashm el Girba 53 F6
Khaskovo 22 D5
Khatanga 30 B8
Khatanga → 30 B8
Khaybar, Harrat 47 F5
Khed Brahma 43 G8
Khemmarat 36 A3
Khenchela 54 A6
Khenifra 54 B3
Kherson 25 D3
Kheta → 30 B8
Khilok 30 D9
Khíos 23 E6
Khiuma = Hiiumaa 24 B1
Khiva 29 E7
Khīyāv 46 C6
Khmelnik 17 D8
Khmelnitskiy = Khmelnytskyy 17 D8
Khmelnytskyy 17 D8
Khmer Rep. = Cambodia ■ 36 B3
Khodoriv 17 D7
Khodzent = Khudzhand 29 E7
Khojak P. 42 D5
Kholm, *Afghan.* 45 B6
Kholm, *Russia* 24 B3
Khomeyn 44 C2
Khon Kaen 36 A2
Khoper → 29 E5
Khóra Sfakíon 23 G5
Khorat = Nakhon Ratchasima 36 B2
Khorramābād 46 D7
Khorrāmshahr 47 E7
Khotyn 17 D8
Khouribga 54 B3
Khowai 41 E8
Khoyniki 17 C9
Khu Khan 36 B2
Khudzhand 29 E7
Khūgīānī 42 D4
Khulna 41 F7
Khulna □ 41 F7
Khūr 44 C4
Khurayṣ 47 F7
Khūrīyā Mūrīyā, Jazā 'ir 48 D6
Khush 42 C3
Khushab 42 C8
Khust 17 D6
Khuzdar 42 F5
Khvor 44 C3
Khvormūj 44 D2
Khvoy 46 C6
Khyber Pass 42 B7
Kiama 63 B5
Kiamba 38 C2
Kiangsi = Jiangxi □ 35 D6
Kiangsu = Jiangsu □ 35 C6
Kibangou 56 E2
Kibombo 57 E5
Kibondo 57 E6
Kibwesa 57 F5
Kibwezi 57 E7
Kicking Horse Pass 71 C8
Kidal 55 E5
Kidnappers, C. 64 C7
Kiel 14 A6
Kiel Canal = Nord-Ostsee-Kanal → 14 A5
Kielce 16 C5
Kieler Bucht 14 A6
Kiev = Kyyiv 17 C10
Kiffa 55 E2
Kifrī 46 D6
Kigali 57 E6
Kigoma-Ujiji 57 E5
Kihee 62 A3
Kii-Suidō 32 C4
Kikinda 22 B3
Kikládhes 23 F5
Kikwit 56 E3
Kilcoy 63 A5
Kilimanjaro 57 E7
Kilindini 57 E7
Kilis 46 C4
Kiliya 17 F9
Kilkenny 11 E3
Kilkís 23 D4
Killarney, *Australia* 63 A5
Killarney, *Ireland* 11 E2
Killeen 78 D5
Killíni 23 F4
Kilmarnock 10 D4
Kilmore 63 C3
Kilosa 57 F7
Kilrush 11 E2
Kilwa Kivinje 57 F7
Kimaam 39 F5
Kimba 62 B2
Kimberley 58 D4
Kimberley Plateau 60 D4
Kimry 24 B4
Kinabalu, Gunong 36 C5
Kindia 55 G2
Kindu 57 E5
Kineshma 24 B5
King George B. 95 G4
King George I. 96 A4
King George Is. 69 C2
King I. = Kadan Kyun 36 B1
King I. 62 C3
King William I. 70 B10
King William's Town 59 E5
Kingaroy 63 A5
Kingoonya 62 B2
Kings Canyon National Park 82 B3
King's Lynn 11 E7
Kingscote 62 C2
Kingsport 75 A6
Kingston, *Canada* 69 D3
Kingston, *Jamaica* 86 C4
Kingston, *N.Z.* 65 F3
Kingston South East 62 C2
Kingston upon Hull 11 E6
Kingstown 87 D7
Kingsville 78 F5
Kınık 23 E6
Kinkala 56 E2
Kinleith 64 C6
Kinsale 11 F2
Kinshasa 56 E3
Kinston 75 B9
Kintampo 55 G4
Kintap 37 E5
Kiparissía 23 F3
Kiparissiakós Kólpos 23 F3
Kipembawe 57 F6
Kipili 57 F6
Kipushi 59 A5
Kirghizia ■ = Kyrgyzstan ■ 29 E8
Kirghizstan = Kyrgyzstan ■ 29 E8
Kiri 56 E3
Kiribati ■ 64 K12
Kırıkkale 46 C3
Kirillov 24 B4
Kirin = Jilin 35 B7
Kiritimati 65 J15
Kirkcaldy 10 C5
Kirkcudbright 11 D4
Kirkee 43 K8
Kirkenes 8 E14
Kirkland Lake 69 D2
Kırklareli 22 D6
Kirkūk 46 D6
Kirkwall 10 B5
Kirov 28 D5
Kirovabad = Gäncä 25 E6
Kirovakan = Vanadzor 25 E5
Kirovograd = Kirovohrad 25 D3
Kirovohrad 25 D3
Kirovsk = Babadayhan 29 F7
Kirovsk 28 C4
Kirsanov 24 C5
Kırşehir 46 C3
Kīrteh 45 C5
Kirthar Range 42 F5
Kiruna 8 E12
Kirundu 57 E5
Kiryū 32 A6
Kisangani 57 D5
Kisar 39 F3
Kiselevsk 29 D9
Kishanganj 40 D7
Kishangarh 42 F7
Kishinev = Chişinău 17 E9
Kishiwada 32 B4
Kishtwar 42 C9
Kisii 57 E6
Kisiju 57 F7
Kiska I. 71 C1
Kiskőrös 16 E4
Kiskunfélegyháza 16 E4
Kiskunhalas 16 E4
Kislovodsk 25 E5
Kiso-Sammyaku 32 B5
Kissidougou 55 G2
Kisumu 57 E6
Kita 55 F3
Kitab 29 F7
Kitakami-Gawa → 33 G12
Kitakyūshū 32 C2
Kitale 57 D7
Kitchener 69 D2
Kitega = Gitega 57 E5
Kitgum 57 D6
Kíthira 23 F4
Kíthnos 23 F5
Kittakittaooloo, L. 62 A2
Kitui 57 E7
Kitwe 59 A5
Kivertsi 17 C7
Kivu, L. 57 E5
Kiyev = Kyyiv 17 C10
Kiyevskoye Vdkhr. = Kyyivske Vdskh. 17 C10
Kızıl Irmak → 25 E4
Kizlyar 25 E6
Kizyl-Arvat = Gyzylarbat 29 F6
Kladno 16 C2
Klagenfurt 15 E8
Klaìpeda 24 B1
Klamath Falls 80 D3
Klamath Mts. 80 E2
Klarälven → 9 G10
Klatovy 16 D1
Klawer 58 E3
Klerksdorp 59 D5
Kletsk = Klyetsk 17 B8
Klin 28 D4
Kłodzko 16 C3
Klondike 70 B6
Klouto 55 G5
Kluane L. 70 B6
Kluczbork 16 C4
Klyetsk 17 B8
Knossós 23 G5
Knox Coast 96 A12
Knoxville 75 B6
Koartac = Quaqtaq 68 B4
Koba, *Aru, Indonesia* 39 F4
Koba, *Bangka, Indonesia* 37 E3
Kobarid 20 A4
Kobdo = Hovd 34 B4
Kōbe 32 B4
København 9 G10
Koblenz 14 C4
Kobroor, Kepulauan 39 F4
Kobryn 17 B7
Kocaeli = İzmit 25 E2
Kočani 22 D4
Koch Bihar 41 D7
Kōchi 32 C3
Kochiu = Gejiu 34 D5
Kodiak 71 C4
Kodiak I. 71 C4
Koes 58 D3
Kofiau 39 E3
Koforidua 55 G4
Kōfu 32 B6
Kogan 63 A5
Koh-i-Bābā 42 B5
Kohat 42 C7
Kohima 41 E10
Kohkīlūyeh va Būyer Aḥmadi □ 44 D2
Kohler Ra. 96 B1
Kokand = Qūqon 29 E8
Kokas 39 E4
Kokchetav = Kökshetaū 29 D7
Koko Kyunzu 41 K9
Kokomo 72 D2
Kokonau 39 E5
Kökshetaū 29 D7
Koksoak → 68 C4
Kokstad 59 E5
Kola, *Indonesia* 39 F4
Kola, *Russia* 28 C4
Kola Pen. = Kolskiy Poluostrov 28 C4

Kolaka 39 E2
Kolar 43 N11
Kolar Gold Fields 43 N11
Kolayat 42 F8
Kolchugino = Leninsk-Kuznetskiy 29 D9
Kolda 55 F2
Kole 56 E4
Kolepom = Yos Sudarso, Pulau 39 F5
Kolguyev, Ostrov 28 C5
Kolhapur 43 L9
Kolín 16 C2
Köln 14 C4
Koło 16 B4
Kołobrzeg 16 A2
Kolokani 55 F3
Kolomna 24 B4
Kolomyya 17 D7
Kolonodale 39 E2
Kolosib 41 E9
Kolpashevo 29 D9
Kolpino 24 B3
Kolskiy Poluostrov 28 C4
Kolwezi 57 G5
Kolyma → 31 C13
Komárno 16 E4
Komatsu 32 A5
Komi □ 28 C6
Kommunarsk = Alchevsk 25 D4
Kommunizma, Pik 29 F8
Komodo 39 F1
Komono 56 E2
Komoran, Pulau 39 F5
Komotini 22 D5
Kompong Cham 36 B3
Kompong Chhnang 36 B2
Kompong Som 36 B2
Komrat = Comrat 17 E9
Komsomolets, Ostrov 30 A7
Konarhá □ 42 B7
Konch 42 G11
Kondoa 57 E7
Konduga 53 F1
Köneürgench 29 E6
Kong 55 G4
Kong, Koh 36 B2
Konglu 41 D11
Kongolo 57 F5
Kongor 53 G5
Königsberg = Kaliningrad 24 C1
Konin 16 B4
Konjic 20 C6
Konosha 28 C5
Konotop 24 C3
Konqi He → 34 B4
Końskie 16 C5
Konstanz 14 E5
Kontagora 55 F6
Kontum 36 B3
Konya 46 C3
Konya Ovası 46 C3
Konza 57 E7
Kooloonong 62 B3
Koondrook 63 C3
Koonibba 62 B1
Koorawatha 63 B4
Kootenay L. 71 D8
Kopaonik 22 C3
Koper 20 B4
Kopeysk 29 D7
Kopi 62 B2
Koprivnica 20 A6
Kopychyntsi 17 D7
Korab 22 D3
Korça 23 D3
Korce = Korça 23 D3
Korčula 20 C6
Kordestan 46 D5
Kordestān □ 46 D6
Kordofân 53 F4
Korea, North ■ 35 C7
Korea, South ■ 35 C7
Korea Bay 35 C7
Korea Strait 35 C7
Korets 17 C8
Korhogo 55 G3
Korim 39 E5
Korinthiakós Kólpos 23 E4
Kórinthos 23 F4
Kōriyama 33 G12
Korneshty = Corneşti 17 E9
Koro, *Ivory C.* 55 G3
Koro, *Mali* 55 F4
Korogwe 57 F7
Koroit 62 C3
Koror 38 C4
Körös → 16 E5
Korosten 17 C9
Korostyshev 17 C9
Korti 53 E5
Kortrijk 14 C2
Kos 23 F6
Kościan 16 B3
Kosciuszko, Mt. 63 C4
Kosha 52 D5
K'oshih = Kashi 34 C2
Košice 16 D5
Kosovo □ 22 C3
Kosovska-Mitrovica 22 C3
Kôstî 53 F5
Kostopil 17 C8
Kostroma 24 B5
Kostrzyn 16 B2
Koszalin 16 A3
Kota 43 G9
Kota Baharu 36 C2
Kota Belud 36 C5
Kota Kinabalu 36 C5
Kota Tinggi 37 D2
Kotaagung 37 F2
Kotabaru 37 E5
Kotabumi 37 E2
Kotamobagu 39 D2
Kotawaringin 37 E4
Kotelnich 24 B6
Kotelnyy, Ostrov 31 B11
Kotka 9 F13
Kotlas 28 C5
Kotli 42 C8
Kotor 22 C2
Kotovsk 17 E9
Kotri 42 G6
Kottayam 43 Q10
Kotturu 43 M10
Kotuy → 30 B8
Kotzebue 71 B3
Kouango 56 D4
Koudougou 55 F4
Kouilou → 56 E2
Kouki 56 C3
Koula Moutou 56 E2
Koulen 36 B2
Koulikoro 55 F3
Koumra 53 G2
Kounradskiy 29 E8
Kouroussa 55 F3
Kousseri 53 F1
Koutiala 55 F3
Kovel 17 C7
Kovrov 24 B5
Kowloon 35 D6
Köyceğiz 23 F7
Koyuk 71 B3
Koyukuk → 71 B4
Kozan 46 C3
Kozáni 23 D3
Kozhikode = Calicut 43 P9
Kozyatyn 17 D9
Kpalimé 55 G5
Kra, Isthmus of = Kra, Kho Khot 36 B1
Kra, Kho Khot 36 B1
Kragujevac 22 B3
Krajina 20 B6
Krakatau = Rakata, Pulau 37 F3
Kraków 16 C4
Kraljevo 22 C3
Kramatorsk 25 D4
Kranj 20 A5
Kraśnik 16 C6
Krasnoarmeysk 29 D5
Krasnodar 25 D4
Krasnoperekopsk 25 D3
Krasnoselkupsk 28 C9
Krasnoturinsk 28 D7
Krasnoufimsk 29 D6
Krasnouralsk 29 D7
Krasnovodsk = Krasnowodsk 29 E6
Krasnowodsk 29 E6
Krasnoyarsk 30 D7
Krasnyy Luch 25 D4
Krasnyy Yar 25 D6
Kratie 36 B3
Krau 39 E6
Krefeld 14 C4
Kremen 20 B5
Kremenchug = Kremenchuk 24 D3
Kremenchuk 24 D3
Kremenchuksk Vdskh. 24 D3
Kremenets 17 C7
Krems 15 D8
Kribi 56 D1
Krichev = Krychaw 17 B10
Krishna → 40 K3
Krishnanagar 41 F7
Kristiansand 9 G9
Kristiansund 8 F9
Kríti 23 G5
Krivoy Rog = Kryvyy Rih 25 D3
Krk 20 B5
Kronprins Olav Kyst 96 A9
Kronshtadt 24 B2
Kroonstad 59 D5
Kropotkin, *Irkutsk, Russia* 30 D9
Kropotkin, *Krasnodar, Russia* 25 D5
Krosno 16 D5
Krotoszyn 16 C3
Krugersdorp 59 D5
Krung Thep = Bangkok 36 B2
Krupki 17 A9
Kruševac 22 C3
Krychaw 17 B10
Krymskiy Poluostrov = Krymskyy Pivostriv 25 D3
Krymskyy Pivostriv 25 D3
Kryvyy Rih 25 D3
Ksar el Boukhari 54 A5
Ksar el Kebir 54 B3
Ksar es Souk = Ar Rachidiya 54 B4
Kuala 37 D3
Kuala Kubu Baharu 37 D2
Kuala Lipis 37 D2
Kuala Lumpur 37 D2
Kuala Terengganu 36 C2
Kualajelai 37 E4
Kualakapuas 37 E4
Kualakurun 37 E4
Kualapembuang 37 E4
Kualasimpang 37 D1
Kuandang 39 D2
Kuangchou = Guangzhou 35 D6
Kuantan 37 D2
Kuba = Quba 25 E6
Kuban → 25 D4
Kucing 37 D4
Kuda 43 H7
Kudat 36 C5
Kudymkar 28 D6
Kueiyang = Guiyang 35 D5
Kufra Oasis = Al Kufrah 52 D3
Kufstein 15 E7
Kugluktuk 70 B8
Kūh-e 'Alijūq 44 D2
Kūh-e-Hazārām 44 D4
Kūh-e Sorkh 44 C4
Kūh-e Taftān 45 D5
Kūhak 42 F3
Kūhhā-ye-Bashākerd 45 E4
Kūhpāyeh 44 C3
Kuito 58 A3
Kujū-San 32 C2
Kukawa 53 F1
Kukësi 22 C3
Kula 23 E7
Kulasekarappattinam 43 Q11
Kuldja = Yining 34 B3
Kŭlob 29 F7
Kulsary 29 E6
Kulunda 29 D8
Kulwin 62 C3
Kulyab = Kŭlob 29 F7
Kum Tekei 29 E8
Kuma → 25 E6
Kumagaya 32 A6
Kumai 37 E4
Kumamba, Kepulauan 39 E5
Kumamoto 32 C2
Kumanovo 22 C3
Kumara 65 E4
Kumasi 55 G4
Kumayri = Gyumri 25 E5
Kumba 56 D1
Kumbakonam 43 P11

Kumbarilla 63 A5
Kumo 55 F7
Kumon Bum 41 D11
Kunama 63 C4
Kungala 63 A5
Kungrad = Qŭnghirot 29 E6
Kungur 29 D6
Kunlong 41 F12
Kunlun Shan 34 C3
Kunming 34 D5
Kunsan 35 C7
Kunya-Urgench = Köneürgench 29 E6
Kuopio 8 F13
Kupa → 20 B6
Kupyansk 28 E4
Kuqa 34 B3
Kür → 25 E6
Kura = Kür → 25 E6
Kurashiki 32 B3
Kurayoshi 32 B3
Kŭrdzhali 22 D5
Kure 32 B3
Kurgaldzhinskiy 29 D8
Kurgan 29 D7
Kuria Maria Is. = Khūrīyā Mūrīyā, Jazā 'ir 48 D6
Kurigram 41 E7
Kuril Is. = Kurilskiye Ostrova 31 E12
Kurilskiye Ostrova 31 E12
Kurmuk 53 F5
Kurnool 43 L11
Kurow 65 F4
Kurrajong 63 B5
Kurri Kurri 63 B5
Kursk 24 C4
Kuruktag 34 B3
Kuruman 58 D4
Kurume 32 C2
Kus Gölü 23 D6
Kuşadası 23 F6
Kushiro 32 F12
Kushtia 41 F7
Kuskokwim → 71 B3
Kuskokwim B. 71 C3
Kustanay = Qostanay 29 D7
Kütahya 46 C2
Kutaisi 25 E5
Kutaraja = Banda Aceh 36 C1
Kutch, Gulf of = Kachchh, Gulf of 43 H6
Kutch, Rann of = Kachchh, Rann of 43 G6
Kutno 16 B4
Kutu 56 E3
Kutum 53 F3
Kuujjuaq 68 C4
Kuwait = Al Kuwayt 47 E7
Kuwait ■ 47 E6
Kuwana 32 B5
Kuybyshev = Samara 24 C7
Kuybyshev 29 D8
Kuybyshevskoye Vdkhr. 24 B6
Kūysanjaq 46 C6
Kuyumba 30 C7
Kuzey Anadolu Dağları 46 B3
Kuznetsk 24 C6
Kvarner 20 B5
Kvarnerič 20 B5
Kwakoegron 92 A2
Kwamouth 56 E3
Kwando → 58 B4
Kwangju 35 C7
Kwangsi-Chuang = Guangxi Zhuangzu Zizhiqu □ 35 D5
Kwangtung = Guangdong □ 35 D6
Kwatisore 39 E4
Kweichow = Guizhou □ 35 D5
Kwekwe 59 B5
Kwidzyn 16 B4
Kwoka 39 E4
Kyabé 53 G2
Kyabra Cr. → 63 A3
Kyabram 63 C4
Kyancutta 62 B2
Kyangin 41 H10
Kyaukpadaung 41 G10
Kyaukpyu 41 H9
Kyaukse 41 G11
Kyle Dam 59 C6
Kyneton 63 C3
Kyō-ga-Saki 32 B4
Kyoga, L. 57 D6
Kyogle 63 A5
Kyongpyaw 41 J10
Kyōto 32 B4
Kyrenia 46 D3
Kyrgyzstan ■ 29 E8
Kystatyam 30 C10
Kytal Ktakh 31 C10
Kyunhla 41 F10
Kyūshū 32 C2
Kyūshū-Sanchi 32 C2
Kyustendil 22 C4
Kyusyur 30 B10
Kywong 63 B4
Kyyiv 17 C10
Kyyivske Vdskh. 17 C10
Kyzyl Kum 29 E7
Kyzyl-Kyya 29 E8
Kzyl-Orda = Qyzylorda 29 E7

L

La Albufera 19 C5
La Alcarria 19 B4
La Asunción 90 A6
La Banda 94 B4
La Calera 94 C2
La Carlota 94 C4
La Ceiba 85 D7
La Chaux de Fonds 13 C7
La Cocha 94 B3
La Coruña 18 A1
La Crosse 77 D9
La Dorada 90 B4
La Estrada 18 A1
La Grange 74 C5
La Guaira 90 A5
La Güera 54 D1
La Habana 86 B3
La Línea de la Concepción 18 D3
La Mancha 19 C4
La Palma, *Canary Is.* 54 C1
La Palma, *Panama* 86 E4
La Palma del Condado 18 D2
La Paragua 90 B6
La Paz, *Entre Ríos, Argentina* 94 C5
La Paz, *San Luis, Argentina* 94 C3
La Paz, *Bolivia* 91 G5
La Paz, *Mexico* 84 C2
La Pedrera 90 D5
La Plata 94 D5
La Quiaca 94 A3
La Rioja 94 B3
La Rioja □ 19 A4
La Robla 18 A3
La Roche-sur-Yon 12 C3
La Rochelle 12 C3
La Roda 19 C4
La Romana 87 C6
La Serena 94 B2
La Seyne-sur-Mer 13 E6
La Spézia 20 B2
La Tortuga 87 D6
La Tuque 69 D3
La Unión 95 E2
La Urbana 90 B5
La Vega 87 C5
Labe = Elbe → 14 B5
Labé 55 F2
Labis 37 D2
Laboulaye 94 C4
Labrador, Coast of □ 69 C4
Lábrea 91 E6
Labuan, Pulau 36 C5
Labuha 39 E3
Labuhanbajo 39 F2
Labuk, Telok 36 C5
Labyrinth, L. 62 B2
Labytnangi 28 C7
Lac La Biche 71 C8
Lac la Martre 70 B8
Lacanau 12 D3
Laccadive Is. = Lakshadweep Is. 26 H11
Lacepede B. 62 C2
Lachine 69 D3
Lachlan → 63 B3
Lackawanna 73 C6
Lacombe 71 C8
Ladakh Ra. 42 B10
Lādīz 45 D5
Ladoga, L. = Ladozhskoye Ozero 28 C4
Ladozhskoye Ozero 28 C4
Ladysmith, *Canada* 71 D7
Ladysmith, *S. Africa* 59 D5
Lae 61 B8
Lafayette 79 D7
Lafia 55 G6
Laghmān □ 45 C7
Laghouat 54 B5
Lagonoy Gulf 38 B2
Lagos, *Nigeria* 55 G5
Lagos, *Portugal* 18 D1
Laguna 94 B7
Lagunas, *Chile* 91 H5
Lagunas, *Peru* 90 E3
Lahad Datu 38 C1
Lahat 37 E2
Lahewa 37 D1
Lāhījān 46 C7
Lahn → 14 C4
Lahore 42 D9
Lahti 8 F13
Lahtis = Lahti 8 F13
Laï 53 G2
Laibin 35 D5
Laidley 63 A5
Laila = Laylá 47 G6
Lairg 10 B4
Lajere 55 F7
Lajes 94 B6
Lake Cargelligo 63 B4
Lake Charles 79 D7
Lake City 75 D6
Lake Harbour 68 B4
Lake Worth 75 F7
Lakeland 75 E7
Lakes Entrance 63 C4
Lakewood 72 D5
Lakonikós Kólpos 23 F4
Lakor 39 F3
Lakota 55 G3
Lakshadweep Is. 26 H11
Lala Ghat 41 E9
Lalibela 53 F6
Lalín 18 A1
Lalitapur = Patan 40 D5
Lamaing 41 K11
Lamas 91 E3
Lambaréné 56 E2
Lambert Glacier 96 B10
Lame 55 F6
Lamego 18 B2
Lameroo 62 C3
Lamía 23 E4
Lamon Bay 38 B2
Lampa 91 G4
Lampedusa 21 G4
Lampione 21 G4
Lampung □ 37 F2
Lamu 57 E8
Lanai I. 82 H12
Lanak La 42 B11
Lanak'o Shank'ou = Lanak La 42 B11
Lanao, L. 38 C2
Lancaster, *U.K.* 11 D5
Lancaster, *U.S.A.* 73 D7
Lancaster Sd. 68 A2
Lanchow = Lanzhou 35 C5
Lanciano 20 C5
Landeck 14 E6
Landes 12 D3
Landi Kotal 42 B7
Land's End 11 F4
Landshut 15 D7
La'nga Co 40 B3
Langkawi, P. 36 C1
Langkon 36 C5
Langres 13 C6
Langres, Plateau de 13 C6
Langsa 36 D1
Languedoc 13 E5
Langzhong 35 C5
Lannion 12 B2
Lansdowne 63 B5
Lansing 72 C3
Lanusei 21 E2

Lanzarote 54 C2
Lanzhou 35 C5
Laoag 38 A2
Laoang 38 B3
Laon 13 B5
Laos ■ 36 A3
Lapa 94 B7
Laparan 38 C1
Lapland = Lappland 8 E12
Lappland 8 E12
Lapseki 23 D6
Laptev Sea 30 B10
L'Áquila 20 C4
Lār 44 E3
Larache 54 A3
Laramie 76 E2
Larantuka 39 F2
Larap 38 B2
Larat 39 F4
Laredo 78 F4
Lariang 39 E1
Lárisa 23 E4
Larnaca 46 D3
Larne 11 D4
Larrimah 60 D5
Larsen Ice Shelf 96 A3
Larvik 9 G9
Laryak 29 C8
Las Anod 49 F4
Las Cruces 83 D9
Las Flores 94 D5
Las Khoreh 49 E4
Las Lajas 94 D2
Las Lomitas 94 A4
Las Palmas 54 C1
Las Pipinas 94 D5
Las Plumas 95 E3
Las Rosas 94 C4
Las Varillas 94 C4
Las Vegas 82 B5
Lashio 41 F11
Lassen Pk. 80 E3
Lastoursville 56 E2
Lastovo 20 C6
Latacunga 90 D3
Latakia = Al Lādhiqīyah 46 D3
Latina 20 D4
Latium = Lazio □ 20 C4
Latrobe 62 D4
Latvia ■ 24 B1
Lauchhammer 15 C7
Launceston 62 D4
Laurel 79 D9
Lauria 21 D5
Laurium 69 D2
Lausanne 13 C7
Laut 36 D3
Laut Kecil, Kepulauan 37 E5
Laval 12 B3
Lávrion 23 F5
Lawas 36 D5
Lawele 39 F2
Lawng Pit 41 E11
Lawrence, *N.Z.* 65 F3
Lawrence, *U.S.A.* 77 F7
Lawton 78 B4
Laylá 47 G6
Lazio □ 20 C4
Le Creusot 13 C6
Le Havre 12 B4
Le Mans 12 C4
Le Mont-St.-Michel 12 B3
Le Moule 87 C7
Le Puy-en-Velay 13 D5
Le Touquet-Paris-Plage 12 A4
Le Tréport 12 A4
Le Verdon-sur-Mer 12 D3
Leamington Spa = Royal Leamington Spa 11 E6
Leandro Norte Alem 94 B5
Leavenworth 77 F7
Lebak 38 C2
Lebanon ■ 46 D3
Lębork 16 A3
Lebrija 18 D2
Lebu 94 D2
Lecce 23 D2
Lecco 20 B2
Lech → 14 D6
Łęczyca 16 B4
Leduc 71 C8
Leeds 11 E6
Leer 14 B4
Leeton 63 B4
Leeuwarden 14 B3
Leeuwin, C. 60 G2
Leeward Is. 87 C7
Leganés 18 B4
Legazpi 38 B2
Leghorn = Livorno 20 C3
Legionowo 16 B5
Legnago 20 B3
Legnica 16 C3
Legume 63 A5
Leh 42 B10
Leicester 11 E6
Leiden 14 B3
Leie → 14 C2
Leine → 14 B5
Leinster □ 11 E3
Leipzig 15 C7
Leiria 18 C1
Leitrim 11 D2
Leizhou Bandao 35 D6
Leksula 39 E3
Lékva Ori 23 G5
Leleque 95 E2
Léman, L. 13 C7
Lemhi Ra. 81 C7
Lena → 30 B10
Leninabad = Khudzhand 29 E7
Leninakan = Gyumri 25 E5
Leningrad = Sankt-Peterburg 24 B3
Leninogorsk = Ridder 29 D9
Leninsk 25 D6
Leninsk-Kuznetskiy 29 D9
Lenmalu 39 E4
Lens 13 A5
Lentini 21 F5
Leoben 15 E8
Leodhas = Lewis 10 B3
León, *Mexico* 84 C4
León, *Nic.* 85 E7
León, *Spain* 18 A3
León, Montañas de 18 A2
Leongatha 63 C4
Léopold II, Lac = Mai-Ndombe, L. 56 E3
Léopoldville = Kinshasa 56 E3
Leova 17 E9
Lepel = Lyepyel 24 C2
Lepikha 31 C10
Léré 53 G1
Lérida 19 B6
Lerwick 10 A6
Les Cayes 86 C5
Les Sables-d'Olonne 12 C3
Lesbos = Lésvos 23 E6
Leskovac 22 C3
Lesotho ■ 59 D5
Lesser Antilles 87 D7
Lesser Sunda Is. 39 F2
Lésvos 23 E6
Leszno 16 C3
Lethbridge 71 D8
Leti, Kepulauan 39 F3
Leti Is. = Leti, Kepulauan 39 F3
Leticia 90 D4
Letpadan 41 J10
Letpan 41 H10
Letterkenny 11 D3
Leuser, G. 37 D1
Leuven 14 C3
Levádhia 23 E4
Levice 16 D4
Levin 64 D6
Lévis 69 D3
Levkás 23 E3
Levkôsia = Nicosia 46 D3
Levskigrad = Karlovo 22 C5
Lewis 10 B3
Lewisporte 69 D5
Lewiston, *Idaho, U.S.A.* 80 B5
Lewiston, *Maine, U.S.A.* 73 B10
Lexington, *Ky., U.S.A.* 72 E3
Lexington, *N.C., U.S.A.* 75 B7
Leyte 38 B2
Lezha 22 D2
Lhasa 34 D4
Lhazê 34 D3
Lhokkruet 36 D1
Lhokseumawe 36 C1
Lhuntsi Dzong 41 D8
Lianga 38 C3
Lianyungang 35 C6
Liaoning □ 35 B7
Liaoyuan 35 B7
Liard → 70 B7
Libau = Liepāja 24 B1
Libenge 56 D3
Liberal 78 A3
Liberec 16 C2
Liberia ■ 55 G3
Lîbîya, Sahrâ' 52 C4
Libobo, Tanjung 39 E3
Libonda 58 A4
Libourne 12 D3
Libreville 56 D1
Libya ■ 52 C2
Libyan Desert = Lîbîya, Sahrâ' 52 C4
Licantén 94 D2
Licata 21 F4
Lichinga 59 A7
Lichtenburg 59 D5
Lida 17 B7
Liechtenstein ■ 14 E5
Liège 14 C3
Liegnitz = Legnica 16 C3
Lienyünchiangshih = Lianyungang 35 C6
Lienz 15 E7
Liepāja 24 B1
Liffey → 11 E3
Lifford 11 D3
Lightning Ridge 63 A4
Liguria □ 20 B2
Ligurian Sea 20 C2
Lijiang 34 D5
Likasi 57 G5
Lille 13 A5
Lillehammer 8 F10
Lilongwe 59 A6
Liloy 38 C2
Lim → 20 C7
Lima, *Indonesia* 39 E3
Lima, *Peru* 91 F3
Lima, *U.S.A.* 72 D3
Lima → 18 B1
Limassol 46 D3
Limay Mahuida 94 D3
Limbang 36 D5
Limbe 56 D1
Limbri 63 B5
Limburg 14 C5
Limeira 94 A7
Limerick 11 E2
Limfjorden 9 G9
Limia = Lima → 18 B1
Límnos 23 E5
Limoeiro do Norte 92 D6
Limoges 12 D4
Limón 86 E3
Limousin 12 D4
Limoux 12 E5
Limpopo → 59 D6
Limuru 57 E7
Linares, *Chile* 94 D2
Linares, *Mexico* 84 C5
Linares, *Spain* 18 C4
Linchuan 35 D6
Lincoln, *Argentina* 94 C4
Lincoln, *N.Z.* 65 E5
Lincoln, *U.K.* 11 E6
Lincoln, *U.S.A.* 77 E6
Linden 90 B7
Líndhos 23 F7
Lindi 57 F7
Lingayen 38 A2
Lingayen G. 38 A2
Lingen 14 B4
Lingga 37 E2
Lingga, Kepulauan 37 E2
Lingga Arch. = Lingga, Kepulauan 37 E2
Linguéré 55 E1
Lingyun 35 D5
Linhai 35 D7
Linhares 93 F5
Linköping 9 G11
Linosa, I. 21 G4
Lins 94 A7
Linville 63 A5
Linxia 34 C5
Linz 15 D8
Lion, G. du 13 E6
Lions, G. of = Lion, G. du 13 E6
Lipa 38 B2

Lípari 21 E5
Lípari, Is. = Eólie, Ís. 21 E5
Lipcani 17 D8
Lipetsk 24 C4
Lipkany = Lipcani 17 D8
Lipovets 17 D9
Lippe → 14 C4
Liptrap C. 63 C4
Lira 57 D6
Liria 19 C5
Lisala 56 D4
Lisboa 18 C1
Lisbon = Lisboa 18 C1
Lisburn 11 D3
Lisburne, C. 71 B3
Lishui 35 D6
Lisichansk = Lysychansk 25 D4
Lisieux 12 B4
Liski 24 C4
Lismore 63 A5
Lister, Mt. 96 B15
Liston 63 A5
Listowel 11 E2
Litang 38 C1
Litani → 46 D3
Lithgow 63 B5
Líthinon, Ákra 23 G5
Lithuania ■ 24 B1
Litoměřice 16 C2
Little Barrier I. 64 B6
Little Laut Is. = Laut Kecil, Kepulauan 37 E5
Little Missouri → 76 B3
Little River 65 E5
Little Rock 79 B7
Liukang Tenggaja 39 F1
Liuwa Plain 58 A4
Liuzhou 35 D5
Liverpool, *Australia* 63 B5
Liverpool, *Canada* 69 D4
Liverpool, *U.K.* 11 E5
Liverpool Plains 63 B5
Liverpool Ra. 63 B5
Livingstone 59 B5
Livingstonia 57 G6
Livny 24 C4
Livorno 20 C3
Livramento 94 C5
Liwale 57 F7
Ljubljana 20 A5
Ljungan → 8 F11
Ljusnan → 8 F11
Llancanelo, Salina 94 D3
Llanelli 11 F4
Llanes 18 A3
Llano Estacado 78 C2
Llanos 90 C4
Lleida = Lérida 19 B6
Llobregat → 19 B7
Lloret de Mar 19 B7
Lluchmayor 19 C7
Llullaillaco, Volcán 94 A3
Loa → 94 A2
Lobatse 59 D5
Lobería 94 D5
Lobito 58 A2
Locarno 13 C8
Loch Garman = Wexford 11 E3
Loches 12 C4
Lock 62 B2
Lodhran 42 E7
Lodi, *Italy* 20 B2
Lodi, *U.S.A.* 80 F3
Lodja 56 E4
Lodwar 57 D7
Łódź 16 C4
Lofoten 8 E10
Logan 81 E8
Logan, Mt. 70 B5
Logone → 53 F2
Logroño 19 A4
Lohardaga 40 F5
Loi-kaw 41 H11
Loir → 12 C3
Loire → 12 C2
Loja, *Ecuador* 90 D3
Loja, *Spain* 18 D3
Loji 39 E3
Lokandu 57 E5
Lokitaung 57 D7
Lokoja 55 G6
Lokolama 56 E3
Loliondo 57 E7
Lom 22 C4
Lomami → 56 D4
Lombárdia □ 20 B2
Lombardy = Lombárdia □ 20 B2
Lomblen 39 F2
Lombok 37 F5
Lomé 55 G5
Lomela 56 E4
Lomela → 56 E4
Lomié 56 D2
Lomond, L. 10 C4
Lompobatang 39 F1
Łomza 16 B6
Loncoche 95 D2
Londa 43 M9
London 11 F6
Londonderry 11 D3
Londonderry, C. 60 C4
Londonderry, I. 95 H2
Londrina 94 A6
Long Beach 82 D3
Long I., *Bahamas* 86 B4
Long I., *U.S.A.* 73 D9
Long Xuyen 36 B3
Longford, *Australia* 62 D4
Longford, *Ireland* 11 E3
Longiram 37 E5
Longlac 69 D2
Longnawan 37 D4
Longreach 61 E7
Longview, *Tex., U.S.A.* 79 C6
Longview, *Wash., U.S.A.* 80 B2
Lons-le-Saunier 13 C6
Lop Nor = Lop Nur 34 B4
Lop Nur 34 B4
Lopez, C. 56 E1
Lora → 42 D4
Lora, Hamun-i- 42 E4
Lora Cr. → 62 A2
Lora del Río 18 D3
Lorain 72 D4
Loralai 42 D6
Lorca 19 D5
Lorestān □ 46 D6
Loreto 92 D4
Lorient 12 C2
Lorne 62 C3
Lorraine 13 B7
Los Alamos 83 C9
Los Andes 94 C2
Los Angeles, *Chile* 94 D2
Los Angeles, *U.S.A.* 82 C3
Los Blancos 94 A4
Los Hermanos 90 A6
Los Mochis 84 B3
Los Roques 90 A5
Los Testigos 90 A6
Los Vilos 94 C2
Lošinj 20 B5
Lot → 12 D4
Lota 94 D2
Loubomo 56 E2
Louga 55 E1
Louis Trichardt 59 C5
Louis XIV, Pte. 69 C3
Louisiade Arch. 61 C9
Louisiana □ 79 D8
Louisville 72 E3
Loulé 18 D1
Lourdes 12 E3
Louth, *Australia* 63 B4
Louth, *U.K.* 11 E6
Louvain = Leuven 14 C3
Lovech 22 C5
Low Tatra = Nízké Tatry 16 D4
Lowell 73 C10
Lower California = Baja California 84 A1
Lower Hutt 65 D6
Lower Saxony = Niedersachsen □ 14 B5
Lower Tunguska = Tunguska, Nizhnyaya → 30 C6
Lowestoft 11 E7
Łowicz 16 B4
Lowyar □ 45 C7
Loxton 62 B3
Loyalty Is. = Loyauté, Is. 64 M11
Loyang = Luoyang 35 C6
Loyauté, Is. 64 M11
Loyev = Loyew 17 C10
Loyew 17 C10
Luachimo 56 F4
Luacono 56 G4
Lualaba → 57 D5
Luanda 56 F2
Luangwa 59 B6
Luangwa → 59 A6
Luanshya 59 A5
Luapula → 57 F5
Luarca 18 A2
Luashi 56 G4
Luau 56 G4
Lubalo 56 F3
Lubang Is. 38 B2
Lubbock 78 C3
Lübeck 15 B6
Lubefu 56 E4
Lubero = Luofu 57 E5
Lubin 16 C3
Lublin 17 C6
Lubuagan 38 A2
Lubuk Antu 37 D4
Lubuklinggau 37 E2
Lubuksikaping 37 D2
Lubumbashi 59 A5
Lubutu 57 E5
Lucca 20 C3
Lucena, *Phil.* 38 B2
Lucena, *Spain* 18 D3
Lučenec 16 D4
Lucerne = Luzern 13 C8
Lucira 58 A2
Luckenwalde 15 B7
Lucknow 40 D3
Lüda = Dalian 35 C7
Lüderitz 58 D3
Ludhiana 42 D9
Ludwigsburg 14 D5
Ludwigshafen 14 D5
Luebo 56 F4
Lufira → 57 F5
Lufkin 79 D6
Luga 24 B2
Lugano 13 C8
Lugansk = Luhansk 25 D4
Lugh Ganana 49 G3
Lugo, *Italy* 20 B3
Lugo, *Spain* 18 A2
Lugoj 17 F5
Lugovoy 29 E8
Luhansk 25 D4
Luiana 58 B4
Luimneach = Limerick 11 E2
Luís Correia 92 C5
Luitpold Coast 96 B5
Luiza 56 F4
Luján 94 C5
Lukanga Swamp 59 A5
Lukenie → 56 E3
Lukolela 56 E3
Łuków 17 C6
Lule älv → 8 E12
Luleå 8 E12
Lüleburgaz 22 D6
Lulonga → 56 D3
Lulua → 56 E4
Luluabourg = Kananga 56 F4
Lumai 58 A4
Lumbala N'guimbo 58 A4
Lumsden 65 F3
Lumut, Tg. 37 E3
Lundazi 59 A6
Lundu 37 D3
Lüneburg 14 B6
Lüneburg Heath = Lüneburger Heide 14 B6
Lüneburger Heide 14 B6
Lunéville 13 B7
Lunglei 41 F9
Luni 42 G8
Luni → 43 G7
Luninets = Luninyets 17 B8
Luninyets 17 B8
Luofu 57 E5
Luoyang 35 C6
Luozi 56 E2
Luremo 56 F3
Lurgan 11 D3
Lusaka 59 B5
Lusambo 56 E4
Lushnja 23 D2
Lushoto 57 E7
Luta = Dalian 35 C7
Luton 11 F6
Lutong 36 D4
Lutsk 17 C7

Lützow Holmbukta 96 A8
Luwuk 39 E2
Luxembourg 13 B7
Luxembourg ■ 14 D4
Luxor = El Uqsur 52 C5
Luza 24 A6
Luzern 13 C8
Luzhou 35 D5
Luziânia 93 F4
Luzon 38 A2
Lviv 17 D7
Lvov = Lviv 17 D7
Lyakhavichy 17 B8
Lyakhovskiye, Ostrova 31 B12
Lyallpur = Faisalabad 42 D8
Lydenburg 59 D6
Lydia 23 E7
Lyell 65 D5
Lyepyel 24 C2
Łyna → 16 A5
Lynchburg 73 F6
Lynd Ra. 63 A4
Lyndhurst 62 B2
Lynn Lake 71 C9
Lyon 13 D6
Lyonnais 13 D6
Lyons = Lyon 13 D6
Lys = Leie → 14 C2
Lysychansk 25 D4
Lyttelton 65 E5
Lyubertsy 24 B4
Lyuboml 17 C7

M

Ma'alah 47 F6
Ma'ān 47 E3
Ma'anshan 35 C6
Ma'arrat an Nu'mān 46 D4
Maas → 14 C3
Maastricht 13 A6
Mabrouk 55 E4
Macaé 93 G5
McAllen 78 F4
Macao = Macau ■ 35 D6
Macapá 92 B3
Macau 92 D6
Macau ■ 35 D6
M'Clintock Chan. 70 A9
McComb 79 D8
Macdonnell Ras. 60 E5
McDouall Peak 62 A1
Macdougall L. 70 B10
Macedonia = Makedhonía □ 23 D4
Macedonia ■ 22 D3
Maceió 93 D6
Macenta 55 G3
Macerata 20 C4
Macfarlane, L. 62 B2
Macgillycuddy's Reeks 11 F2
McGregor Ra. 62 A3
Mach 42 E5
Machado = Jiparaná → 91 E6
Machakos 57 E7
Machala 90 D3
Machilipatnam 40 J3
Machiques 90 A4
Machupicchu 91 F4
Macintyre → 63 A5
Mackay 61 E8
Mackay, L. 60 E4
Mackenzie → 70 B6
Mackenzie City = Linden 90 B7
Mackenzie Mts. 70 B6
McKinley, Mt. 71 B4
McKinney 79 C5
Macksville 63 B5
Maclean 63 A5
Maclear 59 E5
Macleay → 63 B5
McMurdo Sd. 96 B15
Mâcon, *France* 13 C6
Macon, *U.S.A.* 75 C6
Macondo 58 A4
McPherson Ra. 63 A5
Macquarie Harbour 62 D4
MacRobertson Land 96 B10
Madagali 53 F1
Madagascar ■ 59 J9
Madā'in Sālih 47 F4
Madama 52 D1
Madang 61 B8
Madaoua 55 F6
Madaripur 41 F8
Madauk 41 J11
Madaya 41 F11
Maddalena 20 D2
Madeira 54 B1
Madeira → 90 D7
Madha 43 L9
Madhya Pradesh □ 43 H10
Madikeri 43 N9
Madimba 56 E3
Madīnat ash Sha'b 49 E3
Madingou 56 E2
Madison 77 D10
Madiun 37 F4
Madras = Tamil Nadu □ 43 P10
Madras 43 N12
Madre, Laguna 78 F5
Madre, Sierra 38 A2
Madre de Dios → 91 F5
Madre de Dios, I. 95 G1
Madre Occidental, Sierra 84 B3
Madrid 18 B4
Madurai 43 Q11
Madurantakam 43 N11
Mae Sot 36 A1
Maebashi 32 A6
Maestrazgo, Mts. del 19 B5
Maevatanana 59 H9
Mafeking = Mafikeng 59 D5
Maffra 63 C4
Mafia I. 57 F7
Mafikeng 59 D5
Mafra, *Brazil* 94 B7
Mafra, *Portugal* 18 C1
Magadan 31 D13
Magadi 57 E7
Magallanes, Estrecho de 95 G2
Magangué 90 B4
Magburaka 55 G2
Magdalena, *Argentina* 94 D5
Magdalena, *Bolivia* 91 F6
Magdalena, *Malaysia* 36 D5
Magdalena → 90 A4
Magdeburg 15 B6
Magelang 37 F4
Magellan's Str. = Magallanes, Estrecho de 95 G2
Maggiore, L. 20 B2
Magnetic Pole (South) = South Magnetic Pole 96 A13
Magnitogorsk 29 D6
Magosa = Famagusta 46 D3
Maguarinho, C. 92 C4
Mağusa = Famagusta 46 D3
Magwe 41 G10
Mahābād 46 C6
Mahabo 59 J8
Mahagi 57 D6
Mahajanga 59 H9
Mahakam → 37 E5
Mahalapye 59 C5
Maḩallāt 44 C2
Mahanadi → 40 G6
Mahanoro 59 H9
Maharashtra □ 43 J9
Mahbubnagar 43 L10
Mahdia 52 A1
Mahenge 57 F7
Maheno 65 F4
Mahesana 43 H8
Mahia Pen. 64 C7
Mahilyow 17 B10
Mahón 19 C8
Mai-Ndombe, L. 56 E3
Maicurú → 92 C3
Maidstone 11 F7
Maiduguri 53 F1
Maijdi 41 F8
Maikala Ra. 40 G3
Main → 14 D5
Maine 12 C3
Maingkwan 41 D11
Mainit, L. 38 C3
Mainland, *Orkney, U.K.* 10 B5
Mainland, *Shet., U.K.* 10 A6
Maintirano 59 H8
Mainz 14 C5
Maipú 94 D5
Maiquetía 90 A5
Mairabari 41 D9
Maitland, *N.S.W., Australia* 63 B5
Maitland, *S. Austral., Australia* 62 B2
Maizuru 32 B4
Majene 39 E1
Maji 53 G6
Majorca = Mallorca 19 C7
Maka 55 F2
Makale 39 E1
Makari 56 B2
Makarikari = Makgadikgadi Salt Pans 59 C5
Makasar = Ujung Pandang 39 F1
Makasar, Selat 39 E1
Makasar, Str. of = Makasar, Selat 39 E1
Makat 29 E6
Makedhonía □ 23 D4
Makedonija = Macedonia ■ 22 D3
Makeni 55 G2
Makeyevka = Makiyivka 25 D4
Makgadikgadi Salt Pans 59 C5
Makhachkala 25 E6
Makian 39 D3
Makindu 57 E7
Makinsk 29 D8
Makiyivka 25 D4
Makkah 47 G4
Makó 16 E5
Makokou 56 D2
Makoua 56 E3
Makrai 43 H10
Makran 45 E5
Makran Coast Range 42 G4
Maksimkin Yar 29 D9
Mākū 46 C6
Makumbi 56 F4
Makurazaki 33 D2
Makurdi 55 G6
Malabang 38 C2
Malabar Coast 43 P9
Malabo = Rey Malabo 56 D1
Malacca, Str. of 36 D1
Maladzyechna 17 A8
Málaga 18 D3
Malakâl 53 G5
Malakand 42 B7
Malang 37 F4
Malanje 56 F3
Mälaren 9 G11
Malargüe 94 D3
Malaryta 17 C7
Malatya 46 C4
Malawi ■ 59 A6
Malawi, L. 59 A6
Malaybalay 38 C3
Malāyer 46 D7
Malaysia ■ 36 D4
Malazgirt 46 C5
Malbooma 62 B1
Malbork 16 A4
Malden I. 65 K15
Maldives ■ 26 J11
Maldonado 94 C6
Malé Karpaty 16 D3
Maléa, Ákra 23 F4
Malegaon 43 J9
Malema 59 A7
Malha 53 E4
Mali ■ 55 E4
Mali → 41 E11
Malik 39 E2
Malili 39 E2
Malin Hd. 10 D3
Malindi 57 E8
Malines = Mechelen 14 C3
Malino 39 D2
Malita 38 C3
Malkara 22 D6
Mallacoota 63 C4
Mallacoota Inlet 63 C4
Mallaig 10 C4
Mallawi 52 C5
Mallorca 19 C7
Mallow 11 E2

Malmö 9 G10
Malolos 38 B2
Malpelo 90 C2
Malta ■ 21 G5
Maltahöhe 58 C3
Maluku 39 E3
Maluku □ 39 E3
Maluku Sea = Molucca Sea 39 E2
Malvan 43 L8
Malvinas, Is. = Falkland Is. □ 95 G5
Malyn 17 C9
Malyy Lyakhovskiy, Ostrov 31 B12
Mamahatun 46 C5
Mamanguape 92 D6
Mamasa 39 E1
Mamberamo → 39 E5
Mambilima Falls 57 G5
Mamburao 38 B2
Mamfe 55 G6
Mamoré → 91 F5
Mamou 55 F2
Mamuju 39 E1
Man 55 G3
Man, I. of 11 D4
Man Na 41 F11
Mana 92 A3
Manaar, G. of = Mannar, G. of 43 Q11
Manacapuru 90 D6
Manacor 19 C7
Manado 39 D2
Managua 85 E7
Manakara 59 J9
Manama = Al Manāmah 44 E2
Mananara 59 H9
Mananjary 59 J9
Manaos = Manaus 90 D7
Manapouri 65 F2
Manapouri, L. 65 F2
Manas 34 B3
Manas → 41 D8
Manasir 44 E2
Manaung 41 H9
Manaus 90 D7
Manay 38 C3
Manchester, *U.K.* 11 E5
Manchester, *U.S.A.* 73 C10
Mand → 44 D3
Manda 57 G6
Mandal 9 G9
Mandalay 41 F11
Mandale = Mandalay 41 F11
Mandalī 46 D6
Mandar, Teluk 39 E1
Mandaue 38 B2
Mandi 42 D10
Mandimba 59 A7
Mandioli 39 E3
Mandla 40 F3
Mandritsara 59 H9
Mandsaur 43 G9
Mandvi 43 H6
Mandya 43 N10
Manfalût 52 C5
Manfred 63 B3
Manfredónia 20 D5
Mangalia 22 C7
Mangalore 43 N9
Mangaweka 64 C6
Manggar 37 E3
Manggawitu 39 E4
Mangkalihat, Tanjung 39 D1
Mangla Dam 42 C8
Mangnai 34 C4
Mango 55 F5
Mangoche 59 A7
Mangole 39 E3
Mangonui 64 A5
Mangueigne 53 F3
Mangueira, L. da 94 C6
Mangyshlak Poluostrov 29 E6
Manhuaçu 93 G5
Manica 59 B6
Manicoré 91 E6
Manicouagan → 69 D4
Manīfah 47 F7
Manihiki 65 L14
Manila 38 B2
Manila B. 38 B2
Manilla 63 B5
Manipur □ 41 E9
Manipur → 41 F10
Manisa 23 E6
Manitoba □ 71 C10
Manitoba, L. 71 C10
Manitowoc 72 B2
Manizales 90 B3
Manja 59 J8
Manjacaze 59 C6
Manjhand 42 G6
Manjil 46 C7
Manjra → 43 K10
Mankono 55 G3
Manly 63 B5
Manmad 43 J9
Manna 37 E2
Mannahill 62 B3
Mannar 43 Q11
Mannar, G. of 43 Q11
Mannar I. 43 Q11
Mannheim 14 D5
Mannum 62 B2
Mano 55 G2
Manokwari 39 E4
Manombo 59 J8
Manono 57 F5
Manosque 13 E6
Manresa 19 B6
Mansa 57 G5
Mansel I. 68 B2
Mansfield, *Australia* 63 C4
Mansfield, *U.K.* 11 E6
Mansfield, *U.S.A.* 72 D4
Manta 90 D2
Mantalingajan, Mt. 36 C5
Mantes-la-Jolie 12 B4
Manthani 43 K11
Mantiqueira, Serra da 93 G5
Mántova 20 B3
Mantua = Mántova 20 B3
Manu 91 F4
Manuae 65 L15
Manuel Alves → 93 E4
Manui 39 E2
Manyara, L. 57 E7
Manych-Gudilo, Ozero 25 D5
Manyoni 57 F6
Manzai 42 C7
Manzanares 18 C4
Manzanillo, *Cuba* 86 B4
Manzanillo, *Mexico* 84 D4
Manzhouli 35 B6
Mao 53 F2
Maoke, Pegunungan 39 E5
Maoming 35 D6
Mapam Yumco 40 B3
Mapia, Kepulauan 39 D4
Mapuera → 90 D7
Maputo 59 D6
Maqnā 47 E3
Maquela do Zombo 56 F3
Maquinchao 95 E3
Mar, Serra do 94 B7
Mar Chiquita, L. 94 C4
Mar del Plata 94 D5
Mar Menor 19 D5
Maraã 90 D5
Marabá 92 D4
Maracá, I. de 92 B3
Maracaibo 90 A4
Maracaibo, L. de 90 B4
Maracay 90 A5
Marādah 52 C2
Maradi 55 F6
Marāgheh 46 C6
Marāh 47 F6
Marajó, I. de 92 C4
Maralal 57 D7
Marama 62 C3
Marampa 55 G2
Marand 46 C6
Maranguape 92 C6
Maranhão = São Luís 92 C5
Maranhão □ 92 D4
Maranoa → 63 A4
Marañón → 90 D4
Marão 59 C6
Maraş = Kahramanmaraş 46 C4
Maratua 39 D1
Marbella 18 D3
Marburg 14 C5
Marche 12 C4
Marchena 18 D3
Mardan 42 B8
Mardin 46 C5
Marek = Stanke Dimitrov 22 C4
Marek 39 E2
Margarita, I. de 90 A6
Margate 11 F7
Margelan = Marghilon 29 E8
Marghilon 29 E8
Mari El □ 24 B6
Mari Republic □ = Mari El □ 24 B6
Maria I. 62 D4
Maria van Diemen, C. 64 A5
Mariana Trench 64 H9
Marianao 86 B3
Ma'rib 49 D4
Maribor 20 A5
Marîdî 53 H4
Marie Byrd Land 96 B18
Marie-Galante 87 C7
Mariecourt = Kangiqsujuaq 68 B3
Mariental 58 C3
Mariinsk 29 D9
Marília 93 G3
Marín 18 A1
Marinduque 38 B2
Maringá 94 A6
Marion 79 A9
Mariscal Estigarribia 91 H6
Maritime Alps = Maritimes, Alpes 13 D7
Maritimes, Alpes 13 D7
Maritsa = Évros → 22 D6
Mariupol 25 D4
Marīvān 46 D6
Markazī □ 44 C2
Markham, Mt. 96 C15
Marks 24 C6
Marla 62 A1
Marmagao 43 M8
Marmara 23 D6
Marmara, Sea of = Marmara Denizi 22 D7
Marmara Denizi 22 D7
Marmaris 23 F7
Marmolada, Mte. 20 A3
Marne → 12 B5
Maroantsetra 59 H9
Marondera 59 B6
Maroni → 92 A3
Maroochydore 63 A5
Maroona 62 C3
Maroua 53 F1
Marovoay 59 H9
Marquesas Is. = Marquises, Is. 65 K17
Marquette 69 D2
Marquises, Is. 65 K17
Marrakech 54 B3
Marrawah 62 D3
Marree 62 A2
Marromeu 59 B7
Marrowie Cr. → 63 B4
Marrupa 59 A7
Marsá Matrûh 52 B4
Marsá Susah 52 B3
Marsabit 57 D7
Marsala 21 F4
Marsden 63 B4
Marseille 13 E6
Marseilles = Marseille 13 E6
Marshall, *Liberia* 55 G2
Marshall, *U.S.A.* 79 C6
Marshall Is. ■ 64 J12
Marshalltown 77 D8
Martaban 41 J11
Martaban, G. of 41 J11
Martapura, *Kalimantan, Indonesia* 37 E4
Martapura, *Sumatera, Indonesia* 37 E2
Marte 53 F1
Martigny 13 C7
Martigues 13 E6
Martin 16 D4
Martina Franca 21 D6
Martinborough 65 D6
Martinique ■ 87 D7
Martinique Passage 87 C7
Martinsville 75 A8
Marton 64 D6
Martos 18 D4
Marudi 37 D4

Ma'ruf 42 D5
Marugame 32 B3
Marulan 63 B5
Marwar 42 G8
Mary 29 F7
Maryborough = Port Laoise 11 E3
Maryborough, *Queens., Australia* 63 A5
Maryborough, *Vic., Australia* 62 C3
Maryland □ 73 E7
Maryvale 63 A5
Marzūq 52 C1
Masaka 57 E6
Masalembo, Kepulauan 37 F4
Masalima, Kepulauan 37 F5
Masamba 39 E2
Masan 35 C7
Masandam, Ras 44 E4
Masasi 57 G7
Masaya 85 E7
Masbate 38 B2
Mascara 54 A5
Masela 39 F3
Maseru 59 D5
Mashābih 47 F4
Mashhad 44 B4
Mashike 32 F12
Mashkel, Hamun-i- 42 E3
Mashki Chāh 42 E3
Masi Manimba 56 E3
Masindi 57 D6
Masisea 91 E4
Masjed Soleyman 47 E7
Mask, L. 11 E2
Masohi 39 E3
Mason City 77 D8
Masqat 45 F4
Massa 20 B3
Massachusetts □ 73 C9
Massaguet 53 F2
Massakory 53 F2
Massangena 59 C6
Massawa = Mitsiwa 53 E6
Massena 73 B8
Massénya 53 F2
Massif Central 13 D5
Massinga 59 C7
Masson I. 96 A11
Mastanli = Momchilgrad 22 D5
Masterton 65 D6
Mastuj 42 A8
Mastung 42 E5
Masty 17 B7
Masuda 32 B2
Masvingo 59 C6
Mataboor 39 E5
Matad 35 B6
Matadi 56 F2
Matagalpa 85 E7
Matagami, L. 69 D3
Matak, P. 37 D3
Matakana 63 B4
Matam 55 E2
Matamoros, *Coahuila, Mexico* 84 B4
Matamoros, *Tamaulipas, Mexico* 84 B5
Ma'ṭan as Sarra 52 D3
Matane 69 D4
Matanzas 86 B3
Matapan, C. = Taínaron, Ákra 23 F4
Mataram 37 F5
Matarani 91 G4
Mataró 19 B7
Mataura 65 G3
Matehuala 84 C4
Matera 21 D6
Mathura 42 F10
Mati 38 C3
Matiri Ra. 65 D5
Matmata 54 B6
Mato Grosso □ 93 E3
Mato Grosso, Planalto do 93 F3
Mato Grosso do Sul □ 93 F3
Matochkin Shar 28 B6
Matosinhos 18 B1
Matrah 45 F4
Matsue 32 B3
Matsumoto 32 A6
Matsusaka 32 B5
Matsuyama 32 C3
Mattagami → 69 C2
Mattancheri 43 Q10
Matterhorn 13 D7
Matthew's Ridge 90 B6
Matucana 91 F3
Matun 42 C6
Maturín 90 B6
Mau Ranipur 43 G11
Maubeuge 13 A5
Maude 63 B3
Maudin Sun 41 K10
Maués 90 D7
Mauganj 40 E3
Maui 82 H12
Maulamyaing = Moulmein 41 J11
Maumere 39 F2
Maun 58 B4
Maungmagan Kyunzu 41 K11
Mauritania ■ 55 D2
Mauritius ■ 51 H9
Mavinga 58 B4
Mawk Mai 41 G11
Mawlaik 41 F10
Mawson Coast 96 A10
Maxixe 59 C7
Mayaguana 87 B5
Mayagüez 87 C6
Maydena 62 D4
Mayenne → 12 C3
Maykop 25 E5
Mayo 70 B6
Mayo L. 70 B6
Mayon Volcano 38 B2
Mayor I. 64 B7
Mayu 39 D3
Mazabuka 59 B5
Mazagán = El Jadida 54 B3
Mazagão 92 C3
Mazán 90 D4
Māzandarān □ 44 B3
Mazar-e Sharīf 45 B6
Mazara del Vallo 21 F4
Mazarredo 95 F3
Mazarrón 19 D5
Mazaruni → 90 B7
Mazatlán 84 C3
Māzhān 44 C4
Mazīnān 44 B4
Mazoe → 59 B6
Mazurian Lakes = Mazurski, Pojezierze 16 B5
Mazurski, Pojezierze 16 B5
Mazyr 17 C9
Mbabane 59 D6
Mbaïki 56 D3
Mbala 57 F6
Mbale 57 D6
Mbalmayo 56 D2
Mbamba Bay 57 G6
Mbandaka 56 D3
Mbanza Congo 56 F2
Mbanza Ngungu 56 F2
Mbarara 57 E6
Mbeya 57 F6
Mbini □ 56 D2
Mbour 55 F1
Mbout 55 E2
Mbuji-Mayi 56 F4
Mbulu 57 E7
Mchinji 59 A6
Mead, L. 82 B5
Mearim → 92 C5
Meaux 13 B5
Mecca = Makkah 47 G4
Mechelen 14 C3
Mecheria 54 B4
Mecklenburg 15 B6
Mecklenburger Bucht 15 A6
Meconta 59 A7
Medan 37 D1
Medanosa, Pta. 95 F3
Medéa 54 A5
Medellín 90 B3
Mederdra 55 E1
Medford 80 D2
Medgidia 22 B7
Mediaş 17 E7
Medicine Bow Ra. 81 E10
Medicine Hat 71 C8
Medina = Al Madīnah 47 F4
Medina del Campo 18 B3
Medina-Sidonia 18 D3
Medinipur 40 F6
Mediterranean Sea 50 C5
Médoc 12 D3
Medveditsa → 24 D5
Medvezhyegorsk 28 C4
Meekatharra 60 F2
Meerut 42 E10
Mega 53 H6
Mégara 23 F4
Meghalaya □ 41 E8
Mei Xian 35 D6
Meiganga 56 C2
Meiktila 41 G10
Meissen 15 C7
Mejillones 94 A2
Mékambo 56 D2
Mekdela 53 F6
Mekhtar 42 D6
Meknès 54 B3
Mekong → 36 C3
Mekongga 39 E2
Mekvari = Kür → 25 E6
Melagiri Hills 43 N10
Melaka 37 D2
Melalap 36 C5
Melanesia 64 K10
Melbourne, *Australia* 63 C3
Melbourne, *U.S.A.* 75 E7
Mélèzes → 68 C3
Melfi 53 F2
Melfort 71 C9
Melilla 19 E4
Melitopol 25 D4
Melk 15 D8
Melo 94 C6
Melolo 39 F2
Melrose 63 B4
Melun 13 B5
Melut 53 F5
Melville 71 C9
Melville I. 60 C5
Melville Pen. 68 B2
Memba 59 G8
Memboro 39 F1
Memel = Klaipėda 24 B1
Memmingen 14 E6
Mempawah 37 D3
Memphis, *Tenn., U.S.A.* 74 B3
Memphis, *Tex., U.S.A.* 78 B3
Ménaka 55 E5
Menan = Chao Phraya → 36 B2
Menate 37 E4
Mendawai → 37 E4
Mende 13 D5
Mendocino, C. 80 E1
Mendoza 94 C3
Mene Grande 90 B4
Menemen 23 E6
Menggala 37 E3
Mengzi 34 D5
Menindee 62 B3
Menindee L. 62 B3
Meningie 62 C2
Menominee 72 B2
Menongue 58 A3
Menorca 19 C7
Mentawai, Kepulauan 37 E1
Menton 13 E7
Meppel 14 B4
Merabéllou, Kólpos 23 G5
Meran = Merano 20 A3
Merano 20 A3
Merauke 39 F6
Merbein 62 B3
Merca 49 G3
Merced 82 B2
Mercedes, *Buenos Aires, Argentina* 94 C5
Mercedes, *Corrientes, Argentina* 94 B5
Mercedes, *San Luis, Argentina* 94 C3
Mercedes, *Uruguay* 94 C5
Merceditas 94 B2
Mercer 64 B6
Mercy C. 68 B4
Meredith, C. 95 G4
Merga = Nukheila 53 E4
Mergui Arch. = Myeik Kyunzu 36 B1
Mérida, *Mexico* 85 C7
Mérida, *Spain* 18 C2

Mérida, *Venezuela* . . . **90 B4**
Mérida, Cord. de **87 E5**
Meridian **74 C3**
Meriruma **92 B3**
Merowe **53 E5**
Merriwa **63 B5**
Merriwagga . . . **63 B4**
Merrygoen **63 B4**
Mersa Fatma . . **49 E3**
Merseburg **15 C6**
Mersin **46 C3**
Mersing **37 D2**
Merthyr Tydfil . **11 F5**
Mértola **18 D2**
Meru **57 D7**
Mesa **83 D7**
Meshed = Mashhad . . . **44 B4**
Meshra er Req **53 G4**
Mesolóngion . . **23 E3**
Mesopotamia = Al Jazirah . . . **46 D5**
Messina, *Italy* . **21 E5**
Messina, *S. Africa* **59 C6**
Messina, Str. di **21 E5**
Messíni **23 F4**
Messiniakós Kólpos **23 F4**
Mesta → **22 D5**
Meta → **90 B5**
Metairie **79 E8**
Metán **94 B4**
Metangula **59 A6**
Metema **53 F6**
Methven **65 E4**
Metil **59 B7**
Metlakatla **71 C6**
Mettur Dam . . . **43 P10**
Metz **13 B7**
Meulaboh **37 D1**
Meureudu **36 C1**
Meuse → **13 A6**
Mexiana, I. **92 C4**
Mexicali **84 A1**
México **84 D5**
México □ **84 D5**
Mexico ■ **84 C4**
Mexico, G. of . . **85 B7**
Meymaneh . . . **42 B4**
Mezen **28 C5**
Mezen → **28 C5**
Mézene **13 D6**
Mezökövesd . . **16 E5**
Mezötúr **16 E5**
Mhow **43 H9**
Miami **75 G7**
Miami Beach . . **75 G7**
Mīāndowāb . . . **46 C6**
Miandrivazo . . . **59 H9**
Mīāneh **46 C6**
Mianwali **42 C7**
Miaoli **35 D7**
Miarinarivo . . . **59 H9**
Miass **29 D7**
Michalovce . . . **17 D5**
Michigan □ . . . **72 C3**
Michigan, L. . . . **72 C2**
Michipicoten . . **69 D2**
Michurin **22 C6**
Michurinsk **24 C5**
Micronesia, Federated States of ■ . . **64 J10**
Middelburg . . . **58 E5**
Middlesbrough **11 D6**
Midi, Canal du → **12 E4**
Midland **78 D3**
Midyat **46 C5**
Midzŏr **22 C4**
Międzychód . . . **16 B2**
Międzyrzec Podlaski **17 C6**
Mielec **16 C5**
Miercurea Ciuc **17 E7**
Mieres **18 A3**
Miguel Alves . . **92 C5**
Mihara **32 B3**
Mikhaylovgrad **22 C4**
Míkonos **23 F5**
Mikura-Jima . . **32 C6**
Milagro **90 D3**
Milan = Milano **20 B2**
Milang **62 B2**
Milano **20 B2**
Milâs **23 F6**
Milazzo **21 E5**
Mildura **62 B3**
Miles **63 A5**
Miletus **23 F6**
Milford Haven . **11 F4**
Milford Sd. . . . **65 F2**
Milḩ, Baḩr al . . **47 D5**
Miliana **54 C5**
Mill I. **96 A12**
Millau **13 D5**
Millicent **62 C3**
Millinocket **73 B11**
Millmerran **63 A5**
Milne Inlet **68 A2**
Mílos **23 F5**
Milparinka P.O. **62 A3**
Milton **65 G3**
Milton Keynes . **11 E6**
Miltou **53 F2**
Milwaukee **72 C2**
Min Chiang → **35 D6**
Min Jiang → . **35 D5**
Mina Pirquitas . **94 A3**
Mīnā Su'ud . . . **47 E7**
Mīnā'al Aḩmadī **47 E7**
Mīnāb **44 E4**
Minamata **32 C2**
Minas **94 C5**
Minas Gerais □ **93 F4**
Minbu **41 G10**
Mindanao **38 C2**
Mindanao Sea = Bohol Sea . . **38 C2**
Mindanao Trench **38 B3**
Minden **14 B5**
Mindiptana . . . **39 F6**
Mindoro **38 B2**
Mindoro Str. . . **38 B2**
Mindouli **56 E2**
Mingäçevir Su Anbarı **25 E6**
Mingan **69 C4**
Mingechaurskoye Vdkhr. = Mingäçevir Su Anbarı **25 E6**
Mingin **41 F10**
Mingt'iehkaitafan = Mintaka Pass **42 A9**
Minho = Miño → **18 B1**
Minho **18 B1**
Minna **55 G6**
Minneapolis . . **77 C8**
Minnedosa **71 C10**
Minnesota □ . . **77 B7**
Minnipa **62 B2**
Miño → **18 B1**
Minorca = Menorca **19 C7**
Minore **63 B4**
Minot **76 A4**
Minsk **24 C2**
Mińsk Mazowiecki . **16 B5**
Mintaka Pass . . **42 A9**
Minto **71 B5**
Minutang **41 C11**
Minvoul **56 D2**
Mir **53 F1**
Mira **20 B4**
Miraj **43 L9**
Miram Shah . . **42 C7**
Miranda **93 G2**
Miranda de Ebro **19 A4**
Miranda do Douro **18 B2**
Miri **36 D4**
Mirim, L. **94 C6**
Mirpur Khas . . **42 G6**
Mirzapur **40 E4**
Mirzapur-cum-Vindhyachal = Mirzapur **40 E4**
Mish'āb, Ra'as al **47 E7**
Mishan **35 B8**
Miskīn **44 F4**
Miskolc **16 D5**
Misool **39 E4**
Misrātah **52 B2**
Misriç **46 C5**
Missinaibi → . **69 C2**
Mississippi □ . **79 C9**
Mississippi → **79 E9**
Mississippi River Delta **79 E9**
Missoula **81 B6**
Missouri □ **77 F8**
Missouri → . . **77 F9**
Mistassini L. . . **69 C3**
Misurata = Misrātah **52 B2**
Mitchell, *Australia* **63 A4**
Mitchell, *U.S.A.* **76 D5**
Mitchell → . . . **61 D7**
Mitilíni **23 E6**
Mito **32 A7**
Mitrovica = Titova-Mitrovica . . . **22 C3**
Mitsinjo **59 H9**
Mitsiwa **53 E6**
Mittagong **63 B5**
Mitú **90 C4**
Mitumba, Chaîne des . . **57 F5**
Mitumba Mts. = Mitumba, Chaîne des . . **57 F5**
Mitwaba **57 F5**
Mitzic **56 D2**
Miyake-Jima . . **32 B6**
Miyako **33 G12**
Miyakonojō . . . **32 D2**
Miyazaki **32 D2**
Miyet, Bahr el = Dead Sea . . . **47 E3**
Mizal **47 G6**
Mizdah **52 B1**
Mizoram □ . . . **41 F9**
Mjøsa **8 F10**
Mladá Boleslav **16 C2**
Mława **16 B5**
Mljet **20 C6**
Mmabatho **59 D5**
Moa **39 F3**
Moabi **56 E2**
Moalie Park . . . **62 A3**
Moba **57 F5**
Mobaye **56 D4**
Mobayi **56 D4**
Mobile **74 D3**
Mobutu Sese Seko, L. = Albert L. **57 D6**
Moçambique . . **59 H8**
Moçâmedes = Namibe **58 B2**
Mochudi **59 C5**
Mocimboa da Praia **57 G8**
Mocoa **90 C3**
Mocuba **59 B7**
Modane **13 D7**
Módena **20 B3**
Modesto **82 B2**
Módica **21 F5**
Moe **63 C4**
Moengo **92 A3**
Mogadishu = Muqdisho . . . **49 G4**
Mogador = Essaouira . . . **54 B3**
Mogami → . . . **33 G12**
Mogaung **41 E11**
Mogi das Cruzes **94 A7**
Mogi-Mirim . . . **94 A7**
Mogilev = Mahilyow . . . **17 B10**
Mogilev-Podolskiy = Mohyliv-Podilskyy . . . **17 D8**
Mogoi **39 E4**
Mogok **41 F11**
Mohács **16 F4**
Moḩammadābād **44 B4**
Mohoro **57 F7**
Mohyliv-Podilskyy . . . **17 D8**
Mointy **29 E8**
Moisie **69 C4**
Moisie → **69 C4**
Moïssala **53 G2**
Mojave Desert . **82 C4**
Mokai **64 C6**
Mokokchung . . **41 D10**
Mokra Gora . . . **22 C3**
Molchanovo . . **29 D9**
Moldavia ■ = Moldova ■ . . **17 E9**
Molde **8 F9**
Moldova ■ . . . **17 E9**
Moldoveana . . **17 F7**
Molepolole . . . **59 C5**
Molfetta **20 D6**
Moline **77 E9**
Moliro **57 F6**
Mollendo **91 G4**
Molodechno = Maladzyechna **17 A8**
Molokai **82 H12**
Molong **63 B4**
Molopo → . . . **58 D4**
Molotov = Perm **29 D6**
Moloundou . . . **56 D3**
Molu **39 F4**
Molucca Sea . . **39 E2**
Moluccas = Maluku **39 E3**
Moma **59 B7**
Mombasa **57 E7**
Momchilgrad . . **22 D5**

Mompós 90 B4
Mon → 41 G10
Mona, Canal de la 87 C6
Monaco ■ 13 E7
Monahans 78 D2
Monastir = Bitola 22 D3
Monastir 52 A1
Moncayo, Sierra del 19 B5
Mönchengladbach 14 C4
Monchique 18 D1
Monclova 84 B4
Mondego → 18 B1
Mondeodo 39 E2
Mondovì 20 B1
Monforte de Lemos 18 A2
Mong Hsu 41 G12
Mong Kung 41 G11
Mong Nai 41 G11
Mong Pawk 41 F12
Mong Ton 41 G12
Mong Wa 41 G13
Mong Yai 41 F12
Mongalla 53 G5
Monghyr = Munger 40 E6
Mongibello = Etna 21 F5
Mongo 53 F2
Mongolia ■ 35 B5
Mongororo 53 F3
Mongu 58 B4
Monkoto 56 E4
Monópoli 21 D6
Monqoumba 56 D3
Monroe, *La., U.S.A.* 79 C7
Monroe, *N.C., U.S.A.* 75 B7
Monrovia 55 G2
Mons 14 C2
Monse 39 E2
Mont-de-Marsan 12 E3
Mont-St.-Michel, Le = Le Mont-St.-Michel 12 B3
Montalbán 19 B5
Montana □ 81 B9
Montargis 13 C5
Montauban 12 D4
Montbéliard 13 C7
Montceau-les-Mines 13 C6
Monte Alegre 92 C3
Monte Azul 93 F5
Monte-Carlo 20 C1
Monte Caseros 94 C5
Monte Comán 94 C3
Monte Santu, C. di 21 D2
Montecristi 90 D2
Montecristo 20 C3
Montego Bay 86 C4
Montélimar 13 D6
Montemorelos 84 B5
Montenegro □ 22 C2
Montepuez 59 A7
Monterey 82 B2
Montería 90 B3
Monterrey 84 B4
Montes Claros 93 F5
Montesilvano Marina 20 C5
Montevideo 94 C5
Montgomery = Sahiwal 42 D8
Montgomery 74 C4
Montijo 18 C2
Montilla 18 D3
Montluçon 13 C5
Montmorillon 12 C4
Montoro 18 C3
Montpellier 13 E5
Montréal 69 D3
Montreux 13 C7
Montrose, *U.K.* 10 C5
Montrose, *U.S.A.* 83 A9
Montserrat ■ 87 C7
Monveda 56 D4
Monywa 41 F10
Monza 20 B2
Monze 59 B5
Monze, C. 43 G5
Monzón 19 B6
Moolawatana 62 A2
Moomin Cr. → 63 A4
Moonie 63 A5
Moonie → 63 A4
Moonta 62 B2
Mooroopna 63 C4
Moose Jaw 71 C9
Moosomin 71 C9
Moosonee 69 C2
Mopeia Velha 59 B7
Mopti 55 F4
Moquegua 91 G4
Mora 8 F10
Moradabad 42 E11
Morafenobe 59 H8
Moramanga 59 H9
Moratuwa 43 R11
Morava →, *Serbia, Yug.* 22 B3
Morava →, *Slovak Rep.* 16 D3
Moravian Hts. = Ceskomoravská Vrchovina 16 D2
Morawhanna 90 B7
Moray Firth 10 C5
Morden 71 D10
Mordovian Republic □ = Mordvinia □ 24 C5
Mordvinia □ 24 C5
Morea 62 C3
Moree 63 A4
Morelia 84 D4
Morella 19 B5
Morena, Sierra 18 C3
Moreton I. 63 A5
Morgan 62 B2
Morgan City 79 E8
Morioka 33 G12
Morlaix 12 B2
Mornington 63 C4
Mornington, I. 95 F1
Moro G. 38 C2
Morocco ■ 54 B3
Morococha 91 F3
Morogoro 57 F7
Morombe 59 J8
Morón 86 B4
Mörön → 35 B6
Morón de la Frontera 18 D3
Morondava 59 J8
Morotai 39 D3
Moroto 57 D6
Morphou 46 D3
Morrinhos 93 F4
Morrinsville 64 B6
Morristown 75 A6
Morrumbene 59 C7
Morshansk 24 C5
Morteros 94 C4
Mortes, R. das → 93 E3
Mortlake 62 C3
Morundah 63 B4
Moruya 63 C5
Morvan 13 C6
Morven 63 A4
Morwell 63 C4
Moscos Is. 41 L11
Moscow = Moskva 24 B4
Moscow 80 B5
Mosel → 13 A7
Moselle = Mosel → 13 A7
Mosgiel 65 F4
Moshi 57 E7
Moskva 24 B4
Moskva → 24 B4
Moson-magyaróvar 16 E3
Mosquera 90 C3
Moss Vale 63 B5
Mossaka 56 E3
Mossburn 65 F3
Mosselbaai 58 E4
Mossendjo 56 E2
Mossgiel 63 B3
Mossoró 92 D6
Mossuril 59 G8
Most 16 C1
Mostaganem 54 A5
Mostar 20 C6
Mostardas 94 C6
Mostiska = Mostyska 17 D6
Mosty = Masty 17 B7
Mostyska 17 D6
Mosul = Al Mawşil 46 C5
Motihari 40 D5
Motril 18 D4
Motueka 65 D5
Motueka → 65 D5
Mouanda 56 E2
Moúdhros 23 E5
Moudjeria 55 E2
Mouila 56 E2
Moulamein 63 C3
Moulins 13 C5
Moulmein 41 J11
Moundou 53 G2
Mount Barker 62 C2
Mount Darwin 59 B6
Mount Eba 62 B2
Mount Gambier 62 C3
Mount Hope, *N.S.W., Australia* 63 B4
Mount Hope, *S. Austral., Australia* 62 B2
Mount Howitt 62 A3
Mount Isa 61 E6
Mount Lofty Ra. 62 B2
Mount McKinley National Park 71 B4
Mount Margaret 63 A3
Mount Maunganui 64 B7
Mount Olympus = Uludağ 23 D7
Mount Perry 63 A5
Mount Vernon 73 D9
Mountain View 82 B1
Moura, *Brazil* 90 D6
Moura, *Portugal* 18 C2
Mourdi, Dépression du 53 E3
Mourdiah 55 F3
Moussoro 53 F2
Moutohara 64 C7
Moutong 39 D2
Moyale 57 D7
Moyamba 55 G2
Moyen Atlas 54 B3
Moyo 37 F5
Moyyero → 30 C8
Mozambique = Moçambique 59 H8
Mozambique ■ 59 B7
Mozambique Chan. 59 H8
Mozdok 25 E5
Mozyr = Mazyr 17 C9
Mpanda 57 F6
Mpika 59 A6
Mpwapwa 57 F7
Msaken 52 A1
Msoro 59 A6
Mu Us Shamo 35 C5
Muaná 92 C4
Muar 37 D2
Muarabungo 37 E2
Muaraenim 37 E2
Muarajuloi 37 E4
Muarakaman 37 E5
Muaratebo 37 E2
Muaratembesi 37 E2
Muaratewe 37 E4
Mubarraz = Al Mubarraz 47 F7
Mubende 57 D6
Mubi 53 F1
Muckadilla 63 A4
Muconda 56 G4
Mucuri 93 F6
Mudanjiang 35 B7
Mudanya 23 D7
Mudgee 63 B4
Mufulira 59 A5
Muğla 23 F7
Mugu 40 C4
Muhammad Qol 52 D6
Mühlhausen 14 C6
Mühlig Hofmann fjell 96 B7
Mukacheve 17 D6
Mukachevo = Mukacheve 17 D6
Mukah 37 D4
Mukden = Shenyang 35 B7
Mukomuko 37 E2
Muktsar 42 D9
Mukur 42 C5
Mula 19 C5
Mulchén 94 D2
Mulde → 15 C7
Mulgathing 62 B1
Mulgrave 69 D4
Mulhacén 18 D4
Mulhouse 13 C7
Mull 10 C4
Mullengudgery 63 B4
Muller, Pegunungan 37 D4
Mullingar 11 E3
Mullumbimby 63 A5
Multan 42 D7
Mulwala 63 C4
Mumbaī = Bombay 43 K8
Mumbwa 59 A5
Muna 39 F2
München 15 D6

Munchen-Gladbach = Mönchengladbach 14 C4
Muncie 72 D3
Mundala 39 E6
Münden 14 C5
Mundo Novo 93 E5
Mungallala 63 A4
Mungallala Cr. → 63 A4
Mungbere 57 D5
Munger 40 E6
Mungindi 63 A4
Munhango 58 A3
Munich = München 15 D6
Muñoz Gamero, Pen. 95 G2
Münster 14 C4
Munster □ 11 E2
Muntok 37 E3
Mupa 58 B3
Muqdisho 49 G4
Murallón, Cuerro 95 F2
Murang'a 57 E7
Murashi 24 B6
Muratlı 22 D6
Murchison → 60 F1
Murchison, Mt. 96 B15
Murchison Falls = Kabarega Falls 57 D6
Murcia 19 C5
Murcia □ 19 D5
Mureş → 16 E5
Mureşul = Mureş → 16 E5
Murfreesboro 74 B4
Murgab = Murghob 29 F8
Murghob 29 F8
Murgon 63 A5
Müritz-see 15 B7
Murmansk 28 C4
Murom 24 B5
Muroran 32 F12
Muroto-Misaki 32 C4
Murray → 62 C2
Murray Bridge 62 C2
Murree 42 C8
Murrumbidgee → 62 B3
Murrumburrah 63 B4
Murrurundi 63 B5
Murtoa 62 C3
Murwara 40 F3
Murwillumbah 63 A5
Mürzzuschlag 15 E8
Muş 46 C5
Mûsa, G. 47 E3
Musa Khel 42 D6
Mūsá Qal'eh 42 C4
Musaffargarh 42 D7
Musala, *Bulgaria* 22 C4
Musala, *Indonesia* 37 D1
Musay'īd 44 E2
Muscat = Masqat 45 F4
Muscat & Oman = Oman ■ 48 C6
Muscatine 77 E9
Musgrave Ras. 60 F5
Mushie 56 E3
Musi → 37 E2
Muskogee 79 B6
Musmar 53 E6
Musoma 57 E6
Mussoorie 42 D11
Mustafakemalpaşa 23 D7
Mustang 40 C4
Musters, L. 95 F3
Muswellbrook 63 B5
Mût, *Egypt* 52 C4
Mut, *Turkey* 46 C3
Mutare 59 B6
Muting 39 F6
Mutoray 30 C8
Muxima 56 F2
Muynak 29 E6
Muzaffarabad 42 B8
Muzaffarnagar 42 E10
Muzaffarpur 40 D5
Muzhi 28 C7
Muztag 34 C3
Mvuma 59 B6
Mwanza, *Tanzania* 57 E6
Mwanza, *Dem. Rep. of the Congo* 57 F5
Mweka 56 E4
Mwenezi 59 C6
Mwenga 57 E5
Mweru, L. 57 F5
Mwinilunga 58 A4
My Tho 36 B3
Myanaung 41 H10
Myanmar = Burma ■ 41 G11
Myaungmya 41 J10
Mycenæ 23 F4
Myeik Kyunzu 36 B1
Myingyan 41 G10
Myitkyina 41 E11
Mykolayiv 25 D3
Mymensingh 41 E8
Mysia 23 E6
Mysore = Karnataka □ 43 N10
Mysore 43 N10
Myszków 16 C4
Mytishchi 24 B4

N

Na Hearadh = Harris 10 C3
Naab → 15 D7
Naberezhnyye Chelny 29 D6
Nabeul 52 A1
Nabire 39 E5
Nablus = Nābulus 46 D3
Nābulus 46 D3
Nachingwea 57 G7
Nackara 62 B2
Nacogdoches 79 D6
Nacozari 84 A3
Nadiad 43 H8
Nadūshan 44 C3
Nadvirna 17 D7
Nadvornaya = Nadvirna 17 D7
Nadym 28 C8
Nadym → 28 C8
Nafada 55 F7
Nafūd ad Dahy 47 G6
Nafud Desert = An Nafūd 47 E5
Naga 38 B2
Nagaland □ 41 E10
Nagano 32 A6
Nagaoka 33 G11
Nagappattinam 43 P11
Nagar Parkar 43 G7
Nagasaki 32 C1
Nagaur 42 F8
Nagercoil 43 Q10
Nagīneh 44 C4
Nagoya 32 B5
Nagpur 43 J11
Nagykanizsa 16 E3
Nagykörös 16 E4
Nahanni Butte 70 B7
Nahāvand 46 D7
Nā'ifah 48 D5
Nain, *Canada* 68 C4
Nā'īn, *Iran* 44 C3
Nairn 10 C5
Nairobi 57 E7
Naivasha 57 E7
Najafābād 44 C2
Najd 47 F5
Najibabad 42 E11
Nakamura 32 C3
Nakfa 53 E6
Nakhichevan = Naxçıvan 25 F6
Nakhichevan Republic □ = Naxçıvan □ 25 F6
Nakhodka 31 E11
Nakhon Phanom 36 A2
Nakhon Ratchasima 36 B2
Nakhon Sawan 36 A2
Nakhon Si Thammarat 36 C2
Nakina 69 C2
Nakuru 57 E7
Nal → 42 G4
Nalchik 25 E5
Nalgonda 43 L11
Nallamalai Hills 43 M11
Nālūt 52 B1
Nam Co 34 C4
Nam-Phan 36 B3
Namacurra 59 B7
Namak, Daryācheh-ye 44 C3
Namak, Kavir-e 44 C4
Namaland 58 C3
Namangan 29 E8
Namapa 59 A7
Namber 39 E4
Nambour 63 A5
Nambucca Heads 63 B5
Nameh 37 D5
Namib Desert = Namibwoestyn 58 C2
Namibe 58 B2
Namibia ■ 58 C3
Namibwoestyn 58 C2
Namlea 39 E3
Namoi → 63 B4
Nampa 80 D5
Nampula 59 B7
Namrole 39 E3
Namse Shankou 40 C4
Namtu 41 F11
Namur 14 C3
Namutoni 58 B3
Namwala 59 B5
Nanaimo 71 D7
Nanango 63 A5
Nanao 32 A5
Nanchang 35 D6
Nanching = Nanjing 35 C6
Nanchong 35 C5
Nancy 13 B7
Nanda Devi 42 D11
Nanded 43 K10
Nandewar Ra. 63 B5
Nandurbar 43 J9
Nandyal 43 M11
Nanga-Eboko 56 D2
Nanga Parbat 42 B9
Nangapinoh 37 E4
Nangarhár □ 42 B7
Nangatayap 37 E4
Nanjing 35 C6
Nanking = Nanjing 35 C6
Nanning 35 D5
Nanping 35 D6
Nansei-Shotō = Ryūkyū-rettō 35 D7
Nantes 12 C3
Nanuque 93 F5
Nanusa, Kepulauan 38 D3
Nanyang 35 C6
Nanyuki 57 D7
Nao, C. de la 19 C6
Naoetsu 32 A6
Napa 80 F2
Napier 64 C7
Naples = Nápoli 21 D5
Naples 75 F7
Napo → 90 D4
Nápoli 21 D5
Nappa Merrie 62 A3
Nara, *Japan* 32 B4
Nara, *Mali* 55 E3
Naracoorte 62 C3
Naradhan 63 B4
Narasapur 40 J3
Narathiwat 36 C2
Narayanganj 41 F8
Narayanpet 43 L10
Narbonne 13 E5
Nardò 23 D2
Narew → 16 B5
Narin 42 A6
Narmada → 43 J8
Narooma 63 C5
Narrabri 63 B4
Narran → 63 A4
Narrandera 63 B4
Narromine 63 B4
Narsimhapur 43 H11
Narva 24 B2
Narvik 8 E11
Naryan-Mar 28 C6
Naryilco 62 A3
Narym 29 D9
Narymskoye 29 E9
Naryn 29 E8
Nasarawa 55 G6
Naseby 65 F4
Naser, Buheirat en 52 D5
Nashville 74 A4
Nasik 43 K8
Nasirabad 42 F9
Nassau 86 A4
Nassau, B. 95 H3
Nasser, L. = Naser, Buheirat en 52 D5
Nat Kyizin 41 K11
Nata 59 C5
Natagaima 90 C3
Natal, *Brazil* 92 D6
Natal, *Indonesia* 37 D1

Naţanz 44 C2
Natashquan 69 C4
Natashquan → 69 C4
Natchez 79 D8
Nathalia 63 C4
Nathdwara 43 G8
Natitingou 55 F5
Natron, L. 57 E7
Natuna Besar, Kepulauan 37 D3
Natuna Is. = Natuna Besar, Kepulauan 37 D3
Natuna Selatan, Kepulauan 37 D3
Naturaliste, C. 62 D4
Naumburg 15 C6
Nauru ■ 64 K11
Naushahra = Nowshera 42 B8
Nauta 90 D4
Nautanwa 40 D4
Navahrudak 17 B7
Navalmoral de la Mata 18 C3
Navarino, I. 95 H3
Navarra □ 19 A5
Năvodari 22 B7
Navoi = Nawoiy 29 E7
Navojoa 84 B3
Návpaktos 23 E3
Návplion 23 F4
Navsari 43 J8
Nawabshah 42 F6
Nawakot 40 D5
Nawalgarh 42 F9
Nawāṣīf, Harrat 47 G5
Nawoiy 29 E7
Naxçıvan 25 F6
Naxçıvan □ 25 F6
Náxos 23 F5
Nāy Band 44 E3
Nazas → 84 B4
Nazilli 23 F7
Nazir Hat 41 F8
Ncheu 59 A6
Ndalatando 56 F2
Ndélé 56 C4
Ndendé 56 E2
Ndjamena 53 F1
Ndjolé 56 E2
Ndola 59 A5
Neagh, Lough 11 D3
Near Is. 71 C1
Neath 11 F5
Nebine Cr. → 63 A4
Nebitdag 29 F6
Nebraska □ 76 E5
Nébrodi, Monti 21 F5
Neckar → 14 D5
Necochea 94 D5
Neemuch = Nimach 43 G9
Neepawa 71 C10
Nefta 54 B6
Neftçala 46 C7
Negapatam = Nagappattinam 43 P11
Negele 49 F2
Negombo 43 R11
Negotin 22 B4
Negra Pt. 38 A2
Negrais, C. = Maudin Sun 41 K10
Negro →, *Argentina* 95 E4
Negro →, *Brazil* 90 D6
Negro →, *Uruguay* 94 C5
Negros 38 C2
Nehbandān 45 D5
Nei Monggol Zizhiqu □ 35 B6
Neijiang 35 D5
Neiva 90 C3
Nejd = Najd 47 F5
Nekemte 53 G6
Nellore 43 M11
Nelson, *Canada* 71 D8
Nelson, *N.Z.* 65 D5
Nelson → 71 C10
Nelson, C. 62 C3
Nelson, Estrecho 95 G2
Nelspruit 59 D6
Néma 55 E3
Neman → 24 B1
Nemunas = Neman → 24 B1
Nemuro 32 F13
Nemuro-Kaikyō 32 F13
Nenagh 11 E2
Nenana 71 B5
Nenjiang 35 B7
Nepal ■ 40 D5
Nepalganj 40 C3
Neretva → 20 C6
Ness, L. 10 C4
Nesterov 17 C6
Nesvizh = Nyasvizh 17 B8
Netherlands ■ 14 B3
Netherlands Antilles ■ 87 D6
Nettilling L. 68 B3
Neubrandenburg 15 B7
Neuchâtel 13 C7
Neuchâtel, Lac de 13 C7
Neumünster 14 A5
Neunkirchen 14 D4
Neuquén 94 D3
Neuruppin 15 B7
Neustrelitz 15 B7
Neva → 24 B3
Nevada □ 80 F5
Nevada, Sierra, *Spain* 18 D4
Nevada, Sierra, *U.S.A.* 80 F3
Nevers 13 C5
Nevertire 63 B4
Nevinnomyssk 25 E5
Nevis 87 C7
Nevşehir 46 C3
New Amsterdam 90 B7
New Angledool 63 A4
New Bedford 73 D10
New Bern 75 B9
New Brighton 65 E5
New Britain, *Papua N. G.* 64 K10
New Britain, *U.S.A.* 73 D9
New Brunswick □ 69 D4
New Caledonia ■ 64 M11
New Delhi 42 E10
New England Ra. 63 B5
New Glasgow 69 D4
New Guinea 64
New Hampshire □ 73 C10
New Haven 73 D9
New Hebrides = Vanuatu ■ 64 L11
New Ireland 64 K10
New Jersey □ 73 E9
New London 73 D9
New Mexico □ 83 C9
New Norfolk 62 D4
New Orleans 79 E8
New Plymouth 64 C6
New Providence 86 A4
New Siberian Is. = Novosibirskiye Ostrova 31 B12
New South Wales □ 63 B4
New Westminster 71 D7
New York □ 73 C8
New York City 73 D9
New Zealand ■ 64 D7
Newala 57 G7
Newark 73 D8
Newburgh 73 D8
Newbury 11 F6
Newcastle, *Australia* 63 B5
Newcastle, *S. Africa* 59 D5
Newcastle-upon-Tyne 11 D6
Newfoundland □ 69 C5
Newman 60 E2
Newport, *I. of W., U.K.* 11 F6
Newport, *Newp., U.K.* 11 F5
Newport, *U.S.A.* 73 D10
Newport News 73 F7
Newquay 11 F4
Newry 11 D3
Newton Boyd 63 A5
Neya 24 B5
Neyrīz 44 D3
Neyshābūr 44 B4
Nezhin = Nizhyn 24 C3
Ngabang 37 D3
Ngabordamlu, Tanjung 39 F4
Ngami Depression 58 C4
Nganglong Kangri 40 A3
Ngaoundéré 56 C2
Ngapara 65 F4
Ngoring Hu 34 C4
Ngudu 57 E6
Nguigmi 53 F1
Nguru 55 F7
Nha Trang 36 B3
Nhill 62 C3
Niafounké 55 E4
Niagara Falls, *Canada* 69 D3
Niagara Falls, *U.S.A.* 73 C6
Niah 37 D4
Niamey 55 F5
Niangara 57 D5
Nias 37 D1
Nicaragua ■ 85 E7
Nicaragua, L. de 85 E7
Nicastro 21 E6
Nice 13 E7
Nichinan 33 D2
Nicobar Is. 27 J13
Nicosia 46 D3
Nicoya, Pen. de 85 F7
Niedersachsen □ 14 B5
Niemen = Neman → 24 B1
Nienburg 14 B5
Nieuw Amsterdam 92 A2
Nieuw Nickerie 92 A2
Niğde 46 C3
Niger ■ 55 E6
Niger → 55 G6
Nigeria ■ 55 G6
Nightcaps 65 F3
Nii-Jima 32 B6
Niigata 33 G11
Niihama 32 C3
Niihau 82
Nijmegen 14 C3
Nikiniki 39 F2
Nikki 55 G5
Nikolayev = Mykolayiv 25 D3
Nikolayevsk 24 C6
Nikopol 25 D3
Nīkshahr 45 E5
Nikšić 22 C2
Nîl, Nahr en → 52 B5
Nîl el Abyad → 53 E5
Nîl el Azraq → 53 E5
Nile = Nîl, Nahr en → 52 B5
Nimach 43 G9
Nîmes 13 E6
Nimfaíon, Ákra = Pínnes, Ákra 23 D5
Nimmitabel 63 C4
Nīmrūz □ 45 D5
Nimule 57 D6
Nīnawá 46 C5
Nindigully 63 A4
Nineveh = Nīnawá 46 C5
Ningbo 35 D7
Ningde 35 D6
Ningpo = Ningbo 35 D7
Ningsia Hui A.R. = Ningxia Huizu Zizhiqu □ 35 C5
Ningxia Huizu Zizhiqu □ 35 C5
Niobrara → 76 D5
Nioro du Sahel 55 E3
Niort 12 C3
Nipawin 71 C9
Nipigon, L. 69 D2
Niquelândia 93 E4
Nirmal 43 K11
Nirmali 40 D6
Niš 22 C3
Nişāb, *Si. Arabia* 47 E6
Nişāb, *Yemen* 49 E4
Nishinomiya 32 B4
Nistru = Dnister → 17 E10
Niţā' 47 F7
Niterói 93 G5
Nitra 16 D4
Nitra → 16 E4
Niue 65 L14
Niut 37 D4
Nivernais 13 C5
Nizamabad 43 K11
Nizamghat 41 C10
Nizhne-Vartovsk 29 C8
Nizhneyansk 31 B11
Nizhniy Novgorod 24 B5

Nizhniy Tagil 29 D6
Nizhyn 24 C3
Nizip 46 C4
Nízké Tatry 16 D4
Njombe 57 F6
Nkambe 55 G7
Nkawkaw 55 G4
Nkhata Bay 57 G6
Nkhota Kota 59 A6
Nkongsamba 56 D1
Nmai → 41 E11
Noakhali = Maijdi 41 F8
Noatak 71 B3
Nobeoka 32 C2
Nocera Inferiore 21 D5
Nockatunga 62 A3
Nogales, *Mexico* 84 A2
Nogales, *U.S.A.* 83 E7
Nōgata 32 C2
Noginsk 30 C7
Noire, Mts. 12 B2
Noirmoutier, I. de 12 C2
Nok Kundi 42 E3
Nokhtuysk 30 C9
Nokomis 71 C9
Nola 56 D3
Nome 71 B3
Nong Khai 36 A2
Noondoo 63 A4
Nóqui 56 F2
Noranda 69 D3
Nord-Ostsee-Kanal → 14 A5
Nordegg 71 C8
Norderney 14 B4
Norderstedt 14 B5
Nordfriesische Inseln 14 A5
Nordhausen 14 C6
Nordkapp 8 D13
Nordrhein-Westfalen □ 14 C4
Nordvik 30 B9
Norfolk 73 F7
Norfolk I. 64 M11
Norilsk 30 C6
Norley 63 A3
Norman 78 B5
Norman Wells 70 B7
Normandie 12 B4
Normandy = Normandie 12 B4
Normanton 61 D7
Norquinco 95 E2
Norrköping 9 G11
Norrland 8 F11
Norseman 60 G3
North Battleford 71 C9
North Bay 69 D3
North Bend 80 D1
North C. 64 A5
North Cape = Nordkapp 8 D13
North Carolina □ 75 B7
North Channel, *Canada* 69 D2
North Channel, *U.K.* 11 D4
North Dakota □ 76 B4
North Frisian Is. = Nordfriesische Inseln 14 A5
North I. 64 B5
North Korea ■ 35 C7
North Lakhimpur 41 D10
North Minch 10 B4
North Ossetia □ 25 E5
North Pagai, I. = Pagai Utara 37 E2
North Platte 76 E4
North Platte → 76 E4
North Rhine Westphalia □ = Nordrhein-Westfalen □ 14 C4
North Saskatchewan → 71 C8
North Sea 10 D8
North Sporades = Voríai Sporádhes 23 E4
North Taranaki Bight 64 C6
North Thompson → 71 C7
North Uist 10 C3
North West C. 60 E1
North West Frontier □ 42 B8
North West Highlands 10 C4
North West River 69 C4
North West Territories □ 70 B7
Northampton 11 E6
Northern Circars 40 J4
Northern Ireland □ 11 D3
Northern Marianas ■ 64 H9
Northern Territory □ 60 D5
Northland □ 64 A5
Northumberland, C. 62 C3
Northumberland Str. 69 D4
Norton Sd. 71 B3
Norway ■ 8 F10
Norway House 71 C10
Norwegian Sea 6 B5
Norwich 11 E7
Nosok 28 B9
Noşratābād 45 D4
Nossob → 58 D4
Nosy Bé 59 G9
Nosy Boraha 59 H9
Nosy Mitsio 59 G9
Nosy Varika 59 J9
Noteć → 16 B2
Noto-Hanto 33 G11
Notre Dame B. 69 D5
Notre Dame de Koartac = Quaqtaq 68 B4
Notre Dame d'Ivugivic = Ivujivik 68 B3
Nottaway → 69 C3
Nottingham 11 E6
Nouâdhibou 54 D1
Nouâdhibou, Ras 54 D1
Nouakchott 55 E1
Nouméa 64 M11
Noupoort 58 E4
Nouveau Comptoir = Wemindji 69 C3
Nouvelle-Calédonie = New Caledonia ■ 64 M11
Nova Casa Nova 93 D5
Nova Cruz 92 D6
Nova Friburgo 93 G5
Nova Gaia = Cambundi-Catembo 56 G3
Nova Iguaçu 93 G5
Nova Iorque 92 D5
Nova Lima 93 F5
Nova Mambone 59 C7
Nova Scotia □ 69 D4
Nova Sofala 59 C6
Nova Venécia 93 F5
Nova Zagora 22 C5
Novara 20 B2
Novaya Ladoga 24 A3
Novaya Lyalya 29 D7
Novaya Zemlya 28 B6
Nové Zámky 16 D4
Novgorod 24 B3
Novgorod-Severskiy = Novhorod-Siverskyy 24 C3
Novhorod-Siverskyy 24 C3
Novi Lígure 20 B2
Novi Pazar 22 C3
Novi Sad 22 B2
Novo Mesto 20 B5
Novo Remanso 93 D5
Novoataysk 29 D9
Novocherkassk 25 D5
Novogrudok = Navahrudak 17 B7
Novohrad-Volynskyy 17 C8
Novokazalinsk = Zhangaqazaly 29 E7
Novokuybyshevsk 24 C6
Novokuznetsk 29 D9
Novomoskovsk 24 C4
Novorossiysk 25 E4
Novorybnoye 30 B8
Novoselytsya 17 D8
Novoshakhtinsk 25 D4
Novosibirsk 29 D9
Novosibirskiye Ostrova 31 B12
Novotroitsk 29 D6
Novouzensk 24 C6
Novovolynsk 17 C7
Novska 20 B6
Novyy Port 28 C8
Now Shahr 44 B2
Nowa Sól 16 C2
Nowgong 41 D9
Nowra 63 B5
Nowshera 42 B8
Nowy Sącz 16 D5
Nowy Targ 16 D5
Nowy Tomyśl 16 B3
Noyon 13 B5
Nsanje 59 B7
Nsawam 55 G4
Nsukka 55 G6
Nubian Desert = Nûbîya, Es Sahrâ En 52 D5
Nûbîya, Es Sahrâ En 52 D5
Nuboai 39 E5
Nueltin L. 70 B10
Nueva Imperial 94 D2
Nueva Rosita 84 B4
Nuéve de Julio 94 D4
Nuevitas 86 B4
Nuevo, G. 95 E4
Nuevo Laredo 84 B5
Nugget Pt. 65 G3
Nuhaka 64 C7
Nukey Bluff 62 B2
Nukheila 53 E4
Nukus 29 E6
Nulato 71 B4
Nullarbor Plain 60 G4
Numalla, L. 63 A3
Numan 53 G1
Numazu 32 B6
Numfoor 39 E4
Numurkah 63 C4
Nunavut □ 66 C10
Nuneaton 11 E6
Nunivak I. 71 B3
Nunkun 42 C10
Núoro 21 D2
Nuremberg = Nürnberg 15 D6
Nuriootpa 62 B2
Nürnberg 15 D6
Nurran, L. = Terewah, L. 63 A4
Nusa Tenggara Barat □ 37 F5
Nusa Tenggara Timur □ 39 F2
Nushki 42 E5
Nutak 68 C4
Nuuk = Godthåb 68 B5
Nuwakot 40 C4
Nuweveldberge 58 E4
Nuyts Arch. 62 B1
Nyah West 62 C3
Nyahanga 57 E6
Nyahururu 57 D7
Nyainqentanglha Shan 34 C4
Nyâlâ 53 F3
Nyasa, L. = Malawi, L. 59 A6
Nyasvizh 17 B8
Nyda 28 C8
Nyeri 57 E7
Nyíregyháza 17 E5
Nylstroom 59 C5
Nymagee 63 B4
Nyngan 63 B4
Nyoman = Neman → 24 B1
Nysa 16 C3
Nysa → 16 B2
Nyurbe 30 C9
Nzega 57 E6
N'Zérékoré 55 G3
Nzeto 56 F2

O

Ō-Shima 32 B6
Oahe, L. 76 C4
Oahu 82 H12
Oak Ridge 75 A5
Oakbank 62 B3
Oakey 63 A5
Oakland 82 B1
Oamaru 65 F4
Oates Land 96 A15
Oaxaca 84 D5
Ob → 28 C7

Oba **69 D2**
Oban **10 C4**
Obbia **49 F4**
Oberhausen **14 C4**
Oberon **63 B4**
Obi, Kepulauan **39 E3**
Obi Is. = Obi, Kepulauan **39 E3**
Óbidos **92 C2**
Obihiro **32 F12**
Obilatu **39 E3**
Obo **57 C5**
Obozerskaya = Obozerskiy **28 C5**
Obozerskiy **28 C5**
Obskaya Guba **28 C8**
Obuasi **55 G4**
Ocala **75 E6**
Ocaña **18 C4**
Occidental, Cordillera **90 C3**
Ocean I. = Banaba **64 K11**
Oceanside **82 D4**
Ocniţa **17 D8**
Ocumare del Tuy **90 A5**
Odate **33 F12**
Odawara **32 B6**
Oddur **49 G3**
Ödemiş **23 E7**
Odense **9 G10**
Oder → **15 B8**
Odesa **25 D3**
Odessa = Odesa **25 D3**
Odessa **78 D2**
Odienné **55 G3**
Odintsovo **24 B4**
Odorheiu Secuiesc **17 E7**
Odra = Oder → **15 B8**
Odra → **16 B2**
Oeiras **92 D5**
Ofanto → **20 D6**
Offa **55 G5**
Offenbach **14 C5**
Offenburg **14 D4**
Oga-Hantō **33 G11**
Ōgaki **32 B5**
Ogbomosho **55 G5**
Ogden **81 E8**
Ogdensburg **73 B8**
Oglio → **20 B3**
Ogooué → **56 E1**
Ogowe = Ogooué → **56 E1**
Ohai **65 F2**
Ohakune **64 C6**
Ohanet **54 C6**
Ohau, L. **65 F3**
Ohio □ **72 D4**
Ohio → **72 F1**
Ohre → **16 C2**
Ohrid **22 D3**
Ohridsko Jezero **23 D3**
Oise → **12 B5**
Ōita **32 C2**
Oiticica **92 D5**
Ojos del Salado, Cerro **94 B3**
Oka → **28 D5**
Okaba **39 F5**
Okahandja **58 C3**
Okahukura **64 C6**
Okandja **56 E2**
Okanogan → **80 A4**
Okara **42 D8**
Okarito **65 E4**
Okaukuejo **58 B3**
Okavango Swamps **58 B4**
Okaya **32 A6**
Okayama **32 B3**
Okazaki **32 B5**
Okeechobee, L. **75 F7**
Okefenokee Swamp **75 D6**
Okhotsk, Sea of **31 D12**
Oki-Shotō **32 A3**
Okiep **58 D3**
Okinawa-Jima **35 D7**
Oklahoma □ **78 B5**
Oklahoma City **78 B5**
Okmulgee **79 B6**
Oknitsa = Ocniţa **17 D8**
Okrika **55 H6**
Oktabrsk = Oktyabrsk **29 E6**
Oktyabrsk **29 E6**
Oktyabrskiy = Aktsyabrski **17 B9**
Oktyabrskoy Revolyutsii, Os. **30 B7**
Oktyabrskoye **28 C7**
Okuru **65 E3**
Okushiri-Tō **32 F11**
Öland **9 G11**
Olary **62 B3**
Olavarría **94 D4**
Oława **16 C3**
Ólbia **20 D2**
Old Crow **70 B6**
Oldenburg **14 B5**
Oldham **11 E5**
Olekma → **31 C10**
Olekminsk **31 C10**
Oleksandriya **17 C8**
Olenek **30 C9**
Olenek → **30 B10**
Oléron, I. d' **12 D3**
Oleśnica **16 C3**
Olevsk **17 C8**
Olhão **18 D2**
Olifants → **59 C6**
Ólimbos, Óros **23 D4**
Olinda **92 D7**
Oliveira **93 G5**
Olivenza **18 C2**
Ollagüe **91 H5**
Olomouc **16 D3**
Olongapo **38 B2**
Olot **19 A7**
Olsztyn **16 B5**
Olt → **22 C5**
Olteniţa **22 B6**
Oltu **46 B5**
Olympia, *Greece* **23 F3**
Olympia, *U.S.A.* **80 B2**
Olympic Mts. **80 B2**
Olympus, Mt. = Ólimbos, Óros **23 D4**
Om → **29 D8**
Omagh **11 D3**
Omaha **77 E7**
Oman ■ **48 C6**
Oman, G. of **45 E4**
Omaruru **58 C3**
Omate **91 G4**
Ombai, Selat **39 F2**
Omboué **56 E1**
Ombrone → **20 C3**
Omdurmân **53 E5**
Ometepec **84 D5**
Ōmiya **32 B6**
Omo → **53 G6**
Omsk **29 D8**
Omul, Vf. **17 F7**
Ōmura **32 C1**
Omuramba Omatako → **58 B4**
Ōmuta **32 C2**
Onang **39 E1**
Oncócua **58 B2**
Onda **19 C5**
Ondangua **58 B3**
Ondo **55 G5**
Öndörhaan **35 B6**
Onega **28 C4**
Onega → **8 F15**
Onega, G. of = Onezhskaya Guba **28 C4**
Onega, L. = Onezhskoye Ozero **28 C4**
Onehunga **64 B6**
Oneşti **17 E8**
Onezhskaya Guba **28 C4**
Onezhskoye Ozero **28 C4**
Ongarue **64 C6**
Onilahy → **59 J8**
Onitsha **55 G6**
Onoda **32 B2**
Ontario □ **69 D2**
Ontario, L. **73 C7**
Oodnadatta **62 A2**
Oostende **14 C2**
Ootacamund **43 P10**
Opala **56 E4**
Opava **16 D3**
Opole **16 C3**
Oporto = Porto **18 B1**
Opotiki **64 C7**
Opua **64 A6**
Opunake **64 C5**
Oradea **17 E5**
Orai **42 G11**
Oral = Zhayyq → **29 E6**
Oral **24 C7**
Oran, *Algeria* **54 A4**
Oran, *Argentina* **94 A4**
Orange = Oranje → **58 D3**
Orange, *Australia* **63 B4**
Orange, *France* **13 D6**
Orange, *U.S.A.* **79 D7**
Orange, C. **92 B3**
Orangeburg **75 C7**
Oranienburg **15 B7**
Oranje → **58 D3**
Oranjemund **58 D3**
Oras **38 B3**
Oraşul Stalin = Braşov **17 F7**
Orbetello **20 C3**
Orbost **63 C4**
Orchila, I. **90 A5**
Ordos = Mu Us Shamo **35 C5**
Ordu **46 B4**
Ordzhonikidze = Vladikavkaz **25 E5**
Ore Mts. = Erzgebirge **15 C7**
Örebro **9 G11**
Oregon □ **80 C3**
Orekhovo-Zuyevo **24 B4**
Orel **24 C4**
Ören **23 F6**
Orenburg **29 D6**
Orense **18 A2**
Orepuki **65 G2**
Øresund **9 G10**
Orgaz **18 C4**
Orgeyev = Orhei **17 E9**
Orgūn **45 C7**
Orhaneli **23 E7**
Orhangazi **23 D7**
Orhei **17 E9**
Orhon Gol → **35 A5**
Orient **62 A3**
Oriental, Cordillera **90 B4**
Orihuela **19 C5**
Orinoco → **90 B6**
Orissa □ **40 G5**
Oristano **21 E2**
Oristano, G. di **21 E2**
Orizaba **84 D5**
Orkney Is. **10 B5**
Orlando **75 E7**
Orléanais **12 C5**
Orléans **12 C4**
Ormara **42 G4**
Ormoc **38 B2**
Ormond **64 C7**
Örnsköldsvik **8 F11**
Orocué **90 C4**
Orol Dengizi = Aral Sea **29 E6**
Oroquieta **38 C2**
Orós **92 D6**
Orosháza **16 E5**
Orroroo **62 B2**
Orsha **24 C3**
Orsk **29 D6**
Orşova **22 B4**
Ortaca **23 F7**
Ortegal, C. **18 A2**
Orthez **12 E3**
Ortigueira **18 A2**
Ortles **20 A3**
Ortón → **91 F5**
Orūmīyeh **46 C6**
Orūmīyeh, Daryācheh-ye **46 C6**
Oruro **91 G5**
Oruzgān □ **42 C5**
Orvieto **20 C4**
Oryakhovo **22 C4**
Ōsaka **32 B4**
Ösel = Saaremaa **24 B1**
Osh **29 E8**
Oshawa **69 D3**
Oshkosh **76 E3**
Oshmyany = Ashmyany **17 A7**
Oshogbo **55 G5**
Oshwe **56 E3**
Osijek **20 B7**
Osipenko = Berdyansk **25 D4**
Osipovichi = Asipovichy **17 B9**
Oskarshamn **9 G11**
Öskemen **29 E9**
Oslo **9 G10**
Oslob **38 C2**
Oslofjorden **9 G10**
Osmanabad **43 K10**
Osmaniye **46 C4**
Osnabrück **14 B5**
Osorio **94 B6**
Osorno **95 E2**
Ossa, Mt. **62 D4**
Óssa, Oros **23 E4**
Ostend = Oostende **14 C2**

Oster 17 C10
Österdalälven 8 F10
Östersund 8 F10
Ostfriesische Inseln 14 B4
Ostrava 16 D4
Ostróda 16 B4
Ostroh 17 C8
Ostrołęka 16 B5
Ostrów Mazowiecka 16 B5
Ostrów Wielkopolski 16 C3
Ostrowiec-Świętokrzyski 16 C5
Ostuni 21 D6
Ōsumi-Kaikyō 33 D2
Osuna 18 D3
Oswego 73 C7
Oświęcim 16 C4
Otago □ 65 F3
Otago Harbour 65 F4
Ōtake 32 B3
Otaki 64 D6
Otaru 32 F12
Otaru-Wan = Ishikari-Wan 32 F12
Otavalo 90 C3
Otavi 58 B3
Otira Gorge 65 E4
Otjiwarongo 58 C3
Otorohanga 64 C6
Otranto 23 D2
Otranto, C. d' 23 D2
Otranto, Str. of 23 D2
Ōtsu 32 B4
Ottawa 69 D3
Ottawa Is. 68 C2
Ottumwa 77 E8
Oturkpo 55 G6
Otway, B. 95 G2
Otway, C. 62 C3
Otwock 16 B5
Ouachita Mts. 79 B6
Ouadâne 54 D2
Ouadda 56 C4
Ouagadougou 55 F4
Ouahran = Oran 54 A4
Ouallene 54 D5
Ouanda Djallé 56 C4
Ouango 56 D4
Ouargla 54 B6
Ouarzazate 54 B3
Oubangi → 56 E3
Oudtshoorn 58 E4
Ouessant, I. d' 12 B1
Ouesso 56 D3
Ouezzane 54 B3
Ouidah 55 G5
Oujda 54 B4
Oujeft 55 D2
Ouled Djellal 54 B6
Oulu 8 E13
Oulujärvi 8 F13
Oulujoki → 8 E13
Oum Chalouba 53 E3
Ounianga-Kébir 53 E3
Ounianga Sérir 53 E3
Ourense = Orense 18 A2
Ouricuri 92 D5
Ouro Prêto 93 G5
Ouse 62 D4
Outer Hebrides 10 C3
Outjo 58 C3
Ouyen 62 C3
Ovalle 94 C2
Ovamboland 58 B3
Oviedo 18 A3
Ovruch 17 C9
Owaka 65 G3
Owambo = Ovamboland 58 B3
Owase 32 B5
Owbeh 42 B3
Owen Sound 69 D2
Owen Stanley Ra. 61 B8
Owendo 56 D1
Owo 55 G6
Owyhee → 80 D5
Oxford, *N.Z.* 65 E5
Oxford, *U.K.* 11 F6
Oxley 63 B3
Oxnard 82 C3
Oxus = Amudarya → 29 E6
Oya 37 D4
Oyama 32 A6
Oyem 56 D2
Oyo 55 G5
Ozamiz 38 C2
Ozark Plateau 79 A8
Ózd 16 D5

P

Pa-an 41 J11
Paarl 58 E3
Pab Hills 42 F5
Pabianice 16 C4
Pabna 41 E7
Pacaja → 92 C3
Pacaraima, Sierra 90 C6
Pacasmayo 91 E3
Pachpadra 42 G8
Pachuca 84 C5
Padaido, Kepulauan 39 E5
Padang 37 E2
Padangpanjang 37 E2
Padangsidempuan 37 D1
Paderborn 14 C5
Padloping Island 68 B4
Pádova 20 B3
Padua = Pádova 20 B3
Paducah 72 F1
Paeroa 64 B6
Pafúri 59 C6
Pag 20 B5
Pagadian 38 C2
Pagai Selatan, P. 37 E2
Pagai Utara 37 E2
Pagalu = Annobón 51 G4
Pagastikós Kólpos 23 E4
Pagatan 37 E5
Pahiatua 64 D6
Painan 37 E2
Paint Hills = Wemindji 69 C3
Painted Desert 83 C7
País Vasco □ 19 A4
Paisley 10 D4
Paita 90 E2
Pajares, Puerto de 18 A3
Pakaraima Mts. 90 B6
Pakistan ■ 42 E7
Pakokku 41 G10
Pakse 36 A3
Paktīā □ 42 C6
Pala 53 G2
Palagruža 20 C6
Palam 43 K10
Palampur 42 C10
Palana 62 C4
Palanan 38 A2
Palanan Pt. 38 A2
Palangkaraya 37 E4
Palani Hills 43 P10
Palanpur 43 G8
Palanro 39 E1
Palapye 59 C5
Palau ■ 38 C4
Palawan 36 C5
Palayankottai 43 Q10
Paleleh 39 D2
Palembang 37 E2
Palencia 18 A3
Palermo 21 E4
Palestine 79 D6
Paletwa 41 G9
Palghat 43 P10
Pali 42 G8
Palioúrion, Ákra 23 E4
Palitana 43 J7
Palk Bay 43 Q11
Palk Strait 43 Q11
Pallanza = Verbánia 20 B2
Palm Springs 82 D4
Palma 57 G8
Palma → 93 E4
Palma, B. de 19 C7
Palma de Mallorca 19 C7
Palmares 92 D6
Palmas, C. 55 H3
Pálmas, G. di 21 E2
Palmeira dos Índios 93 D6
Palmeirinhas, Pta. das 56 F2
Palmer 71 B5
Palmer Arch. 96 A3
Palmer Land 96 B3
Palmerston 65 F4
Palmerston North 64 D6
Palmi 21 E5
Palmira 90 C3
Palmyra = Tudmur 46 D4
Palopo 39 E2
Palos, C. de 19 D5
Palu, *Indonesia* 39 E1
Palu, *Turkey* 46 C5
Paluan 38 B2
Pama 55 F5
Pamiers 12 E4
Pamirs 29 F8
Pamlico Sd. 75 B10
Pampa 78 B3
Pampa de las Salinas 94 C3
Pampanua 39 E2
Pampas, *Argentina* 94 D4
Pampas, *Peru* 91 F4
Pamplona, *Colombia* 90 B4
Pamplona, *Spain* 19 A5
Panaji 43 M8
Panamá 85 F9
Panama ■ 86 E4
Panamá, G. de 86 E4
Panama City 74 D5
Panão 91 E3
Panay 38 B2
Panay, G. 38 B2
Pančevo 22 B3
Pandan 38 B2
Pandharpur 43 L9
Pando 94 C5
Pando, L. = Hope, L. 62 A2
Panevėžys 24 B1
Panfilov 29 E8
Pang-Long 41 F12
Pang-Yang 41 F12
Pangani 57 F7
Pangfou = Bengbu 35 C6
Pangkajene 39 E1
Pangkalanbrandan 37 D1
Pangkalanbuun 37 E4
Pangkalansusu 37 D1
Pangkalpinang 37 E3
Pangkoh 37 E4
Pangnirtung 68 B4
Pangutaran Group 38 C2
Panjgur 42 F4
Panjim = Panaji 43 M8
Panjinad Barrage 42 E7
Panorama 94 A6
Pantar 39 F2
Pante Macassar 39 F2
Pantelleria 21 F3
Pánuco 84 C5
Panyam 55 G6
Paoting = Baoding 35 C6
Paot'ou = Baotou 35 B6
Paoua 56 C3
Pápa 16 E3
Papakura 64 B6
Papantla 84 C5
Papar 36 C5
Papua New Guinea ■ 61 B8
Papudo 94 C2
Papun 41 H11
Pará = Belém 92 C4
Pará □ 92 C3
Paracatu 93 F4
Paracel Is. = Hsisha Chuntao 36 A4
Parachilna 62 B2
Parachinar 42 C7
Paradip 40 G6
Parado 39 F1
Paragua → 90 B6
Paraguaçu → 93 E6
Paraguaná, Pen. de 90 A4
Paraguarí 94 B5
Paraguay ■ 94 A5
Paraguay → 94 B5
Paraíba = João Pessoa 92 D7
Paraíba □ 92 D6
Paraíba do Sul → 93 G5
Parakou 55 G5
Paramaribo 92 A2
Paraná, *Argentina* 94 C4
Paranã, *Brazil* 93 E4
Paraná □ 94 A6
Paraná → 94 C5
Paranaguá 94 B7
Paranaíba → 93 G3

Paranapanema → 94 A6
Paranapiacaba, Serra do 94 A7
Parang, *Jolo, Phil.* 38 C2
Parang, *Mindanao, Phil.* 38 C2
Paratinga 93 E5
Paratoo 62 B2
Parattah 62 D4
Parbhani 43 K10
Parchim 15 B6
Pardo →, *Bahia, Brazil* 93 F6
Pardo →, *Mato Grosso, Brazil* 93 G3
Pardo →, *São Paulo, Brazil* 93 G4
Pardubice 16 C2
Parecis, Serra dos 91 F7
Parepare 39 E1
Párga 23 E3
Pariaguán 90 B6
Pariaman 37 E2
Parigi 39 E2
Parika 90 B7
Parima, Serra 90 C6
Parinari 90 D4
Parîngul Mare 17 F6
Parintins 92 C2
Pariparit Kyun 41 K9
Paris, *France* 12 B5
Paris, *U.S.A.* 79 C6
Park Range 81 F10
Parkersburg 72 E5
Parkes 63 B4
Parla 18 B4
Parma 20 B3
Parnaguá 93 E5
Parnaíba, *Piauí, Brazil* 92 C5
Parnaíba, *São Paulo, Brazil* 93 F3
Parnaíba → 92 C5
Parnassós 23 E4
Parnu 24 B1
Paroo → 63 B3
Páros 23 F5
Parral 94 D2
Parramatta 63 B5
Parry Sound 69 D3
Partinico 21 E4
Paru → 92 C3
Paruro 91 F4
Parvān □ 42 B6
Parvatipuram 40 H4
Pasadena, *Calif., U.S.A.* 82 C3
Pasadena, *Tex., U.S.A.* 79 E6
Pasaje 90 D3
Pascagoula 79 D9
Paşcani 17 E8
Pasco 80 B4
Pasco, Cerro de 91 F3
Pashmakli = Smolyan 22 D5
Pašman 20 C5
Pasni 42 G3
Paso de Indios 95 E3
Passau 15 D7
Passero, C. 21 F5
Passo Fundo 94 B6
Passos 93 G4
Pastaza → 90 D3
Pasto 90 C3
Patagonia 95 F3
Patan, *India* 43 H8
Patan, *Nepal* 40 D5
Patani 39 D3
Patchewollock 62 C3
Patea 64 C6
Pategi 55 G6
Paternò 21 F5
Paterson 73 D8
Pathankot 42 C9
Patiala 42 D10
Patkai Bum 41 D10
Pátmos 23 F6
Patna 40 E5
Patos, L. dos 94 C6
Patos de Minas 93 F4
Patquía 94 C3
Pátrai 23 E3
Pátraikós Kólpos 23 E3
Patras = Pátrai 23 E3
Patrocínio 93 F4
Pattani 36 C2
Patuakhali 41 F8
Pau 12 E3
Pauini → 90 D6
Pauk 41 G10
Paulis = Isiro 57 D5
Paulistana 92 D5
Paulo Afonso 93 D6
Pavia 20 B2
Pavlodar 29 D8
Pavlograd = Pavlohrad 25 D4
Pavlohrad 25 D4
Pavlovo 24 B5
Pavlovsk 24 C5
Pawtucket 73 D10
Paxoí 23 E3
Payakumbuh 37 E2
Payne Bay = Kangirsuk 68 C4
Paysandú 94 C5
Paz, B. la 84 C2
Pazar 46 B5
Pazardzhik 22 C5
Peace → 70 C8
Peak Hill 63 B4
Peake 62 C2
Peake Cr. → 62 A2
Pebane 59 B7
Pebas 90 D4
Peć 22 C3
Pechenga 28 C4
Pechenizhyn 17 D7
Pechora → 28 C6
Pechorskaya Guba 28 C6
Pecos → 78 E3
Pécs 16 E4
Pedder, L. 62 D4
Pedirka 62 A2
Pedra Azul 93 F5
Pedreiras 92 C5
Pedro Afonso 93 D4
Pedro Juan Caballero 94 A5
Peebinga 62 B3
Peel →, *Australia* 63 B5
Peel →, *Canada* 70 B6
Peera Peera Poolanna L. 62 A2
Pegasus Bay 65 E5
Pegu 41 J11
Pegu Yoma 41 H10
Pehuajó 94 D4
Peine 14 B6
Peip'ing = Beijing 35 C6
Peipus, L. = Chudskoye, Oz. 24 B2
Peixe 93 E4
Pekalongan 37 F3
Pekanbaru 37 D2
Pekin 77 E10
Peking = Beijing 35 C6
Pelagie, Is. 21 G4
Pelaihari 37 E4
Peleaga, Vf. 17 F6
Peleng 39 E2
Pelješac 20 C6
Pelly → 70 B6
Pelly Bay 68 B2
Pelly L. 70 B9
Peloponnese = Pelopónnisos □ 23 F4
Pelopónnisos □ 23 F4
Peloro, C. 21 E5
Pelorus Sd. 65 D5
Pelotas 94 C6
Pelvoux, Massif du 13 D7
Pematangsiantar 37 D1
Pemba I. 57 F7
Pembroke, *Canada* 69 D3
Pembroke, *U.K.* 11 F4
Penang = Pinang 36 C2
Penápolis 94 A6
Peñarroya-Pueblonuevo 18 C3
Peñas, C. de 18 A3
Penas, G. de 95 F2
Pench'i = Benxi 35 B7
Pend Oreille L. 80 A5
Pendembu 55 G2
Pendleton 80 C4
Penedo 93 E6
Penguin 62 D4
Peniche 18 C1
Penida 37 F5
Peninsular Malaysia □ 37 D2
Penmarch, Pte. de 12 C1
Pennines 11 D5
Pennsylvania □ 73 D7
Penola 62 C3
Penong 60 G5
Penrith 63 B5
Pensacola 74 D4
Pensacola Mts. 96 C4
Penshurst 62 C3
Penticton 71 D8
Pentland Firth 10 B5
Penza 24 C6
Penzance 11 F4
Peoria 77 E10
Perabumulih 37 E2
Perche, Collines du 12 B4
Perdido, Mte. 19 A6
Perdu, Mt. = Perdido, Mte. 19 A6
Pereira 90 C3
Perekerten 62 B3
Pereyaslav-Khmelnytskyy 24 C3
Pergamino 94 C4
Péribonca → 69 D3
Perico 94 A3
Périgueux 12 D4
Perijá, Sierra de 90 B4
Perlas, Arch. de las 86 E4
Perm 29 D6
Pernambuco = Recife 92 D7
Pernatty Lagoon 62 B2
Pernik 22 C4
Perpendicular Pt. 63 B5
Perpignan 13 E5
Persepolis 44 D3
Pershotravensk 17 C8
Persian Gulf = Gulf, The 44 E2
Perth, *Australia* 60 G2
Perth, *U.K.* 10 C5
Perth Amboy 73 D8
Peru ■ 90 C3
Perúgia 20 C4
Pervomaysk 25 D3
Pervouralsk 29 D6
Pésaro 20 C4
Pescara 20 C5
Peshawar 42 B7
Peshkopi 22 D3
Pesqueira 92 D6
Petah Tiqwa 46 D3
Petauke 59 A6
Peter I.s Øy 96 A2
Peterborough, *Australia* 62 B2
Peterborough, *Canada* 69 D3
Peterborough, *U.K.* 11 E6
Peterhead 10 C6
Petersburg, *Alaska, U.S.A.* 71 C6
Petersburg, *Va., U.S.A.* 73 F7
Petitsikapau, L. 69 C4
Petlad 43 H8
Peto 85 C7
Petone 65 D6
Petrich 22 D4
Petrikov = Pyetrikaw 17 B9
Petrograd = Sankt-Peterburg 24 B3
Petrolândia 93 D6
Petrolina 93 D5
Petropavl 29 D7
Petropavlovsk = Petropavl 29 D7
Petropavlovsk-Kamchatskiy 31 D13
Petrópolis 93 G5
Petroşani 17 F6
Petrovaradin 22 B2
Petrovsk 24 C6
Petrozavodsk 28 C4
Peureulak 36 D1
Pforzheim 14 D5
Phagwara 42 D9
Phalodi 42 F8
Phan Rang 36 B3
Phangan, Ko 36 C2
Phangnga 36 C1
Phanh Bho Ho Chi Minh 36 B3
Phatthalung 36 C2
Phetchabun 36 A2
Philadelphia 73 E8
Philippines ■ 38 B2
Philippopolis = Plovdiv 22 C5
Phillip I. 63 C4

Phillott 63 A4
Phitsanulok 36 A2
Phnom Dangrek 36 B2
Phnom Penh 36 B2
Phoenix 83 D6
Phra Nakhon Si Ayutthaya 36 B2
Phuket 36 C1
Phumiphon, Khuan 36 A1
Piacenza 20 B2
Pialba 63 A5
Pian Cr. → 63 B4
Pianosa 20 C3
Piatra Neamţ 17 E8
Piauí □ 92 D5
Piave → 20 B4
Pibor Post 53 G5
Pica 91 H5
Picardie 13 B5
Picardy = Picardie 13 B5
Pichilemu 94 C2
Pico Truncado 95 F3
Picton, *Australia* 63 B5
Picton, *N.Z.* 65 D6
Pictou 69 D4
Picún Leufú 95 D3
Piedmont = Piemonte □ 20 B1
Piedras, R. de las → 91 F5
Piedras Negras 84 B4
Piemonte □ 20 B1
Piet Retief 59 D6
Pietermaritzburg 59 D6
Pietersburg 59 C5
Pietrosul, *Romania* 17 E7
Pietrosul, *Romania* 17 E7
Pigüe 94 D4
Piketberg 58 E3
Piła 16 B3
Pilar, *Brazil* 93 D6
Pilar, *Paraguay* 94 B5
Pilas Group 38 C2
Pilcomayo → 94 B5
Pilibhit 42 E11
Pilica → 16 C5
Pílos 23 F3
Pilsen = Plzeň 16 D1
Pimba 62 B2
Pimenta Bueno 91 F6
Pimentel 91 E3
Pinang 36 C2
Pinar del Río 86 B3
Pınarhisar 22 D6
Pińczów 16 C5
Pindiga 55 G7
Pindos Óros 23 E3
Pindus Mts. = Pindos Óros 23 E3
Pine Bluff 79 B7
Pine Point 70 B8
Pinega → 28 C5
Pinerolo 20 B1
Pinetown 59 D6
Ping → 36 A2
Pingdong 35 D7
Pingliang 35 C5
Pingwu 35 C5
Pingxiang 35 D5
Pinhel 18 B2
Pini 37 D1
Piniós → 23 E4
Pinnaroo 62 C3
Pínnes, Ákra 23 D5
Pinrang 39 E1
Pinsk 17 B8
Pintados 91 H5
Pinyug 24 A6
Piombino 20 C3
Pioner, Os. 30 B7
Piorini, L. 90 D6
Piotrków Trybunalski 16 C4
Pīp 45 E5
Piquiri → 94 A6
Piracicaba 94 A7
Piracuruca 92 C5
Piræus = Piraiévs 23 F4
Piraiévs 23 F4
Piranè 94 B5
Pirapora 93 F5
Pírgos 23 F3
Pirin Planina 22 D4
Piripiri 92 C5
Pirmasens 14 D4
Pirot 22 C4
Piru 39 E3
Pisa 20 C3
Pisagua 91 G4
Pisciotta 21 D5
Pisco 91 F3
Písek 16 D2
Pishan 34 C2
Pising 39 F2
Pistóia 20 C3
Pisuerga → 18 B3
Pitarpunga, L. 62 B3
Pitcairn I. 65 M17
Piteå 8 E12
Piteşti 22 B5
Pithapuram 40 J4
Pittsburg 79 A6
Pittsburgh 73 D5
Pittsworth 63 A5
Piura 90 E2
Placentia 69 D5
Placentia B. 69 D5
Plainview 78 B3
Pláka, Ákra 23 G6
Plakhino 28 C9
Plasencia 18 B2
Plata, Río de la 94 C5
Platani → 21 F4
Plato 90 B4
Platte → 77 F7
Plauen 15 C7
Pleiku 36 B3
Plenty, B. of 64 B7
Pleven 22 C5
Plevlja 22 C2
Płock 16 B4
Plöckenstein 15 D7
Ploieşti 22 B6
Plovdiv 22 C5
Plumtree 59 C5
Plymouth 11 F4
Plzeň 16 D1
Po → 20 B4
Po Hai = Bo Hai 35 C6
Pobedy Pik 29 E8
Pocatello 81 D7
Poços de Caldas 93 G4
Podgorica 22 C2
Podilska Vysochyna 17 D8
Podkamennaya Tunguska → 30 C7
Podolsk 24 B4
Podor 55 E1
Pofadder 58 D3
Poh 39 E2
Pohnpei 64 J10
Poinsett, C. 96 A12
Pointe-à-Pitre 87 C7
Pointe Noire 56 E2
Poitiers 12 C4
Poitou 12 C3
Pokaran 42 F7
Pokataroo 63 A4
Pokrovsk = Engels 24 C6
Pola = Pula 20 B4
Polan 45 E5
Poland ■ 16 B5
Polatsk 24 B2
Polcura 94 D2
Polesye = Pripet Marshes 17 B9
Poli 56 C2
Police 16 B2
Polillo Is. 38 B2
Políyiros 23 D4
Pollachi 43 P10
Polnovat 28 C7
Polonne 17 C8
Polonnoye = Polonne 17 C8
Poltava 24 D3
Polunochnoye 28 C7
Polynesia 65 L15
Polynésie française = French Polynesia ■ 65 M16
Pombal, *Brazil* 92 D6
Pombal, *Portugal* 18 C1
Pomézia 20 D4
Pomorski, Pojezierze 16 B3
Ponape = Pohnpei 64 J10
Ponca City 78 A5
Ponce 87 C6
Pond Inlet 68 A3
Pondicherry 43 P11
Ponferrada 18 A2
Ponnani 43 P9
Ponnyadaung 41 F10
Ponoy → 28 C5
Ponta Grossa 94 B6
Ponta Pora 94 A5
Pontarlier 13 C7
Pontchartrain L. 79 D8
Ponte Nova 93 G5
Pontevedra 18 A1
Pontiac 72 C4
Pontianak 37 E3
Pontine Is. = Ponziane, Ísole 21 D4
Pontine Mts. = Kuzey Anadolu Dağları 46 B3
Pontivy 12 B2
Pontoise 12 B5
Ponziane, Ísole 21 D4
Poochera 62 B1
Poole 11 F6
Poona = Pune 43 K8
Pooncarie 62 B3
Poopelloe L. 63 B3
Poopó, L. de 91 G5
Popayán 90 C3
Popigay 30 B9
Popilta, L. 62 B3
Popio L. 62 B3
Poplar Bluff 79 A8
Popocatépetl, Volcán 84 D5
Popokabaka 56 F3
Poprád 16 D5
Porbandar 43 J6
Porcupine → 71 B5
Pordenone 20 B4
Pori 8 F12
Porkkala 9 G12
Porlamar 90 A6
Poroshiri-Dake 32 F12
Porpoise B. 96 A13
Porretta, Passo di 20 B3
Port Adelaide 62 B2
Port Alberni 71 D7
Port Alfred 59 E5
Port Angeles 80 A2
Port Antonio 86 C4
Port Arthur, *Australia* 62 D4
Port Arthur, *U.S.A.* 79 E7
Port-au-Prince 87 C5
Port Augusta 62 B2
Port Augusta West 62 B2
Port Bergé Vaovao 59 H9
Port Bou 19 A7
Port Broughton 62 B2
Port-Cartier 69 C4
Port Chalmers 65 F4
Port Darwin 95 G5
Port Davey 62 D4
Port Dickson 37 D2
Port Elizabeth 59 E5
Port Fairy 62 C3
Port-Gentil 56 E1
Port Harcourt 55 H6
Port Harrison = Inukjuak 68 C3
Port Hawkesbury 69 D4
Port Hedland 60 E2
Port Huron 72 C4
Port Kembla 63 B5
Port Kenny 62 B1
Port Lairge = Waterford 11 E3
Port Laoise 11 E3
Port Lincoln 62 B2
Port Loko 55 G2
Port MacDonnell 62 C3
Port Macquarie 63 B5
Port Moresby 61 B8
Port Nelson 71 C10
Port Nolloth 58 D3
Port Nouveau-Québec = Kangiqsualujjuaq 68 C4
Port of Spain 87 D7
Port Pegasus 65 G2
Port Phillip B. 63 C3
Port Pirie 62 B2
Port Safaga = Bûr Safâga 52 C5
Port Said = Bûr Sa'îd 52 B5
Port Shepstone 59 E6
Port Stanley = Stanley 95 G5
Port Sudan = Bûr Sûdân 53 E6
Port Talbot 11 F5
Port-Vendres 13 E5
Port Wakefield 62 B2
Port Weld 36 D2
Porta Orientalis 22 B4

Portachuelo 91 G6
Portadown 11 D3
Portage La Prairie 71 D10
Portalegre 18 C2
Portile de Fier 22 B4
Portimão 18 D1
Portland, *N.S.W., Australia* 63 B4
Portland, *Vic., Australia* 62 C3
Portland, *Maine, U.S.A.* 73 C10
Portland, *Oreg., U.S.A.* 80 C2
Portland B. 62 C3
Portland Prom. 68 C3
Porto 18 B1
Pôrto Alegre 94 C6
Porto Amboim = Gunza 56 G2
Pôrto de Móz 92 C3
Porto Empédocle 21 F4
Pôrto Esperança 91 G7
Pôrto Franco 92 D4
Porto Mendes 94 A6
Pôrto Murtinho 91 H7
Pôrto Nacional 93 E4
Porto Novo 55 G5
Porto Santo 54 B1
Pôrto Seguro 93 F6
Porto Tórres 20 D2
Pôrto Uniâo 94 B6
Pôrto Válter 91 E4
Porto-Vecchio 13 F8
Pôrto Velho 91 E6
Portoferráio 20 C3
Portoscuso 21 E2
Portovíejo 90 D2
Portree 10 C3
Portsmouth, *U.K.* 11 F6
Portsmouth, *U.S.A.* 73 F7
Porttipahtan tekojärvi 8 E13
Portugal ■ 18 C1
Porvenir 95 G2
Posadas 94 B5
Poshan = Boshan 35 C6
Poso 39 E2
Posse 93 E4
Possel 56 C3
Possession I. 96 B15
Poste Maurice Cortier 54 D5
Postojna 20 B5
Potchefstroom 59 D5
Potenza 21 D5
Poteriteri, L. 65 G2
Potgietersrus 59 C5
Poti 25 E5
Potiskum 55 F7
Potomac → 73 E7
Potosí 91 G5
Pototan 38 B2
Potrerillos 94 B3
Potsdam 15 B7
Poughkeepsie 73 D9
Pouso Alegre 93 E2
Považská Bystrica 16 D4
Povenets 28 C4
Poverty B. 64 C8
Póvoa de Varzim 18 B1
Powder → 76 B2
Powell L. 83 B7
Poyang Hu 35 D6
Požarevac 22 B3
Poznań 16 B3
Pozo Almonte 91 H5
Pozoblanco 18 C3
Pozzuoli 21 D5
Prachuap Khiri Khan 36 B1
Prado 93 F6
Prague = Praha 16 C2
Praha 16 C2
Prainha, *Amazonas, Brazil* 91 E6
Prainha, *Pará, Brazil* 92 C3
Prairies 71 C9
Prapat 37 D1
Prata 93 F4
Prato 20 C3
Pravia 18 A2
Praya 37 F5
Preparis North Channel 41 K9
Preparis South Channel 41 K9
Přerov 16 D3
Preservation Inlet 65 G2
Presidencia Roque Saenz Peña 94 B4
Presidente Epitácio 93 G3
Presidente Hermes 91 F6
Presidente Prudente 93 G3
Prešov 16 D5
Prespa, L. = Prespansko Jezero 23 D3
Prespansko Jezero 23 D3
Presque Isle 73 A11
Preston 11 E5
Pretoria 59 D5
Préveza 23 E3
Příbram 16 D2
Prichard 74 D3
Prieska 58 D4
Prievidza 16 D4
Prilep 22 D3
Priluki = Pryluky 24 C3
Prime Seal I. 62 D4
Prince Albert 71 C9
Prince Albert Mts. 96 B15
Prince Albert Pen. 70 A8
Prince Albert Sd. 70 A8
Prince Charles I. 68 B3
Prince Charles Mts. 96 B10
Prince Edward I. □ 69 D4
Prince of Wales I., *Canada* 70 A10
Prince of Wales I., *U.S.A.* 71 C6
Principe da Beira 91 F6
Prins Harald Kyst 96 B8
Prinsesse Astrid Kyst 96 B7
Prinsesse Ragnhild Kyst 96 B8
Pripet → = Prypyat → 17 C10
Pripet Marshes 17 B9
Pripyat Marshes = Pripet Marshes 17 B9
Pripyats = Prypyat → 17 C10
Priština 22 C3
Privas 13 D6
Privolzhskaya Vozvyshennost 24 C6
Prizren 22 C3
Proddatur 43 M11
Progreso 85 C7
Prokopyevsk 29 D9
Prokuplje 22 C3
Prome = Pyè 41 H10
Propriá 93 E6
Prostějov 16 D3
Proston 63 A5
Provence 13 E6
Providence 73 D10
Providencia, I. de 86 D3
Provins 13 B5
Provo 81 E8
Prozna → 16 B3
Pruszków 16 B5
Prut → 17 F9
Pruzhany 17 B7
Prydz B. 96 A10
Pryluky 24 C3
Prypyat → 17 C10
Przemyśl 17 D6
Przhevalsk 29 E8
Psará 23 E5
Pskov 24 B2
Ptich = Ptsich → 17 B9
Ptsich → 17 B9
Puán 94 D4
Pucallpa 91 E4
Pudukkottai 43 P11
Puebla 84 D5
Pueblo 76 F2
Pueblo Hundido 94 B2
Puelches 94 D3
Puente Alto 94 C2
Puente-Genil 18 D3
Puerto Aisén 95 F2
Puerto Ayacucho 90 B5
Puerto Barrios 85 D7
Puerto Bermejo 94 B5
Puerto Bermúdez 91 F4
Puerto Bolívar 90 D3
Puerto Cabello 90 A5
Puerto Cabezas 86 D3
Puerto Carreño 90 B5
Puerto Chicama 91 E3
Puerto Coig 95 G3
Puerto Cortés 85 D7
Puerto Cumarebo 90 A5
Puerto del Rosario 54 C2
Puerto Deseado 95 F3
Puerto Heath 91 F5
Puerto La Cruz 90 A6
Puerto Leguízamo 90 D4
Puerto Lobos 95 E3
Puerto Madryn 95 E3
Puerto Maldonado 91 F5
Puerto Montt 95 E2
Puerto Morelos 85 C7
Puerto Natales 95 G2
Puerto Páez 90 B5
Puerto Pinasco 94 A5
Puerto Pirámides 95 E4
Puerto Plata 87 C5
Puerto Princesa 38 C1
Puerto Quellón 95 E2
Puerto Rico ■ 87 C6
Puerto Sastre 91 H7
Puerto Suárez 91 G7
Puerto Wilches 90 B4
Puertollano 18 C3
Pueyrredón, L. 95 F2
Pugachev 24 C6
Puget Sound 80 B2
Puigcerdá 19 A6
Pukaki L. 65 F4
Pukapuka 65 L14
Pukekohe 64 B6
Pula 20 B4
Puławy 16 C5
Pullman 80 B5
Pulog 38 A2
Pułtusk 16 B5
Puna 91 G5
Puná, I. 90 D2
Punakha 41 D7
Punata 91 G5
Punch 42 C9
Pune 43 K8
Punjab □, *India* 42 D9
Punjab □, *Pakistan* 42 D8
Puno 91 G4
Punta Alta 94 D4
Punta Arenas 95 G2
Punta de Díaz 94 B2
Puntabie 62 B1
Puntarenas 86 E3
Punto Fijo 90 A4
Puquio 91 F4
Pur → 28 C8
Purace, Vol. 90 C3
Puralia = Puruliya 40 F6
Puri 40 H5
Purnia 40 E6
Purukcahu 37 E4
Puruliya 40 F6
Purus → 90 D6
Pusan 35 C7
Pushkino 24 C6
Putao 41 D11
Putaruru 64 C6
Puthein Myit → 41 K10
Putignano 21 D6
Puting, Tanjung 37 E4
Putorana, Gory 30 C7
Puttalam 43 Q11
Puttgarden 15 A6
Putumayo → 90 D5
Putussibau 37 D4
Puy-de-Dôme 13 D5
Pweto 57 F5
Pwllheli 11 E4
Pyapon 41 J10
Pyasina → 30 B6
Pyatigorsk 25 E5
Pyè 41 H10
Pyetrikaw 17 B9
Pyinmana 41 H11
P'yŏngyang 35 C7
Pyrénées 19 A6
Pyu 41 H11

Q

Qādib 49 E5
Qā'emshahr . . . 44 B3
Qahremānshahr = Bākhtarān . 46 D6
Qaidam Pendi . 34 C4
Qalāt 45 C6
Qal'at al Akhḍar 47 E4
Qal'eh Shaharak 42 B4
Qal'eh-ye Now 45 C5
Qamar, Ghubbat al 49 D5
Qamruddin Karez 42 D6
Qandahār 42 D4
Qandahār □ . . . 42 D4
Qapshaghay . . 29 E8
Qâra 52 C4
Qarabutaq 29 E7
Qarachuk 46 C5
Qaraghandy . . . 29 E8
Qārah 47 E5
Qarataū 29 E8
Qarqan 34 C3
Qarqan He ⟶ . 34 C3
Qarqaraly 29 E8
Qarshi 29 F7
Qaşr-e Qand . . 45 E5
Qasr Farâfra . . 52 C4
Qatar ■ 44 E2
Qattâra, Munkhafed el 52 C4
Qattâra Depression = Qattâra, Munkhafed el 52 C4
Qāyen 44 C4
Qazaqstan = Kazakstan ■ . 29 E7
Qazvin 46 C7
Qena 52 C5
Qeshm 44 E4
Qila Safed 42 E2
Qila Saifullāh . . 42 D6
Qilian Shan . . . 34 C4
Qingdao 35 C7
Qinghai □ 34 C4
Qinghai Hu . . . 34 C5
Qinhuangdao . 35 C6
Qinzhou 35 D5
Qiqihar 35 B7
Qitai 34 B3
Qom 44 C2
Qomsheh 44 C2
Qondūz 45 B7
Qondūz □ 45 B7
Qostanay 29 D7
Qu Xian, *Sichuan, China* 35 C5
Qu Xian, *Zhejiang, China* 35 D6
Quambatook . . 62 C3
Quambone 63 B4
Quan Long 36 C3
Quandialla 63 B4
Quang Ngai . . . 36 A3
Quanzhou 35 D6
Quaqtaq 68 B4
Quaraí 94 C5
Quartu Sant'Elena . . 21 E2
Quatsino 71 C7
Quba 25 E6
Qūchān 44 B4
Queanbeyan . . 63 C4
Québec 69 D3
Québec □ 69 D3
Queen Alexandra Ra. 96 C15
Queen Charlotte Is. 70 C6
Queen Charlotte Str. 71 C7
Queen Elizabeth Is. 66 B9
Queen Mary Land 96 B11
Queen Maud G. 70 B9
Queen Maud Land 96 B7
Queen Maud Mts. 96 C16
Queenscliff . . . 63 C3
Queensland □ . 61 E7
Queenstown, *Australia* 62 D4
Queenstown, *N.Z.* 65 F3
Queenstown, *S. Africa* 59 E5
Queimadas . . . 93 E6
Quela 56 F3
Quelimane 59 B7
Quelpart = Cheju Do . . . 35 C7
Quequén 94 D5
Querétaro 84 C4
Quetta 42 D5
Quezon City . . . 38 B2
Qui Nhon 36 B3
Quibaxe 56 F2
Quibdo 90 B3
Quiberon 12 C2
Quilán, C. 95 E2
Quilengues . . . 58 A2
Quillabamba . . 91 F4
Quillagua 91 H5
Quillota 94 C2
Quilon 43 Q10
Quilpie 63 A3
Quimilí 94 B4
Quimper 12 B1
Quimperlé 12 C2
Quincy 77 F9
Quines 94 C3
Quinga 59 H8
Quintanar de la Orden 18 C4
Quintero 94 C2
Quinyambie . . . 62 B3
Quipungo 58 A2
Quirindi 63 B5
Quissanga 59 G8
Quitilipi 94 B4
Quito 90 D3
Quixadá 92 C6
Qŭnghirot 29 E6
Quondong 62 B3
Quorn 62 B2
Qŭqon 29 E8
Qûs 52 C5
Quseir 52 C5
Qyzylorda 29 E7

R

Raahe 8 F12
Raba 39 F1
Rába ⟶ 16 E3
Rabat, *Malta* . . 21 G5
Rabat, *Morocco* 54 B3
Rabaul 64 K10
Rābigh 47 G4
Race, C. 69 D5
Rach Gia 36 B3
Racibórz 16 C4
Racine 72 C2
Rădăuţi 17 E7
Radekhiv 17 C7
Radekhov = Radekhiv . . . 17 C7
Radhwa, Jabal 47 F4
Radom 16 C5
Radomsko 16 C4
Radomyshl . . . 17 C9
Radstock, C. . . . 62 B1
Rae 70 B8
Rae Bareli 40 D3
Rae Isthmus . . 68 B2
Raetihi 64 C6
Rafaela 94 C4
Rafai 56 D4
Rafḩā 47 E5
Rafsanjān 44 D4
Ragachow 17 B10
Ragama 43 R11
Raglan 64 B6
Ragusa 21 F5
Raha 39 E2
Rahad al Bardī 53 F3
Rahaeng = Tak 36 A1
Rahimyar Khan 42 E7
Raichur 43 L10
Raigarh 40 G4
Railton 62 D4
Rainier, Mt. . . . 80 B3
Raipur 40 G3
Ra'is 47 G4
Raj Nandgaon . 40 G3
Raja, Ujung . . . 37 D1
Raja Ampat, Kepulauan . . 39 E3
Rajahmundry . . 40 J3
Rajang ⟶ 37 D4
Rajapalaiyam . . 43 Q10
Rajasthan □ . . . 42 F8
Rajasthan Canal 42 F8
Rajgarh 43 G10
Rajkot 43 H7
Rajpipla 43 J8
Rajshahi 41 E7
Rakaia 65 E5
Rakaia ⟶ 65 E5
Rakan, Ra's . . . 44 E2
Rakaposhi 42 A9
Rakata, Pulau . 37 F3
Rakhiv 17 D7
Raleigh 75 B8
Ram Hd. 63 C4
Ramanathapuram 43 Q11
Ramechhap . . . 40 D6
Ramelau 39 F3
Ramgarh, *Bihar, India* 40 F5
Ramgarh, *Raj., India* 42 F7
Rāmhormoz . . . 47 E7
Ramnad = Ramanathapuram 43 Q11
Rampur 42 E11
Rampur Hat . . . 40 E6
Ramree I. = Ramree Kyun 41 H9
Ramree Kyun . 41 H9
Ramtek 43 J11
Ranaghat 41 F7
Ranau 36 C5
Rancagua 94 C2
Ranchi 40 F5
Randers 9 G10
Rangaunu B. . . 64 A5
Rangia 41 D8
Rangiora 65 E5
Rangitaiki ⟶ . 64 B7
Rangitata ⟶ . . 65 E4
Rangon ⟶ . . . 41 J11
Rangoon 41 J11
Rangpur 41 E7
Ranibennur . . . 43 M9
Raniganj 40 F6
Raniwara 43 G8
Rankin Inlet . . . 70 B10
Rankins Springs 63 B4
Ranong 36 C1
Ransiki 39 E4
Rantau 37 E5
Rantauprapat . . 37 D1
Rantemario . . . 39 E1
Rapa 65 M16
Rapallo 20 B2
Rāpch 45 E4
Rapid City 76 C3
Rarotonga 65 M14
Ra's al Khaymah 44 E4
Ra's al-Unuf . . . 52 B2
Ras Bânâs 52 D6
Ras Dashen . . . 57 B7
Râs Timirist . . . 55 E1
Rasa, Punta . . . 95 E4
Rashad 53 F5
Rashîd 52 B5
Rasht 46 C7
Rat Islands 71 C1
Ratangarh 42 E9
Rathenow 15 B7
Ratibor = Racibórz 16 C4
Ratlam 43 H9
Ratnagiri 43 L8
Raukumara Ra. 64 C7
Raurkela 40 F5
Rava-Ruska . . . 17 C6
Rava Russkaya = Rava-Ruska 17 C6
Rāvar 44 D4
Ravenna 20 B4
Ravensburg . . . 14 E5
Ravi ⟶ 42 D7
Rawalpindi 42 C8
Rawāndūz 46 C6
Rawene 64 A5
Rawlins 81 E10
Rawson 95 E3
Ray, C. 69 D5
Rayadurg 43 M10
Rayagada 40 H4
Raymond 71 D8
Raz, Pte. du . . . 12 B1
Razdel'naya = Rozdilna 17 E10
Razelm, Lacul . 22 B7
Razgrad 22 C6
Ré, I. de 12 C3
Reading, *U.K.* . 11 F6
Reading, *U.S.A.* 73 D8
Realicó 94 D4
Rebi 39 F4
Rebiana 52 D3
Rebun-Tō 32 E12
Rechytsa 17 B10
Recife 92 D7
Reconquista . . . 94 B5
Recreo 94 B3
Red ⟶, *La., U.S.A.* 79 D8
Red ⟶, *N. Dak., U.S.A.* 76 A6
Red Cliffs 62 B3

Red Deer 71 C8
Red Sea 48 C2
Red Tower Pass = Turnu Roşu, P. 17 F7
Redcar 11 D6
Redcliffe 63 A5
Redding 80 E2
Redditch 11 E6
Redon 12 C2
Redondela 18 A1
Redwood City 82 B1
Ree, L. 11 E3
Reefton 65 E4
Regensburg 15 D7
Réggio di Calábria 21 E5
Réggio nell'Emília 20 B3
Reghin 17 E7
Regina 71 C9
Rehoboth 58 C3
Rehovot 46 E3
Rei-Bouba 53 G1
Reichenbach 15 C7
Reidsville 75 A8
Reigate 11 F6
Reims 13 B6
Reina Adelaida, Arch. 95 G2
Reindeer L. 71 C9
Reinga, C. 64 A5
Reinosa 18 A3
Reliance 70 B9
Remarkable, Mt. 62 B2
Remeshk 45 E4
Rendsburg 14 A5
Rengat 37 E2
Reni 17 F9
Renk 53 F5
Renmark 62 B3
Rennes 12 B3
Reno 80 F4
Reno → 20 B4
Rentería 19 A5
Republican → 76 F6
Repulse Bay 68 B2
Requena, *Peru* 90 E4
Requena, *Spain* 19 C5
Resadiye = Datça 23 F6
Resht = Rasht 46 C7
Resistencia 94 B5
Reşiţa 17 F5
Resolution I., *Canada* 68 B4
Resolution I., *N.Z.* 65 F2
Réthímnon 23 G5
Réunion ■ 51 J9
Reus 19 B6
Reutlingen 14 D5
Reval = Tallinn 24 B1
Revelstoke 71 C8
Rewa 40 E3
Rewari 42 E10
Rey Malabo 56 D1
Reykjavík 8 B2
Reynosa 84 B5
Rhein → 14 C4
Rhein-Main-Donau-Kanal → 15 D6
Rheine 14 B4
Rheinland-Pfalz □ 14 C4
Rhin = Rhein → 14 C4
Rhine = Rhein → 14 C4
Rhineland-Palatinate □ = Rheinland-Pfalz □ 14 C4
Rhode Island □ 73 D10
Rhodes = Ródhos 23 F7
Rhodope Mts. = Rhodopi Planina 22 D5
Rhodopi Planina 22 D5
Rhön = Hohe Rhön 14 C5
Rhondda 11 F5
Rhône → 13 E6
Rhum 10 C3
Riachão 92 D4
Riasi 42 C9
Riau □ 37 E2
Riau, Kepulauan 37 D2
Riau Arch. = Riau, Kepulauan 37 D2
Ribadeo 18 A2
Ribeirão Prêto 93 G4
Riberalta 91 F5
Rîbniţa 17 E9
Riccarton 65 E5
Richland 80 B4
Richmond, *Australia* 63 B5
Richmond, *N.Z.* 65 D5
Richmond, *Calif., U.S.A.* 80 G2
Richmond, *Va., U.S.A.* 73 F7
Richmond Ra. 63 A5
Ridder 29 D9
Ried 15 D7
Riesa 15 C7
Rieti 20 C4
Rig Rig 53 F1
Rīga 24 B1
Riga, G. of 24 B1
Rīgas Jūras Līcis = Riga, G. of 24 B1
Rīgestān □ 42 D4
Rigolet 68 C5
Riiser-Larsen-halvøya 96 A8
Rijeka 20 B5
Rimah, Wadi ar → 47 F5
Rímini 20 B4
Rîmnicu Sărat 17 F8
Rîmnicu Vîlcea 17 F7
Rimouski 69 D4
Rinca 39 F1
Rinconada 94 A3
Rinjani 37 F5
Rio Branco, *Brazil* 91 E5
Río Branco, *Uruguay* 94 C6
Río Cuarto 94 C4
Rio de Janeiro 93 G5
Rio de Janeiro □ 93 G5
Rio do Sul 94 B7
Río Gallegos 95 G3
Río Grande, *Argentina* 95 G3
Rio Grande, *Brazil* 94 C6
Rio Grande → 78
Rio Grande do Norte □ 92 D6
Rio Grande do Sul □ 94 B6
Rio Largo 93 D6
Río Mulatos 91 G5
Río Muni = Mbini □ 56 D2
Rio Negro 94 B7
Rio Verde 93 F3
Ríobamba 90 D3
Ríohacha 90 A4
Ríosucio, *Caldas, Colombia* 90 B3
Ríosucio, *Choco, Colombia* 90 B3
Rishiri-Tō 32 E12
Riva del Garda 20 B3
Rivadavia 94 B2
Rivera 94 C5
Riversdale 58 E4
Riverside 82 D4
Riverton, *Australia* 62 B2
Riverton, *Canada* 71 C10
Riverton, *N.Z.* 65 G2
Riviera di Levante 20 B2
Riviera di Ponente 20 B2
Rivière-du-Loup 69 D4
Rivne 17 C8
Rívoli 20 B1
Rivoli B. 62 C3
Riyadh = Ar Riyāḑ 47 F6
Rize 46 B5
Rizzuto, C. 21 E6
Roanne 13 C6
Roanoke 73 F6
Robbins I. 62 D4
Robertson 58 E3
Robertson I. 96 A4
Robertsport 55 G2
Robertstown 62 B2
Robinvale 62 B3
Roboré 91 G7
Robson, Mt. 71 C8
Roca, C. da 18 C1
Rocas, I. 92 C7
Rocha 94 C6
Rochefort 12 D3
Rochester, *Minn., U.S.A.* 77 C8
Rochester, *N.Y., U.S.A.* 73 C7
Rock Hill 75 B7
Rock Island 77 E9
Rock Springs 81 E9
Rockefeller Plateau 96 C18
Rockford 77 D10
Rockhampton 61 E9
Rocky Mount 75 B9
Rocky Mts. 70 C7
Rod 42 E3
Rodez 13 D5
Ródhos 23 F7
Rodney, C. 64 B6
Roes Welcome Sd. 68 B2
Rogachev = Ragachow 17 B10
Rogagua, L. 91 F5
Rogatyn 17 D7
Rogoaguado, L. 91 F5
Rohri 42 F6
Rohtak 42 E10
Roi Et 36 A2
Rojas 94 C4
Rojo, C. 84 C5
Rokan → 37 D2
Rolândia 94 A6
Roma, *Australia* 63 A4
Roma, *Italy* 20 D4
Roman 17 E8
Romang 39 F3
Romania ■ 22 B5
Romanovka = Basarabeasca 17 E9
Romans-sur-Isère 13 D6
Romblon 38 B2
Rome = Roma 20 D4
Rome 74 B5
Romorantin-Lanthenay 12 C4
Roncador, Serra do 93 E3
Ronda 18 D3
Rondônia □ 91 F6
Rondonópolis 93 F3
Ronge, L. la 71 C9
Ronne Ice Shelf 96 B3
Roodepoort 59 D5
Roorkee 42 E10
Roosevelt → 91 E6
Roosevelt I. 96 B16
Roquetas de Mar 19 D4
Roraima □ 90 C6
Roraima, Mt. 90 B6
Rosa 57 F6
Rosa, Monte 13 D7
Rosario, *Argentina* 94 C4
Rosário, *Brazil* 92 C5
Rosario, *Mexico* 84 C3
Rosario, *Paraguay* 94 A5
Rosario de la Frontera 94 B3
Rosário do Sul 94 C6
Rosas, G. de 19 A7
Roscommon 11 E2
Roseau, *Domin.* 87 C7
Roseau, *U.S.A.* 77 A7
Rosebery 62 D4
Roseburg 80 D2
Rosenheim 15 E7
Rosetown 71 C9
Rosetta = Rashîd 52 B5
Roseville 80 F3
Rosewood 63 A5
Rosignano Maríttimo 20 C3
Rosignol 90 B7
Roşiori-de-Vede 22 B5
Roslavl 24 C3
Roslyn 63 B4
Ross, *Australia* 62 D4
Ross, *N.Z.* 65 E4
Ross I. 96 B15
Ross Ice Shelf 96 C16
Ross Sea 96 B15
Rossano Cálabro 21 E6
Rossland 71 D8
Rosslare 11 E3
Rosso 55 E1
Rossosh 24 C4
Rosthern 71 C9
Rostock 15 A7
Rostov, *Don, Russia* 25 D4
Rostov, *Yarosl., Russia* 24 B4
Roswell 78 C1
Rotherham 11 E6
Roto 63 B4

Rotondo Mte. 13 E8
Rotorua 64 C7
Rotorua, L. 64 C7
Rotterdam 14 C3
Rottweil 14 D5
Rotuma 64 L12
Roubaix 13 A5
Rouen 12 B4
Round Mt. 63 B5
Roussillon 13 E5
Rouyn 69 D3
Rovaniemi 8 E13
Rovereto 20 B3
Rovigo 20 B3
Rovinj 20 B4
Rovno = Rivne 17 C8
Rovuma → 57 G8
Rowena 63 A4
Roxas 38 B2
Roxburgh 65 F3
Royal Leamington Spa 11 E6
Royan 12 D3
Rozdilna 17 E10
Rozhyshche 17 C7
Rtishchevo 24 C5
Ruahine Ra. 64 C7
Ruapehu 64 C6
Ruapuke I. 65 G3
Rub' al Khali 48 D4
Rubio 90 B4
Rubtsovsk 29 D9
Rudall 62 B2
Rudolf, Ostrov 28 A6
Rufa'a 53 F5
Rufiji → 57 F7
Rufino 94 C4
Rufisque 55 F1
Rugby 11 E6
Rügen 15 A7
Ruhr → 14 C4
Rukwa L. 57 F6
Rum = Rhum 10 C3
Rumāḩ 47 F6
Rumania = Romania ■ 22 B5
Rumbêk 53 G4
Rumia 16 A4
Rumoi 32 F12
Runanga 65 E4
Runaway, C. 64 B7
Rungwa 57 F6
Ruoqiang 34 C3
Rupa 41 D9
Rupat 37 D2
Rupert → 69 C3
Rupert House = Waskaganish 69 C3
Rurrenabaque 91 F5
Rusape 59 B6
Ruschuk = Ruse 22 C5
Ruse 22 C5
Rushworth 63 C4
Russas 92 C6
Russellkonda 40 H5
Russkaya Polyana 29 D8
Rustavi 25 E6
Rustenburg 59 D5
Ruteng 39 F2
Rutshuru 57 E5
Ruwenzori 57 D5
Ružomberok 16 D4
Rwanda ■ 57 E6
Ryazan 24 C4
Ryazhsk 24 C5
Rybache = Rybachye 29 E9
Rybachye 29 E9
Rybinsk 24 B4
Rybinskoye Vdkhr. 24 B4
Rybnitsa = Rîbniţa 17 E9
Rylstone 63 B4
Rypin 16 B4
Ryūkyū Is. = Ryūkyū-rettō 35 D7
Ryūkyū-rettō 35 D7
Rzeszów 16 C5
Rzhev 24 B3

S

Sa Dec 36 B3
Sa'ādatābād 44 D3
Saale → 15 C6
Saalfeld 15 C6
Saar → 13 B7
Saarbrücken 14 D4
Saaremaa 24 B1
Šabac 22 B2
Sabadell 19 B7
Sabah □ 36 C5
Şabāḩ, Wadi → 47 G7
Sabalān, Kūhhā-ye 46 C6
Sábanalarga 90 A4
Sabang 36 C1
Sabará 93 F5
Saberania 39 E5
Sabhah 52 C1
Sabinas 84 B4
Sabinas Hidalgo 84 B4
Sablayan 38 B2
Sable, C., *Canada* 69 D4
Sable, C., *U.S.A.* 86 A3
Sable I. 69 D5
Sabrina Coast 96 A12
Sabulubek 37 E1
Sabzevār 44 B4
Sabzvārān 44 D4
Săcele 17 F7
Sachsen □ 15 C7
Sachsen-Anhalt □ 15 C7
Sacramento 80 F3
Sacramento → 80 F3
Sacramento Mts. 83 D10
Sadani 57 F7
Sadd el Aali 52 D5
Sado 33 G11
Sadon 41 E11
Safi 54 B3
Safīd Kūh 42 B3
Saga, *Indonesia* 39 E4
Saga, *Japan* 32 C2
Sagala 55 F3
Sagar 43 M9
Sagil 34 A4
Saginaw 72 C4
Şagīr, Zāb aş → 46 D5
Saglouc = Salluit 68 B3
Sagua la Grande 86 B3
Saguenay → 69 D3
Sagunto 19 C5
Sahagún 18 A3
Sahand, Kūh-e 46 C6
Sahara 54 D6
Saharan Atlas = Saharien, Atlas 54 B5
Saharanpur 42 E10
Saharien, Atlas 54 B5
Sahiwal 42 D8
Sa'id Bundas 53 G3
Saïda 54 B5
Sa'īdābād 44 D3
Sa'īdīyeh 46 C7
Saidpur 41 E7
Saidu 42 B8
Saigon = Phanh Bho Ho Chi Minh 36 B3
Saijō 32 C3
Saikhoa Ghat 41 D10
Saiki 32 C2
Sailolof 39 E4
St. Andrews 10 C5
St. Arnaud 62 C3
St-Augustin-Saguenay 69 C5
St. Augustine 75 E7
St. Austell 11 F4
St. Boniface 71 D10
St.-Brieuc 12 B2
St. Catharines 69 D3
St.-Chamond 13 D6
St. Christopher-Nevis ■ = St. Kitts & Nevis 87 C7
St. Cloud 77 C7
St. Croix 87 C7
St.-Denis 12 B5
St.-Dizier 13 B6
St. Elias, Mt. 70 B5
St.-Étienne 13 D6
St.-Flour 13 D5
St. Francis, C. 58 E4
St. Gallen = Sankt Gallen 13 C8
St.-Gaudens 12 E4
St. George 63 A4
St.-Georges, *Fr. Guiana* 92 B3
St. George's, *Grenada* 87 D7
St. George's Channel 11 F3
St. Georges Hd. 63 C5
St. Gotthard P. = San Gottardo, P. del 13 C8
St. Helena ■ 51 H3
St. Helena B. 58 E3
St. Helens 62 D4
St. Helier 11 G5
St-Hyacinthe 69 D3
St. John 69 D4
St. John's, *Antigua* 87 C7
St. John's, *Canada* 69 D5
St. Johns → 75 D7
St. Joseph 77 F7
St. Joseph, L. 69 C1
St. Kilda, *N.Z.* 65 F4
St. Kilda, *U.K.* 10 C2
St. Kitts & Nevis 87 C7
St.-Laurent 92 A3
St. Lawrence → 69 D4
St. Lawrence, Gulf of 69 D4
St. Lawrence I. 71 B2
St. Leonard 69 D4
St.-Lô 12 B3
St-Louis 55 E1
St. Louis 77 F9
St. Lucia ■ 87 D7
St. Lucia, L. 59 D6
St. Maarten 87 C7
St.-Malo 12 B2
St-Marc 87 C5
St. Mary Pk. 62 B2
St. Marys 62 D4
St.-Mathieu, Pte. 12 B1
St. Matthews, I. = Zadetkyi Kyun 36 C1
St.-Nazaire 12 C2
St.-Omer 12 A5
St. Paul 77 C8
St. Peter Port 11 G5
St. Petersburg = Sankt-Peterburg 24 B3
St. Petersburg 75 F6
St.-Pierre et Miquelon □ 69 D5
St.-Quentin 13 B5
St. Thomas I. 87 C7
St.-Tropez 13 E7
St. Vincent, G. 62 C2
St. Vincent & the Grenadines ■ 87 D7
Saintes 12 D3
Saintonge 12 D3
Saipan 64 H9
Sairang 41 F9
Sairecábur, Cerro 94 A3
Sajama 91 G5
Sajó 16 D5
Sakai 32 B4
Sakākah 47 E5
Sakakawea, L. 76 B4
Sakarya = Adapazarı 46 B2
Sakarya → 25 E3
Sakata 33 G11
Sakhalin 31 D12
Sakon Nakhon 36 A2
Sala 9 G11
Sala Consilina 21 D5
Saladillo 94 D5
Salado →, *Buenos Aires, Argentina* 94 D5
Salado →, *La Pampa, Argentina* 94 D3
Salado →, *Santa Fe, Argentina* 94 C4
Salaga 55 G4
Salālah 49 D5
Salamanca, *Chile* 94 C2
Salamanca, *Spain* 18 B3
Salamís 23 F4
Salar de Atacama 94 A3
Salar de Uyuni 91 H5
Salaverry 91 E3
Salawati 39 E4
Salayar 39 F2
Saldanha 58 E3
Sale, *Australia* 63 C4
Salé, *Morocco* 54 B3
Salekhard 28 C7
Salem, *India* 43 P11
Salem, *U.S.A.* 80 C2
Salerno 21 D5
Salgótarján 16 D4
Salihli 23 E7
Salihorsk 17 B8
Salima 59 A6

Salina, *Italy* **21 E5**
Salina, *U.S.A.* **76 F6**
Salina Cruz **85 D5**
Salinas, *Brazil* **93 F5**
Salinas, *Ecuador* **90 D2**
Salinas, *U.S.A.* **82 B2**
Salinas Grandes **94 C3**
Salinópolis **92 C4**
Salisbury, *Australia* **62 B2**
Salisbury, *U.K.* **11 F6**
Salisbury, *U.S.A.* **75 B7**
Salliq **68 B2**
Salluit **68 B3**
Salmās **46 C6**
Salmon → **80 C5**
Salmon River Mts. **81 C6**
Salon-de-Provence **13 E6**
Salonica = Thessaloníki **23 D4**
Salonta **16 E5**
Salsk **25 D5**
Salso → **21 F4**
Salt Creek **62 C2**
Salt Lake City **81 E8**
Salta **94 A3**
Saltillo **84 B4**
Salto **94 C5**
Salto → **20 C4**
Salton Sea **82 D5**
Saltpond **55 G4**
Salûm **52 B4**
Salûm, Khâlig el **52 B4**
Salur **40 H4**
Salvador **93 E6**
Salwa **44 E2**
Salween → **41 J11**
Salyan **25 F6**
Salzach → **15 D7**
Salzburg **15 E7**
Salzgitter **14 B6**
Salzwedel **15 B6**
Sama **28 C7**
Sama de Langreo **18 A3**
Samales Group **38 C2**
Samangán □ **45 B7**
Samar **38 B3**
Samara **24 C7**
Samarinda **37 E5**
Samarkand = Samarqand **29 F7**
Samarqand **29 F7**
Sāmarrā **46 D5**
Sambalpur **40 G5**
Sambar, Tanjung **37 E4**
Sambas **37 D3**
Sambava **59 G10**
Sambhal **42 E11**
Sambhar **42 F9**
Sambiase **21 E6**
Sambir **17 D6**
Same **57 E7**
Samokov **22 C4**
Sámos **23 F6**
Samothráki, *Évros, Greece* **23 D5**
Samothráki, *Kérkira, Greece* **23 E2**
Sampacho **94 C4**
Sampit **37 E4**
Sampit, Teluk **37 E4**
Samra **47 F5**
Samsun **46 B4**
Samui, Ko **36 C2**
Samut Prakan **36 B2**
Samut Songkhram → **36 B2**
San **55 F4**
San → **16 C5**
San Agustin, C. **38 C3**
San Andrés, I. de **86 D3**
San Andrés Tuxtla **85 D5**
San Angelo **78 D3**
San Antonio, *Chile* **94 C2**
San Antonio, *Spain* **19 C6**
San Antonio, *U.S.A.* **78 E4**
San Antonio, C., *Argentina* **94 D5**
San Antonio, C., *Cuba* **85 C8**
San Antonio Oeste **95 E4**
San Benedetto del Tronto **20 C4**
San Bernardino **82 C4**
San Bernardino Str. **38 B2**
San Bernardo **94 C2**
San Bernardo, I. de **90 B3**
San Borja **91 F5**
San Carlos, *Argentina* **94 C3**
San Carlos, *Chile* **94 D2**
San Carlos, *Phil.* **38 B2**
San Carlos, *Amazonas, Venezuela* **90 C5**
San Carlos, *Cojedes, Venezuela* **90 B5**
San Carlos de Bariloche **95 E2**
San Carlos del Zulia **90 B4**
San Cristóbal, *Argentina* **94 C4**
San Cristóbal, *Mexico* **85 D6**
San Cristóbal, *Venezuela* **90 B4**
San Diego **82 D4**
San Diego, C. **95 G3**
San Felipe, *Chile* **94 C2**
San Felipe, *Venezuela* **90 A5**
San Felíu de Guíxols **19 B7**
San Fernando, *Chile* **94 C2**
San Fernando, *La Union, Phil.* **38 A2**
San Fernando, *Pampanga, Phil.* **38 A2**
San Fernando, *Spain* **18 D2**
San Fernando, *Trin. & Tob.* **87 D7**
San Fernando, *U.S.A.* **82 C3**
San Fernando de Apure **90 B5**
San Fernando de Atabapo **90 C5**
San Francisco, *Argentina* **94 C4**
San Francisco, *U.S.A.* **82 B1**
San Francisco de Macorîs **87 C5**
San Francisco del Monte de Oro **94 C3**
San Gil **90 B4**
San Gottardo, P. del **13 C8**
San Ignacio, *Bolivia* **91 G6**
San Ignacio, *Paraguay* **94 B5**
San Ildefonso, C. **38 A2**
San Javier, *Argentina* **94 C5**
San Javier, *Bolivia* **91 G6**
San Joaquin → **82 A2**
San Jorge, B. de **84 A2**
San Jorge, G. **95 F3**
San Jorge, G. de **19 B6**
San José, *Bolivia* **91 G6**
San José, *Costa Rica* **86 E3**
San José, *Guatemala* **85 E6**
San Jose, *Phil.* **38 A2**
San Jose, *U.S.A.* **82 B2**
San Jose de Buenovista **38 B2**
San José de Jáchal **94 C3**
San José de Mayo **94 C5**
San José de Ocune **90 C4**
San José del Guaviare **90 C4**
San Juan, *Argentina* **94 C3**
San Juan, *Phil.* **38 C3**
San Juan, *Puerto Rico* **87 C6**
San Juan → **86 D3**
San Juan, C. **56 D1**
San Juan de los Morros **90 B5**
San Juan Mts. **83 B9**
San Julián **95 F3**
San Justo **94 C4**
San Leandro **82 B1**
San Lorenzo **90 C3**
San Lorenzo, I. **91 F3**
San Lorenzo, Mt. **95 F2**
San Lucas **91 H5**
San Lucas, C. **84 C2**
San Luis **94 C3**
San Luis Obispo **82 C2**
San Luis Potosí **84 C4**
San Marino **20 C4**
San Marino ■ **20 C4**
San Martín, L. **95 F2**
San Matías **91 G7**
San Matías, G. **95 E4**
San Miguel **85 E7**
San Miguel → **91 F6**
San Miguel de Tucumán **94 B3**
San Narciso **38 A2**
San Nicolás de los Arroyas **94 C4**
San-Pédro **55 H3**
San Pedro de las Colonias **84 B4**
San Pedro de Lloc **91 E3**
San Pedro de Macorís **87 C6**
San Pedro del Paraná **94 B5**
San Pedro Sula **85 D7**
San Pieto **21 E2**
San Rafael, *Argentina* **94 C3**
San Rafael, *U.S.A.* **80 G2**
San Ramón de la Nueva Orán **94 A4**
San Remo **20 C1**
San Roque, *Argentina* **94 B5**
San Roque, *Spain* **18 D3**
San Rosendo **94 D2**
San Salvador, *Bahamas* **86 B5**
San Salvador, *El Salv.* **85 E7**
San Salvador de Jujuy **94 A4**
San Sebastián, *Argentina* **95 G3**
San Sebastián, *Spain* **19 A5**
San Severo **20 D5**
San Valentin, Mte. **95 F2**
San Vicente de la Barquera **18 A3**
Sana' **49 D3**
Sana → **20 B6**
Sanaga → **56 D1**
Sanana **39 E3**
Sanandaj **46 D6**
Sanco Pt. **38 C3**
Sancti-Spíritus **86 B4**
Sancy, Puy de **13 D5**
Sandakan **36 C5**
Sandanski **22 D4**
Sanday **10 B5**
Sandgate **63 A5**
Sandía **91 F5**
Sandıklı **46 C2**
Sandoa **56 F4**
Sandomierz **16 C5**
Sandoway **41 H10**
Sandusky **72 D4**
Sandwip Chan. **41 F8**
Sandy C. **62 D3**
Sandy L. **71 C10**
Sanford, *Fla., U.S.A.* **75 E7**
Sanford, *N.C., U.S.A.* **75 B8**
Sanford, Mt. **71 B5**
Sanga → **56 E3**
Sangamner **43 K9**
Sangar **31 C10**
Sangasangadalam **37 E5**
Sangeang **39 F1**
Sangerhausen **15 C6**
Sanggau **37 D4**
Sangihe, P. **39 D3**
Sangkapura **37 F4**
Sangli **43 L9**
Sangmélina **56 D2**
Sangre de Cristo Mts. **78 A1**
Sanirajak **68 B2**
Sankt Gallen **13 C8**
Sankt Moritz **13 C8**
Sankt-Peterburg **24 B3**

Sankt Pölten 15 D8
Sankuru → 56 E4
Sanliurfa 46 C4
Sanlúcar de Barrameda 18 D2
Sannicandro Gargánico 20 D5
Sanok 17 D6
Sanshui 35 D6
Santa Ana, *Bolivia* 91 F5
Santa Ana, *Ecuador* 90 D2
Santa Ana, *El Salv.* 85 E7
Santa Ana, *U.S.A.* 82 D4
Santa Barbara 82 C3
Santa Catalina I. 82 D3
Santa Catarina □ 94 B7
Santa Clara 86 B4
Santa Clotilde 90 D4
Santa Coloma de Gramanet 19 B7
Santa Cruz, *Argentina* 95 G3
Santa Cruz, *Bolivia* 91 G6
Santa Cruz, *Phil.* 38 B2
Santa Cruz, *U.S.A.* 82 B1
Santa Cruz → 95 G3
Santa Cruz de Tenerife 54 C1
Santa Cruz do Sul 94 B6
Santa Cruz I. 64 L11
Santa Elena 90 D2
Santa Eugenia, Pta. 84 B1
Santa Fe, *Argentina* 94 C4
Santa Fe, *U.S.A.* 83 C10
Santa Filomena 93 D4
Santa Inés, I. 95 G2
Santa Isabel = Rey Malabo 56 D1
Santa Isabel, *Argentina* 94 D3
Santa Isabel, *Brazil* 93 E3
Santa Lucia Range 82 C2
Santa Maria, *Brazil* 94 B6
Santa Maria, *U.S.A.* 82 C2
Santa María → 84 A3
Santa Maria da Vitória 93 E5
Santa Maria di Leuca, C. 23 E2
Santa Marta 90 A4
Santa Marta, Sierra Nevada de 90 A4
Santa Maura = Levkás 23 E3
Santa Rosa, *La Pampa, Argentina* 94 D4
Santa Rosa, *San Luis, Argentina* 94 C3
Santa Rosa, *Bolivia* 91 F5
Santa Rosa, *Brazil* 94 B6
Santa Rosa, *U.S.A.* 80 F2
Santa Rosa de Copán 85 E7
Santa Vitória do Palmar 94 C6
Santai 35 C5
Santana, Coxilha de 94 C5
Santana do Livramento 94 C5
Santander 18 A4
Sant'Antíoco 21 E2
Santarém, *Brazil* 92 C3
Santarém, *Portugal* 18 C1
Santiago, *Brazil* 94 B6
Santiago, *Chile* 94 C2
Santiago → 90 D3
Santiago de Compostela 18 A1
Santiago de Cuba 86 C4
Santiago de los Cabelleros 87 C5
Santiago del Estero 94 B4
Santo Amaro 93 E6
Santo Ângelo 94 B6
Santo Antonio 93 F2
Santo Corazón 91 G7
Santo Domingo 87 C6
Santo Tomás 91 F4
Santo Tomé 94 B5
Santo Tomé de Guayana = Ciudad Guayana 90 B6
Santoña 18 A4
Santoríni = Thíra 23 F5
Santos 94 A7
Santos Dumont 94 A8
Sanza Pombo 56 F3
São Anastácio 94 A6
São Bernado de Campo 93 G4
São Borja 94 B5
São Carlos 94 A7
São Cristóvão 93 E6
São Domingos 93 E4
São Francisco 93 F5
São Francisco → 93 E6
São Francisco do Sul 94 B7
São Gabriel 94 C6
São João da Madeira 18 B1
São João del Rei 93 G5
São João do Araguaia 92 D4
São João do Piauí 92 D5
São José do Rio Prêto 94 A7
São Leopoldo 94 B6
São Lourenço 93 G4
São Lourenço → 93 F2
São Luís 92 C5
São Marcos → 93 F4
São Marcos, B. de 92 C5
São Mateus 93 F6
São Paulo 94 A7
São Paulo □ 94 A7
São Roque, C. de 92 D6
São Sebastião, I. de 94 A7
São Tomé & Principe ■ 51 F4
São Vicente, C. de 18 D1
Saône → 13 D6
Saonek 39 E4
Saparua 39 E3
Sapele 55 G6
Saposoa 91 E3
Sapporo 32 F12
Sapulpa 79 B5
Saqqez 46 C6
Sar-e Pol 45 B6
Sar-e Pol □ 45 B6
Sar Planina 22 C3
Sarāb 46 C6
Sarada → 40 D3
Saragossa = Zaragoza 19 B5
Saraguro 90 D3
Sarajevo 20 C7
Saran, G. 37 E4
Sarandí del Yi 94 C5
Sarangani B. 38 C3
Sarangani Is. 38 C3
Sarangarh 40 G4
Saransk 24 C6
Sarapul 29 D6
Sarasota 75 F6
Saratov 24 C6
Saravane 36 A3
Sarawak □ 37 D4
Saray 22 D6
Sarayköy 23 F7
Sarbāz 45 E5
Sarbīsheh 45 C4
Sarda → = Sarada → 40 D3
Sardalas 54 C7
Sardarshahr 42 E9
Sardegna □ 21 D2
Sardinia = Sardegna □ 21 D2
Sardis 23 E7
Sargodha 42 C8
Sarh 53 G2
Sārī 44 B3
Sarıgöl 23 E7
Sarikamiş 46 B5
Sarikei 37 D4
Sark 11 G5
Şarköy 23 D6
Sarlat-la-Canéda 12 D4
Sarmi 39 E5
Sarmiento 95 F3
Sarnia 69 D2
Sarny 24 C2
Sarolangun 37 E2
Saronikós Kólpos 23 F4
Sarre = Saar → 13 B7
Sarreguemines 13 B7
Sarro 55 F3
Sarthe → 12 C3
Sartynya 28 C7
Sarvestān 44 D3
Sary-Tash 29 F8
Saryshagan 29 E8
Sasabeneh 49 F3
Sasaram 40 E5
Sasebo 32 C1
Saser 42 B10
Saskatchewan □ 71 C9
Saskatchewan → 71 C9
Saskatoon 71 C9
Saskylakh 30 B9
Sasovo 24 C5
Sassandra 55 H3
Sassandra → 55 H3
Sássari 21 D2
Sassnitz 15 A7
Sassuolo 20 B3
Sasyk, Ozero 17 F9
Sata-Misaki 33 D2
Satadougou 55 F2
Satara 43 L8
Satmala Hills 43 J9
Satna 40 E3
Sátoraljaújhely 16 D5
Satpura Ra. 43 J10
Satu Mare 17 E6
Satui 37 E5
Saturnina → 91 F7
Saudi Arabia ■ 47 F6
Sauerland 14 C4
Sault Ste. Marie, *Canada* 69 D2
Sault Ste. Marie, *U.S.A.* 72 A3
Saumlaki 39 F4
Saumur 12 C3
Saunders C. 65 F4
Sauri 55 F6
Saurimo 56 F4
Sava → 22 B3
Savage I. = Niue 65 L14
Savalou 55 G5
Savanna la Mar 86 C4
Savannah 75 C7
Savannah → 75 C7
Savannakhet 36 A2
Savanur 43 M9
Savé 55 G5
Save → 59 C6
Sāveh 46 D7
Savelugu 55 G4
Savoie □ 13 D7
Savona 20 B2
Sawahlunto 37 E2
Sawai 39 E3
Sawai Madhopur 42 F10
Sawara 32 B7
Sawatch Mts. 83 A9
Sawmills 59 B5
Sawu 39 F2
Sawu Sea 39 F2
Saxony, Lower = Niedersachsen □ 14 B5
Say 55 F5
Sayán 91 F3
Sayan, Zapadnyy 30 D7
Saydā 46 D3
Sayghān 45 C6
Sayḩut 49 D5
Saynshand 35 B6
Sazanit 23 D2
Săzava → 16 D2
Sazin 42 B8
Scandicci 20 C3
Scandinavia 8 F10
Scarborough 11 D6
Scebeli, Wabi → 49 G3
Schaffhausen 13 C8
Schefferville 69 C4
Schelde → 14 C3
Schenectady 73 C9
Schiermonnikoog 14 B4
Schio 20 B3

Schleswig	14	A5
Schleswig-Holstein □	14	A5
Schouten I.	62	D4
Schouten Is. = Supiori	39	E5
Schwäbische Alb	14	D5
Schwaner, Pegunungan	37	E4
Schwarzwald	14	D5
Schwedt	15	B8
Schweinfurt	14	C6
Schwenningen = Villingen-Schwenningen	14	D5
Schwerin	15	B6
Schwyz	13	C8
Sciacca	21	F4
Scilla	21	E5
Scilly, Isles of	11	G3
Scone	63	B5
Scotland □	10	C4
Scott Glacier	96	A12
Scott Inlet	68	A3
Scottsbluff	76	E3
Scottsdale	62	D4
Scranton	73	D8
Scunthorpe	11	E6
Scusciuban	49	E5
Scutari = Üsküdar	25	E2
Seaspray	63	C4
Seattle	80	B2
Sebastopol = Sevastopol	25	E3
Sebha = Sabhah	52	C1
Şebinkarahisar	46	B4
Sebta = Ceuta	18	E3
Sebuku	37	E5
Sebuku, Teluk	37	D5
Secretary I.	65	F2
Secunderabad	43	L11
Sedalia	77	F8
Sedan, *Australia*	62	B2
Sedan, *France*	13	B6
Seddon	65	D6
Seddonville	65	D5
Sedhiou	55	F1
Sedova, Pik	28	B6
Seeheim	58	D3
Seferihisar	23	E6
Segamat	37	D2
Segesta	21	F4
Seget	39	E4
Ségou	55	F3
Segovia = Coco →	86	D3
Segovia	18	B3
Segre →	19	B6
Séguéla	55	G3
Segura →	19	C5
Sehitwa	58	C4
Sehore	43	H10
Seine →	12	B4
Seistan	45	D5
Seistan, Daryācheh-ye	45	D5
Sekayu	37	E2
Sekondi-Takoradi	55	H4
Selaru	39	F4
Selçuk	23	F6
Sele →	21	D5
Selenga = Selenge Mörön →	35	A5
Selenge Mörön →	35	A5
Seletan, Tg.	37	E4
Sélibabi	55	E2
Selîma, El Wâhât el	52	D4
Selkirk	71	C10
Selkirk Mts.	71	C8
Selma	75	B8
Selpele	39	E4
Selu	39	F4
Selva	94	B4
Selvas	91	E5
Semani →	23	D2
Semarang	37	F4
Semey	29	D9
Semiozernoye	29	D7
Semipalatinsk = Semey	29	D9
Semirara Is.	38	B2
Semisopochnoi I.	71	C1
Semitau	37	D4
Semiyarka	29	D8
Semiyarskoye = Semiyarka	29	D8
Semmering P.	15	E8
Semnān	44	C3
Semnān □	44	C3
Semporna	38	D1
Semuda	37	E4
Sena Madureira	91	E5
Senador Pompeu	92	D6
Senaja	36	C5
Senanga	58	B4
Sendai, *Kagoshima, Japan*	32	D2
Sendai, *Miyagi, Japan*	33	G12
Senegal ■	55	F2
Senegal →	55	E1
Senge Khambab = Indus →	43	G5
Sengkang	39	E2
Senhor-do-Bonfim	93	E5
Senigállia	20	C4
Senj	20	B5
Senja	8	E11
Senlis	13	B5
Senmonorom	36	B3
Sennâr	53	F5
Senneterre	69	D3
Sens	13	B5
Senta	22	B3
Sentani	39	E6
Seo de Urgel	19	A6
Seoul = Sŏul	35	C7
Sepīdān	44	D3
Sept-Îles	69	C4
Sequoia National Park	82	B3
Seram	39	E3
Seram Laut, Kepulauan	39	E4
Seram Sea	39	E3
Serasan	37	D3
Serbia □	22	C3
Serdobsk	24	C5
Seremban	37	D2
Serenje	59	A6
Sereth = Siret →	17	F9
Sergino	28	C7
Sergipe □	93	E6
Sergiyev Posad	24	B4
Seria	36	D4
Serian	37	D4
Seribu, Kepulauan	37	F3
Sérifos	23	F5
Sermata	39	F3
Serny Zavod	29	F6
Serov	28	D7
Serowe	59	C5
Serpukhov	24	C4
Sérrai	22	D4
Serrezuela	94	C3
Serrinha	93	E6
Sertânia	92	D6
Serua	39	F4
Serui	39	E5
Serule	59	C5
Sesepe	39	E3
Sesfontein	58	B2
Sesheke	58	B4
Sète	13	E5
Sete Lagôas	93	F5
Sétif	54	A6
Seto	32	B5
Settat	54	B3
Setté-Cama	56	E1
Setúbal	18	C1
Setúbal, B. de	18	C1
Seulimeum	36	C1
Sevan, Ozero = Sevana Lich	25	E6
Sevana Lich	25	E6
Sevastopol	25	E3
Severn →, *Canada*	69	C2
Severn →, *U.K.*	11	F5
Severnaya Zemlya	30	B7
Severnyye Uvaly	24	B6
Severo-Yeniseyskiy	30	C7
Severodvinsk	28	C4
Sevilla	18	D2
Seville = Sevilla	18	D2
Sevlievo	22	C5
Seward	71	B5
Seward Pen.	71	B3
Sewer	39	F4
Seychelles ■	26	K9
Seymour	63	C4
Sfax	52	B1
Sfîntu Gheorghe	17	F7
Shaanxi □	35	C5
Shaba □	57	F4
Shabunda	57	E5
Shache	34	C2
Shackleton Ice Shelf	96	A11
Shackleton Inlet	96	C15
Shadrinsk	29	D7
Shāhābād	44	B4
Shahdād	44	D4
Shahdād, Namakzār-e	44	D4
Shahdadkot	42	F5
Shahgarh	42	F6
Shaḩḩāt	52	B3
Shahjahanpur	42	F11
Shahr Kord	44	C2
Shahrig	42	D5
Shaikhabad	42	B6
Shajapur	43	H10
Shakhty	25	D5
Shakhunya	24	B6
Shaki	55	G5
Shala, L.	53	G6
Shalqar	29	E6
Sham, J. ash	44	F4
Shamīl	44	E4
Shammar, Jabal	47	F5
Shamo = Gobi	35	B6
Shamo, L.	53	G6
Shamva	59	B6
Shan □	41	G12
Shandong □	35	C6
Shanghai	35	C7
Shangqiu	35	C6
Shangrao	35	D6
Shangshui	35	C6
Shannon	64	D6
Shannon →	11	E2
Shansi = Shanxi □	35	C6
Shantou	35	D6
Shantung = Shandong □	35	C6
Shanxi □	35	C6
Shaoguan	35	D6
Shaowu	35	D6
Shaoxing	35	C7
Shaoyang	35	D6
Shaqra', *Si. Arabia*	47	F6
Shaqrā', *Yemen*	49	E4
Sharjah = Ash Shāriqah	44	E3
Sharon	72	D5
Sharya	24	B6
Shashi, *Botswana*	59	C5
Shashi, *China*	35	C6
Shasta, Mt.	80	E2
Shatt al'Arab →	47	E7
Shaunavon	71	D9
Shawan	34	B3
Shawinigan	69	D3
Shcherbakov = Rybinsk	24	B4
Shchuchinsk	29	D8
Shebele = Scebeli, Wabi →	49	G3
Sheboygan	72	C2
Sheffield	11	E6
Shekhupura	42	D8
Shelburne	69	D4
Shelby	75	B7
Shelbyville	74	B4
Shellharbour	63	B5
Shenandoah →	73	E7
Shendam	55	G6
Shendî	53	E5
Shensi = Shaanxi □	35	C5
Shenyang	35	B7
Sheopur Kalan	42	G10
Shepetivka	17	C8
Shepetovka = Shepetivka	17	C8
Shepparton	63	C4
Sherbro I.	55	G2
Sherbrooke	69	D3
Sheridan	81	C10
Sherman	79	C5
Sherridon	71	C9
Shetland Is.	10	A6
Shibām	49	D4
Shigaib	53	E3
Shihchiachuangi = Shijiazhuang	35	C6
Shijiazhuang	35	C6
Shikarpur	42	F6
Shikoku	32	C3
Shikoku □	33	H10
Shikoku-Sanchi	32	C3
Shilabo	49	F3
Shiliguri	40	D7
Shillong	41	E8
Shilong	35	D6
Shimada	32	B6
Shimizu	32	B6

Shimoga 43 N9
Shimonoseki 32 C2
Shinano → 32 A6
Shīndand 42 C3
Shingū 32 C4
Shinyanga 57 E6
Shipehenski Prokhod 22 C5
Shipki La 42 D11
Shīr Kūh 44 D3
Shirane-San 32 A6
Shīrāz 44 D3
Shire → 59 B7
Shiretoko-Misaki 32 F13
Shiriya-Zaki 32 F12
Shīrvān 44 B4
Shirwa, L. = Chilwa, L. 59 B7
Shivpuri 43 G10
Shizuoka 32 B6
Shklov = Shklow 17 A10
Shklow 17 A10
Shkoder = Shkodra 22 C2
Shkodra 22 C2
Shkumbini → 23 D2
Shmidta, O. 30 A7
Sholapur = Solapur 43 L9
Shoshone Mts. 80 F5
Shoshong 59 C5
Shreveport 79 C7
Shrewsbury 11 E5
Shrirampur 40 F7
Shu 29 E8
Shuangyashan 35 B8
Shule 34 C2
Shumagin Is. 71 C4
Shungnak 71 B4
Shūr → 44 D3
Shurugwi 59 B5
Shūsf 45 D5
Shūshtar 47 D7
Shwebo 41 F10
Shwegu 41 E11
Shweli → 41 F11
Shymkent 29 E7
Shyok 42 B11
Shyok → 42 B9
Si Kiang = Xi Jiang → 35 D6
Si-ngan = Xi'an 35 C5
Si Racha 36 B2
Siah 47 G6
Siahan Range 42 F4
Siaksriindrapura 37 D2
Sialkot 42 C9
Siantan, P. 37 D3
Sīāreh 45 D5
Siargao 38 C3
Siasi 38 C2
Siau 39 D3
Šiauliai 24 B1
Šibenik 20 C5
Siberut 37 E1
Sibi 42 E5
Sibil 39 E6
Sibiti 56 E2
Sibiu 17 F7
Sibolga 37 D1
Sibsagar 41 D10
Sibu 37 D4
Sibuco 38 C2
Sibuguey B. 38 C2
Sibut 56 C3
Sibutu 38 D1
Sibutu Passage 38 D1
Sibuyan 38 B2
Sibuyan Sea 38 B2
Sichuan □ 34 C5
Sicilia 21 F5
Sicily = Sicilia 21 F5
Sicuani 91 F4
Siddipet 43 K11
Sidéradougou 55 F4
Sîdi Barrâni 52 B4
Sidi-bel-Abbès 54 A4
Sidley, Mt. 96 B18
Sidon = Saydā 46 D3
Sidra, G. of = Surt, Khalīj 52 B2
Siedlce 17 B6
Sieg → 14 C4
Siegen 14 C5
Siem Reap 36 B2
Siena 20 C3
Sieradz 16 C4
Sierra Colorada 95 E3
Sierra Gorda 94 A3
Sierra Leone ■ 55 G2
Sífnos 23 F5
Sighetu-Marmatiei 17 E6
Sighişoara 17 E7
Sigli 36 C1
Sigsig 90 D3
Sigüenza 19 B4
Siguiri 55 F3
Sihanoukville = Kompong Som 36 B2
Siirt 46 C5
Sikar 42 F9
Sikasso 55 F3
Sikhote Alin, Khrebet 31 E11
Sikhote Alin Ra. = Sikhote Alin, Khrebet 31 E11
Síkinos 23 F5
Sikkim □ 40 D7
Sil → 18 A2
Silchar 41 E9
Silesia = Śląsk 16 C3
Silgarhi Doti 40 C3
Silghat 41 D9
Silifke 46 C3
Siliguri = Shiliguri 40 D7
Siling Co 34 C3
Silistra 22 B6
Silivri 22 D7
Sillajhuay, Cordillera 91 G5
Silva Porto = Kuito 58 A3
Simanggang 37 D4
Simav 23 E7
Simbirsk 24 C6
Simeria 17 F6
Simeulue 37 D1
Simferopol 25 E3
Sími 23 F6
Simikot 40 C3
Simla 42 D10
Simplon P. 13 C8
Simpson Desert 60 F6
Simunjan 37 D4
Sinabang 37 D1
Sinadogo 49 F4
Sinai = Es Sînâ' 52 C5
Sinai, Mt. = Mûsa, G. 47 E3
Sinaloa de Levya 84 B3
Sīnāwan 54 B7
Sincelejo 90 B3
Sincorá, Serra do 93 E5
Sind □ 42 F6
Sind Sagar Doab 42 D7
Sindangan 38 C2
Sines 18 D1
Sines, C. de 18 D1
Singa 53 F5
Singapore ■ 37 D2
Singaraja 37 F5
Singida 57 E6
Singitikós Kólpos 23 D5
Singkaling Hkamti 41 E10
Singkawang 37 D3
Singleton 63 B5
Singora = Songkhla 36 C2
Sinjai 39 F2
Sinjār 46 C5
Sinkat 53 E6
Sinkiang Uighur = Xinjiang Uygur Zizhiqu □ 34 B3
Sinni → 21 D6
Sinnuris 52 C5
Sinop 46 B3
Sintang 37 D4
Sintra 18 C1
Sinŭiju 35 B7
Siocon 38 C2
Siófok 16 E4
Sioma 58 B4
Sion 13 C7
Sioux City 77 D6
Sioux Falls 76 D6
Sioux Lookout 71 C10
Siping 35 B7
Sipura 37 E1
Siquijor 38 C2
Siracusa 21 F5
Sirajganj 41 E7
Sirdaryo = Syrdarya → 29 E7
Siret → 17 F9
Sirohi 43 G8
Sironj 43 G10
Síros 23 F5
Sirsa 42 E9
Sisak 20 B6
Sisaket 36 A2
Sisophon 36 B2
Sīstān va Balūchestān □ 45 E5
Sitapur 40 D3
Sitges 19 B6
Sitía 23 G6
Sitka 71 C6
Sittang Myit → 41 J11
Sittwe 41 G9
Siuri 40 F6
Sīvand 44 D3
Sivas 46 C4
Siverek 46 C4
Sivrihisar 46 C2
Sîwa 52 C4
Siwalik Range 40 D4
Siwan 40 D5
Sjælland 9 G10
Sjumen = Šumen 22 C6
Skadarsko Jezero 22 C2
Skagerrak 9 G9
Skagway 71 C6
Skala-Podilska 17 D8
Skala Podolskaya = Skala-Podilska 17 D8
Skalat 17 D7
Skardu 42 B9
Skarzysko-Kamienna 16 C5
Skeena → 70 C6
Skegness 11 E7
Skeldon 90 B7
Skellefte älv → 8 F12
Skellefteå 8 F12
Skíathos 23 E4
Skien 9 G9
Skierniewice 16 C5
Skikda 54 A6
Skipton 62 C3
Skíros 23 E5
Skole 17 D6
Skópelos 23 E4
Skopje 22 C3
Skvyra 17 D9
Skye 10 C3
Skyros = Skíros 23 E5
Slamet 37 F3
Śląsk 16 C3
Slatina 22 B5
Slave → 70 B8
Slavgorod 29 D8
Slavonski Brod 20 B7
Slavuta 17 C8
Slavyansk = Slovyansk 25 D4
Slawharad 17 B10
Sleaford B. 62 B2
Sleeper Is. 68 C2
Sligeach = Sligo 11 D2
Sligo 11 D2
Sliven 22 C6
Slobodskoy 24 B7
Slobozia 22 B6
Slonim 17 B7
Slough 11 F6
Slovak Rep. ■ 16 D5
Slovakia = Slovak Rep. ■ 16 D5
Slovakian Ore Mts. = Slovenské Rudohorie 16 D4
Slovenia ■ 20 B5
Slovenija = Slovenia ■ 20 B5
Slovenská Republika = Slovak Rep. ■ 16 D5
Slovenské Rudohorie 16 D4
Slovyansk 25 D4
Sluch → 17 C8
Słupsk 16 A3
Slutsk 17 B8
Smara 54 B3
Smarhon 17 A8
Smederevo 22 B3
Smith Arm 70 B7
Smithton 62 D4
Smithtown 63 B5
Smoky Bay 62 B1
Smolensk 24 C3
Smolikas, Óros 23 D3
Smolyan 22 D5
Smorgon = Smarhon 17 A8
Smyrna = İzmir 23 E6
Snake → 80 B4
Snake I. 63 C4
Snake River Plain 81 D7

Sneek 14 B3
Sněžka 16 C2
Snøhetta 8 F9
Snowdon 11 E4
Snowdrift 70 B8
Snowtown 62 B2
Snowy → 63 C4
Snowy Mts. . . . 63 C4
Snyatyn 17 D7
Snyder 78 C3
Soalala 59 H9
Sobat, Nahr → 53 G5
Sobral 92 C5
Soc Trang 36 C3
Soch'e = Shache 34 C2
Sochi 25 E4
Société, Is. de la 65 L15
Society Is. = Société, Is. de la 65 L15
Socompa, Portezuelo de 94 A3
Socorro 90 B4
Socotra 49 E5
Soda Plains . . . 42 B11
Söderhamn . . . 8 F11
Sodiri 53 F4
Sodo 53 G6
Sofia = Sofiya . 22 C4
Sofia → 59 H9
Sofiya 22 C4
Sogamoso 90 B4
Sognefjorden . 8 F9
Sohâg 52 C5
Soissons 13 B5
Sokal 17 C7
Söke 23 F6
Sokhumi 25 E5
Sokodé 55 G5
Sokol 24 B5
Sokółka 17 B6
Sokolo 55 F3
Sokolów Podlaski 17 B6
Sokoto 55 F6
Solano 38 A2
Solapur 43 L9
Soledad 90 B6
Soligalich 24 B5
Soligorsk = Salihorsk . . . 17 B8
Solikamsk 28 D6
Solimões = Amazonas → 92 C3
Solingen 14 C4
Sóller 19 C7
Sologne 12 C4
Solok 37 E2
Solomon Is. ■ . 64 K10
Solomon Sea . 61 B9
Solon 35 B7
Solor 39 F2
Solothurn 13 C7
Šolta 20 C6
Solţānābād . . . 44 B4
Solunska Glava 22 D3
Solwezi 59 A5
Soma 23 E6
Somali Rep. ■ . 49 F4
Somalia = Somali Rep. ■ 49 F4
Sombor 22 B2
Sombrerete . . . 84 C4
Sombrero 87 C7
Somerset East . 59 E5
Somerset I. . . . 70 A10
Someş → 17 E6
Sommariva . . . 63 A4
Somme → . . . 12 A4
Somosierra, Puerto de . . . 18 B4
Somport, Puerto de 12 E3
Søndre Strømfjord . . 68 B5
Sóndrio 20 A2
Sonepur 40 G4
Song Cau 36 B3
Songea 57 G7
Songhua Jiang → . . . 35 B8
Songkhla 36 C2
Songpan 34 C5
Sonipat 42 E10
Sonmiani 42 G5
Sono → 93 D4
Sonora → 84 B2
Sonsonate 85 E7
Soochow = Suzhou 35 C7
Sopi 39 D3
Sopot 16 A4
Sopron 16 E3
Sør-Rondane . . 96 B8
Sorata 91 G5
Sorel 69 D3
Sorgono 21 D2
Soria 19 B4
Sorkh, Kuh-e . . 44 C4
Soroca 17 D9
Sorocaba 94 A7
Soroki = Soroca 17 D9
Sorong 39 E4
Soroti 57 D6
Sørøya 8 D12
Sorrento 63 C3
Sorsogon 38 B2
Sosnowiec 16 C4
Souanké 56 D2
Soúdhas, Kólpos 23 G5
Sŏul 35 C7
Sound, The = Øresund 9 G10
Sources, Mt. aux 59 D5
Soure 92 C4
Souris 71 D9
Souris → 71 D10
Sousa 92 D6
Sousel 92 C3
Sousse 52 A1
South Africa ■ 58 E4
South Australia □ . . 62 B2
South Bend . . . 72 D2
South Carolina □ . . 75 C7
South China Sea 36 C4
South Dakota □ 76 C4
South East C. . 62 D4
South Horr 57 D7
South I. 65 E3
South Invercargill . . 65 G3
South Korea ■ 35 C7
South Magnetic Pole 96 A13
South Nahanni → . 70 B7
South Natuna Is. = Natuna Selatan, Kepulauan . . 37 D3
South Orkney Is. 96 A4
South Pagai, I. = Pagai Selatan, P. . . 37 E2
South Platte → 76 E4
South Pole . . . . 96 C
South Ronaldsay . . 10 B5
South Saskatchewan → 71 C9
South Shetland Is. 96 A4
South Shields . 11 D6
South Taranaki Bight 64 C6
South Uist 10 C3
South West C. . 62 D4
Southampton . 11 F6
Southampton I. 68 B2
Southbridge . . 65 E5
Southend-on-Sea 11 F7
Southern Alps . 65 E4
Southern Indian L. 71 C10
Southern Ocean 96 A9
Southern Uplands 10 D5
Southport 63 A5
Southwest C. . . 65 G2
Soutpansberg . 59 C5
Sovetsk, *Kaliningd., Russia* 24 B1
Sovetsk, *Kirov, Russia* 24 B6
Sōya-Misaki . . . 32 E12
Soyo 56 F2
Sozh → 17 C10
Spain ■ 18 C4
Spalding 62 B2
Spanish Town . 86 C4
Sparta = Spárti 23 F4
Spartanburg . . 75 B7
Spárti 23 F4
Spartivento, C., *Calabria, Italy* 21 F6
Spartivento, C., *Sard., Italy* . . 21 E2
Spátha, Ákra . . 23 G4
Spence Bay . . . 70 B10
Spencer, C. . . . 62 C2
Spencer G. 62 B2
Spenser Mts. . . 65 E5
Spey → 10 C5
Speyer 14 D5
Split 20 C6
Spokane 80 B5
Spoleto 20 C4
Sporyy Navolok, Mys 28 B7
Spratly I. 36 C4
Spree → 15 B7
Springbok 58 D3
Springfield, *N.Z.* 65 E4
Springfield, *Ill., U.S.A.* 77 F10
Springfield, *Mass., U.S.A.* 73 C9
Springfield, *Mo., U.S.A.* 79 A7
Springfield, *Ohio, U.S.A.* . 72 E4
Springfield, *Oreg., U.S.A.* 80 C2
Springfontein . 59 E5
Springhill 69 D4
Springhurst . . . 63 C4
Springs 59 D5
Squamish 71 D7
Srbija = Serbia □ 22 C3
Sre Umbell . . . 36 B2
Srebrnica 20 B7
Sredinny Ra. = Sredinnyy Khrebet 31 D14
Sredinnyy Khrebet 31 D14
Srednevilyuysk 31 C10
Śrem 16 B3
Sremska Mitrovica . . . 22 B2
Sri Lanka ■ . . . 43 R12
Srikakulam 40 H4
Srinagar 42 B9
Stade 14 B5
Stadlandet 8 F9
Stafford 11 E5
Stakhanov 25 D4
Stalingrad = Volgograd . . 25 D5
Staliniri = Tskhinvali . . . 25 E5
Stalino = Donetsk 25 D4
Stalinogorsk = Novomoskovsk 24 C4
Stalowa Wola . 17 C6
Stamford 73 D9
Stanislav = Ivano-Frankivsk . . . 17 D7
Stanke Dimitrov 22 C4
Stanley, *Australia* 62 D4
Stanley, *Canada* 71 C9
Stanley, *Falk. Is.* 95 G5
Stanovoy Khrebet 31 D10
Stanovoy Ra. = Stanovoy Khrebet 31 D10
Stanthorpe 63 A5
Stara Planina . . 22 C4
Stara Zagora . . 22 C5
Starachowice . . 16 C5
Staraya Russa . 24 B3
Starbuck I. 65 K15
Stargard Szczeciński . . 16 B2
Staritsa 24 B3
Starogard Gdański 16 B4
Starokonstantinov = Starokonstyantyniv 17 D8
Starokonstyantyniv 17 D8
Staryy Chartoriysk . . 17 C7
Staryy Oskol . . 24 C4
State College . . 73 D7
Staten, I. = Estados, I. de Los 95 G4
Statesville 75 B7
Stavanger 9 G9
Staveley 65 E4
Stavropol 25 D5
Stawell 62 C3
Steenkool = Bintuni 39 E4
Stefanie L. = Chew Bahir . 53 H6
Stefansson Bay 96 A9
Steiermark □ . . 15 E8
Steinkjer 8 F10
Stellenbosch . . 58 E3
Stendal 15 B6

Steornabhaigh = Stornoway 10 B3
Stepanakert = Xankändi 25 F6
Stephens Creek 62 B3
Stepnoi = Elista 25 D5
Stepnyak 29 D8
Sterlitamak 29 D6
Stettin = Szczecin 16 B2
Stettiner Haff 15 B8
Stettler 71 C8
Steubenville 72 D5
Stevenage 11 F6
Stewart 70 B6
Stewart, I. 95 G2
Stewart I. 65 G2
Steyr 15 D8
Stillwater, *N.Z.* 65 E4
Stillwater, *U.S.A.* 78 A5
Štip 22 D4
Stirling 10 C5
Stockerau 15 D9
Stockholm 9 G11
Stockport 11 E5
Stockton 82 B2
Stockton-on-Tees 11 D6
Stoke on Trent 11 E5
Stokes Pt. 62 D3
Stolac 20 C6
Stolbovoy, Ostrov 30 B11
Stolbtsy = Stowbtsy 17 B8
Stolin 17 C8
Stonehaven 10 C5
Stonewall 71 C10
Stony Tunguska = Podkamennaya Tunguska → 30 C7
Stora Lulevatten 8 E11
Storavan 8 E11
Store Bælt 9 G10
Store Creek 63 B4
Storm B. 62 D4
Stormberge 59 E5
Stornoway 10 B3
Storozhinets = Storozhynets 17 D7
Storozhynets 17 D7
Storsjön 8 F10
Storuman 8 E11
Stowbtsy 17 B8
Strahan 62 D4
Stralsund 15 A7
Strand 58 E3
Stranraer 11 D4
Strasbourg 13 B7
Stratford, *Canada* 69 D2
Stratford, *N.Z.* 64 C6
Strathalbyn 62 C2
Straubing 15 D7
Streaky B. 62 B1
Streaky Bay 62 B1
Strelka 30 D7
Strezhevoy 29 C8
Strimón → 23 D4
Strimonikós Kólpos 23 D5
Strómboli 21 E5
Stronsay 10 B5
Stroud Road 63 B5
Strumica 22 D4
Stryy 17 D6
Strzelecki Cr. → 62 A2
Stuart Ra. 62 A1
Stung Treng 36 B3
Stutterheim 59 E5
Stuttgart 14 D5
Styria = Steiermark □ 15 E8
Suakin 53 E6
Subansiri → 41 D9
Subi 37 D3
Subotica 16 E4
Suceava 17 E8
Suchou = Suzhou 35 C7
Süchow = Xuzhou 35 C6
Sucre 91 G5
Sudair 47 F6
Sudan ■ 53 E4
Sudbury 69 D2
Sûdd 53 G4
Sudeten Mts. = Sudety 16 C3
Sudety 16 C3
Sudirman, Pegunungan 39 E5
Sueca 19 C5
Suez = El Suweis 52 C5
Suez, G. of = Suweis, Khalîg el 52 C5
Sugluk = Salluit 68 B3
Suhār 44 E4
Suhbaatar 35 A5
Suhl 14 C6
Suihua 35 B7
Sukadana, *Kalimantan, Indonesia* 37 E3
Sukadana, *Sumatera, Indonesia* 37 F3
Sukaraja 37 E4
Sukarnapura = Jayapura 39 E6
Sukhona → 28 C5
Sukhumi = Sokhumi 25 E5
Sukkur 42 F6
Sukkur Barrage 42 F6
Sula, Kepulauan 39 E3
Sulaiman Range 42 D6
Sulawesi □ 39 E2
Sulawesi Sea = Celebes Sea 39 D2
Sulima 55 G2
Sulina 17 F9
Sulitjelma 8 E11
Sullana 90 D2
Sultanpur 40 D4
Sulu Arch. 38 C2
Sulu Sea 38 C2
Suluq 52 B3
Sulzberger Ice Shelf 96 B17
Sumalata 39 D2
Sumatera □ 37 D2
Sumatra = Sumatera □ 37 D2
Sumba 39 F1
Sumba, Selat 39 F1
Sumbawa 37 F5
Sumbawa Besar 37 F5
Sumbe 56 G2
Šumen 22 C6
Sumgait = Sumqayıt 25 E6
Summerside 69 D4
Sumperk 16 D3
Sumqayıt 25 E6
Sumter 75 C7
Sumy 24 C3
Sunbury 63 C3
Sunda, Selat 37 F3
Sunda Str. = Sunda, Selat 37 F3
Sundarbans, The 41 G7
Sundargarh 40 F5
Sunderland 11 D6
Sundsvall 8 F11
Sungaigerong 37 E2
Sungailiat 37 E3
Sungaipakning 37 D2
Sungaipenuh 37 E2
Sungaitiram 37 E5
Sungari = Songhua Jiang → 35 B8
Sungguminasa 39 F1
Sunghua Chiang = Songhua Jiang → 35 B8
Sungurlu 46 B3
Sunnyvale 82 B1
Suntar 30 C9
Supaul 40 D6
Superior 77 B8
Superior, L. 69 D2
Suphan Dağı 46 C5
Supiori 39 E5
Sūr, *Lebanon* 46 D3
Sūr, *Oman* 45 F4
Sura → 24 B6
Surabaja = Surabaya 37 F4
Surabaya 37 F4
Surakarta 37 F4
Surat, *Australia* 63 A4
Surat, *India* 43 J8
Surat Thani 36 C1
Suratgarh 42 E8
Surgut 29 C8
Suriapet 43 L11
Surigao 38 C3
Surinam ■ 92 B2
Suriname ■ = Surinam ■ 92 B2
Suriname → 92 A2
Surt 52 B2
Surt, Khalīj 52 B2
Suruga-Wan 32 B6
Sūsangerd 47 E7
Susanville 80 E3
Susquehanna → 73 E7
Susques 94 A3
Susunu 39 E4
Susurluk 23 E7
Sutherland Falls 65 F2
Sutlej → 42 E7
Suva 64 L12
Suva Planina 22 C4
Suvorov Is. = Suwarrow Is. 65 L14
Suwałki 17 A6
Suwarrow Is. 65 L14
Suweis, Khalîg el 52 C5
Suzdal 24 B5
Suzhou 35 C7
Suzu-Misaki 32 A5
Svealand □ 9 G10
Sverdlovsk = Yekaterinburg 29 D7
Svetlogorsk = Svyetlahorsk 17 B9
Svetozarevo 22 B3
Svishtov 22 C5
Svislach 17 B7
Svyetlahorsk 17 B9
Swabian Alps = Schwäbische Alb 14 D5
Swakopmund 58 C2
Swan Hill 62 C3
Swansea, *Australia* 63 B5
Swansea, *U.K.* 11 F5
Swatow = Shantou 35 D6
Swaziland ■ 59 D6
Sweden ■ 9 G10
Sweetwater 78 C3
Swellendam 58 E4
Świdnica 16 C3
Świdnik 17 C6
Świebodzin 16 B2
Świecie 16 B4
Swift Current 71 C9
Swindon 11 F6
Swinemünde = Świnoujście 16 B2
Świnoujście 16 B2
Switzerland ■ 13 C8
Sydney, *Australia* 63 B5
Sydney, *Canada* 69 D4
Sydra, G. of = Surt, Khalīj 52 B2
Syktyvkar 28 C6
Sylhet 41 E8
Sylt 14 A5
Sym 29 C9
Syracuse 73 C7
Syrdarya → 29 E7
Syria ■ 46 D4
Syrian Desert = Ash Shām, Bādiyat 47 D4
Syzran 24 C6
Szczecin 16 B2
Szczecinek 16 B3
Szczytno 16 B5
Szechwan = Sichuan □ 34 C5
Szeged 16 E5
Székesfehérvár 16 E4
Szekszárd 16 E4
Szentes 16 E5
Szolnok 16 E5
Szombathely 16 E3

T

Tabacal 94 A4
Tabaco 38 B2
Ţābah 47 F5
Tabarka 54 A6
Ţabas, *Khorāsān, Iran* 44 C4
Ţabas, *Khorāsān, Iran* 45 C5
Tabatinga, Serra da 93 E5
Tablas 38 B2
Table B. = Tafelbaai 58 E3
Table Mt. 58 E3
Tábor 16 D2
Tabora 57 F6
Tabou 55 H3
Tabrīz 46 C6
Tabūk 47 E4

Tacheng 34 B3
Tacloban 38 B2
Tacna 91 G4
Tacoma 80 B2
Tacuarembó 94 C5
Tademaït, Plateau du 54 C5
Tadjoura 49 E3
Tadmor 65 D5
Tadoussac 69 D4
Tadzhikistan = Tajikistan ■ 29 F8
Taegu 35 C7
Taejŏn 35 C7
Tafalla 19 A5
Tafelbaai 58 E3
Tafermaar 39 F4
Taft 38 B3
Taga Dzong 41 D7
Taganrog 25 D4
Tagbilaran 38 C2
Tagish 70 B6
Tagish L. 70 B6
Tagliamento → 20 B4
Taguatinga 93 E5
Tagum 38 C3
Tagus = Tejo → 18 C1
Tahakopa 65 G3
Tahan, Gunong 36 D2
Tahat 54 D6
Tāherī 44 E3
Tahiti 65 L16
Tahoe, L. 80 F3
Tahoua 55 F6
Tahta 52 C5
Tahulandang 39 D3
Tahuna 39 D3
Taï 55 G3
Tai Hu 35 C7
Taibei 35 D7
T'aichung = Taizhong 35 D7
Taidong 35 D7
Taieri → 65 G4
Taihape 64 C6
Tailem Bend 62 C2
Taimyr Peninsula = Taymyr, Poluostrov 30 B7
Tain 10 C4
Tainan 35 D7
Taínaron, Ákra 23 F4
T'aipei = Taibei 35 D7
Taiping 36 D2
Taitao, Pen. de 95 F1
Taiwan ■ 35 D7
Taïyetos Óros 23 F4
Taiyuan 35 C6
Taizhong 35 D7
Ta'izz 49 E3
Tajikistan ■ 29 F8
Tajo = Tejo → 18 C1
Tājūrā 52 B1
Tak 36 A1
Takada 32 A6
Takaka 65 D5
Takamatsu 32 B4
Takaoka 32 A5
Takapuna 64 B6
Takasaki 32 A6
Takatsuki 32 B4
Takaungu 57 E7
Takayama 32 A5
Takefu 32 B5
Takengon 36 D1
Takeo 36 B2
Tākestān 46 D7
Takhār □ 45 B7
Takum 55 G6
Talara 90 D2
Talas 29 E8
Talaud, Kepulauan 38 D3
Talaud Is. = Talaud, Kepulauan 38 D3
Talavera de la Reina 18 C3
Talayan 38 C2
Talbragar → 63 B4
Talca 94 D2
Talcahuano 94 D2
Talcher 40 G5
Taldy Kurgan = Taldyqorghan 29 E8
Taldyqorghan 29 E8
Ṭalesh, Kūhhā-ye 46 C7
Tali Post 53 G5
Talibon 38 B2
Taliwang 37 F5
Tall 'Afar 46 C5
Talladega 74 C4
Tallahassee 75 D5
Tallangatta 63 C4
Tallarook 63 C4
Tallinn 24 B1
Talodi 53 F5
Taltal 94 B2
Talwood 63 A4
Talyawalka Cr. → 62 B3
Tamale 55 G4
Tamanrasset 54 D6
Tamarang 63 B5
Tamaské 55 F6
Tambacounda 55 F2
Tambelan, Kepulauan 37 D3
Tambo de Mora 91 F3
Tambora 37 F5
Tambov 24 C5
Tamburâ 53 G4
Tâmchekket 55 E2
Tamega → 18 B1
Tamenglong 41 E9
Tamgak, Mts. 55 E6
Tamil Nadu □ 43 P10
Tammerfors = Tampere 8 F12
Tamo Abu, Pegunungan 37 D5
Tampa 75 F6
Tampere 8 F12
Tampico 84 C5
Tamrida = Qādib 49 E5
Tamsagbulag 35 B6
Tamu 41 E10
Tamworth 63 B5
Tana →, *Kenya* 57 E8
Tana →, *Norway* 8 D13
Tana, L. 53 F6
Tanahbala 37 E1
Tanahgrogot 37 E5
Tanahjampea 39 F2
Tanahmasa 37 E1
Tanahmerah 39 F6
Tanami Desert 60 D5
Tanana 71 B4
Tanana → 71 B4
Tananarive = Antananarivo 59 H9
Tánaro → 20 B2
Tandag 38 C3
Tandil 94 D5
Tandil, Sa. del 94 D5
Tando Adam 42 G6
Tandou L. 62 B3
Tane-ga-Shima 33 D2
Taneatua 64 C7
Tanen Tong Dan 41 J12
Tanezrouft 54 D5
Tanga 57 F7
Tanganyika, L. 57 F5
Tanger = Tangier 54 A3
Tanggula Shan 34 C4
Tangier 54 A3
Tangshan 35 C6
Tanimbar, Kepulauan 39 F4
Tanimbar Is. = Tanimbar, Kepulauan 39 F4
Tanjay 38 C2
Tanjore = Thanjavur 43 P11
Tanjung 37 E5
Tanjungbalai 37 D1
Tanjungbatu 37 D5
Tanjungkarang Telukbetung 37 F3
Tanjungpandan 37 E3
Tanjungpinang 37 D2
Tanjungredeb 37 D5
Tanjungselor 37 D5
Tanout 55 F6
Tanta 52 B5
Tantung = Dandong 35 B7
Tanunda 62 B2
Tanzania ■ 57 F6
Taolanaro 59 K9
Taoudenni 54 D4
Taourirt 54 B4
Tapa Shan = Daba Shan 35 C5
Tapah 37 D2
Tapajós → 92 C3
Tapaktuan 37 D1
Tapanui 65 F3
Tapauá → 91 E6
Tapeta 55 G3
Tapi → 43 J8
Tapirapecó, Serra 90 C6
Tapuaenuku, Mt. 65 D5
Tapul Group 38 C2
Taquari → 91 G7
Tara, *Australia* 63 A5
Tara, *Russia* 29 D8
Tara →, *Montenegro, Yug.* 22 C2
Tara →, *Russia* 29 D8
Tarabagatay, Khrebet 29 E9
Tarābulus, *Lebanon* 46 D3
Tarābulus, *Libya* 52 B1
Tarakan 37 D5
Taralga 63 B4
Taranaki □ 64 C6
Tarancón 19 B4
Taranga Hill 43 H8
Táranto 21 D6
Táranto, G. di 21 D6
Tarapacá 90 D5
Tararua Ra. 64 D6
Tarashcha 17 D10
Tarauacá 91 E4
Tarauacá → 91 E5
Tarawera 64 C7
Tarawera L. 64 C7
Tarazona 19 B5
Tarbela Dam 42 B8
Tarbes 12 E4
Tarcoola 62 B1
Tarcoon 63 B4
Taree 63 B5
Tarfaya 54 C2
Tarifa 18 D3
Tarija 94 A4
Tariku → 39 E5
Tarim Basin = Tarim Pendi 34 C3
Tarim He → 34 C3
Tarim Pendi 34 C3
Taritatu → 39 E5
Tarkhankut, Mys 25 D3
Tarko Sale 28 C8
Tarkwa 55 G4
Tarlac 38 A2
Tarma 91 F3
Tarn → 12 D4
Tarnobrzeg 16 C5
Tarnów 16 C5
Tarnowskie Góry 16 C4
Taroom 63 A4
Taroudannt 54 B3
Tarragona 19 B6
Tarrasa 19 B7
Tarso Emissi 52 D2
Tarsus 46 C3
Tartagal 94 A4
Tartu 24 B2
Tarṭūs 46 D3
Tarutung 37 D1
Tasāwah 52 C1
Taschereau 69 D3
Tash-Kömür 29 E8
Tash-Kumyr = Tash-Kömür 29 E8
Tashauz = Dashhowuz 29 E6
Tashi Chho Dzong = Thimphu 41 D7
Tashkent = Toshkent 29 E7
Tashtagol 29 D9
Tasman B. 65 D5
Tasman Mts. 65 D5
Tasman Pen. 62 D4
Tasmania □ 62 D4
Tatabánya 16 E4
Tatar Republic □ = Tatarstan □ 29 D6
Tatarbunary 17 F9
Tatarsk 29 D8
Tatarstan □ 29 D6
Tateyama 32 B6
Tathra 63 C4
Tatra = Tatry 16 D4
Tatry 16 D4
Tatta 43 G5
Tatuī 94 A7
Tat'ung = Datong 35 B6
Tatvan 46 C5
Taubaté 94 A7
Tauern 15 E7
Taumarunui 64 C6
Taumaturgo 91 E4
Taungdwingyi 41 G10
Taunggyi 41 G11
Taungup 41 H10
Taungup Pass 41 H10
Taungup Taunggya 41 H9
Taunton 11 F5

Taunus 14 C5
Taupo 64 C7
Taupo, L. 64 C6
Tauranga 64 B7
Tauranga Harb. 64 B7
Taurianova . . . 21 E6
Taurus Mts. = Toros Dağları 46 C3
Tavda 29 D7
Tavda ➝ 29 D7
Taveta 57 E7
Tavira 18 D2
Tavoy 36 B1
Tawau 36 D5
Tawitawi 38 C2
Tay ➝ 10 C5
Tayabamba . . . 91 E3
Taylakova 29 D8
Taylakovy = Taylakova . . . 29 D8
Taymā 47 F4
Taymyr, Oz. . . . 30 B8
Taymyr, Poluostrov . . 30 B7
Taytay 38 B1
Taz ➝ 28 C8
Taza 54 B4
Tazovskiy 28 C8
Tbilisi 25 E5
Tchad = Chad ■ 53 E2
Tchad, L. 53 F1
Tch'eng-tou = Chengdu 35 C5
Tchibanga 56 E2
Tch'ong-k'ing = Chongqing . . 35 D5
Tczew 16 A4
Te Anau, L. . . . 65 F2
Te Aroha 64 B6
Te Awamutu . . 64 C6
Te Kuiti 64 C6
Te Puke 64 B7
Te Waewae B. . 65 G2
Tebakang 37 D4
Tébessa 54 A6
Tebicuary ➝ . 94 B5
Tebingtinggi . . 37 D1
Tecuci 22 B6
Tedzhen = Tejen 29 F7
Tefé 90 D6
Tegal 37 F3
Tegina 55 F6
Tegucigalpa . . . 85 E7
Tehachapi 82 C3
Tehrān 44 C2
Tehuantepec . . 85 D5
Tehuantepec, G. de 85 D5
Tehuantepec, Istmo de 85 D6
Tejen 29 F7
Tejo ➝ 18 C1
Tekapo, L. 65 E4
Tekeli 29 E8
Tekirdağ 22 D6
Tekkali 40 H5
Tel Aviv-Yafo . . 46 D3
Tela 85 D7
Telanaipura = Jambi 37 E2
Telavi 25 E6
Telekhany = Tsyelyakhany 17 B7
Teles Pires ➝ . 91 E7
Telford 11 E5
Télimélé 55 F2
Tellicherry 43 P9
Telsen 95 E3
Teluk Anson . . 37 D2
Teluk Betung = Tanjungkarang Telukbetung . 37 F3
Teluk Intan = Teluk Anson . 37 D2
Telukbutun . . . 37 D3
Telukdalem . . . 37 D1
Tema 55 G4
Temax 85 C7
Temerloh 37 D2
Temir 29 E6
Temirtau, *Kazakstan* . . . 29 D8
Temirtau, *Russia* 29 D9
Temma 62 D3
Temora 63 B4
Tempe 83 D7
Temple 78 D5
Temuco 94 D2
Temuka 65 F4
Tenali 40 J3
Tenasserim . . . 36 B1
Tenda, Col di . . 20 B1
Tendaho 49 E3
Tenerife 54 C1
Teng Xian 35 C6
Tengah □ 39 E2
Tengah Kepulauan . . 37 F5
Tengchong . . . 34 D4
Tenggara □ . . . 39 E2
Tenggarong . . . 37 E5
Tengiz, Ozero . 29 D7
Tenkasi 43 Q10
Tenke 57 G5
Tenkodogo . . . 55 F4
Tennessee □ . . 74 B4
Tennessee ➝ . 72 F1
Tenom 36 C5
Tenryū-Gawa ➝ . . . 32 B5
Tenterfield 63 A5
Teófilo Otoni . . 93 F5
Tepa 39 F3
Tepic 84 C4
Teplice 16 C1
Ter ➝ 19 A7
Téra 55 F5
Téramo 20 C4
Terang 62 C3
Terebovlya 17 D7
Terek ➝ 25 E6
Teresina 92 D5
Terewah, L. . . . 63 A4
Terhazza 54 D3
Teridgerie Cr. ➝ 63 B4
Termez = Termiz 29 F7
Términi Imerese 21 F4
Termiz 29 F7
Térmoli 20 C5
Ternate 39 D3
Terni 20 C4
Ternopil 17 D7
Ternopol = Ternopil 17 D7
Terowie, *N.S.W., Australia* 63 B4
Terowie, *S. Austral., Australia* 62 B2
Terracina 20 D4
Terralba 21 E2
Terranova = Ólbia 20 D2
Terrassa = Tarrasa 19 B7
Terre Haute . . . 72 E2
Terschelling . . . 14 B3
Teruel 19 B5
Teryaweyna L. . 62 B3
Teshio-Gawa ➝ 32 F12
Tesiyn Gol ➝ . 34 A4
Teslin 70 B6
Tessalit 54 D5
Tessaoua 55 F6
Tetas, Pta. 94 A2
Tete 59 B6
Teterev ➝ . . . 17 C10
Teteven 22 C5
Tetiyev 17 D9
Tétouan 54 A3
Tetovo 22 C3
Teuco ➝ 94 B4
Teun 39 F3
Teutoburger Wald 14 B5
Tévere ➝ 20 D4
Tewantin 63 A5
Texarkana 79 C6
Texas 63 A5
Texas □ 78 D4
Texas City 79 E6
Texel 14 B3
Teyvareh 45 C6
Tezpur 41 D9
Thabana Ntlenyana . . . 59 D5
Thabazimbi . . . 59 C5
Thailand ■ 36 A2
Thailand, G. of 36 B2
Thakhek 36 A2
Thal 42 C7
Thala La 41 C11
Thallon 63 A4
Thames 64 B6
Thames ➝ . . . 11 F7
Thane 43 K8
Thanh Pho Ho Chi Minh = Phanh Bho Ho Chi Minh . . . 36 B3
Thanjavur 43 P11
Thar Desert . . . 42 F7
Tharad 43 G7
Thargomindah 63 A3
Tharrawaddy . . 41 J10
Thásos 23 D5
Thaton 41 J11
Thaungdut 41 E10
Thayetmyo . . . 41 H10
Thazi 41 G11
The Alberga ➝ 62 A2
The Coorong . . 62 C2
The Frome ➝ . 62 A2
The Grampians 62 C3
The Great Divide = Great Dividing Ra. . 61 E8
The Hague = 's-Gravenhage . 14 B3
The Hamilton ➝ 62 A2
The Macumba ➝ 62 A2
The Neales ➝ 62 A2
The Pas 71 C9
The Rock 63 C4
The Salt L. 62 B3
The Stevenson ➝ 62 A2
The Warburton ➝ 62 A2
Thebes = Thívai 23 E4
Theebine 63 A5
Thermaïkós Kólpos 23 D4
Thermopylae P. 23 E4
Thessaloníki . . 23 D4
Thessaloniki, Gulf of = Thermaïkós Kólpos 23 D4
Thetford 11 E7
Thetford Mines 69 D3
Thevenard 62 B1
Thiel Mts. 96 C2
Thiers 13 D5
Thies 55 F1
Thika 57 E7
Thimphu 41 D7
Thionville 13 B7
Thíra 23 F5
Thistle I. 62 C2
Thívai 23 E4
Thomas, L. 62 A2
Thomasville, *Ga., U.S.A.* . . 75 D6
Thomasville, *N.C., U.S.A.* . 75 B7
Thompson 71 C10
Thomson's Falls = Nyahururu 57 D7
Thrace 22 D6
Three Hummock I. 62 D3
Three Points, C. 55 H4
Thun 13 C7
Thunder Bay . . 69 D2
Thung Song . . 36 C1
Thunkar 41 D8
Thüringer Wald 14 C6
Thurles 11 E3
Thurloo Downs 63 A3
Thurso 10 B5
Thurston I. 96 B2
Thylungra 63 A3
Tia 63 B5
Tian Shan 34 B3
Tianjin 35 C6
Tianshui 35 C5
Tiaret 54 A5
Tiassalé 55 G4
Tibati 53 G1
Tiber = Tévere ➝ . . 20 D4
Tiberias, L. = Yam Kinneret 46 D3
Tibesti 52 D2
Tibet = Xizang □ . . . 34 C3
Tibooburra 62 A3
Tiburón 84 B2
Tîchît 55 E3
Ticino ➝ 20 B2
Tiddim 41 F9
Tidjikja 55 E2
Tidore 39 D3
Tiel 55 F1
Tierra de Campos 18 A3
Tierra del Fuego, I. Gr. de 95 G3
Tiétar ➝ 18 C2
Tieyon 62 A1
Tiflis = Tbilisi . 25 E5
Tifu 39 E3
Tighina 17 E9
Tignish 69 D4
Tigre ➝ 90 D4
Tigris = Dijlah, Nahr ➝ 47 E6
Tigyaing 41 F11

Tîh, Gebel el .. 52 C5
Tijuana 84 A1
Tikamgarh 43 G11
Tikhoretsk 25 D5
Tikrīt 46 D5
Tiksi 30 B10
Tilamuta 39 D2
Tilburg 14 C3
Tillabéri 55 F5
Tílos 23 F6
Tilpa 63 B3
Tilsit = Sovetsk 24 B1
Timaru 65 F4
Timbedgha ... 55 E3
Timboon 62 C3
Timbuktu = Tombouctou 55 E4
Timimoun 54 C5
Timişoara 16 F5
Timmins 69 D2
Timok → 22 B4
Timon 92 D5
Timor 39 F2
Tinaca Pt. 38 C3
Tindouf 54 C3
Tingo Maria ... 91 E3
Tinjoub 54 C3
Tinnevelly = Tirunelveli .. 43 Q10
Tinogasta 94 B3
Tínos 23 F5
Tintinara 62 C3
Tioman, Pulau . 37 D2
Tipongpani ... 41 D10
Tipperary 11 E2
Tīrān 44 C2
Tirana 22 D2
Tiranë = Tirana 22 D2
Tiraspol 17 E9
Tire 23 E6
Tirebolu 46 B4
Tiree 10 C3
Tîrgovişte 22 B5
Tîrgu-Jiu 17 F6
Tîrgu Mureş ... 17 E7
Tirich Mir 42 A7
Tîrnăveni 17 E7
Tírnavos 23 E4
Tirodi 43 J11
Tirol □ 14 E6
Tirso → 21 E2
Tiruchchirappalli 43 P11
Tirunelveli 43 Q10
Tirupati 43 N11
Tiruppur 43 P10
Tiruvannamalai 43 N11
Tisa → 22 B3
Tisdale 71 C9
Tisza = Tisa → 22 B3
Tit-Ary 30 B10
Titicaca, L. 91 G5
Titograd = Podgorica ... 22 C2
Titov Veles 22 D3
Titova-Mitrovica = Kosovska-Mitrovica ... 22 C3
Titovo Užice .. 22 C2
Titule 57 D5
Tivaouane 55 F1
Tívoli 20 D4
Tiwī 45 F4
Tizi-Ouzou 54 A5
Tiznit 54 C3
Tjirebon = Cirebon 37 F3
Tlaxcala 84 D5
Tlaxiaco 84 D5
Tlemcen 54 B4
Tmassah 52 C2
Toamasina 59 H9
Toay 94 D4
Toba 32 B5
Toba Kakar ... 42 D6
Tobago 87 D7
Tobelo 39 D3
Tobermory 10 C3
Toboali 37 E3
Tobol → 29 D7
Toboli 39 E2
Tobolsk 29 D7
Tobruk = Tubruq 52 B3
Tobyl = Tobol → ... 29 D7
Tocantinópolis 92 D4
Tocantins □ ... 93 E4
Tocantins → .. 92 C4
Tochigi 32 A6
Tocopilla 94 A2
Tocumwal 63 C4
Tocuyo → 90 A5
Todeli 39 E2
Todenyang ... 57 D7
Todos os Santos, B. de 93 E6
Togba 55 E2
Togian, Kepulauan .. 39 E2
Togliatti 24 C6
Togo ■ 55 G5
Toinya 53 G4
Tojikiston = Tajikistan ■ . 29 F8
Tojo 39 E2
Tokala 39 E2
Tōkamachi 32 A6
Tokanui 65 G3
Tokar 53 E6
Tokarahi 65 F4
Tokat 46 B4
Tokelau Is. 65 K13
Tokmak 29 E8
Tokushima 32 B4
Tokuyama 32 B2
Tōkyō 32 B6
Tolaga Bay ... 64 C8
Tolbukhin = Dobrich 22 C6
Toledo, *Spain* . 18 C3
Toledo, *U.S.A.* . 72 D4
Toledo, Montes de 18 C3
Tolga 54 B6
Toliara 59 J8
Tolima 90 C3
Tolitoli 39 D2
Tolo 56 E3
Tolo, Teluk 39 E2
Toluca 84 D5
Tomakomai ... 32 F12
Tomar 18 C1
Tomaszów Mazowiecki . 16 C4
Tombé 53 G5
Tombouctou .. 55 E4
Tombua 58 B2
Tomelloso 18 C4
Tomingley 63 B4
Tomini 39 D2
Tomini, Teluk . 39 E2
Tomorit 23 D3
Tomsk 29 D9
Tonantins 90 D5
Tonawanda ... 73 C6
Tondano 39 D2
Tonekābon 44 B2
Tong Xian 35 C6
Tonga ■ 65 L13
Tonga Trench . 65 L13
Tongareva 65 K15
Tongchuan ... 35 C5
Tonghua 35 B7
Tongjiang 35 B8
Tongking, G. of = Tonkin, G. of 35 D5
Tongoy 94 C2
Tongren 35 D5
Tongsa Dzong . 41 D8
Tongue → ... 76 B2
Tonk 42 F9
Tonkin, G. of .. 35 D5
Tonlé Sap 36 B2
Toompine 63 A3
Toora 63 C4
Toowoomba .. 63 A5
Topeka 77 F7
Topki 29 D9
Topol'čany 16 D4
Topolobampo . 84 B3
Torata 91 G4
Torbalı 23 E6
Torbat-e Heydārīyeh .. 44 C4
Torbat-e Jām .. 45 C5
Torbay 11 F5
Tordesillas 18 B3
Torgau 15 C7
Torino 20 B1
Torit 53 H5
Tormes → ... 18 B2
Torne älv → .. 8 E12
Torneå = Tornio 8 E12
Torneträsk 8 E11
Tornio 8 E12
Tornquist 94 D4
Toro, Cerro del 94 B3
Toroníios Kólpos 23 D4
Toronto, *Australia* 63 B5
Toronto, *Canada* 69 D3
Toropets 24 B3
Tororo 57 D6
Toros Dağları .. 46 C3
Tôrre de Moncorvo ... 18 B2
Torre del Greco 21 D5
Torrejón de Ardoz 18 B4
Torrelavega ... 18 A3
Torremolinos .. 18 D3
Torrens, L. 62 B2
Torrente 19 C5
Torreón 84 B4
Torres 84 B2
Torres Vedras . 18 C1
Torrevieja 19 D5
Tortosa 19 B6
Tortosa, C. de . 19 B6
Ţorūd 44 C3
Toruń 16 B4
Tosa-Wan 32 C3
Toscana □ 20 C3
Toshkent 29 E7
Tostado 94 B4
Tosya 46 B3
Toteng 58 C4
Totma 24 A5
Totten Glacier . 96 A12
Tottenham 63 B4
Tottori 32 B4
Touba 55 G3
Toubkal, Djebel 54 B3
Tougan 55 F4
Touggourt 54 B6
Tougué 55 F2
Toul 13 B6
Toulepleu 55 G3
Toulon 13 E6
Toulouse 12 E4
Toummo 52 D1
Toungoo 41 H11
Touraine 12 C4
Tourane = Da Nang 36 A3
Tourcoing 13 A5
Touriñán, C. ... 18 A1
Tournai 14 C2
Tournon 13 D6
Tours 12 C4
Towamba 63 C4
Towang 41 D8
Townsville 61 D8
Toyama 32 A5
Toyohashi 32 B5
Toyonaka 32 B4
Toyooka 32 B4
Toyota 32 B5
Tozeur 54 B6
Trá Li = Tralee 11 E2
Trabzon 46 B4
Trafalgar, C. ... 18 D2
Trail 71 D8
Tralee 11 E2
Trancas 94 B3
Trang 36 C1
Trangan 39 F4
Trangie 63 B4
Trani 20 D6
Transantarctic Mts. 96 C3
Transilvania ... 17 F7
Transilvanian Alps = Carpaţii Meridionali .. 17 F7
Transylvania = Transilvania . 17 F7
Trápani 21 E4
Traralgon 63 C4
Trasimeno, L. . 20 C4
Traun 15 D8
Travemünde .. 15 B6
Travers, Mt. ... 65 E5
Travnik 20 B6
Trébbia → ... 20 B2
Třebíč 16 D2
Trebinje 20 C7
Treinta y Tres . 94 C6
Trelew 95 E3
Tremp 19 A6
Trenčín 16 D4
Trenque Lauquen 94 D4
Trent → 11 E6
Trento 20 A3
Trenton 73 D8
Trepassey 69 D5
Tres Arroyos .. 94 D4
Três Corações . 93 G4
Três Lagoas ... 93 G3
Tres Montes, C. 95 F1
Tres Puentes .. 94 B2
Tres Puntas, C. 95 F3
Três Rios 93 G5
Treviso 20 B4
Triabunna 62 D4
Trichinopoly = Tiruchchirappalli 43 P11
Trichur 43 P10
Trida 63 B4
Trier 14 D4
Trieste 20 B4

Triglav 20 A4
Tríkkala 23 E3
Trikora, Puncak 39 E5
Trinidad, *Bolivia* 91 F6
Trinidad, *Colombia* 90 B4
Trinidad, *Cuba* 86 B3
Trinidad, *Uruguay* 94 C5
Trinidad, *U.S.A.* 78 A1
Trinidad, I. 95 D4
Trinidad & Tobago ■ 87 D7
Trinity → 79 E6
Trinity B. 69 D5
Trinity Range 80 E4
Trinkitat 53 E6
Tripoli = Tarābulus, *Lebanon* 46 D3
Tripoli = Tarābulus, *Libya* 52 B1
Trípolis 23 F4
Tripura □ 41 F8
Trivandrum 43 Q10
Trnava 16 D3
Troglav 20 C6
Trois-Rivières 69 D3
Troitsko Pechorsk 28 C6
Trollhättan 9 G10
Tronador 95 E2
Trondheim 8 F10
Trondheimsfjorden 8 F10
Trout L. 70 B7
Trouville-sur-Mer 12 B4
Troy, *Turkey* 23 E6
Troy, *Ala., U.S.A.* 74 D5
Troy, *N.Y., U.S.A.* 73 C9
Troyes 13 B6
Trucial States = United Arab Emirates ■ 44 F3
Trujillo, *Honduras* 85 D7
Trujillo, *Peru* 91 E3
Trujillo, *Spain* 18 C3
Trujillo, *Venezuela* 90 B4
Truk 64 J10
Trundle 63 B4
Truro, *Canada* 69 D4
Truro, *U.K.* 11 F4
Truskavets 17 D6
Trutnov 16 C2
Tsaratanana 59 H9
Tsarevo = Michurin 22 C6
Tsau 58 C4
Tselinograd = Astana 29 D8
Tsetserleg 34 B5
Tshabong 58 D4
Tshane 58 C4
Tshela 56 E2
Tshikapa 56 F4
Tshofa 57 F5
Tshwane 58 C4
Tsihombe 59 K9
Tsimlyansk Res. = Tsimlyanskoye Vdkhr. 25 D5
Tsimlyanskoye Vdkhr. 25 D5
Tsinan = Jinan 35 C6
Tsinghai = Qinghai □ 34 C4
Tsingtao = Qingdao 35 C7
Tskhinvali 25 E5
Tsna → 24 C5
Tsu 32 B5
Tsuchiura 32 A7
Tsugaru-Kaikyō 32 F12
Tsumeb 58 B3
Tsumis 58 C3
Tsuruga 32 B5
Tsurugi-San 32 C4
Tsuruoka 33 G11
Tsyelyakhany 17 B7
Tual 39 F4
Tuamotu Arch. = Tuamotu Is. 65 L16
Tuamotu Is. 65 L16
Tuamotu Ridge 65 M17
Tuao 38 A2
Tuapse 25 E4
Tuatapere 65 G2
Tubarão 94 B7
Tubau 37 D4
Tübingen 14 D5
Tubruq 52 B3
Tubuai Is. 65 M16
Tucacas 90 A5
Tucson 83 D7
Tucumcari 78 B2
Tucupita 90 B6
Tucuruí 92 C4
Tucuruí, Represa de 92 C4
Tudela 19 A5
Tudmur 46 D4
Tuen 63 A4
Tuguegarao 38 A2
Tukangbesi, Kepulauan 39 F2
Tūkrah 52 B3
Tuktoyaktuk 70 B6
Tukuyu 57 F6
Tula, *Mexico* 84 C5
Tula, *Russia* 24 C4
Tulak 45 C5
Tulancingo 84 C5
Tulare 82 B3
Tulcán 90 C3
Tulcea 17 F9
Tulchyn 17 D9
Tuli, *Indonesia* 39 E2
Tuli, *Zimbabwe* 59 C5
Tullamore, *Australia* 63 B4
Tullamore, *Ireland* 11 E3
Tulle 12 D4
Tullibigeal 63 B4
Ţulmaythah 52 B3
Tulsa 79 A6
Tulua 90 C3
Tulungagung 37 F4
Tum 39 E4
Tumaco 90 C3
Tumatumari 90 B7
Tumba, L. 56 E3
Tumbarumba 63 C4
Túmbes 90 D2
Tumby Bay 62 B2
Tumeremo 90 B6
Tumkur 43 N10
Tump 42 F3
Tumpat 36 C2
Tumu 55 F4
Tumucumaque, Serra 92 B3
Tumut 63 C4
Tuncurry 63 B5
Tunduru 57 G7
Tundzha → 22 D6
Tunga Pass 41 C10
Tungabhadra → 43 M11
Tungaru 53 F5
Tunguska, Nizhnyaya → 30 C6
Tunis 54 A7
Tunisia ■ 54 B6
Tunja 90 B4
Tunuyán → 94 C3
Tunxi 35 D6
Tupelo 74 B3
Tupinambaranas 90 D7
Tupiza 94 A3
Tupungato, Cerro 94 C3
Túquerres 90 C3
Tura 30 C8
Turabah 47 E5
Tūrān 44 C4
Turayf 47 E4
Turda 17 E6
Turek 16 B4
Turfan = Turpan 34 B3
Turfan Depression = Turpan Hami 34 B3
Tŭrgovishte 22 C6
Turgutlu 23 E6
Turhal 46 B4
Turia → 19 C5
Turiaçu 92 C4
Turiaçu → 92 C4
Turin = Torino 20 B1
Turkana, L. 57 D7
Turkestan = Türkistan 29 E7
Turkey ■ 46 C3
Türkistan 29 E7
Turkmenistan ■ 29 F6
Turks & Caicos Is. ■ 87 B5
Turku 9 F12
Turnagain, C. 64 D7
Turneffe Is. 85 D7
Turnhout 14 C3
Tŭrnovo = Veliko Tŭrnovo 22 C5
Turnu Măgurele 22 C5
Turnu Roşu, P. 17 F7
Turpan 34 B3
Turpan Hami 34 B3
Turukhansk 30 C6
Tuscaloosa 74 C4
Tuscany = Toscana □ 20 C3
Tuticorin 43 Q11
Tutóia 92 C5
Tutong 36 D4
Tutrakan 22 B6
Tuttlingen 14 E5
Tutuala 39 F3
Tutuila 65 L13
Tuvalu ■ 64 K12
Tuxpan 84 C5
Tuxtla Gutiérrez 85 D6
Tuy 18 A1
Tuz Gölü 46 C3
Ţūz Khurmātū 46 D6
Tuzla 20 B7
Tver 24 B4
Tweed Heads 63 A5
Twillingate 69 D5
Twin Falls 81 D6
Twofold B. 63 C4
Tyachiv 17 D6
Tychy 16 C4
Tyler 79 C6
Tyre = Sūr 46 D3
Tyrol = Tirol □ 14 E6
Tyrrell → 62 C3
Tyrrell, L. 62 C3
Tyrrhenian Sea 21 E4
Tyumen 29 D7
Tzaneen 59 C6
Tzukong = Zigong 35 D5

U

U.S.A. = United States of America ■ 67 F10
Uarsciek 49 G4
Uato-Udo 39 F3
Uatumã → 90 D7
Uaupés 90 D5
Uaupés → 90 C5
Ubá 93 G5
Ubaitaba 93 E6
Ubangi = Oubangi → 56 E3
Ubauro 42 E6
Ube 32 C2
Ubeda 18 C4
Uberaba 93 F4
Uberlândia 93 F4
Ubon Ratchathani 36 A2
Ubort → 17 B9
Ubundu 57 E5
Ucayali → 90 D4
Uchiura-Wan 32 F12
Udaipur 43 G8
Udaipur Garhi 40 D6
Udgir 43 K10
Udhampur 42 C9
Udi 55 G6
Údine 20 A4
Udmurtia □ 28 D6
Udon Thani 36 A2
Udupi 43 N9
Ueda 32 A6
Uele → 57 D4
Uelzen 14 B6
Ufa 29 D6
Ugab → 58 C2
Ugalla → 57 F6
Uganda ■ 57 D6
Ugljane 20 B5
Ugolyak 30 C10
Uibhist a Deas = South Uist 10 C3
Uibhist a Tuath = North Uist 10 C3
Uíge 56 F2
Uinta Mts. 81 E8
Uitenhage 59 E5
Ujjain 43 H9
Ujung Pandang 39 F1
Ukerewe I. 57 E6
Ukhrul 41 E10
Ukhta 28 C6
Ukraine ■ 25 D3
Ulaanbaatar 35 B5
Ulaangom 34 A4
Ulan Bator = Ulaanbaatar 35 B5
Ulan Ude 30 D8
Ulcinj 22 D2

Ulhasnagar 43 K8
Ulladulla 63 C5
Ullapool 10 C4
Ulm 14 D5
Ulmarra 63 A5
Ulonguè 59 A6
Ulster □ 11 D3
Ulubat Gölü 23 D7
Uludağ 23 D7
Ulungur He → 34 B3
Uluru = Ayers Rock 60 F5
Ulutau 29 E7
Ulverstone 62 D4
Ulyanovsk = Simbirsk 24 C6
Ulyasutay 34 B4
Umala 91 G5
Uman 17 D10
Umaria 40 F3
Umarkot 43 G6
Umba 28 C4
Umbrella Mts. 65 F3
Ume älv → 8 F12
Umeå 8 F12
Umera 39 E3
Umm al Qaywayn 44 E3
Umm Bel 53 F4
Umm Lajj 47 F4
Umm Ruwaba 53 F5
Umnak I. 71 C3
Umniati → 59 B5
Umtata 59 E5
Umuarama 93 G3
Una → 20 B6
Unalaska 71 C3
Uncía 91 G5
Underbool 62 C3
Ungarie 63 B4
Ungarra 62 B2
Ungava B. 68 C4
Ungava Pen. 68 B3
Ungeny = Ungheni 17 E8
Ungheni 17 E8
União da Vitória 94 B6
Unimak I. 71 C3
United Arab Emirates ■ 44 F3
United Kingdom ■ 11 E5
United States of America ■ 67 F10
Unnao 40 D3
Unst 10 A6
Ünye 46 B4
Upata 90 B6
Upemba, L. 57 F5
Upington 58 D4
Upper Hutt 65 D6
Upper Volta = Burkina Faso ■ 55 F4
Uppsala 9 G11
Ur 47 E6
Uracara 90 D7
Ural = Zhayyq → 29 E6
Ural 63 B4
Ural Mts. = Uralskie Gory 28 D6
Uralla 63 B5
Uralsk = Oral 24 C7
Uralskie Gory 28 D6
Uranquinty 63 C4
Urawa 32 B6
Uray 29 C7
Urbana 72 D1
Urbino 20 C4
Urbión, Picos de 19 A4
Urcos 91 F4
Urda 25 D6
Urdzhar 29 E9
Ures 84 B2
Urfa = Sanliurfa 46 C4
Urganch 29 E7
Urgench = Urganch 29 E7
Uribia 90 A4
Urla 23 E6
Urmia = Orūmīyeh 46 C6
Urmia, L. = Orūmīyeh, Daryācheh-ye 46 C6
Uroševac 22 C3
Uruana 93 F4
Urubamba 91 F4
Urubamba → 91 F4
Uruçuí 92 D5
Uruguai → 94 B6
Uruguaiana 94 B5
Uruguay ■ 94 C5
Uruguay → 94 C5
Urumchi = Ürümqi 34 B3
Ürümqi 34 B3
Usakos 58 C3
Usedom 15 B8
Ush-Tobe 29 E8
Ushant = Ouessant, I. d' 12 B1
Ushuaia 95 G3
Üsküdar 25 E2
Usman 24 C4
Usoke 57 F6
Uspallata, P. de 94 C3
Uspenskiy 29 E8
Ussuriysk 31 E11
Ust-Aldan = Batamay 31 C10
Ust Ilimpeya = Yukti 30 C8
Ust Ishim 29 D8
Ust-Kamenogorsk = Öskemen 29 E9
Ust-Karenga 31 D9
Ust Kuyga 31 B11
Ust Muya 30 D9
Ust Olenek 30 B10
Ust Port 28 C9
Ust Tsilma 28 C6
Ust Urt = Ustyurt, Plateau 29 E6
Ust Vorkuta 28 C7
Ústí nad Labem 16 C2
Ustica 21 E4
Ustinov = Izhevsk 28 D6
Ustye 30 D7
Ustyurt, Plateau 29 E6
Usu 34 B3
Usuki 32 C2
Usumacinta → 85 D6
Usumbura = Bujumbura 57 E5
Uta 39 E5
Utah □ 81 F8
Utete 57 F7
Utiariti 91 F7
Utica 73 C8
Utrecht 14 B3
Utrera 18 D3
Utsunomiya 32 A6
Uttar Pradesh □ 42 F11
Uttaradit 36 A2
Uummannarsuaq = Farvel, Kap 68 C6
Uusikaupunki 8 F12
Uvat 29 D7
Uvinza 57 F6
Uvira 57 E5
Uvs Nuur 34 A4
Uwajima 32 C3
Uyuni 91 H5
Uzbekistan ■ 29 E7
Uzerche 12 D4
Uzh → 17 C10
Uzhgorod = Uzhhorod 17 D6
Uzhhorod 17 D6
Uzunköprü 22 D6

V

Vaal → 58 D4
Vaasa 8 F12
Vác 16 E4
Vach → = Vakh → 29 C8
Vadodara 43 H8
Vadsø 8 D13
Vaduz 13 C8
Váh → 16 E4
Vahsel B. 96 B5
Vaigach 28 B6
Vakh → 29 C8
Val d'Or 69 D3
Valahia 22 B5
Valandovo 22 D4
Valcheta 95 E3
Valdayskaya Vozvyshennost 24 B3
Valdepeñas 18 C4
Valdés, Pen. 95 E4
Valdez 71 B5
Valdivia 95 D2
Valdosta 75 D6
Valença 93 E6
Valença do Piauí 92 D5
Valence 13 D6
Valencia, *Spain* 19 C5
Valencia, *Venezuela* 90 A5
Valencia □ 19 C5
Valencia, G. de 19 C6
Valencia de Alcántara 18 C2
Valencia I. 11 F1
Valenciennes 13 A5
Valentim, Sa. do 92 D5
Valera 90 B4
Valjevo 22 B2
Vall de Uxó 19 C5
Valladolid, *Mexico* 85 C7
Valladolid, *Spain* 18 B3
Valle de la Pascua 90 B5
Valledupar 90 A4
Vallejo 80 F2
Vallenar 94 B2
Valletta 21 G5
Valls 19 B6
Valognes 12 B3
Valona = Vlóra 23 D2
Valozhyn 17 A8
Valparaíso 94 C2
Vals, Tanjung 39 F5
Valsad 43 J8
Valverde del Camino 18 D2
Van 46 C5
Van, L. = Van Gölü 46 C5
Van Gölü 46 C5
Van Rees, Pegunungan 39 E5
Vanadzor 25 E5
Vancouver, *Canada* 71 D7
Vancouver, *U.S.A.* 80 C2
Vancouver I. 71 D7
Vänern 9 G10
Vanga 57 E7
Vangaindrano 59 J9
Vännäs 8 F11
Vannes 12 C2
Vanrhynsdorp 58 E3
Vanua Levu 64 L12
Vanuatu ■ 64 L11
Vapnyarka 17 D9
Varanasi 40 E4
Varangerfjorden 8 D13
Varaždin 20 A6
Varberg 9 G10
Vardak □ 45 C7
Vardar = Axiós → 23 D4
Varese 20 B2
Varna 22 C6
Varzaneh 44 C3
Vasa Barris → 93 E6
Vascongadas = País Vasco □ 19 A4
Vasht = Khāsh 42 E2
Vasilevichi 17 B9
Vasilkov = Vasylkiv 17 C10
Vaslui 17 E8
Västerås 9 G11
Västervik 9 G11
Vasto 20 C5
Vasylkiv 17 C10
Vatican City ■ 20 D4
Vatomandry 59 H9
Vatra-Dornei 17 E7
Vättern 9 G10
Vaupés = Uaupés → 90 C5
Vawkavysk 17 B7
Vaygach, Ostrov 28 C6
Vedea → 22 C5
Vega 8 E10
Vegreville 71 C8
Vejer de la Frontera 18 D3
Velebit Planina 20 B5
Vélez 90 B4
Vélez Málaga 18 D3
Vélez Rubio 19 D4
Velhas → 93 F5
Velika Kapela 20 B5
Velikaya → 24 B2
Veliki Ustyug 24 A6
Velikiye Luki 24 B3
Veliko Tŭrnovo 22 C5
Velikonda Range 43 M11
Velletri 20 D4
Vellore 43 N11
Venado Tuerto 94 C4
Vendée □ 12 C3
Vendôme 12 C4
Venézia 20 B4
Venézia, G. di 20 B4

Venezuela ■ 90 B5
Venezuela, G. de 90 A4
Vengurla 43 M8
Venice = Venézia 20 B4
Venkatapuram 40 H3
Ventotene 21 D4
Ventoux, Mt. 13 D6
Ventspils 24 B1
Ventuarí → 90 C5
Ventura 82 C3
Venus B. 63 C4
Vera, *Argentina* 94 B4
Vera, *Spain* 19 D5
Veracruz 84 D5
Veraval 43 J7
Verbánia 20 B2
Vercelli 20 B2
Verde → 95 E3
Verden 14 B5
Verdun 13 B6
Vereeniging 59 D5
Verga, C. 55 F2
Verín 18 B2
Verkhnevilyuysk 30 C10
Verkhniy Baskunchak 25 D6
Verkhoyansk 31 C11
Verkhoyansk Ra. = Verkhoyanskiy Khrebet 31 C10
Verkhoyanskiy Khrebet 31 C10
Vermilion 71 C8
Vermont □ 73 C9
Vernon, *Canada* 71 C8
Vernon, *U.S.A.* 78 B4
Véroia 23 D4
Verona 20 B3
Versailles 12 B5
Vert, C. 55 F1
Verviers 14 C3
Veselovskoye Vdkhr. 25 D5
Vesoul 13 C7
Vesterålen 8 E11
Vestfjorden 8 E10
Vesuvio 21 D5
Vesuvius, Mt. = Vesuvio 21 D5
Veszprém 16 E3
Vetlugu → 28 D5
Vettore, Mte. 20 C4
Veys 47 E7
Vezhen 22 C5
Viacha 91 G5
Viamão 94 C6
Viana 92 C5
Viana do Alentejo 18 C2
Viana do Castelo 18 B1
Vianópolis 93 F4
Viaréggio 20 C3
Vibo Valéntia 21 E6
Vicenza 20 B3
Vich 19 B7
Vichy 13 C5
Vicksburg 79 C8
Viçosa 93 D6
Victor 43 J7
Victor Harbor 62 C2
Victoria, *Canada* 71 D7
Victoria, *Chile* 94 D2
Victoria, *Guinea* 55 F2
Victoria, *Malaysia* 36 C5
Victoria □ 62 C3
Victoria, L., *Africa* 57 E6
Victoria, L., *Australia* 62 B3
Victoria Beach 71 C10
Victoria de Durango = Durango 84 C4
Victoria Falls 59 B5
Victoria I. 70 A8
Victoria Ld. 96 B14
Victoria Taungdeik 41 G9
Victoria West 58 E4
Victorica 94 D3
Vicuña 94 C2
Vidin 22 C4
Vidisha 43 H10
Viedma 95 E4
Viedma, L. 95 F2
Vienna = Wien 15 D9
Vienne 13 D6
Vienne → 12 C4
Vientiane 36 A2
Vierzon 12 C5
Vietnam ■ 36 A3
Vigan 38 A2
Vigévano 20 B2
Vigia 92 C4
Vigo 18 A1
Vijayawada 40 J3
Vikeke 39 F3
Vikna 8 F10
Vila da Maganja 59 B7
Vila de João Belo = Xai-Xai 59 D6
Vila do Bispo 18 D1
Vila Franca de Xira 18 C1
Vila Machado 59 B6
Vila Nova de Gaia 18 B1
Vila Real 18 B2
Vila Real de Santo António 18 D2
Vila Velha 93 G5
Vilaine → 12 C2
Vilanculos 59 C7
Vileyka 17 A8
Vilhelmina 8 F11
Vilhena 91 F6
Vilkitskogo, Proliv 30 B8
Vilkovo = Vylkove 17 F9
Villa Ahumada 84 A3
Villa Ángela 94 B4
Villa Bella 91 F5
Villa Bens = Tarfaya 54 C2
Villa Colón 94 C3
Villa de María 94 B4
Villa Dolores 94 C3
Villa Hayes 94 B5
Villa María 94 C4
Villa Mazán 94 B3
Villa Montes 94 A4
Villa Ocampo 94 B5
Villacarrillo 18 C4
Villach 15 E7
Villagarcía de Arosa 18 A1
Villaguay 94 C5
Villahermosa 85 D6
Villajoyosa 19 C5
Villalba 18 A2
Villanueva de la Serena 18 C3
Villanueva y Geltrú 19 B6
Villarreal 19 C5
Villarrica, *Chile* 95 D2
Villarrica, *Paraguay* 94 B5
Villarrobledo 19 C4
Villavicencio 90 C4
Villaviciosa 18 A3
Villazón 94 A3
Villena 19 C5
Villeneuve-d'Ascq 13 A5
Villeneuve-sur-Lot 12 D4
Villingen-Schwenningen 14 D5
Vilnius 24 C2
Vilyuy → 31 C10
Vilyuysk 31 C10
Viña del Mar 94 C2
Vinaroz 19 B6
Vindhya Ra. 43 H10
Vineland 73 E8
Vinkovci 20 B7
Vinnitsa = Vinnytsya 17 D9
Vinnytsya 17 D9
Virac 38 B2
Viramgam 43 H8
Viranşehir 46 C4
Virden 71 D9
Vire 12 B3
Vírgenes, C. 95 G3
Virgin Is. (British) ■ 87 C7
Virginia □ 73 F6
Virginia Beach 73 F8
Virovitica 20 B6
Virudunagar 43 Q10
Vis 20 C6
Visalia 82 B3
Visayan Sea 38 B2
Visby 9 G11
Višegrad 20 C7
Viseu, *Brazil* 92 C4
Viseu, *Portugal* 18 B2
Vishakhapatnam 40 J4
Viso, Mte. 20 B1
Vistula = Wisła → 16 A4
Vitebsk = Vitsyebsk 24 B3
Viterbo 20 C4
Viti Levu 64 L12
Vitigudino 18 B2
Vitória, *Brazil* 93 G5
Vitoria, *Spain* 19 A4
Vitória da Conquista 93 E5
Vitsyebsk 24 B3
Vittória 21 F5
Vittório Véneto 20 B4
Vivero 18 A2
Vize 22 D6
Vizianagaram 40 H4
Vjosa → 23 D2
Vladikavkaz 25 E5
Vladimir 24 B5
Vladimir Volynskiy = Volodymyr-Volynskyy 17 C7
Vladivostok 31 E11
Vlissingen 14 C2
Vlóra 23 D2
Vltava → 16 C2
Vogelsberg 14 C5
Voghera 20 B2
Vohibinany 59 H9
Vohimarina 59 G10
Vohimena, Tanjon' i 59 K9
Vohipeno 59 J9
Voi 57 E7
Voiron 13 D6
Vojvodina □ 22 B2
Volga → 25 D6
Volga Hts. = Privolzhskaya Vozvyshennost 24 C6
Volgodonsk 25 D5
Volgograd 25 D5
Volgogradskoye Vdkhr. 24 C6
Volkhov → 24 A3
Volkovysk = Vawkavysk 17 B7
Volochanka 30 B7
Volodymyr-Volynskyy 17 C7
Vologda 24 B4
Vólos 23 E4
Volovets 17 D6
Volozhin = Valozhyn 17 A8
Volsk 24 C6
Volta → 55 G5
Volta, L. 55 G5
Volta Redonda 93 G5
Volterra 20 C3
Volturno → 20 D4
Volzhskiy 25 D5
Voríai Sporádhes 23 E4
Vorkuta 28 C7
Voronezh 24 C4
Voroshilovgrad = Luhansk 25 D4
Voroshilovsk = Alchevsk 25 D4
Vosges 13 B7
Vostok I. 65 L15
Vouga → 18 B1
Voznesensk 25 D3
Voznesenye 28 C4
Vrangelya, Ostrov 31 B15
Vranje 22 C3
Vratsa 22 C4
Vrbas → 20 B6
Vrede 59 D5
Vredenburg 58 E3
Vršac 22 B3
Vryburg 58 D4
Vryheid 59 D6
Vukovar 20 B7
Vulcan 17 F6
Vulcaneşti 17 F9
Vulcano 21 E5
Vulkaneshty = Vulcaneşti 17 F9
Vung Tau 36 B3
Vyatka = Kirov 28 D5
Vyatskiye Polyany 24 B7
Vyazma 24 B3
Vyborg 28 C3
Vychegda → 28 C5
Vychodné Beskydy 17 D5
Vylkove 17 F9
Vynohradiv 17 D6
Vyshniy Volochek 24 B3
Vyškov 16 D3

W

Wa **55 F4**
Waal → **14 C3**
Wabash → **72 F1**
Waco **78 D5**
Wad Banda **53 F4**
Wad Hamid **53 E5**
Wâd Medanî **53 F5**
Waddington, Mt. **71 C7**
Waddy Pt. **63**
Wadi Halfa **52 D5**
Wafrah **47 E6**
Wager B. **68 B2**
Wager Bay **68 B1**
Wagga Wagga **63 C4**
Waghete **39 E5**
Wah **42 C8**
Wahai **39 E3**
Waiau → **65 E5**
Waibeem **39 E4**
Waigeo **39 E4**
Waihi **64 B6**
Waihou → **64 B6**
Waikabubak **39 F1**
Waikari **65 E5**
Waikato → **64 B6**
Waikerie **62 B2**
Waikokopu **64 C7**
Waikouaiti **65 F4**
Waimakariri → **65 E5**
Waimate **65 F4**
Wainganga → **43 K11**
Waingapu **39 F2**
Wainwright, *Canada* **71 C8**
Wainwright, *U.S.A.* **71 A3**
Waiouru **64 C6**
Waipara **65 E5**
Waipawa **64 C7**
Waipiro **64 C8**
Waipu **64 A6**
Waipukurau **64 D7**
Wairakei **64 C7**
Wairarapa, L. **65 D6**
Wairoa **64 C7**
Waitaki → **65 F4**
Waitara **64 C6**
Waiuku **64 B6**
Wajima **32 A5**
Wajir **57 D8**
Wakasa-Wan **32 B4**
Wakatipu, L. **65 F3**
Wakayama **32 B4**
Wakefield **65 D5**
Wakema **41 J10**
Wakkanai **32 E12**
Wakool **63 C3**
Wakool → **62 C3**
Wakre **39 E4**
Wałbrzych **16 C3**
Walcha **63 B5**
Wałcz **16 B3**
Wales □ **11 E4**
Walgett **63 A4**
Walgreen Coast **96 B1**
Walhalla **63 C4**
Walla Walla **80 B4**
Wallachia = Valahia **22 B5**
Wallal **63 A4**
Wallaroo **62 B2**
Wallerawang **63 B5**
Wallis & Futuna, Is. **64 L13**
Wallowa Mts. **80 C5**
Wallsend **63 B5**
Wallumbilla **63 A4**
Walvisbaai **58 C2**
Wamba **57 D5**
Wamena **39 E5**
Wamulan **39 E3**
Wana **42 C6**
Wanaaring **63 A3**
Wanaka **65 F3**
Wanaka L. **65 F3**
Wanapiri **39 E5**
Wanbi **62 B3**
Wandoan **63 A4**
Wangal **39 F4**
Wanganella **63 C3**
Wanganui **64 C6**
Wangaratta **63 C4**
Wangary **62 B2**
Wangerooge **14 B4**
Wangiwangi **39 F2**
Wanxian **35 C5**
Warangal **43 L11**
Waratah **62 D4**
Waratah B. **63 C4**
Warburton **63 C4**
Ward **65 D6**
Ward → **63 A4**
Wardha **43 J11**
Wardha → **43 K11**
Warialda **63 A5**
Wariap **39 E4**
Warkopi **39 E4**
Warmbad, *Namibia* **58 D3**
Warmbad, *S. Africa* **59 C5**
Warner Mts. **80 E3**
Warracknabeal **62 C3**
Warragul **63 C4**
Warrego → **63 B4**
Warren **63 B4**
Warrenton **58 D4**
Warrenville **63 A4**
Warri **55 G6**
Warrina **62 A2**
Warrington, *U.K.* **11 E5**
Warrington, *U.S.A.* **74 D4**
Warrnambool **62 C3**
Warsa **39 E5**
Warsaw = Warszawa **16 B5**
Warszawa **16 B5**
Warta → **16 B2**
Warthe = Warta → **16 B2**
Waru **39 E4**
Warwick **63 A5**
Wasatch Ra. **81 E8**
Wash, The **11 E7**
Washim **43 J10**
Washington **73 E7**
Washington □ **80 B3**
Washington, Mt. **73 B10**
Wasian **39 E4**
Wasior **39 E4**
Waskaganish **69 C3**
Wasserkuppe **14 C5**
Watangpone **39 E2**
Waterbury **73 D9**
Waterford **11 E3**
Waterloo, *S. Leone* **55 G2**
Waterloo, *U.S.A.* **77 D8**
Waterton-Glacier International Peace Park **81 A6**
Watertown **73 C8**
Waterville **73 B11**
Watford **11 F6**
Watling I. = San Salvador **86 B5**
Watrous **71 C9**
Watsa **57 D5**
Watson Lake **70 B7**
Watsonville **82 B2**
Wattiwarriganna Cr. → **62 A2**
Watuata = Batuata **39 F2**
Watubela, Kepulauan **39 E4**
Watubela Is. = Watubela, Kepulauan **39 E4**
Wauchope **63 B5**
Waukegan **72 C2**
Waukesha **72 C1**
Wausau **77 C10**
Wauwatosa **72 C2**
Waverley **64 C6**
Wâw **53 G4**
Wāw al Kabīr **52 C2**
Waxahachie **79 C5**
Wayabula Rau **39 D3**
Wayatinah **62 D4**
Waycross **75 D6**
Wazirabad **42 C9**
We **36 C1**
Weda **39 D3**
Weda, Teluk **39 D3**
Weddell I. **95 G4**
Weddell Sea **96 A4**
Wedderburn **62 C3**
Wee Waa **63 B4**
Weemelah **63 A4**
Weiden **15 D7**
Weifang **35 C6**
Weimar **15 C6**
Weipa **61 C7**
Weir → **63 A4**
Wejherowo **16 A4**
Welbourn Hill **62 A1**
Welkom **59 D5**
Wellesley Is. **60 D6**
Wellington, *Australia* **63 B4**
Wellington, *N.Z.* **65 D6**
Wellington, I. **95 F1**
Wellington, L. **63 C4**
Wels **15 D8**
Welshpool **11 E5**
Wemindji **69 C3**
Wenatchee **80 B3**
Wenchi **55 G4**
Wenchow = Wenzhou **35 D7**
Wendesi **39 E4**
Wensu **34 B3**
Wentworth **62 B3**
Wenut **39 E4**
Wenzhou **35 D7**
Werda **58 D4**
Werder **49 F4**
Weri **39 E4**
Werra → **14 C5**
Werribee **63 C3**
Werrimull **62 B3**
Werris Creek **63 B5**
Wersar **39 E4**
Weser → **14 B5**
Wesiri **39 F3**
West Bengal □ **40 F7**
West Beskids = Západné Beskydy **16 D4**
West Falkland **95 G4**
West Fjord = Vestfjorden **8 E10**
West Ice Shelf **96 A11**
West Nicholson **59 C5**
West Palm Beach **75 F7**
West Pt. **62 C2**
West Virginia □ **72 E5**
West Wyalong **63 B4**
Westall Pt. **62 B1**
Westbury **62 D4**
Westerland **14 A5**
Western Australia □ **60 F3**
Western Dvina = Daugava → **24 B1**
Western Ghats **43 N9**
Western Sahara ■ **54 D2**
Western Samoa ■ **65 L13**
Westerwald **14 C4**
Westland Bight **65 E4**
Weston **36 C5**
Weston-super-Mare **11 F5**
Westport, *Ireland* **11 E2**
Westport, *N.Z.* **65 D4**
Westray **10 B5**
Wetar **39 F3**
Wetaskiwin **71 C8**
Wetzlar **14 C5**
Wewak **61**
Wexford **11 E3**
Weyburn **71 D9**
Weymouth **11 F5**
Whakatane **64 B7**
Whale → **68 C4**
Whale Cove **70 B10**
Whales, B. of **96 B16**
Whangamomona **64 C6**
Whangarei **64 A6**
Whangarei Harb. **64 A6**
Wheeling **72 D5**
White →, *Ark., U.S.A.* **79 C8**
White →, *Ind., U.S.A.* **72 E2**
White Cliffs **62 B3**
White I. **64 B7**
White Nile = Nîl el Abyad → **53 E5**
White Russia = Belarus ■ **24 C2**
White Sea = Beloye More **28 C4**
Whitecliffs **65 E4**
Whitehaven **11 D5**
Whitehorse **70 B6**
Whitemark **62 D4**
Whitfield **63 C4**
Whitianga **64 B6**
Whitney, Mt. **82 B3**
Whittlesea **63 C4**
Wholdaia L. **70 B9**
Whyalla **62 B2**
Whyjonta **62 A3**
Wichita **78 A5**
Wichita Falls **78 C4**
Wick **10 B5**
Wickham, C. **62 C3**
Wicklow Mts. **11 E3**
Wieluń **16 C4**
Wien **15 D9**
Wiener Neustadt **15 E9**
Wiesbaden **14 C5**
Wilcannia **62 B3**
Wildspitze **14 E6**
Wilhelm, Mt. **61 B8**
Wilhelm II Coast **96 A11**

Wilhelmshaven 14 B5
Wilkes-Barre 73 D8
Wilkie 71 C9
Willandra Billabong Creek → 63 B4
Willemstad 87 D6
William Creek 62 A2
Williams Lake 71 C7
Williamsburg 73 F7
Williamsport 73 D7
Williamstown 63 C3
Williston 76 A3
Willowmore 58 E4
Willunga 62 C2
Wilmington, *Australia* 62 B2
Wilmington, *Del., U.S.A.* 73 E8
Wilmington, *N.C., U.S.A.* 75 B9
Wilpena Cr. → 62 B2
Wilson 75 B9
Wilson → 62 A3
Wilsons Promontory 63 C4
Wimmera → 62 C3
Winchester 11 F6
Wind River Range 81 D9
Windau = Ventspils 24 B1
Windhoek 58 C3
Windsor, *Australia* 63 B5
Windsor, *N.S., Canada* 69 D4
Windsor, *Ont., Canada* 69 D2
Windward Is. 87
Wingen 63 B5
Wingham 63 B5
Winisk → 69 C2
Winneba 55 G4
Winnipeg 71 D10
Winnipeg, L. 71 C10
Winnipegosis L. 71 C9
Winona 77 C9
Winston-Salem 75 A7
Winterthur 13 C8
Winton, *Australia* 61 E7
Winton, *N.Z.* 65 G3
Wirrulla 62 B1
Wisconsin □ 77 C10
Wisła → 16 A4
Wismar 15 B6
Witbank 59 D5
Wittenberg 15 C7
Wittenberge 15 B6
Wkra → 16 B5
Włocławek 16 B4
Włodawa 17 C6
Wodonga 63 C4
Wokam 39 F4
Wolfsberg 15 E8
Wolfsburg 15 B6
Wolin 16 B2
Wollaston, Is. 95 H3
Wollaston Pen. 70 B8
Wollongong 63 B5
Wolseley 62 C3
Wolverhampton 11 E5
Wondai 63 A5
Wongalarroo L. 63 B3
Wŏnsan 35 C7
Wonthaggi 63 C4
Woocalla 62 B2
Woodburn 63 A5
Woodenbong 63 A5
Woodend 63 C3
Woodland 80 F3
Woodroffe, Mt. 60 F5
Woods, L. of the 71 D10
Woodstock 69 D4
Woodville 64 D6
Woolamai, C. 63 C4
Woolgoolga 63 B5
Woombye 63 A5
Woomera 62 B2
Worcester, *S. Africa* 58 E3
Worcester, *U.K.* 11 E5
Worcester, *U.S.A.* 73 C10
Workington 11 D5
Worms 14 D5
Worthing 11 F6
Wosi 39 E3
Wou-han = Wuhan 35 C6
Wour 52 D2
Wousi = Wuxi 35 C7
Wowoni 39 E2
Woy Woy 63 B5
Wrangel I. = Vrangelya, Ostrov 31 B15
Wrangell 71 C6
Wrangell Mts. 71 B5
Wrath, C. 10 B4
Wrexham 11 E5
Wright 38 B3
Wrigley 70 B7
Wrocław 16 C3
Września 16 B3
Wu Jiang → 35 D5
Wuhan 35 C6
Wuhsi = Wuxi 35 C7
Wuhu 35 C6
Wukari 55 G6
Wuliaru 39 F4
Wulumuchi = Ürümqi 34 B3
Wum 55 G7
Wuntho 41 F10
Wuppertal 14 C4
Würzburg 14 D5
Wutongqiao 34 D5
Wuwei 34 C5
Wuxi 35 C7
Wuyi Shan 35 D6
Wuzhi Shan 35 E5
Wuzhong 35 C5
Wuzhou 35 D6
Wyandotte 72 C4
Wyandra 63 A4
Wyangala Res. 63 B4
Wyara, L. 63 A3
Wycheproof 62 C3
Wynbring 62 B1
Wyndham, *Australia* 60 D4
Wyndham, *N.Z.* 65 G3
Wynnum 63 A5
Wynyard 62 D4
Wyoming □ 81 D10
Wyong 63 B5

X

Xai-Xai 59 D6
Xainza 34 C3
Xangongo 58 B3
Xankändi 25 F6
Xánthi 22 D5
Xapuri 91 F5
Xi Jiang → 35 D6
Xiaguan 34 D5
Xiamen 35 D6
Xi'an 35 C5
Xiang Jiang → 35 D6
Xiangfan 35 C6
Xiangtan 35 D6
Xiao Hinggan Ling 35 B7
Xiapu 35 D6
Xichang 34 D5
Xigazê 34 D3
Xinavane 59 D6
Xing'an 35 D6
Xingren 35 D5
Xingtai 35 C6
Xingu → 92 C3
Xining 34 C5
Xinjiang Uygur Zizhiqu □ 34 B3
Xinjin 35 C7
Xinxiang 35 C6
Xinyang 35 C6
Xinzhu 35 D7
Xique-Xique 93 E5
Xisha Qundao = Hsisha Chuntao 36 A4
Xixabangma Feng 40 C5
Xizang □ 34 C3
Xuanhua 35 B6
Xuchang 35 C6
Xuzhou 35 C6

Y

Ya'an 34 D5
Yaapeet 62 C3
Yabelo 53 H6
Yablonovy Ra. = Yablonovyy Khrebet 30 D9
Yablonovyy Khrebet 30 D9
Yacuiba 94 A4
Yadgir 43 L10
Yagoua 56 B3
Yahuma 56 D4
Yakima 80 B3
Yakutat 71 C6
Yakutsk 31 C10
Yala 36 C2
Yalinga 56 C4
Yalong Jiang → 34 D5
Yalova 22 D7
Yalta 25 E3
Yalutorovsk 29 D7
Yam Ha Melah = Dead Sea 47 E3
Yam Kinneret 46 D3
Yamagata 33 G12
Yamaguchi 32 B2
Yamal, Poluostrov 28 B8
Yamal Pen. = Yamal, Poluostrov 28 B8
Yamantau, Gora 29 D6
Yamba, *N.S.W., Australia* 63 A5
Yamba, *S. Austral., Australia* 62 B3
Yâmbiô 53 H4
Yambol 22 C6
Yamdena 39 F4
Yamethin 41 G11
Yamma-Yamma, L. 62 A3
Yamoussoukro 55 G3
Yampil 17 D9
Yampol = Yampil 17 D9
Yamuna → 40 E3
Yamzho Yumco 34 D4
Yana → 31 B11
Yanac 62 C3
Yanbu 'al Baḩr 47 F4
Yancannia 62 B3
Yanco Cr. → 63 C4
Yandoon 41 J10
Yangambi 56 D4
Yangch'ü = Taiyuan 35 C6
Yangchun 35 D6
Yangjiang 35 D6
Yangon = Rangoon 41 J11
Yangquan 35 C6
Yanji 35 B7
Yanna 63 A4
Yanqi 34 B3
Yantabulla 63 A4
Yantai 35 C7
Yanykurgan 29 E7
Yao 53 F2
Yaoundé 56 D2
Yapen 39 E5
Yapen, Selat 39 E5
Yaqui → 84 B2
Yar-Sale 28 C8
Yaraka 61 E7
Yaransk 24 B6
Yardea P.O. 62 B2
Yaremcha 17 D7
Yarensk 28 C5
Yarí → 90 D4
Yarkand = Shache 34 C2
Yarkhun → 42 A8
Yaroslavl 24 B4
Yarram 63 C4
Yarraman 63 A5
Yarranvale 63 A4
Yarras 63 B5
Yartsevo 30 C7
Yaselda 17 B8
Yasinya 17 D7
Yass 63 B4
Yatağan 23 F7
Yathkyed L. 70 B10
Yatsushiro 32 C2
Yauyos 91 F3
Yavari → 90 D4
Yavatmal 43 J11
Yavoriv 17 D6
Yavorov = Yavoriv 17 D6
Yawatahama 32 C3
Yazd 44 D3
Yazd □ 44 C3
Yazdān 45 C5
Yazoo → 79 C8
Ye Xian 35 C6
Yebyu 41 K12
Yecla 19 C5
Yedintsy = Edinița 17 D8
Yeelanna 62 B2
Yegros 94 B5
Yei 53 H5
Yekaterinburg 29 D7
Yekaterinodar = Krasnodar 25 D4

Yelarbon 63 A5
Yelets 24 C4
Yelizavetgrad = Kirovohrad 25 D3
Yell 10 A6
Yellow Sea 35 C7
Yellowhead Pass 71 C8
Yellowknife 70 B8
Yellowknife → 70 B8
Yellowstone → 76 B3
Yellowstone National Park 81 C8
Yelsk 17 C9
Yemen ■ 49 E3
Yenangyaung 41 G10
Yenbo = Yanbu 'al Baḩr 47 F4
Yenda 63 B4
Yenice 23 E6
Yenisey → 28 B9
Yeniseysk 30 D7
Yeniseyskiy Zaliv 28 B9
Yenyuka 31 D10
Yeola 43 J9
Yeovil 11 F5
Yerbent 29 F6
Yerevan 25 E5
Yermak 29 D8
Yershov 24 C6
Yerushalayim = Jerusalem 47 E3
Yessey 30 C8
Yeu, I. d' 12 C2
Yevpatoriya 25 D3
Yeysk 25 D4
Yezd = Yazd 44 D3
Yiannitsa 23 D4
Yibin 35 D5
Yichang 35 C6
Yichun 35 B7
Yilan 35 D7
Yinchuan 35 C5
Yingkou 35 B7
Yingtan 35 D6
Yining 34 B3
Yinmabin 41 F10
Yishan 35 D5
Yíthion 23 F4
Yiyang 35 D6
Yog Pt. 38 B2
Yogyakarta 37 F4
Yokadouma 56 D2
Yokkaichi 32 B5
Yoko 53 G1
Yokohama 32 B6
Yokosuka 32 B6
Yola 53 G1
Yonago 32 B3
Yongji 35 C6
Yonibana 55 G2
Yonkers 73 D9
Yonne → 13 B5
York, *U.K.* 11 E6
York, *U.S.A.* 73 E7
York, C. 61 C7
Yorke Pen. 62 B2
Yorkton 71 C9
Yos Sudarso, Pulau 39 F5
Yosemite National Park 82 B3
Yoshkar Ola 24 B6
Youghal 11 F3
Young 63 B4
Younghusband, L. 62 B2
Younghusband Pen. 62 C2
Youngstown 72 D5
Yozgat 46 C3
Ysyk-Köl, Ozero 29 E8
Yu Jiang → 35 D6
Yu Shan 35 D7
Yuan Jiang → 35 D6
Yuanling 35 D6
Yuanyang 34 D5
Yuba City 80 F3
Yūbari 32 F12
Yucatán □ 85 C7
Yucatán, Canal de 85 C7
Yucatán, Península de 85 D7
Yucatan Str. = Yucatán, Canal de 85 C7
Yuci 35 C6
Yugoslavia ■ 22 B3
Yukon → 71 B3
Yukon Territory □ 70 B6
Yukti 30 C8
Yuma 82 D5
Yumen 34 C4
Yun Xian 35 C6
Yungas 91 G5
Yunnan □ 34 D5
Yunta 62 B2
Yurgao 29 D9
Yuribei 28 B8
Yurimaguas 91 E3
Yuryung Kaya 30 B9
Yushu 34 C4
Yuzhno-Sakhalinsk 31 E12
Yvetot 12 B4

Z

Zabid 49 E3
Zābol 45 D5
Zābol □ 45 D6
Zābolī 45 E5
Zabrze 16 C4
Zacapa 85 E7
Zacatecas 84 C4
Zacoalco 84 C4
Zadar 20 B5
Zadetkyi Kyun 36 C1
Zafra 18 C2
Żagań 16 C2
Zagazig 52 B5
Zagorsk = Sergiyev Posad 24 B4
Zagreb 20 B6
Zāgros, Kūhhā-ye 44 C2
Zagros Mts. = Zāgros, Kūhhā-ye 44 C2
Zāhedān 45 D5
Zahlah 46 D3
Zaïre = Congo → 56 F2
Zaïre = Congo, Dem. Rep. of the ■ 56 E4
Zaječar 22 C4
Zakhodnaya Dzvina = Daugava → 24 B1
Zākhū 46 C5
Zákinthos 23 F3
Zakopane 16 D4
Zalaegerszeg 16 E3
Zalău 17 E6
Zaleshchiki = Zalishchyky 17 D7
Zalew Wiślany 16 A4
Zalingei 53 F3
Zalishchyky 17 D7
Zambeze → 59 B7
Zambezi = Zambeze → 59 B7
Zambezi 58 A4
Zambia ■ 59 B5
Zamboanga 38 C2
Zamora, *Mexico* 84 D4
Zamora, *Spain* 18 B3
Zamość 17 C6
Zanaga 56 E2
Zanesville 72 E4
Zanjān 46 C7
Zanjān □ 46 C7
Zante = Zákinthos 23 F3
Zanzibar 57 F7
Zaouiet El-Kala = Bordj Omar Driss 54 C6
Zaouiet Reggane 54 C5
Zap Suyu = Kabīr, Zab al → 46 C5
Zapadnaya Dvina 28 D4
Zapadnaya Dvina → = Daugava → 24 B1
Západné Beskydy 16 D4
Zaporizhzhya 25 D4
Zaporozhye = Zaporizhzhya 25 D4
Zara 46 C4
Zaragoza 19 B5
Zarand 44 D4
Zaranj 42 D2
Zaria 55 F6
Zaruma 90 D3
Żary 16 C2
Zarzis 52 B1
Zaskar Mts. 42 C10
Zavāreh 44 C3
Zawiercie 16 C4
Zāyandeh → 44 C3
Zaysan 29 E9
Zaysan, Oz. 29 E9
Zbarazh 17 D7
Zdolbuniv 17 C8
Zduńska Wola 16 C4
Zeebrugge 14 C2
Zeehan 62 D4
Zeerust 59 D5
Zeila 49 E3
Zeitz 15 C7
Zelenograd 24 B4
Zémio 57 C5
Zemun 22 B3
Zenica 20 B6
Žepce 20 B7
Zêzere → 18 C1
Zgorzelec 16 C2
Zhabinka 17 B7
Zhailma 29 D7
Zhambyl 29 E8
Zhangaqazaly 29 E7
Zhanghua 35 D7
Zhangjiakou 35 B6
Zhangye 34 C5
Zhangzhou 35 D6
Zhanjiang 35 D6
Zhanyi 34 D5
Zhaotong 34 D5
Zhashkiv 17 D10
Zhayyq → 29 E6
Zhdanov = Mariupol 25 D4
Zhejiang □ 35 D7
Zhengzhou 35 C6
Zhenjiang 35 C6
Zhenyuan 35 D5
Zhezqazghan 29 E7
Zhigansk 30 C10
Zhijiang 35 D5
Zhilinda 30 B9
Zhitomir = Zhytomyr 17 C9
Zhlobin 17 B10
Zhmerinka = Zhmerynka 17 D9
Zhmerynka 17 D9
Zhodino = Zhodzina 17 A9
Zhodzina 17 A9
Zhongdian 34 D4
Zhumadian 35 C6
Zhuzhou 35 D6
Zhytomyr 17 C9
Zibo 35 C6
Zielona Góra 16 C2
Zigey 53 F2
Zigong 35 D5
Zigui 35 C6
Ziguinchor 55 F1
Zile 46 B3
Žilina 16 D4
Zillah 52 C2
Zimbabwe ■ 59 B5
Zimnicea 22 C5
Zinder 55 F6
Zion National Park 83 B6
Zipaquirá 90 C4
Ziway, L. 53 G6
Zlatograd 22 D5
Zlatoust 29 D6
Zlin 16 D3
Zlītan 52 B1
Zmeinogorsk 29 D9
Znojmo 16 D3
Zolochev = Zolochiv 17 D7
Zolochiv 17 D7
Zomba 59 B7
Zongo 56 D3
Zonguldak 46 B2
Zorritos 90 D2
Zouar 52 D2
Zouérate 54 D2
Zrenjanin 22 B3
Zuetina = Az Zuwaytīnah 52 B3
Zufar 48 D5
Zug 13 C8
Zugspitze 14 E6
Zula 53 E6
Zumbo 59 B6
Zungeru 55 G6
Zunyi 35 D5
Zürich 13 C8
Zuwārah 52 B1
Zvishavane 59 C6
Zvolen 16 D4
Zwettl 15 D8
Zwickau 15 C7
Zwolle 14 B4
Żyrardów 16 B5
Zyryan 29 E9
Zyryanovsk = Zyryan 29 E9
Żywiec 16 D4